AIR FRYER COOKBOOK FOR BEGINNERS:

1200 Air Fryer Recipes

Affordable For Advanced Users And Smart People on a Budget for Quick and Easy Meals.

DEANNA BURNS

ALL RIGHTS RESERVED

This book contains material protected under international and Federal Copyright Laws and Treaties.Any unauthorized reprint or use of this material is prohibited.

No part of this book may be reproduced or transmitted in any form or by any means, electronic or mechanical,including photocopying, recording,or by any information storage and retrieval system without express written permission from the author/publisher

.

Table of Contents

Sommario

1200 Air Fryer Recipes 1

Breackfast & Brunch 34

1. Blueberry Cream Cheese Toasts 35
2. Mediterranean Avocado Toast .. 35
3. Onion & Cheddar Omelet 35
4. Bacon & Egg Sandwich 35
5. Spicy Egg & Bacon Tortilla Wraps 35
6. Grilled Apple & Brie Sandwich . 36
7. Turkey & Mushroom Sandwich 36
8. Air Fried Sourdough Sandwiches 36
9. Grilled Tofu Sandwich with Cabbage 36
10. Sausage & Egg Casserole 36
11. Omelet Bread Cups 37
12. Cheese & Ham Breakfast Egg Cups 37
13. Prosciutto, Mozzarella & Eggs in a Cup 37
14. Prosciutto & Mozzarella Bruschetta 37
15. Crustless Mediterranean Quiche 37
16. Mushroom & Chicken Mini Pizzas 38
17. Air Fried Italian Calzone 38
18. Soppressata Pizza 38
19. Italian Sausage Patties 38
20. Sausage Frittata with Parmesan 38
21. Brioche Toast with Chocolate 39
22. Crustless Broccoli & Mushroom Quiche 39
23. Breakfast Egg Muffins with Shrimp 39
24. Zucchini Muffins 39
25. Kiwi Muffins with Pecans 40
26. Banana & Hazelnut Muffins ... 40
27. Hearty Banana Pastry 40
28. Breakfast Banana Bread 40
29. Mango Bread 40
30. Sweet Bread Pudding with Raisins 41
31. Pumpkin & Sultanas' Bread 41
32. Cherry & Almond Scones 41
33. French Toast with Vanilla Filling 41
34. Toasted Herb & Garlic Bagel .. 42
35. Greek-Style Frittata 42
36. Spanish Chorizo Frittata 42
37. Morning Potato Skins 42
38. Easy Breakfast Potatoes 43
39. Buttered Eggs in Hole 43
40. Air Fried Shirred Eggs 43
41. Loaded Egg Pepper Rings 43
42. Pancake The German Way 43
43. Chili Hash Browns 44
44. Masala Omelet the Indian Way 44
45. Japanese-Style Omelet 44
46. Three Meat Cheesy Omelet 44
47. Baked Kale Omelet 44

48. Orange Creamy Cupcakes 45
49. Baked Avocado with Eggs & Cilantro 45
50. Avocado Tempura 45
51. Coconut & Oat Cookies 45
52. Blueberry Oat Bars 46
53. Paprika Rarebit 46
54. Crispy Croutons 46
55. Quick Feta Triangles 46
56. Roasted Asparagus with Serrano Ham 46
57. Flaxseed Porridge 46
58. Very Berry Breakfast Puffs 47

Snacks and Appetizers 48

59. Italian-Style Tomato Chips 49
60. Pecorino Romano Meatballs . 49
61. Italian-Style Tomato-Parmesan Crisps 49
62. Romano Cheese and Broccoli Balls 49
63. Bruschetta with Fresh Tomato and Basil 49
64. Root Vegetable Chips with Dill Mayonnaise 50
65. Paprika and Cheese French Fries 50
66. Greek-Style Zucchini Rounds 50
67. Hot Cheesy Mushrooms Bites 50
68. Crunchy Wontons with Sausage and Peppers 50
69. Pork Crackling with Sriracha Dip 51
70. Sweet Potato Chips with Chili Mayo 51

71. Cheesy Potato Puffs 51
72. Prosciutto Stuffed Jalapeños 51
73. Pepper and Bacon Mini Skewers 51
74. Hot Roasted Cauliflower Florets 52
75. Wonton Sausage Appetizers .. 52
76. Apple Chips with Walnuts 52
77. Southwestern Caprese Bites .. 52
78. Easy Mexican Elote 52
79. Salmon, Cheese and Cucumber Bites 53
80. Classic Jiaozi (Chinese Dumplings) 53
81. Mint Plantain Bites 53
82. Mexican-Style Corn on the Cob with Bacon 53
83. Paprika Potato Chips 54
84. Mini Plantain Cups 54
85. Sticky Glazed Wings 54
86. Sweet Potato Fries with Spicy Dip 54
87. Asian Twist Chicken Wings 54
88. The Best Calamari Appetizer . 55
89. Mini Turkey and Corn Burritos 55
90. The Best Party Mix Ever 55
91. Cheddar Cheese Lumpia Rolls 55
92. Cocktail Sausage and Veggies on a Stick 55
93. Spicy Korean Short Ribs 56
94. Crunchy Roasted Chickpeas .. 56

95. Crunchy Asparagus with Mediterranean Aioli 56
96. Red Beet Chips with Pizza Sauce 56
97. Cheesy Zucchini Sticks 57
98. Fried Pickle Chips with Greek Yogurt Dip 57
99. Parsnip Chips with Spicy Citrus Aioli 57
100. Parmesan Squash Chips 57
101. Bacon Chips with Chipotle Dipping Sauce 58
102. Hot Paprika Bacon Deviled Eggs 58
103. Fish Sticks with Honey Mustard Sauce 58
104. Kid-Friendly Mozzarella Sticks 58
105. Mustard Brussels Sprout Chips 58
106. Famous Blooming Onion with Mayo Dip 59
107. Avocado Fries with Chipotle Sauce 59
108. Roasted Parsnip Sticks with Salted Caramel 59
109. Spinach Chips with Chili Yogurt Dip 59
110. Sea Scallops and Bacon Skewers 60
111. Crunchy Roasted Pepitas 60
112. Loaded Tater Tot Bites 60
113. Summer Meatball Skewers 60
114. Classic Deviled Eggs 60
115. Chicken Nuggets with Campfire Sauce 61
116. Beer-Battered Vidalia Onion Rings 61
117. Sea Scallops and Bacon Kabobs 61
118. Coconut Banana Chips............. 61
119. Chili-Lime French Fries 61
120. Easy Toasted Nuts 62
121. Eggplant Parm Chips................. 62
122. Cinnamon Pear Chips 62
123. Mexican Crunchy Cheese Straws 62
124. Crunchy Roasted Chickpeas 62
125. Greek-Style Deviled Eggs 63
126. Baked Cheese Crisps............... 63
127. Puerto Rican Tostones.......... 63
128. Hot Roasted Cauliflower Florets 63
129. Green Bean Crisps 63
130. Southern Cheese Straws 64
131. Quick and Easy Popcorn 64
132. Crunchy Broccoli Fries.......... 64
133. Homemade Ranch Tater Tots 64
134. Beer Battered Vidalia Rings 65
135. Barbecue Little Smokies 65
136. Avocado Fries with Lime Sauce 65
137. Baby Carrots with Asian Flair 65
138. Kale Chips with Tahini Sauce 65
139. Greek-Style Squash Chips ... 66

140. Thyme-Roasted Sweet Potatoes 66
141. Cajun Cheese Sticks 66
142. Cocktail Cranberry Meatballs 66
143. Kale Chips with White Horseradish Mayo 67
144. Teriyaki Chicken Drumettes 67
145. Mexican Cheesy Zucchini Bites 67
146. Blue Cheesy Potato Wedges 67
147. Homemade Apple Chips 67
148. Easy and Delicious Pizza Puffs 68
149. Yakitori (Japanese Chicken Skewers) 68
150. Party Greek Keftedes 68
151. Paprika Zucchini Bombs with Goat Cheese 68
152. Cauliflower Bombs with Sweet & Sour Sauce 69

Classic Fried Rice 71

154. Bacon and Cheese Sandwich 71
155. Italian-Style Fried Polenta Slices 71
156. Savory Cheese and Herb Biscuits 71
157. Grilled Garlic and Avocado Toast 71
158. Aromatic Seafood Pilaf 72
159. Smoked Salmon and Rice Rollups 72
160. Pretzel Knots with Cumin Seeds 72
161. Fried Bread Pudding Squares 72
162. Sweet Potato Croquettes 72
163. Shawarma Roasted Chickpeas 73
164. Veggie Fajitas with Simple Guacamole 73
165. The Best Falafel Ever 73
166. Onion Rings with Spicy Ketchup 73
167. Barbecue Roasted Almonds 74
168. Green Beans with Oyster Mushrooms 74
169. Rainbow Roasted Vegetables 74
170. Peppers Provençal with Garbanzo Beans 74
171. Polenta Bites with Wild Mushroom Ragout 75
172. Paella-Style Spanish Rice 75
173. Chocolate Chip Bread Pudding Squares 75
174. Quick and Easy Cornbread . 75
175. Mediterranean Monkey Bread 76
176. Basic Air Fryer Granola 76
177. Easy Mexican Burritos 76
178. Savory Cheesy Cornmeal Biscuits 76
179. Tyrolean Kaiserschmarrn (Austrian Pancakes) 77
180. Famous Everything Bagel Kale Chips 77
181. Delicious Coconut Granola 77

- 182. Almost Famous Four-Cheese Pizza 77
- 183. Asian-Style Brussels Sprouts 77
- 184. Classic Honey Muffins 78
- 185. Healthy Oatmeal Cups 78
- 186. Old-Fashioned Greek Tiganites 78
- 187. Mediterranean Mini Monkey Bread 78
- 188. Traditional Italian Arancini 78
- 189. Spanish-Style Chorizo and Cheese Casserole 79
- 190. Easy Pizza Margherita 79
- 191. Sun-Dried Tomato and Herb Pull-Apart Bread 79
- 192. Last Minute German Franzbrötchen 79
- 193. Japanese Chicken and Rice Salad 80
- 194. Greek-Style Pizza with Spinach and Feta 80
- 195. Crème Brûlée French Toast 80
- 196. Southwestern Fried Apples 80
- 197. Italian Panettone Bread Pudding 81
- 198. Ciabatta Bread Pudding with Walnuts 81
- 199. Old-Fashioned Burritos 81
- 200. Authentic Prosciutto Bruschetta 81
- 201. Taco Stuffed Bread 82
- 202. Cheese and Bacon Ciabatta Sandwich 82
- 203. Ooey-Gooey Dessert Quesadilla 82
- 204. Easy Granola with Raisins and Nuts 82
- 205. Tofu in Sweet & Sour Sauce 83
- 206. Delicious Asparagus and Mushroom Fritters 83
- 207. Mashed Potatoes with Roasted Peppers 83
- 208. Marinated Tofu Bowl with Pearl Onions 83
- 209. Honey Cornbread Muffins 84
- 210. Fluffy Pancake Cups with Sultanas 84
- 211. New York-Style Pizza 84
- 212. Mexican-Style Brown Rice Casserole 84
- 213. Rich Couscous Salad with Goat Cheese 85
- 214. Classic Air Fryer Cornbread 85
- 215. Classic Pancakes with Blueberries 85
- 216. Golden Beet Salad with Tahini Sauce 85
- 217. Decadent Carrot Salad with Sultanas 86
- 218. Pearl Onions with Tahini Sauce 86
- 219. Italian-Style Tomato Cutlets 86
- 220. Authentic Platanos Maduros 86
- 221. The Best Potato Fritters Ever 86
- 222. Traditional Indian Pakora 87

223. Easy Crispy Shawarma Chickpeas 87
224. Famous Buffalo Cauliflower 87
225. Dad's Roasted Pepper Salad 87
226. Classic Baked Banana 88
227. Winter Squash and Tomato Bake 88
228. Barbecue Tofu with Green Beans 88
229. Buffalo Cauliflower Bites 88
230. Italian-Style Pasta Chips 89
231. Cinnamon Pear Chips 89
232. Hoisin-Glazed Bok Choy 89
233. Corn on the Cob with Spicy Avocado Spread 89
234. Rosemary Au Gratin Potatoes 89
235. Tofu and Brown Rice Bake . 90
236. Vegetable Kabobs with Simple Peanut Sauce 90
237. Classic Rizzi Bizzi 90
238. Air Grilled Cheese Roll-Ups 90
239. Favorite Cheese Biscuits 91
240. Favorite Spinach Cheese Pie 91
241. Delicious Sultana Muffins .. 91
242. Japanese Yaki Onigiri 91
243. Louisiana-Style Eggplant Cutlets 92
244. Classic Vegan Chili 92
245. Authentic Churros with Hot Chocolate 92
246. Aromatic Baked Potatoes with Chives 92
247. Warm Farro Salad with Roasted Tomatoes 93
248. Kid-Friendly Vegetable Fritters 93
249. Mediterranean-Style Potato Chips with Vegveeta Dip 93
250. Mom's Favorite Wontons 93
251. Everyday Mac and Cheese... 94
252. Chinese Spring Rolls 94
253. Easy Pizza Margherita 94
254. Authentic Tortilla Española 94
255. Cinnamon Breakfast Muffins 94
256. Polenta Fries with Sriracha Sauce 95
257. Sunday Glazed Cinnamon Rolls 95
258. Baked Tortilla Chips 95
259. Buckwheat and Potato Flat Bread 95
260. Fried Green Beans 95
261. Quinoa-Stuffed Winter Squash 96
262. Old-Fashioned Potato Wedges 96
263. Perfect Shallot Rings 96
264. Swiss Chard and Potato Fritters 96
265. Couscous with Sun-Dried Tomatoes 96
266. Greek-Style Roasted Vegetables 97
267. Easy Vegan "Chicken" 97

#	Title	Page
268.	Spicy Roasted Cashew Nuts	97
269.	Easy Tortilla Chips	97
270.	Famous Greek Tyrompiskota	98
271.	Mexicana Air Grilled Fish Tacos	98
272.	Festive Crescent Ring	98
273.	Apple Cinnamon Rolls	98
274.	Traditional Japanese Onigiri	98
275.	Honey Raisin French Toast	99
276.	Double Cheese Risotto Balls with Arrabbiata Sauce	99
277.	Delicious Turkey Sammies	99
278.	The Best Fish Tacos Ever	99
279.	Cheese and Bacon Crescent Ring	100
280.	Beef and Wild Rice Casserole	100
281.	Golden Cornbread Muffins	100
282.	Caprese Mac and Cheese	100
283.	Stuffed French Toast	101
284.	Broccoli Bruschetta with Romano Cheese	101
285.	Roasted Asparagus Salad	101
286.	Corn on the Cob with Mediterranean Sauce	101
287.	Bell Pepper Fries	102
288.	Crispy Butternut Squash Fries	102
289.	Caribbean-Style Fried Plantains	102
290.	Thai Sweet Potato Balls	102
291.	Gourmet Wasabi Popcorn	102
292.	Hungarian Mushroom Pilaf	103
293.	Healthy Mac and Cheese	103
294.	Ultimate Vegan Calzone	103
295.	Paprika Brussels Sprout Chips	103
296.	Cinnamon French Toast with Neufchâtel cheese	103
297.	Autumn Pear Beignets	104
298.	Oatmeal Pizza Cups	104
299.	Basic Air Grilled Granola	104
300.	Mexican-Style Bubble Loaf	104
301.	Hibachi-Style Fried Rice	105
302.	Classic Italian Arancini	105
303.	Spicy Seafood Risotto	105
304.	Risotto Balls with Bacon and Corn	106
305.	Puff Pastry Meat Strudel	106
306.	Beef Taquito Casserole	106
307.	Couscous and Black Bean Bowl	107
308.	Asian-Style Shrimp Pilaf	107
309.	Mediterranean Pita Pockets	107
310.	Crispy Pork Wontons	107
311.	Mexican Taco Bake	108
312.	Cornmeal Crusted Okra	108
313.	Tex Mex Pasta Bake	108
314.	Air Grilled Tofu	108
315.	Easy Roasted Fennel	109
316.	Korean-Style Broccoli	109

- 317. Cajun Celery Sticks 109
- 318. Cauliflower Oatmeal Fritters 109
- 319. Portobello Mushroom Schnitzel 110
- 320. Fried Parsnip with Mint Yogurt Sauce 110
- 321. Authentic Vegan Ratatouille 110
- 322. Crispy Garlic Tofu with Brussels Sprouts 110
- 323. Baby Potatoes with Garlic-Rosemary Sauce 111
- 324. Paprika Squash Fries 111
- 325. Green Potato Croquettes... 111
- 326. Easy Homemade Falafel.... 111
- 327. Spicy Sesame Cauliflower Steaks 112
- 328. Spicy Bean Burgers 112
- 329. Polish Placki Ziemniaczan 112
- 330. Favorite Lentil Burgers 112
- 331. The Best Crispy Tofu........... 113
- 332. Crunchy Eggplant Rounds 113
- 333. Indian Plantain Chips (Kerala Neenthram) 113
- 334. Garlic-Roasted Brussels Sprouts with Mustard 113
- 335. Italian-Style Risi e Bisi...... 113
- 336. Baked Oatmeal with Berries 114
- 337. Herb Roasted Potatoes and Peppers 114
- 338. Cinnamon Sugar Tortilla Chips 114
- 339. Cauliflower, Broccoli and Chickpea Salad 114
- 340. Butternut Squash Chili 115
- 341. Sunday Potato Fritters 115
- 342. Baked Spicy Tortilla Chips 115

Fish and Sea Food 116

- 343. Old Bay Crab Sticks with Garlic Mayo 117
- 344. Crispy Prawns in Bacon Wraps 117
- 345. Rosemary Cashew Shrimp 117
- 346. Mango Shrimp Skewers with Hot Sauce 117
- 347. Mediterranean Squid Rings with Couscous 117
- 348. American Panko Fish Nuggets 118
- 349. Cod Fillets with Ginger-Cilantro Sauce 118
- 350. Golden Cod Fish Fillets 118
- 351. Gourmet Black Cod with Fennel & Pecans 118
- 352. Tandoori Crispy Salmon.... 118
- 353. Salmon & Spring Onion Balls 119
- 354. Smoked Salmon Taquitos . 119
- 355. Trout with Dill-Yogurt Sauce 119
- 356. Lovely "Blackened" Catfish 119
- 357. Rosemary Catfish 119
- 358. Jamaican Catfish Fillets 120
- 359. Air-Fried Broiled Tilapia... 120
- 360. Hot Sardine Cakes............ 120

361. Japanese Ponzu Marinated Tuna 120
362. Basil White Fish with Cheese 120
363. Delicious Seafood Pie 121
364. Herbed Crab Croquettes.... 121
365. Basil Crab & Potato Patties 121
366. Chinese Garlic Prawns 121
367. Sesame Prawns with Firecracker Sauce 122
368. Cod Cornflakes Nuggets with Avocado Dip 122
369. Wild Salmon with Creamy Parsley Sauce 122
370. Baked Trout en Papillote with Herbs 122
371. Fried Catfish Fillets 122
372. Ale-Battered Fish with Tartar Sauce 123
373. Barramundi Fillets in Lemon Sauce 123
374. Peppery & Lemony Haddock 123
375. Peach Salsa & Beer Halibut Tacos 123
376. Oaty Fishcakes 123
377. Crab Fritters with Sweet Chili Sauce 124
378. Fiery Prawns 124
379. Ale-Battered Scampi with Tartare Sauce 124
380. Buttered Crab Legs 124
381. Herbed Garlic Lobster 124
382. Air-Fried Seafood 124
383. Soy Sauce-Glazed Cod 125
384. Cod Finger Pesto Sandwich 125
385. Pistachio-Crusted Salmon Fillets 125
386. Hot Salmon Fillets with Broccoli 125
387. Smoked Trout Frittata 125
388. Crumbly Haddock Patties .126
389. Effortless Tuna Fritters 126
390. Sesame Halibut Fillets 126
391. Smoked Fish Quiche 126
392. Delicious Coconut Shrimp 126
393. Louisiana-Style Shrimp...... 127
394. Asian Shrimp Medley.......... 127
395. Cajun-Rubbed Jumbo Shrimp 127
396. Breaded Scallops................... 127
397. Herbed Garlic Lobster 127
398. Kimchi-Spiced Salmon 128
399. Salmon Cakes 128
400. Mediterranean Salmon 128
401. Parmesan Tilapia Fillets 128
402. Air Fried Tuna Sandwich... 128
403. Spicy Shrimp with Coconut-Avocado Dip 129
404. Greek-Style Fried Mussels 129
405. Calamari Rings with Olives 129
406. Greek-Style Salmon with Dill Sauce 129
407. Cajun Mango Salmon 129
408. Simple Creole Trout............129

409. Fried Tilapia Bites 130
410. Colorful Salmon and Fennel Salad   130
411. Salmon Bowl with Lime Drizzle   130
412. Fish Sticks with Vidalia Onions   130
413. Classic Calamari with Mediterranean Sauce 131
414. Fish Cakes with Bell Pepper   131
415. Herb and Garlic Grouper Filets   131
416. Cajun Fish Cakes with Cheese   131
417. Crab Cake Burgers 132
418. Monkfish with Sautéed Vegetables and Olives 132
419. Cajun Cod Fillets with Avocado Sauce 132
420. Crispy Mustardy Fish Fingers   132
421. Snapper Casserole with Gruyere Cheese 133
422. Roasted Mediterranean Snapper Fillets 133
423. Halibut with Thai Lemongrass Marinade 133
424. Quick Thai Coconut Fish ... 133
425. Tuna Cake Burgers with Beer Cheese Sauce 134
426. Parmesan Chip-Crusted Tilapia   134
427. Easiest Lobster Tails Ever   134
428. Classic Crab Cakes 134

429. Grouper with Miso-Honey Sauce   135
430. Baked Sardines with Tangy Dipping Sauce 135
431. Southwestern Prawns with Asparagus 135
432. Classic Old Bay Fish with Cherry Tomatoes 135
433. Homemade Fish Fingers ... 135
434. Mom's Lobster Tails 136
435. Dijon Catfish with Eggplant Sauce   136
436. Tuna Steak with Roasted Cherry Tomatoes 136
437. Scallops with Pineapple Salsa and Pickled Onions 136
438. Vermouth and Garlic Shrimp Skewers 137
439. Korean-Style Salmon Patties   137
440. Cod and Shallot Frittata 137
441. Halibut Cakes with Horseradish Mayo 137
442. Authentic Mediterranean Calamari Salad 138
443. Sunday Fish with Sticky Sauce   138
444. Swordfish with Roasted Peppers and Garlic Sauce 138
445. Crusty Catfish with Sweet Potato Fries.. 138
446. Shrimp Kabobs with Cherry Tomatoes 139
447. Easy Creamy Shrimp Nachos   139
448. Keto Cod Fillets 139

449. Famous Tuna Niçoise Salad 139
450. Ginger-Garlic Swordfish with Mushrooms 140
451. Classic Pancetta-Wrapped Scallops 140
452. Melt-in-Your Mouth Salmon with Cilantro Sauce 140
453. Fried Oysters with Kaffir Lime Sauce 140
454. Salmon with Baby Bok Choy 140
455. Spicy Curried King Prawns 141
456. Crispy Tilapia Fillets 141
457. Grilled Salmon Steaks 141
458. Easy Prawns alla Parmigiana 141
459. Indian Famous Fish Curry 141
460. Old Bay Calamari 142
461. Greek-Style Roast Fish 142
462. Grilled Tilapia with Portobello Mushrooms 142
463. Filet of Flounder Cutlets 142
464. Crunchy Topped Fish Bake 143
465. Orange Glazed Scallops 143
466. Beer Battered Fish with Honey Tartar Sauce 143
467. Jamaican-Style Fish and Potato Fritters 143
468. Snapper with Coconut Milk Sauce 144
469. Salmon Fillets with Herbs and Garlic 144

470. Moroccan Harissa Shrimp 144
471. Garlic Butter Scallops 144
472. Anchovy and Cheese Wontons 144
473. Ahi Tuna with Peppers and Tartare Sauce 145
474. Seed-Crusted Codfish Fillets 145
475. Salmon Filets with Fennel Slaw 145
476. Tuna Steaks with Pearl Onions 145
477. Tortilla-Crusted Haddock Fillets 146
478. English-Style Flounder Fillets 146
479. Smoked Halibut and Eggs in Brioche 146
480. Quick-Fix Seafood Breakfast 146
481. Monkfish Fillets with Romano Cheese 146
482. Grilled Hake with Garlic Sauce 147
483. Shrimp Scampi Linguine ... 147
484. Buttermilk Tuna fillets 147
485. Shrimp Scampi Dip with Cheese 147
486. King Prawns with Lemon Butter Sauce 148
487. Creamed Trout Salad 148
488. Sea Bass with French Sauce Tartare 148
489. Double Cheese Fish Casserole 148

490. Rosemary-Infused Butter Scallops 149	511. Avocado & Mango Chicken Breasts 155
491. Italian-Style Crab Bruschetta 149	512. Easy Chicken Enchiladas ... 155
492. Greek Sardeles Psites 149	513. Ham & Cheese Filled Chicken Breasts 155
493. Thai-Style Jumbo Scallops 149	514. Sweet Wasabi Chicken 155
494. Halibut Steak with Cremini Mushrooms 150	515. Tasty Chicken Kiev 156
495. Marinated Flounder Filets 150	516. Tropical Coconut Chicken Thighs 156
496. Greek-Style Sea Bass 150	517. Sweet Mustard Chicken Thighs 156
497. Haddock Steaks with Decadent Mango Salsa 150	518. Crispy Drumsticks with Blue Cheese Sauce 156
498. Classic Fish Tacos 151	519. Thyme-Fried Chicken Legs 157
499. Halibut Steak with Zoodles and Lemon 151	520. Tarragon & Garlic Roasted Chicken 157
500. Easy Lobster Tails 151	521. Honey-Glazed Turkey 157
501. Saucy Garam Masala Fish . 151	522. Turkey Tenderloins with Fattoush Salad 157
502. Coconut Shrimp with Orange Sauce 152	523. Spice-Rubbed Jerk Chicken Wings 157
503. Delicious Snapper en Papillote 152	524. Sweet Chili & Ginger Chicken Wings 158
504. Dilled and Glazed Salmon Steaks 152	525. Sweet Sesame Chicken Wings 158

Poultry 153

505. One-Tray Parmesan Chicken Wings 154	526. Chicken Meatballs with Farfalle Pasta 158
506. South Asian Chicken Strips 154	527. Crispy Breaded Chicken Breasts 158
507. Crunchy Coconut Chicken Dippers 154	528. Spanish-Style Crusted Chicken Fingers 158
508. Buffalo Chicken Tenders ... 154	529. Crispy Chicken Tenderloins 159
509. Chicken Fillets with Sweet Chili Adobo 154	530. Herby Chicken Schnitzels with Mozzarella 159
510. Jamaican Chicken Fajitas . 155	

531. Gluten-Free Crunchy Chicken ... 159
532. Prosciutto-Wrapped Chicken Breasts 159
533. Gingery Chicken Wings ... 159
534. Air Fried Chicken Bowl with Black Beans ... 160
535. Rosemary & Oyster Chicken Breasts 160
536. French-Style Chicken Thighs 160
537. Chicken Thighs with Parmesan Crust ... 160
538. Thai Chicken Satay ... 160
539. Chicken & Baby Potato Traybake ... 161
540. Asian Sticky Chicken Wingettes ... 161
541. Portuguese Roasted Whole Chicken ... 161
542. Turkey Burgers with Cabbage Slaw 161
543. Turkey & Veggie Skewers .. 161
544. Turkey Strips with Garlic Mushrooms ... 162
545. Chipotle Buttered Turkey . 162
546. Thai Tom Yum Wings ... 162
547. Sweet Curried Chicken Cutlets 162
548. Almond-Fried Crispy Chicken ... 162
549. Chicken Thighs with Herby Tomatoes ... 163
550. Chicken Quarters with Broccoli & Rice ... 163
551. BBQ Whole Chicken ... 163
552. Whole Chicken with Prunes 163
553. Thyme Turkey Nuggets ... 163
554. Sticky Chicken Wings with Coleslaw ... 164
555. .Hot Chili Chicken Wings .. 164
556. Italian Parmesan Wings with Herbs 164
557. Homemade Chicken Patties 164
558. Rice Krispies Chicken Goujons ... 164
559. Chicken Pinchos with Salsa Verde 165
560. Crispy Chicken Tenders with Hot Aioli ... 165
561. Juicy Chicken Fillets with Peppers ... 165
562. Jerusalem Matzah & Chicken Schnitzels ... 165
563. Crumbed Sage Chicken Scallopini ... 166
564. Creamy Asiago Chicken ... 166
565. Hawaiian-Style Chicken ... 166
566. Creamy Onion Chicken ... 166
567. Garlicky Chicken on Green Bed 166
568. Cauli-Oat Crusted Drumsticks ... 166
569. Hot Green Curry Chicken Drumsticks ... 167
570. Chicken Asian Lollipop ... 167
571. Whole Chicken with Sage & Garlic ... 167
572. Moroccan Turkey Meatballs 167

573. Parmesan Turkey Meatballs 167
574. Roasted Turkey with Brussels Sprouts 168
575. Turkey Stuffed Bell Peppers 168
576. Greek-Style Chicken Wings 168
577. Authentic Mongolian Chicken Wings 168
578. Chicken & Jalapeño Quesadilla 168
579. Spiced Chicken Tacos 169
580. Chicken Fingers with Red Mayo Dip 169
581. Harissa Chicken Sticks 169
582. Balsamic Chicken with Green Beans 169
583. Chicken Breasts en Papillote 169
584. Chicken Teriyaki 170
585. Paprika Chicken Breasts ... 170
586. Spinach Loaded Chicken Breasts 170
587. Caprese Chicken with Balsamic Sauce 170
588. Double Cheese Marinara Chicken 170
589. Buttermilk Chicken Thighs 171
590. Chicken Thighs with Marinara Sauce 171
591. Sweet & Sticky Chicken Drumsticks 171
592. Whole Roasted Chicken 171
593. Turkey Fingers with Cranberry Glaze 171
594. Quinoa Chicken Nuggets ... 172
595. Chicken Skewers with Yogurt Dip 172
596. Tex-Mex Seasoned Chicken 172
597. Popcorn Chicken Tenders. 172
598. Cajun Chicken Tenders 172
599. Greek Chicken Gyros 173
600. Gruyère Chicken with Lemon 173
601. Lemony Chicken Breast 173
602. Apricot & Garlic Chicken Breasts 173
603. Chicken Cheesy Divan Casserole 173
604. Restaurant-Style Chicken with Yogurt 174
605. Texas BBQ Chicken Thighs 174
606. Luscious Enchilada Chicken Thighs 174
607. Honey Chicken Drumsticks 174
608. Easy Chicken Legs with Rice 174
609. Honey & Lemon-Glazed Stuffed Chicken 175
610. Greek-Style Whole Chicken 175
611. Roasted Chicken with Pancetta & Thyme 175
612. Chicken Parmigiana with Fresh Rosemary 175

Pork Beff & Lamb 176

613. Pork Loin with Roasted Peppers 177
614. Meatballs with Sweet and Sour Sauce 177
615. Korean Pork Bulgogi Bowl 177
616. Pork and Mushroom Kabobs 177
617. Chinese Five-Spice Pork Ribs 178
618. Pork Cutlets with Pearl Onions 178
619. Keto Crispy Pork Chops 178
620. Bacon with Onions Rings and Remoulade Sauce 178
621. Rustic Pizza with Ground Pork 178
622. Easy Pork & Parmesan Meatballs 179
623. Pork Shoulder with Molasses Sauce 179
624. Boston Butt with Salsa Verde 179
625. Blade Steaks with Butter-Fried Broccoli 179
626. Party Pork and Bacon Skewers 180
627. Pork Stuffed Peppers with Cheese 180
628. Festive Pork Fillets with Apples 180
629. Pork Cutlets with Plum Sauce 180
630. Meatloaf Muffins with Sweet Potato Frosting 181
631. Tagliatelle al Ragu 181
632. Greek Pork Loin with Tzatziki 181
633. Pork Ragout with Egg Noodles 182
634. Taco Casserole with Cheese 182
635. Ground Pork and Wild Rice Casserole 182
636. Fried Pork Loin Chops 182
637. Easy Munchy Pork Bites 183
638. Rustic Ground Pork-Stuffed Peppers 183
639. Country-Style Pork Goulash 183
640. Delicious Chifa Chicharonnes 183
641. Pineapple Pork Carnitas 184
642. Pork Sausage with Baby Potatoes 184
643. Easy Pork Pot Stickers 184
644. Chinese Char Siu Pork 184
645. Perfect Meatball Hoagies ... 185
646. Autumn Boston Butt with Acorn Squash 185
647. Pork Cutlets with a Twist ... 185
648. Cheesy Creamy Pork Casserole 185
649. Mexican-Style Ground Pork with Peppers 186
650. Smoky Mini Meatloaves with Cheese 186
651. Egg Noodles with Sausage-Pepper Sauce 186
652. Pork Loin with Mushroom Sauce 187

653. St. Louis-Style Pork Ribs with Roasted Peppers 187
654. Elegant Pork Chops with Applesauce 187
655. Spanish-Style Pork with Padrón Peppers 187
656. Filipino Pork Adobo 188
657. Spanish Pork Skewers (Pinchos Morunos) 188
658. Porterhouse Steak for Two 188
659. Dijon Mustard and Honey Roasted Pork Cutlets 188
660. BBQ-Glazed Meatloaf Muffins 189
661. Pork Tenderloin with Brussels Sprouts 189
662. Perfect Pork Wraps 189
663. Authentic Balkan-Style Cevapi 189
664. Sunday Meatball Sliders ... 190
665. Mexican Pork Quesadillas 190
666. Warm Pork Salad 190
667. Classic Fried Bacon 190
668. Herb-Crusted Pork Roast . 191
669. Balsamic Pork Chops with Asparagus 191
670. Spicy Bacon-Wrapped Tater Tots 191
671. Tender Spare Ribs 191
672. Pork Belly with New Potatoes 191
673. Authentic Spaghetti Bolognese 192
674. Perfect Sloppy Joes 192
675. Sausage and Mushroom Chili 192
676. Cracker Pork Chops with Mustard 192
677. Hawaiian Cheesy Meatball Sliders 193
678. Omelet with Prosciutto and Ricotta Cheese 193
679. Pork Leg with Candy Onions 193
680. Honey and Herb Roasted Pork Tenderloin 193
681. Pork Loin with Greek-Style Sauce 194
682. German-Style Pork with Sauerkraut 194
683. Tacos Al Pastor 194
684. Italian Nonna's Polpette 195
685. Caprese Pork Chops 195
686. The Best BBQ Ribs Ever 195
687. Texas Pulled Pork 195
688. Authentic Greek Pork Gyro 196
689. Pork Koftas with Yoghurt Sauce 196
690. Herbed Pork Loin with Carrot Chips 196
691. Italian-Style Honey Roasted Pork 197
692. Ground Pork and Cheese Casserole 197
693. Asian Sticky Ribs 197
694. Smoked Sausage with Sauerkraut 197
695. Easy Pork Sandwiches 198

#	Title	Page
696.	Sticky Dijon Pork Chops	198
697.	Easy Keto Pork Rinds	198
698.	Sri Lankan Pork Curry	198
699.	Herbed and Garlicky Pork Belly	198
700.	Ranchero Pork Kebabs	199
701.	Enchilada Bake with Corn and Cheese	199
702.	Dijon Ribs with Cherry Tomatoes	199
703.	Country-Style Pork and Mushroom Patties	199
704.	Japanese Ribs (Supearibu no Nikomi)	200
705.	Easy Minty Meatballs	200
706.	Italian Sausage Meatball Casserole	200
707.	Pigs in a Blanket with a Twist	200
708.	Mayo Roasted Sirloin Steak	200
709.	Porterhouse Steak with Tangy Sauce	201
710.	Filet Mignon and Green Bean Salad	201
711.	Grandma's Roast Beef with Harvest Vegetables	201
712.	Mediterranean Burgers with Onion Jam	201
713.	Traditional Italian Beef Braciole	202
714.	Mediterranean-Style Beef Steak and Zucchini	202
715.	Scotch Fillet with Sweet 'n' Sticky Sauce	202
716.	Beef Taco Roll-Ups with Cotija Cheese	202
717.	Meatballs with Cranberry Sauce	203
718.	Kid-Friendly Mini Meatloaves	203
719.	Mayonnaise and Rosemary Grilled Steak	203
720.	New York Strip with Pearl Onions	203
721.	Grilled London Broil with Mustard	204
722.	Beef Skewers with Pearl Onions and Eggplant	204
723.	Beef and Sausage Meatloaf with Peppers	204
724.	Korean Beef Bowl with Rice	204
725.	Birthday Party Cheeseburger Pizza	204
726.	Roasted Blade Steak with Green Beans	205
727.	Polish Sausage and Sourdough Kabobs	205
728.	Grilled Vienna Sausage with Broccoli	205
729.	Steak Fingers with Lime Sauce	205
730.	Classic Beef Ribs	205
731.	Spicy Short Ribs with Red Wine Sauce	206
732.	Beef Nuggets with Cheesy Mushrooms	206
733.	Asian-Style Beef Dumplings	206
734.	Paprika Porterhouse Steak with Cauliflower	206

735. Rustic Mini Meatloaves 207
736. Kansas City-Style Ribs 207
737. Greek-Style Roast Beef 207
738. Argentinian Beef Empanadas 207
739. Authentic Greek Souvlaki with Sauce 208
740. BBQ Glazed Beef Riblets ... 208
741. Beef Sausage-Stuffed Zucchini 208
742. Italian-Style Steak with Cremini Mushrooms 208
743. Tex-Mex Taco Pizza 208
744. Doubly Cheesy Meatballs .. 209
745. Taco Stuffed Avocados 209
746. Roasted Ribeye with Garlic Mayo 209
747. Quick Sausage and Veggie Sandwiches 209
748. Tender Marinated Flank Steak 209
749. Korean-Style Breakfast Patties 210
750. Indonesian Beef with Peanut Sauce 210
751. Authentic Dum Kebab with Raita Sauce 210
752. Moroccan-Style Steak Salad 211
753. Best Pretzel Sliders 211
754. Pastrami and Cheddar Quiche 211
755. Hungarian Oven Stew (Marha Pörkölt) 211

756. Ranch Meatloaf with Peppers 212
757. Cube Steak with Cowboy Sauce 212
758. Beef Kofta Sandwich 212
759. Beef Schnitzel with Buttermilk Spaetzle 213
760. Mom's Toad in the Hole 213
761. Chuck Roast with Sweet 'n' Sticky Sauce 213
762. Flank Steak with Dijon Honey Butter 213
763. Ritzy Cheesy Meatballs 213
764. Classic Filet Mignon with Mushrooms 214
765. Masala Dum Kabab 214
766. Marinated London Broil 214
767. Easy Beef Burritos 214
768. Grandma's Meat Tarts 214
769. Beef Parmigiana Sliders 215
770. Dad's Barbecued Ribs 215
771. London Broil with Herb Butter 215
772. American-Style Roast Beef 215
773. Beef and Broccoli Stir-Fry 215
774. Cuban Mojo Beef 216
775. Chicago-Style Beef Sandwich 216
776. Classic Beef Jerky 216
777. Dad's Meatloaf with a Twist . 216
778. Italian Piadina Sandwich .. 216
779. Sunday Beef Schnitzel 217
780. Dijon Top Chuck with Herbs 217

781.	Peperonata with Beef Sausage	217
782.	New York Strip with Mustard Butter	217
783.	Crustless Beef and Cheese Tart	217
784.	Barbecue Skirt Steak	218
785.	Cheesy Beef Burrito	218
786.	Beef and Vegetable Stir Fry	218
787.	Homemade Beef Empanadas	218
788.	Sunday Tender Skirt Steak	219
789.	Beef with Creamed Mushroom Sauce	219
790.	Burgers with Caramelized Onions	219
791.	Easy Asian Gyudon	219
792.	Juicy Strip Steak	219
793.	Filipino Tortang Giniling	220
794.	Minty Tender Filet Mignon	220
795.	Easy Beef Jerky	220
796.	Indian Beef Samosas	220
797.	Aromatic T-Bone Steak with Garlic	220
798.	Sausage Scallion Balls	221
799.	Beef Sausage Goulash	221
800.	Char Siew Pork Ribs	221
801.	Pork & Pear Blue Cheese Patties	221
802.	Maple Mustard Pork Balls	221
803.	Fennel & Sage Pork Sausage Balls	222
804.	Pork, Red Pepper & Mushroom Pinchos	222
805.	Stuffed Pork Tenderloin	222
806.	Sage-Rubbed Pork Loin	222
807.	Pork Chops with Mustard-Apricot Glaze	223
808.	French Pork Chops with Blue Cheese Butter	223
809.	Italian Pork Scaloppini	223
810.	Thyme Pork Escalopes	223
811.	Tangy Pork Belly with Herbs	223
812.	Healthy Burgers	224
813.	Mexican Beef Cabbage Wraps	224
814.	Mexican Chorizo & Beef Empanadas	224
815.	Italian Beef Meatloaf with Basil & Cheese	224
816.	Chimichurri New York Steak	224
817.	Chipotle Rib-Eye Steak with Avocado Salsa	225
818.	Beef Veggie Mix with Hoisin Sauce	225
819.	Korean Beef Bulgogi	225
820.	Spicy Sweet Beef with Veggie Topping	225
821.	Mexican Beef Quesadillas	226
822.	Thyme Lamb Chops with Asparagus	226
823.	LAMB Honey Barbecue Pork Ribs	226
824.	Sweet & Hot Pork Ribs	226
825.	Swedish Meatballs	226

826. Pork Sausage with Butter Bean Ratatouille ... 227
827. Paprika Pork Kabobs ... 227
828. Zesty Breaded Chops ... 227
829. Southeast-Asian Pork Chops 227
830. Roasted Pork Chops with Mushrooms ... 227
831. Juicy Double Cut Pork Chops 228
832. Stuffed Pork Chops ... 228
833. Pork Sandwiches with Bacon & Cheddar ... 228
834. Smoked Beef Burgers with Hoisin Sauce ... 228
835. Beef & Tomato Meatball Bake 228
836. Argentinian-Style Beef Empanadas ... 229
837. Chili Beef & Bean Casserole 229
838. Effortless Beef Short Ribs 229
839. Tender Rib Eye Steak ... 229
840. Sausage-Stuffed Beef Steak 229
841. Spice-Coated Beef Steaks ... 230
842. Thai Roasted Beef ... 230
843. Boeuf Stroganoff ... 230
844. Beef with Cauliflower & Carrots 230
845. Crunchy Beef Escalopes ... 230
846. African Minty Lamb Kofta 231
847. Traditional Lamb Kabobs . 231
848. Thyme Lamb Steaks with Potatoes ... 231
849. Lamb Taquitos ... 231
850. Roasted Pork Rack with Macadamia Nuts ... 231
851. Baby Back Pork Ribs with BBQ Sauce ... 232
852. Pork Meatball Noodle Bowl 232
853. Best Ever Pork Burgers ... 232
854. Pork Kofta Kebabs with Yogurt Sauce ... 232
855. Sausage Sticks Rolled in Bacon 233
856. Spicy Tricolor Pork Kebabs 233
857. Sweet Pork Tenderloin ... 233
858. Pork Lettuce Cups ... 233
859. Hungarian-Style Pork Chops 234
860. Mexican Pork Chops ... 234
861. Apple Pork Chops ... 234
862. Spicy-Sweet Pork Chops ... 234
863. Pork Escalopes with Beet & Cabbage Salad ... 235
864. Crispy Pork Schnitzel ... 235
865. Provençal Pork Medallions 235
866. Pork Belly the Philippine Style 235
867. South American Burgers ... 235
868. Beef Meatballs in Tomato Sauce 236
869. Greek-Style Beef Meatballs 236
870. California-Style Street Beef Taco Rolls ... 236

871. Classic Beef Meatloaf 236
872. Stefania Beef Meatloaf 236
873. Mini Beef Sausage Rolls 237
874. Ginger-Garlic Beef Ribs with Hot Sauce 237
875. Garlic Steak with Mexican Salsa 237
876. Gorgonzola Rib Eye Steak . 237
877. Parsley Crumbed Beef Strips 237
878. Homemade Hot Beef Satay 238
879. Pesto Beef Steaks 238
880. Beef Steak Fingers 238
881. Bloody Mary Beef Steak with Avocado 238
882. Burgundy Beef Casserole .. 238
883. Delicious Beef with Rice & Broccoli 239
884. Simple Roast Beef with Herbs 239
885. Wiener Beef Schnitzel 239
886. Beer-Dredged Corned Beef 239
887. Beef Liver with Onions 239

Vegetables & Side Dishes
.... 240

888. Serve Roasted Tomatoes with Cheese Topping 241
889. Authentic Spanish Patatas Bravas 241
890. Curly Coconut Fries 241
891. Crispy Bell Peppers with Tartare Sauce 241
892. Crunchy Parmesan Zucchini 242
893. Russian-Style Eggplant Caviar 242
894. Avocado Fries with Pico de Gallo 242
895. Cheese & Cauliflower Tater Tot Bites 242
896. Broccoli with Parmesan Cheese 243
897. Spicy Vegetable Skewers 243
898. Roasted Balsamic Veggies . 243
899. Classic French Ratatouille 243
900. Middle Eastern Veggie Kofta 243
901. Chili Falafel with Cheesy Sauce 244
902. African Vegetables with Fontina Cheese 244
903. Italian-Style Stuffed Mushrooms 244
904. Egg & Cauliflower Rice Casserole 244
905. Air Fried Veggie Sushi 245
906. Cheesy English Muffins 245
907. Crispy Mozzarella Rolls 245
908. Romanian Polenta Fries 245
909. Brussels Sprouts with Raisins & Pine Nuts 245
910. Mushroom Balls with Tomato Sauce 246
911. Spicy Sweet Potato French Fries 246
912. Brussels Sprouts with Garlic Aioli 246

- 913. Green Cabbage with Blue Cheese Sauce 246
- 914. Eggplant Steaks with Garlic & Parsley 247
- 915. Eggplant & Zucchini Chips 247
- 916. Breaded Italian Green Beans 247
- 917. Cholula Seasoned Broccoli 247
- 918. Tempura Veggies with Sesame Soy Sauce 248
- 919. Spicy Mixed Veggie Bake ... 248
- 920. Turmeric Crispy Chickpeas 248
- 921. Air Fried Ravioli 248
- 922. Easy Vegetable Croquettes 249
- 923. Hoisin Spring Rolls 249
- 924. Chili Roasted Pumpkin with Orzo 249
- 925. Greek-Style Stuffed Bell Peppers 249
- 926. Vegetable & Goat Cheese Tian 250
- 927. Cheesy Vegetable Quesadilla 250
- 928. Dilled Zucchini Egg Cakes 250
- 929. Cheesy Broccoli & Egg Cups 250
- 930. Vegetable Tortilla Pizza 251
- 931. Potato Filled Bread Rolls .. 251
- 932. Easy Fried Green Tomatoes 251
- 933. Roasted Brussels Sprouts . 251
- 934. Honey Baby Carrots 252
- 935. Sesame Balsamic Asparagus 252
- 936. Homemade Cipollini Onions 252
- 937. Easy Roasted Cauliflower . 252
- 938. Party Crispy Nachos 252
- 939. Winter Vegetable Delight .. 253
- 940. Green Vegetable Rotini Pasta Bake 253
- 941. Roasted Veggies with Penne Pasta 253
- 942. Tomato Sandwiches with Feta & Pesto 253
- 943. Mexican Chile Relleno 254
- 944. Homemade Pie with Root Vegetables 254
- 945. Plantain Fritters 254
- 946. Baked Mediterranean Shakshuka 254
- 947. Spanish-Style Huevos Rotos (Broken Eggs) 254
- 948. Delicious Potato Patties 255
- 949. Traditional Jacket Potatoes 255
- 950. Cheesy Potatoes & Asparagus 255
- 951. Easy Cabbage Steaks 255
- 952. Bulgarian Red Pepper "Burek" 255
- 953. Zesty Bell Pepper Bites 256
- 954. Green Pea Arancini with Tomato Sauce 256
- 955. Indian Fried Okra 256
- 956. Zucchini Fries with Tabasco Dip 257

- **957.** Cheesy Eggplant Schnitzels 257
- **958.** Effortless Eggplant Cheeseburger 257
- **959.** Air Fried Eggplant Toast 257
- **960.** Quick Beetroot Chips 258
- **961.** Tasty Balsamic Beets 258
- **962.** Aunt's Shallot & Carrot Bake 258
- **963.** Teriyaki Cauliflower 258
- **964.** Air Fried Parmesan Cauliflower 258
- **965.** Chili Corn on the Cob 259
- **966.** Zucchini & Turnip Bake 259
- **967.** Vegetable Bean Burgers 259
- **968.** Roasted Squash with Goat Cheese 259
- **969.** Nutty Pumpkin with Blue Cheese 260
- **970.** Indian Aloo Tikki 260
- **971.** Garlicky Vegetable Spread 260
- **972.** Root Vegetable Medley 260
- **973.** Crispy Fried Tofu 261
- **974.** Cashew & Chickpea Balls 261
- **975.** Fava Bean Falafel with Tzatziki 261
- **976.** Halloumi Cheese with Veggies 261
- **977.** Eggplant Gratin with Mozzarella Crust 262
- **978.** Quinoa & Veggie Stuffed Peppers 262
- **979.** Poblano & Tomato Stuffed Squash 262
- **980.** Chickpea & Spinach Casserole 262
- **981.** Jalapeño & Bean Tacos 263
- **982.** Southern-Style Corn Cakes 263

Desserts 264

- **983.** French Sour Cherry Clafoutis 265
- **984.** Classic Crème Brûlée 265
- **985.** Apple Caramel Relish 265
- **986.** White Chocolate Pudding 265
- **987.** Madrid-Style Almond Meringues 266
- **988.** Cinnamon Grilled Pineapples 266
- **989.** Dark Rum Pear Pie 266
- **990.** Tropical Pineapple Fritters 266
- **991.** Chocolate Soufflé 266
- **992.** Apricot & Lemon Flapjacks 267
- **993.** Molten Lava Cake 267
- **994.** Blueberry Muffins 267
- **995.** Spanish Churros con Chocolate 267
- **996.** Mock Cherry Pie 268
- **997.** Vanilla & Chocolate Brownies 268
- **998.** Orange Sponge Cake 268
- **999.** Chocolate & Raspberry Cake 268
- **1000.** Lemon-Glazed Cupcakes 269
- **1001.** Peach Almond Flour Cake 269
- **1002.** Air Fried Donuts 269

- **1003.** Mom's Lemon Curd 269
- **1004.** Snickerdoodle Poppers 269
- **1005.** Chocolate & Peanut Butter Fondants 270
- **1006.** Awesome Chocolate Fudge 270
- **1007.** Easy Lemony Cheesecake . 270
- **1008.** Oat & Walnut Granola 270
- **1009.** Soft Buttermilk Biscuits 271
- **1010.** Easy Chocolate Squares 271
- **1011.** White Chocolate Cookies .. 271
- **1012.** Effortless Pecan Pie 271
- **1013.** Pineapple Cake 271
- **1014.** Simple Coffee Cake 272
- **1015.** Yummy Moon Pie 272
- **1016.** Honey & Cherry Rice 272
- **1017.** No Flour Lime Cupcakes ... 272
- **1018.** Cheat Apple Pie 272
- **1019.** Fruit Skewers 273
- **1020.** Homemade Chelsea Currant Buns 273
- **1021.** Chocolate Mug Cake 273
- **1022.** Mini Apple and Cranberry Crisp Cakes 273
- **1023.** Old-Fashioned Baked Pears 274
- **1024.** Honey-Drizzled Banana Fritters 274
- **1025.** Easy Monkey Rolls 274
- **1026.** Dessert French Toast with Blackberries 274
- **1027.** Chocolate Apple Chips 274
- **1028.** Peppermint Chocolate Cheesecake 275
- **1029.** Chocolate Biscuit Sandwich Cookies 275
- **1030.** Country Pie with Walnuts . 275
- **1031.** Rustic Baked Apples 275
- **1032.** Coconut Chip Cookies 276
- **1033.** Chocolate Birthday Cake ... 276
- **1034.** Baked Fruit Compote with Coconut Chips 276
- **1035.** Greek-Style Griddle Cakes 277
- **1036.** Coconut Pancake Cups 277
- **1037.** Classic Butter Cake 277
- **1038.** Pop Tarts with Homemade Strawberry Jam 277
- **1039.** Old-Fashioned Plum Dumplings 278
- **1040.** White Chocolate Rum Molten Cake 278
- **1041.** Coconut Cheesecake Bites 278
- **1042.** Old-Fashioned Pinch-Me Cake with Walnuts 278
- **1043.** Air Grilled Peaches with Cinnamon-Sugar Butter 279
- **1044.** Crunchy French Toast Sticks 279
- **1045.** Blueberry Fritters with Cinnamon Sugar 279
- **1046.** Summer Fruit Pie 279
- **1047.** Cinnamon-Streusel Coffeecake 280
- **1048.** Chocolate Chip Banana Crepes 280
- **1049.** Sweet Dough Dippers 280

1050. Baked Banana with Chocolate Glaze ... 280
1051. Classic Brownie Cupcakes 281
1052. Old-Fashioned Donuts ... 281
1053. Apricot and Almond Crumble 281
1054. Greek Roasted Figs with Yiaourti me Meli ... 281
1055. Panettone Pudding Tart ... 282
1056. Banana Chips with Chocolate Glaze 282
1057. Favorite Apple Crisp ... 282
1058. Cinnamon and Sugar Sweet Potato Fries ... 282
1059. Chocolate Raspberry Wontons ... 283
1060. Sunday Banana Chocolate Cookies ... 283
1061. Chocolate and Peanut Butter Brownies ... 283
1062. English-Style Scones with Raisins 283
1063. Spanish-Style Doughnut Tejeringos ... 284
1064. Banana Crepes with Apple Topping ... 284
1065. Butter Rum Cookies with Walnuts ... 284
1066. Fall Harvest Apple Cinnamon Buns 285
1067. Summer Fruit Pie with Cinnamon Streusel ... 285
1068. Authentic Swedish Kärleksmums ... 285
1069. Strawberry Dessert Dumplings ... 286
1070. Old-Fashioned Apple Crumble ... 286
1071. Banana and Pecan Muffins 286
1072. Air Grilled Apricots with Mascarpone ... 286
1073. Lemon-Glazed Crescent Ring 287
1074. Authentic Spanish Churros 287
1075. Indian-Style Donuts (Gulgulas) ... 287
1076. Perfect English-Style Scones 287
1077. Sherry Roasted Sweet Cherries ... 288
1078. Apple Fries with Snickerdoodle Dip ... 288
1079. Classic Vanilla Mini Cheesecakes ... 288
1080. Light and Fluffy Chocolate Cake 288
1081. Cocktail Party Fruit Kabobs 289
1082. The Ultimate Berry Crumble 289
1083. Easy Chocolate and Coconut Cake 289
1084. Baked Peaches with Oatmeal Pecan Streusel ... 289
1085. Nana's Famous Apple Fritters 290
1086. Salted Caramel Cheesecake 290
1087. Pecan Fudge Brownies ... 290
1088. Pear Fritters with Cinnamon and Ginger ... 291

1089. Mom's Orange Rolls 291
1090. Sweet Potato Boats 291
1091. Classic Flourless Cake 292
1092. Mini Molten Lava Cakes 292
1093. Chocolate Peppermint Cream Pie 292
1094. Fluffy Chocolate Chip Cookies 292
1095. Baked Fruit Salad 293
1096. Chocolate Puff Pastry Sticks 293
1097. Red Velvet Pancakes 293
1098. Chocolate Lava Cake 293
1099. Grandma's Butter Cookies 294
1100. Cinnamon Dough Dippers 294
1101. Baked Coconut Doughnuts 294
1102. Bakery-Style Hazelnut Cookies 294
1103. Easy Chocolate Brownies .. 295
1104. Easy Blueberry Muffins 295
1105. Mocha Chocolate Espresso Cake 295
1106. Grilled Banana Boats 295
1107. Favorite New York Cheesecake 296
1108. Red Velvet Pancakes 296
1109. Summer Peach Crisp 296
1110. Authentic Indian Gulgulas 296
1111. Apricot and Walnut Crumble 297
1112. Fried Honey Banana 297
1113. Almond Chocolate CupCakes 297

Other Air Fryer Favorites
.... 298

1114. Air-Fried Guacamole Balls 299
1115. Greek-Style Frittata 299
1116. Cornbread Muffins with Raisins 299
1117. Classic French Potato Galette 299
1118. Taco Rolls with A Twist 300
1119. Easy Greek Revithokeftedes 300
1120. Rosemary Roasted Mixed Nuts 300
1121. Jamaican Cornmeal Pudding 300
1122. Traditional Onion Bhaji 301
1123. Baked Eggs Florentine 301
1124. Classic Egg Salad 301
1125. Southwest Bean Potpie 301
1126. French Toast with Blueberries and Honey 301
1127. Famous Western Eggs 302
1128. Easy Roasted Hot Dogs 302
1129. Bourbon Glazed Mango with Walnuts 302
1130. Salted Pretzel Crescents 302
1131. Party Pancake Kabobs 302
1132. Red Currant Cupcakes 303
1133. Cranberry Cornbread Muffins 303
1134. Sweet Corn and Kernel Fritters 303
1135. Creamed Cajun Chicken 303

1136.	Grilled Chicken Tikka Masala 304	1159.	Farmer's Breakfast Deviled Eggs 309
1137.	Tangy Paprika Chicken 304	1160.	Brown Rice Bowl 309
1138.	Roasted Turkey Sausage with Potatoes 304	1161.	Delicious Hot Fruit Bake ... 309
1139.	Super Easy Sage and Lime Wings 304	1162.	Country-Style Apple Fries .309
1140.	Cajun Turkey Meatloaf 305	1163.	Italian Sausage and Veggie Bake 309
1141.	Cornbread with Pulled Pork 305	1164.	Quinoa with Baked Eggs and Bacon 310
1142.	Easiest Pork Chops Ever 305	1165.	English Muffins with a Twist 310
1143.	Sausage, Pepper and Fontina Frittata 305	1166.	Mediterranean Roasted Vegetable and Bean Salad 310
1144.	The Best London Broil Ever 306	1167.	Crunch-Crunch Party Mix .310
1145.	All-In-One Spicy Spaghetti with Beef 306	1168.	Easy Fried Button Mushrooms 310
1146.	Beef and Kale Omelet 306	1169.	Creamed Asparagus and Egg Salad 311
1147.	Spanish Bolitas de Queso .. 306	1170.	Spring Chocolate Doughnuts 311
1148.	Pumpkin Griddle Cake 306		
1149.	Coconut Chip Cookies 307	1171.	Scrambled Eggs with Spinach and Tomato 311
1150.	Apple Oatmeal Cups 307		
1151.	Mini Banana Bread Loaves 307	1172.	Potato Appetizer with Garlic-Mayo Sauce 311
1152.	Air-Fried Popcorn 307	1173.	Potato and Kale Croquettes 312
1153.	Spicy Polenta Fries 307		
1154.	Salted Pretzel Croissants .. 308	1174.	Cheese and Chive Stuffed Chicken Rolls 312
1155.	Air-Grilled Sweet English Muffin 308	1175.	Dinner Avocado Chicken Sliders 312
1156.	Mediterranean Keto Bread 308	1176.	Cheesy Pasilla Turkey 312
1157.	Baked Eggs in Dinner Rolls 308	1177.	Creamy Lemon Turkey 313
		1178.	Easy Pork Burgers with Blue Cheese 313
1158.	Mini Raspberry Pies 308	1179.	Grilled Lemony Pork Chops 313

1180. Old-Fashioned Beef Stroganoff 313
1181. Beer-Braised Short Loin ... 314
1182. Traditional Greek Revithokeftedes 314
1183. Malaysian Sweet Potato Balls 314
1184. Broccoli and Ham Croquettes 314
1185. Easy Fluffy Flapjacks 314
1186. Air-Grilled Fruit Skewers . 315
1187. Air Grilled Yam Skewers ... 315
1188. Mini Espresso Brownies ... 315
1189. Philadelphia Mushroom Omelet 315
1190. Fingerling Potatoes with Cashew Sauce 316
1191. Grilled Cheese Sandwich .. 316
1192. Scrambled Eggs with Sausage 316
1193. Easiest Vegan Burrito Ever 316
1194. Mozzarella Stick Nachos ... 317
1195. Easy Zucchini Chips 317
1196. Sweet Mini Monkey Rolls . 317

1197. Crispy Wontons with Asian Dipping Sauce 317
1198. Spicy Cheesy Risotto Balls 318
1199. Spicy Potato Wedges 318
1200. Lamb Meat Balls whit Roasted Veggie Salad 318
1201. Sweet & Sour Lamb Strips 318
1202. Italian Sausage Peperonata Pomodoro 319
1203. Easy Homemade Hamburgers 319

Introduction

The air fryer has become the most popular and trendy kitchen appliance this year. But why are people excited about it? Why has it become favorite of people who love fried food? Why is it promoting frying being healthy?

The air fryer is nothing like a typical deep fryer. This cooking utensil is much more like a small, stylish and self-contained oven that uses convection cooking method. It uses electrical element that heats the air in the fryer and then circulates it evenly around the food for its cooking. As a result, this hot air cooks the food in the fryer quickly and brings out the well-cooked food that is evenly browned and crunchy on the outside, but the inside of food stays moist and tasty.

With air fryer, frying your food is healthy. How? Air fryer only needs just a tiny sprit of oil or no oil at all to cook your cook. You can easily cook fries, chicken wings, onion rings and much more and still get crispy foods without the extra oil. And, compare to oven and deep-frying cooking, the foods from the air fryer especially fries are crispier and not dried out, making the food even more impressive.

Since air fryer is small than the oven, it circulates hot air around its fan quickly that cooks the food faster. Air fryer takes less time to reach the cooking temperature compare to an oven which may take 20 minutes or more to properly preheat and begin cooking. So, if you need to make your meals in a hurry, you will love the air fryer time-saving features.

Air fryer doesn't only just do frying. You can do so much more cooking with it! The air fryer can also roast, grill, stir-fry, broil and bakes, even cakes.

You can make fresh or frozen food in it or reheat the leftovers. Make use of air fryer additional accessories like cake pan, pizza pan, rotisserie rack, frill pan, steamer inserts to cook variety of foods.

If you live in a dorm, share house, or have a small kitchen, then you will surely appreciate the small size of air fryer. The air fryer comes in different sizes, but its small size can be of a coffee maker size, which won't take too much room on your kitchen counter. Hence, air fryer is easy to move or store away. The air fryer is also handy to take it on your travel ventures and placing it in your office kitchen to cook fresh food.

Most of the cooks don't enjoy the cleanup of kitchen utensils, but with air fryer, this won't be a trouble for you in any way. Air fryer just has a fryer basket and pan to clean, which is dishwasher safe and takes few minutes to wash up after cooking. And, the cooking basket or pan is non-stick, so food usually doesn't stick to it and instead, slides onto the plate easil

Before we move on, you might be wondering what an air fryer is exactly. Having made its debut in 2010, the air fryer is basically a kitchen appliance that fries without oil. Or, if need be, as little oil as possible. It does this by circulating hot

air quickly with a built-in fan, a process that builds temperatures high enough to mimic conventional frying. Because of this, air fryers can fry food without the hazards of traditional oil frying – such as oil burns or fire damage – and can do it in a more systematic, controlled manner.

Since an air fryer uses hot air, some may argue that it works the same as a conventional oven. One, however, must remember that the two appliances produce different results, often due to their differences in technology. While ovens apply the dry air and heat directly onto the dish and take longer cooking times, air fryers contain a technology that rapidly spirals air around the dish, resulting in faster cooking times and a more fried appearance. How to use an air fryer

Since 2010, there have been countless versions of the air fryer, often with different styles and mechanisms. That said, it's usually best to consult your service provider when it comes to how to use it, and if you're looking to replace your current brand with another, how it differs from your newer appliance. There are, however, some similarities:

Use the right attachment. Before anything else, clarify with the recipe what attachment you'll be needing for the dish. Do you need a mixer? A grill? And extra pan? Ensure that you have everything ready.

Unstick your pan. While air fryers don't need oil to work, not using oil often means a larger chance of certain dishes sticking to the pan or basket. That said, you can either mist the pan lightly with oil to keep your food from sticking or add parchment paper to it for a true oil-free alternative. Nonetheless, unsticking your pan is crucial.

Set the temperature. Whether you're using fahrenheit, celsius, or amount of wattage, be sure you set your fryer at the right temperature or power level, so it doesn't over or undercook your dish. Some air fryers also provide "modes," or cooking options, for certain types of food like fries and pastries.

Set the timer. Once you're done with your temperature, just set the timer as indicated in the recipe and let it fly. You can experiment a little with this. Also, you can also take out the pan every now and then to add more ingredients: or to check your cooking; all you need is to pause the machine.

Benefits of the air fryer

Use less fat and oil

Perhaps the top reason for using an air fryer is so you can cook using less fat and oil. No more cooking fries or spring rolls in a deep fryer filled with all that fattening oil. Now you can cook them in your air fryer using no more than a tablespoon of oil! The circulating hot oil cooks the fries, keeping the inside tender and the outside nice and crisp.

Your air fryer not only cuts down the amount of fat and oil you use, but it also reduces your daily calorie intake. When you use the air fryer, you'll be able to enjoy the foods you love while still eating a healthy diet. French fries when you're watching your weight? Absolutely! Eating healthy is all about consuming nutritious foods and still being able to enjoy those treats you love.

Fits perfectly on your kitchen countertop

You'll be using your air fryer a lot, so it's a good thing it fits so perfectly on any countertop in your kitchen. Air fryers only take up a small amount of room – leaving your kitchen neat and tidy. You'll be able to cook all kinds of delicious meals without making a mess in your kitchen. And all the air fryer accessories can be stored within the air fryer, keeping your kitchen uncluttered.

Ease and versatility

Depending on what model air fryer you have, there are many different features you can use. In fact, there are so many functions;

you'll never use your microwave or oven again to cook a meal. And all these functions are easy to use. This means you'll be able to cook with ease, without the hassle of using other kitchen appliances. All you need to do is get all the ingredients together for a recipe, pop them into the air fryer, and set the function, temperature, and timer. Then wait until your meal is cooked to perfection.

How to use your air fryer

Air fryers are designed to be super easy to use. Here's a little guide to get you started.

Choose a recipe

Choose a recipe that you can cook in your air fryer. Remember that most foods that you cook in your microwave or oven, or on the stovetop, can be prepared in the air fryer – except for those recipes that have a lot of fat or liquids.

Prepare the air fryer

Read through the recipe to the end, so you know what accessories you need for cooking. Some recipes call for using the basket, rack, or rotisserie that comes with the air fryer. Other recipes use cake or muffin pans that you can insert into the air fryer. Just be sure these pans fit into the fryer and are safe to use.

Prepare the ingredients

Gather the ingredients for the recipe and prep them according to the instructions. When prepped, put the ingredients into the air fryer or in the basket, rack, or pans within the air fryer. Use parchment baking paper or a light mist of oil spray to prevent food from sticking.

Never crowd food in the air fryer or over-fill. Food that is crowded in the air fryer won't cook evenly and can be raw and under-cooked. If you're preparing for a crowd, you may have to cook more than one batch.

Setting the temperature and time

Check the recipe for the correct temperature and time setting. You can set manually, or you can use the digital setting for the temperature and time needed for the recipe. Most air fryers also have preset functions that make it easy to set according to each recipe.

Check food during cooking

Many air fryer recipes require you to check the food while it's cooking so that it cooks evenly and doesn't over-cook. All you need to do is shake, flip, or toss the food to distribute it. Or for some recipes, you'll need to turn the food about halfway through when cooking so that it cooks and crisps thoroughly all the way through.

Cleaning the air fryer

Once the food is cooked, remove, and unplug the air fryer. Let it cool completely before cleaning. Follow the instructions that come with the fryer for proper cleaning. Never scrub or use abrasive cleaners when cleaning the fryer or the fryer accessories.

Cooking, Frying, Baking & Co. - What's The Difference?

Idfferent dishes require different preparation methods. But why are certain foods cooked, grilled, fried or steamed? And what else is there for new preparation methods? We introduce you to the most important methods.

Dampen

When steaming food is not prepared directly in the water but in steam. There are special pots with sieve insert, in which the food is put into it. You then cook with the lid closed. Even pressure cookers are suitable for steaming. Even more comfortable is the preparation in special dampfgargeräten. The beauty: the method is not only suitable for vegetables, but also for fish, meat and fruit.

The following advantages are offered by steaming:

Vitamins and nutrients are largely retained as the food does not come into direct contact with boiling water

Especially ideal for preserving the taste, shape and color of the food

Cook

When cooking food is placed directly in 100 ° c hot water. As a result, they cook quickly, but it is also the vitamins and nutrients to the collar. Because the higher the temperature, the more nutrients are lost. In addition, some foods change when in contact with boiling liquids. For example, the protein found in animal foods is solidified (e.g. In fish or eggs) and starch contained in foodstuffs.

When cooking food is heated in 100 ° c hot water Deep-fry

When frying foods are cooked in 180 to 220 ° c hot fat and thus quickly get an intense taste. The fryer is best suited for this, but theoretically, it can also be fried in a saucepan. It is important to use a fat with a high smoke point (e.g. Lard or coconut fat). In addition, the fat must be hot enough. Otherwise, the food will absorb too much of it and become a calorie bomb. The hot fat can be used up to three times but should be filtered after each use.

If you like it healthier and still do not want to do without fried food, you should resort to a hot air fryer. Here are usually a few drops of fat, because the food is cooked in the hot air. Your meals will not only have a much lower fat content compared to the traditional fryer - but your kitchen will also be spared the typical frying smell.

Frying is a popular preparation method - even for sweet potatoes

Roast

Whether almonds, coffee or nuts - when roasting pleasant flavors rise in the nose. In addition, the food obtained by the roasting a particularly good taste. It can be roasted with both fat and fat.

But beware: roasting also causes unwanted substances, such as furan. This was classified by the world health organization (who) as potentially carcinogenic. However, the furan content can be reduced by reducing food browning (for example, toasting toast).

To bake

The cooking in hot air normally takes place in the oven at temperatures between 100 and 250 ° c instead. Due to the dry heat, the food on the surface usually gets a tan or a crust. In addition to cakes, bread and pastries, casseroles are also prepared in this way. By the way: did you know that dough tans faster in dark ovens than in light ovens?

The oven is cooking food with hot air Stew

If food is cooked only in its own juice or with little liquid such as water, wine or broth, it is called stewing. Steaming can be done both in the oven (for example in aluminum foil or in the roasting pan) but also on the hotplate. In the latter case, you should use a shallow and large pot or pan with lid. A roman pot is also suitable for steaming. The browning of the food remains in the process. Since the foods are only exposed to medium heat while steaming, they retain more vitamins and minerals compared to cooking or grilling.

Stew

.

When stewing, foods such as meat are first sautéed in hot fat, quenched and then cooked in the sauce. Ideal for this is pots or roasters, each with a lid. The method is particularly suitable for meat and vegetables.

Grilling

At temperatures between 250 and 300 ° c, foods are cooked on a grill at high heat. Grilling is popular on charcoal, gas or electric grills, but also ovens have a grill function. You should be careful with dripping fat. If this meets the heat source, harmful substances can form.

When grilling caution with dripping grease is required Roast meat

When roasting, a distinction is made between long-term roasting with temperatures between 140 and 250 ° c, short-time roasting at 120 to 200 ° c and low-temperature roasting at 100 ° c:

Long-term roast: food, such as meat, is first seared with or without fat at high temperatures and then cooked.

Short-time roast: first, the food is fried in hot fat and then cooked at low temperatures ready. By the way, one variant of short-term roasting is sautéing, in which thinly cut foods are sautéed and then pivoted at high temperatures, for example in a wok.

Low-temperature cooking: the gentlest method of cooking, which takes place in the oven at a constant 80 ° c. A special form is vacuum cooking, or sous vide. Here, the food is first sealed in plastic bags and vacuumed before they are cooked at 50 to 85 ° c

Breakfast & Brunch

1. Blueberry Cream Cheese Toasts
INGREDIENTS (2 Servings)

2 eggs, beaten	1 ½ cups corn flakes	1 tbsp blueberry preserves
4 bread slices	⅓ cup milk ¼ tsp ground nutmeg	
1 tbsp sugar	4 tbsp whipped cream cheese	

DIRECTIONS (Prep + Cook Time: 15 minutes)

Preheat air fryer to 390 F. In a bowl, mix sugar, eggs, nutmeg, and milk. In a separate bowl, whisk the cream cheese and blueberry preserves. Spread the blueberry mixture on 2 bread slices. Cover with the remaining 2 slices to make sandwiches. Dip in the egg mixture, then thoroughly coat in cornflakes. Lay the sandwiches in the air fryer's basket and cook for 8 minutes, flipping once. Serve immediately.

2. Mediterranean Avocado Toast
INGREDIENTS (2 Serving)

2 slices thick whole grain bread	1 ripe avocado, pitted, peeled, and sliced	1 tbsp pinch of salt
4 thin tomato slices	1 tbsp olive oil	½ tsp chili flakes

DIRECTIONS (Prep + Cook Time: 7 minutes)

Preheat air fryer to 370 F. Arrange the bread slices on the fryer and toast on Bake mode. Add the avocado to a bowl and mash it up with a fork until smooth. Season with salt.

When the toasted bread is ready, remove it to a plate. Drizzle with olive oil and arrange the thin tomato slices on top. Spread the avocado mash on top. Sprinkle the toasts with chili flakes and serve

3. Onion & Cheddar Omelet
INGREDIENTS (2 Servings)

4 eggs	1 tsp soy sauce
3 tbsp cheddar cheese, grated	½ onion, sliced

DIRECTIONS (Prep + Cook Time: 20 minutes)

Preheat air fryer to 350 F. Whisk the eggs with soy sauce and mix in onion. Pour the egg mixture into a greased baking pan and place it in the fryer's basket. Bake for 12-14 minutes. Top with the grated cheddar cheese and serve right away. Best served with a tomato salad or freshly chopped scallions.

4. Bacon & Egg Sandwich
INGREDIENTS (1 Serving)

1 egg, fried	Salt and black pepper to taste	½ tbsp butter, softened
1 slice English bacon	2 bread slices	

DIRECTIONS (Prep + Cook Time: 10 minutes)

Preheat air fryer to 400 F. Spread butter on one side of the bread slices. Add the fried egg on top and season with salt and black pepper. Top with bacon and cover with the other slice of bread. Place in the fryer's cooking basket and AirFry for 4-6 minutes. Serve warm.

5. Spicy Egg & Bacon Tortilla Wraps
INGREDIENTS (3 Servings)

3 flour tortillas	3 slices bacon, cut into strips	3 tbsp cream cheese
2 eggs, scrambled	3 tbsp salsa	1 cup Pepper Jack cheese, grated

DIRECTIONS (Prep + Cook Time: 15 minutes)

Preheat air fryer to 390 F. Spread the cream cheese on the tortillas. Add the eggs and bacon and top with salsa. Scatter over the grated cheese and roll up tightly. Place in the fryer's basket and AirFry for 10 minutes or until golden. Cut in half and serve warm.

6. Grilled Apple & Brie Sandwich
INGREDIENTS (1 Serving)

2 bread slices	2 tsp butter
½ apple, thinly sliced	2 oz brie cheese, thinly sliced

DIRECTIONS (Prep + Cook Time: 10 minutes)

Spread butter on the outside of the bread slices and top with apple slices. Place brie slices on top of the apple and cover with the other slice of bread. Bake in the fryer for 5 minutes at 350 F. When ready, remove and cut diagonally to serve.

7. Turkey & Mushroom Sandwich
INGREDIENTS (1 Serving)

⅓ cup leftover turkey, shredded	2 tomato slices	1 hamburger bun, halved
⅓ cup sliced mushrooms, sauteed	½ tsp red pepper flakes	
½ tbsp butter, softened	Salt and black pepper to taste	

DIRECTIONS (Prep + Cook Time: 10 minutes)

Preheat air fryer to 350 F. Brush the bottom half with butter and top with shredded turkey. Arrange mushroom slices on top of the turkey. Cover with tomato slices and sprinkle with salt, black pepper, and red flakes. Top with the other bun half and AirFry in the fryer for 5-8 minutes until crispy.

8. Air Fried Sourdough Sandwiches
INGREDIENTS (2 Servings)

4 slices sourdough bread	2 slices ham	1 tomato, sliced
2 tbsp mayonnaise	2 lettuce leaves	2 slices mozzarella chees

DIRECTIONS (Prep + Cook Time: 20 minutes)

Preheat air fryer to 350 F. On a clean working board, lay the bread slices and spread them with mayonnaise. Top 2 of the slices with ham, lettuce leaves, tomato slices, and mozzarella. Cover with the remaining bread slices to form two sandwiches. AirFry for 12 minutes, flipping once. Serve hot.

9. Grilled Tofu Sandwich with Cabbage
INGREDIENTS (1 Serving)

2 slices of bread	¼ cup red cabbage, shredded	¼ tsp vinegar
1 slice tofu, 1-inch thick	2 tsp olive oil	Salt and black pepper to taste

DIRECTIONS (Prep + Cook Time: 20 minutes)

Preheat air fryer to 350 F. Add the bread slices to the air fryer basket and toast for 3 minutes; set aside. Brush the tofu with some olive oil and place in the air fryer to Bake for 5 minutes on each side.

Mix the cabbage, remaining olive oil, and vinegar. Season with salt. Place the tofu on top of one bread slice, place the cabbage over, and top with the other bread slice. Serve with cream cheese-mustard dip.

10. Sausage & Egg Casserole
INGREDIENTS (6 Servings)

1 lb ground sausages	1 green pepper, diced	1 cup cheddar cheese, shredded
6 eggs	1 yellow pepper, diced	Salt and black pepper to taste
1 red pepper, diced	1 sweet onion, diced	2 tbsp fresh parsley, chopped

DIRECTIONS (Prep + Cook Time: 20 minutes)

Place a skillet over medium heat on a stovetop. Add the sausages and cook until brown, turning occasionally, about 5 minutes. Once done, drain any excess fat derived from cooking and set aside.

Arrange the sausages on the bottom of a greased casserole dish that fits in your air fryer. Top with onion, red pepper, green pepper, and yellow pepper. Sprinkle the cheese on top.

In a bowl, beat the eggs with salt and pepper. Pour the mixture over the cheese. Place the casserole dish in the air fryer basket and bake at 360 F for 15 minutes. Serve warm garnished with fresh parsley.

11. Omelet Bread Cups
INGREDIENTS (4 Servings)

4 crusty rolls	½ tsp thyme, dried	2 tbsp heavy cream
5 eggs, beaten	3 strips cooked bacon, chopped	4 Gouda cheese thin slices

DIRECTIONS (Prep + Cook Time: 25 minutes)

Preheat air fryer to 330 F. Cut the tops off the rolls and remove the inside with your fingers. Line the rolls with a slice of cheese and press down, so the cheese conforms to the inside of the roll.

In a bowl, mix the eggs, heavy cream, bacon, and thyme. Stuff the rolls with the egg mixture. Lay them in the greased air fryer's basket and bake for 8-10 minutes or until the eggs become puffy, and the roll shows a golden brown texture. Remove and serve immediately.

12. Cheese & Ham Breakfast Egg Cups
INGREDIENTS (6 Servings)

4 eggs, beaten	½ cup Colby cheese, shredded	1 cup smoked ham, chopped
1 tbsp olive oil	2 ¼ cups frozen hash browns, thawed	½ tsp Cajun seasoning

DIRECTIONS (Prep + Cook Time: 20 minutes)

Preheat air fryer to 360 F. Gather 12 silicone muffin cups and coat with olive oil. Whisk the eggs, hash browns, smoked ham, Colby cheese, and Cajun seasoning in a medium bowl and add a heaping spoonful into each muffin cup.

Put the muffin cups in the fryer basket and AirFry 8-10 minutes until golden brown and the center is set. Transfer to a wire rack to cool completely. Serve.

13. Prosciutto, Mozzarella & Eggs in a Cup
INGREDIENTS (2 Servings)

2 bread slices	¼ tsp balsamic vinegar	Salt and black pepper to taste
2 prosciutto slices, chopped	2 tbsp mozzarella cheese, grated	Cooking spray
2 eggs	¼ tsp maple syrup	
4 tomato slices	2 tbsp mayonnaise	

DIRECTIONS (Prep + Cook Time: 20 minutes)

Preheat air fryer to 350 F. Grease 2 ramekins with cooking spray. Place one bread slice on the bottom of each ramekin. Place 2 tomato slices on top and divide mozzarella cheese between the ramekins. Crack the eggs over the mozzarella cheese. Drizzle with maple syrup and balsamic vinegar. Season with salt and pepper and Bake for 10 minutes in the fryer. Top with mayonnaise and serve.

14. Prosciutto & Mozzarella Bruschetta
INGREDIENTS (2 Servings)

½ cup tomatoes, finely chopped	3 prosciutto slices, chopped	1 tsp dried basil
3 oz mozzarella cheese, grated	1 tbsp olive oil	6 small French bread slices

DIRECTIONS (Prep + Cook Time: 7 minutes)

Preheat air fryer to 350 F. Add in the bread slices and toast for 3 minutes on AirFry mode. Remove and top the bread with tomatoes, prosciutto, and mozzarella cheese. Sprinkle basil all over and drizzle with olive oil. Return to the fryer and cook for 1 more minute, just to heat through. Serve warm.

15. Crustless Mediterranean Quiche
INGREDIENTS (2 Servings)

4 eggs	½ tbsp fresh basil, chopped	¼ cup onions, chopped
½ cup tomatoes, chopped	½ tbsp fresh oregano, chopped	½ cup milk
1 cup feta cheese, crumbled	¼ cup Kalamata olives, sliced	Salt and black pepper to taste

DIRECTIONS (Prep + Cook Time: 40 minutes)

Preheat air fryer to 340 F. Beat the eggs along with the milk, salt, and pepper. Stir in all the remaining ingredients. Pour the egg mixture into a greased baking pan that fits in your air fryer and place in the fryer. Bake for 30 minutes or until lightly golden. Serve warm with a green salad.

16. Mushroom & Chicken Mini Pizzas
INGREDIENTS (1 Serving)

½ cup chicken meat, thinly chopped	1 cup button mushrooms, sliced	1 tsp black pepper
¼ cup tomato-basil sauce	1 tsp Parmesan cheese, grated	½ tsp garlic powder

DIRECTIONS (Prep + Cook Time: 15 minutes)

Preheat air fryer to 400 F. Line a baking dish with parchment paper. In a bowl, combine chicken with garlic and pepper. Place spoonfuls of the chicken into the dish and flatten into rounds. AirFry for 8-10 minutes, remove, turn, and top with tomato-basil sauce, mushrooms, and Parmesan cheese. Slide in the fryer and continue cooking for 5-6 minutes more until golden. Serve.

17. Air Fried Italian Calzone
INGREDIENTS (4 Servings)

1 pizza dough	2 cups cooked turkey, shredded	½ tsp dried oregano
4 oz cheddar cheese, grated	1 egg, beaten	Salt and black pepper to taste
1 oz mozzarella cheese, grated	4 tbsp tomato paste	
1 oz bacon, diced	½ tsp dried basil	

DIRECTIONS (Prep + Cook Time: 20 minutes)

Preheat air fryer to 350 F. Divide the pizza dough into 4 equal pieces, so you have the dough for 4 pizza crusts. Combine the tomato paste, basil, and oregano in a small bowl. Brush the mixture onto the crusts; make sure not to go all the way and avoid brushing near the edges of each crust. Scatter half of the turkey on top and season with salt and pepper. Top with bacon, mozzarella and cheddar cheeses. Brush the edges with the beaten egg. Fold the crusts and seal with a fork. Bake for 10-12 minutes until puffed and golden, turning over halfway through the cooking time. Serve.

18. Soppressata Pizza
INGREDIENTS (2 Servings)

1 pizza crust	½ cup passata	4 oz soppressata, chopped
½ tsp dried oregano	½ cup mozzarella cheese, shredded	4 basil leaves

DIRECTIONS (Prep + Cook Time: 15 minutes)

Preheat air fryer to 370 F. Spread the passata over the pizza crust, sprinkle with oregano, mozzarella cheese, and finish with soppressata. Bake in the fryer for 10 minutes. Top with basil leaves to serve.

19. Italian Sausage Patties
INGREDIENTS (4 Servings)

1 lb ground Italian sausage	1 tsp red pepper flakes	¼ tsp garlic powder
¼ cup breadcrumbs	Salt and black pepper to taste	1 egg, beaten

DIRECTIONS (Prep + Cook Time: 20 minutes)

Preheat air fryer to 350 F. Combine all the ingredients in a large bowl. Make patties out of the mixture and arrange them on a greased baking sheet. Add to the fryer and AirFry for 15 minutes, flipping once.

20. Sausage Frittata with Parmesan
INGREDIENTS (2 Servings)

1 sausage, chopped	4 eggs	2 tbsp Parmesan cheese, shredded
Salt and black pepper to taste	1 tbsp olive oil	
1 tbsp parsley, chopped	4 cherry tomatoes, halved	

DIRECTIONS (Prep + Cook Time: 15 minutes)

Preheat air fryer to 360 F. Place tomatoes and sausages in the air fryer's basket and cook for 5 minutes. Remove them to a bowl and mix in eggs, salt, parsley, Parmesan cheese, olive oil, and black pepper. Add the mixture to a greased baking pan and fit in the fryer. Bake for 8 minutes. Serve hot.

21. Brioche Toast with Chocolate
INGREDIENTS (2 Servings)

- 4 slices of brioche
- 3 eggs
- 4 tbsp butter
- 6 oz milk chocolate, broken into chunks
- ½ cup heavy cream
- 1 tsp vanilla extract
- ½ cup maple syrup
- ½ tsp salt

DIRECTIONS (Prep + Cook Time: 15 minutes)

Preheat air fryer to 350 F. Beat the eggs with heavy cream, salt, and vanilla in a small bowl. Dip the brioche slices in the egg mixture and AirFry in the greased fryer for 7-8 minutes in total, shaking once or twice. Melt the chocolate and butter in the microwave for 60-90 seconds, remove, and whisk with a fork until well combined. Let cool slightly. When the brioches are ready, remove, and dip in the chocolate-butter mixture. Serve with a cup of tea and enjoy!

22. Crustless Broccoli & Mushroom Quiche
INGREDIENTS (4 Servings)

- 4 eggs, beaten
- 1 cup mushrooms, sliced
- 1 cup broccoli florets, steamed
- ½ cup cheddar cheese, shredded
- ½ cup mozzarella cheese, shredded
- 2 tbsp olive oil
- ¼ tsp ground allspice
- Salt and black pepper to tast

DIRECTIONS (Prep + Cook Time: 25 minutes)

Preheat air fryer to 360 F. Warm the olive oil in a pan over medium heat. Sauté the mushrooms for 3-4 minutes or until soft. Stir the broccoli for 1 minute; set aside. Put the eggs, cheddar cheese, mozzarella cheese, allspice, salt, and pepper in a medium bowl and whisk well. Pour the mushroom/broccoli concoction into the egg mixture and gently fold it in. Transfer the batter to a greased baking pan. Air fry for 5 minutes, then stir the mixture and air fry until the eggs are done, about 3-5 more minutes. Cut into wedges and serve.

23. Breakfast Egg Muffins with Shrimp
INGREDIENTS (4 Servings)

- 4 eggs, beaten
- 2 tbsp olive oil
- ½ small red bell pepper, finely diced
- 1 garlic clove, minced
- 4 oz shrimp, cooked, chopped
- 4 tsp ricotta cheese, crumbled
- 1 tsp dry dill
- Salt and black pepper to taste

DIRECTIONS (Prep + Cook Time: 35 minutes)

Preheat air fryer to 360 F. Warm the olive oil in a skillet over medium heat. Sauté the bell pepper and garlic until the pepper is soft, then add the shrimp. Season with dill, salt, and pepper and cook for about 5 minutes. Remove from the heat and mix in the eggs. Grease 4 ramekins with cooking spray. Divide the mixture between the ramekins. Place them in the fryer and cook for 6 minutes. Remove and stir the mixture. Sprinkle with ricotta and return to the fryer. Cook for 5 minutes until the eggs are set, and the top is lightly browned. Let sit for 2 minutes, invert on a plate, while warm and serve.

24. Zucchini Muffins
INGREDIENTS (4 Servings)

- 1 ½ cups flour
- 1 tsp cinnamon
- 3 eggs
- 2 tsp baking powder
- ½ tsp sugar 1 cup milk
- 2 tbsp butter, melted
- 1 tbsp yogurt
- 1 zucchini, shredded
- A pinch of salt
- 2 tbsp cream cheese

DIRECTIONS (Prep + Cook Time: 25 minutes)

Preheat air fryer to 350 F. In a bowl, whisk the eggs with sugar, salt, cinnamon, cream cheese, flour, and baking powder. In another bowl, combine the remaining ingredients, except for the zucchini. Gently combine the dry and liquid mixtures. Stir in zucchini. Grease the muffin tins with cooking spray and pour the batter inside them. Place in the air fryer and cook for 18 minutes. Serve warm or chilled.

25. Kiwi Muffins with Pecans
INGREDIENTS (4 Servings)

1 cup flour	1 tsp milk	¼ cup oats
1 kiwi, mashed	1 tbsp pecans, chopped	¼ cup butter, room temperature
¼ cup powdered sugar	½ tsp baking powder	

DIRECTIONS (Prep + Cook Time: 25 minutes)

Preheat air fryer to 350 F. Place the sugar, pecans, kiwi, and butter in a bowl and mix well. In another bowl, mix the flour, baking powder, and oats and stir well. Combine the two mixtures and stir in the milk. Pour the batter into a greased muffin tin that fits in the fryer and Bake for 15 minutes. Remove to a wire rack and leave to cool for a few minutes before removing from the muffin tin. Enjoy!

26. Banana & Hazelnut Muffins
INGREDIENTS (6 Servings)

¼ cup butter, melted	½ tsp vanilla extract	¼ cup hazelnuts, chopped
¼ cup honey	1 cup flour	¼ cup dark chocolate chips
1 egg, lightly beaten	½ tsp baking powder	
2 ripe bananas, mashed	½ tsp ground cinnamon	

DIRECTIONS (Prep + Cook Time: 30 minutes)

Spray a muffin tin that fits in your air fryer with cooking spray. In a bowl, whisk butter, honey, eggs, bananas, and vanilla until well combined. Sift in flour, baking powder, and cinnamon without overmixing. Stir in the hazelnuts and chocolate. Pour the batter into the muffin holes and fit in the air fryer. Cook for 20 minutes at 350 F on Bake, checking them around the 15-minute mark. Serve chilled.

27. Hearty Banana Pastry
INGREDIENTS (2 Servings)

3 bananas, sliced	2 puff pastry sheets, cut into thin strips
3 tbsp honey	1 cup fresh berries to serve

DIRECTIONS (Prep + Cook Time: 20 minutes)

Preheat air fryer to 340 F. Place the banana slices into a greased baking dish. Cover with pastry strips and drizzle with honey. Bake in the air fryer for 12 minutes until golden. Serve with berries.

28. Breakfast Banana Bread
INGREDIENTS (2 Servings)

1 cup flour	2 mashed bananas	¾ cup chopped walnuts
¼ tsp baking soda	¼ cup vegetable oil	¼ tsp salt
1 tsp baking powder	1 egg, beaten	2 tbsp peanut butter, softened
⅓ cup sugar	1 tsp vanilla extract	2 tbsp sour cream

DIRECTIONS (Prep + Cook Time: 30 minutes)

Preheat air fryer to 350 F. Sift the flour into a large bowl and add salt, baking powder, and baking soda; stir to combine. In another bowl, combine the bananas, vegetable oil, egg, peanut butter, vanilla, sugar, and sour cream; stir. Mix both mixtures and fold in the chopped walnuts. Pour the batter into a greased baking dish and fit in the fryer. Bake for 20-25 minutes until nice and golden. Serve chilled.

29. Mango Bread
INGREDIENTS (6 Servings)

½ cup butter, melted	1 tsp vanilla extract	1 tsp baking powder
1 egg, lightly beaten	3 ripe mangoes, mashed	½ tsp grated nutmeg
½ cup brown sugar	1 ½ cups flour	½ tsp ground cinnamon

DIRECTIONS (Prep + Cook Time: 30 minutes)

Line a loaf tin with baking paper. In a bowl, whisk melted butter, egg, sugar, vanilla, and mangoes. Sift in flour, baking powder, nutmeg, and ground cinnamon and stir without overmixing. Pour the batter into the tin and place it in the air fryer. Bake for 18-20 minutes at 330 F. Let cool before slicing and serve.

30. Sweet Bread Pudding with Raisins
INGREDIENTS (4 Servings)

8 bread slices, cubed	2 eggs	4 tbsp raisins
½ cup buttermilk	½ tsp vanilla extract	2 tbsp chopped hazelnuts
¼ cup honey	2 tbsp butter, softened	Ground cinnamon for garnish
1 cup milk	¼ cup sugar	

DIRECTIONS (Prep + Cook Time: 45 minutes)

Preheat air fryer to 350 F. Beat the eggs with buttermilk, honey, milk, vanilla, sugar, and butter in a bowl. Stir in raisins and hazelnuts, then add in the bread cubes to soak, about 10 minutes. Transfer to a greased tin and Bake the pudding in fryer for 25 minutes. Dust with ground cinnamon and serve.

31. Pumpkin & Sultanas' Bread
INGREDIENTS (6 Servings)

1 cup pumpkin, peeled and shredded	2 eggs	2 tbsp sultanas, soaked
1 cup flour	½ cup sugar	1 tbsp honey
1 tsp ground nutmeg	¼ cup milk	1 tbsp canola oil
½ tsp salt	2 tbsp butter, melted	
¼ tsp baking powder	½ tsp vanilla extract	

DIRECTIONS (Prep + Cook Time: 30 minutes + cooling time)

Preheat air fryer to 350 F. In a bowl, beat the eggs and add in pumpkin, sugar, milk, canola oil, sultanas, and vanilla. In a separate bowl, sift the flour and mix in nutmeg, salt, butter, and baking powder. Combine the 2 mixtures and stir until a thick cake mixture forms. Spoon the batter into a greased baking dish and place it in the air fryer. Bake for 25 minutes until a toothpick inserted in the center comes out clean and dry. Remove to a wire rack to cool completely. Drizzle with honey and serve.

32. Cherry & Almond Scones
INGREDIENTS (4 Servings)

2 cups flour + some more	½ cup sliced almonds	½ cup milk
⅓ cup sugar	¾ cup chopped cherries, dried	1 egg
2 tsp baking powder	¼ cup cold butter, cut into cubes	1 tsp vanilla extract

DIRECTIONS (Prep + Cook Time: 25 minutes)

Line the air fryer basket with baking paper. Mix together flour, sugar, baking powder, sliced almonds, and dried cherries in a bowl. Rub the butter into the dry ingredients with hands to form a sandy, crumbly texture. Whisk together egg, milk, and vanilla extract. Pour into the dry ingredients and stir to combine. Sprinkle a working board with flour, lay the dough onto the board, and give it a few kneads. Shape into a rectangle and cut into 9 squares. Arrange the squares in the air fryer's basket and cook for 14 minutes at 390 F. Work in batches if needed. Serve immediately.

33. French Toast with Vanilla Filling
INGREDIENTS (3 Servings)

6 slices white bread	¼ cup heavy cream	1 tsp ground cinnamon	1 tsp vanilla extract
2 eggs	⅓ cup sugar mixed with	6 tbsp caramel	Cooking spray

DIRECTIONS (Prep + Cook Time: 15 minutes)

In a bowl, whisk eggs, and heavy cream. Dip each piece of bread into the egg mixture. Coat the bread with sugar and cinnamon mixture. On a clean board, lay the coated slices and spread three of the slices with about 2 tbsp of caramel each around the center. Place the remaining three slices on top to form three sandwiches. Spray the air fryer basket with some cooking spray. Arrange the sandwiches into the fryer and cook for 10 minutes at 340 F, turning once

34. Toasted Herb & Garlic Bagel
INGREDIENTS (1 Serving)

1 tbsp butter, softened

¼ tsp dried basil

¼ tsp dried parsley

¼ tsp garlic powder

1 tbsp Parmesan cheese, grated

Salt and black pepper to taste

1 bagel, halved

DIRECTIONS (Prep + Cook Time: 10 minutes)

Preheat air fryer to 370 degrees. Place the bagel halves in the fryer and toast for 3 minutes on AirFry mode. Mix butter, Parmesan cheese, garlic, basil, and parsley in a bowl. Season with salt and pepper. Spread the mixture onto the toasted bagel and return to the fryer to AirFry for 3 more minutes. Serve.

35. Greek-Style Frittata
INGREDIENTS (4 Servings)

5 eggs

1 cup baby spinach

½ cup grape tomatoes, halved

½ cup feta cheese, crumbled

10 Kalamata olives, sliced

Salt and black pepper to taste

2 tbsp fresh parsley, chopped

DIRECTIONS (Prep + Cook Time: 30 minutes)

Preheat air fryer to 360 F. Beat the eggs, salt, and pepper in a bowl, combining well before adding the spinach and stirring until all is mixed. Pour half the mixture into a greased baking pan. On top of the mixture, add half of the tomatoes, olives, and feta. Cover the pan with foil, making sure to close it tightly around the edges, then place the pan in the air fryer and cook for 12 minutes. Remove the foil and cook for an additional 5-7 minutes, until the eggs are fully cooked. Place the finished frittata on a serving plate and repeat the above instructions for the remainder of the ingredients. Decorate with parsley and cut into wedges. Serve hot or at room temperature.

36. Spanish Chorizo Frittata
INGREDIENTS (2 Servings)

4 eggs

1 large potato, boiled and cubed

½ cup sweet corn

½ cup feta cheese, crumbled

1 tbsp parsley, chopped

1 chorizo sausage, sliced

2 tbsp olive oil

Salt and black pepper to taste

DIRECTIONS (Prep + Cook Time: 20 minutes)

Preheat air fryer to 330 F. Heat olive oil in a skillet over medium heat and cook the chorizo until slightly browned, about 4 minutes; set aside. In a bowl, beat the eggs with salt and black pepper. Stir in all of the remaining ingredients, except for the parsley. Grease a baking pan that fits your air fryer with the chorizo fat and pour in the egg mixture. Insert into the air fryer and Bake for 8-10 minutes until golden. Serve topped with parsley. Enjoy!

37. Morning Potato Skins
INGREDIENTS (4 Servings)

4 eggs

2 large russet potatoes, scrubbed

1 tbsp olive oil

2 tbsp cooked bacon, chopped

1 cup cheddar cheese, shredded

1 tbsp chopped chives

¼ tsp red pepper flakes

Salt and black pepper to taste

DIRECTIONS (Prep + Cook Time: 35 minutes)

Preheat air fryer to 360 F. Using a fork, poke holes in all sides of the potatoes, then cook them in the microwave on high for 5 minutes. Flip the potatoes and cook in the microwave for another 3-5 minutes. Test with a fork to make sure they are tender. Halve the potatoes lengthwise and scoop out most of the 'meat,' leaving enough potato, so the sides of the 'boat' don't collapse. Coat the skin side of the potatoes with olive oil, salt, and pepper for taste. Arrange the potatoes, skin down, in the lightly greased air fryer basket. Crack an egg and put it in the scooped potato, one egg for each half. Divide the bacon and cheddar cheese between the potatoes and sprinkle with salt and pepper. For a runny yolk, air fry for 5-6 minutes, and for a solid yolk, air fry for 7-10 minutes. Sprinkle with red pepper flakes and chives. Serve immediately.

38. Easy Breakfast Potatoes
INGREDIENTS (6 Servings)

- 4 large potatoes, cubed
- 2 bell peppers, cut into 1-inch chunks
- ½ onion, diced
- 2 tsp olive oil
- 1 garlic clove, minced
- ½ tsp dried thyme
- ½ tsp cayenne pepper
- Salt to taste

DIRECTIONS (Prep + Cook Time: 35 minutes)

Preheat air fryer to 390 F. Place the potato cubes in a bowl and sprinkle with garlic, cayenne pepper, and salt. Drizzle with some olive oil and toss to coat. Arrange the potatoes on an even layer on the greased air fryer basket. Air Fry for 10 minutes, shaking the basket once during the cooking time. In the meantime, add the remaining olive oil, garlic, thyme, and salt in a mixing bowl. Add in the bell peppers and onion and mix well. Pour the veggies over the potatoes and continue cooking in the air fryer for 5 minutes. At the 5-minute mark, shake the basket and cook for 5 minutes. Serve warm.

39. Buttered Eggs in Hole
INGREDIENTS (2 Servings)

- 2 bread slices
- 2 eggs
- Salt and black pepper to taste
- 2 tbsp butter

DIRECTIONS (Prep + Cook Time: 15 minutes)

Preheat air fryer to 360 F. Place a heatproof bowl in the fryer's basket and brush with butter. Make a hole in the middle of the bread slices with a bread knife and place on the heatproof bowl in 2 batches. Crack an egg into the center of each hole; season. Bake in the air fryer for 4 minutes. Turn the bread with a spatula and cook for another 4 minutes. Serve warm.

40. Air Fried Shirred Eggs
INGREDIENTS (2 Servings)

- 2 tsp butter
- 4 eggs
- 2 tbsp heavy cream
- 4 slices ham
- 3 tbsp Parmesan cheese, grated
- ¼ tsp paprika
- Salt and black pepper to taste
- 2 tsp chopped chives

DIRECTIONS (Prep + Cook Time: 20 minutes)

Preheat air fryer to 320 F. Arrange the ham slices on the bottom of a greased pie pan to cover it completely. Whisk one egg along with the heavy cream, salt, and pepper in a small bowl. Pour the mixture over the ham slices. Crack the other eggs on top and sprinkle with Parmesan cheese. AirFry for 14 minutes. Garnish with paprika and fresh chives and serve.

41. Loaded Egg Pepper Rings
INGREDIENTS (4 Servings)

- 4 eggs
- 1 bell pepper, cut into four ¾-inch rings
- 5 cherry tomatoes, halved
- Salt and black pepper to taste

DIRECTIONS (Prep + Cook Time: 15 minutes)

Preheat air fryer to 360 F. Put the bell pepper rings in a greased baking pan and crack an egg into each one. Season with salt and pepper. Top with the halved cherry tomatoes. Put the pan into the air fryer and air fry for 6-9 minutes, or until the eggs are have set. Serve and enjoy!

42. Pancake The German Way
INGREDIENTS (4 Servings)

- 3 eggs, beaten
- 2 tbsp butter, melted
- 1 cup flour
- 2 tbsp sugar, powdered
- ½ cup milk
- 1 cup fresh strawberries, sliced

DIRECTIONS (Prep + Cook Time: 30 minutes)

Preheat air fryer to 330 F. In a bowl, mix flour, milk, and eggs until fully incorporated. Grease a baking pan that fits in your air fryer with the butter and pour in the mixture. Place the pan in the air fryer's basket and AirFry for 12-16 minutes until the pancake is fluffy and golden brown. Drizzle powdered sugar and arrange sliced strawberries on top to serve.

43. Chili Hash Browns
INGREDIENTS (4 Servings)

1 lb potatoes, peeled and shredded	1 tsp chili flakes	Cooking spray
Salt and black pepper to taste	1 tsp onion powder 1 egg, beaten	
1 tsp garlic powder	1 tbsp olive oil	

DIRECTIONS (Prep + Cook Time: 25 minutes + cooling time)

Heat olive oil in a skillet over medium heat and sauté potatoes for 10 minutes; transfer to a bowl. After they have cooled, add in the egg, pepper, salt, chili flakes, onion powder, and garlic powder and mix well. On a flat plate, spread the mixture and pat it firmly with your fingers. Refrigerate for 20 minutes. Preheat air fryer to 350 F. Shape the cooled into patties. Grease the air fryer basket with cooking spray and arrange the patties in. Cook for 12 minutes on AirFry mode, flipping once. Serve warm.

44. Masala Omelet the Indian Way
INGREDIENTS (1 Serving)

1 garlic clove, crushed	½ tsp garam masala	1 tbsp fresh cilantro, chopped
2 green onions	2 eggs	Salt and black pepper to taste
½ chili powder	1 tbsp olive oil	

DIRECTIONS (Prep + Cook Time: 15 minutes)

Warm the olive oil in a skillet over medium. Add and sauté the spring onions and garlic for 2 minutes until softened. Sprinkle with chili powder, garam masala, salt, and pepper. Set aside. Preheat air fryer to 340 F. In a bowl, mix the eggs with salt and black pepper. Add in the masala mixture and stir well. Transfer to a greased baking that fits into your air fryer. Bake in the fryer for 8 minutes until golden, flipping once. Scatter your omelet with cilantro and serve immediately.

45. Japanese-Style Omelet
INGREDIENTS (1 Serving)

1 cup cubed tofu	¼ tsp ground coriander	1 tbsp green onions, chopped
3 whole eggs	¼ tsp cumin	¼ onion, chopped
Salt and black pepper to taste	1 tsp soy sauce	

DIRECTIONS (Prep + Cook Time: 20 minutes)

In a bowl, mix eggs, onion, soy sauce, coriander, cumin, black pepper, and salt. Add in cubed tofu and pour the mixture into a greased baking tray. Place in the air fryer and Bake for 8 minutes at 400 F. When ready, remove, and sprinkle with green onions to serve.

46. Three Meat Cheesy Omelet
INGREDIENTS (2 Servings)

1 beef sausage, chopped	1 cup mozzarella cheese, grated	1 tbsp ketchup
4 slices prosciutto, chopped	4 eggs	1 tsp fresh parsley, chopped
3 oz salami, chopped	1 green onion, chopped	

DIRECTIONS (Prep + Cook Time: 20 minutes)

Preheat air fryer to 350 F. Whisk the eggs with ketchup in a bowl. Stir in green onion, mozzarella, salami, and prosciutto. AirFry the sausage in a greased baking tray in the fryer for 2 minutes. Slide-out and pour the egg mixture on top. Cook for another 8 minutes until golden. Serve sliced with parsley.

47. Baked Kale Omelet
INGREDIENTS (2 Servings)

5 eggs	1 cup kale, chopped	½ tbsp fresh parsley, chopped
3 tbsp cottage cheese, crumbled	½ tbsp fresh basil, chopped	Salt and black pepper to taste

DIRECTIONS (Prep + Cook Time: 15 minutes)

Beat the eggs, salt, and pepper in a bowl. Stir in the rest of the ingredients. Pour the mixture into a greased baking pan and fit in the air fryer. Bake for 10 minutes at 330 F until slightly golden and set.

48. Orange Creamy Cupcakes
INGREDIENTS (4 Servings)

Lemon Frosting:

1 cup plain yogurt	1 orange, juiced	7 oz cream cheese
2 tbsp sugar	1 tbsp orange zest	

Cake:

2 lemons, seeded and quartered	¼ tsp salt	
½ cup flour + extra for basing	2 tbsp sugar	
1 tsp baking powder	2 eggs ½ cup butter, softened	
1 tsp vanilla extract	2 tbsp milk	

DIRECTIONS (Prep + Cook Time: 25 minutes)

In a bowl, add yogurt and cream cheese and mix until smooth. Add in orange juice and zest and whisk well. Gradually add the sugar and stir until smooth. Make sure the frost is not runny. Set aside. Place the lemon quarters in a food processor and process until pureed. Add in the flour, baking powder, softened butter, milk, eggs, vanilla extract, sugar, and salt. Process again until smooth. Preheat air fryer to 360 F. Flour the bottom of 4 cupcake cases and spoon the batter into the cases, ¾ way up. Place them in the air fryer and bake for 12 minutes or until the inserted toothpick comes out clean. Once ready, remove and let cool. Design the cupcakes with the frosting and serve.

49. Baked Avocado with Eggs & Cilantro
INGREDIENTS (1 Serving)

1 ripe avocado, pitted and halved	Salt and black pepper, to taste
2 eggs	1 tsp fresh cilantro, chopped

DIRECTIONS (Prep + Cook Time: 10 minutes)

Preheat air fryer to 400 F. Crack one egg into each avocado half and place in the air fryer. Bake for 8-12 minutes until the eggs are cooked through. Sprinkle with salt and black pepper and let cool slightly. Top with freshly chopped cilantro and serve warm.

50. Avocado Tempura
INGREDIENTS (4 Servings)

½ cup breadcrumbs	½ tsp salt 1 avocado, pitted, peeled, and sliced	½ cup liquid from beans

DIRECTIONS (Prep + Cook Time: 10 minutes)

Preheat air fryer to 360 F. In a bowl, add the crumbs and salt and mix to combine. Sprinkle the avocado with the beans' liquid and then coat in the crumbs. Arrange the slices in one layer inside the fryer and AirFry for 8-10 minutes, shaking once or twice. Serve warm

51. Coconut & Oat Cookies
INGREDIENTS (4 Servings)

¾ cup flour	¼ cup coconut flakes	½ cup powdered sugar
4 tbsp sugar	Filling:	1 tsp vanilla extract
½ cup oats	1 tbsp white chocolate, melted	
1 egg	4 tbsp butter	

DIRECTIONS (Prep + Cook Time: 30 minutes)

In a bowl, beat egg, sugar, oats, and coconut flakes with an electric mixer. Fold in the flour. Drop spoonfuls of the batter onto a greased baking sheet and cook in the air fryer at 350 F for 18 minutes on Bake. Let cool to firm up and resemble cookies. Cook in batches if needed. Meanwhile, prepare the filling by beating all ingredients together. Spread the filling on half of the cookies. Top with the other halves to make cookie sandwiches.

52. Blueberry Oat Bars
INGREDIENTS (12 bars)

2 cups rolled oats	½ tsp ground cinnamon	1 tsp vanilla extract
¼ cup ground almonds	2 eggs, lightly beaten	2 cups blueberries
¼ cup sugar	½ cup canola oil	
1 tsp baking powder	½ cup milk	

DIRECTIONS (Prep + Cook Time: 20 minutes)

Spray a baking pan that fits in your air fryer with cooking spray. In a bowl, add oats, almonds, sugar, baking powder, and cinnamon and stir well. In another bowl, whisk eggs, canola oil, milk, and vanilla. Stir the wet ingredients gently into the oat mixture. Fold in the blueberries. Pour the mixture into the pan and place it in the fryer. Cook for 10 minutes at 350 F. Let it cool on a wire rack. Cut into 12 bars.

53. Paprika Rarebit
INGREDIENTS (2 Servings)

4 slices bread, toasted	2 eggs, beaten	4 ½ oz cheddar cheese, grated
1 tsp smoked paprika	1 tsp dijon mustard	Salt and black pepper to taste

DIRECTIONS (Prep + Cook Time: 15 minutes) In a bowl, combine the eggs, mustard, cheddar cheese, and paprika. Season with salt and pepper. Spread the mixture on the toasts. AirFry the slices in the preheated air fryer for 10 minutes at 360 F.

54. Crispy Croutons
INGREDIENTS (4 Servings)

2 cups bread cubes	1 tsp dried parsley
2 tbsp butter, melted	Garlic salt and black pepper to taste

DIRECTIONS (Prep + Cook Time: 20 minutes)

Mix the cubed bread with butter, parsley, garlic salt, and black pepper until well coated. Place in the fryer's basket and AirFry for 6-8 minutes at 380 F, shaking once until golden brown. Use in soups.

55. Quick Feta Triangles
INGREDIENTS (3 Servings)

1 cup feta cheese	2 tbsp parsley, chopped	2 tbsp olive oil
1 onion, chopped	1 egg yolk	3 sheets filo pastry

DIRECTIONS (Prep + Cook Time: 30 minutes)

Cut each of the filo sheets into 3 equal-sized strips. Brush the strips with some olive oil. In a bowl, mix onion, feta, egg yolk, and parsley. Divide the mixture between the strips and fold each diagonally to make triangles. Arrange them on a greased baking pan and brush the tops with the remaining olive oil. Place in the fryer and Bake for 8 minutes at 360 F. Serve warm.

56. Roasted Asparagus with Serrano Ham
INGREDIENTS (4 Servings)

12 spears asparagus, trimmed	¼ cup Parmesan cheese, grated
12 Serrano ham slices	Salt and black pepper to taste

DIRECTIONS (Prep + Cook Time: 15 minutes)

Preheat air fryer to 350 F. Season asparagus with salt and black pepper. Wrap each ham slice around each asparagus spear from one end to the other end to cover completely. Arrange them on the greased air fryer basket and AirFry for 10 minutes, shaking once or twice throughout cooking. When ready, scatter with Parmesan cheese and serve immediately.

57. Flaxseed Porridge
INGREDIENTS (4 Servings)

1 cup steel-cut oats	1 tbsp peanut butter	1 cup milk
1 tbsp flax seeds	1 tbsp butter	2 tbsp honey

DIRECTIONS (Prep + Cook Time: 5 minutes)

Preheat air fryer to 350 F. Combine all ingredients in an ovenproof bowl. Place the bowl in the air fryer and Bake for 10 minutes. Let cool for a few minutes before serving.

58. Very Berry Breakfast Puffs
INGREDIENTS (4 Servings)

1 puff pastry sheet

1 tbsp strawberries, mashed

1 tbsp raspberries, mashed

¼ tsp vanilla extract

1 cup cream cheese

1 tbsp honey

DIRECTIONS (Prep + Cook Time: 20 minutes)

Preheat air fryer to 375 F. Roll the puff pastry out on a lightly floured surface into a 1-inch thick rectangle. Cut into 4 squares. Spread the cream cheese evenly on them. In a bowl, combine the berries, honey, and vanilla. Spoon the mixture onto the pastry squares. Fold in the sides over the filling. Pinch the ends to form a puff. Place the puffs on a lined with waxed paper baking dish. Bake in the air fryer for 15 minutes until the pastry is puffed and golden all over. Let it cool for 10 mins before serving.

Snacks & Appetizers

59. Italian-Style Tomato Chips
INGREDIENTS (2 Servings)

2 tomatoes, cut into thick rounds	Sea salt and fresh ground pepper, to taste	¼ cup Romano cheese, grated
1 teaspoon extra-virgin olive oil	1 teaspoon Italian seasoning mix	

DIRECTIONS (Prep + Cook Time: 20 minutes)

Preheat air fryer to 350 F.Toss the tomato sounds with remaining ingredients. Transfer the tomato rounds to the cooking basket without overlapping. Cook your tomato rounds in the preheated Air Fryer for 5 minutes. Flip them over and cook an additional 5 minutes. Work with batches. Serve warm.

60. Pecorino Romano Meatballs
INGREDIENTS (2 Servings)

½ pound ground turkey	2 tablespoons scallions, chopped	1 egg, beaten
2 tablespoons tomato ketchup	1 garlic clove, minced	½ teaspoon red pepper flakes, crushed
1 teaspoon stone-ground mustard	¼ Pecorino-Romano cheese, grated	Sea salt and ground black pepper, to taste

DIRECTIONS (Prep + Cook Time: 15 minutes)

In a mixing bowl, thoroughly combine all ingredients. Shape the mixture into 6 equal meatballs. Transfer the meatballs to the Air Fryer cooking basket that is previously greased with a nonstick cooking spray. Cook the meatballs at 360 degrees F for 10 to 11 minutes, shaking the basket occasionally to ensure even cooking. An instant thermometer should read 165 degrees F and serve

61. Italian-Style Tomato-Parmesan Crisps
INGREDIENTS (4 Servings)

4 Roma tomatoes, sliced	Sea salt and white pepper, to taste	4 tablespoons Parmesan cheese, grated
2 tablespoons olive oil	1 teaspoon Italian seasoning mix	

DIRECTIONS (Prep + Cook Time: 20 minutes)

Preheat air fryer to 350 F.Generously grease the Air Fryer basket with nonstick cooking oil. Toss the sliced tomatoes with the remaining ingredients. Transfer them to the cooking basket without overlapping. Cook in the preheated Air Fryer for 5 minutes. Shake the cooking basket and cook an additional 5 minutes. Work in batches. Serve with Mediterranean aioli for dipping, if desired. Enjoy!

62. Romano Cheese and Broccoli Balls
INGREDIENTS (4 Servings)

½ pound broccoli	1 shallot, chopped	½ teaspoon paprika
½ cup Romano cheese, grated	4 eggs, beaten	¼ teaspoon dried basil
2 garlic cloves, minced	2 tablespoons butter, at room temperature	Sea salt and ground black pepper, to taste

DIRECTIONS (Prep + Cook Time: 25 minutes)

Add the broccoli to your food processor and pulse until the consistency resembles rice. Stir in the remaining ingredients; mix until everything is well combined. Shape the mixture into bite-sized balls and transfer them to the lightly greased cooking basket. Cook in the preheated Air Fryer at 375 degrees F for 16 minutes, shaking halfway through the cooking time. Serve with cocktail sticks and tomato ketchup on the side.

63. Bruschetta with Fresh Tomato and Basil
INGREDIENTS (3 Servings)

½ Italian bread, sliced	2 ripe tomatoes, chopped
2 garlic cloves, peeled	1 teaspoon dried oregano Salt, to taste
2 tablespoons extra-virgin olive oil	8 fresh basil leaves, roughly chopped

DIRECTIONS (Prep + Cook Time: 15 minutes)

Place the bread slices on the lightly greased Air Fryer grill pan. Bake at 370 degrees F for 3 minutes. Cut a clove of garlic in half and rub over one side of the toast; brush with olive oil. Add the chopped tomatoes. Sprinkle with oregano and salt. Increase the temperature to 380 degrees F. Cook in the preheated Air Fryer for 3 minutes more. Garnish with fresh basil and serve. Serve and enjoy!

64. Root Vegetable Chips with Dill Mayonnaise
INGREDIENTS (4 Servings)

½ pound red beetroot, julienned	Sea salt and ground black pepper, to taste	1 teaspoon garlic, minced
½ pound golden beetroot, julienned	1 teaspoon olive oil	¼ teaspoon dried dill weed
¼ pound carrot, julienned	½ cup mayonnaise	

DIRECTIONS (Prep + Cook Time: 40 minutes)

Toss your veggies with salt, black pepper and olive oil. Arrange the veggie chips in a single layer in the Air Fryer cooking basket. Cook the veggie chips in the preheated Air Fryer at 340 degrees F for 20 minutes; tossing the basket occasionally to ensure even cooking. Work with two batches. Meanwhile, mix the mayonnaise, garlic and dill until well combined. Serve the vegetable chips with the mayo sauce on the side. and serve.

65. Paprika and Cheese French Fries
INGREDIENTS (2 Servings)

8 ounces French fries, frozen	½ cup Monterey-Jack cheese, grated	1 teaspoon paprika Sea salt, to taste

DIRECTIONS (Prep + Cook Time: 15 minutes)

Cook the French fries in your Air Fryer at 400 degrees F for about 7 minutes. Shake the basket and continue to cook for a further 6 minutes. Top the French fries with cheese, paprika and salt cheese. Continue to cook for 1 minute more or until the cheese has melted. Serve warm and enjoy!

66. Greek-Style Zucchini Rounds
INGREDIENTS (3 Servings)

½ pound zucchini, cut into thin rounds	¼ teaspoon ground bay leaf	2 tablespoons mayonnaise
1 teaspoon extra-virgin olive oil	Coarse sea salt and ground black pepper, to taste	½ teaspoon garlic, pressed
½ teaspoon dried sage, crushed	Greek dipping sauce: ½ cup Greek yogurt	
½ teaspoon oregano	½ teaspoon fresh lemon juice	

DIRECTIONS (Prep + Cook Time: 15 minutes)

Toss the zucchini rounds with olive oil and spices and place them in the Air Fryer cooking basket. Cook in the preheated Air Fryer at 400 degrees F for 10 minutes; shaking the basket halfway through the cooking time. Let it cool slightly and cook an additional minute or so until crispy and golden brown. Meanwhile, make the sauce by whisking all the sauce ingredients; place the sauce in the refrigerator until ready to serve. Serve the crispy zucchini rounds with Greek dipping sauce on the side. Serve warm.

67. Hot Cheesy Mushrooms Bites
INGREDIENTS (3 Servings)

1 teaspoon butter, melted	1 tablespoon fresh coriander, chopped	Sea salt and ground black pepper, to taste
1 teaspoon fresh garlic, finely minced	½ teaspoon hot sauce	
4 ounces cheddar cheese, grated	12 button mushrooms, stalks removed and chopped	
4 tablespoons tortilla chips, crushed		

DIRECTIONS (Prep + Cook Time: 10 minutes)

In a mixing bowl, thoroughly combine the butter, garlic, cheddar cheese, tortilla chips, coriander, hot sauce and chopped mushrooms. Divide the filling among mushroom caps and transfer them to the air Fryer cooking basket; season them with salt and black pepper. Cook your mushrooms in the preheated Air Fryer at 400 degrees F for 5 minutes. Transfer the warm mushrooms to a serving platter and serve at room temperature. Serve and enjoy!

68. Crunchy Wontons with Sausage and Peppers
INGREDIENTS (3 Servings)

20 (3-½-inch) wonton wrappers	½ teaspoon granulated garlic	1 teaspoon Sriracha sauce
½ pound beef sausage crumbled	1 tablespoon soy sauce	1 teaspoon sesame seeds, toasted
1 bell pepper, deveined and chopped	1 tablespoon rice wine vinegar	
1 teaspoon sesame oil	1 tablespoon honey	

DIRECTIONS (Prep + Cook Time: 20 minutes)

Mix the crumbled sausage with the chopped pepper and set it aside. Place wonton wrappers on a clean work surface. Divide the sausage filling between the wrappers. Wet the edge of each wrapper with water, fold the top half over the bottom half and pinch the border to seal. Place the wontons in the cooking basket and brush them with a little bit of olive oil. Cook the wontons at 400 degrees F for 8 minutes. Work with batches. In the meantime, whisk the sauce ingredients and set it aside. Serve the warm wontons with the sauce for dipping. Enjoy!

69. Pork Crackling with Sriracha Dip
INGREDIENTS (3 Servings)

- ½ pound pork rind
- Sea salt and ground black pepper, to taste
- ½ cup tomato sauce
- 1 teaspoon Sriracha sauce
- ½ teaspoon stone-ground mustard

DIRECTIONS (Prep + Cook Time: 40 minutes)

Rub sea salt and pepper on the skin side of the pork rind. Allow it to sit for 30 minutes. Then, cut the pork rind into chunks using kitchen scissors. Roast the pork rind at 380 degrees F for 8 minutes; turn them over and cook for a further 8 minutes or until blistered. Meanwhile, mix the tomato sauce with the Sriracha sauce and mustard. Serve the pork crackling with the Sriracha dip and enjoy!

70. Sweet Potato Chips with Chili Mayo
INGREDIENTS (3 Servings)

- 1 sweet potato, cut into 1/8-inch-thick slices
- 1 teaspoon olive oil
- Sea salt and cracked mixed peppercorns, to taste
- ½ teaspoon turmeric powder
- ⅓ cup mayonnaise
- 1 teaspoon granulated garlic
- ½ teaspoon red chili flakes

DIRECTIONS (Prep + Cook Time: 35 minutes)

Toss the sweet potato slices with olive oil, salt, cracked peppercorns and turmeric powder. Cook your sweet potatoes at 380 degrees F for 33 to 35 minutes, tossing the basket every 10 minutes to ensure even cooking. Work with batches. Meanwhile, mix the mayonnaise, garlic and red chili flakes to make the sauce. The sweet potato chips will crisp up as it cools. Serve the sweet potato chips with the chili mayo on the side.

71. Cheesy Potato Puffs
INGREDIENTS (4 Servings)

- 8 ounces potato puffs
- 1 teaspoon olive oil
- 4 ounces cheddar cheese, shredded
- ½ cup tomato sauce
- 1 teaspoon Dijon mustard
- ½ teaspoon Italian seasoning mix

DIRECTIONS (Prep + Cook Time: 15 minutes)

Brush the potato puffs with olive oil and transfer them to the Air Fryer cooking basket. Cook the potato puffs at 400 degrees F for 10 minutes, shaking the basket occasionally to ensure even browning. Top them with cheese and continue to cook for 2 minutes more until the cheese melts. Meanwhile, whisk the tomato sauce with the mustard and Italian seasoning mix. Serve the warm potato puffs with cocktail sticks and the sauce on the side. Serve warm.

72. Prosciutto Stuffed Jalapeños
INGREDIENTS (2 Servings)

- 8 fresh jalapeño peppers, deseeded and cut in half lengthwise
- 4 ounces Ricotta cheese, at room temperature
- ¼ teaspoon cayenne pepper
- ½ teaspoon granulated garlic
- 8 slices prosciutto, chopped

DIRECTIONS (Prep + Cook Time: 15 minutes)

Place the fresh jalapeño peppers on a clean surface. Mix the remaining ingredients in a bowl; divide the filling between the jalapeño peppers. Transfer the peppers to the Air Fryer cooking basket. Cook the stuffed peppers at 400 degrees F for 15 minutes. Serve and enjoy!

73. Pepper and Bacon Mini Skewers
INGREDIENTS (4 Servings)

- 4 ounces bacon, diced
- 2 bell peppers, sliced
- ¼ cup barbecue sauce
- 1 teaspoon Ranch seasoning blend
- ½ cup tomato sauce
- 1 teaspoon jalapeno, minced

DIRECTIONS (Prep + Cook Time: 10 minutes)

Assemble the skewers alternating bacon and bell pepper. Toss them with barbecue sauce and Ranch seasoning blend. Cook the mini skewers in the preheated Air Fryer at 400 degrees F for 6 minutes. Mix the tomato sauce and minced jalapeno. Bon appétit!

74. Hot Roasted Cauliflower Florets
INGREDIENTS (3 Servings)

- ½ cup plain flour
- ½ teaspoon shallot powder
- 1 teaspoon garlic powder
- ¼ teaspoon dried dill weed
- ½ teaspoon chipotle powder
- Sea salt and ground black pepper, to taste
- ½ cup rice milk
- 2 tablespoons coconut oil, softened
- 1 pound cauliflower florets

DIRECTIONS (Prep + Cook Time: 20 minutes)

In a mixing bowl, thoroughly combine the flour, spices, rice milk and coconut oil. Mix to combine well. Coat the cauliflower florets with the batter and allow the excess batter to drip back into the bowl. Cook the cauliflower florets at 400 degrees F for 12 minutes, shaking the basket once or twice to ensure even browning. Serve with some extra hot sauce, if desired. Enjoy!

75. Wonton Sausage Appetizers
INGREDIENTS (5 Servings)

- ½ pound ground sausage
- 2 tablespoons scallions, chopped
- 1 garlic clove, minced
- ½ tablespoon fish sauce
- 1 teaspoon Sriracha sauce
- 20 wonton wrappers
- 1 egg, whisked with
- 1 tablespoon water

DIRECTIONS (Prep + Cook Time: 20 minutes)

In a mixing bowl, thoroughly combine the ground sausage, scallions, garlic, fish sauce, and Sriracha. Divide the mixture between the wonton wrappers. Dip your fingers in the egg wash Fold the wonton in half. Bring up the 2 ends of the wonton and use the egg wash to stick them together. Pinch the edges and coat each wonton with the egg wash. Place the folded wontons in the lightly greased cooking basket. Cook at 360 degrees F for 10 minutes. Work in batches and serve warm. Serve warm.

76. Apple Chips with Walnuts
INGREDIENTS (2 Servings)

- 2 apples, peeled, cored and sliced
- ½ teaspoon ground cloves
- 1 teaspoon cinnamon
- ¼ cup walnuts

DIRECTIONS (Prep + Cook Time: 35 minutes)

Toss the apple slices with ground cloves and cinnamon. Place the apple slices in the Air Fryer cooking basket and cook at 360 degrees F for 10 minutes or until crisp. Reserve. Then, toast the walnuts at 300 degrees F for 10 minutes; now, shake the basket and cook for another 10 minutes. Chop the walnuts and scatter them over the apple slices and serve.

77. Southwestern Caprese Bites
INGREDIENTS (2 Servings)

- ½ pound cherry tomatoes
- 1 tablespoon extra-virgin olive oil
- ½ pound bocconcini, drained
- 2 tablespoon fresh basil leaves
- ½ teaspoon chili powder
- ½ teaspoon ground cumin
- ¼ teaspoon garlic powder
- Sea salt and ground black pepper, to taste

DIRECTIONS (Prep + Cook Time: 10 minutes)

Brush the cherry tomatoes with olive oil and transfer them to the cooking basket. Bake the cherry tomatoes at 400 degrees F for 4 minutes. Assemble the bites by using a toothpick and skewer cherry tomatoes, bocconcini and fresh basil leaves. Season with chili powder, cumin, garlic powder, salt and black pepper. Arrange on a nice serving platter Serve and enjoy!

78. Easy Mexican Elote
INGREDIENTS (2 Servings)

- 2 ears of corn, husked
- 4 tablespoons Mexican crema
- 4 tablespoons Mexican cheese blend, crumbled
- 1 teaspoon fresh lime juice
- Sea salt and chili powder, to taste
- 1 tablespoon fresh cilantro, chopped

DIRECTIONS (Prep + Cook Time: 10 minutes)

Cook the corn in the preheated Air Fryer at 390 degrees F for about 6 minutes. Mix the Mexican crema, Mexican cheese blend, lime juice, salt and chili powder in a bowl. Afterwards, insert a wooden stick into the core as a handle. Rub each ear of corn with the topping mixture. Garnish with fresh chopped cilantro. Serve immediately.

79. Salmon, Cheese and Cucumber Bites
INGREDIENTS (3 Servings)

- ½ pound salmon
- 1 teaspoon extra-virgin olive oil
- ½ teaspoon onion powder
- ¼ teaspoon cumin powder
- 1 teaspoon granulated garlic
- Sea salt and ground black pepper, to taste
- 2 ounces cream cheese
- 1 English cucumber, cut into 1-inch rounds

DIRECTIONS (Prep + Cook Time: 15 minutes)

Pat the salmon dry and drizzle it with olive oil. Season the salmon with onion powder, cumin, granulated garlic, salt and black pepper. Transfer the salmon to the Air Fryer cooking basket. Cook the salmon at 400 degrees F for 5 minutes; turn the salmon over and continue to cook for 5 minutes more or until opaque. Cut the salmon into bite-sized pieces. Spread 1 teaspoon of cream cheese on top of each cucumber slice; top each slice with a piece of salmon. Insert a tiny party fork down the center to keep in place. Enjoy!

80. Classic Jiaozi (Chinese Dumplings)
INGREDIENTS (3 Servings)

- ½ pound ground pork
- 1 cup Napa cabbage, shredded
- 2 scallion stalks, chopped
- 1 ounce bamboo shoots, shredded
- ½ teaspoon garlic paste
- 1 teaspoon fresh ginger, peeled and grated
- 8 ounces round wheat dumpling

Sauce:

- 2 tablespoons rice vinegar
- ¼ cup soy sauce
- 1 tablespoon ketchup
- 1 teaspoon deli mustard
- 1 teaspoon honey
- 1 teaspoon sesame seeds, lightly toasted

DIRECTIONS (Prep + Cook Time: 15 minutes)

Cook the pork in a wok that is preheated over medium-high heat; cook until no longer pink and stir in the Napa cabbage, scallions, bamboo shoots, garlic paste and ginger; salt to taste and stir to combine well. Divide the pork mixture between dumplings. Moisten the edge of each dumpling with water, fold the top half over the bottom half and press together firmly. Place your dumplings in the Air Fryer cooking basket and spritz them with cooking spray. Cook your dumplings at 400 degrees F for 8 minutes. Work with batches. While your dumplings are cooking, whisk the sauce ingredients. Serve the warm dumplings with the sauce for dipping. Enjoy!

81. Mint Plantain Bites
INGREDIENTS (3 Servings)

- 1 pound plantains, peeled and cut into rounds
- 1 teaspoon coconut oil
- A pinch of coarse sea salt
- 1 tablespoon mint leaves, chopped

DIRECTIONS (Prep + Cook Time: 10 minutes)

Start by preheating your Air Fryer to 350 degrees F. Brush the plantain rounds with coconut oil and sprinkle with coarse sea salt. Cook the plantain rounds in the preheated Air Fryer for 5 minutes; shake the basket and cook for a further 5 minutes or until golden on the top. Garnish with roughly chopped mint and serve. Enjoy!

82. Mexican-Style Corn on the Cob with Bacon
INGREDIENTS (3 Servings)

- 2 slices bacon
- 4 ears fresh corn, shucked and cut into halves
- 1 avocado, pitted, peeled and mashed
- 1 teaspoon ancho chili powder
- 2 garlic cloves
- 2 tablespoons cilantro, chopped
- 1 teaspoon lime juice
- Salt and black pepper, to taste

DIRECTIONS (Prep + Cook Time: 20 minutes)

Start by preheating your Air Fryer to 400 degrees F. Cook the bacon for 6 to 7 minutes; chop into small chunks and reserve. Spritz the corn with cooking spray. Cook at 395 degrees F for 8 minutes, turning them over halfway through the cooking time. Mix the reserved bacon with the remaining ingredients. Spoon the bacon mixture over the corn on the cob and serve immediately.

83. Paprika Potato Chips
INGREDIENTS (3 Servings)

3 potatoes, thinly sliced

1 teaspoon sea salt

1 teaspoon garlic powder

1 teaspoon paprika

¼ cup ketchup

Directions (Prep + Cook Time: 50 minutes)

Add the sliced potatoes to a bowl with salted water. Let them soak for 30 minutes. Drain and rinse your potatoes. Pat dry and toss with salt. Cook in the preheated Air Fryer at 400 degrees F for 15 minutes, shaking the basket occasionally. Work in batches. Toss with the garlic powder and paprika. Serve with ketchup. Enjoy!

84. Mini Plantain Cups
INGREDIENTS (3 Servings)

2 blackened plantains, chopped

¼ cup all-purpose flour

½ cup cornmeal

½ cup milk

1 tablespoon coconut oil

1 teaspoon fresh ginger, peeled and minced

A pinch of salt

A pinch of ground cinnamon

DIRECTIONS (Prep + Cook Time: 10 minutes)

In a mixing bowl, thoroughly combine all ingredients until everything is well incorporated. Spoon the batter into a greased mini muffin tin. Bake the mini plantain cups in your Air Fryer at 330 degrees F for 6 to 7 minutes or until golden brown. Enjoy!

85. Sticky Glazed Wings
INGREDIENTS (2 Servings)

½ pound chicken wings

1 tablespoon sesame oil

2 tablespoons brown sugar

1 tablespoon Worcestershire sauce

1 tablespoon hot sauce

1 tablespoon balsamic vinegar

DIRECTIONS (Prep + Cook Time: 30 minutes)

Brush the chicken wings with sesame oil and transfer them to the Air Fryer cooking basket. Cook the chicken wings at 370 degrees F for 12 minutes; turn them over and cook for a further 10 minutes. Meanwhile, bring the other ingredients to a boil in a saucepan; cook for 2 to 3 minutes or until thoroughly cooked. Toss the warm chicken wings with the sauce and place them on a serving platter. Serve and enjoy!

86. Sweet Potato Fries with Spicy Dip
INGREDIENTS (3 Servings)

3 medium sweet potatoes, cut into ⅓-inch sticks

Spicy Dip:

¼ cup mayonnaise

¼ cup Greek yogurt

2 tablespoons olive oil

1 teaspoon kosher salt

¼ teaspoon Dijon mustard

1 teaspoon hot sauce

DIRECTIONS (Prep + Cook Time: 50 minutes)

Soak the sweet potato in icy cold water for 30 minutes. Drain the sweet potatoes and pat them dry with paper towels. Toss the sweet potatoes with olive oil and salt. Place in the lightly greased cooking basket. Cook in the preheated Air Fryer at 360 degrees F for 14 minutes. Wok in batches. While the sweet potatoes are cooking, make the spicy dip by whisking the remaining ingredients. Place in the refrigerator until ready to serve. Enjoy!

87. Asian Twist Chicken Wings
INGREDIENTS (6 Servings)

1 ½ pounds chicken wings

2 teaspoons sesame oil

Kosher salt and ground black pepper, to taste

2 tablespoons tamari sauce

1 tablespoon rice vinegar

2 garlic clove, minced

2 tablespoons honey

2 sun-dried tomatoes, minced

DIRECTIONS (Prep + Cook Time: 20 minutes)

Toss the chicken wings with the sesame oil, salt, and pepper. Add chicken wings to a lightly greased baking pan. Roast the chicken wings in the preheated Air Fryer at 390 degrees F for 7 minutes.Turn them over once or twice to ensure even cooking. In a mixing dish, thoroughly combine the tamari sauce, vinegar, garlic, honey, and sun-dried tomatoes. Pour the sauce all over the chicken wings; bake an additional 5 minutes. Serve warm.

88. The Best Calamari Appetizer
INGREDIENTS (6 Servings)

- 1 ½ pounds calamari tubes, cleaned, cut into rings
- Sea salt and ground black pepper, to taste
- 2 tablespoons lemon juice
- 1 cup cornmeal
- 1 cup all-purpose flour
- 1 teaspoon paprika
- 1 egg, whisked
- ¼ cup buttermilk

DIRECTIONS (Prep + Cook Time: 20 minutes)

Preheat your Air Fryer to 390 degrees F. Rinse the calamari and pat it dry. Season with salt and black pepper. Drizzle lemon juice all over the calamari. Now, combine the cornmeal, flour, and paprika in a bowl; add the whisked egg and buttermilk. Dredge the calamari in the egg/flour mixture. Arrange them in the cooking basket. Spritz with cooking oil and cook for 9 to 12 minutes, shaking the basket occasionally. Work in batches. Serve with toothpicks. Enjoy!

89. Mini Turkey and Corn Burritos
INGREDIENTS (6 Servings)

- 1 tablespoon olive oil
- ½ pound ground turkey
- 2 tablespoons shallot, minced
- 1 garlic clove, smashed
- 1 red bell pepper, seeded and chopped
- 1 ancho chili pepper, seeded and minced
- ½ teaspoon ground cumin
- Sea salt and freshly ground black pepper, to taste
- ⅓ cup salsa
- 6 ounces sweet corn kernels
- 12 (8-inch) tortilla shells
- 1 tablespoon butter, melted
- ½ cup sour cream, for serving

DIRECTIONS (Prep + Cook Time: 25 minutes)

Heat the olive oil in a sauté pan over medium-high heat. Cook the ground meat and shallots for 3 to 4 minutes. Add the garlic and peppers and cook an additional 3 minutes or until fragrant. After that, add the spices, salsa, and corn. Stir until everything is well combined. Place about 2 tablespoons of the meat mixture in the center of each tortilla. Roll your tortillas to seal the edges and make the burritos. Brush each burrito with melted butter and place them in the lightly greased cooking basket. Bake at 395 degrees F for 10 minutes, turning them over halfway through the cooking time. Garnish each burrito with a dollop of sour cream and serve.

90. The Best Party Mix Ever
INGREDIENTS (10 Servings)

- 2 cups mini pretzels
- 1 cup mini crackers
- 1 cup peanuts
- 1 tablespoon Creole seasoning
- 2 tablespoons butter, melted

DIRECTIONS (Prep + Cook Time: 15 minutes)

Toss all ingredients in the Air Fryer basket. Cook in the preheated Air Fryer at 360 degrees F approximately 9 minutes until lightly toasted. Shake the basket periodically. Enjoy!

91. Cheddar Cheese Lumpia Rolls
INGREDIENTS (5 Servings)

- 5 ounces mature cheddar cheese, cut into 15 sticks
- 15 pieces spring roll lumpia wrappers
- 2 tablespoons sesame oil

DIRECTIONS (Prep + Cook Time: 20 minutes)

Wrap the cheese sticks in the lumpia wrappers. Transfer to the Air Fryer basket. Brush with sesame oil. Bake in the preheated Air Fryer at 395 degrees for 10 minutes or until the lumpia wrappers turn golden brown. Work in batches. Shake the Air Fryer basket occasionally to ensure even cooking. Enjoy!

92. Cocktail Sausage and Veggies on a Stick
INGREDIENTS (6 Servings)

- 16 cocktail sausages, halved
- 16 pearl onions
- 1 red bell pepper, cut into 1 ½-inch pieces
- 1 green bell pepper, cut into 1 ½-inch pieces
- Salt and cracked black pepper, to taste
- ½ cup tomato chili sauce

Directions (Prep + Cook Time: 25 minutes)

Thread the cocktail sausages, pearl onions, and peppers alternately onto skewers. Sprinkle with salt and black pepper. Cook in the preheated Air Fryer at 380 degrees for 15 minutes, turning the skewers over once or twice to ensure even cooking. Serve with the tomato chili sauce on the side. Enjoy!

93. Spicy Korean Short Ribs
INGREDIENTS (4 Servings)

- 1 pound meaty short ribs
- ½ rice vinegar
- ½ cup soy sauce
- 1 tablespoon brown sugar
- 1 tablespoons Sriracha sauce
- 2 garlic cloves, minced
- 1 tablespoon daenjang (soybean paste)
- 1 teaspoon kochukaru (chili pepper flakes)
- Sea salt and ground black pepper, to taste
- 1 tablespoon sesame oil
- ¼ cup green onions, roughly chopped

DIRECTIONS (Prep + Cook Time: 35 minutes)

Place the short ribs, vinegar, soy sauce, sugar, Sriracha, garlic, and spices in Ziploc bag; let it marinate overnight. Rub the sides and bottom of the Air Fryer basket with sesame oil. Discard the marinade and transfer the ribs to the prepared cooking basket. Cook the marinated ribs in the preheated Air Fryer at 365 degrees for 17 minutes. Turn the ribs over, brush with the reserved marinade, and cook an additional 15 minutes. Garnish with green onions. Serve and enjoy!

94. Crunchy Roasted Chickpeas
INGREDIENTS (4 Servings)

- 1 (15-ounce) can chickpeas, drained and patted dry
- 1 tablespoon sesame oil
- 1/8 cup Romano cheese, grated
- ¼ teaspoon mustard powder
- ½ teaspoon shallot powder
- ½ teaspoon garlic powder
- 1 teaspoon coriander, minced
- ½ teaspoon red pepper flakes, crushed
- Coarse sea salt and ground black pepper, to taste

DIRECTIONS (Prep + Cook Time: 25 minutes)

Toss all ingredients in a mixing bowl. Roast in the preheated Air Fryer at 380 degrees F for 10 minutes, shaking the basket halfway through the cooking time. Work in batches. Bon appétit!

95. Crunchy Asparagus with Mediterranean Aioli
INGREDIENTS (4 Servings)

Crunchy Asparagus:
- 2 eggs
- ¾ cup breadcrumbs

Mediterranean Aioli:
- 4 garlic cloves, minced
- 4 tablespoons olive oil mayonnaise

- 2 tablespoons Parmesan cheese
- Sea salt and ground white pepper, to taste

- 1 tablespoons lemon juice, freshly squeezed

- ½ pound asparagus, cleaned and trimmed
- Cooking spray

DIRECTIONS (Prep + Cook Time: 50 minutes)

Start by preheating your Air Fryer to 400 degrees F. In a shallow bowl, thoroughly combine the eggs, breadcrumbs, Parmesan cheese, salt, and white pepper. Dip the asparagus spears in the egg mixture; roll to coat well. Cook in the preheated Air Fryer for 5 to 6 minutes; work in two batches. Place the garlic on a piece of aluminum foil and spritz with cooking spray. Wrap the garlic in the foil. Cook in the preheated Air Fryer at 400 degrees for 12 minutes. Check the garlic, open the top of the foil and continue to cook for 10 minutes more. Let it cool for 10 to 15 minutes; remove the cloves by squeezing them out of the skins; mash the garlic and add the mayo and fresh lemon juice; whisk until everything is well combined. Serve the asparagus with the chilled aioli on the side. Enjoy!

96. Red Beet Chips with Pizza Sauce
INGREDIENTS (4 Servings)

- 2 red beets, thinly sliced
- 1 tablespoon grapeseed oil
- 1 teaspoon seasoned salt
- ½ teaspoon ground black pepper
- ¼ teaspoon cumin powder
- ½ cup pizza sauce

DIRECTIONS (Prep + Cook Time: 30 minutes)

Toss the red beets with the oil, salt, black pepper, and cumin powder. Arrange the beet slices in a single layer in the Air Fryer basket. Cook in the preheated Air Fryer at 330 degrees F for 13 minutes. Serve with the pizza sauce and enjoy!

97. Cheesy Zucchini Sticks
INGREDIENTS (2 Servings)

- 1 zucchini, slice into strips
- 2 tablespoons mayonnaise
- ¼ cup tortilla chips, crushed
- ¼ cup Romano cheese, shredded
- Sea salt and black pepper, to your liking
- 1 tablespoon garlic powder
- ½ teaspoon red pepper flakes

DIRECTIONS (Prep + Cook Time: 20 minutes)

Coat the zucchini with mayonnaise. Mix the crushed tortilla chips, cheese and spices in a shallow dish. Then, coat the zucchini sticks with the cheese/chips mixture. Cook in the preheated Air Fryer at 400 degrees F for 12 minutes, shaking the basket halfway through the cooking time. Work in batches until the sticks are crispy and golden brown. Serve and enjoy!

98. Fried Pickle Chips with Greek Yogurt Dip
INGREDIENTS (5 Servings)

- ½ cup cornmeal
- ½ cup all-purpose flour
- 1 teaspoon cayenne pepper
- ½ teaspoon shallot powder
- 1 teaspoon garlic powder
- ½ teaspoon porcini powder
- Kosher salt and ground black pepper, to taste
- 2 eggs
- 2 cups pickle chips, pat dry with kitchen towels

Greek Yogurt Dip:
- ½ cup Greek yogurt
- 1 clove garlic, minced
- ¼ teaspoon ground black pepper
- 1 tablespoon fresh chives, chopped

DIRECTIONS (Prep + Cook Time: 20 minutes)

In a shallow bowl, mix the cornmeal and flour; add the seasonings and mix to combine well. Beat the eggs in a separate shallow bowl. Dredge the pickle chips in the flour mixture, then, in the egg mixture. Press the pickle chips into the flour mixture again, coating evenly. Cook in the preheated Air Fryer at 400 degrees F for 5 minutes; shake the basket and cook for 5 minutes more. Work in batches. Meanwhile, mix all the sauce ingredients until well combined. Serve the fried pickles with the Greek yogurt dip and enjoy.

99. Parsnip Chips with Spicy Citrus Aioli
INGREDIENTS (4 Servings)

- 1 pound parsnips, peel long strips
- 2 tablespoons sesame oil
- Sea salt and ground black pepper, to taste
- 1 teaspoon red pepper flakes, crushed
- ½ teaspoon curry powder
- ½ teaspoon mustard seeds

Spicy Citrus Aioli:
- ¼ cup mayonnaise
- 1 tablespoon fresh lime juice
- 1 clove garlic, smashed
- Salt and black pepper, to taste

DIRECTIONS (Prep + Cook Time: 20 minutes)

Start by preheating the Air Fryer to 380 degrees F. Toss the parsnip chips with the sesame oil, salt, black pepper, red pepper, curry powder, and mustard seeds. Cook for 15 minutes, shaking the Air Fryer basket periodically. Meanwhile, make the sauce by whisking the mayonnaise, lime juice, garlic, salt, and pepper. Place in the refrigerator until ready to use. Enjoy!

100. Parmesan Squash Chips
INGREDIENTS (3 Servings)

- ¾ pound butternut squash, cut into thin rounds
- ½ cup Parmesan cheese, grated
- Sea salt and ground black pepper, to taste
- 1 teaspoon butter
- ½ cup ketchup
- 1 teaspoon Sriracha sauce

DIRECTIONS (Prep + Cook Time: 20 minutes)

Toss the butternut squash with Parmesan cheese, salt, black pepper and butter. Transfer the butternut squash rounds to the Air Fryer cooking basket. Air Fryer at 400 degrees F for 12 minutes. Shake the Air Fryer basket periodically to ensure even cooking. Work with batches. While the parmesan squash chips are baking, whisk the ketchup and sriracha and set it aside. Serve the parmesan squash chips with Sriracha ketchup and enjoy!

101. Bacon Chips with Chipotle Dipping Sauce
INGREDIENTS (3 Servings)

6 ounces bacon, cut into strips	6 tablespoons sour cream	
Chipotle Dipping Sauce:	½ teaspoon chipotle chili powder	

DIRECTIONS (Prep + Cook Time: 15 minutes)

Place the bacon strips in the Air Fryer cooking basket. Cook the bacon strips at 360 degrees F for 5 minutes; turn them over and cook for another 5 minutes. Meanwhile, make the chipotle dipping sauce by whisking the sour cream and chipotle chili powder; reserve. Serve the bacon chips with the chipotle dipping sauce and enjoy!

102. Hot Paprika Bacon Deviled Eggs
INGREDIENTS (4 Servings)

4 eggs	2 tablespoons cream cheese	1 tablespoon pickle relish
2 ounces bacon bits	1 teaspoon hot sauce	½ teaspoon hot paprika
2 tablespoons mayonnaise	½ teaspoon garlic, minced	Salt and ground black pepper, to taste

DIRECTIONS (Prep + Cook Time: 15 minutes)

Place the wire rack in the Air Fryer basket and lower the eggs onto the rack. Cook the eggs at 260 degrees F for 15 minutes. Transfer the eggs to an ice-cold water bath to stop cooking. Peel the eggs under cold running water; slice them into halves, separating the whites and yolks. Mash the egg yolks; add in the remaining ingredients and stir to combine; spoon the yolk mixture into the egg whites. Serve and enjoy!

103. Fish Sticks with Honey Mustard Sauce
INGREDIENTS (3 Servings)

10 ounces fish sticks	2 teaspoons yellow mustard
½ cup mayonnaise	2 teaspoons honey

DIRECTIONS (Prep + Cook Time: 10 minutes)

Add the fish sticks to the Air Fryer cooking basket; drizzle the fish sticks with a nonstick cooking spray. Cook the fish sticks at 400 degrees F for 5 minutes; turn them over and cook for another 5 minutes. Meanwhile, mix the mayonnaise, yellow mustard and honey until well combined. Serve the fish sticks with the honey mustard sauce for dipping. Enjoy!

104. Kid-Friendly Mozzarella Sticks
INGREDIENTS (3 Servings)

2 eggs	1 cup Italian-style dried breadcrumbs	½-inch sticks
¼ cup corn flour	1 teaspoon Italian seasoning mix	1 cup marinara sauce
¼ cup plain flour	10 ounces mozzarella, cut into	

DIRECTIONS (Prep + Cook Time: 10 minutes)

Beat the eggs in a shallow bowl until pale and frothy. Then, in a second bowl, place both types of flour. In a third bowl, mix breadcrumbs with Italian seasoning mix. Dip the mozzarella sticks in the beaten eggs and allow the excess egg to drip back into the bowl. Then, dip the mozzarella sticks in the flour mixture. Lastly, roll them over the seasoned breadcrumbs. Cook the mozzarella sticks in the preheated Air Fryer at 370 degrees F for 4 minutes. Flip them over and continue to cook for 2 to 3 minutes more. Serve the mozzarella sticks with marinara sauce. Enjoy!

105. Mustard Brussels Sprout Chips
INGREDIENTS (2 Servings)

½ pound Brussels sprouts, cut into small pieces	1 teaspoon champagne vinegar	Coarse sea salt and ground black pepper, to taste
1 teaspoon deli mustard	¼ teaspoon paprika	
1 teaspoon sesame oil	¼ teaspoon cayenne pepper	

DIRECTIONS (Prep + Cook Time: 25 minutes)

Start by preheating your Air Fryer to 360 degrees F. Toss the Brussels sprouts with the other ingredients until well coated. Transfer the Brussels sprouts to the Air Fryer cooking basket. Cook the Brussels sprout chips in the preheated Air Fryer for about 20 minutes, shaking the basket every 6 to 7 minutes. Serve with your favorite sauce for dipping. Enjoy!

106. Famous Blooming Onion with Mayo Dip
INGREDIENTS (3 Servings)

1 large Vidalia onion	1 teaspoon cayenne pepper	2 eggs
½ cup all-purpose flour	½ teaspoon dried thyme	¼ cup milk
1 teaspoon salt	½ teaspoon dried oregano	
½ teaspoon ground black pepper	½ teaspoon ground cumin	

Mayo Dip:

3 tablespoons mayonnaise	1 tablespoon horseradish, drained
3 tablespoons sour cream	Kosher salt and freshly ground black pepper, to taste

DIRECTIONS (Prep + Cook Time: 25 minutes)

Cut off the top ½ inch of the Vidalia onion; peel your onion and place it cut-side down. Starting ½ inch from the root, cut the onion in half. Make a second cut that splits each half in two. You will have 4 quarters held together by the root. Repeat these cuts, splitting the 4 quarters to yield eighths; then, you should split them again until you have 16 evenly spaced cuts. Turn the onion over and gently separate the outer pieces using your fingers. In a mixing bowl, thoroughly combine the flour and spices. In a separate bowl, whisk the eggs and milk. Dip the onion into the egg mixture, followed by the flour mixture. Spritz the onion with cooking spray and transfer to the lightly greased cooking basket. Cook for 370 degrees F for 12 to 15 minutes. Meanwhile, make the mayo dip by whisking the remaining ingredients. Serve and enjoy!

107. Avocado Fries with Chipotle Sauce
INGREDIENTS (3 Servings)

2 tablespoons fresh lime juice	¼ cup flour	¼ cup light mayonnaise
1 avocado, pitted, peeled, and sliced	1 egg	¼ cup plain Greek yogurt
Pink Himalayan salt and ground white pepper, to taste	½ cup breadcrumbs	
	1 chipotle chili in adobo sauce	

DIRECTIONS (Prep + Cook Time: about 20 minutes)

Drizzle lime juice all over the avocado slices and set aside. Then, set up your breading station. Mix the salt, pepper, and all-purpose flour in a shallow dish. In a separate dish, whisk the egg. Finally, place your breadcrumbs in a third dish. Start by dredging the avocado slices in the flour mixture; then, dip them into the egg. Press the avocado slices into the breadcrumbs, coating evenly. Cook in the preheating Air Fryer at 380 degrees F for 11 minutes, shaking the cooking basket halfway through the cooking time. Meanwhile, blend the chipotle chili, mayo, and Greek yogurt in your food processor until the sauce is creamy and uniform. Serve the warm avocado slices with the sauce on the side. Enjoy!

108. Roasted Parsnip Sticks with Salted Caramel
INGREDIENTS (4 Servings)

1 pound parsnip, trimmed, scrubbed, cut into sticks	2 tablespoons granulated sugar	½ teaspoon coarse salt
	2 tablespoons butter	
2 tablespoon avocado oil	¼ teaspoon ground allspice	

DIRECTIONS (Prep + Cook Time: 25 minutes)

Toss the parsnip with the avocado oil; bake in the preheated Air Fryer at 380 degrees F for 15 minutes, shaking the cooking basket occasionally to ensure even cooking. Then, heat the sugar and 1 tablespoon of water in a small pan over medium heat. Cook until the sugar has dissolved; bring to a boil. Keep swirling the pan around until the sugar reaches a rich caramel color. Pour in 2 tablespoons of cold water. Now, add the butter, allspice, and salt. The mixture should be runny. Afterwards, drizzle the salted caramel over the roasted parsnip sticks and enjoy!

109. Spinach Chips with Chili Yogurt Dip
INGREDIENTS (3 Servings)

3 cups fresh spinach leaves	½ teaspoon cayenne pepper	¼ cup yogurt
1 tablespoon extra-virgin olive oil	1 teaspoon garlic powder	2 tablespoons mayonnaise
1 teaspoon sea salt	Chili Yogurt Dip:	½ teaspoon chili powder

DIRECTIONS (Prep + Cook Time: 20 minutes)

Toss the spinach leaves with the olive oil and seasonings. Bake in the preheated Air Fryer at 350 degrees F for 10 minutes, shaking the cooking basket occasionally. Bake until the edges brown, working in batches. In the meantime, make the sauce by whisking all ingredients in a mixing dish. Serve immediately.

110. Sea Scallops and Bacon Skewers
INGREDIENTS (6 Servings)

- ½ pound sea scallops
- ½ cup coconut milk
- 6 ounces orange juice
- 1 tablespoon vermouth
- Sea salt and ground black pepper, to taste
- ½ pound bacon, diced
- 1 shallot, diced
- 1 teaspoon garlic powder
- 1 teaspoon paprika

DIRECTIONS (Prep + Cook Time: 50 minutes)

In a ceramic bowl, place the sea scallops, coconut milk, orange juice, vermouth, salt, and black pepper; let it marinate for 30 minutes. Assemble the skewers alternating the scallops, bacon, and shallots. Sprinkle garlic powder and paprika all over the skewers. Bake in the preheated air Fryer at 400 degrees F for 6 minutes. Serve warm and enjoy!

111. Crunchy Roasted Pepitas
INGREDIENTS (4 Servings)

- 2 cups fresh pumpkin seeds with shells
- 1 tablespoon olive oil
- 1 teaspoon sea salt
- 1 teaspoon ground coriander
- 1 teaspoon cayenne pepper

DIRECTIONS (Prep + Cook Time: 20 minutes)

Toss the pumpkin seeds with the olive oil. Spread in an even layer in the Air Fryer basket; roast the seeds at 350 degrees F for 15 minutes, shaking the basket every 5 minutes. Immediately toss the seeds with the salt, coriander, salt, and cayenne pepper. Enjoy!

112. Loaded Tater Tot Bites
INGREDIENTS (6 Servings)

- 24 tater tots, frozen
- 1 cup Swiss cheese, grated
- 6 tablespoons
- Canadian bacon, cooked and chopped
- ¼ cup Ranch dressing

DIRECTIONS (Prep + Cook Time: 20 minutes)

Spritz the silicone muffin cups with non-stick cooking spray. Now, press the tater tots down into each cup. Divide the cheese, bacon, and Ranch dressing between tater tot cups. Cook in the preheated Air Fryer at 395 degrees for 10 minutes. Serve in paper cake cups. Enjoy!

113. Summer Meatball Skewers
INGREDIENTS (6 Servings)

- ½ pound ground pork
- ½ pound ground beef
- 1 teaspoon dried onion flakes
- 1 teaspoon fresh garlic, minced
- 1 teaspoon dried parsley flakes
- Salt and black pepper, to taste 1 red pepper,
- 1-inch pieces
- 1 cup pearl onions
- ½ cup barbecue sauce

DIRECTIONS (Prep + Cook Time: 20 minutes)

Mix the ground meat with the onion flakes, garlic, parsley flakes, salt, and black pepper. Shape the mixture into 1-inch balls. Thread the meatballs, pearl onions, and peppers alternately onto skewers. Microwave the barbecue sauce for 10 seconds. Cook in the preheated Air Fryer at 380 degrees for 5 minutes. Turn the skewers over halfway through the cooking time. Brush with the sauce and cook for a further 5 minutes. Work in batches. Serve with the remaining barbecue sauce and enjoy!

114. Classic Deviled Eggs
INGREDIENTS (3 Servings)

- 5 eggs
- 2 tablespoons mayonnaise
- 2 tablespoons sweet pickle relish
- Sea salt, to taste
- ½ teaspoon mixed peppercorns, crushed

DIRECTIONS (Prep + Cook Time: 20 minutes)

Place the wire rack in the Air Fryer basket; lower the eggs onto the wire rack. Cook at 270 degrees F for 15 minutes. Transfer them to an ice-cold water bath to stop the cooking. Peel the eggs under cold running water; slice them into halves. Mash the egg yolks with the mayo, sweet pickle relish, and salt; spoon yolk mixture into egg whites. Arrange on a nice serving platter and garnish with the mixed peppercorns. Enjoy!

115. Chicken Nuggets with Campfire Sauce
INGREDIENTS (6 Servings)

- 1 pound chicken breasts, slice into tenders
- ½ teaspoon cayenne pepper
- Salt and black pepper, to taste
- ¼ cup cornmeal
- 1 egg, whisked
- ½ cup seasoned breadcrumbs
- ¼ cup mayo
- ¼ cup barbecue sauce

DIRECTIONS (Prep + Cook Time: 20 minutes)

Pat the chicken tenders dry with a kitchen towel. Season with the cayenne pepper, salt, and black pepper. Dip the chicken tenders into the cornmeal, followed by the egg. Press the chicken tenders into the breadcrumbs, coating evenly. Place the chicken tenders in the lightly greased Air Fryer basket. Cook at 360 degrees for 9 to 12 minutes, turning them over to cook evenly. In a mixing bowl, thoroughly combine the mayonnaise with the barbecue sauce. Serve the chicken nuggets with the sauce for dipping. Enjoy!

116. Beer-Battered Vidalia Onion Rings
INGREDIENTS (2 Servings)

- ½ cup all-purpose flour
- ½ teaspoon baking powder
- ¼ teaspoon cayenne pepper
- ¼ teaspoon dried oregano
- Kosher salt and ground black pepper, to taste
- 1 large egg, beaten
- ¼ cup beer
- 1 cup crushed tortilla chips
- ½ pound Vidalia onions, cut into rings

DIRECTIONS (Prep + Cook Time: 15 minutes)

In a mixing bowl, thoroughly combine the flour, baking powder, cayenne pepper, oregano, salt, black pepper, egg and beer; mix to combine well. In another shallow bowl, place the crushed tortilla chips. Dip the Vidalia rings in the beer mixture; then, coat the rings with the crushed tortilla chips, pressing to adhere. Transfer the onion rings to the Air Fryer cooking basket and spritz them with a nonstick spray. Cook the onion rings at 380 degrees F for about 8 minutes, shaking the basket halfway through the cooking time to ensure even browning. Serve and enjoy!

117. Sea Scallops and Bacon Kabobs
INGREDIENTS (2 Servings)

- 10 sea scallops, frozen
- 4 ounces bacon, diced
- 1 teaspoon garlic powder
- 1 teaspoon paprika
- Sea salt and ground black pepper, to taste

DIRECTIONS (Prep + Cook Time: 10 minutes)

Assemble the skewers alternating sea scallops and bacon. Sprinkle the garlic powder, paprika, salt and black pepper all over your kabobs. Bake your kabobs in the preheated Air Fryer at 400 degrees F for 6 minutes. Serve warm with your favorite sauce for dipping. Enjoy!

118. Coconut Banana Chips
INGREDIENTS (2 Servings)

- 1 large banana, peeled and sliced
- 1 teaspoon coconut oil
- ¼ teaspoon ground cinnamon
- A pinch of coarse salt
- 2 tablespoons coconut flakes

DIRECTIONS (Prep + Cook Time: 10 minutes)

Toss the banana slices with the coconut oil, cinnamon and salt. Transfer banana slices to the Air Fryer cooking basket. Cook the banana slices at 375 degrees F for about 8 minutes, shaking the basket every 2 minutes. Scatter coconut flakes over the banana slices and let banana chips cool slightly before serving. Enjoy!

119. Chili-Lime French Fries
INGREDIENTS (3 Servings)

- 1 pound potatoes, peeled and cut into matchsticks
- 1 teaspoon olive oil
- 1 lime, freshly squeezed
- 1 teaspoon chili powder
- Sea salt and ground black pepper, to taste

DIRECTIONS (Prep + Cook Time: 20 minutes)

Toss your potatoes with the remaining ingredients until well coated. Transfer your potatoes to the Air Fryer cooking basket. Cook the French fries at 370 degrees F for 9 minutes. Shake the cooking basket and continue to cook for about 9 minutes. Serve immediately. Enjoy!

120. Easy Toasted Nuts
INGREDIENTS (4 Servings)

½ cup pecans

1 cup almonds

2 tablespoons egg white

1 tablespoon granulated sugar

A pinch of coarse sea salt

DIRECTIONS (Prep + Cook Time: 10 minutes)

Toss the pecans and almonds with the egg white, granulated sugar and salt until well coated. Transfer the pecans and almonds to the Air Fryer cooking basket. Roast the pecans and almonds at 360 degrees F for about 6 to 7 minutes, shaking the basket once or twice. Taste and adjust seasonings. Enjoy!

121. Eggplant Parm Chips
INGREDIENTS (2 Servings)

½ pound eggplant, cut into rounds

Kosher salt and ground black pepper, to taste

½ teaspoon shallot powder

½ teaspoon porcini powder

½ teaspoon garlic powder

¼ teaspoon cayenne pepper

½ cup Parmesan cheese, grated

DIRECTIONS (Prep + Cook Time: 30 minutes)

Toss the eggplant rounds with the remaining ingredients until well coated on both sides. Bake the eggplant chips at 400 degrees F for 15 minutes; shake the basket and continue to cook for 15 minutes more. Let cool slightly, eggplant chips will crisp up as it cools. Enjoy!

122. Cinnamon Pear Chips
INGREDIENTS (2 Servings)

1 large pear, cored and sliced

1 teaspoon apple pie spice blend

1 teaspoon coconut oil

1 teaspoon honey

DIRECTIONS (Prep + Cook Time: 10 minutes)

Toss the pear slices with the spice blend, coconut oil and honey. Then, place the pear slices in the Air Fryer cooking basket and cook at 360 degrees F for about 8 minutes. Shake the basket once or twice to ensure even cooking. Pear chips will crisp up as it cools. Enjoy!

123. Mexican Crunchy Cheese Straws
INGREDIENTS (3 Servings)

½ cup almond flour

¼ teaspoon xanthan gum

¼ teaspoon shallot powder

¼ teaspoon garlic powder

¼ teaspoon ground cumin

1 egg yolk, whisked

1 ounce Manchego cheese, grated

2 ounces Cotija cheese, grated

DIRECTIONS (Prep + Cook Time: 15 minutes)

Mix all ingredients until everything is well incorporated. Twist the batter into straw strips and place them on a baking mat inside your Air Fryer.

Cook the cheese straws in your Air Fryer at 360 degrees F for 5 minutes; turn them over and cook an additional 5 minutes. Let the cheese straws cool before serving. Enjoy!

124. Crunchy Roasted Chickpeas
INGREDIENTS (2 Servings)

1 tablespoon extra-virgin olive oil

8 ounces can chickpeas, drained

½ teaspoon smoked paprika

½ teaspoon ground cumin

½ teaspoon garlic powder Sea salt, to taste

DIRECTIONS (Prep + Cook Time: 20 minutes)

Drizzle olive oil over the drained chickpeas and transfer them to the Air Fryer cooking basket. Cook your chickpeas in the preheated Air Fryer at 395 degrees F for 13 minutes. Turn your Air Fryer to 350 degrees F and cook an additional 6 minutes. Toss the warm chickpeas with smoked paprika, cumin, garlic and salt. Enjoy!

125. Greek-Style Deviled Eggs
INGREDIENTS (2 Servings)

- 4 eggs
- 1 tablespoon chives, chopped
- 1 tablespoon parsley, chopped
- 2 tablespoons Kalamata olives, pitted and chopped
- 1 tablespoon Greek-style yogurt
- 1 teaspoon habanero pepper, seeded and chopped
- Sea salt and crushed red pepper flakes, to taste

DIRECTIONS (Prep + Cook Time: 20 minutes)

Place the wire rack in the Air Fryer basket and lower the eggs onto the rack. Cook the eggs at 260 degrees F for 15 minutes. Transfer the eggs to an ice-cold water bath to stop cooking. Peel the eggs under cold running water; slice them into halves, separating the whites and yolks. Mash the egg yolks with the remaining ingredients and mix to combine. Spoon the yolk mixture into the egg whites and serve well chilled. Enjoy!

126. Baked Cheese Crisps
INGREDIENTS (4 Servings)

- ½ cup Parmesan cheese, shredded
- 1 cup Cheddar cheese, shredded
- 1 teaspoon Italian seasoning
- ½ cup marinara sauce

DIRECTIONS (Prep + Cook Time: 15 minutes)

Start by preheating your Air Fryer to 350 degrees F. Place a piece of parchment paper in the cooking basket. Mix the cheese with the Italian seasoning. Add about 1 tablespoon of the cheese mixture (per crisp) to the basket, making sure they are not touching. Bake for 6 minutes or until browned to your liking. Work in batches and place them on a large tray to cool slightly. Serve with the marinara sauce. Enjoy!

127. Puerto Rican Tostones
INGREDIENTS (2 Servings)

- 1 ripe plantain, sliced
- 1 tablespoon sunflower oil
- A pinch of grated nutmeg
- A pinch of kosher salt

DIRECTIONS (Prep + Cook Time: 15 minutes)

Toss the plantains with the oil, nutmeg, and salt in a bowl. Cook in the preheated Air Fryer at 400 degrees F for 10 minutes, shaking the cooking basket halfway through the cooking time. Adjust the seasonings to taste and serve immediately.

128. Hot Roasted Cauliflower Florets
INGREDIENTS (3 Servings)

- ½ cup plain flour
- ½ teaspoon shallot powder
- 1 teaspoon garlic powder
- ¼ teaspoon dried dill weed
- ½ teaspoon chipotle powder
- Sea salt and ground black pepper, to taste
- ½ cup rice milk
- 2 tablespoons coconut oil, softened
- 1 pound cauliflower florets

DIRECTIONS (Prep + Cook Time: 20 minutes)

In a mixing bowl, thoroughly combine the flour, spices, rice milk and coconut oil. Mix to combine well. Coat the cauliflower florets with the batter and allow the excess batter to drip back into the bowl. Cook the cauliflower florets at 400 degrees F for 12 minutes, shaking the basket once or twice to ensure even browning. Serve with some extra hot sauce, if desired. Serve warm.

129. Green Bean Crisps
INGREDIENTS (4 Servings)

- 1 egg, beaten
- ¼ cup cornmeal
- ¼ cup parmesan, grated
- 1 teaspoon sea salt
- ½ teaspoon red pepper flakes, crushed
- 1 pound green beans
- 2 tablespoons grapeseed oil

DIRECTIONS (Prep + Cook Time: 20 minutes)

In a mixing bowl, combine together the egg, cornmeal, parmesan, salt, and red pepper flakes; mix to combine well. Dip the green beans into the batter and transfer them to the cooking basket. Brush with the grapeseed oil. Cook in the preheated Air Fryer at 390 degrees F for 4 minutes. Shake the basket and cook for a further 3 minutes. Work in batches. Taste, adjust the seasonings and serve. Serve warm.

130. Southern Cheese Straws
INGREDIENTS (6 Servings)

1 cup all-purpose flour

Sea salt and ground black pepper, to taste

¼ teaspoon smoked paprika

½ teaspoon celery seeds

4 ounces mature Cheddar, cold, freshly grated

1 sticks butter

DIRECTIONS (Prep + Cook Time: 30 minutes)

Start by preheating your air Fryer to 330 degrees F. Line the Air Fryer basket with parchment paper. In a mixing bowl, thoroughly combine the flour, salt, black pepper, paprika, and celery seeds. Then, combine the cheese and butter in the bowl of a stand mixer. Slowly stir in the flour mixture and mix to combine well. Then, pack the dough into a cookie press fitted with a star disk. Pipe the long ribbons of dough across the parchment paper. Then cut into six-inch lengths. Bake in the preheated Air Fryer for 15 minutes. Repeat with the remaining dough. Let the cheese straws cool on a rack. You can store them between sheets of parchment in an airtight container. Enjoy!

131. Quick and Easy Popcorn
INGREDIENTS (4 Servings)

2 tablespoons dried corn kernels

1 teaspoon safflower oil

Kosher salt, to taste

1 teaspoon red pepper flakes, crushed

DIRECTIONS (Prep + Cook Time: 20 minutes)

Add the dried corn kernels to the Air Fryer basket; brush with safflower oil. Cook at 395 degrees F for 15 minutes, shaking the basket every 5 minutes. Sprinkle with salt and red pepper flakes. Enjoy!

132. Crunchy Broccoli Fries
INGREDIENTS (4 Servings)

1 pound broccoli florets

½ teaspoon onion powder

1 teaspoon granulated garlic

½ teaspoon cayenne pepper

Sea salt and ground black pepper, to taste

2 tablespoons sesame oil

4 tablespoons parmesan cheese, preferably freshly grated

DIRECTIONS (Prep + Cook Time: 15 minutes)

Start by preheating the Air Fryer to 400 degrees F. Blanch the broccoli in salted boiling water until al dente, about 3 to 4 minutes. Drain well and transfer to the lightly greased Air Fryer basket. Add the onion powder, garlic, cayenne pepper, salt, black pepper, and sesame oil. Cook for 6 minutes, tossing halfway through the cooking time. Serve and enjoy!

133. Homemade Ranch Tater Tots
INGREDIENTS (2 Servings)

½ pound potatoes, peeled and shredded

½ teaspoon hot paprika

½ teaspoon dried marjoram

1 teaspoon Ranch seasoning mix

2 tablespoons Colby cheese, finely grated (about ⅓ cup)

1 teaspoon butter, melted

Sea salt and ground black pepper, to taste

DIRECTIONS (Prep + Cook Time: 15 minutes)

In a mixing bowl, thoroughly combine all ingredients until everything is well incorporated. Transfer your tater tots to a lightly greased Air Fryer cooking basket. Cook your tater tots in the preheated Air Fryer at 400 degrees F for 12 minutes, shaking the basket halfway through the cooking time to ensure even browning. Serve and enjoy!

134. Beer Battered Vidalia Rings
INGREDIENTS (4 Servings)

- ½ pound Vidalia onions, sliced into rings
- ½ cup all-purpose flour
- ¼ cup cornmeal
- ½ teaspoon baking powder
- Sea salt and freshly cracked black pepper, to taste
- ¼ teaspoon garlic powder
- 2 eggs, beaten
- ½ cup lager-style beer
- 1 cup plain breadcrumbs
- 2 tablespoons peanut oil

DIRECTIONS (Prep + Cook Time: 30 minutes)

Place the onion rings in the bowl with icy cold water; let them soak approximately 20 minutes; drain the onion rings and pat them dry. In a shallow bowl, mix the flour, cornmeal, baking powder, salt, and black pepper. Add the garlic powder, eggs and beer; mix well to combine. In another shallow bowl, mix the breadcrumbs with the peanut oil. Dip the onion rings in the flour/egg mixture; then, dredge in the breadcrumb mixture. Roll to coat them evenly. Spritz the Air Fryer basket with cooking spray; arrange the breaded onion rings in the basket. Cook in the preheated Air Fryer at 400 degrees F for 4 to 5 minutes, turning them over halfway through the cooking time. Enjoy!

135. Barbecue Little Smokies
INGREDIENTS (6 Servings)

- 1 pound beef cocktail wieners
- 10 ounces barbecue sauce

DIRECTIONS (Prep + Cook Time: 20 minutes)

Start by preheating your Air Fryer to 380 degrees F. Prick holes into your sausages using a fork and transfer them to the baking pan. Cook for 13 minutes. Spoon the barbecue sauce into the pan and cook an additional 2 minutes. Serve with toothpicks. Enjoy!

136. Avocado Fries with Lime Sauce
INGREDIENTS (4 Servings)

- ½ cup plain flour
- ½ milk
- ½ cup tortilla chips, crushed
- ½ teaspoon red pepper flakes, crushed
- Sea salt and ground black pepper, to taste
- 2 avocados, peeled, pitted and sliced
- ½ cup Greek yogurt
- 4 tablespoons mayonnaise
- 1 teaspoon fresh lime juice
- ½ teaspoon lime chili seasoning salt

DIRECTIONS (Prep + Cook Time: 15 minutes)

Mix the plain flour and milk in a plate. Add the crushed tortilla chips, red pepper flakes, salt and black pepper to another rimmed plate. Dredge the avocado slices in the flour mixture and then, coat them in the crushed tortilla chips. Cook the avocado at 390 degrees F for about 8 minutes, shaking the basket halfway through the cooking time. In the meantime, mix the remaining ingredients, until well combined. Serve warm avocado fries with the lime sauce. Enjoy!

137. Baby Carrots with Asian Flair
INGREDIENTS (3 Servings)

- 1 pound baby carrots
- 2 tablespoons sesame oil
- ½ teaspoon Szechuan pepper
- 1 teaspoon Wuxiang powder (Five-spice powder)
- 1 tablespoon honey
- 1 large garlic clove, crushed
- 1 (1-inch) piece fresh ginger root, peeled and grated
- 2 tablespoons tamari sauce

DIRECTIONS (Prep + Cook Time: 20 minutes)

Start by preheating your Air Fryer to 380 degrees F. Toss all ingredients together and place them in the Air Fryer basket. Cook for 15 minutes, shaking the basket halfway through the cooking time. Enjoy!

138. Kale Chips with Tahini Sauce
INGREDIENTS (4 Servings)

- 5 cups kale leaves, torn into 1-inch pieces
- 1 ½ tablespoons sesame oil
- ½ teaspoon shallot powder
- 1 teaspoon garlic powder
- ¼ teaspoon porcini powder
- ½ teaspoon mustard seeds
- 1 teaspoon salt
- ⅓ cup tahini (sesame butter)
- 1 tablespoon fresh lemon juice
- 2 cloves garlic, minced

DIRECTIONS (Prep + Cook Time: 15 minutes)

Toss the kale with the sesame oil and seasonings. Bake in the preheated Air Fryer at 350 degrees F for 10 minutes, shaking the cooking basket occasionally. Bake until the edges are brown. Work in batches. Meanwhile, make the sauce by whisking all ingredients in a small mixing bowl. Serve and enjoy!

139. Greek-Style Squash Chips
INGREDIENTS (4 Servings)

- ½ cup seasoned breadcrumbs
- ½ cup Parmesan cheese, grated
- Sea salt and ground black pepper, to taste
- ¼ teaspoon oregano
- 2 yellow squash, cut into slices
- 2 tablespoons grapeseed oil

Sauce:
- ½ cup Greek-style yogurt
- 1 tablespoon fresh cilantro, chopped
- 1 garlic clove, minced
- Freshly ground black pepper, to your liking

DIRECTIONS (Prep + Cook Time: 25 minutes)

In a shallow bowl, thoroughly combine the seasoned breadcrumbs, Parmesan, salt, black pepper, and oregano. Dip the yellow squash slices in the prepared batter, pressing to adhere. Brush with the grapeseed oil and cook in the preheated Air Fryer at 400 degrees F for 12 minutes. Shake the Air Fryer basket periodically to ensure even cooking. Work in batches. While the chips are baking, whisk the sauce ingredients; place in your refrigerator until ready to serve. Enjoy!

140. Thyme-Roasted Sweet Potatoes
INGREDIENTS (3 Servings)

- 1 pound sweet potatoes, peeled, cut into bite-sized pieces
- 2 tablespoons olive oil
- 1 teaspoon sea salt
- ¼ teaspoon freshly ground black pepper
- ½ teaspoon cayenne pepper
- 2 fresh thyme sprigs

DIRECTIONS (Prep + Cook Time: 35 minutes)

Arrange the potato slices in a single layer in the lightly greased cooking basket. Add the olive oil, salt, black pepper, and cayenne pepper; toss to coat. Bake at 380 degrees F for 30 minutes, shaking the cooking basket occasionally. Bake until tender and slightly browned, working in batches. Serve warm, garnished with thyme sprigs.

141. Cajun Cheese Sticks
INGREDIENTS (4 Servings)

- ½ cup all-purpose flour
- 2 eggs
- ½ cup parmesan cheese, grated
- 1 tablespoon Cajun seasonings
- 8 cheese sticks, kid-friendly
- ¼ cup ketchup

DIRECTIONS (Prep + Cook Time: 15 minutes)

To begin, set up your breading station. Place the all-purpose flour in a shallow dish. In a separate dish, whisk the eggs. Finally, mix the parmesan cheese and Cajun seasoning in a third dish. Start by dredging the cheese sticks in the flour; then, dip them into the egg. Press the cheese sticks into the parmesan mixture, coating evenly. Place the breaded cheese sticks in the lightly greased Air Fryer basket. Cook at 380 degrees F for 6 minutes. Serve with ketchup and enjoy!

142. Cocktail Cranberry Meatballs
INGREDIENTS (5 Servings)

- ½ pound ground beef
- ½ pound ground turkey
- ¼ cup Parmesan cheese, grated
- ¼ cup breadcrumbs
- 1 small shallot, chopped
- 2 eggs, whisked
- ½ teaspoon garlic powder
- ½ teaspoon porcini powder
- Sea salt and ground black pepper, to taste
- 1 teaspoon red pepper flakes, crushed
- 1 tablespoon soy sauce
- 1 (8-ounce) can jellied cranberry sauce
- 6 ounces tomato-based chili sauce

DIRECTIONS (Prep + Cook Time: 15 minutes)

In a mixing bowl, combine the ground meat together with the cheese, breadcrumbs, shallot, eggs, and spices. Shape the mixture into 1-inch balls. Cook the meatballs in the preheated Air Fryer at 380 degrees for 5 minutes. Shake halfway through the cooking time. Work in batches. Whisk the soy sauce, cranberry sauce, and chili sauce in a mixing bowl. Pour the sauce over the meatballs and bake an additional 2 minutes. Serve with cocktail sticks. Enjoy!

143. Kale Chips with White Horseradish Mayo
INGREDIENTS (1 Servings)

2 cups loosely packed kale	Sea salt and ground black pepper, to taste	1 ounce mayonnaise
1 teaspoon sesame oil	1 teaspoon sesame seeds, lightly toasted	1 teaspoon prepared white horseradish

DIRECTIONS (Prep + Cook Time: 10 minutes)

Toss the kale pieces with sesame oil, salt and black pepper. Cook the kale pieces at 370 degrees F for 2 minutes; shake the basket and continue to cook for 2 minutes more. Meanwhile, make the horseradish mayo by whisking the mayonnaise and prepared horseradish. Let cool slightly, kale chips will crisp up as it cools. Sprinkle toasted sesame seeds over the kale chips. Serve the kale chips with the horseradish mayo. Enjoy!

144. Teriyaki Chicken Drumettes
INGREDIENTS (6 Servings)

1 ½ pounds chicken drumettes	¼ cup soy sauce	2 tablespoons rice wine vinegar
Sea salt and cracked black pepper, to taste	½ cup water	½ teaspoon fresh ginger, grated
2 tablespoons fresh chives, roughly chopped	¼ cup honey	2 cloves garlic, crushed
Teriyaki Sauce:	½ teaspoon Five-spice powder	1 tablespoon corn starch dissolved in 3 tablespoons of water
1 tablespoon sesame oil		

DIRECTIONS (Prep + Cook Time: 40 minutes)

Start by preheating your Air Fryer to 380 degrees F. Rub the chicken drumettes with salt and cracked black pepper. Cook in the preheated Air Fryer approximately 15 minutes. Turn them over and cook an additional 7 minutes. While the chicken drumettes are roasting, combine the sesame oil, soy sauce, water, honey, Five-spice powder, vinegar, ginger, and garlic in a pan over medium heat. Cook for 5 minutes, stirring occasionally. Add the cornstarch slurry, reduce the heat, and let it simmer until the glaze thickens. After that, brush the glaze all over the chicken drumettes. Air-fry for a further 6 minutes or until the surface is crispy. Serve topped with the remaining glaze and garnished with fresh chives. Enjoy!

145. Mexican Cheesy Zucchini Bites
INGREDIENTS (4 Servings)

1 large-sized zucchini, thinly sliced	1 egg, whisked	Salt and cracked pepper, to taste
½ cup flour	½ cup tortilla chips, crushed	
¼ cup yellow cornmeal	½ cup Queso Añejo, grated	

DIRECTIONS (Prep + Cook Time: 25 minutes)

Pat dry the zucchini slices with a kitchen towel. Mix the remaining ingredients in a shallow bowl; mix until everything is well combined. Dip each zucchini slice in the prepared batter. Cook in the preheated Air Fryer at 400 degrees F for 12 minutes, shaking the basket halfway through the cooking time. Work in batches until the zucchini slices are crispy and golden brown. Enjoy!

146. Blue Cheesy Potato Wedges
INGREDIENTS (4 Servings)

2 Yukon Gold potatoes, peeled and cut into wedges	Kosher salt, to taste
2 tablespoons ranch seasoning	½ cup blue cheese, crumbled

DIRECTIONS (Prep + Cook Time: 20 minutes)

Sprinkle the potato wedges with the ranch seasoning and salt. Grease generously the Air Fryer basket. Place the potatoes in the cooking basket. Roast in the preheated Air Fryer at 400 degrees for 12 minutes. Top with the cheese and roast an additional 3 minutes or until cheese begins to melt. Serve and enjoy!

147. Homemade Apple Chips
INGREDIENTS (4 Servings)

2 cooking apples, cored and thinly sliced	¼ teaspoon ground cloves	1 tablespoon smooth peanut butter
1 teaspoon peanut oil	¼ teaspoon ground cinnamon	

DIRECTIONS (Prep + Cook Time: 20 minutes)

Toss the apple slices with the peanut oil. Bake at 350 degrees F for 5 minutes; shake the basket to ensure even cooking and continue to cook an additional 5 minutes. Spread each apple slice with a little peanut butter and sprinkle with ground cloves and cinnamon. Serve and enjoy!

148. Easy and Delicious Pizza Puffs
INGREDIENTS (6 Servings)

- 6 ounces crescent roll dough
- ½ cup mozzarella cheese, shredded
- 3 ounces pepperoni
- 3 ounces mushrooms, chopped
- 1 teaspoon oregano
- 1 teaspoon garlic powder
- ¼ cup Marina sauce, for dipping

DIRECTIONS (Prep + Cook Time: 15 minutes)

Unroll the crescent dough. Roll out the dough using a rolling pin; cut into 6 pieces. Place the cheese, pepperoni, and mushrooms in the center of each pizza puff. Sprinkle with oregano and garlic powder. Fold each corner over the filling using wet hands. Press together to cover the filling entirely and seal the edges. Now, spritz the bottom of the Air Fryer basket with cooking oil. Lay the pizza puffs in a single layer in the cooking basket. Work in batches. Bake at 370 degrees F for 5 to 6 minutes or until golden brown. Serve with the marinara sauce for dipping.

149. Yakitori (Japanese Chicken Skewers)
INGREDIENTS (4 Servings)

- ½ pound chicken tenders, cut bite sized pieces
- 1 clove garlic, minced
- 1 teaspoon coriander seeds
- Sea salt and ground pepper, to taste
- 2 tablespoons Shoyu sauce
- 2 tablespoons sake
- 1 tablespoon fresh lemon juice
- 1 teaspoon sesame oil

DIRECTIONS (Prep + Cook Time: 15 minutes)

Place the chicken tenders, garlic, coriander, salt, black pepper, Shoyu sauce, sake, and lemon juice in a ceramic dish; cover and let it marinate for 2 hours. Then, discard the marinade and tread the chicken tenders onto bamboo skewers. Place the skewered chicken in the lightly greased Air Fryer basket. Drizzle sesame oil all over the skewered chicken. Cook at 360 degrees for 6 minutes. Turn the skewered chicken over; brush with the reserved marinade and cook for a further 6 minutes. Enjoy!

150. Party Greek Keftedes
INGREDIENTS (6 Servings)

Greek Keftedes:

- ½ pound mushrooms, chopped
- ½ pound pork sausage, chopped
- 1 teaspoon shallot powder
- 1 teaspoon granulated garlic
- 1 teaspoon dried rosemary
- 1 teaspoon dried basil
- 1 teaspoon dried oregano
- 2 eggs
- 2 tablespoons cornbread crumbs

Tzatziki Dip:

- 1 Lebanese cucumbers, grated, juice squeezed out
- 1 cup full-fat Greek yogurt
- 1 tablespoon fresh lemon juice
- 1 garlic clove, minced
- 1 tablespoon extra-virgin olive oil
- ½ teaspoon salt

DIRECTIONS (Prep + Cook Time: 20 minutes)

In a mixing bowl, thoroughly combine all ingredients for the Greek keftedes. Shape the meat mixture into bite-sized balls. Cook in the preheated Air Fryer at 380 degrees for 10 minutes, shaking the cooking basket once or twice to ensure even cooking. Meanwhile, make the tzatziki dip by mixing all ingredients. Serve the keftedes with cocktail sticks and tzatziki dip on the side. Enjoy!

151. Paprika Zucchini Bombs with Goat Cheese
INGREDIENTS (4 ervings)

- 1 cup zucchini, grated, juice squeezed out
- 1 egg 1 garlic clove, minced
- ½ cup all-purpose flour
- ½ cup cornbread crumbs
- ½ cup parmesan cheese, grated
- ½ cup goat cheese, grated
- Salt and black pepper, to taste
- 1 teaspoon paprika

DIRECTIONS (Prep + Cook Time: 20 minutes)

Start by preheating your Air Fryer to 330 degrees F. Spritz the cooking basket with nonstick cooking oil. Mix all ingredients until everything is well incorporated. Shape the zucchini mixture into golf sized balls and place them in the cooking basket. Cook in the preheated Air Fryer for 15 to 18 minutes, shaking the basket periodically to ensure even cooking. Garnish with some extra paprika if desired and serve at room temperature. Enjoy!

152. Cauliflower Bombs with Sweet & Sour Sauce
INGREDIENTS (4 Servings)

Cauliflower Bombs:

½ pound cauliflower	⅓ cup Swiss cheese	1 tablespoon Italian seasoning mix
2 ounces Ricotta cheese	1 egg	

Sweet & Sour Sauce:

1 red bell pepper, jarred	1 teaspoon sherry vinegar	2 tablespoons olive oil
1 clove garlic, minced	1 tablespoon tomato puree	Salt and black pepper, to taste

DIRECTIONS (Prep + Cook Time: 25 minutes)

Blanch the cauliflower in salted boiling water about 3 to 4 minutes until al dente. Drain well and pulse in a food processor. Add the remaining ingredients for the cauliflower bombs; mix to combine well. Bake in the preheated Air Fryer at 375 degrees F for 16 minutes, shaking halfway through the cooking time. In the meantime, pulse all ingredients for the sauce in your food processor until combined. Season to taste. Serve the cauliflower bombs with the Sweet & Sour Sauce on the side. Serve and enjoy!

Classic Fried Rice

153. Classic Fried Rice
INGREDIENTS (2 Servings)

- 1 cup white rice
- 1 tablespoon sesame oil
- Himalayan sea salt and ground black pepper, to taste
- 1 teaspoon hot paprika
- 2 tablespoons vegetable broth
- 2 tablespoons tamari sauce
- 1 egg, whisked

DIRECTIONS (Prep + Cook Time: 40 minutes)

Bring 2 cups of a lightly salted water to a boil in a medium saucepan over medium-high heat. Add in the rice, turn to a simmer and cook, covered, for about 18 minutes until water is absorbed. Let your rice stand, covered, for 5 to 7 minutes; fluff with a fork and transfer to a lightly greased Air Fryer safe pan. Stir in the sesame oil, salt, black pepper, paprika and broth; stir until everything is well incorporated. Cook the rice at 350 degrees F for about 10 minutes. Stir in the tamari sauce and egg and continue to cook for a further 5 minutes. Serve immediately

154. Bacon and Cheese Sandwich
INGREDIENTS (1 Servings)

- 2 slices whole-wheat bread
- 1 tablespoon ketchup
- ½ teaspoon Dijon mustard
- 2 ounces bacon, sliced
- 1 ounce cheddar cheese, sliced

DIRECTIONS (Prep + Cook Time: 15 minutes)

Spread the ketchup and mustard on a slice of bread. Add the bacon and cheese and top with another slice of bread. Place your sandwich in the lightly buttered Air Fryer cooking basket. Now, bake your sandwich at 380 degrees F for 10 minutes or until the cheese has melted. Make sure to turn it over halfway through the cooking time. Enjoy!

155. Italian-Style Fried Polenta Slices
INGREDIENTS (3 Servings)

- 9 ounces pre-cooked polenta roll
- 1 teaspoon sesame oil
- 2 ounces prosciutto, chopped
- 1 teaspoon Italian seasoning blend

DIRECTIONS (Prep + Cook Time: 35 minutes)

Cut the pre-cooked polenta roll into nine equal slices. Brush them with sesame oil on all sides. Then, transfer the polenta slices to the lightly oiled Air Fryer cooking basket. Cook the polenta slices at 395 degrees F for about 30 minutes; then, top them with chopped prosciutto and Italian seasoning blend. Continue to cook for another 5 minutes until cooked through. Serve with marinara sauce, if desired. Enjoy!

156. Savory Cheese and Herb Biscuits
INGREDIENTS (3 Servings)

- 1 cup self-rising flour
- ½ teaspoon baking powder
- ½ teaspoon honey
- ½ stick butter, melted
- ½ cup Colby cheese, grated
- ½ cup buttermilk
- ¼ teaspoon kosher salt
- 1 teaspoon dried parsley
- 1 teaspoon dried rosemary

DIRECTIONS (Prep + Cook Time: 30 minutes)

Preheat your Air Fryer to 360 degrees F. Line the cooking basket with a piece of parchment paper. In a mixing bowl, thoroughly combine the flour, baking powder, honey, and butter. Gradually stir in the remaining ingredients. Bake in the preheated Air Fryer for 15 minutes. Work in batches. Serve at room temperature. Enjoy!

157. Grilled Garlic and Avocado Toast
INGREDIENTS (2 Servings)

- 4 slices artisan bread
- 1 garlic clove, halved
- 2 tablespoons olive oil
- 1 avocado, seeded, peeled and mashed
- ½ teaspoon sea salt
- ¼ teaspoon ground black pepper

DIRECTIONS (Prep + Cook Time: 15 minutes)

Rub 1 side of each bread slice with garlic. Brush with olive oil. Place the bread slices on the Air Fryer grill pan. Bake in the preheated Air Fryer at 400 degrees F for 3 to 4 minutes. Slather the mashed avocado on top of the toast and season with salt and pepper. Enjoy!

158. Aromatic Seafood Pilaf
INGREDIENTS (2 Servings)

1 cup jasmine rice

Salt and black pepper, to taste

1 bay leaf

1 small yellow onion, chopped

1 small garlic clove, finely chopped

1 teaspoon butter, melted

4 tablespoons cream of mushroom soup

½ pound shrimp, divined and sliced

DIRECTIONS (Prep + Cook Time: 45 minutes)

Bring 2 cups of a lightly salted water to a boil in a medium saucepan over medium-high heat. Add in the jasmine rice, turn to a simmer and cook, covered, for about 18 minutes until water is absorbed. Let the jasmine rice stand covered for 5 to 6 minutes; fluff with a fork and transfer to a lightly greased Air Fryer safe pan. Stir in the salt, black pepper, bay leaf, yellow onion, garlic, butter and cream of mushroom soup; stir until everything is well incorporated. Cook the rice at 350 degrees F for about 13 minutes. Stir in the shrimp and continue to cook for a further 5 minutes. Check the rice for softness. If necessary, cook for a few minutes more. Enjoy!

159. Smoked Salmon and Rice Rollups
INGREDIENTS (3 Servings)

1 tablespoon fresh lemon juice

6 slices smoked salmon

1 tablespoon extra-virgin olive oil

½ cup cooked rice

1 tablespoon whole-grain mustard

3 tablespoons shallots, chopped

1 garlic clove, minced

1 teaspoon capers, rinsed and chopped

Sea salt and ground black pepper, to taste

3 ounces sour cream

DIRECTIONS (Prep + Cook Time: 25 minutes)

Drizzle the lemon juice all over the smoked salmon. Then, spread each salmon strip with olive oil. In a mixing bowl, thoroughly combine the cooked rice, mustard, shallots, garlic, and capers. Spread the rice mixture over the olive oil. Roll the slices into individual rollups and secure with a toothpick. Season with salt and black pepper. Place in the lightly greased Air Fryer basket. Bake at 370 degrees F for 16 minutes, turning them over halfway through the cooking time. Serve with sour cream and enjoy!

160. Pretzel Knots with Cumin Seeds
INGREDIENTS (6 Servings)

1 package crescent refrigerator rolls

2 eggs, whisked with 4 tablespoons of water

1 teaspoon cumin seeds

DIRECTIONS (Prep + Cook Time: 25 minutes)

Roll the dough out into a rectangle. Slice the dough into 6 pieces. Roll each piece into a log and tie each rope into a knot. Cover and let it rest for 10 minutes. Brush the top of the pretzel knots with the egg wash; sprinkle with the cumin seeds. Arrange the pretzel knots in the lightly greased Air Fryer basket. Bake in the preheated Air Fryer at 340 degrees for 7 minutes until golden brown. Serve and enjoy!

161. Fried Bread Pudding Squares
INGREDIENTS (4 Servings)

6 slices bread, cubed

1 cup sugar

2 cups milk

2 large eggs, beaten

½ teaspoon vanilla extract

½ teaspoon ground cinnamon

2 tablespoons dark rum

2 tablespoons icing sugar

DIRECTIONS (Prep + Cook Time: 40 minutes)

Place the bread cubes in a lightly greased baking dish. In a mixing bowl, thoroughly combine the sugar, milk, eggs, vanilla, cinnamon, and rum. Pour the custard over the bread cubes. Let stand for 30 minutes, occasionally pressing with a wide spatula to submerge. Cook in the preheated Air Fryer at 370 degrees F degrees for 7 minutes; check to ensure even cooking and cook an additional 5 to 6 minutes. Place your bread pudding in the refrigerator to cool completely; cut into 1 ½-inch squares. Bake at 330 degrees F for 2 minutes in the lightly buttered Air Fryer basket. Dust with icing sugar and serve. Enjoy!

162. Sweet Potato Croquettes
INGREDIENTS (3 Servings)

½ pound sweet potatoes

¼ cup wheat flour

¼ cup glutinous rice flour

1 teaspoon baking powder

1 tablespoon brown sugar

¼ teaspoon cayenne pepper

A pinch of grated nutmeg

Kosher salt and ground black pepper, to taste

DIRECTIONS (Prep + Cook Time: 20 minutes)

Mix all ingredients in a bowl; stir until everything is well combined. Transfer the sweet potato balls to the Air Fryer cooking basket and spritz them with a nonstick cooking oil. Bake the sweet potato balls in the preheated Air Fryer at 360 degrees F for 15 minutes or until thoroughly cooked and crispy. Enjoy!

163. Shawarma Roasted Chickpeas
INGREDIENTS (2 Servings)

- 8 ounces canned chickpeas
- ¼ teaspoon turmeric powder
- ¼ teaspoon cinnamon
- ¼ teaspoon allspice
- ½ teaspoon ground coriander
- ¼ teaspoon ground ginger
- ¼ teaspoon smoked paprika
- Coarse sea salt and freshly ground black pepper, to taste

DIRECTIONS (Prep + Cook Time: 20 minutes)

Rinse your chickpeas with cold running water and pat it dry using kitchen towels. Place the spices in a plastic bag; add in the chickpeas and shake until all the chickpeas are coated with the spices. Spritz the spiced chickpeas with a nonstick cooking oil and transfer them to the Air Fryer cooking basket. Cook your chickpeas in the preheated Air Fryer at 395 degrees F for 13 minutes. Turn your Air Fryer to 350 degrees F and cook an additional 6 minutes. Enjoy!

164. Veggie Fajitas with Simple Guacamole
INGREDIENTS (4 Servings)

- 1 tablespoon canola oil
- ½ cup scallions, thinly sliced
- 2 bell peppers, seeded and sliced into strips
- 1 habanero pepper, seeded and minced
- 1 garlic clove, minced
- 4 large Portobello mushrooms, thinly sliced
- ¼ cup salsa 1 tablespoon yellow mustard
- Kosher salt and ground black pepper, to taste
- ½ teaspoon Mexican oregano
- 1 medium ripe avocado, peeled, pitted and mashed
- 1 tablespoon fresh lemon juice
- ½ teaspoon onion powder
- ½ teaspoon garlic powder
- 1 teaspoon red pepper flakes
- 4 (8-inch) flour tortillas

DIRECTIONS (Prep + Cook Time: 25 minutes)

Brush the sides and bottom of the cooking basket with canola oil. Add the scallions and cook for 1 to 2 minutes or until aromatic. Then, add the peppers, garlic, and mushrooms to the cooking basket. Cook for 2 to 3 minutes or until tender. Stir in the salsa, mustard, salt, black pepper, and oregano. Cook in the preheated Air Fryer at 380 degrees F for 15 minutes, stirring occasionally. In the meantime, make your guacamole by mixing mashed avocado together with the lemon juice, garlic powder, onion powder, and red pepper flakes. Divide between the tortillas and garnish with guacamole. Roll up your tortillas and enjoy!

165. The Best Falafel Ever
INGREDIENTS (2 Servings)

- 1 cup dried chickpeas, soaked overnight
- 1 small-sized onion, chopped
- 2 cloves garlic, minced
- 2 tablespoons fresh cilantro leaves, chopped
- 1 tablespoon flour
- ½ teaspoon baking powder
- 1 teaspoon cumin powder
- A pinch of ground cardamom
- Sea salt and ground black pepper, to taste

DIRECTIONS (Prep + Cook Time: 20 minutes)

Pulse all the ingredients in your food processor until the chickpeas are ground. Form the falafel mixture into balls and place them in the lightly greased Air Fryer basket. Cook at 380 degrees F for about 15 minutes, shaking the basket occasionally to ensure even cooking. Serve in pita bread with toppings of your choice. Enjoy!

166. Onion Rings with Spicy Ketchup
INGREDIENTS (2 Servings)

- 1 onion, sliced into rings
- ⅓ cup all-purpose flour
- ½ cup oat milk
- 1 teaspoon curry powder
- 1 teaspoon cayenne pepper
- Salt and ground black pepper, to your liking
- ½ cup cornmeal
- 4 tablespoons vegan parmesan
- ¼ cup spicy ketchup

DIRECTIONS (Prep + Cook Time: 30 minutes)

Place the onion rings in the bowl with cold water; let them soak approximately 20 minutes; drain the onion rings and pat dry using a kitchen towel. In a shallow bowl, mix the flour, milk, curry powder, cayenne pepper, salt, and black pepper. Mix to combine well. Mix the cornmeal and vegan parmesan in another shallow bowl. Dip the onion rings in the flour/milk mixture; then, dredge in the cornmeal mixture. Spritz the Air Fryer basket with cooking spray; arrange the breaded onion rings in the Air Fryer basket. Cook in the preheated Air Fryer at 400 degrees F for 4 to 5 minutes, turning them over halfway through the cooking time. Serve with spicy ketchup. Enjoy!

167. Barbecue Roasted Almonds
INGREDIENTS (6 Servings)

- 1 ½ cups raw almonds
- Sea salt and ground black pepper, to taste
- ¼ teaspoon garlic powder
- ¼ teaspoon mustard powder
- ½ teaspoon cumin powder
- ¼ teaspoon smoked paprika
- 1 tablespoon olive oil

DIRECTIONS (Prep + Cook Time: 20 minutes)

Toss all ingredients in a mixing bowl. Line the Air Fryer basket with baking parchment. Spread out the coated almonds in a single layer in the basket. Roast at 350 degrees F for 6 to 8 minutes, shaking the basket once or twice. Work in batches. Enjoy!

168. Green Beans with Oyster Mushrooms
INGREDIENTS (3 Servings)

1 tablespoon extra-virgin olive oil 2 garlic cloves, minced ½ cup scallions, chopped 2 cups oyster mushrooms, sliced 12 ounces fresh green beans, trimmed 1 tablespoon soy sauce Sea salt and ground black pepper, to taste

DIRECTIONS (Prep + Cook Time: 20 minutes)

Start by preheating your Air Fryer to 390 degrees F. Heat the oil and sauté the garlic and scallions until tender and fragrant, about 5 minutes. Add the remaining ingredients and stir to combine well. Increase the temperature to 400 degrees F and cook for a further 5 minutes. Serve warm.

169. Rainbow Roasted Vegetables
INGREDIENTS (4 Servings)

- 1 red bell pepper, seeded and cut into ½-inch chunks
- 1 cup squash, peeled and cut into ½-inch chunks
- 1 yellow bell pepper, seeded and cut into ½-inch chunks
- 1 yellow onion, quartered
- 1 green bell pepper, seeded and cut into ½-inch chunks
- 1 cup broccoli, broken into ½-inch florets
- 2 parsnips, trimmed and cut into ½-inch chunks
- 2 garlic cloves, minced
- Pink Himalayan salt and ground black pepper, to taste
- ½ teaspoon marjoram
- ½ teaspoon dried oregano
- ¼ cup dry white wine
- ¼ cup vegetable broth
- ½ cup Kalamata olives, pitted and sliced

DIRECTIONS (Prep + Cook Time: 25 minutes)

Arrange your vegetables in a single layer in the baking pan in the order of the rainbow (red, orange, yellow, and green). Scatter the minced garlic around the vegetables. Season with salt, black pepper, marjoram, and oregano. Drizzle the white wine and vegetable broth over the vegetables. Roast in the preheated Air Fryer at 390 degrees F for 15 minutes, rotating the pan once or twice. Scatter the Kalamata olives all over your vegetables and serve warm. Enjoy!

170. Peppers Provençal with Garbanzo Beans
INGREDIENTS (3 Servings)

- 1 pound bell peppers, deseeded and sliced
- 2 teaspoons olive oil
- 1 teaspoon Herbs de Provence
- 1 onion, chopped
- 10 ounces canned tomato sauce
- 1 teaspoon red wine vinegar
- 9 ounces canned garbanzo beans

DIRECTIONS (Prep + Cook Time: 25 minutes)

Drizzle the bell peppers with 1 teaspoon of olive oil; sprinkle them with Herbs de Provence and transfer to the Air Fryer cooking basket. Cook the peppers in the preheated Air Fryer at 400 degrees F for 15 minutes, shaking the basket halfway through the cooking time. Meanwhile, heat the remaining teaspoon of olive oil in a saucepan over medium-high heat. Once hot, sauté the onion until just tender and translucent. Then, add in the tomato sauce and let it simmer, partially covered, for about 10 minutes until the sauce has thickened. Remove from the heat and add in the vinegar and garbanzo beans; stir to combine. Serve the roasted peppers with the saucy garbanzo beans. Enjoy!

171. Polenta Bites with Wild Mushroom Ragout
INGREDIENTS (3 Servings)

- 2 cups water
- 1 teaspoon salt
- ½ cup polenta
- 2 tablespoons butter, melted
- 1 tablespoon olive oil
- 6 ounces wild mushrooms, sliced
- ½ red onion, chopped
- ½ teaspoon fresh garlic, minced
- Sea salt and freshly ground black pepper, to taste
- 1 teaspoon cayenne pepper
- ½ cup dry white wine

DIRECTIONS (Prep + Cook Time: 50 minutes)

Bring 2 cups of water and 1 teaspoon salt to a boil in a saucepan over medium-high heat. Slowly and gradually, stir in the polenta, whisking constantly. Reduce the heat to medium-low and continue to cook for 5 to 6 minutes more. Stir in the butter and mix to combine. Pour the prepared polenta into a parchment-lined baking pan, cover and let stand for 15 to 20 minutes or until set. In the meantime, preheat your Air Fryer to 360 degrees F. Heat the olive oil until sizzling. Then, add the mushrooms, onion, and garlic to the baking pan. Cook for 5 minutes, stirring occasionally. Season with salt, black pepper, cayenne pepper, and wine; cook an additional 5 minutes and reserve. Cut the polenta into 18 squares. Transfer to the lightly greased cooking basket. Cook in the preheated Air Fryer at 395 degrees F for about 8 minutes. Top with the wild mushroom ragout and bake an additional 3 minutes. Serve warm.

172. Paella-Style Spanish Rice
INGREDIENTS (2 Servings)

- 2 cups water
- 1 cup white rice, rinsed and drained
- 1 cube vegetable stock
- 1 chorizo, sliced
- 2 cups brown mushrooms, cleaned and sliced
- 2 cloves garlic, finely chopped
- ½ teaspoon fresh ginger, ground
- 1 long red chili, minced
- ¼ cup dry white wine
- ½ cup tomato sauce
- 1 teaspoon smoked paprika
- Kosher salt and ground black pepper, to taste
- 1 cup green beans

DIRECTIONS (Prep + Cook Time: 35 minutes)

In a medium saucepan, bring the water to a boil. Add the rice and vegetable stock cube. Stir and reduce the heat. Cover and let it simmer for 20 minutes. Then, place the chorizo, mushrooms, garlic, ginger, and red chili in the baking pan. Cook at 380 degrees F for 6 minutes, stirring periodically. Add the prepared rice to the casserole dish. Add the remaining ingredients and gently stir to combine. Cook for 6 minutes, checking periodically to ensure even cooking. Serve in individual bowls and enjoy!

173. Chocolate Chip Bread Pudding Squares
INGREDIENTS (3 Servings)

- 3 thick slices bread, cut into cubes
- 1 egg
- 1 cup heavy cream
- 1 tablespoon agave nectar
- ¼ teaspoon ground cinnamon
- ¼ teaspoon ground cloves
- 2 tablespoons chocolate chips
- 2 tablespoons icing sugar

DIRECTIONS (Prep + Cook Time: 20 minutes)

Add the bread chunks to a lightly oiled baking dish. In a mixing dish, whisk the egg, heavy cream, agave nectar, cinnamon and cloves. Pour the custard over the bread chunks and press to soak well. Fold in the chocolate chips. Cook in the preheated Air Fryer at 370 degrees F for about 13 minutes. Place the bread pudding in the refrigerator until it is chilled completely; cut into 1 ½-inch squares. Bake the squares at 330 degrees F for 2 minutes until golden on the top. Dust with icing sugar and serve. Enjoy!

174. Quick and Easy Cornbread
INGREDIENTS (4 Servings)

- ½ cup self-rising cornmeal mix
- A dash of salt
- A dash of grated nutmeg
- A dash of granulated sugar
- 1 tablespoon honey
- 4 tablespoons butter, melted
- ½ cup full-fat milk

DIRECTIONS (Prep + Cook Time: 20 minutes)

In a mixing bowl, thoroughly combine the dry ingredients. In another bowl, mix the wet ingredients. Then, stir the wet mixture into the dry mixture. Pour the batter into a lightly buttered baking pan. Now, bake your cornbread at 340 degrees F for about 15 minutes. Check for doneness and transfer to a wire rack to cool slightly before cutting and serving. Enjoy!

175. Mediterranean Monkey Bread
INGREDIENTS (6 Servings)

- 1 (16-ounce) can refrigerated buttermilk biscuits
- 3 tablespoons olive oil
- 1 cup Provolone cheese, grated
- ¼ cup black olives, pitted and chopped
- 4 tablespoons basil pesto
- ¼ cup pine nuts, chopped
- 1 tablespoon
- Mediterranean herb mix

DIRECTIONS (Prep + Cook Time: 20 minutes)

Separate your dough into the biscuits and cut each of them in half; roll them into balls. Dip each ball into the olive oil and begin layering in a nonstick Bundt pan. Cover the bottom of the pan with one layer of dough balls. Prepare the coating mixtures. In a shallow bowl, place the provolone cheese and olives, add the basil pesto to a second bowl and add the pine nuts to a third bowl. Roll the dough balls in the coating mixtures; then, arrange them in the Bundt pan so the various coatings are alternated. Top with Mediterranean herb mix Cook the monkey bread in the Air Fryer at 320 degrees for 13 to 16 minutes. Serve and enjoy!

176. Basic Air Fryer Granola
INGREDIENTS (12 Servings)

- ½ cup rolled oats
- 1 cup walnuts, chopped
- 3 tablespoons sunflower seeds
- 3 tablespoons pumpkin seeds
- 1 teaspoon coarse sea salt
- 2 tablespoons honey

DIRECTIONS (Prep + Cook Time: 45 minutes)

Thoroughly combine all ingredients and spread the mixture onto the Air Fryer trays. Spritz with nonstick cooking spray. Bake at 230 degrees F for 25 minutes; rotate the trays and bake 10 to 15 minutes more. This granola can be kept in an airtight container for up to 2 weeks. Enjoy!

177. Easy Mexican Burritos
INGREDIENTS (4 Servings)

- 1 tablespoon olive oil
- 1 cup ground beef
- 1 teaspoon fresh garlic, minced
- 2 tablespoons scallions, chopped
- 1 habanero pepper, seeded and chopped
- 2 (8-ounce) cans refrigerated crescent dinner rolls
- ½ cup canned pinto beans, rinsed and drained
- 1 tablespoon taco seasoning mix
- 1 cup Colby cheese, shredded

DIRECTIONS (Prep + Cook Time: 25 minutes)

Heat the olive oil in a skillet over medium heat. Now, cook the ground beef, garlic, scallions, and habanero pepper until the beef is no longer pink and the onion is translucent and fragrant. Separate the crescent dinner rolls into 8 rectangles. Divide the beef mixture between rectangles; add the pinto beans and taco seasoning mix; top with the shredded cheese. Roll up and pinch the edge to seal. Place the seam side down on the parchment-lined Air Fryer basket. Bake in the preheated Air Fryer at 355 degrees F for 20 minutes. Enjoy!

178. Savory Cheesy Cornmeal Biscuits
INGREDIENTS (6 Servings)

- 2 cups all-purpose flour
- 1 teaspoon baking soda
- 1 teaspoon baking powder
- 1 teaspoon granulated sugar
- ¼ teaspoon ground chipotle
- Sea salt, to taste
- A pinch of grated nutmeg
- 1 stick butter, cold
- 6 ounces canned whole corn kernels
- 1 cup Colby cheese, shredded
- 2 tablespoons sour cream
- 2 eggs, beaten

DIRECTIONS (Prep + Cook Time: 35 minutes)

In a mixing bowl, combine the flour, baking soda, baking powder, sugar, ground chipotle, salt, and a pinch of nutmeg. Cut in the butter until the mixture resembles coarse crumbs. Stir in the corn, Colby cheese, sour cream, and eggs; stir until everything is well incorporated. Turn the dough out onto a floured surface. Knead the dough with your hands and roll it out to 1-inch thickness. Using 3-inch round cutter, cut out the biscuits. Transfer the cornmeal biscuits to the lightly greased Air Fryer basket. Brush the biscuits with cooking oil. Bake in the preheated Air Fryer at 400 degrees F for 17 minutes. Continue cooking until all the batter is used. Enjoy!

179. Tyrolean Kaiserschmarrn (Austrian Pancakes)
INGREDIENTS (4 Servings)

- ½ cup flour
- A pinch of salt
- A pinch of sugar
- ½ cup whole milk
- 3 eggs
- 1 shot of rum
- 4 tablespoons raisins
- ½ cup icing sugar
- ½ cup stewed plums

DIRECTIONS (Prep + Cook Time: 30 minutes)

Mix the flour, salt, sugar, and milk in a bowl until the batter becomes semi-solid. Fold in the eggs; add the rum and whisk to combine well. Let it stand for 20 minutes. Spritz the Air Fryer baking pan with cooking spray. Pour the batter into the pan using a measuring cup. Scatter the raisins over the top. Cook at 230 degrees F for 4 to 5 minutes or until golden brown. Repeat with the remaining batter. Cut the pancake into pieces, sprinkle over the icing sugar, and serve with the stewed plums. Enjoy!

180. Famous Everything Bagel Kale Chips
INGREDIENTS (1 Servings)

- 2 cups loosely packed kale leaves, stems removed
- 1 teaspoon olive oil
- 1 tablespoon nutritional yeast flakes
- Coarse salt and ground black pepper, to taste
- 1 teaspoon sesame seeds, lightly toasted
- ½ teaspoon poppy seeds, lightly toasted
- ¼ teaspoon garlic powder

DIRECTIONS (Prep + Cook Time: 12 minutes)

Toss the kale leaves with olive oil, nutritional yeast, salt and black pepper. Cook your kale at 250 degrees F for 12 minutes, shaking the basket every 4 minutes to promote even cooking. Place the kale leaves on a platter and sprinkle evenly with sesame seeds, poppy seeds and garlic powder while still hot. Enjoy!

181. Delicious Coconut Granola
INGREDIENTS (12 Servings)

- 2 cups rolled oats
- 2 tablespoons butter
- 1 cup honey
- ½ teaspoon coconut extract
- ½ teaspoon vanilla extract
- ¼ cup sesame seeds
- ¼ cup pumpkin seeds
- ½ cup coconut flakes

DIRECTIONS (Prep + Cook Time: 40 minutes)

Thoroughly combine all ingredients, except the coconut flakes; mix well. Spread the mixture onto the Air Fryer trays. Spritz with nonstick cooking spray. Bake at 230 degrees F for 25 minutes; rotate the trays, add the coconut flakes, and bake for a further 10 to 15 minutes. This granola can be stored in an airtight container for up to 3 weeks. Enjoy!

182. Almost Famous Four-Cheese Pizza
INGREDIENTS (4 Servings)

- 1 (11-ounce) can refrigerated thin pizza crust
- ½ cup tomato pasta sauce
- 2 tablespoons scallions, chopped
- ¼ cup Parmesan cheese, grated
- 1 cup provolone cheese, shredded
- 1 cup mozzarella cheese, sliced
- 4 slices cheddar cheese
- 1 tablespoon olive oil

DIRECTIONS (Prep + Cook Time: 15 minutes)

Stretch the dough on a work surface lightly dusted with flour. Spread with a layer of tomato pasta sauce. Top with the scallions and cheese. Place on the baking tray that is previously greased with olive oil. Bake in the preheated Air Fryer at 395 degrees F for 5 minutes. Rotate the baking tray and bake for a further 5 minutes. Serve immediately.

183. Asian-Style Brussels Sprouts
INGREDIENTS (3 Servings)

- 1 pound Brussels sprouts, trimmed and halved
- 1 teaspoon coconut oil
- 2 tablespoons Shoyu sauce
- 1 tablespoon agave syrup
- 1 teaspoon rice vinegar
- ½ teaspoon Gochujang paste
- 1 clove garlic, minced
- 2 scallion stalks, chopped
- 1 tablespoon sesame seeds, toasted

DIRECTIONS (Prep + Cook Time: 20 minutes)

Toss the Brussels sprouts with coconut oil, Shoyu sauce, agave syrup, rice vinegar, Gochujang paste and garlic. Cook the Brussels sprouts in the preheated Air Fryer at 380 degrees F for 15 minutes, shaking the basket halfway through the cooking time. Place the roasted Brussels sprouts on a serving platter and garnish with scallions and sesame seeds. Serve immediately!

184. Classic Honey Muffins
INGREDIENTS (3 Servings)

2 ½ ounces all-purpose flour	A pinch of coarse salt	1 egg
1 teaspoon baking powder	½ teaspoon vanilla extract	2 ounces milk
A pinch of ground cloves	2 tablespoons honey	2 tablespoons butter, melted

DIRECTIONS (Prep + Cook Time: 20 minutes)

In a mixing bowl, combine the ingredients in the order listed above. Spritz a silicone muffin tin with a nonstick cooking spray. Divide the batter between cups. Bake in the preheated Air Fryer at 330 degrees F for 12 to 15 minutes. Rotate the muffin tin halfway through the cooking time. Enjoy!

185. Healthy Oatmeal Cups
INGREDIENTS (2 Servings)

1 large banana, mashed	1 tablespoon agave syrup	1 cup coconut milk
1 cup quick-cooking steel cut oats	1 egg, well beaten	3 ounces mixed berries

DIRECTIONS (Prep + Cook Time: 15 minutes)

In a mixing bowl, thoroughly combine the banana, oats, agave syrup, beaten egg and coconut milk. Spoon the mixture into an Air Fryer safe baking dish. Bake in the preheated Air Fryer at 395 degrees F for about 7 minutes. Top with berries and continue to bake an additional 2 minutes. Spoon into individual bowls and serve with a splash of coconut milk if desired. Enjoy!

186. Old-Fashioned Greek Tiganites
INGREDIENTS (3 Servings)

½ cup plain flour	A pinch of cinnamon	3 tablespoons honey
½ cup barley flour	1 egg	3 tablespoons walnuts, chopped
1 teaspoon baking powder	½ cup milk	3 tablespoons Greek yogurt
A pinch of salt	½ cup carbonated water	
A pinch of sugar	1 tablespoon butter, melted	

DIRECTIONS (Prep + Cook Time: 50 minutes)

Thoroughly combine the flour, baking powder, salt, sugar and cinnamon in a large bowl. Fold in the egg and mix again. Gradually pour in the milk, water and melted butter, whisking continuously, until well combined. Let the batter stand for about 30 minutes. Spritz the Air Fryer baking pan with a cooking spray. Pour the batter into the pan using a measuring cup. Cook at 230 degrees F for 6 to 8 minutes or until golden brown. Repeat with the remaining batter. Serve your tiganites with the honey, walnuts and Greek yogurt. Enjoy!

187. Mediterranean Mini Monkey Bread
INGREDIENTS (3 Servings)

6 ounces refrigerated crescent rolls	¼ cup pesto sauce	2 cloves garlic, minced	½ teaspoon dried parsley flakes
¼ cup ketchup	½ cup provolone cheese, shredded	½ teaspoon dried oregano	
		½ teaspoon dried basil	

DIRECTIONS (Prep + Cook Time: 15 minutes)

Start by preheating your Air Fryer to 350 degrees F. Roll out crescent rolls. Divide the ingredients between crescent rolls and roll them up. Using your fingertips, gently press them to seal the edges. Bake the mini monkey bread for 12 minutes or until the top is golden brown. Enjoy!

188. Traditional Italian Arancini
INGREDIENTS (3 Servings)

3 cups vegetable broth	1 ounce Ricotta cheese, at room temperature	1 large egg
1 cup white rice	1 tablespoon fresh cilantro, chopped	½ cup Italian seasoned breadcrumbs
2 ounces Colby cheese, grated	Sea salt and ground black pepper, to taste	

DIRECTIONS (Prep + Cook Time: 35 minutes) Bring the vegetable broth to a boil in a saucepan over medium-high heat. Stir in the rice and reduce the heat to simmer; cook about 20 minutes. Add in the cheese and cilantro. Season with salt and pepper and shape the mixture into bite-sized balls. Beat the egg in a shallow bowl; in another shallow bowl, place the seasoned breadcrumbs. Dip each rice ball into the beaten egg, then, roll in the seasoned breadcrumbs, gently pressing to coat well. Bake the rice balls in the preheated Air Fryer at 350 degrees F for about 10 minutes, shaking the basket halfway through the cooking time to ensure even browning. Enjoy!

189. Spanish-Style Chorizo and Cheese Casserole
INGREDIENTS (3 Servings)

- 8 slices white bread, cubed
- 1 tablespoon butter, softened
- 3 ounces chorizo sausage, crumbled
- 1 Spanish pepper, deveined and chopped
- 1 habanero pepper, deveined and chopped
- 1 cup Mexican cheese blend, shredded
- 2 tablespoons fresh cilantro, chopped
- 3 eggs
- 1 cup double cream
- ¼ teaspoon cayenne pepper
- ¼ teaspoon Mexican oregano
- Sea salt and freshly ground black pepper

DIRECTIONS (Prep + Cook Time: 20 minutes)

Add the bread chunks to a greased Air Fryer safe dish. Add in the butter, sausage, peppers, cheese and cilantro; stir to combine well. In a mixing dish, thoroughly combine the remaining ingredients and stir to combine well. Spoon the custard into the baking dish and press with a spatula to soak. Cook in the preheated Air Fryer at 370 degrees F for about 15 minutes until golden on the top. Serve and enjoy!

190. Easy Pizza Margherita
INGREDIENTS (1 Servings)

- 6-inch dough
- 2 tablespoons tomato sauce
- 2 ounces mozzarella
- 1 teaspoon extra-virgin olive oil
- Coarse sea salt, to taste
- 2-3 fresh basil leaves

DIRECTIONS (Prep + Cook Time: 15 minutes)

Start by preheating your Air Fryer to 380 degrees F. Stretch the dough on a pizza peel lightly dusted with flour. Spread with a layer of tomato sauce. Add mozzarella to the crust and drizzle with olive oil. Salt to taste. Bake in the preheated Air Fryer for 4 minutes. Rotate the baking tray and bake for a further 4 minutes. Garnish with fresh basil leaves and serve immediately.

191. Sun-Dried Tomato and Herb Pull-Apart Bread
INGREDIENTS (6 Servings)

- 1 (16-ounce) can refrigerated buttermilk biscuits
- ½ cup stick butter, melted
- ⅓ cup parmesan cheese, grated
- ¼ cup sun-dried tomatoes
- 1 teaspoon rosemary
- 1 teaspoon basil
- 1 teaspoon oregano
- ½ teaspoon sage
- 1 teaspoon parsley
- 2 garlic cloves very finely minced

DIRECTIONS (Prep + Cook Time: 20 minutes)

Separate your dough into the biscuits and cut each of them in half; roll them into balls. Dip each ball into the butter and begin layering in a nonstick Bundt pan. Cover the bottom of the pan with one layer of dough balls; then, top the dough balls with half of the cheese and half of the sun-dried tomatoes. Repeat for another layer. In a small mixing bowl, thoroughly combine the garlic with herbs. Finish with a third layer of dough and top it with the herb/garlic mixture. Cook the pull-apart bread in the Air Fryer at 320 degrees for 13 to 16 minutes. Serve and enjoy!

192. Last Minute German Franzbrötchen
INGREDIENTS (6 Servings)

- 6 slices white bread
- 1 tablespoon butter, melted
- Glaze:
- ½ cup icing sugar
- ¼ cup brown sugar
- 1 tablespoon ground cinnamon
- ½ teaspoon vanilla paste
- 1 tablespoon milk

DIRECTIONS (Prep + Cook Time: 15 minutes)

Flatten the bread slices to ¼-inch thickness using a rolling pin. In a small mixing bowl, thoroughly combine the butter, brown sugar and ground cinnamon. Spread the butter mixture on top of each slice of bread; roll them up. Bake the rolls at 350 degrees F for 10 minutes, flipping them halfway through the cooking time. Meanwhile, whisk the icing sugar, vanilla paste and milk until everything is well incorporated. Drizzle the glaze over the top of the slightly cooled rolls. Let the glaze set before serving. Enjoy!

193. Japanese Chicken and Rice Salad
INGREDIENTS (4 Servings)

1 pound chicken tenderloins	1 cup baby spinach	1 tablespoon liquid from pickled ginger
2 ablespoons shallots, chopped	½ cup snow peas	1 teaspoon agave syrup
1 garlic clove, minced	2 tablespoons soy sauce	2 tablespoons black sesame seeds, to serve
1 red bell pepper, chopped	1 teaspoon yellow mustard	¼ cup Mandarin orange segments
1 ½ cups brown rice	1 tablespoon rice vinegar	

DIRECTIONS (Prep + Cook Time: 45 minutes)

Start by preheating your Air Fryer to 380 degrees F. Then, add the chicken tenderloins to the baking pan and cook until it starts to get crisp or about 6 minutes. Add the shallots, garlic, and bell pepper. Cook for 6 minutes more. Wait for the chicken mixture to cool down completely and transfer to a salad bowl. Bring 3 cups of water and 1 teaspoon of salt to a boil in a saucepan over medium-high heat. Stir in the rice and reduce the heat to simmer; cook about 20 minutes. Let your rice sit in the covered saucepan for another 10 minutes. Drain the rice and allow it to cool completely. Stir the cold rice into the salad bowl; add the baby spinach and snow peas. In a small mixing dish, whisk the soy sauce, mustard, rice vinegar, liquid from pickled ginger, and agave syrup. Dress the salad and stir well to combine. Garnish with black sesame seeds and Mandarin orange. Enjoy!

194. Greek-Style Pizza with Spinach and Feta
INGREDIENTS (2 Servings)

2 ounces frozen chopped spinach	¼ cup tomato sauce	½ feta cheese, crumbled
Coarse sea salt, to taste	2 tablespoons fresh basil, roughly chopped	
2 personal pizza crusts		
1 tablespoon olive oil	½ teaspoon dried oregano	

DIRECTIONS (Prep + Cook Time: 20 minutes)

Add the frozen spinach to the saucepan and cook until all the liquid has evaporated, about 6 minutes. Season with sea salt to taste. Preheat the Air Fryer to 395 degrees F. Unroll the pizza dough on the Air Fryer baking tray; brush with olive oil. Spread the tomato sauce over the pizza crust. Add the sautéed spinach, basil, and oregano. Sprinkle the feta cheese, covering the pizza crust to the edges. Cook for 10 minutes, rotating your pizza halfway through the cooking time. Repeat with another pizza and serve warm.

195. Crème Brûlée French Toast
INGREDIENTS (2 Servings)

4 slices bread, about 1-inch thick	2 ounces brown sugar	2 ounces Neufchâtel cheese, softened
2 tablespoons butter, softened	½ teaspoon vanilla paste	
1 teaspoon ground cinnamon	A pinch of sea salt	

DIRECTIONS (Prep + Cook Time: 10 minutes)

In a mixing dish, combine the butter, cinnamon, brown sugar, vanilla, and salt. Spread the cinnamon butter on both sides of the bread slices. Arrange in the cooking basket. Cook at 390 degrees F for 2 minutes; turn over and cook an additional 2 minutes. Serve with softened Neufchâtel cheese on individual plates. Serve and enjoy!

196. Southwestern Fried Apples
INGREDIENTS (3 Servings)

2 granny smith apples, peeled, cored and sliced	1 teaspoon fresh lemon juice	1 teaspoon apple pie seasoning mix
1 tablespoon coconut oil	¼ cup brown sugar	

DIRECTIONS (Prep + Cook Time: 10 minutes)

Toss the apple slices with the coconut oil, lemon juice, brown sugar and apple pie seasoning mix. Place the apple slices in the Air Fryer cooking basket and cook them at 360 degrees F for about 8 minutes, shaking the cooking basket halfway through the cooking time. Serve and enjoy!

197. Italian Panettone Bread Pudding
INGREDIENTS (3 Servings)

- 4 slices of panettone bread, crusts trimmed, bread cut into 1-inch cubes
- 4 tablespoons dried cranberries
- 2 tablespoons amaretto liqueur
- 1 cup coconut milk
- ½ cup whipping cream
- 2 eggs
- 1 tablespoon agave syrup
- ½ vanilla extract
- ½ teaspoon ground cloves
- ½ teaspoon ground cinnamon

DIRECTIONS (Prep + Cook Time: 45 minutes)

Place the panettone bread cubes in a lightly greased baking dish. Scatter the dried cranberry over the top. In a mixing bowl, thoroughly combine the remaining ingredients. Pour the custard over the bread cubes. Let it stand for 30 minutes, occasionally pressing with a wide spatula to submerge. Cook in the preheated Air Fryer at 370 degrees F degrees for 7 minutes; check to ensure even cooking and cook an additional 5 to 6 minutes. Serve and enjoy!

198. Ciabatta Bread Pudding with Walnuts
INGREDIENTS (4 Servings)

- 4 cups ciabatta bread cubes
- 2 eggs, slightly beaten
- 1 cup milk
- 2 tablespoons butter
- 4 tablespoons honey
- 1 teaspoon vanilla extract
- ½ teaspoon ground cloves
- ½ teaspoon ground cinnamon
- A pinch of salt
- A pinch of grated nutmeg
- ⅓ cup walnuts, chopped

DIRECTIONS (Prep + Cook Time: 45 minutes)

Place the ciabatta bread cubes in a lightly greased baking dish. In a mixing bowl, thoroughly combine the eggs, milk, butter, honey, vanilla, ground cloves, cinnamon, salt, and nutmeg. Pour the custard over the bread cubes. Scatter the chopped walnuts over the top of your bread pudding. Let stand for 30 minutes, occasionally pressing with a wide spatula to submerge. Cook in the preheated Air Fryer at 370 degrees F degrees for 7 minutes; check to ensure even cooking and cook an additional 5 to 6 minutes. Serve and enjoy!

199. Old-Fashioned Burritos
INGREDIENTS (3 Servings)

- ½ pound ground turkey
- 1 teaspoon taco seasoning blend
- 1 teaspoon deli mustard
- 8 ounces canned black beans
- ½ red onion, sliced
- Sea salt and ground black pepper, to taste
- 3 (12-inch) whole-wheat tortillas, warmed
- ½ cup Cotija cheese, crumbled
- 1 cup butterhead lettuce, torn into pieces
- 1 teaspoon olive oil

DIRECTIONS (Prep + Cook Time: 20 minutes)

Cook the ground turkey in a nonstick skillet for about 4 minutes, crumbling with a fork. Stir the taco seasoning blend, mustard, beans, onion, salt and pepper into the skillet. Place the meat mixture in the center of each tortilla. Top with cheese and lettuce. Roll your tortillas to make burritos. Brush each burrito with olive oil and place them in the lightly greased cooking basket. Bake your burritos at 395 degrees F for 10 minutes, turning them over halfway through the cooking time. Serve immediately with salsa on the side, if desired.

200. Authentic Prosciutto Bruschetta
INGREDIENTS (3 Servings)

- 3 slices sourdough bread
- ½ cup marinara sauce
- 3 slices mozzarella
- 6 slices prosciutto
- 6 fresh basil leaves

DIRECTIONS (Prep + Cook Time: 10 minutes)

Using a rolling pin, flatten the bread slightly. Spread the marinara sauce on top of each slice of bread, then, top with mozzarella and prosciutto. Now, bake your bruschetta at 360 degrees F for about 8 minutes until the cheese is melted and golden. Garnish with basil leaves and serve.

201. Taco Stuffed Bread
INGREDIENTS (4 Servings)

- 1 loaf French bread
- ½ pound ground beef
- 1 onion, chopped
- 1 teaspoon garlic, minced
- 1 package taco seasoning
- 1 ½ cups Queso Panela, sliced
- Salt and ground black pepper, to taste
- 3 tablespoons tomato paste
- 2 tablespoons fresh cilantro leaves, chopped

DIRECTIONS (Prep + Cook Time: 15 minutes)

Cut the top off of the loaf of bread; remove some of the bread from the middle creating a well and reserve. In a large skillet, cook the ground beef with the onion and garlic until the beef is no longer pink and the onion is translucent. Add the taco seasoning, cheese, salt, black pepper, and tomato paste. Place the taco mixture into your bread. Bake in the preheated Air Fryer at 380 degrees F for 5 minutes. Garnish with fresh cilantro leaves. Enjoy!

202. Cheese and Bacon Ciabatta Sandwich
INGREDIENTS (2 Servings)

- 2 ciabatta sandwich buns, split
- 2 tablespoons butter
- 2 teaspoons Dijon mustard
- 4 slices Canadian bacon
- 4 slices Monterey Jack cheese

DIRECTIONS (Prep + Cook Time: 10 minutes)

Place the bottom halves of buns, cut sides up in the parchment lined Air Fryer basket. Spread the butter and mustard on the buns. Top with the bacon and cheese. Bake in the preheated Air Fryer at 400 degrees F for 3 minutes. Flip the sandwiches over and cook for 3 minutes longer or until the cheese has melted. Serve with some extra ketchup or salsa sauce. Enjoy!

203. Ooey-Gooey Dessert Quesadilla
INGREDIENTS (2 Servings)

- ¼ cup blueberries
- ¼ cup fresh orange juice
- ½ tablespoon maple syrup
- ½ cup vegan cream cheese
- 1 teaspoon vanilla extract
- 2 (6-inch) tortillas
- 2 teaspoons coconut oil
- ¼ cup vegan dark chocolate

DIRECTIONS (Prep + Cook Time: 25 minutes)

Bring the blueberries, orange juice, and maple syrup to a boil in a saucepan. Reduce the heat and let it simmer until the sauce thickens, about 10 minutes. In a mixing dish, combine the cream cheese with the vanilla extract; spread on the tortillas. Add the blueberry filling on top. Fold in half. Place the quesadillas in the greased Air Fryer basket. Cook at 390 degrees F for 10 minutes, until tortillas are golden brown and filling is melted. Make sure to turn them over halfway through the cooking. Heat the coconut oil in a small pan and add the chocolate; whisk to combine well. Drizzle the chocolate sauce over the quesadilla and serve. Enjoy!

204. Easy Granola with Raisins and Nuts
INGREDIENTS (8 Servings)

- 2 cups rolled oats
- ½ cup walnuts, chopped
- ⅓ cup almonds chopped
- ¼ cup raisins
- ¼ cup whole wheat pastry flour
- ½ teaspoon cinnamon
- ¼ teaspoon nutmeg, preferably freshly grated
- ½ teaspoon salt
- ⅓ cup coconut oil, melted
- ⅓ cup agave nectar
- ½ teaspoon coconut extract
- ½ teaspoon vanilla extract

DIRECTIONS (Prep + Cook Time: 40 minutes)

Thoroughly combine all ingredients. Then, spread the mixture onto the Air Fryer trays. Spritz with cooking spray. Bake at 230 degrees F for 25 minutes; rotate the trays and bake 10 to 15 minutes more. This granola can be stored in an airtight container for up to 2 weeks. Enjoy!

205. Tofu in Sweet & Sour Sauce
INGREDIENTS (3 Servings)

- 2 tablespoons Shoyu sauce
- 16 ounces extra-firm tofu, drained, pressed and cubed
- ½ cup water
- ¼ cup pineapple juice
- 2 garlic cloves, minced
- ½ teaspoon fresh ginger, grated
- 1 teaspoon cayenne pepper
- ¼ teaspoon ground black pepper
- ½ teaspoon salt
- 1 teaspoon honey
- 1 tablespoon arrowroot powder

DIRECTIONS (Prep + Cook Time: 25 minutes)

Drizzle the Shoyu sauce all over the tofu cubes. Cook in the preheated Air Fryer at 380 degrees F for 6 minutes; shake the basket and cook for a further 5 minutes. Meanwhile, cook the remaining ingredients in a heavy skillet over medium heat for 10 minutes, until the sauce has slightly thickened. Stir the fried tofu into the sauce and continue cooking for 4 minutes more or until the tofu is thoroughly heated. Serve warm and enjoy!

206. Delicious Asparagus and Mushroom Fritters
INGREDIENTS (4 Servings)

- 1 pound asparagus spears
- 1 tablespoon canola oil
- 1 teaspoon paprika
- Sea salt and freshly ground black pepper, to taste
- 1 teaspoon garlic powder
- 3 tablespoons scallions, chopped
- 1 cup button mushrooms, chopped
- ½ cup fresh breadcrumbs
- 1 tablespoon flax seeds, soaked in 2 tablespoons of water (vegan "egg")
- 4 tablespoons sun-dried tomato hummus

DIRECTIONS (Prep + Cook Time: 15 minutes)

Place the asparagus spears in the lightly greased cooking basket. Toss the asparagus with the canola oil, paprika, salt, and black pepper. Cook in the preheated Air Fryer at 400 degrees F for 5 minutes. Chop the asparagus spears and add the garlic powder, scallions, mushrooms, breadcrumbs, and vegan "egg". Mix until everything is well incorporated and form the asparagus mixture into patties. Cook in the preheated Air Fryer at 400 degrees F for 5 minutes, flipping halfway through the cooking time. Serve with sun-dried tomato hummus. Enjoy!

207. Mashed Potatoes with Roasted Peppers
INGREDIENTS (4 Servings)

- 4 potatoes
- 1 tablespoon vegan margarine
- 1 teaspoon garlic powder
- 1 pound bell peppers, seeded and quartered lengthwise
- 2 Fresno peppers, seeded and halved lengthwise
- 4 tablespoons olive oil
- 2 tablespoons cider vinegar
- 4 garlic cloves, pressed
- Kosher salt, to taste
- ½ teaspoon freshly ground black pepper
- ½ teaspoon dried dill

DIRECTIONS (Prep + Cook Time: 1 hour)

Place the potatoes in the Air Fryer basket and cook at 400 degrees F for 40 minutes. Discard the skin and mash the potatoes with the vegan margarine and garlic powder. Then, roast the peppers at 400 degrees F for 5 minutes. Give the peppers a half turn; place them back in the cooking basket and roast for another 5 minutes. Turn them one more time and roast until the skin is charred and soft or 5 more minutes. Peel the peppers and let them cool to room temperature. Toss your peppers with the remaining ingredients and serve with the mashed potatoes. Enjoy!

208. Marinated Tofu Bowl with Pearl Onions
INGREDIENTS (4 Servings)

- 16 ounces firm tofu, pressed and cut into 1-inch pieces
- 2 tablespoons vegan Worcestershire sauce
- 1 tablespoon apple cider vinegar
- 1 tablespoon maple syrup
- ½ teaspoon shallot powder
- ½ teaspoon porcini powder
- ½ teaspoon garlic powder
- 2 tablespoons peanut oil
- 1 cup pearl onions, peeled

DIRECTIONS (Prep + Cook Time: 20 minutes)

Place the tofu, Worcestershire sauce, vinegar, maple syrup, shallot powder, porcini powder, and garlic powder in a ceramic dish. Let it marinate in your refrigerator for 1 hour. Transfer the tofu to the lightly greased Air Fryer basket. Add the peanut oil and pearl onions; toss to combine. Cook the tofu with the pearl onions in the preheated Air Fryer at 380 degrees F for 6 minutes; pause and brush with the reserved marinade; cook for a further 5 minutes. Serve immediately. Enjoy!

209. Honey Cornbread Muffins
INGREDIENTS (3 Servings)

- ½ cup cornmeal
- ½ cup plain flour
- 1 tablespoon flaxseed meal
- 1 teaspoon baking powder
- 3 tablespoons honey
- A pinch of coarse sea salt
- A pinch of grated nutmeg
- ½ teaspoon ground cinnamon
- 1 egg, whisked
- 3/4 cup milk
- 2 tablespoons butter, melted

DIRECTIONS (Prep + Cook Time: 20 minutes)

In a mixing bowl, thoroughly combine the dry ingredients. In another bowl, mix the wet ingredients. Then, stir the wet mixture into the dry mixture. Pour the batter into a lightly buttered muffin tin. Now, bake your cornbread muffins at 350 degrees F for about 20 minutes. Check for doneness with a toothpick and transfer to a wire rack to cool slightly before serving. Enjoy!

210. Fluffy Pancake Cups with Sultanas
INGREDIENTS (3 Servings)

- ½ cup all-purpose flour
- ½ cup coconut flour
- ⅓ cup carbonated water
- ⅓ cup coconut milk
- 1 tablespoon dark rum
- 2 eggs
- ½ teaspoon vanilla
- ¼ teaspoon cardamom
- ½ cup Sultanas, soaked for 15 minutes

DIRECTIONS (Prep + Cook Time: 30 minutes)

In a mixing bowl, thoroughly combine the dry ingredients; in another bowl, mix the wet ingredients. Then, stir the wet mixture into the dry mixture and stir again to combine well. Let the batter sit for 20 minutes in your refrigerator. Spoon the batter into a greased muffin tin. Bake the pancake cups in your Air Fryer at 330 degrees F for 6 to 7 minutes or until golden brown. Repeat with the remaining batter. Enjoy!

211. New York-Style Pizza
INGREDIENTS (4 Servings)

- 1 pizza dough
- 1 cup tomato sauce
- 14 ounces mozzarella cheese, freshly grated
- 2 ounces parmesan, freshly grated

DIRECTIONS (Prep + Cook Time: 15 minutes)

Stretch your dough on a pizza peel lightly dusted with flour. Spread with a layer of tomato sauce. Top with cheese. Place on the baking tray. Bake in the preheated Air Fryer at 395 degrees F for 5 minutes. Rotate the baking tray and bake for a further 5 minutes. Serve immediately.

212. Mexican-Style Brown Rice Casserole
INGREDIENTS (4 Servings)

- 1 tablespoon olive oil
- 1 shallot, chopped
- 2 cloves garlic, minced
- 1 habanero pepper, minced
- 2 cups brown rice
- 3 cups chicken broth
- 1 cup water
- 2 ripe tomatoes, pureed
- Sea salt and ground black pepper, to taste
- ½ teaspoon dried
- Mexican oregano
- 1 teaspoon red pepper flakes
- 1 cup Mexican Cotija cheese, crumbled

DIRECTIONS (Prep + Cook Time: 50 minutes)

In a nonstick skillet, heat the olive oil over a moderate flame. Once hot, cook the shallot, garlic, and habanero pepper until tender and fragrant; reserve. Heat the brown rice, vegetable broth and water in a pot over high heat. Bring it to a boil; turn the stove down to simmer and cook for 35 minutes. Grease a baking pan with nonstick cooking spray. Spoon the cooked rice into the baking pan. Add the sautéed mixture. Spoon the tomato puree over the sautéed mixture. Sprinkle with salt, black pepper, oregano, and red pepper. Cook in the preheated Air Fryer at 380 degrees F for 8 minutes. Top with the Cotija cheese and bake for 5 minutes longer or until cheese is melted. Enjoy!

213. Rich Couscous Salad with Goat Cheese
INGREDIENTS (4 Servings)

- ½ cup couscous
- 4 teaspoons olive oil
- ½ lemon, juiced, zested
- 1 tablespoon honey
- Sea salt and freshly ground black pepper, to your liking
- 2 tomatoes, sliced
- 1 red onion, thinly sliced
- ½ English cucumber, thinly sliced
- 2 ounces goat cheese, crumbled
- 1 teaspoon ghee
- 2 tablespoons pine nuts
- ½ cup loosely packed Italian parsley, finely chopped

DIRECTIONS (Prep + Cook Time: 45 minutes)

Put the couscous in a bowl; now, pour the boiling water over it. Cover and set aside for 5 to 8 minutes; fluff with a fork. Place the couscous in a cake pan. Transfer the pan to the Air Fryer basket and cook at 360 digress F about 20 minutes. Make sure to stir every 5 minutes to ensure even cooking. Meanwhile, in a small mixing bowl, whisk the olive oil, lemon juice and zest, honey, salt, and black pepper. Toss the couscous with this dressing. Add the tomatoes, red onion, English cucumber, and goat cheese; gently stir to combine. Rub the ghee in the pine nuts, using your hands and place them in the Air Fryer basket. Roast for 4 minutes; give the nuts a good toss. Put the cooking basket back again and roast for a further 3 to 4 minutes. Scatter the toasted nuts over your salad and garnish with parsley. Enjoy!

214. Classic Air Fryer Cornbread
INGREDIENTS (4 Servings)

- 3/4 cup cornmeal
- 1 cup flour
- 2 teaspoons baking powder
- ½ tablespoon brown sugar
- ½ teaspoon salt
- 5 tablespoons butter, melted
- 3 eggs, beaten
- 1 cup full-fat milk

DIRECTIONS (Prep + Cook Time: 30 minutes)

Start by preheating your Air Fryer to 370 degrees F. Then, spritz a baking pan with cooking oil. In a mixing bowl, combine the flour, cornmeal, baking powder, brown sugar, and salt. In a separate bowl, mix the butter, eggs, and milk. Pour the egg mixture into the dry cornmeal mixture; mix to combine well. Pour the batter into the baking pan; cover with aluminum foil and poke tiny little holes all over the foil. Now, bake for 15 minutes. Remove the foil and bake for 10 minutes more. Transfer to a wire rack to cool slightly before cutting and serving. Enjoy!

215. Classic Pancakes with Blueberries
INGREDIENTS (4 Servings)

- 1 cup flour
- 1 teaspoon baking powder
- 1 teaspoon baking soda
- ½ teaspoon salt
- 1 teaspoon granulated sugar
- 2 eggs, beaten
- ½ cup milk
- 2 tablespoons butter melted
- 4 tablespoons maple syrup
- ½ cup fresh blueberries

DIRECTIONS (Prep + Cook Time: 30 minutes)

Mix the flour, baking powder, baking soda, salt, sugar, and eggs in a large bowl. Gradually add the milk and the melted butter, whisking continuously, until well combined. Let it stand for 20 minutes. Spritz the Air Fryer baking pan with cooking spray. Pour the batter into the pan using a measuring cup. Cook at 230 degrees F for 4 to 5 minutes or until golden brown. Repeat with the remaining batter. Serve with maple syrup and fresh blueberries. Enjoy!

216. Golden Beet Salad with Tahini Sauce
INGREDIENTS (2 Servings)

- 2 golden beets
- 1 tablespoon sesame oil
- Sea salt and ground black pepper, to taste
- 2 cups baby spinach
- 2 tablespoons tahini
- 2 tablespoons soy sauce
- 1 tablespoon white vinegar
- 1 clove garlic, pressed
- ½ jalapeno pepper, chopped
- ¼ teaspoon ground cumin

DIRECTIONS (Prep + Cook Time: 40 minutes)

Toss the golden beets with sesame oil. Cook the golden beets in the preheated Air Fryer at 400 degrees F for 40 minutes, turning them over once or twice to ensure even cooking. Let your beets cool completely and then, slice them with a sharp knife. Place the beets in a salad bowl and add in salt, pepper and baby spinach. In a small mixing dish, whisk the remaining ingredients until well combined. Spoon the sauce over your beets, toss to combine and serve immediately. Enjoy!

217. Decadent Carrot Salad with Sultanas
INGREDIENTS (3 Servings)

1 pound carrots, cut into ½-inch slices	2 tablespoons maple syrup	6 ounces baby spinach
¼ teaspoon dried dill	2 tablespoons Sultanas	¼ cup pine nuts, roughly chopped
½ teaspoon dried parsley flakes	½ cup orange juice	
	1 tablespoon champagne vinegar	

DIRECTIONS (Prep + Cook Time: 20 minutes)

Toss your carrots with dried dill and dried parsley flakes; brush them with a nonstick cooking spray. Cook your carrots in the preheated Air Fryer at 380 degrees F for about 15 minutes, shaking the basket halfway through the cooking time. Meanwhile, add the maple syrup, Sultanas, orange juice and champagne vinegar to a saucepan; let it simmer over a moderate heat until the sauce has thickened. Spoon the sauce over the roasted carrots and stir in the baby spinach. Top with chopped pine nuts and serve at room temperature. Enjoy!

218. Pearl Onions with Tahini Sauce
INGREDIENTS (2 Servings)

3/4 pound pearl onions	½ teaspoon thyme	1 tablespoon balsamic vinegar
1 teaspoon olive oil	2 tablespoons tahini	
Sea salt and ground black pepper, to taste	2 tablespoons soy sauce	

DIRECTIONS (Prep + Cook Time: 10 minutes)

Toss the pearl onions with olive oil, salt, black pepper and thyme. Cook the pearl onions in the preheated Air Fryer at 400 degrees F for 5 minutes. Shake the basket and continue to cook for another 5 minutes. Meanwhile, make the tahini sauce by whisking the remaining ingredients; whisk to combine well. Spoon the tahini sauce over the pearl onions and enjoy!

219. Italian-Style Tomato Cutlets
INGREDIENTS (2 Servings)

1 beefsteak tomato – sliced into halves	½ cup almond milk	1 teaspoon Italian seasoning mix
½ cup all-purpose flour	½ cup breadcrumbs	

DIRECTIONS (Prep + Cook Time: 10 minutes)

Pat the beefsteak tomato dry and set it aside. In a shallow bowl, mix the all-purpose flour with almond milk. In another bowl, mix breadcrumbs with Italian seasoning mix. Dip the beefsteak tomatoes in the flour mixture; then, coat the beefsteak tomatoes with the breadcrumb mixture, pressing to adhere to both sides. Cook your tomatoes at 360 degrees F for about 5 minutes; turn them over and cook on the other side for 5 minutes longer. Serve at room temperature and enjoy!

220. Authentic Platanos Maduros
INGREDIENTS (2 Servings)

1 very ripe, sweet plantain	1 teaspoon Caribbean Sorrel Rum Spice Mix	1 teaspoon coconut oil, melted

DIRECTIONS (Prep + Cook Time: 15 minutes)

Cut your plantain into slices. Toss your plantain with Caribbean Sorrel Rum Spice Mix and coconut oil. Cook your plantain in the preheated Air Fryer at 400 degrees F for 10 minutes, shaking the cooking basket halfway through the cooking time. Serve immediately and enjoy!

221. The Best Potato Fritters Ever
INGREDIENTS (3 Servings)

3 medium-sized potatoes, peeled	½ teaspoon cayenne pepper	1 tablespoon olive oil
1 tablespoon flax seeds, ground	¼ teaspoon dried dill weed	1 tablespoon fresh chives, chopped
½ cup plain flour	Sea salt and ground black pepper, to taste	

DIRECTIONS (Prep + Cook Time: 55 minutes)

Place your potatoes in the Air Fryer cooking basket and cook them at 400 degrees F for about 40 minutes, shaking the basket occasionally to promote even cooking. Mash your potatoes with a fork or potato masher. Make a vegan egg by mixing 1 tablespoon of ground flax seeds with 1 ½ tablespoons of water. Let it stand for 5 minutes. Stir in the mashed potatoes, flour and spices; form the mixture into equal patties and brush them with olive oil. Cook your fritters at 390 degrees F for about 10 minutes, flipping them halfway through the cooking time. Garnish with fresh, chopped chives and serve warm. Enjoy!

222. Traditional Indian Pakora
INGREDIENTS (2 Servings)

- 1 large zucchini, grated
- ½ cup besan flour
- ½ teaspoon baking powder
- 2 scallion stalks, chopped
- ½ teaspoon paprika
- ¼ teaspoon curry powder
- 14 teaspoon ginger-garlic paste
- Sea salt and ground black pepper, to taste
- 1 teaspoon olive oil

DIRECTIONS (Prep + Cook Time: 35 minutes)

Sprinkle the salt over the grated zucchini and leave it for 20 minutes. Then, squeeze the zucchini and drain off the excess liquid. Mix the grated zucchini with the flour, baking powder, scallions, paprika, curry powder and ginger-garlic paste. Salt and pepper to taste. Shape the mixture into patties and transfer them to the Air Fryer cooking basket. Brush the zucchini patties with 1 teaspoon of olive oil. Cook the pakora at 380 degrees F for about 12 minutes, flipping them halfway through the cooking time. Serve on dinner rolls and enjoy!

223. Easy Crispy Shawarma Chickpeas
INGREDIENTS (4 Servings)

- 1 (12-ounce) can chickpeas, drained and rinsed
- 2 tablespoons canola oil
- 1 teaspoon cayenne pepper
- 1 teaspoon sea salt
- 1 tablespoon Shawarma spice blend

DIRECTIONS (Prep + Cook Time: 25 minutes)

Toss all ingredients in a mixing bowl. Roast in the preheated Air Fryer at 380 degrees F for 10 minutes, shaking the basket halfway through the cooking time. Work in batches. Serve and enjoy!

224. Famous Buffalo Cauliflower
INGREDIENTS (4 Servings)

- 1 pound cauliflower florets
- ½ cup all-purpose flour
- ½ cup rice flour
- Sea salt and cracked black pepper, to taste
- ½ teaspoon cayenne pepper
- ½ teaspoon chili powder
- ½ cup soy milk
- 2 tablespoons soy sauce
- 2 tablespoons tahini
- 1 teaspoon vegetable oil
- 2 cloves garlic, minced
- 6 scotch bonnet peppers, seeded and sliced
- 1 small-sized onion, minced
- ½ teaspoon salt
- 1 cup water
- 2 tablespoons white vinegar
- 1 tablespoon granulated sugar

DIRECTIONS (Prep + Cook Time: 30 minutes)

Rinse the cauliflower florets and pat them dry. Spritz the Air Fryer basket with cooking spray. In a mixing bowl, combine the all purpose flour and rice flour; add the salt, black pepper, cayenne pepper, and chili powder. Add the soy milk, soy sauce, and tahini. Stir until a thick batter is formed. Dip the cauliflower florets in the batter. Cook the cauliflower at 400 degrees F for 16 minutes, turning them over halfway through the cooking time. Meanwhile, heat the vegetable oil in a saucepan over medium-high heat; then, sauté the garlic, peppers, and onion for a minute or so or until they are fragrant. Add the remaining ingredients and bring the mixture to a rapid boil. Now, reduce the heat to simmer, and continue cooking for 10 minutes more or until the sauce has reduced by half. Pour the sauce over the prepared cauliflower and serve. Enjoy!

225. Dad's Roasted Pepper Salad
INGREDIENTS (4 Servings)

- 2 yellow bell peppers
- 2 red bell peppers
- 2 green bell peppers
- 1 Serrano pepper
- 4 tablespoons olive oil
- 2 tablespoons cider vinegar
- 2 garlic cloves, peeled and pressed
- 1 teaspoon cayenne pepper
- Sea salt, to taste
- ½ teaspoon mixed peppercorns, freshly crushed
- ½ cup pine nuts
- ¼ cup loosely packed fresh Italian parsley leaves, roughly chopped

DIRECTIONS (Prep + Cook Time: 25 minutes + Chilling Time)

Start by preheating your Air Fryer to 400 degrees F. Brush the Air Fryer basket lightly with cooking oil. Then, roast the peppers for 5 minutes. Give the peppers a half turn; place them back in the cooking basket and roast for another 5 minutes. Turn them one more time and roast until the skin is charred and soft or 5 more minutes. Peel the peppers and let them cool to room temperature. In a small mixing dish, whisk the olive oil, vinegar, garlic, cayenne pepper, salt, and crushed peppercorns. Dress the salad and set aside. Add the pine nuts to the cooking basket. Roast at 360 degrees F for 4 minutes; give the nuts a good toss. Put the cooking basket back again and roast for a further 3 to 4 minutes. Scatter the toasted nuts over the peppers and garnish with parsley. Serve and enjoy!

226. Classic Baked Banana
INGREDIENTS (2 Servings)

- 2 just-ripe bananas
- 2 teaspoons lime juice
- 2 tablespoons honey
- ¼ teaspoon grated nutmeg
- ½ teaspoon ground cinnamon
- A pinch of salt

DIRECTIONS (Prep + Cook Time: 20 minutes)

Toss the banana with all ingredients until well coated. Transfer your bananas to the parchment-lined cooking basket. Bake in the preheated Air Fryer at 370 degrees F for 12 minutes, turning them over halfway through the cooking time. Enjoy!

227. Winter Squash and Tomato Bake
INGREDIENTS (4 Servings)

Cashew Cream:
- ½ cup sunflower seeds, soaked overnight, rinsed and drained
- ¼ cup lime juice
- Sea salt, to taste
- 2 teaspoons nutritional yeast
- 1 tablespoon tahini
- ½ cup water

Squash:
- 1 pound winter squash, peeled and sliced
- 2 tablespoons olive oil
- Sea salt and ground black pepper, to taste

Sauce:
- 2 tablespoons olive oil
- 2 ripe tomatoes, crushed
- 6 ounces spinach, torn into small pieces
- 2 garlic cloves, minced
- 1 cup vegetable broth
- ½ teaspoon dried rosemary
- ½ teaspoon dried basil

DIRECTIONS (Prep + Cook Time: 30 minutes)

Mix the ingredients for the cashew cream in your food processor until creamy and uniform. Reserve. Place the squash slices in the lightly greased casserole dish. Add the olive oil, salt, and black pepper. Mix all the ingredients for the sauce. Pour the sauce over the vegetables. Bake in the preheated Air Fryer at 390 degrees F for 15 minutes. Top with the cashew cream and bake an additional 5 minutes or until everything is thoroughly heated. Transfer to a wire rack to cool slightly before sling and serving.

228. Barbecue Tofu with Green Beans
INGREDIENTS (3 Servings)

- 12 ounces super firm tofu, pressed and cubed
- ¼ cup ketchup
- 1 tablespoon white vinegar
- 1 tablespoon coconut sugar
- 1 tablespoon mustard
- ¼ teaspoon ground black pepper
- ½ teaspoon sea salt
- ¼ teaspoon smoked paprika
- ½ teaspoon freshly grated ginger
- 2 cloves garlic, minced
- 2 tablespoons olive oil
- 1 pound green beans

DIRECTIONS (Prep + Cook Time: 1 hour)

Toss the tofu with the ketchup, white vinegar, coconut sugar, mustard, black pepper, sea salt, paprika, ginger, garlic, and olive oil. Let it marinate for 30 minutes. Cook at 360 degrees F for 10 minutes; turn them over and cook for 12 minutes more. Reserve. Place the green beans in the lightly greased Air Fryer basket. Roast at 400 degrees F for 5 minutes. Enjoy!

229. Buffalo Cauliflower Bites
INGREDIENTS (2 Servings)

- ½ pound cauliflower florets
- ½ cup all-purpose flour
- ½ cup rice milk
- ½ teaspoon chili powder
- 1 teaspoon garlic powder
- Sea salt and ground black pepper, to taste

DIRECTIONS (Prep + Cook Time: 35 minutes)

Pat the cauliflower florets dry and reserve. In a mixing bowl, thoroughly combine the flour, rice milk, chili powder, garlic powder, salt and black pepper. Dip the cauliflower florets in the batter until well coated on all sides. Place the cauliflower florets in your freezer for 15 minutes. Cook the cauliflower in the preheated Air Fryer at 390 degrees F for about 10 minutes; turn them over and cook for another 10 minutes. Taste, adjust the seasonings and serve warm.

230. Italian-Style Pasta Chips
INGREDIENTS (2 Servings)

- 1 cup dry rice pasta
- 1 teaspoon olive oil
- 1 tablespoon nutritional yeast
- ½ teaspoon dried oregano
- ½ teaspoon dried basil
- 1 teaspoon dried parsley flakes
- Kosher salt and ground black pepper, to taste

DIRECTIONS (Prep + Cook Time: 15 minutes)

Cook the pasta according to the manufacturer's instructions. Drain your pasta and toss it with the remaining ingredients. Cook the pasta chips at 390 degrees F for about 10 minutes, shaking the cooking basket halfway through the cooking time. The pasta chips will crisp up as it cools. Serve with tomato ketchup if desired. Serve and enjoy!

231. Cinnamon Pear Chips
INGREDIENTS (1 Servings)

- 1 medium pear, cored and thinly sliced
- 2 tablespoons cinnamon & sugar mixture

DIRECTIONS (Prep + Cook Time: 25 minutes)

Toss the pear slices with the cinnamon & sugar mixture. Transfer them to the lightly greased Air Fryer basket. Bake in the preheated Air Fryer at 380 degrees F for 8 minutes, turning them over halfway through the cooking time. Transfer to wire rack to cool. Serve and enjoy!

232. Hoisin-Glazed Bok Choy
INGREDIENTS (4 Servings)

- 1 pound baby Bok choy, bottoms removed, leaves separated
- 2 garlic cloves, minced
- 1 teaspoon onion powder
- ½ teaspoon sage
- 2 tablespoons hoisin sauce
- 2 tablespoons sesame oil
- 1 tablespoon all-purpose flour

DIRECTIONS (Prep + Cook Time: 10 minutes)

Place the Bok choy, garlic, onion powder, and sage in the lightly greased Air Fryer basket. Cook in the preheated Air Fryer at 350 degrees F for 3 minutes. In a small mixing dish, whisk the hoisin sauce, sesame oil, and flour. Drizzle the sauce over the Bok choy. Cook for a further 3 minutes. Serve and enjoy!

233. Corn on the Cob with Spicy Avocado Spread
INGREDIENTS (4 Servings)

- 4 corn cobs
- 1 avocado, pitted, peeled and mashed
- 1 clove garlic, pressed
- 1 tablespoon fresh lime juice
- 1 tablespoon soy sauce
- 4 teaspoons nutritional yeast
- ½ teaspoon cayenne pepper
- ½ teaspoon dried dill
- Sea salt and ground black pepper, to taste
- 1 teaspoon hot sauce
- 2 heaping tablespoons fresh cilantro leaves, roughly chopped

DIRECTIONS (Prep + Cook Time: 15 minutes)

Spritz the corn with cooking spray. Cook at 390 degrees F for 6 minutes, turning them over halfway through the cooking time. In the meantime, mix the avocado, lime juice, soy sauce, nutritional yeast, cayenne pepper, dill, salt, black pepper, and hot sauce. Spread the avocado mixture all over the corn on the cob. Garnish with fresh cilantro leaves. Enjoy!

234. Rosemary Au Gratin Potatoes
INGREDIENTS (4 Servings)

- 2 pounds potatoes
- ¼ cup sunflower kernels, soaked overnight
- ½ cup almonds, soaked overnight
- 1 cup unsweetened almond milk
- 2 tablespoons nutritional yeast
- 1 teaspoon shallot powder
- 2 fresh garlic cloves, minced
- ½ cup water
- Kosher salt and ground black pepper, to taste
- 1 teaspoon cayenne pepper
- 1 tablespoon fresh rosemary

DIRECTIONS (Prep + Cook Time: 45 minutes)

Bring a large pan of water to a boil. Cook the whole potatoes for about 20 minutes. Drain the potatoes and let sit until cool enough to handle. Peel your potatoes and slice into 1/8-inch rounds. Add the sunflower kernels, almonds, almond milk, nutritional yeast, shallot powder, and garlic to your food processor; blend until uniform, smooth, and creamy. Add the water and blend for 30 seconds more. Place ½ of the potatoes overlapping in a single layer in the lightly greased casserole dish. Spoon ½ of the sauce on top of the potatoes. Repeat the layers, ending with the sauce. Top with salt, black pepper, cayenne pepper, and fresh rosemary. Bake in the preheated Air Fryer at 325 degrees F for 20 minutes. Serve warm.

235. Tofu and Brown Rice Bake
INGREDIENTS (4 Servings)

1 cup brown rice

16 ounces extra firm tofu, pressed, drained, and cut into bite-sized cubes

Marinade:

2 tablespoons sesame oil

1 tablespoon white vinegar

Salt and black pepper, to taste

½ cup tamari sauce

1 teaspoon hot sauce

2 tablespoons maple syrup

4 tablespoons cornstarch

DIRECTIONS (Prep + Cook Time: 55 minutes +Marinating Time)
Heat the brown rice and 2 ½ cups of water in a saucepan over high heat. Bring it to a boil; turn the stove down to simmer and cook for 35 minutes. Place the tofu in a ceramic dish; add the remaining ingredients for the marinade and whisk to combine well. Allow it to marinate for 1 hour in your refrigerator. Grease a baking pan with nonstick cooking spray. Add the hot rice and place the tofu on the top. Stir in the reserved marinade. Cook at 370 degrees F for 15 minutes, checking occasionally to ensure even cooking. Enjoy!

236. Vegetable Kabobs with Simple Peanut Sauce
INGREDIENTS (4 Servings)

8 whole baby potatoes, diced into 1-inch pieces

8 pearl onions, halved

1 teaspoon red pepper flakes, crushed

8 small button mushrooms, cleaned

1 teaspoon dried rosemary, crushed

2 bell peppers, diced into 1-inch pieces

2 tablespoons extra-virgin olive oil

⅓ teaspoon granulated garlic

Sea salt and ground black pepper, to taste

Peanut Sauce:

2 tablespoons peanut butter

1 tablespoon soy sauce

1 tablespoon balsamic vinegar

½ teaspoon garlic salt

DIRECTIONS (Prep + Cook Time: 30 minutes)
Soak the wooden skewers in water for 15 minutes. Thread the vegetables on skewers; drizzle the olive oil all over the vegetable skewers; sprinkle with spices. Cook in the preheated Air Fryer at 400 degrees F for 13 minutes. Meanwhile, in a small dish, whisk the peanut butter with the balsamic vinegar, soy sauce, and garlic salt. Serve your kabobs with the peanut sauce on the side. Enjoy!

237. Classic Rizzi Bizzi
INGREDIENTS (2 Servings)

1 cup long-grain brown rice, soaked overnight

1 cup green peas, fresh or thawed

1 teaspoon sesame oil

¼ cup Shoyu sauce

1 carrot, grated

DIRECTIONS (Prep + Cook Time: 35 minutes)
Add the brown rice and 2 cups of water to a saucepan. Bring to a boil. Cover and reduce the heat to a slow simmer. Cook your rice for 30 minutes, then, fluff it with a fork. Combine your rice with the remaining ingredients and transfer it to the cooking basket. Cook your rizzi bizzi at 340 degrees F for about 13 minutes, stirring halfway through the cooking time. Serve immediately!

238. Air Grilled Cheese Roll-Ups
INGREDIENTS (3 Servings)

6 slices bread

6 slices Colby cheese

2 tablespoons butter

A pinch of ground black pepper

DIRECTIONS (Prep + Cook Time: 10 minutes)
Flatten the bread slices to ¼ -inch thickness using a rolling pin. Spread the melted butter on top of each slice of bread. Place a cheese slice on top of each slice of bread; sprinkle with black pepper and roll them up tightly. Bake the cheese roll-ups at 390 degrees F for about 8 minutes. Enjoy!

239. Favorite Cheese Biscuits
INGREDIENTS (4 Servings)

- 1 ½ cups all-purpose flour
- ⅓ cup butter, room temperature
- 1 teaspoon baking powder
- 1 teaspoon baking soda
- ½ cup buttermilk
- 2 eggs, beaten
- 1 cup Swiss cheese, shredded

DIRECTIONS (Prep + Cook Time: 30 minutes)

In a mixing bowl, thoroughly combine the flour and butter. Gradually stir in the remaining ingredients. Divide the mixture into 12 balls. Bake in the preheated Air Fryer at 360 degrees F for 15 minutes. Work in two batches. Serve at room temperature. Enjoy!

240. Favorite Spinach Cheese Pie
INGREDIENTS (4 Servings)

- 1 (16-ounce) refrigerated rolled pie crusts
- 4 eggs, beaten
- ½ cup buttermilk
- ½ teaspoon salt
- ½ teaspoon garlic powder
- ¼ teaspoon cayenne pepper
- 2 cups spinach, torn into pieces
- 1 cup Swiss cheese, shredded
- 2 tablespoons scallions, chopped

DIRECTIONS (Prep + Cook Time: 30 minutes)

Unroll the pie crust and press it into a cake pan, crimping the top edges if desired. In a mixing dish, whisk together the eggs, buttermilk, salt, garlic, powder, and cayenne pepper. Add the spinach, ½ of Swiss cheese, and scallions into the pie crust; pour the egg mixture over the top. Sprinkle the remaining ½ cup of Swiss cheese on top of the egg mixture. Bake in the preheated Air Fryer at 350 degrees F for 10 minutes. Rotate the cake pan and bake an additional 10 minutes. Transfer to a wire rack to cool for 5 to 10 minutes. Serve warm.

241. Delicious Sultana Muffins
INGREDIENTS (4 Servings)

- 1 cup flour
- 1 teaspoon baking powder
- 1 tablespoon honey
- 1 egg
- ½ teaspoon star anise, ground
- 1 teaspoon vanilla extract
- 1 egg
- ½ cup milk
- 2 tablespoons melted butter
- 1 cup dried Sultanas, soaked in 2 tablespoons of rum

DIRECTIONS (Prep + Cook Time: 20 minutes)

Mix all the ingredients until everything is well incorporated. Spritz a silicone muffin tin with cooking spray. Pour the batter into the silicone muffin tin. Bake in the preheated Air Fryer at 330 degrees F for 12 to 15 minutes. Rotate the silicone muffin tin halfway through the cooking time to ensure even cooking. Serve and enjoy!

242. Japanese Yaki Onigiri
INGREDIENTS (2 Servings)

- ½ cup sushi rice, cooked
- 1 cup canned green peas, drained
- ¼ cup cream cheese
- ¼ cup Colby cheese, shredded
- 2 tablespoons dashi
- Salt and cracked black pepper, to taste
- 2 tablespoons scallions, chopped
- 1 cup all-purpose flour
- 1 egg, whisked
- 2 tablespoons soy sauce (unagi)

DIRECTIONS (Prep + Cook Time: 50 minutes)

In a bowl, combine the rice, green peas, cheese, dashi, salt, black pepper, and scallions. Add the flour and egg and mix to combine well. Refrigerate for 20 to 40 minutes. Then, put some salt in your hands and rub to spread all around. Form the rice mixture into triangles. Cook in the preheated Air Fryer at 370 degrees F for 7 to 10 minutes. Brush with the unagi sauce and serve immediately. Enjoy!

243. Louisiana-Style Eggplant Cutlets
INGREDIENTS (3 Servings)

- 1 pound eggplant, cut lengthwise into ½-inch thick slices
- ¼ cup plain flour
- ¼ cup almond milk
- 1 cup fresh bread crumbs
- 1 teaspoon Cajun seasoning mix
- Sea salt and ground black pepper, to taste
- 1 cup tomato sauce
- 1 teaspoon brown mustard
- ½ teaspoon chili powder

DIRECTIONS (Prep + Cook Time: 45 minutes) Toss your eggplant with 1 teaspoon of salt and leave it for 30 minutes; drain and rinse the eggplant and set it aside. In a shallow bowl, mix the flour with almond milk until well combined. In a separate bowl, mix the breadcrumbs with Cajun seasoning mix, salt and black pepper. Dip your eggplant in the flour mixture, then, coat each slice with the breadcrumb mixture, pressing to adhere. Cook the breaded eggplant at 400 degrees F for 10 minutes, flipping them halfway through the cooking time to ensure even browning. In the meantime, mix the remaining ingredients for the sauce. Divide the tomato mixture between eggplant cutlets and continue to cook for another 5 minutes or until thoroughly cooked. Transfer the warm eggplant cutlets to a wire rack to stay crispy. Enjoy!

244. Classic Vegan Chili
INGREDIENTS (3 Servings)

- 1 tablespoon olive oil
- ½ yellow onion, chopped
- 2 garlic cloves, minced
- 2 red bell peppers, seeded and chopped
- 1 red chili pepper, seeded and minced
- Sea salt and ground black pepper, to taste
- 1 teaspoon ground cumin
- 1 teaspoon cayenne pepper
- 1 teaspoon Mexican oregano
- ½ teaspoon mustard seeds
- ½ teaspoon celery seeds
- 1 can (28-ounces) diced tomatoes with juice
- 1 cup vegetable broth
- 1 (15-ounce) can black beans, rinsed and drained
- 1 bay leaf 1 teaspoon cider vinegar
- 1 avocado, sliced

DIRECTIONS (Prep + Cook Time: 40 minutes)

Start by preheating your Air Fryer to 365 degrees F. Heat the olive oil in a baking pan until sizzling. Then, sauté the onion, garlic, and peppers in the baking pan. Cook for 4 to 6 minutes. Now, add the salt, black pepper, cumin, cayenne pepper, oregano, mustard seeds, celery seeds, tomatoes, and broth. Cook for 20 minutes, stirring every 4 minutes. Stir in the canned beans, bay leaf, cider vinegar; let it cook for a further 8 minutes, stirring halfway through the cooking time. Serve in individual bowls garnished with the avocado slices. Enjoy!

245. Authentic Churros with Hot Chocolate
INGREDIENTS (3 Servings)

- ½ cup water
- 2 tablespoons granulated sugar
- ¼ teaspoon sea salt
- 1 teaspoon lemon zest
- 1 tablespoon canola oil
- 1 cup all-purpose flour
- 2 ounces dark chocolate
- 1 cup milk
- 1 tablespoon cornstarch
- ⅓ cup sugar
- 1 teaspoon ground cinnamon

DIRECTIONS (Prep + Cook Time: 25 minutes)

To make the churro dough, boil the water in a pan over medium-high heat; now, add the sugar, salt and lemon zest; cook until dissolved. Add the canola oil and remove the pan from the heat. Gradually stir in the flour, whisking continuously until the mixture forms a ball. Pour the mixture into a piping bag with a large star tip. Squeeze 4-inch strips of dough into the greased Air Fryer pan. Cook at 410 degrees F for 6 minutes. Meanwhile, prepare the hot chocolate for dipping. Melt the chocolate and ½ cup of milk in a pan over low heat. Dissolve the cornstarch in the remaining ½ cup of milk; stir into the hot chocolate mixture. Cook on low heat approximately 5 minutes. Mix the sugar and cinnamon; roll the churros in this mixture. Serve with the hot chocolate on the side. Enjoy!

246. Aromatic Baked Potatoes with Chives
INGREDIENTS (2 Servings)

- 4 medium baking potatoes, peeled
- 2 tablespoons olive oil
- ¼ teaspoon red pepper flakes
- ¼ teaspoon smoked paprika
- 1 tablespoon sea salt
- 2 garlic cloves, minced
- 2 tablespoons chives, chopped

DIRECTIONS (Prep + Cook Time: 45 minutes)

Toss the potatoes with the olive oil, seasoning, and garlic. Place them in the Air Fryer basket. Cook in the preheated Air Fryer at 400 degrees F for 40 minutes or until fork tender. Garnish with fresh chopped chives. Enjoy!

247. Warm Farro Salad with Roasted Tomatoes
INGREDIENTS (2 Servings)

3/4 cup farro	2 spring onions, chopped	2 tablespoons white wine
3 cups water	2 carrots, grated	2 tablespoons extra-virgin olive oil
1 tablespoon sea salt	2 heaping tablespoons fresh parsley leaves	1 teaspoon red pepper flakes
1 pound cherry tomatoes	2 tablespoons champagne vinegar	

DIRECTIONS (Prep + Cook Time: 40 minutes)

Place the farro, water, and salt in a saucepan and bring it to a rapid boil. Turn the heat down to medium-low, and simmer, covered, for 30 minutes or until the farro has softened. Drain well and transfer to an air fryer-safe pan. Meanwhile, place the cherry tomatoes in the lightly greased Air Fryer basket. Roast at 400 degrees F for 4 minutes. Add the roasted tomatoes to the pan with the cooked farro, Toss the salad ingredients with the spring onions, carrots, parsley, vinegar, white wine, and olive oil. Bake at 360 degrees F an additional 5 minutes. Serve garnished with red pepper flakes and enjoy!

248. Kid-Friendly Vegetable Fritters
INGREDIENTS (4 Servings)

1 pound broccoli florets	1 carrot, grated	½ cup all-purpose flour
1 tablespoon ground flaxseeds	2 garlic cloves, pressed	½ cup cornmeal
1 yellow onion, finely chopped	1 teaspoon turmeric powder	Salt and ground black pepper, to taste
1 sweet pepper, seeded and chopped	½ teaspoon ground cumin	2 tablespoons olive oil

DIRECTIONS (Prep + Cook Time: 20 minutes)

Blanch the broccoli in salted boiling water until al dente, about 3 to 4 minutes. Drain well and transfer to a mixing bowl; mash the broccoli florets with the remaining ingredients. Form the mixture into patties and place them in the lightly greased Air Fryer basket. Cook at 400 degrees F for 6 minutes, turning them over halfway through the cooking time; work in batches. Serve warm with your favorite Vegenaise. Enjoy!

249. Mediterranean-Style Potato Chips with Vegveeta Dip
INGREDIENTS (4 Servings)

1 large potato, cut into 1/8 inch thick slices	Sea salt, to taste	½ teaspoon fresh sage
	½ teaspoon red pepper flakes, crushed	½ teaspoon fresh basil
1 tablespoon olive oil	1 teaspoon fresh rosemary	
Dipping Sauce:		
⅓ cup raw cashews	1 ½ tablespoons olive oil	¼ teaspoon prepared yellow mustard
1 tablespoon tahini	¼ cup raw almonds	

DIRECTIONS (Prep + Cook Time: 1 hour)

Soak the potatoes in a large bowl of cold water for 20 to 30 minutes. Drain the potatoes and pat them dry with a kitchen towel. Toss with olive oil and seasonings. Place in the lightly greased cooking basket and cook at 380 degrees F for 30 minutes. Work in batches. Meanwhile, puree the sauce ingredients in your food processor until smooth. Serve the potato chips with the Vegveeta sauce for dipping. Enjoy!

250. Mom's Favorite Wontons
INGREDIENTS (2 Servings)

½ pound ground turkey	1 tablespoon tomato paste	Seas salt and ground black pepper, to taste
1 teaspoon shallot powder	1 teaspoon soy sauce	
1 teaspoon instant dashi granules	1 teaspoon sesame oil	20 wonton wrappers, defrosted
1 teaspoon fish sauce		

DIRECTIONS (Prep + Cook Time: 10 minutes)

Brush a nonstick skillet with cooking spray. Once hot, cook the ground turkey until no longer pink, crumbling with a fork. Stir in the other ingredients, except for the wonton wrappers; stir to combine well. Place the wonton wrappers on a clean work surface. Divide the filling between wrappers. Wet the edge of each wrapper with water, fold top half over bottom half and pinch border to seal. Cook your wontons at 400 degrees F for 8 minutes; working in batches. Enjoy!

251. Everyday Mac and Cheese
INGREDIENTS (2 Servings)

- 3/4 cup cavatappi
- ¼ cup double cream
- 4 ounces Colby cheese, shredded
- ½ teaspoon granulated garlic
- Sea salt and ground black pepper, to taste
- ¼ teaspoon cayenne pepper

DIRECTIONS (Prep + Cook Time: 25 minutes)

Bring a pot of salted water to a boil over high heat; turn the heat down to medium and add the cavatappi. Let it simmer about 8 minutes. Drain cavatappi, reserving ¼ cup of the cooking water; add them to a lightly greased baking pan. Add in ¼ cup of the cooking water, double cream, cheese and spices to the baking pan; gently stir to combine. Bake your mac and cheese in the preheated Air Fryer at 360 degrees F for 15 minutes. Garnish with fresh basil leaves if desired. Enjoy!

252. Chinese Spring Rolls
INGREDIENTS (2 Servings)

- 1 tablespoon sesame oil, divided
- 1 cup Chinese cabbage, shredded
- 1 bell pepper, deveined and cut into sticks
- 3 ounces prawns, deveined and chopped
- 1 garlic clove, minced
- 1 teaspoon fresh coriander, minced
- 1 tablespoon rice vinegar
- 2 tablespoons soy sauce
- 4 (8-inch-square) spring roll wrappers
- ½ cup hot sauce

DIRECTIONS (Prep + Cook Time: 15 minutes)

In a wok, heat the sesame oil over medium-high heat. Then, sauté the Chinese cabbage and bell pepper for 2 to 3 minutes. Add in the prawns and garlic and continue to sauté an additional minute or so until aromatic. Remove from heat and add in coriander, vinegar and soy sauce. Divide the filling between spring roll wrappers. Fold the top corner over the filling; fold in the two side corners; brush with water to seal the edges. Place the spring rolls in the cooking basket and brush them with nonstick cooking oil. Cook the spring rolls at 380 degrees F for 5 minutes; turn them over and continue to cook for a further 2 to 3 minutes until they are crisped and lightly browned. Serve with hot sauce. Enjoy!

253. Easy Pizza Margherita
INGREDIENTS (1 Servings)

- 6-inch dough
- 2 tablespoons tomato sauce
- 2 ounces mozzarella
- 1 teaspoon extra-virgin olive oil
- Coarse sea salt, to taste
- 2-3 fresh basil leaves

DIRECTIONS (Prep + Cook Time: 15 minutes)

Start by preheating your Air Fryer to 380 degrees F. Stretch the dough on a pizza peel lightly dusted with flour. Spread with a layer of tomato sauce. Add mozzarella to the crust and drizzle with olive oil. Salt to taste. Bake in the preheated Air Fryer for 4 minutes. Rotate the baking tray and bake for a further 4 minutes. Garnish with fresh basil leaves and serve immediately. Enjoy!

254. Authentic Tortilla Española
INGREDIENTS (2 Servings)

- ½ pound medium-starch potatoes, peeled and cut into wedges
- ⅓ cup shallots
- ¼ teaspoon cayenne pepper
- Kosher salt and black pepper, to season
- 1 clove garlic, minced
- 3 large eggs
- ½ cup heavy cream
- 4 ounces Cotija cheese, shredded
- 1 teaspoon olive oil

DIRECTIONS (Prep + Cook Time: 20 minutes)

Cook your potatoes in a saucepan for about 10 minutes; drain and transfer to a bowl of your food processor. Add in the shallots and process them until smooth. Transfer the mixture to a mixing bowl; add in the other ingredients and mix to combine. Spoon the pancake batter into an Air Fryer baking pan. Cook the Spanish tortilla at 370 degrees for 5 minutes; turn over and cook for a further 5 minutes. Repeat until you run out of the pancake batter. Serve warm and enjoy!

255. Cinnamon Breakfast Muffins
INGREDIENTS (4 Servings)

- 1 cup all-purpose flour
- 1 teaspoon baking powder
- 1 tablespoon brown sugar
- 2 eggs 1 teaspoon cinnamon powder
- 1 teaspoon vanilla paste
- ¼ cup milk
- 4 tablespoons butter, melted

DIRECTIONS (Prep + Cook Time: 20 minutes)

Start by preheating your Air Fryer to 330 degrees F. Now, spritz the silicone muffin tins with cooking spray. Thoroughly combine all ingredients in a mixing dish. Fill the muffin cups with batter. Cook in the preheated Air Fryer approximately 13 minutes. Check with a toothpick; when the toothpick comes out clean, your muffins are done. Place on a rack to cool slightly before removing from the muffin tins. Enjoy!

256. Polenta Fries with Sriracha Sauce
INGREDIENTS (3 Servings)

Polenta Fries:

- 1 ½ cups water
- 1 teaspoon sea salt
- ½ cup polenta
- 1 tablespoon butter, room temperature
- A pinch of grated nutmeg
- 1 teaspoon dried Italian herb mix

Sriracha Sauce:

- 1 red jalapeno pepper, minced
- 1 garlic clove, minced
- 1 tablespoon cider vinegar
- 2 tablespoons tomato paste
- 1 tablespoon honey

DIRECTIONS (Prep + Cook Time: 45 minutes + Chilling Time)

Bring the water and 1 teaspoon sea salt to a boil in a saucepan; slowly and gradually stir in the polenta, whisking continuously until there are no lumps. Reduce the heat to simmer and cook for 5 to 6 minutes until the polenta starts to thicken. Cover and continue to simmer for 25 minutes or until you have a thick mixture, whisking periodically. Stir in the butter, nutmeg, and Italian herbs. Pour your polenta into a parchment-lined rimmed baking tray, spreading the mixture evenly. Cover with plastic wrap; let it stand in your refrigerator for about 2 hours to firm up. Then, slice the polenta into strips and place them in the greased Air Fryer basket. Cook in the preheated Air Fryer at 395 degrees F for about 11 minutes. Meanwhile, make the Sriracha sauce by whisking all ingredients. Serve the warm polenta fries with the Sriracha sauce on the side. Enjoy!

257. Sunday Glazed Cinnamon Rolls
INGREDIENTS (4 Servings)

- 1 can cinnamon rolls
- 2 tablespoons butter
- 1 cup powdered sugar
- 1 teaspoon vanilla extract
- 3 tablespoons hot water

DIRECTIONS (Prep + Cook Time: 15 minutes)

Place the cinnamon rolls in the Air Fryer basket. Bake at 300 degrees F for 10 minutes, flipping them halfway through the cooking time. Meanwhile, mix the butter, sugar, and vanilla. Pour in water, 1 tablespoon at a time, until the glaze reaches desired consistency. Spread over the slightly cooled cinnamon rolls. Enjoy!

258. Baked Tortilla Chips
INGREDIENTS (3 Servings)

- ½ (12-ounce) package corn tortillas
- 1 tablespoon canola oil
- ½ teaspoon chili powder
- 1 teaspoon salt

DIRECTIONS (Prep + Cook Time: 15 minutes)

Cut the tortillas into small rounds using a cookie cutter. Brush the rounds with canola oil. Sprinkle them with chili powder and salt. Transfer to the lightly greased Air Fryer basket and bake at 360 degrees F for 5 minutes, shaking the basket halfway through. Bake until the chips are crisp, working in batches. Serve with salsa or guacamole. Enjoy!

259. Buckwheat and Potato Flat Bread
INGREDIENTS (4 Servings)

- 4 potatoes, medium-sized
- 1 cup buckwheat flour
- ½ teaspoon salt
- ½ teaspoon red chili powder
- ¼ cup honey

DIRECTIONS (Prep + Cook Time: 20 minutes)

Put the potatoes into a large saucepan; add water to cover by about 1 inch. Bring to a boil. Then, lower the heat, and let your potatoes simmer about 8 minutes until they are fork tender. Mash the potatoes and add the flour, salt, and chili powder. Create 4 balls and flatten them with a rolling pin Bake in the preheated Air Fryer at 390 degrees F for 6 minutes. Serve warm with honey.

260. Fried Green Beans
INGREDIENTS (2 Servings)

- ½ pound green beans, cleaned and trimmed
- 1 teaspoon extra-virgin olive oil
- ½ teaspoon onion powder
- ½ teaspoon shallot powder
- ¼ teaspoon cumin powder
- ½ teaspoon cayenne pepper
- ½ teaspoon garlic powder
- Himalayan salt and freshly ground black pepper, to taste
- 1 tablespoon lime juice
- 1 tablespoon soy sauce
- ¼ cup pecans, roughly chopped

DIRECTIONS (Prep + Cook Time: 10 minutes)

Toss the green beans with olive oil, spices and lime juice. Cook the green beans in your Air Fryer at 400 degrees F for 5 minutes, shaking the basket halfway through the cooking time to promote even cooking. Toss the green beans with soy sauce and serve garnished with chopped pecans. Enjoy!

261. Quinoa-Stuffed Winter Squash
INGREDIENTS (2 Servings)

- ½ cup quinoa
- 1 cup loosely mixed greens, torn into small pieces
- 1 teaspoon sesame oil
- 1 clove garlic, pressed
- 1 small winter squash, halved lengthwise, seeds removed
- Sea salt and ground black pepper, to taste
- 1 tablespoon fresh parsley, roughly chopped

DIRECTIONS (Prep + Cook Time: 30 minutes)

Rinse your quinoa, drain it and transfer to a pot with 1 cup of lightly salted water; bring to a boil. Turn the heat to a simmer and continue to cook, covered, for about 10 minutes; add in the mixed greens and continue to cook for 5 minutes longer. Stir in the sesame oil and garlic and stir to combine. Divide the quinoa mixture between the winter squash halves and sprinkle it with the salt and pepper. Cook your squash in the preheated Air Fryer at 400 degrees F for about 12 minutes. Place the stuffed squash on individual plates, garnish with fresh parsley and serve. Enjoy!

262. Old-Fashioned Potato Wedges
INGREDIENTS (2 Servings)

- 2 medium potatoes, scrubbed and cut into wedges
- 1 teaspoon olive oil
- 1 teaspoon garlic powder
- 1 teaspoon shallot powder
- ¼ teaspoon cayenne pepper
- Kosher salt and ground black pepper, to season

DIRECTIONS (Prep + Cook Time: 15 minutes)

Toss the potato wedges with olive oil and spices and transfer them to the Air Fryer cooking basket. Cook the potato wedges at 400 degrees F for 6 minutes; shake the basket and cook for another 6 to 8 minutes. Serve with your favorite vegan dip. Enjoy!

263. Perfect Shallot Rings
INGREDIENTS (2 Servings)

- ½ cup all-purpose flour
- ¼ cup cornflour
- ½ cup rice milk
- ¼ cup fizzy water
- ¼ teaspoon turmeric powder
- Sea salt and red pepper, to taste
- ½ cup seasoned breadcrumbs
- 2 shallots, sliced into rings

DIRECTIONS (Prep + Cook Time: 15 minutes)

In a shallow bowl, thoroughly combine the flour, milk, fizzy water, turmeric, salt and pepper. In another bowl, place seasoned breadcrumbs. Dip the shallot rings in the flour mixture; then, coat the rings with the seasoned breadcrumbs, pressing to adhere. Transfer the shallot rings to the Air Fryer cooking basket and spritz them with a nonstick spray. Cook the shallot rings at 380 degrees F for about 10 minutes, shaking the basket halfway through the cooking time to ensure even browning. Enjoy!

264. Swiss Chard and Potato Fritters
INGREDIENTS (4 Servings)

- 8 baby potatoes
- 2 tablespoons olive oil
- 1 garlic clove, pressed
- ½ cup leeks, chopped
- 1 cup Swiss chard, torn into small pieces
- Sea salt and ground black pepper, to your liking
- 1 tablespoon flax seed, soaked in
- 3 tablespoon water (vegan egg)
- 1 cup vegan cheese, shredded
- ¼ cup chickpea flour

DIRECTIONS (Prep + Cook Time: 35 minutes)

Start by preheating your Air Fryer to 400 degrees F. Drizzle olive oil all over the potatoes. Place the potatoes in the Air Fryer basket and cook approximately 15 minutes, shaking the basket periodically. Lightly crush the potatoes to split; mash the potatoes with the other ingredients. Form the potato mixture into patties. Bake in the preheated Air Fryer at 380 degrees F for 14 minutes, flipping them halfway through the cooking time. Enjoy!

265. Couscous with Sun-Dried Tomatoes
INGREDIENTS (4 Servings)

- 1 cup couscous
- 1 cup boiled water
- 2 garlic cloves, pressed
- ⅓ cup coriander, chopped
- 1 cup shallots, chopped
- 4 ounces sun-dried tomato strips in oil
- 1 cup arugula lettuce, torn into pieces
- 2 tablespoons apple cider vinegar
- Sea salt and ground black pepper, to taste

DIRECTIONS (Prep + Cook Time: 30 minutes) Put the couscous in a bowl; pour the boiling water, cover and set aside for 5 to 8 minutes; fluff with a fork. Place the couscous in a lightly greased cake pan. Transfer the pan to the Air Fryer basket and cook at 360 digress F about 20 minutes. Make sure to stir every 5 minutes to ensure even cooking. Transfer the prepared couscous to a nice salad bowl. Add the remaining ingredients; stir to combine and enjoy!

266. Greek-Style Roasted Vegetables
INGREDIENTS (3 Servings)

½ pound butternut squash, peeled and cut into 1-inch chunks

½ pound cauliflower, cut into 1-inch florets

½ pound zucchini, cut into 1-inch chunks

1 red onion, sliced

2 bell peppers, cut into 1-inch chunks

2 tablespoons extra-virgin olive oil

1 cup dry white wine

1 teaspoon dried rosemary

Sea salt and freshly cracked black pepper, to taste

½ teaspoon dried basil

1 (28-ounce) canned diced tomatoes with juice

½ cup Kalamata olives, pitted

DIRECTIONS (Prep + Cook Time: 25 minutes)

Toss the vegetables with the olive oil, wine, rosemary, salt, black pepper, and basil until well coated. Pour ½ of the canned diced tomatoes into a lightly greased baking dish; spread to cover the bottom of the baking dish. Add the vegetables and top with the remaining diced tomatoes. Scatter the Kalamata olives over the top. Bake in the preheated Air Fryer at 390 degrees F for 20 minutes, rotating the dish halfway through the cooking time. Serve warm and enjoy!

267. Easy Vegan "Chicken"
INGREDIENTS (4 Servings)

8 ounces soy chunks

½ cup cornmeal

¼ cup all-purpose flour

1 teaspoon cayenne pepper

½ teaspoon mustard powder

1 teaspoon celery seeds

Sea salt and ground black pepper, to taste

DIRECTIONS (Prep + Cook Time: 20 minutes)

Boil the soya chunks in lots of water in a saucepan over medium-high heat. Remove from the heat and let them soak for 10 minutes. Drain, rinse, and squeeze off the excess water. Mix the remaining ingredients in a bowl. Roll the soy chunks over the breading mixture, pressing to adhere. Arrange the soy chunks in the lightly greased Air Fryer basket. Cook in the preheated Air Fryer at 390 degrees for 10 minutes, turning them over halfway through the cooking time; work in batches. enjoy!

268. Spicy Roasted Cashew Nuts
INGREDIENTS (4 Servings)

1 cup whole cashews

1 teaspoon olive oil

Salt and ground black pepper, to taste

½ teaspoon smoked paprika

½ teaspoon ancho chili powder

DIRECTIONS (Prep + Cook Time: 20 minutes)

Toss all ingredients in the mixing bowl. Line the Air Fryer basket with baking parchment. Spread out the spiced cashews in a single layer in the basket. Roast at 350 degrees F for 6 to 8 minutes, shaking the basket once or twice. Work in batches. Enjoy!

269. Easy Tortilla Chips
INGREDIENTS (3 Servings)

½ (12-ounce) package corn tortillas

1 teaspoon olive oil

1 teaspoon lime juice

½ teaspoon chili powder

Coarse sea salt, to taste

DIRECTIONS (Prep + Cook Time: 15 minutes)

Cut the tortillas into chip-sized wedges using a cookie cutter. Brush your chips with olive oil, lime juice, chili powder and sea salt. Transfer the tortilla chips to the lightly greased Air Fryer basket and bake at 360 degrees F for 5 minutes, shaking the basket halfway through; work with batches. Serve with salsa or guacamole. Enjoy!

270. Famous Greek Tyrompiskota
INGREDIENTS (3 Servings)

1 cup all-purpose flour	½ stick butter	1 teaspoon Greek spice blend
1 tablespoon flaxseed meal	½ cup halloumi cheese, grated	Salt to taste
1 teaspoon baking powder	1 egg	

DIRECTIONS (Prep + Cook Time: 45 minutes)

In a mixing bowl, combine the flour, flaxseed meal and baking powder. In another bowl, mix the butter, cheese and egg. Add the cheese mixture to the dry flour mixture. Mix with your hands and stir in the Greek spice blend; salt to taste and stir again to combine well. Shape the batter into a log, wrap in cling film and refrigerate for about 30 minutes. Cut the chilled log into thin slices using a sharp knife. Cook your biscuits in the preheated Air Fryer at 360 degrees F for 15 minutes. Work with batches. Enjoy!

271. Mexicana Air Grilled Fish Tacos
INGREDIENTS (3 Servings)

1 pound tilapia filets	1 teaspoon extra-virgin olive oil	
1 teaspoon chipotle powder	1 teaspoon taco seasoning mix	
1 teaspoon fresh coriander, finely chopped	1 cup pickled cabbage, drained and shredded	
1 teaspoon fresh garlic, minced	6 mini taco shells	

DIRECTIONS (Prep + Cook Time: 15 minutes)

Toss the tilapia filets with the chipotle powder, coriander, garlic, olive oil and taco seasoning mix. Cook the fish in your Air Fryer at 400 degrees F for 10 minutes, flipping halfway through the cooking time. Remove the tilapia filets to a cutting board then flake into pieces. To assemble the tacos, divide the fish and pickled cabbage between taco shells. Roll them up and transfer to the Air Fryer cooking basket. Bake your tacos at 360 degrees F for 5 minutes until thoroughly warmed. Enjoy!

272. Festive Crescent Ring
INGREDIENTS (3 Servings)

½ (8-ounce) can crescent dough sheet	2 ounces capocollo, sliced	½ teaspoon dried basil
3 slices Colby cheese, cut into half	4 tablespoons tomato sauce	1 teaspoon dried oregano
2 ounces bacon, sliced	⅓ teaspoon dried rosemary	

DIRECTIONS (Prep + Cook Time: 25 minutes)

Separate the crescent dough sheet into 8 triangles. Then, arrange the triangles in a sunburst pattern so it should look like the sun. Place the cheese, bacon, capocollo and tomato sauce on the bottom of each triangle. Sprinkle with dried herbs. Now, fold the triangle tips over the filling and tuck under the base to secure. Bake the ring at 360 degrees F for 20 minutes until the dough is golden and the cheese has melted. Enjoy!

273. Apple Cinnamon Rolls
INGREDIENTS (4 Servings)

1 (10-ounces) can buttermilk biscuits	¼ cup powdered sugar	1 tablespoon coconut oil, melted
1 apple, cored and chopped	1 teaspoon cinnamon	

DIRECTIONS (Prep + Cook Time: 20 minutes)

Line the bottom of the Air Fryer cooking basket with a parchment paper. Separate the dough into biscuits and cut each of them into 2 layers. Mix the remaining ingredients in a bowl. Divide the apple/cinnamon mixture between biscuits and roll them up. Brush the biscuits with coconut oil and transfer them to the Air Fryer cooking basket. Cook the rolls at 330 degrees F for about 13 minutes, turning them over halfway through the cooking time. Enjoy!

274. Traditional Japanese Onigiri
INGREDIENTS (3 Servings)

3 cups water	½ cup cheddar cheese, grated	½ teaspoon cumin seeds
1 cup white Japanese rice	½ teaspoon kinako	1 teaspoon sesame oil
1 teaspoon dashi granules	1 tablespoon fish sauce	¼ cup shallots, chopped
1 egg, beaten	½ teaspoon coriander seeds	Sea salt, to taste

DIRECTIONS (Prep + Cook Time: 30 minutes) Bring the vegetable broth to a boil in a saucepan over medium-high heat. Stir in the rice and reduce the heat to simmer; cook about 20 minutes and fluff with a fork. Mix the cooked rice with the remaining ingredients and stir until everything is well incorporated. Then, shape and press the mixture into triangle-shape cakes. Bake the rice cakes in the preheated Air Fryer at 350 degrees F for about 10 minutes, turning them over halfway through the cooking time. Serve with seasoned nori, if desired. Enjoy!

275. Honey Raisin French Toast
INGREDIENTS (2 Servings)

- 2 eggs
- ¼ cup full-fat milk
- ¼ teaspoon ground cloves
- ½ teaspoon ground cinnamon
- 4 tablespoons honey
- 2 tablespoons coconut oil, melted
- 4 slices sweet raisin bread

DIRECTIONS (Prep + Cook Time: 5 minutes)

Thoroughly combine the eggs, mink, ground cloves, cinnamon, honey and coconut oil. Spread the mixture on both sides of the bread slices. Arrange the bread slices in the cooking basket and cook them at 390 degrees F for 2 minutes; flip and cook on the other side for 2 to 3 minutes more. Serve with some extra honey if desired. Enjoy!

276. Double Cheese Risotto Balls with Arrabbiata Sauce
INGREDIENTS (3 Servings)

- 1 cup Arborio rice
- 2 tablespoons butter
- 2 ounces Provolone cheese, grated
- 2 ounces Asiago cheese, grated
- 1 egg, whisked
- ⅓ cup seasoned breadcrumbs, passed through a sieve
- 1 tablespoon olive oil
- ¼ cup leeks, chopped
- 9 ounces canned San Marzano tomatoes
- 1 teaspoon red pepper flakes, crushed
- 2 tablespoons fresh basil leaves, roughly chopped
- Sea salt and freshly cracked black pepper, to taste

DIRECTIONS (Prep + Cook Time: 35 minutes)

Bring 3 cups of water to a boil in a saucepan over medium-high heat. Stir in the rice and reduce the heat to simmer; cook for about 20 minutes. Fluff your rice in a mixing bowl; stir in the butter and cheese. Salt and pepper to taste; shape the mixture into equal balls. Beat the egg in a shallow bowl; in another shallow bowl, place the seasoned breadcrumbs. Dip each rice ball into the beaten egg, then, roll in the seasoned breadcrumbs, gently pressing to adhere. Bake the rice balls in the preheated Air Fryer at 350 degrees F for about 10 minutes, shaking the basket halfway through the cooking time to ensure even cooking. Meanwhile, heat the olive oil in a saucepan over a moderate flame. Once hot, sauté the leeks until just tender and fragrant. Now, add in the tomatoes and spices and let it simmer for about 25 minutes, breaking your tomatoes with a spatula. Serve the warm risotto balls with Arrabbiata sauce for dipping. Enjoy!

277. Delicious Turkey Sammies
INGREDIENTS (4 Servings)

- ½ pound turkey tenderloins
- 1 tablespoon olive oil
- Salt and ground black pepper, to your liking
- 4 slices bread
- ¼ cup tomato paste
- ¼ cup pesto sauce
- 1 yellow onion, thinly sliced
- 1 cup mozzarella cheese, shredded

DIRECTIONS (Prep + Cook Time: 50 minutes)

Brush the turkey tenderloins with olive oil. Season with salt and black pepper. Cook the turkey tenderloins at 350 degrees F for 30 minutes, flipping them over halfway through. Let them rest for 5 to 9 minutes before slicing. Cut the turkey tenderloins into thin slices. Make your sandwiches with bread, tomato paste, pesto, and onion. Place the turkey slices on top. Add the cheese and place the sandwiches in the Air Fryer basket. Then, preheat your Air Fryer to 390 degrees F. Bake for 7 minutes or until cheese is melted. Serve immediately.

278. The Best Fish Tacos Ever
INGREDIENTS (3 Servings)

- 1 tablespoon mayonnaise
- 1 teaspoon Dijon mustard
- 1 tablespoon sour cream
- ½ teaspoon fresh garlic, minced
- ¼ teaspoon red pepper flakes
- Sea salt, to taste
- 2 bell peppers, seeded and sliced
- 1 shallot, thinly sliced
- 1 egg
- 1 tablespoon water
- 1 tablespoon taco seasoning mix
- ⅓ cup tortilla chips, crushed
- ¼ cup parmesan cheese, grated
- 1 halibut fillets, cut into 1-inch strips
- 6 mini flour taco shells
- 6 lime wedges, for serving

DIRECTIONS (Prep + Cook Time: 25 minutes)

Thoroughly combine the mayonnaise, mustard, sour cream, garlic, red pepper flakes, and salt. Add the bell peppers and shallots; toss to coat well. Place in your refrigerator until ready to serve. Line the Air Fryer basket with a piece of parchment paper. In a shallow bowl, mix the egg, water, and taco seasoning mix. In a separate shallow bowl, mix the crushed tortilla chips and parmesan. Dip the fish into the egg mixture, then coat with the parmesan mixture, pressing to adhere. Bake in the preheated Air Fryer at 380 degrees F for 13 minutes, flipping halfway through the cooking time. Divide the creamed pepper mixture among the taco shells. Top with the fish, and serve with lime wedges. Enjoy!

279. Cheese and Bacon Crescent Ring
INGREDIENTS (4 Servings)

1 (8-ounce) can crescent dough sheet	4 slices bacon, cut chopped	1 teaspoon dried oregano
1 ½ cups Monterey Jack cheese, shredded	4 tablespoons tomato sauce	

DIRECTIONS (Prep + Cook Time: 25 minutes)

Unroll the crescent dough sheet and separate into 8 triangles. Arrange the triangles on a piece of parchment paper; place the triangles in the ring so it should look like the sun. Place the shredded Monterey Jack cheese, bacon, and tomato sauce on the half of each triangle, at the center of the ring. Sprinkle with oregano. Bring each triangle up over the filling. Press the overlapping dough to flatten. Transfer the parchment paper with the crescent ring to the Air Fryer basket. Bake at 355 degrees F for 20 minutes or until the ring is golden brown. Enjoy!

280. Beef and Wild Rice Casserole
INGREDIENTS (3 Servings)

3 cups beef stock	1 carrot, chopped	Kosher salt and ground black pepper, to your liking
1 cup wild rice, rinsed well	1 medium-sized leek, chopped	
1 tablespoon olive oil	2 garlic cloves, minced	
½ pound steak, cut into strips	1 chili pepper, minced	

DIRECTIONS (Prep + Cook Time: 50 minutes)

Place beef stock and rice in a saucepan over medium-high heat. Cover and bring it to a boil. Reduce the heat and let it simmer about 40 minutes. Drain the excess liquid and reserve. Heat the olive oil in a heavy skillet over moderate heat. Cook the steak until no longer pink; place in the lightly greased baking pan. Add carrot, leek, garlic, chili pepper, salt, and black pepper. Stir in the reserved wild rice. Stir to combine well. Cook in the preheated Air Fryer at 360 degrees for 9 to 10 minutes. Serve immediately and enjoy!

281. Golden Cornbread Muffins
INGREDIENTS (4 Servings)

½ cup sorghum flour	A pinch of salt	4 tablespoons butter, melted
½ cup yellow cornmeal	A pinch of grated nutmeg	4 tablespoons honey
¼ cup white sugar	2 eggs, beaten	
2 teaspoons baking powder	½ cup milk	

DIRECTIONS (Prep + Cook Time: 30 minutes)

Start by preheating your Air Fryer to 370 degrees F. Then, line the muffin cups with the paper baking cups. In a mixing bowl, combine the flour, cornmeal, sugar, baking powder, salt, and nutmeg. In a separate bowl, mix the eggs, milk, and butter. Pour the egg mixture into the dry cornmeal mixture; mix to combine well. Pour the batter into the prepared muffin cups. Bake for 15 minutes. Rotate the pan and bake for 10 minutes more. Transfer to a wire rack to cool slightly before cutting and serving. Serve with honey and enjoy!

282. Caprese Mac and Cheese
INGREDIENTS (3 Servings)

½ pound cavatappi	2 cups mozzarella cheese, grated	2 tomatoes, sliced
1 cup cauliflower florets	½ teaspoon Italian seasoning	1 cup Parmesan cheese, grated
1 cup milk	Salt and ground black pepper, to taste	1 tablespoon fresh basil leaves

DIRECTIONS (Prep + Cook Time: 25 minutes)

Bring a pot of salted water to a boil over high heat; turn the heat down to medium and add the cavatappi and cauliflower. Let it simmer about 8 minutes. Drain the cavatappi and cauliflower; place them in a lightly greased baking pan. Add the milk and mozzarella cheese to the baking pan; gently stir to combine. Add the Italian seasoning, salt, and black pepper. Top with the tomatoes and parmesan cheese. Bake in the preheated Air Fryer at 360 degrees F for 15 minutes. Serve garnished with fresh basil leaves. Enjoy!

283. Stuffed French Toast
INGREDIENTS (3 Servings)

- 6 slices of challah bread, without crusts
- ¼ cup Mascarpone cheese
- 3 tablespoons fig jam
- 1 egg
- 4 tablespoons milk
- ½ teaspoon grated nutmeg
- 1 teaspoon ground cinnamon
- ½ teaspoon vanilla paste
- ¼ cup butter, melted
- ½ cup brown sugar

DIRECTIONS (Prep + Cook Time: 15 minutes) Spread the three slices of bread with the mascarpone cheese, leaving ½-inch border at the edges. Spread the three slices of bread with ½ tablespoon of fig jam; then, invert them onto the slices with the cheese in order to make sandwiches. Mix the egg, milk, nutmeg, cinnamon, and vanilla in a shallow dish. Dip your sandwiches in the egg mixture. Cook in the preheated Air Fryer at 340 degrees F for 4 minutes. Dip in the melted butter, then, roll in the brown sugar. Serve warm.

284. Broccoli Bruschetta with Romano Cheese
INGREDIENTS (3 Servings)

- 6 slices of panini bread
- 1 teaspoon garlic puree
- 3 tablespoons extra-virgin olive oil
- 6 tablespoons passata di pomodoro (tomato passata)
- 1 cup small broccoli florets
- ½ cup Romano cheese, grated

DIRECTIONS (Prep + Cook Time: 20 minutes)

Place the slices of panini bread on a flat surface. In a small mixing bowl, combine together the garlic puree and extra-virgin olive oil. Brush one side of each bread slice with the garlic/oil mixture. Place in the Air Fryer grill pan. Add the tomato passata, broccoli, and cheese. Cook in the preheated Air Fryer at 370 degrees F for 10 minutes. Enjoy!

285. Roasted Asparagus Salad
INGREDIENTS (4 Servings)

- 1 pound asparagus spears, trimmed and sliced into 1-inch chunks
- ½ teaspoon turmeric powder
- 1 cup canned chickpeas, drained
- ½ cup canned white beans, drained
- ¼ cup shallots, chopped
- 1 clove garlic, pressed
- 2 tablespoons champagne vinegar
- 2 tablespoons extra-virgin olive oil
- ¼ teaspoon cayenne pepper
- Kosher salt and freshly ground black pepper, to taste

DIRECTIONS (Prep + Cook Time: 10 minutes)

Toss the asparagus with turmeric powder and brush with a nonstick cooking spray. Air fry your asparagus at 400 degrees F for 5 minutes, tossing halfway through the cooking time to promote even cooking. Allow your asparagus to cool slightly and transfer to a salad bowl. Toss your asparagus with the chickpeas, white beans, shallots and garlic. In a small bowl, whisk the remaining ingredients to make the dressing. Dress the salad and serve at room temperature. Enjoy!

286. Corn on the Cob with Mediterranean Sauce
INGREDIENTS (2 Servings)

- 2 ears corn, husked
- ⅓ cup raw cashews, soaked
- 2 cloves garlic, minced
- ½ teaspoon nutritional yeast
- ½ teaspoon Dijon mustard
- 4 tablespoons oat milk
- 1 tablespoon extra-virgin olive oil
- 1 teaspoon freshly squeezed lemon juice
- Sea salt and ground black pepper, to taste

DIRECTIONS (Prep + Cook Time: 10 minutes)

Cook your corn in the preheated Air Fryer at 390 degrees F for about 6 minutes. Meanwhile, blitz the remaining ingredients in your food processor or blender until smooth, creamy and uniform. Rub each ear of corn with the Mediterranean spread and serve immediately. Enjoy!

287. Bell Pepper Fries
INGREDIENTS (2 Servings)

- 1 cup flour
- 1 cup oat milk
- ½ teaspoon dried marjoram
- ½ teaspoon turmeric powder
- Sea salt and ground black pepper, to taste
- 1 cup seasoned breadcrumbs
- 2 large bell peppers

DIRECTIONS (Prep + Cook Time: 15 minutes)

In a shallow bowl, thoroughly combine the flour, milk, marjoram, turmeric, salt and black pepper. In another bowl, place seasoned breadcrumbs. Dip the pepper rings in the flour mixture; then, coat the rings with the seasoned breadcrumbs, pressing to adhere. Transfer the pepper rings to the Air Fryer cooking basket and spritz them with a nonstick spray. Cook the pepper rings at 380 degrees F for about 10 minutes, shaking the basket halfway through the cooking time to promote even cooking. Enjoy!

288. Crispy Butternut Squash Fries
INGREDIENTS (4 Servings)

- 1 cup all-purpose flour
- Salt and ground black pepper, to taste
- 3 tablespoons nutritional yeast flakes
- ½ cup almond milk
- ½ cup almond meal
- ½ cup bread crumbs
- 1 tablespoon herbs (oregano, basil, rosemary), chopped
- 1 pound butternut squash, peeled and cut into French fry shapes

DIRECTIONS (Prep + Cook Time: 25 minutes)

In a shallow bowl, combine the flour, salt, and black pepper. In another shallow dish, mix the nutritional yeast flakes with the almond milk until well combined. Mix the almond meal, breadcrumbs, and herbs in a third shallow dish. Dredge the butternut squash in the flour mixture, shaking off the excess. Then, dip in the milk mixture; lastly, dredge in the breadcrumb mixture. Spritz the butternut squash fries with cooking oil on all sides. Cook in the preheated Air Fryer at 400 degrees F approximately 12 minutes, turning them over halfway through the cooking time. Serve with your favorite sauce for dipping. Enjoy!

289. Caribbean-Style Fried Plantains
INGREDIENTS (2 Servings)

- 2 plantains, peeled and cut into slices
- 2 tablespoons avocado oil
- 2 teaspoons Caribbean Sorrel Rum Spice Mix

DIRECTIONS (Prep + Cook Time: 20 minutes)

Toss the plantains with the avocado oil and spice mix. Cook in the preheated Air Fryer at 400 degrees F for 10 minutes, shaking the cooking basket halfway through the cooking time. Adjust the seasonings to taste and enjoy!

290. Thai Sweet Potato Balls
INGREDIENTS (4 Servings)

- 1 pound sweet potatoes
- 1 cup brown sugar
- 1 tablespoon orange juice
- 2 teaspoons orange zest
- ½ teaspoon ground cinnamon
- ¼ teaspoon ground cloves
- ½ cup almond meal
- 1 teaspoon baking powder
- 1 cup coconut flakes

DIRECTIONS (Prep + Cook Time: 50 minutes)

Bake the sweet potatoes at 380 degrees F for 30 to 35 minutes until tender; peel and mash them. Add the brown sugar, orange juice, orange zest, ground cinnamon, cloves, almond meal, and baking powder; mix to combine well. Roll the balls in the coconut flakes. Bake in the preheated Air Fryer at 360 degrees F for 15 minutes or until thoroughly cooked and crispy. Repeat the process until you run out of ingredients. Enjoy!

291. Gourmet Wasabi Popcorn
INGREDIENTS (2 Servings)

- ½ teaspoon brown sugar
- 1 teaspoon salt
- ½ teaspoon wasabi powder, sifted
- 1 tablespoon avocado oil
- 3 tablespoons popcorn kernels

DIRECTIONS (Prep + Cook Time: 30 minutes)

Add the dried corn kernels to the Air Fryer basket; toss with the remaining ingredients. Cook at 395 degrees F for 15 minutes, shaking the basket every 5 minutes. Work in two batches. Taste, adjust the seasonings and serve immediately. Enjoy!

292. Hungarian Mushroom Pilaf
INGREDIENTS (4 Servings)

- 1 ½ cups white rice
- 3 cups vegetable broth
- 2 tablespoons olive oil
- 1 pound fresh porcini mushrooms, sliced
- 2 tablespoons olive oil
- 2 garlic cloves
- 1 onion, chopped
- ¼ cup dry vermouth
- 1 teaspoon dried thyme
- ½ teaspoon dried tarragon
- 1 teaspoon sweet Hungarian paprika

DIRECTIONS (Prep + Cook Time: 50 minutes)

Place the rice and broth in a large saucepan, add water; and bring to a boil. Cover, turn the heat down to low, and continue cooking for 16 to 18 minutes more. Set aside for 5 to 10 minutes. Now, stir the hot cooked rice with the remaining ingredients in a lightly greased baking dish. Cook in the preheated Air Fryer at 370 degrees for 20 minutes, checking periodically to ensure even cooking. Serve in individual bowls. Enjoy!

293. Healthy Mac and Cheese
INGREDIENTS (4 Servings)

- 12 ounces elbow pasta
- 2 garlic cloves, minced
- ⅓ cup vegan margarine
- ⅓ cup chickpea flour
- 3/4 cup unsweetened almond milk
- 2 heaping tablespoons nutritional yeast
- ½ teaspoon curry powder
- ½ teaspoon mustard powder
- ½ teaspoon celery seeds
- Sea salt and white pepper, to taste
- 1 ½ cups pasta water
- ½ cup seasoned breadcrumbs
- 1 heaping tablespoon Italian parsley, roughly chopped

DIRECTIONS (Prep + Cook Time: 30 minutes)

Bring a pot of salted water to a boil over high heat; turn the heat down to medium and add the elbow pasta. Let it cook approximately 8 minutes. Drain and transfer to the lightly greased baking pan. In a mixing dish, thoroughly combine the garlic, margarine, chickpea flour, milk, nutritional yeast, and spices. Add the pasta water and mix to combine well. Pour the milk mixture into the baking pan; gently stir to combine. Top with the seasoned breadcrumbs. Bake in the preheated Air Fryer at 360 degrees F for 15 minutes. Serve garnished with fresh parsley leaves. Enjoy!

294. Ultimate Vegan Calzone
INGREDIENTS (1 Servings)

- 1 teaspoon olive oil
- ½ small onion, chopped
- 2 sweet peppers, seeded and sliced
- Sea salt, to taste
- ¼ teaspoon ground black pepper
- ¼ teaspoon dried oregano
- 4 ounces prepared Italian pizza dough
- ¼ cup marinara sauce
- 2 ounces plant-based cheese Mozzarella-style, shredded

DIRECTIONS (Prep + Cook Time: 25 minutes)

Heat the olive oil in a nonstick skillet. Once hot, cook the onion and peppers until tender and fragrant, about 5 minutes. Add salt, black pepper, and oregano. Sprinkle some flour on a kitchen counter and roll out the pizza dough. Spoon the marinara sauce over half of the dough; add the sautéed mixture and sprinkle with the vegan cheese. Now, gently fold over the dough to create a pocket; make sure to seal the edges. Use a fork to poke the dough in a few spots. Add a few drizzles of olive oil and place in the lightly greased cooking basket. Bake in the preheated Air Fryer at 330 degrees F for 12 minutes, turning the calzones over halfway through the cooking time. Enjoy!

295. Paprika Brussels Sprout Chips
INGREDIENTS (2 Servings)

- 10 Brussels sprouts
- 1 teaspoon canola oil
- 1 teaspoon coarse sea salt
- 1 teaspoon paprika

DIRECTIONS (Prep + Cook Time: 20 minutes) Toss all ingredients in the lightly greased Air Fryer basket. Bake at 380 degrees F for 15 minutes, shaking the basket halfway through the cooking time to ensure even cooking. Serve and enjoy!

296. Cinnamon French Toast with Neufchâtel cheese
INGREDIENTS (2 Servings)

- 2 tablespoons butter
- ½ teaspoon ground cinnamon
- ¼ teaspoon ground anise
- A pinch of ground cloves
- 2 tablespoons brown sugar
- A pinch of sea salt
- 3 tablespoons milk
- 2 slices bread, about 1-inch thick
- 2 ounces Neufchâtel cheese, softened

DIRECTIONS (Prep + Cook Time: 10 minutes) Thoroughly combine the butter, cinnamon, anise, cloves, brown sugar, salt and milk. Spread the cinnamon butter on both sides of the bread slices. Arrange the bread slices in the cooking basket and cook them at 390 degrees F for 2 minutes; flip and cook on the other side for 2 to 3 minutes more. Serve with Neufchâtel cheese. Enjoy!

297. Autumn Pear Beignets
INGREDIENTS (3 Servings)

- 1 medium-sized pear, peeled, cored and chopped
- ¼ cup powdered sugar
- 2 tablespoons walnuts, ground
- ¼ teaspoon ground cloves
- ½ teaspoon vanilla paste
- ¼ teaspoon ground cinnamon
- 5 ounces refrigerated buttermilk biscuits
- 2 tablespoons coconut oil, at room temperature

DIRECTIONS (Prep + Cook Time: 15 minutes)

In a mixing bowl, thoroughly combine the pear, sugar, walnuts, cloves, vanilla and cinnamon. Separate the dough into 3 biscuits and then, divide each of them into 2 layers. Shape the biscuits into rounds. Divide the pear mixture between the biscuits and roll them up. Brush the biscuits with coconut oil and transfer them to the Air Fryer cooking basket. Cook your beignets at 330 degrees F for about 13 minutes, turning them over halfway through the cooking time. Serve with some extra powdered sugar if desired. Enjoy!

298. Oatmeal Pizza Cups
INGREDIENTS (3 Servings)

- 1 egg
- ½ cup oat milk
- 1 cup rolled oats
- ½ teaspoon baking soda
- ¼ teaspoon salt
- 1/8 teaspoon ground black pepper
- 2 tablespoons butter, melted
- 3 ounces smoked ham, chopped
- 3 ounces mozzarella cheese, shredded
- 4 tablespoons ketchup

DIRECTIONS (Prep + Cook Time: 25 minutes)

In a mixing bowl, beat the egg and milk until pale and frothy. In a separate bowl, mix the rolled oats, baking soda, salt, pepper and butter; mix to combine well. Fold in the smoked ham and mozzarella; gently stir to combine and top with ketchup. Spoon the mixture into a lightly greased muffin tin. Bake in the preheated Air Fryer at 330 degrees F for 20 minutes until a toothpick inserted comes out clean. Enjoy!

299. Basic Air Grilled Granola
INGREDIENTS (3 Servings)

- 1 cup rolled oats
- A pinch of salt
- A pinch of grated nutmeg
- ¼ teaspoon ground cinnamon
- 1 tablespoon honey
- 1 tablespoon coconut oil
- ¼ cup walnuts, chopped
- 1 tablespoon sunflower seeds
- 1 tablespoon pumpkin seeds

DIRECTIONS (Prep + Cook Time: 20 minutes)

In a mixing bowl, thoroughly combine the rolled oats, salt, nutmeg, cinnamon, honey and coconut oil. Spread the mixture into an Air Fryer baking pan and bake at 330 degrees F for about 15 minutes. Stir in the walnuts, sunflower seeds and pumpkin seeds. Continue to cook for a further 5 minutes. Store your granola in an airtight container for up to 2 weeks. Enjoy!

300. Mexican-Style Bubble Loaf
INGREDIENTS (4 Servings)

- 1 (16-ounce) can flaky buttermilk biscuits
- 4 tablespoons olive oil, melted
- ½ cup Manchego cheese, grated
- ½ teaspoon granulated garlic
- 1 tablespoon fresh cilantro, chopped
- ½ teaspoon Mexican oregano
- 1 teaspoon chili pepper flakes
- Kosher salt and ground black pepper, to taste

DIRECTIONS (Prep + Cook Time: 20 minutes)

Open a can of biscuits and cut each biscuit into quarters. Brush each piece of biscuit with the olive oil and begin layering in a lightly greased Bundt pan. Cover the bottom of the pan with one layer of biscuits. Next, top the first layer with half of the cheese, spices and granulated garlic. Repeat for another layer. Finish with a third layer of dough. Cook your bubble loaf in the Air Fryer at 330 degrees for about 15 minutes until the cheese is bubbly. Enjoy!

301. Hibachi-Style Fried Rice
INGREDIENTS (2 Servings)

- 1 ¾ cups leftover jasmine rice
- 2 teaspoons butter, melted
- Sea salt and freshly ground black pepper, to your liking
- 2 eggs, beaten
- 2 scallions, white and green parts separated, chopped
- 1 cup snow peas
- 1 tablespoon Shoyu sauce
- 1 tablespoon sake
- 2 tablespoons Kewpie Japanese mayonnaise

DIRECTIONS (Prep + Cook Time: 30 minutes)

Thoroughly combine the rice, butter, salt, and pepper in a baking dish. Cook at 340 degrees F about 13 minutes, stirring halfway through the cooking time. Pour the eggs over the rice and continue to cook about 5 minutes. Next, add the scallions and snow peas and stir to combine. Continue to cook 2 to 3 minutes longer or until everything is heated through. Meanwhile, make the sauce by whisking the Shoyu sauce, sake, and Japanese mayonnaise in a mixing bowl. Divide the fried rice between individual bowls and serve with the prepared sauce. Enjoy!

---

302. Classic Italian Arancini
INGREDIENTS (2 Servings)

- 1 ½ cups chicken broth
- ½ cup white rice
- 2 tablespoons parmesan cheese, grated
- Sea salt and cracked black pepper, to your liking
- 2 eggs
- 1 cup fresh bread crumbs
- ½ teaspoon oregano
- 1 teaspoon basil

DIRECTIONS (Prep + Cook Time: 35 minutes)

Bring the chicken broth to a boil in a saucepan over medium-high heat. Stir in the rice and reduce the heat to simmer; cook about 20 minutes. Drain the rice and allow it to cool completely. Add the parmesan, salt, and black pepper. Shape the mixture into bite-sized balls. In a shallow bowl, beat the eggs; in another shallow bowl, mix bread crumbs with oregano and basil. Dip each rice ball into the beaten eggs, then, roll in the breadcrumb mixture, gently pressing to adhere. Bake in the preheated Air Fryer at 350 degrees F for 10 to 12 minutes, flipping them halfway through the cooking time. Enjoy!

---

303. Spicy Seafood Risotto
INGREDIENTS (3 Servings)

- 1 ½ cups cooked rice, cold
- 3 tablespoons shallots, minced
- 2 garlic cloves, minced
- 1 tablespoon oyster sauce
- 2 tablespoons dry white wine
- 2 tablespoons sesame oil
- Salt and ground black pepper, to taste
- 2 eggs
- 4 ounces lump crab meat
- 1 teaspoon ancho chili powder
- 2 tablespoons fresh parsley, roughly chopped

DIRECTIONS (Prep + Cook Time: 25 minutes)

Mix the cold rice, shallots, garlic, oyster sauce, dry white wine, sesame oil, salt, and black pepper in a lightly greased baking pan. Stir in the whisked eggs. Cook in the preheated Air Fryer at 370 degrees for 13 to 16 minutes. Add the crab and ancho chili powder to the baking dish; stir until everything is well combined. Cook for 6 minutes more. Serve at room temperature, garnished with fresh parsley. Enjoy!

304. Risotto Balls with Bacon and Corn
INGREDIENTS (6 Servings)

- 4 slices Canadian bacon
- 1 tablespoon olive oil
- ½ medium-sized leek, chopped
- 1 teaspoon fresh garlic, minced
- Sea salt and freshly ground pepper, to taste
- 1 cup white rice
- 4 cups vegetable broth
- ⅓ cup dry white wine
- 2 tablespoons tamari sauce
- 1 tablespoon oyster sauce
- 1 tablespoon butter
- 1 cup sweet corn kernels
- 1 bell pepper, seeded and chopped
- 2 eggs lightly beaten
- 1 cup bread crumbs
- 1 cup parmesan cheese, preferably freshly grated

DIRECTIONS (Prep + Cook Time: 30 minutes + Chilling Time) Cook the Canadian bacon in a nonstick skillet over medium-high heat. Let it cool, finely chop and reserve. Heat the olive oil in a saucepan over medium heat. Now, sauté the leeks and garlic, stirring occasionally, about 5 minutes. Add the salt and pepper. Stir in the white rice. Continue to cook approximately 3 minutes or until translucent. Add the warm broth, wine, tamari sauce, and oyster sauce; cook until the liquid is absorbed. Remove the saucepan from the heat; stir in the butter, corn, bell pepper, and reserved Canadian bacon. Let it cool completely. Then, shape the mixture into small balls. In a shallow bowl, combine the eggs with the breadcrumbs and parmesan cheese. Dip each ball in the eggs/crumb mixture. Cook in the preheated Air Fryer at 395 degrees F for 10 to 12 minutes, shaking the basket periodically. Serve warm.

305. Puff Pastry Meat Strudel
INGREDIENTS (8 Servings)

- 1 tablespoon olive oil
- 1 small onion, chopped
- 2 garlic cloves, minced
- ⅓ pound ground beef
- ⅓ pound ground pork
- 2 tablespoons tomato puree
- 2 tablespoons matzo meal
- Sea salt and ground black pepper, to taste
- ½ teaspoon cayenne pepper
- ¼ teaspoon dried marjoram
- 2 cans (8-ounces) refrigerated crescent rolls
- 1 egg, whisked with
- 1 tablespoon of water
- 2 tablespoons sesame seeds
- ½ cup marinara sauce
- 1 cup sour cream

DIRECTIONS (Prep + Cook Time: 40 minutes)

Heat the oil in a heavy skillet over medium flame. Sauté the onion just until soft and translucent. Add the garlic and sauté for 1 minute more. Add the ground beef and pork and continue to cook for 3 minutes more or until the meat is no longer pink. Remove from the heat. Add the tomato puree and matzo meal. Roll out the puff pastry and spread the meat mixture lengthwise on the dough. Sprinkle with salt, black pepper, cayenne pepper, and marjoram. Fold in the sides of the dough over the meat mixture. Pinch the edges to seal. Place the strudel on the parchment lined Air Fryer basket. Brush the strudel with the egg wash; sprinkle with sesame seeds. Bake in the preheated Air Fryer at 330 degrees F for 18 to 20 minutes or until the pastry is puffed and golden and the filling is thoroughly cooked. Allow your strudel to rest for 5 to 10 minutes before cutting and serving. Serve with the marinara sauce and sour cream on the side. Enjoy!

306. Beef Taquito Casserole
INGREDIENTS (4 Servings)

- ½ (15-ounce) can black beans, drained and rinsed well
- 1 tablespoon taco seasoning mix
- 4 ounces mild enchilada sauce
- 1 cup Mexican cheese blend, shredded
- ½ (20-ounce) box frozen taquitos (chicken and cheese in tortillas)
- 2 tablespoons fresh chives, roughly chopped

DIRECTIONS (Prep + Cook Time: 20 minutes)

Start by preheating your Air Fryer to 350 degrees F. Spritz the baking pan with cooking spray. Mix the beans, taco seasoning mix, enchilada sauce and ½ cups of shredded cheese in the baking dish. Top the mixture with taquitos. Bake for 15 minutes. Top with the remaining ½ cup of shredded cheese and bake for a further 15 minutes. Serve garnished with chopped chives. Enjoy!

307. Couscous and Black Bean Bowl
INGREDIENTS (4 Servings)

- 1 cup couscous
- 1 cup canned black beans, drained and rinsed
- 1 tablespoon fresh cilantro, chopped
- 1 bell pepper, sliced
- 2 tomatoes, sliced
- 2 cups baby spinach
- 1 red onion, sliced
- Sea salt and ground black pepper, to taste
- 1 teaspoon lemon juice
- 1 teaspoon lemon zest
- 1 tablespoon olive oil
- 4 tablespoons tahini

DIRECTIONS (Prep + Cook Time: 35 minutes)

Put the couscous in a bowl; pour the boiling water to cover by about 1 inch. Cover and set aside for 5 to 8 minutes; fluff with a fork. Place the couscous in a lightly greased cake pan. Transfer the pan to the Air Fryer basket and cook at 360 digress F about 20 minutes. Make sure to stir every 5 minutes to ensure even cooking. Transfer the prepared couscous to a mixing bowl. Add the remaining ingredients; gently stir to combine. Enjoy!

308. Asian-Style Shrimp Pilaf
INGREDIENTS (3 Servings)

- 1 cup koshihikari rice, rinsed
- 1 yellow onion, chopped
- 2 garlic cloves, minced
- ½ teaspoon fresh ginger, grated
- 1 tablespoon Shoyu sauce
- 2 tablespoons rice wine
- 1 tablespoon sushi seasoning
- 1 tablespoon caster sugar
- ½ teaspoon sea salt
- 5 ounces frozen shrimp, thawed
- 2 tablespoons katsuobushi flakes, for serving

DIRECTIONS (Prep + Cook Time: 45 minutes)

Place the koshihikari rice and 2 cups of water in a large saucepan and bring to a boil. Cover, turn the heat down to low, and continue cooking for 15 minutes more. Set aside for 10 minutes. Mix the rice, onion, garlic, ginger, Shoyu sauce, wine, sushi seasoning, sugar, and salt in a lightly greased baking dish. Cook in the preheated Air Fryer at 370 degrees for 13 to 16 minutes. Add the shrimp to the baking dish and gently stir until everything is well combined. Cook for 6 minutes more. Serve at room temperature, garnished with katsuobushi flakes. Enjoy!

309. Mediterranean Pita Pockets
INGREDIENTS (4 Servings)

- 1 teaspoon olive oil
- 1 onion
- 2 garlic cloves, minced
- 3/4 pound ground turkey
- Salt and ground black pepper, to taste
- ½ teaspoon mustard seeds
- 4 small pitas Tzatziki
- ½ cup Greek-style yogurt
- ½ cucumber, peeled
- 1 clove garlic, minced
- 2 tablespoons fresh lemon juice
- Sea salt, to taste
- ¼ teaspoon dried oregano

DIRECTIONS (Prep + Cook Time: 25 minutes)

Mix the olive oil, onion, garlic, turkey, salt, black pepper, and mustard seeds; shape the mixture into four patties. Cook in the preheated Air Fryer at 370 degrees F for 10 minutes, turning them over once or twice. Meanwhile, mix all ingredients for the tzatziki and place in the refrigerator until ready to use. Warm the pita pockets in the preheated Air Fryer at 360 degrees F for 4 to 5 minutes or until thoroughly heated. Spread the tzatziki in pita pockets and add the turkey patties. Enjoy!

310. Crispy Pork Wontons
INGREDIENTS (3 Servings)

- 1 tablespoon olive oil
- 3/4 pound ground pork
- 1 red bell pepper, seeded and chopped
- 1 green bell pepper, seeded and chopped
- 1 habanero pepper, minced
- 3 tablespoons onion, finely chopped
- Salt and ground black pepper, to taste
- ½ teaspoon dried parsley flakes
- 1 teaspoon dried thyme
- 6 wonton wrappers

DIRECTIONS (Prep + Cook Time: 20 minutes)

Heat the olive oil in a heavy skillet over medium heat. Cook the ground pork, peppers, and onion until tender and fragrant or about 4 minutes. Add the seasonings and stir to combine. Lay a piece of the wonton wrapper on your palm; add the filling in the middle of the wrapper. Then, fold it up to form a triangle; pinch the edges to seal tight. Place the folded wontons in the lightly greased cooking basket. Cook at 360 degrees F for 10 minutes. Work in batches and serve warm. Enjoy!

311. Mexican Taco Bake
INGREDIENTS (4 Servings)

- 1 tablespoon olive oil
- ¼ pound ground beef
- ½ pound ground pork
- 1 shallot, minced
- 1 garlic, minced
- ½ cup beef broth
- 1 bell pepper, seeded and chopped
- 1 Mexican chili pepper, seeded and minced
- 1 ½ cups tomato sauce
- 4 flour tortillas for fajitas
- 1 cup Mexican cheese blend, shredded

DIRECTIONS (Prep + Cook Time: 40 minutes)

Heat the olive oil in a heavy skillet over a moderate flame. Cook the ground meat with the shallots and garlic until no longer pink. Then, add the beef broth, peppers, and tomato sauce to the skillet. Continue to cook on low heat for 3 minutes, stirring continuously. Spritz a baking dish with nonstick cooking spray. Cut the tortillas in half; place 2 tortilla halves in the bottom of the baking dish. Top with half of the meat mixture. Sprinkle with ½ cup of the cheese and the remaining tortilla halves. Top with the remaining meat mixture and cheese. Cover with a piece of aluminum foil and bake in the preheated Air Fryer at 330 degrees F for 20 minutes. Remove the foil and bake for a further 12 minutes or until thoroughly heated. Enjoy!

312. Cornmeal Crusted Okra
INGREDIENTS (2 Servings)

- 3/4 cup cornmeal
- ¼ cup parmesan cheese, grated
- Sea salt and ground black pepper, to taste
- 1 teaspoon cayenne pepper
- 1 teaspoon garlic powder
- ½ teaspoon cumin seeds
- ½ pound of okra, cut into small chunks
- 2 teaspoons sesame oil

DIRECTIONS (Prep + Cook Time: 30 minutes)

In a mixing bowl, thoroughly combine the cornmeal, parmesan, salt, black pepper, cayenne pepper, garlic powder, and cumin seeds. Stir well to combine. Roll the okra pods over the cornmeal mixture, pressing to adhere. Drizzle with sesame oil. Cook in the preheated Air Fryer at 370 digress F for 20 minutes, shaking the basket periodically to ensure even cooking. Enjoy!

313. Tex Mex Pasta Bake
INGREDIENTS (4 Servings)

- 3/4 pound pasta noodles
- 1 tablespoon olive oil
- 3/4 pound ground beef
- 1 medium-sized onion, chopped
- 1 teaspoon fresh garlic, minced
- 1 bell pepper, seeded and sliced
- 1 jalapeno, seeded and minced
- Sea salt and cracked black pepper, to taste
- 1 ½ cups enchilada sauce
- 1 cup Mexican cheese blend, shredded
- ⅓ cup tomato paste
- ½ teaspoon Mexican oregano
- ½ cup nacho chips
- 2 tablespoons fresh coriander, chopped

DIRECTIONS (Prep + Cook Time: 40 minutes)

Boil the pasta noodles for 3 minutes less than mentioned on the package; drain, rinse and place in the lightly greased casserole dish. In a saucepan, heat the olive oil until sizzling. Add the ground beef and cook for 2 to 3 minutes or until slightly brown. Now, add the onion, garlic, and peppers and continue to cook until tender and fragrant or about 2 minutes. Season with salt and black pepper. Add the enchilada sauce to the casserole dish. Add the beef mixture and ½ cup of the Mexican cheese blend. Gently stir to combine. Add the tomato paste, Mexican oregano, nacho chips, and the remaining ½ cup of cheese blend. Cover with foil. Bake in the preheated Air Fryer at 350 degrees F for 20 minutes; remove the foil and bake for a further 10 to 12 minutes. Serve garnished with fresh coriander and enjoy!

314. Air Grilled Tofu
INGREDIENTS (3 Servings)

- 8 ounces firm tofu, pressed and cut into bite-sized cubes
- 1 tablespoon tamari sauce
- 1 teaspoon peanut oil
- ½ teaspoon garlic powder
- ½ teaspoon onion powder

DIRECTIONS (Prep + Cook Time: 15 minutes)

Toss the tofu cubes with tamari sauce, peanut oil, garlic powder and onion powder. Cook your tofu in the preheated Air Fryer at 380 degrees F for about 13 minutes, shaking the basket once or twice to ensure even browning. Enjoy!

315. Easy Roasted Fennel
INGREDIENTS (3 Servings)

1 pound fennel bulbs, sliced

1 tablespoon olive oil

½ teaspoon dried basil

½ teaspoon dried marjoram

Sea salt and ground black pepper, to taste

¼ cup vegan mayonnaise

DIRECTIONS (Prep + Cook Time: 25 minutes)

Toss the fennel slices with the olive oil and spices and transfer them to the Air Fryer cooking basket. Roast the fennel at 370 degrees F for about 20 minutes, shaking the basket once or twice to promote even cooking. Serve the fennel slice with mayonnaise and enjoy!

316. Korean-Style Broccoli
INGREDIENTS (2 Servings)

½ pound broccoli florets

1 tablespoon sesame oil

1 tablespoon soy sauce

¼ teaspoon coriander seeds

½ teaspoon garlic powder

1 tablespoon brown sugar

½ teaspoon gochukaru (Korean red chili powder)

Sea salt and ground black pepper, to taste

DIRECTIONS (Prep + Cook Time: 12 minutes)

Toss the broccoli florets with the other ingredients until well coated. Air fry your broccoli at 390 degrees F for about 10 minutes, shaking the basket halfway through the cooking time. Serve with your favorite vegan dip. Enjoy!

317. Cajun Celery Sticks
INGREDIENTS (3 Servings)

½ pound celery root, peeled and cut into ½-inch sticks

1 teaspoon Cajun seasoning mix

Salt and white pepper, to taste

Sauce:

⅓ cup tofu mayonnaise

1 teaspoon lime juice

1 teaspoon deli mustard

1 teaspoon agave nectar

DIRECTIONS (Prep + Cook Time: 20 minutes)

Toss the celery sticks with the Cajun seasoning mix, salt and white pepper and place them in the Air Fryer cooking basket. Now, cook the celery sticks at 400 degrees F for about 17 minutes, shaking the basket halfway through the cooking time. In the meantime, mix the mayonnaise with the lime juice, deli mustard and agave nectar. Serve the celery sticks with the mayo sauce on the side. Enjoy!

318. Cauliflower Oatmeal Fritters
INGREDIENTS (3 Servings)

½ pound cauliflower florets

1 cup rolled oats

2 tablespoons flaxseed meal

2 tablespoons sunflower seeds

2 tablespoons hemp hearts

4 tablespoons pumpkin seeds butter

1 glove garlic, chopped

1 small yellow onion

½ teaspoon smoked paprika

Kosher salt and freshly ground black pepper, to taste

1 tablespoon canola oil

DIRECTIONS (Prep + Cook Time: 20 minutes)

Place all ingredients in the bowl of your food processor or blender; mix until well combined. Then, shape the mixture into small patties and transfer them to the Air Fryer cooking basket. Cook the cauliflower patties in the preheated Air Fryer at 375 degrees F for 16 minutes, shaking the basket halfway through the cooking time to ensure even browning. Enjoy!

319. Portobello Mushroom Schnitzel
INGREDIENTS (2 Servings)

- 7 ounces Portobello mushrooms
- ¼ cup chickpea flour
- ¼ cup plain flour
- ⅓ cup beer
- 1 cup breadcrumbs
- ½ teaspoon porcini powder
- ½ teaspoon dried basil
- ¼ teaspoon dried oregano
- ¼ teaspoon ground cumin
- ¼ teaspoon ground bay leaf
- ½ teaspoon garlic powder
- ½ teaspoon shallot powder
- Kosher salt and ground black pepper, to taste

DIRECTIONS (Prep + Cook Time: 10 minutes)

Pat dry the Portobello mushrooms and set them aside. Then, add the flour and beer to a rimmed plate and mix to combine well. In another bowl, mix the breadcrumbs with spices. Dip your mushrooms in the flour mixture, then, coat them with the breadcrumb mixture. Cook the breaded mushrooms in the preheated Air Fryer at 380 degrees F for 6 to 7 minutes, flipping them over halfway through the cooking time. Eat warm.

320. Fried Parsnip with Mint Yogurt Sauce
INGREDIENTS (2 Servings)

- ½ parsnip, peeled and sliced into sticks
- 1 teaspoon olive oil
- Sea salt and ground black pepper, to taste
- 3 ounces Greek-style dairy-free yogurt, unsweetened
- 1 teaspoon juice
- ½ teaspoon fresh garlic, pressed
- 1 teaspoon fresh mint, chopped

DIRECTIONS (Prep + Cook Time: 10 minutes)

Toss your parsnip with olive oil, salt and black pepper. Cook the parsnip in the preheated Air Fryer at 390 degrees F for 15 minutes, shaking the basket halfway through the cooking time. In the meantime, mix the remaining ingredients until well combined. Serve the warm parsnip with the mint yogurt for dipping. Serve and enjoy!

321. Authentic Vegan Ratatouille
INGREDIENTS (2 Servings)

- 4 ounces courgette, sliced
- 4 ounces eggplant, sliced
- 1 bell pepper, sliced
- 4 ounces tomatoes, peeled and quartered
- 1 yellow onion, peeled and sliced
- 1 teaspoon fresh garlic, minced
- ½ teaspoon oregano
- ½ teaspoon basil
- Coarse sea salt and ground black pepper, to taste
- 1 tablespoon olive oil

DIRECTIONS (Prep + Cook Time: 15 minutes)

Place the sliced veggies in the Air Fryer cooking basket. Season your veggies with oregano, basil, salt and black pepper. Drizzle olive oil over the top. Cook your veggies at 400 degrees F for about 15 minutes, shaking the basket halfway through the cooking time to promote even cooking. Arrange the sliced veggies in alternating patterns and serve warm.

322. Crispy Garlic Tofu with Brussels Sprouts
INGREDIENTS (2 Servings)

- 8 ounces firm tofu, pressed and cut into bite-sized cubes
- 1 teaspoon garlic paste
- 1 tablespoons arrowroot powder
- 1 teaspoon peanut oil
- ½ pound Brussels sprouts, halved
- Sea salt and ground black pepper, to taste

DIRECTIONS (Prep + Cook Time: 20 minutes)

Toss the tofu cubes with the garlic paste, arrowroot powder and peanut oil. Transfer your tofu to the Air Fryer cooking basket; add in the Brussels sprouts and season everything with salt and black pepper. Cook the tofu cubes and Brussels sprouts at 380 degrees F for 15 minutes, shaking the basket halfway through the cooking time. Enjoy!

323. Baby Potatoes with Garlic-Rosemary Sauce
INGREDIENTS (3 Servings)

- 1 pound baby potatoes, scrubbed
- 1 tablespoon olive oil
- ½ garlic bulb, slice the top
- ¼ -inch off the garlic head
- 1 tablespoon fresh rosemary leaves, chopped
- 1 teaspoon sherry vinegar
- ½ cup white wine
- Salt and freshly ground black pepper

DIRECTIONS (Prep + Cook Time: 50 minutes)

Brush the baby potatoes with olive oil and transfer them to the air Fryer cooking basket. Cook the baby potatoes at 400 degrees F for 12 minutes, shaking the basket halfway through the cooking time. Place the garlic bulb into the center of a piece of aluminum foil. Drizzle the garlic bulb with a nonstick cooking spray and wrap tightly in foil. Cook the garlic at 390 degrees F for about 25 minutes or until the cloves are tender. Let it cool for about 10 minutes; remove the cloves by squeezing them out of the skins; mash the garlic and add it to a saucepan. Stir the remaining ingredients into the saucepan and let it simmer for 10 to 15 minutes until the sauce has reduced by half. Spoon the sauce over the baby potatoes and serve warm. Enjoy!

324. Paprika Squash Fries
INGREDIENTS (3 Servings)

- ¼ cup rice milk
- ¼ cup almond flour
- 2 tablespoons nutritional yeast
- ¼ teaspoon shallot powder
- ½ teaspoon garlic powder
- ½ teaspoon paprika
- Sea salt and ground black pepper, to taste
- 1 pound butternut squash, peeled and into sticks
- 1 cup tortilla chips, crushed

DIRECTIONS (Prep + Cook Time: 15 minutes)

In a bowl, thoroughly combine the milk flour, nutritional yeast and spices. In another shallow bowl, place the crushed tortilla chips. Dip the butternut squash sticks into the batter and then, roll them over the crushed tortilla chips until well coated. Arrange the squash pieces in the Air Fryer cooking basket. Cook the squash fries at 400 degrees F for about 12 minutes, shaking the basket once or twice. Enjoy!

325. Green Potato Croquettes
INGREDIENTS (2 Servings)

- ½ pound cup russet potatoes
- 1 teaspoon olive oil
- ½ teaspoon garlic, pressed
- 2 cups loosely packed mixed greens, torn into pieces
- 2 tablespoons oat milk
- Sea salt and ground black pepper, to taste
- ¼ teaspoon red pepper flakes, crushed

DIRECTIONS (Prep + Cook Time: 45 minutes)

Cook your potatoes for about 30 minutes until they are fork-tender; peel the potatoes and add them to a mixing bowl. Mash your potatoes and stir in the remaining ingredients. Shape the mixture into bite-sized balls and place them in the cooking basket; sprits the balls with a nonstick cooking oil. Cook the croquettes at 390 degrees F for about 13 minutes, shaking the cooking basket halfway through the cooking time. Serve with tomato ketchup if desired. Enjoy!

326. Easy Homemade Falafel
INGREDIENTS (3 Servings)

- 1 cup dry chickpeas, soaked overnight
- 1 small onion, sliced
- 2 tablespoons fresh cilantro
- 2 tablespoons fresh parsley
- 2 cloves garlic
- ½ teaspoon cayenne pepper
- Sea salt and ground black pepper, to taste
- ½ teaspoon ground cumin

DIRECTIONS (Prep + Cook Time: 15 minutes)

Drain and rinse your chickpeas and place them in a bowl of a food processor. Add in the remaining ingredients and blitz until the ingredients form a coarse meal. Roll the mixture into small balls with oiled hands. Cook your falafel in the preheated Air Fryer at 395 degrees F for 5 minutes; turn them over and cook for another 5 to 6 minutes. Serve and enjoy!

327. Spicy Sesame Cauliflower Steaks
INGREDIENTS (2 Servings)

- ½ pound cauliflower, cut into
- 2 slabs
- ½ cup plain flour
- ¼ cup cornstarch
- ½ cup ale
- ½ teaspoon hot sauce
- ¼ teaspoon onion powder
- ½ teaspoon garlic powder
- ½ teaspoon smoked paprika
- 1 tablespoon sesame seeds
- Kosher salt and ground black pepper, to taste
- ¼ cup buffalo sauce

DIRECTIONS (Prep + Cook Time: 25 minutes)

Parboil the cauliflower in the pot with a lightly salted water for about 15 minutes. In a mixing bowl, combine the remaining ingredients, except for the buffalo sauce, until everything is well incorporated. Then, dip the cauliflower steaks into the batter. Cook the cauliflower steaks at 400 degrees F for 10 minutes, flipping them over halfway through the cooking time to promote even cooking. Serve the warm cauliflower steaks with buffalo sauce and enjoy!

328. Spicy Bean Burgers
INGREDIENTS (3 Servings)

- ½ cup old-fashioned oats
- 2 tablespoons red onions, finely chopped
- 2 garlic cloves, finely chopped
- 8 ounces canned beans
- ⅓ cup marinara sauce
- 1 teaspoon tamari sauce
- A few drops of liquid smoke
- Kosher salt and ground black pepper, to taste
- ¼ teaspoon ancho chile powder

DIRECTIONS (Prep + Cook Time: 15 minutes)

Pulse all ingredients in your food processor leaving some larger chunks of beans. Now, form the mixture into patties and place them in the Air Fryer cooking basket. Brush the patties with a nonstick cooking oil. Cook your burgers at 380 degrees F for about 15 minutes, flipping them halfway through the cooking time. Serve on burger buns garnished with your favorite fixings. Serve and enjoy!

329. Polish Placki Ziemniaczan
INGREDIENTS (2 Servings)

- ½ pound potatoes, peeled and finely grated
- ½ small white onion, finely chopped
- ¼ cup all-purpose flour
- ½ teaspoon turmeric powder
- 2 tablespoons breadcrumbs
- Kosher salt and freshly ground black pepper, to taste
- 2 tablespoons granulated sugar
- 2 ounces sour cream

DIRECTIONS (Prep + Cook Time: 10 minutes)

Place the grated potatoes in a triple layer of cheesecloth; now, twist and squeeze the potatoes until no more liquid comes out of them. Place the potatoes in a mixing bowl; stir in the onion, flour, turmeric powder, breadcrumbs, salt and black pepper. Cook them at 380 degrees for about 10 minutes, turning over after 5 minutes. Serve with granulated sugar and sour cream. Enjoy!

330. Favorite Lentil Burgers
INGREDIENTS (3 Servings)

- ½ cup wild rice, cooked
- 1 cup red lentils, cooked
- ½ small onion, quartered
- ½ small beet, peeled and quartered
- 1 garlic clove
- ¼ cup walnuts
- 2 tablespoons breadcrumbs
- ½ teaspoon cayenne pepper
- Sea salt and ground black pepper, to taste
- 1 tablespoon vegan barbecue sauce

DIRECTIONS (Prep + Cook Time: 15 minutes)

In your food processor, pulse all ingredients until a moldable dough forms. Shape the mixture into equal patties and place them in the lightly oiled Air Fryer cooking basket. Cook your burgers at 380 degrees F for about 15 minutes, flipping them halfway through the cooking time. Serve on burger buns and enjoy!

331. The Best Crispy Tofu
INGREDIENTS (4 Servings)

- 16 ounces firm tofu, pressed and cubed
- 1 tablespoon vegan oyster sauce
- 1 tablespoon tamari sauce
- 1 teaspoon cider vinegar
- 1 teaspoon pure maple syrup
- 1 teaspoon sriracha
- ½ teaspoon shallot powder
- ½ teaspoon porcini powder
- 1 teaspoon garlic powder
- 1 tablespoon sesame oil
- 5 tablespoons cornstarch

DIRECTIONS (Prep + Cook Time: 55 minutes)

Toss the tofu with the oyster sauce, tamari sauce, vinegar, maple syrup, sriracha, shallot powder, porcini powder, garlic powder, and sesame oil. Let it marinate for 30 minutes. Toss the marinated tofu with the cornstarch. Cook at 360 degrees F for 10 minutes; turn them over and cook for 12 minutes more. Serve and enjoy!

332. Crunchy Eggplant Rounds
INGREDIENTS (4 Servings)

- 1 (1-pound) eggplant, sliced
- ½ cup flax meal
- ½ cup rice flour
- Coarse sea salt and ground black pepper, to taste
- 1 teaspoon paprika
- 1 cup water
- 1 cup cornbread crumbs, crushed
- ½ cup vegan parmesan

DIRECTIONS (Prep + Cook Time: 55 minutes)

Toss the eggplant with 1 tablespoon of salt and let it stand for 30 minutes. Drain and rinse well. Mix the flax meal, rice flour, salt, black pepper, and paprika in a bowl. Then, pour in the water and whisk to combine well. In another shallow bowl, mix the cornbread crumbs and vegan parmesan. Dip the eggplant slices in the flour mixture, then in the crumb mixture; press to coat on all sides. Transfer to the lightly greased Air Fryer basket. Cook at 370 degrees F for 6 minutes. Turn each slice over and cook an additional 5 minutes. Serve garnished with spicy ketchup if desired. Enjoy!

333. Indian Plantain Chips (Kerala Neenthram)
INGREDIENTS (2 Servings)

- 1 pound plantain, thinly sliced
- 1 tablespoon turmeric
- 2 tablespoons coconut oil

DIRECTIONS (Prep + Cook Time: 30 minutes)

Directions Fill a large enough cup with water and add the turmeric to the water. Soak the plantain slices in the turmeric water for 15 minutes. Brush with coconut oil and transfer to the Air Fryer basket. Cook in the preheated Air Fryer at 400 degrees F for 10 minutes, shaking the cooking basket halfway through the cooking time. Serve at room temperature. Enjoy!

334. Garlic-Roasted Brussels Sprouts with Mustard
INGREDIENTS (3 Servings)

- 1 pound Brussels sprouts, halved
- 2 tablespoons olive oil
- Sea salt and freshly ground black pepper, to taste
- 2 garlic cloves, minced
- 1 tablespoon Dijon mustard

DIRECTIONS (Prep + Cook Time: 20 minutes)

Toss the Brussels sprouts with the olive oil, salt, black pepper, and garlic. Roast in the preheated Air Fryer at 380 degrees F for 15 minutes, shaking the basket occasionally. Serve with Dijon mustard and enjoy!

335. Italian-Style Risi e Bisi
INGREDIENTS (4 Servings)

- 2 cups brown rice
- 4 cups water
- ½ cup frozen green peas
- 3 tablespoons soy sauce
- 1 tablespoon olive oil
- 1 cup brown mushrooms, sliced
- 2 garlic cloves, minced
- 1 small-sized onion, chopped
- 1 tablespoon fresh parsley, chopped

DIRECTIONS (Prep + Cook Time: 20 minutes)

Heat the brown rice and water in a pot over high heat. Bring it to a boil; turn the stove down to simmer and cook for 35 minutes. Allow your rice to cool completely. Transfer the cold cooked rice to the lightly greased Air Fryer pan. Add the remaining ingredients and stir to combine. Cook in the preheated Air Fryer at 360 degrees F for 18 to 22 minutes. Serve warm.

336. Baked Oatmeal with Berries
INGREDIENTS (4 Servings)

- 1 cup fresh strawberries
- ½ cup dried cranberries
- 1 ½ cups rolled oats
- ½ teaspoon baking powder
- A pinch of sea salt
- A pinch of grated nutmeg
- ½ teaspoon ground cinnamon
- ½ teaspoon vanilla extract
- 4 tablespoons agave syrup
- 1 ½ cups coconut milk

DIRECTIONS (Prep + Cook Time: 30 minutes)

Spritz a baking pan with cooking spray. Place ½ cup of strawberries on the bottom of the pan; place the cranberries over that. In a mixing bowl, thoroughly combine the rolled oats, baking powder, salt, nutmeg, cinnamon, vanilla, agave syrup, and milk. Pour the oatmeal mixtures over the fruits; allow it to soak for 15 minutes. Top with the remaining fruits. Bake at 330 degrees F for 12 minutes. Serve warm or at room temperature. Enjoy!

337. Herb Roasted Potatoes and Peppers
INGREDIENTS (4 Servings)

- 1 pound russet potatoes, cut into 1-inch chunks
- 2 bell peppers, seeded and cut into 1-inch chunks
- 2 tablespoons olive oil
- 1 teaspoon dried rosemary
- 1 teaspoon dried basil
- 1 teaspoon dried oregano
- 1 teaspoon dried parsley flakes
- Sea salt and ground black pepper, to taste
- ½ teaspoon smoked paprika

DIRECTIONS (Prep + Cook Time: 30 minutes)

Toss all ingredients in the Air Fryer basket. Roast at 400 degrees F for 15 minutes, tossing the basket occasionally. Work in batches. Serve warm and enjoy!

338. Cinnamon Sugar Tortilla Chips
INGREDIENTS (4 Servings)

- 4 (10-inch) flour tortillas
- ¼ cup vegan margarine, melted
- 1 ½ tablespoons ground cinnamon
- ¼ cup caster sugar

DIRECTIONS (Prep + Cook Time: 20 minutes)

Slice each tortilla into eight slices. Brush the tortilla pieces with the melted margarine. In a mixing bowl, thoroughly combine the cinnamon and sugar. Toss the cinnamon mixture with the tortillas. Transfer to the cooking basket and cook at 360 degrees F for 8 minutes or until lightly golden. Work in batches. They will crisp up as they cool. Serve and enjoy!

339. Cauliflower, Broccoli and Chickpea Salad
INGREDIENTS (4 Servings)

- ½ pound cauliflower florets
- ½ pound broccoli florets
- Sea salt, to taste
- ½ teaspoon red pepper flakes
- 2 tablespoons soy sauce
- 2 tablespoons cider vinegar
- 1 teaspoon Dijon mustard
- 2 tablespoons extra-virgin olive oil
- 1 cup canned or cooked chickpeas, drained
- 1 avocado, pitted, peeled and sliced
- 1 small sized onion, peeled and sliced
- 1 garlic clove, minced
- 2 cups arugula
- 2 tablespoons sesame seeds, lightly toasted

DIRECTIONS (Prep + Cook Time: 20 minutes +Chilling Time)

Start by preheating your Air Fryer to 400 degrees F. Brush the cauliflower and broccoli florets with cooking spray. Cook for 12 minutes, shaking the cooking basket halfway through the cooking time. Season with salt and red pepper. In a mixing dish, whisk the soy sauce, cider vinegar, Dijon mustard, and olive oil. Dress the salad. Add the chickpeas, avocado, onion, garlic, and arugula. Top with sesame seeds. Serve and enjoy!

340. Butternut Squash Chili
INGREDIENTS (4 Servings)

2 tablespoons canola oil

1 cup leeks, chopped

2 garlic cloves, crushed

2 ripe tomatoes, pureed

2 chipotle peppers in adobo, chopped

1 teaspoon ground cumin

1 teaspoon chili powder

Kosher salt and ground black pepper, to your liking

1 cup vegetable broth

1 pound butternut squash, peeled and diced into

½-inch chunks

16 ounces canned kidney beans, drained and rinsed

1 avocado, pitted, peeled and diced

DIRECTIONS (Prep + Cook Time: 35 minutes)

Start by preheating your Air Fryer to 365 degrees F. Heat the oil in a baking pan until sizzling. Then, sauté the leeks and garlic in the baking pan. Cook for 4 to 6 minutes. Now, add the tomatoes, chipotle peppers, cumin, chili powder, salt, pepper, and vegetable broth. Cook for 15 minutes, stirring every 5 minutes. Stir in the the butternut squash and canned beans; let it cook for a further 8 minutes, stirring halfway through the cooking time. Serve in individual bowls, garnished with the avocado. Enjoy!

341. Sunday Potato Fritters
INGREDIENTS (3 Servings)

1 tablespoon olive oil

½ pound potatoes, peeled and cut into chunks

½ cup cashew cream

½ cup chickpea flour

½ teaspoon baking powder

½ onion, chopped

1 garlic clove, minced

Sea salt and ground black pepper, to your liking

1 cup tortilla chips, crushed

DIRECTIONS (Prep + Cook Time: 30 minutes)

Start by preheating your Air Fryer to 400 degrees F. Drizzle the olive oil all over the potatoes. Place the potatoes in the Air Fryer basket and cook approximately 15 minutes, shaking the basket periodically. Lightly crush the potatoes to split; mash the potatoes and combine with the other ingredients. Form the potato mixture into patties. Bake in the preheated Air Fryer at 380 degrees F for 14 minutes, flipping them halfway through the cooking time to ensure even cooking. Enjoy!

342. Baked Spicy Tortilla Chips
INGREDIENTS (3 Servings)

6 (6-inch) corn tortillas

1 teaspoon canola oil 1 teaspoon salt

¼ teaspoon ground white pepper

½ teaspoon ground cumin

½ teaspoon ancho chili powder

DIRECTIONS (Prep + Cook Time: 20 minutes)

Slice the tortillas into quarters. Brush the tortilla pieces with the canola oil until well coated. Toss with the spices and transfer to the Air Fryer basket. Bake at 360 degrees F for 8 minutes or until lightly golden. Work in batches. Enjoy!

Fish & Seafood

343. Old Bay Crab Sticks with Garlic Mayo
INGREDIENTS (4 Servings)

1 lb crab sticks	2 eggs	1 lime, juiced
1 tbsp old bay seasoning	½ cup mayonnaise	1 cup flour
⅓ cup panko breadcrumbs	2 garlic cloves, minced	

DIRECTIONS (Prep + Cook Time: 20 minutes)

Preheat air fryer to 390 F. Beat the eggs in a bowl. In another bowl, mix breadcrumbs with old bay seasoning. In a third bowl, pour the flour. Dip the sticks in the flour, then in the eggs, and finally in the crumbs. Spray with cooking spray and AirFry in the frying basket for 12 minutes, flipping once. Mix mayonnaise with garlic and lime juice. Serve as a dip along with crab sticks.

344. Crispy Prawns in Bacon Wraps
INGREDIENTS (4 Servings)

8 bacon slices	8 jumbo prawns, peeled and deveined

DIRECTIONS (Prep + Cook Time: 30 minutes)

Wrap each prawn from head to tail with each bacon slice overlapping to keep the bacon in place. Secure the ends with toothpicks. Refrigerate for 15 minutes. Preheat air fryer to 400 F. Arrange the bacon-wrapped prawns on the greased frying basket and Bake for 8 minutes, turning once. Serve hot.

345. Rosemary Cashew Shrimp
INGREDIENTS (4 Servings)

3 oz cashews, chopped	1 garlic clove, minced	1 tbsp olive oil
1 tbsp fresh rosemary, chopped	1 tbsp breadcrumbs	Salt and black pepper to taste
1 ½ lb shrimp	1 egg, beaten	

DIRECTIONS (Prep + Cook Time: 35 minutes)

Preheat air fryer to 320 F. Combine olive oil with garlic and brush onto the shrimp. Combine rosemary, cashews, and crumbs in a bowl. Dip shrimp in the egg and coat it in the cashew mixture. Place in the frying basket and Bake for 25 minutes. Increase the temperature to 390 F and cook for 5 more minutes. Cover with a foil and let sit for a couple of minutes before serving.

346. Mango Shrimp Skewers with Hot Sauce
INGREDIENTS (4 Servings)

20 small-sized shrimp, peeled and deveined	2 tbsp fresh lime juice	1 tbsp red chili flakes, crushed
2 tbsp olive oil	Salt and black pepper to taste	4 tbsp olive oil
½ tsp garlic powder	2 tbsp fresh cilantro, chopped	2 tbsp white wine vinegar
1 tsp mango powder	1 garlic clove, minced	
	1 green onion, finely sliced	

DIRECTIONS (Prep + Cook Time: 20 minutes + marinating time)

In a bowl, mix garlic powder, mango powder, lime juice, salt, and black pepper. Add the shrimp and toss to coat. Cover and marinate for 20 minutes. Soak wooden skewers in water for 15 minutes. In a small dish, mix cilantro, minced garlic, green onion, chili flakes, olive oil, and champagne vinegar. Preheat air fryer to 390 F. Thread the marinated shrimp onto the skewers, drizzle with olive oil, and place in the frying basket. AirFry for 5 minutes, shake the shrimp, and cook for 5 more minutes. Serve the skewers with the cilantro sauce.

347. Mediterranean Squid Rings with Couscous
INGREDIENTS (4 Servings)

1 cup couscous	½ cup all-purpose flour	1 tsp cayenne pepper
1 lb squid rings	½ cup semolina	Salt and black pepper to taste
2 large eggs	1 tsp ground coriander seeds	4 lemon wedges to garnish

DIRECTIONS (Prep + Cook Time: 20 minutes)

Place the couscous in a large bowl and cover with boiling water. Season with salt and pepper and stir. Cover and set aside for 5-7 minutes until the water is absorbed. Preheat air fryer to 390 F. Beat the eggs in a bowl. In another bowl, combine the flour, semolina, ground coriander, cayenne pepper, salt, and pepper. Dip the squid rings in the eggs first, then in the flour mixture, and place them in the greased frying basket. AirFry for 15 minutes, until golden brown, shaking once. Transfer the couscous to a large platter and arrange the squid rings on top. Serve.

348. American Panko Fish Nuggets
INGREDIENTS (4 Servings)

1 lb fish fillets	1 tsp dried dill	1 tbsp garlic powder
1 lemon, juiced	4 tbsp mayonnaise	1 cup breadcrumbs
Salt and black pepper to taste	2 eggs, beaten	1 tsp paprika

DIRECTIONS (Prep + Cook Time: 20 minutes)

Preheat air fryer to 400 F. Season the fish with salt and black pepper. In a bowl, mix beaten eggs, lemon juice, and mayonnaise. In a separate bowl, mix breadcrumbs, paprika, dill, and garlic powder. Dredge the fillets in the egg mixture and then in the crumbs. Place the fillets in the greased frying basket and AirFry for 15 minutes, flipping once halfway through. Serve warm.

349. Cod Fillets with Ginger-Cilantro Sauce
INGREDIENTS (4 Servings)

1 lb cod fillets	1 cup water	1 tsp soy sauce
2 tbsp fresh cilantro, chopped	1 tbsp ginger paste	2 cubes rock sugar
Salt to taste	5 tbsp light soy sauce	
4 green onions, chopped	2 tbsp olive oil	

DIRECTIONS (Prep + Cook Time: 20 minutes)

Preheat air fryer to 360 F. Sprinkle cod fillets with salt and some olive oil. Place in the frying basket and AirFry for 15 minutes, flipping once halfway through. Heat the remaining olive oil in a pan over medium heat and stir-fry the remaining ingredients for 4-5 minutes. Pour the sauce over the fish and serve.

350. Golden Cod Fish Fillets
INGREDIENTS (4 Servings)

4 cod fillets	2 eggs, beaten	A pinch of salt
2 tbsp olive oil	1 cup breadcrumbs	1 cup flour

DIRECTIONS (Prep + Cook Time: 20 minutes)

Preheat air fryer to 390 F. Mix breadcrumbs, olive oil, and salt in a bowl. In another bowl, place the eggs. Put the flour into a third bowl. Toss the cod fillets in the flour, then in the eggs, and then in the breadcrumb mixture. Place them in the greased frying basket and AirFry for 9 minutes. At the 5-minute mark, quickly turn the fillets. Once done, remove to a plate and serve with cilantro-yogurt sauce.

351. Gourmet Black Cod with Fennel & Pecans
INGREDIENTS (2 Servings)

2 black cod fillets	1 small fennel bulb, sliced	2 tsp white balsamic vinegar
Salt and black pepper to taste	½ cup pecans	2 tbsp olive oil

DIRECTIONS (Prep + Cook Time: 20 minutes)

Preheat air fryer to 400 F. Season fillets with salt and black pepper and drizzle some olive oil. Place in the air fryer basket and AirFry for 10 minutes, flipping once halfway through. Remove to a plate. Add pecans and fennel slices to a baking dish. Drizzle with olive oil and season with salt and black pepper. Transfer the dish to the fryer and Bake for 5 minutes. When ready, add balsamic vinegar and olive oil to the mixture, season with salt and black pepper. Pour over the black cod and serve.

352. Tandoori Crispy Salmon
INGREDIENTS (2 Serving)

2 salmon fillets	1 tsp sweet paprika, minced	¼ cup yogurt Juice and zest from
1 tsp ginger powder	1 tsp honey	1 lime
1 garlic clove, minced	1 tsp garam masala	
½ green bell pepper, sliced	1 tbsp fresh cilantro, chopped	

DIRECTIONS (Prep + Cook Time: 15 minutes)

In a bowl, mix all the ingredients, except for salmon and yogurt. Season to taste and stir in the yogurt. Top the fillets with the mixture and let sit for 15 minutes. Preheat air fryer to 400 F. Place the fillets into the greased frying basket and Bake for 12-15 minutes until nice and crispy. Serve on a bed of rice.

353. Salmon & Spring Onion Balls
INGREDIENTS (2 Servings)

- 1 cup tinned salmon
- ¼ celery stalk, chopped
- 1 spring onion, sliced
- 4 tbsp wheat germ
- 2 tbsp olive oil
- 1 large egg
- 1 tbsp fresh dill, chopped
- ½ tsp garlic powder

DIRECTIONS (Prep + Cook Time: 15 minutes)

Preheat air fryer to 390 F. In a large bowl, mix tinned salmon, egg, celery, onion, dill, and garlic. Shape the mixture into balls and roll them in wheat germ. Carefully flatten and place in them the greased air fryer basket. AirFry for 8-10 minutes, flipping once halfway through until golden. Serve warm.

354. Smoked Salmon Taquitos
INGREDIENTS (4 Servings)

- 2 tbsp olive oil
- 1 lb smoked salmon, chopped
- Salt to taste
- 1 tbsp taco seasoning
- 1 cup cheddar cheese, shredded
- 1 lime, juiced
- ½ cup fresh cilantro, chopped
- 8 corn tortillas

DIRECTIONS (Prep + Cook Time: 15 minutes)

Preheat air fryer to 390 F. In a bowl, mix salmon, taco seasoning, lime juice, cheddar cheese, salt, and cilantro. Divide the mixture between the tortillas. Wrap the tortillas around the filling and place them in the greased air fryer basket. Bake for 10 minutes, turning once halfway through. Serve with hot salsa.

355. Trout with Dill-Yogurt Sauce
INGREDIENTS (4 Servings)

- 4 trout pieces
- 2 tbsp olive oil
- Salt to taste
- ½ cup greek yogurt
- 2 garlic cloves, minced
- 2 tbsp fresh dill, finely chopped

DIRECTIONS (Prep + Cook Time: 20 minutes)

Preheat air fryer to 380 F. Drizzle the trout with olive oil and season with salt. Place the seasoned trout into the frying basket and AirFry for 12-14 minutes, flipping once. In a bowl, mix Greek yogurt, garlic, chopped dill, and salt. Top the trout with the dill sauce and serve.

356. Lovely "Blackened" Catfish
INGREDIENTS (2 Servings)

- 2 catfish fillets
- 2 tsp blackening seasoning
- Juice of 1 lime
- 2 tbsp butter, melted
- 1 garlic clove, minced
- 2 tbsp fresh cilantro, chopped

DIRECTIONS (Prep + Cook Time: 20 minutes)

Preheat air fryer to 360 F. In a bowl, mix garlic, lime juice, cilantro, and butter. Divide the sauce into two parts, rub 1 part of the sauce onto fish fillets and sprinkle with the seasoning. Place the fillets in the greased frying basket and Bake for 15 minutes, flipping once. Serve with the remaining sauce.

357. Rosemary Catfish
INGREDIENTS (4 Servings)

- 4 catfish fillets
- ¼ cup seasoned fish fry
- 1 tbsp olive oil
- 1 tbsp fresh rosemary, chopped

DIRECTIONS (Prep + Cook Time: 25 minutes)

Preheat air fryer to 400 F. Add the seasoned fish fry and the fillets to a large Ziploc bag; massage well to coat. Place the fillets in the greased frying basket and AirFry for 10-12 minutes. Flip the fillets and cook for 2-3 more minutes until crispy. Top with freshly chopped rosemary and serve.

358. Jamaican Catfish Fillets
INGREDIENTS (4 Servings)

- 4 catfish fillets
- 2 tbsp olive oil
- 1 tsp paprika
- 1 tsp garlic powder
- 1 tsp dried basil
- 1 tbsp ground Jamaican allspice
- ½ lemon, juiced

DIRECTIONS (Prep + Cook Time: 20 minutes)

Preheat air fryer to 390 F. Spray the frying basket with cooking spray. In a bowl, mix paprika, garlic powder, and Jamaican allspice seasoning. Rub the catfish fillets with the spice mixture. Transfer to the frying basket and drizzle the olive oil. AirFry for 8 minutes, slide the basket out and turn the fillets. Cook further for 5 minutes until crispy. Sprinkle with lemon juice to serve.

359. Air-Fried Broiled Tilapia
INGREDIENTS (4 Servings)

- 1 lb tilapia fillets
- 1 tsp old bay seasoning
- 2 tbsp canola oil
- 2 tbsp lemon pepper
- Salt to taste
- 2 butter buds

DIRECTIONS (Prep + Cook Time: 15 minutes)

Preheat air fryer to 400 F. Drizzle canola oil over tilapia. In a bowl, mix salt, lemon pepper, butter buds, and old bay seasoning; spread on the fish. Place the fillets in the fryer to AirFry for 10-12 minutes, turning once, until crispy. Serve with green salad.

360. Hot Sardine Cakes
INGREDIENTS (4 Servings)

- 2 (4-oz) tins sardines, chopped
- 2 eggs, beaten
- ½ cup breadcrumbs
- ⅓ cup green onions, finely chopped
- 2 tbsp fresh parsley, chopped
- 1 tbsp mayonnaise
- 1 tsp sweet chili sauce
- ½ tsp paprika
- Salt and black pepper to taste
- 2 tbsp olive oil

DIRECTIONS (Prep + Cook Time: 20 minutes)

In a bowl, add sardines, eggs, breadcrumbs, green onions, parsley, mayonnaise, chili sauce, paprika, salt, and black pepper. Mix well with hands. Shape into 8 cakes and brush them lightly with olive oil. AirFry in the fryer for 8 minutes at 390 F, shaking once halfway through cooking. Serve warm.

361. Japanese Ponzu Marinated Tuna
INGREDIENTS (4 Servings)

- 4 tuna steaks
- 1 cup Japanese ponzu sauce
- 2 tbsp sesame oil
- 1 tbsp red pepper flakes
- 2 tbsp ginger paste
- ¼ cup scallions, sliced
- Salt and black pepper to taste

DIRECTIONS (Prep + Cook Time: 20 minutes + marinating time)

In a bowl, mix the ponzu sauce, sesame oil, red pepper flakes, ginger paste, salt, and black pepper. Add in the tuna and toss to coat. Cover and marinate for 60 minutes in the fridge. Preheat air fryer to 380 F. Remove tuna from the marinade and arrange on the greased frying basket. AirFry for 14-16 minutes, turning once. Top with scallions and serve with green salad.

362. Basil White Fish with Cheese
INGREDIENTS (4 Servings)

- 2 tbsp fresh basil, chopped
- 1 tsp garlic powder
- 2 tbsp Romano cheese, grated
- Salt and black pepper to taste
- 4 white fish fillets

DIRECTIONS (Prep + Cook Time: 15 minutes)

Preheat air fryer to 350 F. Season fillets with garlic, salt, and black pepper. Place in the greased frying basket and AirFry them for 8-10 minutes, flipping once. Serve topped with Romano cheese and basil.

363. Delicious Seafood Pie
INGREDIENTS (4 Servings)

1 cup seafood mix	2 tbsp fresh parsley, chopped	2 tbsp butter	Salt and black pepper to taste
1 lb russet potatoes, peeled and quartered	10 oz baby spinach	4 tbsp milk	
1 carrot, grated	1 small tomato, diced	½ cup cheddar cheese, grated	
½ fennel bulb, sliced	½ celery stick, grated	1 small red chili, minced	

DIRECTIONS (Prep + Cook Time: 60 minutes + cooling time)

Cover the potatoes with salted water in a pot and cook over medium heat for 18 minutes or until tender. Drain and mash them with butter, milk, salt, and pepper: Mix until smooth and set aside. In a bowl, mix celery, carrot, red chili, fennel, parsley, seafood mix, tomato, spinach, salt, and black pepper; mix well. Preheat air fryer to 330 F. In a casserole baking dish, spread the veggie mixture. Top with potato mash and level. Sprinkle with cheddar cheese and place the dish in the air fryer. Bake for 20-25 minutes until golden and bubbling at the edges. Let cool for 10 minutes, slice, and serve.

364. Herbed Crab Croquettes
INGREDIENTS (4 Servings)

1 ½ lb lump crab meat	½ celery stalk, chopped	1 tsp cayenne pepper	Salt to taste
⅓ cup sour cream	1 tsp fresh tarragon, chopped	1 ½ cups breadcrumbs	Lemon wedges to serve
⅓ cup mayonnaise		2 tsp olive oil	
1 red pepper, finely chopped	1 tsp fresh chives, chopped	1 cup flour	
⅓ cup red onion, chopped	1 tsp fresh parsley, chopped	3 eggs, beaten	

DIRECTIONS (Prep + Cook Time: 25 minutes)

Heat olive oil in a skillet over medium heat and sauté red pepper, onion, and celery for 5 minutes or until sweaty and translucent. Turn off the heat. Pour the breadcrumbs and salt on a plate. In 2 separate bowls, add the flour and beaten eggs, respectively, set aside. In a separate bowl, add crabmeat, mayo, sour cream, tarragon, chives, parsley, cayenne pepper, and vegetable sautéed mix. Form bite-sized oval balls from the mixture and place them onto a plate. Preheat air fryer to 390 F. Dip each crab meatball in the beaten eggs and press them in the breadcrumb mixture. Place the croquettes in the greased fryer basket without overcrowding. Cook for 10 minutes until golden brown, shaking once halfway through. Serve hot with lemon wedges.

365. Basil Crab & Potato Patties
INGREDIENTS (4 Servings)

3 potatoes, boiled and mashed	½ celery stalk, chopped	¼ cup breadcrumbs
1 cup cooked crab meat	½ bell red pepper, chopped	1 tsp old bay seasoning
¼ cup red onions, chopped	1 tbsp Dijon mustard	½ cup mayonnaise
1 tbsp fresh basil, chopped	½ lemon, zested and juiced	Salt and black pepper to taste

DIRECTIONS (Prep + Cook Time: 20 minutes + refrigerating time)

Place mashed potatoes, red onions, old bay seasoning, breadcrumbs, celery, bell pepper, mustard, lemon zest, crab meat, salt, and pepper in a large bowl and mix well. Make patties from the mixture and refrigerate for 30 minutes. Mix the mayonnaise, lemon juice, basil, salt, and pepper and set aside. Preheat air fryer to 390 F. Remove the patties from the fridge and place them in the greased frying basket. AirFry for 12-14 minutes, flipping once until golden. Serve the patties with basil-mayo dip.

366. Chinese Garlic Prawns
INGREDIENTS (4 Servings)

1 lb prawns, peeled and deveined	2 tbsp peanut oil	1 red chili pepper, minced
Juice of 1 lemon	2 tbsp cornstarch	Salt and black pepper to taste
1 tsp sugar	2 scallions, chopped	
	¼ tsp Chinese powder	4 garlic cloves, minced

DIRECTIONS (Prep + Cook Time: 20 minutes + marinating time)

In a Ziploc bag, mix lemon juice, sugar, black pepper, 1 tbsp peanut oil, cornstarch, Chinese powder, and salt. Add in prawns and massage gently to coat. Let sit for 20 minutes. Heat the remaining peanut oil in a pan over medium heat and sauté garlic, scallions, and red chili pepper for 5 minutes. Preheat air fryer to 390 F. Place the marinated prawns in a baking dish and cover with the sautéed vegetables. AirFry for 10 minutes, shaking once halfway through, until nice and crispy. Serve warm.

367. Sesame Prawns with Firecracker Sauce
INGREDIENTS (4 Servings)

1 lb tiger prawns, peeled	2 eggs	¼ cup sesame seeds
Salt and black pepper to taste	½ cup flour	¾ cup seasoned breadcrumbs

Firecracker sauce:

⅓ cup sour cream	¼ cup spicy ketchup
2 tbsp buffalo sauce	1 green onion, chopped

DIRECTIONS (Prep + Cook Time: 20 minutes)

Preheat air fryer to 390 F. Beat the eggs in a bowl with salt. In another bowl, mix breadcrumbs with sesame seeds. In a third bowl, mix flour with salt and pepper. Dip prawns in the flour and then in the eggs, and finally in the crumbs. Spray with cooking spray and AirFry for 10 minutes, flipping once. Meanwhile, mix well all thee sauce ingredients, except for green onion in a bowl. Serve the prawns with firecracker sauce and scatter with freshly chopped green onions.

368. Cod Cornflakes Nuggets with Avocado Dip
INGREDIENTS (4 Servings)

1 ¼ lb cod fillets, cut into 4 chunks each	2 eggs, beaten	Salt and black pepper to taste
	1 cup cornflakes	1 avocado, chopped
½ cup flour	1 tbsp olive oil	1 lime, juiced

DIRECTIONS (Prep + Cook Time: 25 minutes)

Mash the avocado with a fork in a small bowl. Stir in lime juice and salt and set aside. Place olive oil and cornflakes in a food processor and process until crumbed. Season the fish with salt and pepper. Preheat air fryer to 350 F. Place flour, eggs and cornflakes in separate dishes. Toss the fish with flour, dip in eggs, then coat well with cornflakes. AirFry for 15 minutes until golden. Serve with avocado dip.

369. Wild Salmon with Creamy Parsley Sauce
INGREDIENTS (4 Servings)

4 Alaskan wild salmon fillets	½ cup heavy cream	2 tbsp fresh parsley, chopped
2 tsp olive oil Salt to taste	½ cup milk	

DIRECTIONS (Prep + Cook Time: 20 minutes)

Preheat air fryer to 380 F. Drizzle the fillets with olive oil, and season with salt and black pepper. Place salmon in the frying basket and Bake for 15 minutes, turning once until tender and crispy. In a bowl, mix milk, parsley, salt, and whipped cream. Serve the salmon with the sauce.

370. Baked Trout en Papillote with Herbs
INGREDIENTS (2 Servings)

2 whole trout, scaled and cleaned	1 tbsp fresh parsley, chopped	1 lemon, sliced
¼ bulb fennel, sliced	1 tbsp fresh dill, chopped	Salt and black pepper to taste
½ brown onion, sliced	1 tbsp olive oil	

DIRECTIONS (Prep + Cook Time: 20 minutes)

In a bowl, add the onion, parsley, dill, fennel, and garlic. Mix and drizzle with olive oil. Preheat air fryer to 350 F. Open the cavity of the fish and fill with the fennel mixture. Wrap the fish completely in parchment paper and then in foil. Place the fish in the frying basket and Bake for 14 minutes. Remove the paper and foil and top with lemon slices to serve

371. Fried Catfish Fillets
INGREDIENTS (2 Servings)

2 catfish fillets	¼ tsp cayenne pepper	1 tbsp fresh parsley, chopped
½ cup breadcrumbs	¼ tsp fish seasoning	Salt to taste

DIRECTIONS (Prep + Cook Time: 20 minutes)

Preheat air fryer to 400 F. Pour all the dry ingredients, except for the parsley, in a bowl. Add in the fish pieces and toss to coat. Lightly spray the fish with olive oil. Put the fillets in the fryer basket and AirFry for 6-7 minutes. Flip and cook further for 5 minutes. Garnish with freshly chopped parsley and serve.

372. Ale-Battered Fish with Tartar Sauce
INGREDIENTS (4 Servings)

4 lemon wedges	Salt and black pepper to taste	2 dill pickles, chopped
2 eggs	4 white fish fillets	1 tbsp capers
1 cup ale beer	½ cup light mayonnaise	1 tbsp fresh dill, roughly chopped
1 cup flour	½ cup Greek yogurt	Lemon wedges to serve

DIRECTIONS (Prep + Cook Time: 20 minutes)

Preheat air fryer to 390 F. Beat the eggs in a bowl along with ale beer, salt, and black pepper. Pat dry the fish fillets with paper towels and dredge them in the flour. Shake off the excess flour. Dip in the egg mixture and then in the flour again. Spray with cooking spray and add to the frying basket. AirFry for 10 minutes, flipping once. In a bowl, mix mayonnaise, yogurt, capers, salt, and dill pickles. Serve the fish with the sauce and freshly cut lemon wedges.

373. Barramundi Fillets in Lemon Sauce
INGREDIENTS (4 Servings)

4 barramundi fillets	2 tbsp butter	2 cloves garlic, minced
1 lemon, juiced	½ cup white wine	2 shallots, chopped
Salt and black pepper to taste	8 black peppercorns	

DIRECTIONS (Prep + Cook Time: 30 minutes)

Preheat air fryer to 390 F. Season the fillets with salt and pepper. Place in the greased air fryer basket. AirFry for 15 minutes, flipping once halfway through until the edges are golden brown. Remove to a plate. Melt the butter in a pan over low heat. Add in garlic and shallots and stir-fry for 3 minutes. Pour in white wine, lemon juice, and peppercorns. Cook until the liquid is reduced by three quarters, about 3-5 minutes. Adjust the seasoning and strain the sauce. Drizzle the sauce over the fish and serve.

374. Peppery & Lemony Haddock
INGREDIENTS (4 Servings)

4 haddock fillets	Salt and black pepper to taste	¼ cup Parmesan cheese, grated
1 cup breadcrumbs	¼ cup potato flakes	3 tbsp flour
2 tbsp lemon juice	2 eggs, beaten	

DIRECTIONS (Prep + Cook Time: 20 minutes)

In a bowl, combine flour, salt, and pepper. In another bowl, combine breadcrumbs, Parmesan cheese, and potato flakes. Dip fillets in the flour first, then in the eggs, and coat them with the cheese crumbs. Place in the frying basket and AirFry for 14-16 minutes at 370 F, flipping once. Serve with lemon juice.

375. Peach Salsa & Beer Halibut Tacos
INGREDIENTS (4 Servings)

4 corn tortillas	1 ½ cups flour	4 tbsp peach salsa
1 halibut fillet	1 can beer	4 tsp fresh cilantro, chopped
2 tbsp olive oil	A pinch of salt	1 tsp baking powder

DIRECTIONS (Prep + Cook Time: 15 minutes)

Preheat air fryer to 390 F. In a bowl, combine flour, baking powder, and salt. Pour in some of the beer, enough to form a batter-like consistency. Save the rest of the beer to gulp with the tacos. Slice the fillet into 4 strips. Dip them into the beer batter and arrange on a lined baking dish. Place in the fryer and AirFry for 8 minutes. Spread the peach salsa on the tortillas. Top with fish strips and cilantro to serve.

376. Oaty Fishcakes
INGREDIENTS (4 Servings)

4 potatoes, cooked and mashed	1 tsp Dijon mustard	2 tbsp olive oil
2 salmon fillets, cubed	½ cup oats	Salt and black pepper to taste
1 haddock fillet, cubed	2 tbsp fresh dill, chopped	

DIRECTIONS (Prep + Cook Time: 20 minutes)

Preheat air fryer to 400 F. Boil salmon and haddock cubes in a pot filled with salted water over medium heat for 5 minutes. Drain, cool, and pat dry. Flake or shred and add to a bowl. Mix in mashed potatoes, mustard, oats, dill, salt, and pepper. Shape into balls and flatten to make patties. Brush with olive oil and arrange them on the bottom of the frying basket. Bake for 10 minutes, flipping once halfway through. Let cool before serving.

377. Crab Fritters with Sweet Chili Sauce
INGREDIENTS (4 Servings)

1 lb jumbo crabmeat	1 tsp garlic puree	1 egg ¼ cup panko breadcrumbs
1 lime, zested and juiced	1 tbsp fresh cilantro, chopped	1 tsp soy sauce sauce
1 tsp ginger paste	1 red chili, roughly chopped	3 tbsp sweet chili sauce

DIRECTIONS (Prep + Cook Time: 20 minutes)

Preheat air fryer to 400 F. In a bowl, mix crabmeat, lime zest, egg, ginger paste, and garlic puree. Form small cakes out of the mixture and dredge them into breadcrumbs. Place in the greased frying basket and AirFry for 15 minutes, shaking once until golden. In a small bowl, mix the sweet chili sauce with lime juice and soy sauce. Serve the fritters topped with cilantro and sweet chili sauce

378. Fiery Prawns
INGREDIENTS (4 Servings)

8 prawns, cleaned	½ tsp ground cayenne pepper	½ tsp ground cumin
Salt and black pepper to taste	½ tsp red chili flakes	½ tsp garlic powder

DIRECTIONS (Prep + Cook Time: 15 minutes)

In a bowl, season the prawns with salt and black pepper. Sprinkle with cayenne pepper, chili flakes, cumin, and garlic, and stir to coat. Spray the frying basket with oil and lay the prawns in an even layer. AirFry for 8 minutes at 340 F, turning once halfway through. Serve with fresh sweet chili sauce.

379. Ale-Battered Scampi with Tartare Sauce
INGREDIENTS (4 Servings)

1 lb prawns, peeled and deveined	Tartare sauce:	1 pickled cucumber, finely chopped
1 cup plain flour	½ cup mayonnaise	2 tsp lemon juice
1 cup ale beer	2 tbsp capers, roughly chopped	½ tsp Worcestershire sauce
Salt and black pepper to taste	2 tbsp fresh dill, chopped	

DIRECTIONS (Prep + Cook Time: 15 minutes)

Preheat air fryer to 380 F. In a bowl, mix all the sauce ingredients and keep in the fridge. Mix flour, ale beer, salt, and pepper in a large bowl. Dip in the prawns and place them in the frying basket. AirFry for 10 minutes, shaking halfway through the cooking time. Serve with the tartare sauce.

380. Buttered Crab Legs
INGREDIENTS (4 Servings)

3 lb crab legs	2 tbsp butter, melted	1 tbsp fresh parsley

DIRECTIONS (Prep + Cook Time: 15 minutes)

Preheat air fryer to 380 F. Place the crab legs in the greased air fryer basket and AirFry for 10 minutes, shaking once. Pour the butter over crab legs, sprinkle with parsley, and serve.

381. Herbed Garlic Lobster
INGREDIENTS (4 Servings)

4 oz lobster tails, halved	1 tbsp butter	½ tbsp lemon Juice
1 garlic clove, minced	Salt and black pepper to taste	

DIRECTIONS (Prep + Cook Time: 15 minutes)

Blend all ingredients, except for lobster, in a food processor. Clean the skin of the lobster and cover it with the mixture. Preheat air fryer to 380 F. Place the lobster in the frying basket and AirFry for 10 minutes, turning once halfway through. Serve with fresh herbs.

382. Air-Fried Seafood
INGREDIENTS (4 Servings)

1 lb fresh scallops, mussels, fish fillets, prawns, shrimp	Salt and black pepper to taste	1 lemon
2 eggs	1 cup breadcrumbs mixed with the zest of	

DIRECTIONS (Prep + Cook Time: 15 minutes)

Beat the eggs with salt and pepper in a bowl. Dip in each piece of seafood and then coat with breadcrumbs. Place in the greased air fryer basket and AirFry for 10-12 minutes at 400 F, turning once.

383. Soy Sauce-Glazed Cod
INGREDIENTS (2 Servings)

2 cod fillets	1 tbsp soy sauce	¼ tsp honey
1 tbsp olive oil	1 tbsp sesame oil	
Salt and black pepper to taste	¼ tsp ginger powder	

DIRECTIONS (Prep + Cook Time: 15 minutes)

Preheat air fryer to 370 F. In a bowl, combine olive oil, salt, and pepper. Rub the mixture onto the fillets. Place them on a piece of aluminum sheet and then in the greased frying basket. Bake for 6 minutes. Meanwhile, combine the soy sauce, ginger powder, honey, and sesame oil in a small bowl. Flip the fillets and brush them with the glaze. Cook for 3 more minutes. Serve warm.

384. Cod Finger Pesto Sandwich
INGREDIENTS (4 Servings)

4 cod fillets	1 cup breadcrumbs	4 lettuce leaves
4 bread rolls	4 tbsp pesto sauce	Salt and black pepper to taste

DIRECTIONS (Prep + Cook Time: 20 minutes)

Preheat air fryer to 370 F. Season the fillets with salt and black pepper and coat them with breadcrumbs. Arrange them into the greased air fryer basket and Bake for 12-15 minutes, flipping once. Cut the bread rolls in half. Divide lettuce leaves between the bottom halves and place the fillets over. Spread pesto sauce on top of the fillets and cover with the remaining halves to serve.

385. Pistachio-Crusted Salmon Fillets
INGREDIENTS (2 Servings)

2 salmon fillets	Salt and black pepper to taste	2 tbsp Parmesan cheese, grated
1 tsp mustard	1 tsp garlic powder	1 tsp olive oil
4 tbsp pistachios, chopped	2 tsp lemon juice	

DIRECTIONS (Prep + Cook Time: 20 minutes)

Preheat air fryer to 350 F. Whisk together mustard, olive oil, lemon juice, salt, black pepper, and garlic powder in a bowl. Rub the mustard mixture onto salmon fillets. Combine the pistachios with Parmesan cheese; sprinkle on top of the salmon. Place the salmon in the greased frying basket, skin side down, and Bake for 12-13 minutes. Flip at the 7-minute mark. Serve.

386. Hot Salmon Fillets with Broccoli
INGREDIENTS (2 Servings)

2 salmon fillets	1 tsp chili flakes	1 tbsp soy sauce
2 tsp olive oil Juice of	Salt and black pepper to taste	
1 lime	5 oz broccoli florets, steamed	

DIRECTIONS (Prep + Cook Time: 25 minutes)

In a bowl, add half of the olive oil, lime juice, chili flakes, salt, and black pepper; rub the mixture onto fillets. Lay the florets into your air fryer and drizzle with the remaining olive oil. Arrange the fillets on top and Bake at 340 F for 14 minutes, flipping once. Drizzle the florets with soy sauce and serve with fish.

387. Smoked Trout Frittata
INGREDIENTS (4 Servings)

2 tbsp olive oil	6 tbsp crème fraiche	2 tbsp fresh dill, chopped
1 onion, sliced	½ tbsp horseradish sauce	
1 egg, beaten	1 cup smoked trout, diced	

DIRECTIONS (Prep + Cook Time: 25 minutes)

Preheat air fryer to 350 F. Heat olive oil in a pan over medium heat. Stir-fry onion for 3 minutes. In a bowl, mix the egg with crème fraiche and horseradish sauce. Add the onion, dill, and trout and mix well. Pour the mixture into a greased baking dish and Bake in the fryer for 14 minutes until golden

388. Crumbly Haddock Patties
INGREDIENTS (2 Servings)

8 oz haddock, cooked and flaked	2 tbsp green olives, pitted and chopped	1 tsp lemon zest
2 potatoes, cooked and mashed	1 tbsp fresh cilantro, chopped	1 egg, beaten

DIRECTIONS (Prep + Cook Time: 15 minutes + refrigerating time)

Mix haddock, zest, olives, cilantro, egg, and potatoes. Shape into patties and chill for 60 minutes. Preheat air fryer to 350 F. Place the patties in the greased baking basket and AirFry for 12-14 minutes, flipping once halfway through cooking. Serve with green salad.

389. Effortless Tuna Fritters
INGREDIENTS (2 Servings)

5 oz canned tuna	¼ cup flour	2 eggs
1 tsp lime juice	½ cup milk	1 tsp chili powder, optional
½ tsp paprika	1 small onion, diced	½ tsp salt

DIRECTIONS (Prep + Cook Time: 20 minutes + refrigerating time)

Place all ingredients in a bowl and mix well. Make two large patties out of the mixture. Refrigerate them for 30 minutes. Then, remove and AirFry the patties for 13-15 minutes at 350 F in the greased frying basket, flipping once halfway through cooking. Serve warm

390. Sesame Halibut Fillets
INGREDIENTS (4 Servings)

4 halibut fillets	1 egg, beaten	3 tbsp olive oil
4 biscuits, crumbled	Salt and black pepper to taste	2 tbsp sesame seeds
3 tbsp flour	¼ tsp dried rosemary	

DIRECTIONS (Prep + Cook Time: 20 minutes)

Preheat air fryer to 390 F. In a bowl, combine flour, black pepper, and salt. In another bowl, combine sesame seeds, crumbled biscuits, olive oil, and rosemary. Dip the fish fillets into the flour mixture first, then into the beaten egg. Finally, coat them with the sesame mixture. Arrange on the greased frying basket and AirFry for 8 minutes. Flip the fillets and cook for 4-5 more minutes. Serve immediately.

391. Smoked Fish Quiche
INGREDIENTS (4 Servings)

1 pie crust	¼ cup green onions, finely chopped	Salt and black pepper to taste
5 eggs, lightly beaten	2 tbsp fresh parsley, chopped	1 lb smoked salmon, chopped
4 tbsp heavy cream	1 tsp baking powder	1 cup mozzarella cheese, shredded

DIRECTIONS (Prep + Cook Time: 35 minutes)

In a bowl, whisk eggs, heavy cream, green onions, parsley, baking powder, salt, and pepper. Stir in salmon and mozzarella cheese. Roll out the pie crust and press it gently into a greased quiche pan that fits in your air fryer. Prick the pie all over with a fork. Pour in the salmon mixture and place the pan inside the fryer. Bake for 25 minutes at 360 F. Let cool slightly before slicing.

392. Delicious Coconut Shrimp
INGREDIENTS (2 Servings)

8 large shrimp, peeled and deveined	Salt to taste	½ tsp cayenne pepper
½ cup breadcrumbs	½ cup orange jam	¼ tsp hot sauce
8 oz coconut milk	1 tsp mustard	
½ cup coconut, shredded	1 tbsp honey	

DIRECTIONS (Prep + Cook Time: 30 minutes)

Combine breadcrumbs, cayenne pepper, shredded coconut, and salt in a bowl. Dip the shrimp in the coconut milk, and then in the coconut crumbs. Arrange on a lined sheet and Bake in the air fryer for 12 minutes at 350 F. Whisk jam, honey, hot sauce, and mustard in a bowl. Serve with the shrimp.

393. Louisiana-Style Shrimp
INGREDIENTS (4 Servings)

- 1 lb shrimp, peeled and deveined
- 1 egg, beaten
- 1 cup flour
- 1 cup breadcrumbs
- 2 tbsp Cajun seasoning
- Salt and black pepper to taste
- 1 lemon, cut into wedges

DIRECTIONS (Prep + Cook Time: 14 minutes)

Preheat air fryer to 390 F. Spray the air fryer basket with cooking spray. Beat the eggs in a bowl and season with salt and black pepper. In a separate bowl, mix breadcrumbs with Cajun seasoning. In a third bowl, pour the flour. Dip shrimp in flour, then in the eggs, and finally in the crumbs mixture. Spray with cooking spray and AirFry in the frying basket for 5 minutes. Flip and cook for 4 more minutes. Serve with lemon wedges.

394. Asian Shrimp Medley
INGREDIENTS (4 Servings)

- 1 lb shrimp, peeled and deveined
- 2 whole onions, chopped
- 3 tbsp butter
- 1 tbsp sugar
- 2 tbsp soy sauce
- 2 cloves garlic, chopped
- 2 tsp lime juice
- 1 tsp ginger paste

DIRECTIONS (Prep + Cook Time: 20 minutes + marinating time)

Melt butter in a frying pan over medium heat and stir-fry the onions for 3 minutes until translucent. Mix in the lime juice, soy sauce, ginger paste, garlic, and sugar and stir for 1-2 minutes. Let cool and then pour the mixture over the shrimp. Cover and let marinate for 30 minutes in the fridge. Preheat air fryer to 380 F. Transfer the shrimp with marinade to a baking dish and AirFry in the fryer for 12 minutes, shaking once halfway through. Serve warm.

395. Cajun-Rubbed Jumbo Shrimp
INGREDIENTS (2 Servings)

- 1 lb jumbo shrimp, deveined
- Salt to taste
- ¼ tsp old bay seasoning
- ⅓ tsp smoked paprika
- ¼ tsp cayenne pepper
- 1 tbsp olive oil

DIRECTIONS (Prep + Cook Time: 15 minutes)

Preheat air fryer to 390 degrees. In a bowl, add shrimp, paprika, olive oil, salt, old bay seasoning, and cayenne pepper; mix well. Place the shrimp in the fryer and AirFry for 8-10 minutes, shaking once.

396. Breaded Scallops
INGREDIENTS (4 Servings)

- 1 lb fresh scallops
- 3 tbsp flour
- Salt and black pepper to taste
- 1 egg, lightly beaten
- 1 cup breadcrumbs
- 2 tbsp olive oil
- ½ tsp fresh parsley, chopped

DIRECTIONS (Prep + Cook Time: 10 minutes)

Coat the scallops with flour. Dip into the egg, then into the breadcrumbs. Brush with olive oil and place into the frying basket. AirFry for 6-8 minutes at 360 F, shaking once. Serve topped with parsley. Enjoy!

397. Herbed Garlic Lobster
INGREDIENTS (4 Servings)

- 4 oz lobster tails, halved
- 1 garlic clove, minced
- 1 tbsp butter
- Salt and black pepper to taste
- ½ tbsp lemon Juice

DIRECTIONS (Prep + Cook Time: 15 minutes)

Blend all ingredients, except for lobster, in a food processor. Clean the skin of the lobster and cover it with the mixture. Preheat air fryer to 380 F. Place the lobster in the frying basket and AirFry for 10 minutes, turning once halfway through. Serve with fresh herbs. Enjoy!

398. Kimchi-Spiced Salmon
INGREDIENTS (4 Servings)

2 tbsp soy sauce

2 tbsp sesame oil

2 tbsp mirin

1 tbsp ginger puree

1 tsp kimchi spice

1 tsp sriracha sauce

2 lb salmon fillets

1 lime, cut into wedges

DIRECTIONS (Prep + Cook Time: 15 minutes)

Preheat air fryer to 350 F. Grease the air fryer basket with cooking spray. In a bowl, mix together soy sauce, mirin, ginger puree, kimchi spice, and sriracha sauce. Add the salmon fillets and toss to coat. Place in the air fryer basket and drizzle with sesame oil. AirFry for 10 minutes, flipping once halfway through. Garnish with lime wedges and serve

399. Salmon Cakes
INGREDIENTS (4 Servings)

1 lb cooked salmon

4 potatoes, boiled and mashed

½ cup flour

2 tbsp capers, chopped

2 tbsp fresh parsley, chopped

1 tbsp olive oil Zest of

1 lemon

DIRECTIONS (Prep + Cook Time: 15 minutes + marinating time)

Place mashed potatoes in a bowl and flake the salmon over. Stir in capers, parsley, and lemon zest. Shape cakes out of the mixture and dust them with flour. Refrigerate for 1 hour. Preheat the air fryer to 350 F. Remove the cakes and brush them with olive oil. Bake in the greased frying basket for 12-14 minutes, flipping once halfway through cooking. Serve with ketchup. Enjoy!

400. Mediterranean Salmon
INGREDIENTS (2 Servings)

2 salmon fillets

Salt and black pepper to taste

1 lemon, cut into wedges

8 asparagus spears, trimmed

DIRECTIONS (Prep + Cook Time: 15 minutes)

Rinse and pat dry the fillets with a paper towel. Coat the fish generously on both sides with cooking spray. Season fish and asparagus with salt and pepper. Arrange fish in the frying basket and lay the asparagus around the fish. AirFry for 10-12 minutes at 350 F, flipping once. Serve with lemon wedges.

401. Parmesan Tilapia Fillets
INGREDIENTS (4 Servings)

¾ cup Parmesan cheese, grated

2 tbsp olive oil

2 tsp paprika

2 tbsp fresh parsley, chopped

¼ tsp garlic powder

4 tilapia fillets

DIRECTIONS (Prep + Cook Time: 15 minutes)

Preheat air fryer to 350 F. Mix parsley, Parmesan cheese, garlic, and paprika in a shallow bowl. Coat fillets with the Parmesan mixture and brush with the olive oil. Place the filets into the air fryer basket and AirFry for 10-12 minutes, flipping once until golden brown. Serve immediately

402. Air Fried Tuna Sandwich
INGREDIENTS (2 Servings)

4 white bread slices

1 (5-oz) can tuna, drained

½ onion, finely chopped

2 tbsp mayonnaise

1 cup mozzarella cheese, shredded

1 tbsp olive oil

DIRECTIONS (Prep + Cook Time: 10 minutes)

In a small bowl, mix tuna, onion, and mayonnaise. Spoon the mixture over two bread slices, top with mozzarella cheese, and cover with the remaining bread slices. Brush with olive oil and arrange the sandwiches in the air fryer basket. Bake at 360 F for 6-8 minutes, turning once halfway through. Serve and enjoy!

403. Spicy Shrimp with Coconut-Avocado Dip
INGREDIENTS (4 Servings)

1 ¼ lb tiger shrimp, peeled and deveined	1 lime, juiced and zested	1 large avocado, pitted
2 garlic cloves, minced	Salt to taste	¼ cup coconut cream
¼ tsp red chili flakes	1 tbsp fresh cilantro, chopped	2 tablespoons olive oil

DIRECTIONS (Prep + Cook Time: 15 minutes)

Blend avocado, lime juice, coconut cream, cilantro, olive oil, and salt in a food processor until smooth. Transfer to a bowl, cover, and keep in the fridge until ready to use. Preheat air fryer to 390 F. In a bowl, place garlic, chili flakes, lime zest, and salt, and add in the shrimp; toss to coat. Place them in the frying basket and AirFry for 8-10 minutes, shaking once halfway through or until entirely pink. Serve with the chilled avocado dip.

404. Greek-Style Fried Mussels
INGREDIENTS (4 Servings)

4 lb mussels	Salt and black pepper to taste	5 garlic cloves
4 tbsp olive oil	1 tsp Greek seasoning	4 bread slices
1 cup white wine	2 tbsp white wine vinegar	½ cup mixed nuts

DIRECTIONS (Prep + Cook Time: 30 minutes)

Preheat air fryer to 350 F. Add olive oil, garlic, Greek seasoning, vinegar, salt, mixed nuts, black pepper, and bread slices to a food processor and process until you obtain a creamy texture. In a skillet over medium heat, add wine and mussels. Bring to a boil, then lower the heat and simmer until the mussels have opened up. Then, drain and remove from the shells. Add them to the previously prepared mixture and toss to coat. Place in a greased baking dish and Bake in the air fryer for 10 minutes, shaking once. Serve warm.

405. Calamari Rings with Olives
INGREDIENTS (4 Servings)

1 lb calamari rings	1 chili pepper, minced	1 cup pimiento-stuffed green olives
2 tbsp cilantro, chopped	2 tbsp olive oil	Salt and black pepper to taste

DIRECTIONS (Prep + Cook Time: 30 minutes)

In a bowl, add calamari rings, chili pepper, salt, black pepper, olive oil, and fresh cilantro. Marinate for 10 minutes. Pour the calamari into a baking dish and place it inside the fryer. AirFry for 15 minutes, stirring every 5 minutes at 400 F. Serve warm with pimiento-stuffed olives.

406. Greek-Style Salmon with Dill Sauce
INGREDIENTS (4 Servings)

1 lb salmon fillets	2 tsp olive oil	1 cup sour cream
Salt and black pepper to taste	2 tbsp fresh dill, chopped	1 cup Greek yogurt

DIRECTIONS (Prep + Cook Time: 20 minutes)

In a bowl, mix sour cream, yogurt, dill, and salt; set aside. Preheat air fryer to 340 F. Drizzle olive oil over the salmon and rub with salt and black pepper. Arrange the fish in the frying basket and Bake for 10 minutes, flipping once. Top with the yogurt sauce.

407. Cajun Mango Salmon
INGREDIENTS (4 Servings)

4 salmon fillets	1 tbsp Cajun seasoning	1 tbsp fresh parsley, chopped
½ tsp brown sugar	1 lemon, zested and juiced	2 tbsp mango salsa

DIRECTIONS (Prep + Cook Time: 15 minutes)

Preheat air fryer to 350 F. In a bowl, mix sugar, Cajun seasoning, lemon juice and zest, and coat the salmon with the mixture. Line with parchment paper the frying basket and place in the fish. Bake for 12 minutes, turning once halfway through. Top with parsley and mango salsa to serve.

408. Simple Creole Trout
INGREDIENTS (4 Servings)

4 skin-on trout fillets	2 tsp creole seasoning	2 tbsp fresh dill, chopped	1 lemon, sliced

DIRECTIONS (Prep + Cook Time: 15 minutes)

Preheat air fryer to 350 F. Season the trout with creole seasoning on both sides and spray with cooking spray. Place in the frying basket and Bake for 10-12 minutes, flipping once. Serve sprinkled with dill and garnished with lemon slices. Enjoy!

409. Fried Tilapia Bites
INGREDIENTS (4 Servings)

- 1 lb tilapia fillets, cut into chunks
- ½ cup cornflakes
- 1 cup flour
- 2 eggs, beaten
- Salt to taste Lemon wedges for serving

DIRECTIONS (Prep + Cook Time: 20 minutes)

Preheat air fryer to 390 F. Pour the flour, eggs, and cornflakes each into different bowls. Dip the tilapia first in the flour, then in the egg, and lastly, coat with the cornflakes. Lay on the greased air fryer basket and AirFry for 6 minutes. Shake and cook for 4-5 minutes until crispy. Serve with lemon wedges. Enjoy!

410. Colorful Salmon and Fennel Salad
INGREDIENTS (3 Servings)

- 1 pound salmon
- 1 fennel, quartered
- 1 teaspoon olive oil
- Sea salt and ground black pepper, to taste
- 1/2 teaspoon paprika
- 1 tablespoon balsamic vinegar
- 1 tablespoon lime juice
- 1 tablespoon extra-virgin olive oil
- 1 tomato, sliced
- 1 cucumber, sliced
- 1 tablespoon sesame seeds, lightly toasted

DIRECTIONS (Prep + Cook Time: 20 minutes)

Toss the salmon and fennel with 1 teaspoon of olive oil, salt, black pepper and paprika. Cook in the preheated Air Fryer at 380 degrees F for 12 minutes; shaking the basket once or twice. Cut the salmon into bite-sized strips and transfer them to a nice salad bowl.

Add in the fennel, balsamic vinegar, lime juice, 1 tablespoon of extra-virgin olive oil, tomato and cucumber. Toss to combine well and serve garnished with lightly toasted sesame seeds. Enjoy!

411. Salmon Bowl with Lime Drizzle
INGREDIENTS (3 Servings)

- 1 pound salmon steak
- 2 teaspoons sesame oil
- Sea salt and Sichuan pepper, to taste
- 1/2 teaspoon coriander seeds
- 1 lime, juiced
- 2 tablespoons reduced-sodium soy sauce
- 1 teaspoon honey

DIRECTIONS (Prep + Cook Time: 15 minutes)

Pat the salmon dry and drizzle it with 1 teaspoon of sesame oil. Season the salmon with salt, pepper and coriander seeds. Transfer the salmon to the Air Fryer cooking basket. Cook the salmon at 400 degrees F for 5 minutes; turn the salmon over and continue to cook for 5 minutes more or until opaque. Meanwhile, warm the remaining ingredients in a small saucepan to make the lime drizzle. Slice the fish into bite-sized strips, drizzle with the sauce and serve immediately. Enjoy!

412. Fish Sticks with Vidalia Onions
INGREDIENTS (2 Servings)

- 1/2 pound fish sticks, frozen
- 1/2 pound Vidalia onions, halved
- 1 teaspoon sesame oil
- Sea salt and ground black pepper, to taste
- 1/2 teaspoon red pepper flakes
- 4 tablespoons mayonnaise
- 4 tablespoons Greek-style yogurt
- 1/4 teaspoon mustard seeds
- 1 teaspoon chipotle chili in adobo, minced

DIRECTIONS (Prep + Cook Time: 12 minutes)

Drizzle the fish sticks and Vidalia onions with sesame oil. Toss them with salt, black pepper and red pepper flakes. Transfer them to the Air Fryer cooking basket. Cook the fish sticks and onions at 400 degreed F for 5 minutes. Shake the basket and cook an additional 5 minutes or until cooked through. Meanwhile, mix the mayonnaise, Greek-style yogurt, mustard seeds and chipotle chili. Serve the warm fish sticks garnished with Vidalia onions and the sauce on the side. Serve and enjoy!

413. Classic Calamari with Mediterranean Sauce
INGREDIENTS (2 Servings)

- 1/2 pound calamari tubes cut into rings, cleaned
- Sea salt and ground black pepper, to season
- 1/2 cup almond flour
- 1/2 cup all-purpose flour
- 4 tablespoons parmesan cheese, grated
- 1/2 cup ale beer
- 1/4 teaspoon cayenne pepper
- 1/2 cup breadcrumbs
- 1/4 cup mayonnaise
- 1/4 cup Greek-style yogurt
- 1 clove garlic, minced
- 1 tablespoon fresh lemon juice
- 1 teaspoon fresh parsley, chopped
- 1 teaspoon fresh dill, chopped

DIRECTIONS (Prep + Cook Time: 10 minutes)

Sprinkle the calamari with salt and black pepper. Mix the flour, cheese and beer in a bowl until well combined. In another bowl, mix cayenne pepper and breadcrumbs Dip the calamari pieces in the flour mixture, then roll them onto the breadcrumb mixture, pressing to coat on all sides; transfer them to a lightly oiled cooking basket. Cook at 400 degrees F for 4 minutes, shaking the basket halfway through the cooking time. Meanwhile, mix the remaining ingredients until everything is well incorporated. Serve warm calamari with the sauce for dipping. Enjoy!

414. Fish Cakes with Bell Pepper
INGREDIENTS (3 Servings)

- 1 pound haddock
- 1 egg
- 2 tablespoons milk
- 1 bell pepper, deveined and finely chopped
- 2 stalks fresh scallions, minced
- 1/2 teaspoon fresh garlic, minced
- Sea salt and ground black pepper, to taste
- 1/2 teaspoon cumin seeds
- 1/4 teaspoon celery seeds
- 1/2 cup breadcrumbs
- 1 teaspoon olive oil

DIRECTIONS (Prep + Cook Time: 15 minutes)

Thoroughly combine all ingredients, except for the breadcrumbs and olive oil, until everything is blended well. Then, roll the mixture into 3 patties and coat them with breadcrumbs, pressing to adhere. Drizzle olive oil over the patties and transfer them to the Air Fryer cooking basket. Cook the fish cakes at 400 degrees F for 5 minutes; turn them over and continue to cook an additional 5 minutes until cooked through. Serve and enjoy!

415. Herb and Garlic Grouper Filets
INGREDIENTS (3 Servings)

- 1 pound grouper filets
- 1/4 teaspoon shallot powder
- 1/4 teaspoon porcini powder
- 1 teaspoon fresh garlic, minced
- 1/2 teaspoon cayenne pepper
- 1/2 teaspoon hot paprika
- 1/4 teaspoon oregano
- 1/2 teaspoon marjoram
- 1/2 teaspoon sage
- 1 tablespoon butter, melted
- Sea salt and black pepper, to taste

DIRECTIONS (Prep + Cook Time: 15 minutes)

Pat dry the grouper filets using kitchen towels. In a small dish, make the rub by mixing the remaining ingredients until everything is well incorporated. Rub the fish with the mixture, coating well on all sides. Cook the grouper filets in the preheated Air Fryer at 400 degrees F for 5 minutes; turn the filets over and cook on the other side for 5 minutes more. Serve over hot rice if desired. Enjoy!

416. Cajun Fish Cakes with Cheese
INGREDIENTS (4 Servings)

- 2 catfish fillets
- 1 cup all-purpose flour
- 3 ounces butter
- 1 teaspoon baking powder
- 1 teaspoon baking soda
- 1/2 cup buttermilk
- 1 teaspoon Cajun seasoning
- 1 cup Swiss cheese, shredded

DIRECTIONS (Prep + Cook Time: 30 minutes)

Bring a pot of salted water to a boil. Boil the fish fillets for 5 minutes or until it is opaque. Flake the fish into small pieces. Mix the remaining ingredients in a bowl; add the fish and mix until well combined. Shape the fish mixture into 12 patties. Cook in the preheated Air Fryer at 380 degrees F for 15 minutes. Work in batches. Enjoy!

417. Crab Cake Burgers
INGREDIENTS (3 Servings)

- 2 eggs, beaten
- 1 shallot, chopped
- 2 garlic cloves, crushed
- 1 tablespoon olive oil
- 1 teaspoon yellow mustard
- 1 teaspoon fresh cilantro, chopped
- 10 ounces crab meat
- 1 cup tortilla chips, crushed
- 1/2 teaspoon cayenne pepper
- 1/2 teaspoon ground black pepper
- Sea salt, to taste
- 3/4 cup fresh bread crumbs

DIRECTIONS (Prep + Cook Time: 2hours 20 minutes)

In a mixing bowl, thoroughly combine the eggs, shallot, garlic, olive oil, mustard, cilantro, crab meat, tortilla chips, cayenne pepper, black pepper, and salt. Mix until well combined. Shape the mixture into 6 patties. Dip the crab patties into the fresh breadcrumbs, coating well on all sides. Place in your refrigerator for 2 hours. Spritz the crab patties with cooking oil on both sides. Cook in the preheated Air Fryer at 360 degrees F for 14 minutes. Serve on dinner rolls if desired. Enjoy!

418. Monkfish with Sautéed Vegetables and Olives
INGREDIENTS (2 Servings)

- 2 teaspoons olive oil
- 2 carrots, sliced
- 2 bell peppers, sliced
- 1 teaspoon dried thyme
- 1/2 teaspoon dried marjoram
- 1/2 teaspoon dried rosemary
- 2 monkfish fillets
- 1 tablespoon soy sauce
- 2 tablespoons lime juice Coarse
- Salt and ground black pepper, to taste
- 1 teaspoon cayenne pepper
- 1/2 cup Kalamata olives, pitted and sliced

DIRECTIONS (Prep + Cook Time: 20 minutes)

In a nonstick skillet, heat the olive oil for 1 minute. Once hot, sauté the carrots and peppers until tender, about 4 minutes. Sprinkle with thyme, marjoram, and rosemary and set aside. Toss the fish fillets with the soy sauce, lime juice, salt, black pepper, and cayenne pepper. Place the fish fillets in a lightly greased cooking basket and bake at 390 degrees F for 8 minutes. Turn them over, add the olives, and cook an additional 4 minutes. Serve with the sautéed vegetables on the side. Enjoy!

419. Cajun Cod Fillets with Avocado Sauce
INGREDIENTS (2 Servings)

- 2 cod fish fillets
- 1 egg
- Sea salt, to taste
- 1/2 cup tortilla chips, crushed
- 2 teaspoons olive oil
- 1/2 avocado, peeled, pitted, and mashed
- 1 tablespoon mayonnaise
- 3 tablespoons sour cream
- 1/2 teaspoon yellow mustard
- 1 teaspoon lemon juice
- 1 garlic clove, minced
- ¼ teaspoon black pepper
- ¼ teaspoon salt
- ¼ teaspoon hot pepper sauce

DIRECTIONS (Prep + Cook Time: 20 minutes)

Start by preheating your Air Fryer to 360 degrees F. Spritz the Air Fryer basket with cooking oil. Pat dry the fish fillets with a kitchen towel. Beat the egg in a shallow bowl. In a separate bowl, thoroughly combine the salt, crushed tortilla chips, and olive oil. Dip the fish into the egg, then, into the crumb mixture, making sure to coat thoroughly. Cook in the preheated Air Fryer approximately 12 minutes. Meanwhile, make the avocado sauce by mixing the remaining ingredients in a bowl. Place in your refrigerator until ready to serve. Serve the fish fillets with chilled avocado sauce on the side. Enjoy!

420. Crispy Mustardy Fish Fingers
INGREDIENTS (4 Servings)

- 1 ½ pounds tilapia pieces (fingers)
- 1/2 cup all-purpose flour
- 2 eggs
- 1 tablespoon yellow mustard
- 1 cup cornmeal
- 1 teaspoon garlic powder
- 1 teaspoon onion powder
- Sea salt and ground black pepper, to taste
- 1/2 teaspoon celery powder
- 2 tablespoons peanut oil

DIRECTIONS (Prep + Cook Time: 20 minutes)

Pat dry the fish fingers with a kitchen towel. To make a breading station, place the all-purpose flour in a shallow dish. In a separate dish, whisk the eggs with mustard. In a third bowl, mix the remaining ingredients. Dredge the fish fingers in the flour, shaking the excess into the bowl; dip in the egg mixture and turn to coat evenly; then, dredge in the cornmeal mixture, turning a couple of times to coat evenly. Cook in the preheated Air Fryer at 390 degrees F for 5 minutes; turn them over and cook another 5 minutes. Enjoy!

421. Snapper Casserole with Gruyere Cheese
INGREDIENTS (4 Servings)

2 tablespoons olive oil	1 teaspoon cayenne pepper
1 shallot, thinly sliced	1/2 teaspoon dried basil
2 garlic cloves, minced	1/2 cup tomato puree
1 ½ pounds snapper fillets	1/2 cup white wine
Sea salt and ground black pepper, to taste	1 cup Gruyere cheese, shredded

DIRECTIONS (Prep + Cook Time: 25 minutes)

Heat 1 tablespoon of olive oil in a saucepan over medium-high heat. Now, cook the shallot and garlic until tender and aromatic. Preheat your Air Fryer to 370 degrees F. Grease a casserole dish with 1 tablespoon of olive oil. Place the snapper fillet in the casserole dish. Season with salt, black pepper, and cayenne pepper. Add the sautéed shallot mixture. Add the basil, tomato puree and wine to the casserole dish. Cook for 10 minutes in the preheated Air Fryer. Top with the shredded cheese and cook an additional 7 minutes. Serve immediately

422. Roasted Mediterranean Snapper Fillets
INGREDIENTS (3 Servings)

Marinade:

1 tablespoon black olives, chopped	2 tablespoons fresh lemon juice	1/2 teaspoon dried basil	1 tomato, pureed
1/4 cup dry white wine	1/2 teaspoon dried oregano	1 tablespoon parsley leaves, chopped	

Roasted Snapper:

1 pound snapper fillets	Salt and white pepper, to taste
1/2 cup cassava flour	

DIRECTIONS (Prep + Cook Time: 20 minutes + Marinating Time)

Add all ingredients for the marinade to a large ceramic bowl. Add the snapper fillets and let them marinate for 1 hour in your refrigerator. Place the cassava flour on a tray; now, coat the snapper fillets with the cassava flour. Season with salt and pepper. Cook the snapper fillets in the preheated Air Fryer at 395 degrees F for 10 minutes, basting with the marinade and flipping them halfway through the cooking time. Serve and enjoy!

423. Halibut with Thai Lemongrass Marinade
INGREDIENTS (2 Servings)

2 tablespoons tamari sauce	1/2 inch lemongrass, finely chopped	Sea salt and ground black pepper, to taste
2 tablespoons fresh lime juice	1 teaspoon basil	2 halibut steaks
2 tablespoons olive oil	2 cloves garlic, minced	
1 teaspoon Thai curry paste	2 tablespoons shallot, minced	

DIRECTIONS (Prep + Cook Time: 45 minutes)

Place all ingredients in a ceramic dish; let it marinate for 30 minutes. Place the halibut steaks in the lightly greased cooking basket. Bake in the preheated Air Fryer at 400 degrees F for 9 to 10 minutes, basting with the reserved marinade and flipping them halfway through the cooking time. Enjoy!

424. Quick Thai Coconut Fish
INGREDIENTS (2 Servings)

1 cup coconut milk	1 teaspoon turmeric powder	1 pound tilapia
2 tablespoons lime juice	1/2 teaspoon ginger powder	2 tablespoons olive oil
2 tablespoons Shoyu sauce	1/2 Thai Bird's Eye chili, seeded and finely chopped	
Salt and white pepper, to taste		

DIRECTIONS (Prep + Cook Time: 20 minutes + Marinating Time)

In a mixing bowl, thoroughly combine the coconut milk with the lime juice, Shoyu sauce, salt, pepper, turmeric, ginger, and chili pepper. Add tilapia and let it marinate for 1 hour. Brush the Air Fryer basket with olive oil. Discard the marinade and place the tilapia fillets in the Air Fryer basket. Cook the tilapia in the preheated Air Fryer at 400 degrees F for 6 minutes; turn them over and cook for 6 minutes more. Work in batches. Serve with some extra lime wedges if desired. Enjoy!

425. Tuna Cake Burgers with Beer Cheese Sauce
INGREDIENTS (4 Servings)

- 1 pound canned tuna, drained
- 1 egg, whisked
- 1 garlic clove, minced
- 2 tablespoons shallots, minced
- 1 cup fresh breadcrumbs
- Sea salt and ground black pepper, to taste
- 1 tablespoon sesame oil

Beer Cheese Sauce:

- 1 tablespoon butter
- 1 cup beer
- 1 tablespoon rice flour
- 2 tablespoons Colby cheese, grated

DIRECTIONS (Prep + Cook Time: 2hours 20 minutes)

In a mixing bowl, thoroughly combine the tuna, egg, garlic, shallots, breadcrumbs, salt, and black pepper. Shape the tuna mixture into four patties and place in your refrigerator for 2 hours. Brush the patties with sesame oil on both sides. Cook in the preheated Air Fryer at 360 degrees F for 14 minutes. In the meantime, melt the butter in a pan over a moderate heat. Add the beer and flour and whisk until it starts bubbling. Now, stir in the grated cheese and cook for 3 to 4 minutes longer or until the cheese has melted. Spoon the sauce over the fish cake burgers and serve immediately.

426. Parmesan Chip-Crusted Tilapia
INGREDIENTS (3 Servings)

- 1 ½ pounds tilapia, slice into 4 portions
- Sea salt and ground black pepper, to taste
- 1/2 teaspoon cayenne pepper
- 1 teaspoon granulated garlic
- 1/4 cup almond flour
- 1/4 cup parmesan cheese, preferably freshly grated
- 1 egg, beaten
- 2 tablespoons buttermilk
- 1 cup tortilla chips, crushed

DIRECTIONS (Prep + Cook Time: 15 minutes)

Generously season your tilapia with salt, black pepper and cayenne pepper. Prepare a bread station. Add the granulated garlic, almond flour and parmesan cheese to a rimmed plate. Whisk the egg and buttermilk in another bowl and place crushed tortilla chips in the third bowl. Dip the tilapia pieces in the flour mixture, then in the egg/buttermilk mixture and finally roll them in the crushed chips, pressing to adhere well. Cook in your Air Fryer at 400 degrees F for 10 minutes, flipping halfway through the cooking time. Serve with chips if desired. Enjoy!

427. Easiest Lobster Tails Ever
INGREDIENTS (2 Servings)

- 2 (6-ounce) lobster tails
- 1 teaspoon fresh cilantro, minced
- 1/2 teaspoon dried rosemary
- 1/2 teaspoon garlic, pressed
- 1 teaspoon deli mustard
- Sea salt and ground black pepper, to taste
- 1 teaspoon olive oil

DIRECTIONS (Prep + Cook Time: 10 minutes)

Toss the lobster tails with the other ingredients until they are well coated on all sides. Cook the lobster tails at 370 degrees F for 3 minutes. Then, turn them and cook on the other side for 3 to 4 minutes more until they are opaque. Serve warm and enjoy!

428. Classic Crab Cakes
INGREDIENTS (3 Servings)

- 1 egg, beaten
- 2 tablespoons milk
- 2 crustless bread slices
- 1 pound lump crabmeat
- 2 tablespoons scallions, chopped
- 1 garlic clove, minced
- 1 teaspoon deli mustard
- 1 teaspoon Sriracha sauce
- Sea salt and ground black pepper, to taste
- 4 lemon wedges, for serving

DIRECTIONS (Prep + Cook Time: 15 minutes)

Whisk the egg and milk until pale and frothy; add in the bread and let it soak for a few minutes. Stir in the other ingredients, except for the lemon wedges; shape the mixture into 4 equal patties. Place your patties in the Air Fryer cooking basket. Spritz your patties with a nonstick cooking spray. Cook the crab cakes at 400 degrees F for 5 minutes. Turn them over and cook on the other side for 5 minutes. Serve warm, garnished with lemon wedges.Serve and enjoy!

429. Grouper with Miso-Honey Sauce
INGREDIENTS (2 Servings)

- 3/4 pound grouper fillets
- Salt and white pepper, to taste
- 1 tablespoon sesame oil
- 1 teaspoon water
- 1 teaspoon deli mustard or Dijon mustard
- 1/4 cup white miso
- 1 tablespoon mirin
- 1 tablespoon honey
- 1 tablespoon Shoyu sauce

DIRECTIONS (Prep + Cook Time: 15 minutes)

Sprinkle the grouper fillets with salt and white pepper; drizzle them with a nonstick cooking oil. Cook the fish at 400 degrees F for 5 minutes; turn the fish fillets over and cook an additional 5 minutes. Meanwhile, make the sauce by whisking the remaining ingredients. Serve the warm fish with the miso-honey sauce on the side.

430. Baked Sardines with Tangy Dipping Sauce
INGREDIENTS (3 Servings)

- 1 pound fresh sardines
- Sea salt and ground black pepper, to taste
- 1 teaspoon Italian seasoning mix
- 2 cloves garlic, minced 3 tablespoons olive oil
- 1/2 lemon, freshly squeezed

DIRECTIONS (Prep + Cook Time: 45 minutes)

Toss your sardines with salt, black pepper and Italian seasoning mix. Cook in your Air Fryer at 325 degrees F for 35 to 40 minutes until skin is crispy. Meanwhile, make the sauce by whisking the remaining ingredients Serve warm sardines with the sauce on the side. Serve and enjoy!

431. Southwestern Prawns with Asparagus
INGREDIENTS (3 Servings)

- 1 pound prawns, deveined
- 1/2 pound asparagus spears, cut into 1-inch chinks
- 1 teaspoon butter, melted
- 1/4 teaspoon oregano
- 1/2 teaspoon mixed peppercorns, crushed
- Salt, to taste
- 1 ripe avocado
- 1 lemon, sliced
- 1/2 cup chunky-style salsa

DIRECTIONS (Prep + Cook Time: 10 minutes)

Toss your prawns and asparagus with melted butter, oregano, salt and mixed peppercorns. Cook the prawns and asparagus at 400 degrees F for 5 minutes, shaking the basket halfway through the cooking time. Divide the prawns and asparagus between serving plates and garnish with avocado and lemon slices. Serve with the salsa on the side. Enjoy!

432. Classic Old Bay Fish with Cherry Tomatoes
INGREDIENTS (3 Servings)

- 1 pound swordfish steak
- 1/2 cup cornflakes, crushed
- 1 teaspoon Old Bay seasoning
- Salt and black pepper, to season
- 2 teaspoon olive oil
- 1 pound cherry tomatoes

DIRECTIONS (Prep + Cook Time: 15 minutes)

Toss the swordfish steak with cornflakes, Old Bay seasoning, salt, black pepper and 1 teaspoon of olive oil. Cook the swordfish steak in your Air Fryer at 400 degrees F for 6 minutes. Now, turn the fish over, top with tomatoes and drizzle with the remaining teaspoon of olive oil. Continue to cook for 4 minutes. Serve with lemon slices if desired. Enjoy!

433. Homemade Fish Fingers
INGREDIENTS (2 Servings)

- 3/4 pound tilapia
- 1 egg
- 2 tablespoons milk
- 4 tablespoons chickpea flour
- 1/4 cup pork rinds
- 1/2 cup breadcrumbs
- 1/2 teaspoon red chili flakes
- Coarse sea salt and black pepper, to season

DIRECTIONS (Prep + Cook Time: 15 minutes)

Rinse the tilapia and pat it dry using kitchen towels. Then, cut the tilapia into strips. Then, whisk the egg, milk and chickpea flour in a rimmed plate. Add the pork rinds and breadcrumbs to another plate; stir in red chili flakes, salt and black pepper and stir to combine well. Dip the fish strips in the egg mixture, then, roll them over the breadcrumb mixture. Transfer the fish fingers to the Air Fryer cooking basket and spritz them with a nonstick cooking spray. Cook in the preheated Air Fryer at 400 degrees F for 10 minutes, shaking the basket halfway through to ensure even browning. Serve warm and enjoy.

434. Mom's Lobster Tails
INGREDIENTS (2 Servings)

- 1/2 pound lobster tails
- 1 teaspoon olive oil
- 1 teaspoon fresh lime juice
- 1 bell pepper, sliced
- 1 jalapeno pepper, sliced
- 1 carrot, julienned
- 1 cup green cabbage, shredded
- 2 tablespoons mayonnaise
- 2 tablespoons Greek-style yogurt
- Sea salt and ground black pepper, to taste
- 1 teaspoon baby capers, drained
- 4 leaves butterhead lettuce, for serving

DIRECTIONS (Prep + Cook Time: 10 minutes)

Drizzle olive oil over the lobster tails and transfer them to the Air Fryer cooking basket. Cook the lobster tails at 370 degrees F for 3 minutes. Then, turn them over and cook on the other side for 3 to 4 minutes more until they are opaque. Toss the lobster tails with the other ingredients, except for the lettuce leaves; gently stir until well combined. Lay the lettuce leaves on a serving platter and top with the lobster salad. Enjoy!

435. Dijon Catfish with Eggplant Sauce
INGREDIENTS (3 Servings)

- 1 pound catfish fillets
- Sea salt and ground black pepper, to taste
- 1/4 cup Dijon mustard
- 1 tablespoon honey
- 1 tablespoon white vinegar
- 1 pound eggplant, 1 ½-inch cubes
- 2 tablespoons olive oil
- 1 tablespoon tahini
- 1/2 teaspoon garlic, minced
- 1 tablespoon parsley, chopped

DIRECTIONS (Prep + Cook Time: 30 minutes)

Pat the catfish dry with paper towels and generously season with salt and black pepper. In a small mixing bowl, thoroughly combine Dijon mustard, honey and vinegar. Cook the fish in your Air Fryer at 400 degrees F for 5 minutes. Turn the fish over and brush with the Dijon mixture; continue to cook for a further 5 minutes. Then, set your Air Fryer to 400 degrees F. Add the eggplant chunks to the cooking basket and cook for 15 minutes, shaking the basket occasionally to ensure even cooking. Transfer the cooked eggplant to a bowl of your food processor; stir in the remaining ingredients and blitz until everything is well blended and smooth. Serve the warm catfish with the eggplant sauce on the side.

436. Tuna Steak with Roasted Cherry Tomatoes
INGREDIENTS (3 Servings)

- 1 pound tuna steak
- 1 cup cherry tomatoes
- 1 teaspoon extra-virgin olive oil
- 2 sprigs rosemary, leaves picked and crushed
- Sea salt and red pepper flakes, to taste
- 1 teaspoon garlic, finely chopped
- 1 tablespoon lime juice

DIRECTIONS (Prep + Cook Time: 30 minutes)

Toss the tuna steaks and cherry tomatoes with olive oil, rosemary leaves, salt, black pepper and garlic. Place the tuna steaks in a lightly oiled cooking basket; cook tuna steaks at 440 degrees F for about 6 minutes. Turn the tuna steaks over, add in the cherry tomatoes and continue to cook for 4 minutes more. Drizzle the fish with lime juice and serve warm garnished with roasted cherry tomatoes! Enjoy!

437. Scallops with Pineapple Salsa and Pickled Onions
INGREDIENTS (3 Servings)

- 12 scallops
- 1 teaspoon sesame oil
- 1/4 teaspoon dried rosemary
- 1/2 teaspoon dried tarragon
- 1/2 teaspoon dried basil
- 1/4 teaspoon red pepper flakes, crushed
- Coarse sea salt and black pepper, to taste
- 1/2 cup pickled onions, drained

Pineapple Salsa:

- 1 cup pineapple, diced
- 2 tablespoons fresh cilantro, roughly chopped
- 1 jalapeño, deveined and minced
- 1 small-sized red onion, minced
- 1 teaspoon ginger root, peeled and grated
- 1/2 teaspoon coconut sugar
- Sea salt and ground black pepper, to taste

DIRECTIONS (Prep + Cook Time: 15 minutes)

Toss the scallops sesame oil, rosemary, tarragon, basil, red pepper, salt and black pepper. Cook in the preheated Air Fryer at 400 degrees F for 6 to 7 minutes, shaking the basket once or twice to ensure even cooking. Meanwhile, process all the salsa ingredients in your blender; cover and place the salsa in your refrigerator until ready to serve. Serve the warm scallops with pickled onions and pineapple salsa on the side. Enjoy!

438. Vermouth and Garlic Shrimp Skewers
INGREDIENTS (4 Servings)

1 ½ pounds shrimp	Kosher salt, to taste	8 skewers, soaked in water for 30 minutes
1/4 cup vermouth	1/4 teaspoon black pepper, freshly ground	1 lemon, cut into wedges
2 cloves garlic, crushed	2 tablespoons olive oil	
1 teaspoon dry mango powder	4 tablespoons flour	

DIRECTIONS (Prep + Cook Time: 15 minutes + Marinating Time)

Add the shrimp, vermouth, garlic, mango powder, salt, black pepper, and olive oil in a ceramic bowl; let it sit for 1 hour in your refrigerator. Discard the marinade and toss the shrimp with flour. Thread on to skewers and transfer to the lightly greased cooking basket. Cook at 400 degrees F for 5 minutes, tossing halfway through. Serve with lemon wedges. Enjoy!

439. Korean-Style Salmon Patties
INGREDIENTS (4 Servings)

1 pound salmon	1 garlic clove, minced	1/2 cup rolled oats
1 egg	2 green onions, minced	

Sauce:

1 teaspoon rice wine	1 teaspoon honey	1 teaspoon gochugaru (Korean red chili pepper flakes)
1 ½ tablespoons soy sauce	A pinch of salt	

DIRECTIONS (Prep + Cook Time: 15 minutes)

Start by preheating your Air Fryer to 380 degrees F. Spritz the Air Fryer basket with cooking oil. Mix the salmon, egg, garlic, green onions, and rolled oats in a bowl; knead with your hands until everything is well incorporated. Shape the mixture into equally sized patties. Transfer your patties to the Air Fryer basket. Cook the fish patties for 10 minutes, turning them over halfway through. Meanwhile, make the sauce by whisking all ingredients. Serve the warm fish patties with the sauce on the side. Enjoy!

440. Cod and Shallot Frittata
INGREDIENTS (3 Servings)

2 cod fillets	1 shallot, chopped	1/2 teaspoon red pepper flakes, crushed
6 eggs	2 garlic cloves, minced	
1/2 cup milk	Sea salt and ground black pepper, to taste	

DIRECTIONS (Prep + Cook Time: 20 minutes)

Bring a pot of salted water to a boil. Boil the cod fillets for 5 minutes or until it is opaque. Flake the fish into bite-sized pieces. In a mixing bowl, whisk the eggs and milk. Stir in the shallots, garlic, salt, black pepper, and red pepper flakes. Stir in the reserved fish. Pour the mixture into the lightly greased baking pan. Cook in the preheated Air Fryer at 360 degrees F for 9 minutes, flipping over halfway through.

441. Halibut Cakes with Horseradish Mayo
INGREDIENTS (4 Servings)

Halibut Cakes:

1 pound halibut	Salt, to taste	1/2 cup Romano cheese, grated
2 tablespoons olive oil	2 tablespoons cilantro, chopped	1/2 cup breadcrumbs
1/2 teaspoon cayenne pepper	1 shallot, chopped	1 egg, whisked
1/4 teaspoon black pepper	2 garlic cloves, minced	1 tablespoon Worcestershire sauce

Mayo Sauce:

1 teaspoon horseradish, grated	1/2 cup mayonnaise

DIRECTIONS (Prep + Cook Time: 20 minutes)

Start by preheating your Air Fryer to 380 degrees F. Spritz the Air Fryer basket with cooking oil. Mix all ingredients for the halibut cakes in a bowl; knead with your hands until everything is well incorporated. Shape the mixture into equally sized patties. Transfer your patties to the Air Fryer basket. Cook the fish patties for 10 minutes, turning them over halfway through. Mix the horseradish and mayonnaise. Serve the halibut cakes with the horseradish mayo.

442. Authentic Mediterranean Calamari Salad
INGREDIENTS (3 Servings)

- 1 pound squid, cleaned, sliced into rings
- 2 tablespoons sherry wine
- 1/2 teaspoon granulated garlic
- Salt, to taste
- 1/2 teaspoon ground black pepper
- 1/2 teaspoon basil
- 1/2 teaspoon dried rosemary
- 1 cup grape tomatoes
- 1 small red onion, thinly sliced
- 1/3 cup Kalamata olives, pitted and sliced
- 1/2 cup mayonnaise
- 1 teaspoon yellow mustard
- 1/2 cup fresh flat-leaf parsley leaves, coarsely chopped

DIRECTIONS (Prep + Cook Time: 15 minutes)

Start by preheating the Air Fryer to 400 degrees F. Spritz the Air Fryer basket with cooking oil. Toss the squid rings with the sherry wine, garlic, salt, pepper, basil, and rosemary. Cook in the preheated Air Fryer for 5 minutes, shaking the basket halfway through the cooking time. Work in batches and let it cool to room temperature. When the squid is cool enough, add the remaining ingredients. Gently stir to combine and serve well chilled. Enjoy!

443. Sunday Fish with Sticky Sauce
INGREDIENTS (2 Servings)

- 2 pollack fillets
- Salt and black pepper, to taste
- 1 tablespoon olive oil
- 1 cup chicken broth
- 2 tablespoons light soy sauce
- 1 tablespoon brown sugar
- 2 tablespoons butter, melted
- 1 teaspoon fresh ginger, minced
- 1 teaspoon fresh garlic, minced
- 2 corn tortillas

DIRECTIONS (Prep + Cook Time: 20 minutes)

Pat dry the pollack fillets and season them with salt and black pepper; drizzle the sesame oil all over the fish fillets. Preheat the Air Fryer to 380 degrees F and cook your fish for 11 minutes. Slice into bite-sized pieces. Meanwhile, prepare the sauce. Add the broth to a large saucepan and bring to a boil. Add the soy sauce, sugar, butter, ginger, and garlic. Reduce the heat to simmer and cook until it is reduced slightly. Add the fish pieces to the warm sauce. Serve on corn tortillas and enjoy!

444. Swordfish with Roasted Peppers and Garlic Sauce
INGREDIENTS (3 Servings)

- 3 bell peppers
- 3 swordfish steaks
- 1 tablespoon butter, melted
- 2 garlic cloves, minced
- Sea salt and freshly ground black pepper, to taste
- 1/2 teaspoon cayenne pepper
- 1/2 teaspoon ginger powder

DIRECTIONS (Prep + Cook Time: 30 minutes)

Start by preheating your Air Fryer to 400 degrees F. Brush the Air Fryer basket lightly with cooking oil. Then, roast the bell peppers for 5 minutes. Give the peppers a half turn; place them back in the cooking basket and roast for another 5 minutes. Turn them one more time and roast until the skin is charred and soft or 5 more minutes. Peel the peppers and set aside. Then, add the swordfish steaks to the lightly greased cooking basket and cook at 400 degrees F for 10 minutes. Meanwhile, melt the butter in a small saucepan. Cook the garlic until fragrant and add the salt, pepper, cayenne pepper, and ginger powder. Cook until everything is thoroughly heated. Plate the peeled peppers and the roasted swordfish; spoon the sauce over them and serve warm. Enjoy!

445. Crusty Catfish with Sweet Potato Fries
INGREDIENTS (2 Servings)

- 1/2 pound catfish
- 1/2 cup bran cereal
- 1/4 cup parmesan cheese, grated
- Sea salt and ground black pepper, to taste
- 1 teaspoon smoked paprika
- 1 teaspoon garlic powder
- 1/4 teaspoon ground bay leaf
- 1 egg
- 2 tablespoons butter, melted
- 4 sweet potatoes, cut French fries

DIRECTIONS (Prep + Cook Time: 50 minutes)

Pat the catfish dry with a kitchen towel. Combine the bran cereal with the parmesan cheese and all spices in a shallow bowl. Whisk the egg in another shallow bowl. Dip the fish in the egg mixture and turn to coat evenly; then, dredge in the bran cereal mixture, turning a couple of times to coat evenly. Spritz the Air Fryer basket with cooking spray. Cook the catfish in the preheated Air Fryer at 390 degrees F for 10 minutes; turn them over and cook for 4 minutes more. Then, drizzle the melted butter all over the sweet potatoes; cook them in the preheated Air Fryer at 380 degrees F for 30 minutes, shaking occasionally. Serve over the warm fish fillets. Enjoy!

446. Shrimp Kabobs with Cherry Tomatoes
INGREDIENTS (4 Servings)

- 1 ½ pounds jumbo shrimp, cleaned, shelled and deveined
- 1 pound cherry tomatoes
- 2 tablespoons butter, melted
- 1 tablespoons Sriracha sauce
- Sea salt and ground black pepper, to taste
- 1/2 teaspoon dried oregano
- 1/2 teaspoon dried basil
- 1 teaspoon dried parsley flakes
- 1/2 teaspoon marjoram
- 1/2 teaspoon mustard seeds

DIRECTIONS (Prep + Cook Time: 30 minutes)

Toss all ingredients in a mixing bowl until the shrimp and tomatoes are covered on all sides. Soak the wooden skewers in water for 15 minutes. Thread the jumbo shrimp and cherry tomatoes onto skewers. Cook in the preheated Air Fryer at 400 degrees F for 5 minutes, working with batches.

447. Easy Creamy Shrimp Nachos
INGREDIENTS (4 Servings)

- 1 pound shrimp, cleaned and deveined
- 1 tablespoon olive oil
- 2 tablespoons fresh lemon juice
- 1 teaspoon paprika
- 1/4 teaspoon cumin powder
- 1/2 teaspoon shallot powder
- 1/2 teaspoon garlic powder
- Coarse sea salt and ground black pepper, to taste
- 1 (9-ounce) bag corn tortilla chips
- 1/4 cup pickled jalapeño, minced
- 1 cup Pepper Jack cheese, grated
- 1/2 cup sour cream

DIRECTIONS (Prep + Cook Time: 15 minutes)

Toss the shrimp with the olive oil, lemon juice, paprika, cumin powder, shallot powder, garlic powder, salt, and black pepper. Cook in the preheated Air Fryer at 390 degrees F for 5 minutes. Place the tortilla chips on the aluminum foil-lined cooking basket. Top with the shrimp mixture, jalapeño and cheese. Cook another 2 minutes or until cheese has melted. Serve garnished with sour cream and enjoy!

448. Keto Cod Fillets
INGREDIENTS (2 Servings)

- 2 cod fish fillets
- 1 teaspoon butter, melted
- 1 teaspoon Old Bay seasoning
- 1 egg, beaten
- 2 tablespoons coconut milk, unsweetened
- 1/3 cup coconut flour, unsweetened

DIRECTIONS (Prep + Cook Time: 15 minutes)

Place the cod fish fillets, butter and Old Bay seasoning in a Ziplock bag; shake until the fish is well coated on all sides. In a shallow bowl, whisk the egg and coconut milk until frothy. In another bowl, place the coconut flour. Dip the fish fillets in the egg mixture, then, coat them with coconut flour, pressing to adhere. Cook the fish at 390 degrees F for 6 minutes; flip them over and cook an additional 6 minutes until your fish flakes easily when tested with a fork. Serve and enjoy!

449. Famous Tuna Niçoise Salad
INGREDIENTS (3 Servings)

- 1 pound tuna steak
- Sea salt and ground black pepper, to taste
- 1/2 teaspoon red pepper flakes, crushed
- 1/4 teaspoon dried dill weed
- 1/2 teaspoon garlic paste
- 1 pound green beans, trimmed
- 2 handfuls baby spinach
- 2 handfuls iceberg lettuce, torn into pieces
- 1/2 red onion, sliced
- 1 cucumber, sliced
- 2 tablespoons lemon juice
- 1 tablespoon olive oil
- 1 teaspoon Dijon mustard
- 1 tablespoon balsamic vinegar
- 1 tablespoon roasted almonds, coarsely chopped
- 1 tablespoon fresh parsley, coarsely chopped

DIRECTIONS (Prep + Cook Time: 15 minutes)

Pat the tuna steak dry; toss your tuna with salt, black pepper, red pepper, dill and garlic paste. Spritz your tuna with a nonstick cooking spray. Cook the tuna steak at 400 degrees F for 5 minutes; turn your tuna steak over and continue to cook for 4 to 5 minutes more. Then, add the green beans to the cooking basket. Spritz green beans with a nonstick cooking spray. Cook at 400 degrees F for 5 minutes, shaking the basket once or twice. Cut your tuna into thin strips and transfer to a salad bowl; add in the green beans. Then, add in the baby spinach, iceberg lettuce, onion and cucumber and toss to combine. In a mixing bowl, whisk the lemon juice, olive oil, mustard and vinegar. Dress the salad and garnish with roasted almonds and fresh parsley. Serve and enjoy!

450. Ginger-Garlic Swordfish with Mushrooms
INGREDIENTS (3 Servings)

1 pound swordfish steak	Sea salt and ground black pepper, to taste	1/4 teaspoon dried dill weed
1 teaspoon ginger-garlic paste	1/4 teaspoon cayenne pepper	1/2 pound mushrooms

DIRECTIONS (Prep + Cook Time: 15 minutes)

Rub the swordfish steak with ginger-garlic paste; season with salt, black pepper, cayenne pepper and dried dill. Spritz the fish with a nonstick cooking spray and transfer to the Air Fryer cooking basket. Cook at 400 degrees F for 5 minutes. Now, add the mushrooms to the cooking basket and continue to cook for 5 minutes longer until tender and fragrant. Eat warm. Enjoy!

451. Classic Pancetta-Wrapped Scallops
INGREDIENTS (3 Servings)

1 pound sea scallops	1/4 teaspoon shallot powder	Sea salt and ground black pepper, to taste
1 tablespoon deli mustard	1/4 teaspoon garlic powder	4 ounces pancetta slices
2 tablespoons soy sauce	1/2 teaspoon dried dill	

DIRECTIONS (Prep + Cook Time: 10 minutes)

Pat dry the sea scallops and transfer them to a mixing bowl. Toss the sea scallops with the deli mustard, soy sauce, shallot powder, garlic powder, dill, salt and black pepper. Wrap a slice of bacon around each scallop and transfer them to the Air Fryer cooking basket. Cook in your Air Fryer at 400 degrees F for 4 minutes; turn them over and cook an additional 3 minutes. Serve with hot sauce for dipping if desired. Enjoy!

452. Melt-in-Your Mouth Salmon with Cilantro Sauce
INGREDIENTS (2 Servings)

1 pound salmon fillets	Sea salt and ground black pepper, to season	1/2 cup Mexican crema
1 teaspoon coconut oil	2 heaping tablespoons cilantro	1 tablespoon fresh lime juice

DIRECTIONS (Prep + Cook Time: 15 minutes)

Rinse and pat your salmon dry using paper towels. Toss the salmon with coconut oil, salt and black pepper. Cook the salmon filets in your Air Fryer at 380 degrees F for 6 minutes; turn the salmon filets over and cook on the other side for 6 to 7 minutes. Meanwhile, mix the remaining ingredients in your blender or food processor. Spoon the cilantro sauce over the salmon filets and serve immediately.

453. Fried Oysters with Kaffir Lime Sauce
INGREDIENTS (2 Servings)

8 fresh oysters, shucked	1/2 teaspoon Italian seasoning mix 1 lime, freshly squeezed	1 habanero pepper, minced
1/3 cup plain flour		1 teaspoon olive oil
1 egg	1 teaspoon coconut sugar	
3/4 cup breadcrumbs	1 kaffir lime leaf, shredded	

DIRECTIONS (Prep + Cook Time: 10 minutes)

Clean the oysters and set them aside. Add the flour to a rimmed plate. Whisk the egg in another rimmed plate. Mix the breadcrumbs and Italian seasoning mix in a third plate. Dip your oysters in the flour, shaking off the excess. Then, dip them in the egg mixture and finally, coat your oysters with the breadcrumb mixture. Spritz the breaded oysters with a nonstick cooking spray. Cook your oysters in the preheated Air Fryer at 400 degrees F for 2 to 3 minutes, shaking the basket halfway through the cooking time. Meanwhile, blend the remaining ingredients to make the sauce. Serve the warm oysters with the kaffir lime sauce on the side. Enjoy!

454. Salmon with Baby Bok Choy
INGREDIENTS (3 Servings)

1 pound salmon filets	1 tablespoon honey	Kosher salt and black pepper, to taste
1 teaspoon garlic chili paste	1 tablespoon soy sauce	
1 teaspoon sesame oil	1 pound baby Bok choy, bottoms removed	

DIRECTIONS (Prep + Cook Time: 20 minutes)

Start by preheating your Air Fryer to 380 degrees F. Toss the salmon fillets with garlic chili paste, sesame oil, honey, soy sauce, salt and black pepper. Cook the salmon in the preheated Air Fryer for 6 minutes; turn the filets over and cook an additional 6 minutes. Then, cook the baby Bok choy at 350 degrees F for 3 minutes; shake the basket and cook an additional 3 minutes. Salt and pepper to taste. Serve the salmon fillets with the roasted baby Bok choy. Enjoy!

455. Spicy Curried King Prawns
INGREDIENTS (2 Servings)

- 12 king prawns, rinsed
- 1 tablespoon coconut oil
- 1/2 teaspoon piri piri powder
- Salt and ground black pepper, to taste
- 1 teaspoon garlic paste
- 1 teaspoon onion powder
- 1/2 teaspoon cumin powder
- 1 teaspoon curry powder

DIRECTIONS (Prep + Cook Time: 10 minutes)

In a mixing bowl, toss all ingredient until the prawns are well coated on all sides. Cook in the preheated Air Fryer at 360 degrees F for 4 minutes. Shake the basket and cook for 4 minutes more. Serve over hot rice if desired. Enjoy!

456. Crispy Tilapia Fillets
INGREDIENTS (5 Servings)

- 5 tablespoons all-purpose flour
- Sea salt and white pepper, to taste
- 1 teaspoon garlic paste
- 2 tablespoons extra virgin olive oil
- 1/2 cup cornmeal
- 5 tilapia fillets, slice into halves

DIRECTIONS (Prep + Cook Time: 20 minutes)

Combine the flour, salt, white pepper, garlic paste, olive oil, and cornmeal in a Ziploc bag. Add the fish fillets and shake to coat well. Spritz the Air Fryer basket with cooking spray. Cook in the preheated Air Fryer at 400 degrees F for 10 minutes; turn them over and cook for 6 minutes more. Work in batches. Serve with lemon wedges if desired. Enjoy!

457. Grilled Salmon Steaks
INGREDIENTS (4 Servings)

- 2 cloves garlic, minced
- 4 tablespoons butter, melted
- Sea salt and ground black pepper, to taste
- 1 teaspoon smoked paprika
- 1/2 teaspoon onion powder
- 1 tablespoon lime juice
- 1/4 cup dry white wine
- 4 salmon steaks

DIRECTIONS (Prep + Cook Time: 45 minutes)

Place all ingredients in a large ceramic dish. Cover and let it marinate for 30 minutes in the refrigerator. Arrange the salmon steaks on the grill pan. Bake at 390 degrees for 5 minutes, or until the salmon steaks are easily flaked with a fork. Flip the fish steaks, baste with the reserved marinade, and cook another 5 minutes. Serve and enjoy!

458. Easy Prawns alla Parmigiana
INGREDIENTS (4 Servings)

- 2 egg whites
- 1 cup all-purpose flour
- 1 cup Parmigiano-Reggiano, grated
- 1/2 cup fine breadcrumbs
- 1/2 teaspoon celery seeds
- 1/2 teaspoon porcini powder
- 1/2 teaspoon onion powder
- 1 teaspoon garlic powder
- 1/2 teaspoon dried rosemary
- 1/2 teaspoon sea salt
- 1/2 teaspoon ground black pepper
- 1 ½ pounds prawns, deveined

DIRECTIONS (Prep + Cook Time: 20 minutes)

To make a breading station, whisk the egg whites in a shallow dish. In a separate dish, place the all-purpose flour. In a third dish, thoroughly combine the Parmigiano-Reggiano, breadcrumbs, and seasonings; mix to combine well. Dip the prawns in the flour, then, into the egg whites; lastly, dip them in the parm/breadcrumb mixture. Roll until they are covered on all sides. Cook in the preheated Air Fryer at 390 degrees F for 5 to 7 minutes or until golden brown. Work in batches. Serve with lemon wedges if desired. Enjoy!

459. Indian Famous Fish Curry
INGREDIENTS (4 Servings)

- 2 tablespoons sunflower oil
- 1/2 pound fish, chopped
- 2 red chilies, chopped
- 1 tablespoon coriander powder
- 1 teaspoon curry paste
- 1 cup coconut milk
- Salt and white pepper, to taste
- 1/2 teaspoon fenugreek seeds
- 1 shallot, minced
- 1 garlic clove, minced
- 1 ripe tomato, pureed

DIRECTIONS (Prep + Cook Time: 25 minutes)

Preheat your Air Fryer to 380 degrees F; brush the cooking basket with 1 tablespoon of sunflower oil. Cook your fish for 10 minutes on both sides. Transfer to the baking pan that is previously greased with the remaining tablespoon of sunflower oil. Add the remaining ingredients and reduce the heat to 350 degrees F. Continue to cook an additional 10 to 12 minutes or until everything is heated through. Enjoy!

460. Old Bay Calamari
INGREDIENTS (3 Servings)

1 cup beer	2 eggs	1/2 teaspoon ground black pepper
1 pound squid, cleaned and cut into rings	1/2 cup cornstarch	1 tablespoon Old Bay seasoning
1 cup all-purpose flour	Sea salt, to taste	

DIRECTIONS (Prep + Cook Time: 20 minutes + Marinating Time)

Add the beer and squid in a glass bowl, cover and let it sit in your refrigerator for 1 hour. Preheat your Air Fryer to 390 degrees F. Rinse the squid and pat it dry. Place the flour in a shallow bowl. In another bowl, whisk the eggs. Add the cornstarch and seasonings to a third shallow bowl. Dredge the calamari in the flour. Then, dip them into the egg mixture; finally, coat them with the cornstarch on all sided. Arrange them in the cooking basket. Spritz with cooking oil and cook for 9 to 12 minutes, depending on the desired level of doneness. Work in batches. Serve warm with your favorite dipping sauce. Enjoy!

461. Greek-Style Roast Fish
INGREDIENTS (3 Servings)

2 tablespoons olive oil	3 pollock fillets, skinless	1 teaspoon oregano
1 red onion, sliced	2 ripe tomatoes, diced	1 teaspoon rosemary
2 cloves garlic, chopped	12 Kalamata olives, pitted and chopped	Sea salt, to taste
1 Florina pepper, deveined and minced	2 tablespoons capers	1/2 cup white wine

DIRECTIONS (Prep + Cook Time: 20 minutes)

Start by preheating your Air Fryer to 360 degrees F. Heat the oil in a baking pan. Once hot, sauté the onion, garlic, and pepper for 2 to 3 minutes or until fragrant. Add the fish fillets to the baking pan. Top with the tomatoes, olives, and capers. Sprinkle with the oregano, rosemary, and salt. Pour in white wine and transfer to the cooking basket. Turn the temperature to 395 degrees F and bake for 10 minutes. Taste for seasoning and serve on individual plates, garnished with some extra Mediterranean herbs if desired. Enjoy!

462. Grilled Tilapia with Portobello Mushrooms
INGREDIENTS (2 Servings)

2 tilapia fillets	1/2 teaspoon dried sage, crushed	1 teaspoon dried parsley flakes
1 tablespoon avocado oil	1/4 teaspoon lemon pepper	4 medium-sized Portobello mushrooms
1/2 teaspoon red pepper flakes, crushed	1/2 teaspoon sea salt	A few drizzles of liquid smoke

DIRECTIONS (Prep + Cook Time: 20 minutes)

Toss all ingredients in a mixing bowl; except for the mushrooms. Transfer the tilapia fillets to a lightly greased grill pan. Preheat your Air Fryer to 400 degrees F and cook the tilapia fillets for 5 minutes. Now, turn the fillets over and add the Portobello mushrooms. Continue to cook for 5 minutes longer or until mushrooms are tender and the fish is opaque. Serve immediately. Enjoy!

463. Filet of Flounder Cutlets
INGREDIENTS (2 Servings)

1 egg	Sea salt and white pepper, to taste	2 flounder fillets
1/2 cup cracker crumbs	1/2 teaspoon cayenne pepper	
1/2 cup Pecorino Romano cheese, grated	1 teaspoon dried parsley flakes	

DIRECTIONS (Prep + Cook Time: 15 minutes)

To make a breading station, whisk the egg until frothy. In another bowl, mix the cracker crumbs, Pecorino Romano cheese, and spices. Dip the fish in the egg mixture and turn to coat evenly; then, dredge in the cracker crumb mixture, turning a couple of times to coat evenly. Cook in the preheated Air Fryer at 390 degrees F for 5 minutes; turn them over and cook another 5 minutes. Enjoy!

464. Crunchy Topped Fish Bake
INGREDIENTS (4 Servings)

- 1 tablespoon butter, melted
- 1 medium-sized leek, thinly sliced
- 1 tablespoon chicken stock
- 1 tablespoon dry white wine
- 1 pound tuna
- 1/2 teaspoon red pepper flakes, crushed
- Sea salt and ground black pepper, to taste
- 1/2 teaspoon dried rosemary
- 1/2 teaspoon dried basil
- 1/2 teaspoon dried thyme
- 2 ripe tomatoes, pureed
- 1/4 cup breadcrumbs
- 1/4 cup Parmesan cheese, grated

DIRECTIONS (Prep + Cook Time: 20 minutes)

Melt 1/2 tablespoon of butter in a sauté pan over medium-high heat. Now, cook the leek and garlic until tender and aromatic. Add the stock and wine to deglaze the pan. Preheat your Air Fryer to 370 degrees F. Grease a casserole dish with the remaining 1/2 tablespoon of melted butter. Place the fish in the casserole dish. Add the seasonings. Top with the sautéed leek mixture. Add the tomato puree. Cook for 10 minutes in the preheated Air Fryer. Top with the breadcrumbs and cheese; cook an additional 7 minutes until the crumbs are golden. Serve and enjoy!

465. Orange Glazed Scallops
INGREDIENTS (3 Servings)

- 1 pound jumbo sea scallops
- 1 tablespoon soy sauce
- 2 tablespoons orange juice
- 1 teaspoon orange zest
- 1/2 teaspoon fresh parsley, minced
- 1 tablespoon olive oil
- Sea salt, to taste
- 1/2 teaspoon ground black pepper

DIRECTIONS (Prep + Cook Time: 15 minutes)

Start by preheating your Air Fryer to 400 degrees F. Toss all ingredients in mixing bowl. Place the scallops in the lightly greased cooking basket and cook for 7 minutes, shaking the basket halfway through the cooking time. Work in batches. Taste, adjust the seasonings and serve warm. Enjoy!

466. Beer Battered Fish with Honey Tartar Sauce
INGREDIENTS (2 Servings)

- 1/2 pound hoki fillets
- Sea salt and black pepper, to taste
- 1/2 cup flour
- 1 egg
- 1 teaspoon paprika
- 1 (12-ounce) bottle beer
- 1/4 cup mayonnaise
- 1/2 teaspoon honey
- 1 tablespoon fresh lemon juice
- 1 teaspoon Dijon mustard
- 1 teaspoon sweet pickle relish

DIRECTIONS (Prep + Cook Time: 20 minutes)

Rinse the hoki fillets and pat dry. Combine the flour, egg and paprika in a bowl. Gradually pour in beer until a batter is formed. Dip the fish fillets into the batter; then, transfer to the lightly greased cooking basket. Cook in the preheated Air Fryer at 380 degrees F for 12 minutes. In the meantime, whisk the remaining ingredients to make the sauce. Place in the refrigerator until ready to serve. Enjoy!

467. Jamaican-Style Fish and Potato Fritters
INGREDIENTS (2 Servings)

- 1/2 pound sole fillets
- 1/2 pound mashed potatoes
- 1 egg, well beaten
- 1/2 cup red onion, chopped
- 2 garlic cloves, minced
- 2 tablespoons fresh parsley, chopped
- 1 bell pepper, finely chopped
- 1/2 teaspoon scotch bonnet pepper, minced
- 1 tablespoon olive oil
- 1 tablespoon coconut aminos
- 1/2 teaspoon paprika
- Salt and white pepper, to taste

DIRECTIONS (Prep + Cook Time: 30 minutes)

Start by preheating your Air Fryer to 395 degrees F. Spritz the sides and bottom of the cooking basket with cooking spray. Cook the sole fillets in the preheated Air Fryer for 10 minutes, flipping them halfway through the cooking time. In a mixing bowl, mash the sole fillets into flakes. Stir in the remaining ingredients. Shape the fish mixture into patties. Bake in the preheated Air Fryer at 390 degrees F for 14 minutes, flipping them halfway through the cooking time. Serve and enjoy!

468. Snapper with Coconut Milk Sauce
INGREDIENTS (2 Servings)

1/2 cup full-fat coconut milk	1 teaspoon fresh ginger, grated	1 tablespoon olive oil	Salt and white pepper, to taste
2 tablespoons lemon juice	2 snapper fillets	1 tablespoon cornstarch	

DIRECTIONS (Prep + Cook Time: 20 minutes + Marinating Time)
Place the milk, lemon juice, and ginger in a glass bowl; add fish and let it marinate for 1 hour. Removed the fish from the milk mixture and place in the Air Fryer basket. Drizzle olive oil all over the fish fillets. Cook in the preheated Air Fryer at 390 degrees F for 15 minutes. Meanwhile, heat the milk mixture over medium-high heat; bring to a rapid boil, stirring continuously. Reduce to simmer and add the cornstarch, salt, and pepper; continue to cook 12 minutes more. Spoon the sauce over the warm snapper fillets and serve immediately.

469. Salmon Fillets with Herbs and Garlic
INGREDIENTS (3 Servings)

1 pound salmon fillets	1 sprig thyme	1 lemon, sliced
Sea salt and ground black pepper, to taste	2 sprigs rosemary	
1 tablespoon olive oil	2 cloves garlic, minced	

DIRECTIONS (Prep + Cook Time: 15 minutes)
Pat the salmon fillets dry and season them with salt and pepper; drizzle salmon fillets with olive oil and place in the Air Fryer cooking basket. Cook the salmon fillets at 380 degrees F for 7 minutes; turn them over, top with thyme, rosemary and garlic and continue to cook for 5 minutes more. Serve topped with lemon slices and enjoy

470. Moroccan Harissa Shrimp
INGREDIENTS (3 Servings)

1 pound breaded shrimp, frozen	Sea salt and ground black pepper, to taste	1 teaspoon caraway seeds	1 teaspoon fresh garlic, minced
1 teaspoon extra-virgin olive oil	1 teaspoon coriander seeds	1 teaspoon crushed red pepper	

DIRECTIONS (Prep + Cook Time: 10 minutes)
Toss the breaded shrimp with olive oil and transfer to the Air Fryer cooking basket. Cook in the preheated Air Fryer at 400 degrees F for 5 minutes; shake the basket and cook an additional 4 minutes. Meanwhile, mix the remaining ingredients until well combined. Taste and adjust seasonings. Toss the warm shrimp with the harissa sauce and serve immediately. Enjoy!

471. Garlic Butter Scallops
INGREDIENTS (2 Servings)

1/2 pound scallops	1/4 teaspoon cayenne pepper	1/4 teaspoon dried basil	1 teaspoon garlic, minced
Coarse sea salt and ground black pepper, to taste	1/4 teaspoon dried oregano	2 tablespoons butter pieces, cold	1 teaspoon lemon zest

DIRECTIONS (Prep + Cook Time: 10 minutes)
Sprinkle the scallops with salt, black pepper, cayenne pepper, oregano and basil. Spritz your scallops with a nonstick cooking oil and transfer them to the Air Fryer cooking basket. Cook the scallops at 400 degrees F for 6 to 7 minutes, shaking the basket halfway through the cooking time. In the meantime, melt the butter in a small saucepan over medium-high heat. Once hot, add in the garlic and continue to sauté until fragrant, about 1 minute. Add in lemon zest, taste and adjust the seasonings. Spoon the garlic butter over the warm scallops and serve. Enjoy!

472. Anchovy and Cheese Wontons
INGREDIENTS (2 Servings)

½ pound anchovies	1 teaspoon garlic, minced	½ pound wonton wrappers
½ cup cheddar cheese, grated	1 tablespoon Shoyu sauce	1 teaspoon sesame oil
1 cup fresh spinach	Himalayan salt and ground black pepper, to taste	
2 tablespoons scallions, minced		

DIRECTIONS (Prep + Cook Time: 15 minutes)
Mash the anchovies and mix with the cheese, spinach, scallions, garlic and Shoyu sauce; season with salt and black pepper and mix to combine well. Fill your wontons with 1 tablespoon of the filling mixture and fold into triangle shape; brush the side with a bit of oil and water to seal the edges. Cook in your Air Fryer at 390 degrees F for 10 minutes, flipping the wontons for even cooking. Enjoy!

473. Ahi Tuna with Peppers and Tartare Sauce
INGREDIENTS (2 Servings)

- 2 ahi tuna steaks
- 2 Spanish peppers, quartered
- 1 teaspoon olive oil
- 1/2 teaspoon garlic powder
- Salt and freshly ground black pepper, to taste

Tartare sauce:

- 4 tablespoons mayonnaise
- 2 tablespoons sour cream
- 1 tablespoon baby capers, drained
- 1 tablespoon gherkins, drained and chopped
- 2 tablespoons white onion, minced

DIRECTIONS (Prep + Cook Time: 15 minutes)

Pat the ahi tuna dry using kitchen towels. Toss the ahi tuna and Spanish peppers with olive oil, garlic powder, salt and black pepper. Cook the ahi tuna and peppers in the preheated Air Fryer at 400 degrees F for 10 minutes, flipping them halfway through the cooking time. Meanwhile, whisk all the sauce ingredients until well combined. Plate the ahi tuna steaks and arrange Spanish peppers around them. Serve with tartare sauce on the side and enjoy!

474. Seed-Crusted Codfish Fillets
INGREDIENTS (2 Servings)

- 2 codfish fillets
- 1 teaspoon sesame oil
- Sea salt and black pepper, to taste
- 1 teaspoon sesame seeds
- 1 tablespoon chia seeds

DIRECTIONS (Prep + Cook Time: 15 minutes)

Start by preheating your Air Fryer to 380 degrees F. Add the sesame oil, salt, black pepper, sesame seeds and chia seeds to a rimmed plate. Coat the top of the codfish with the seed mixture, pressing it down to adhere. Lower the codfish fillets, seed side down, into the cooking basket and cook for 6 minutes. Turn the fish fillets over and cook for a further 6 minutes. Serve warm and enjoy!

475. Salmon Filets with Fennel Slaw
INGREDIENTS (3 Servings)

- 1 pound salmon filets
- 1 teaspoon Cajun spice mix
- Sea salt and ground black pepper, to taste

Fennel Slaw:

- 1 pound fennel bulb, thinly sliced
- 1 Lebanese cucumber, thinly sliced
- 1/2 red onion, thinly sliced
- 1/2 ounce tarragon
- 2 tablespoons tahini
- 2 tablespoons lemon juice
- 1 tablespoon soy sauce

DIRECTIONS (Prep + Cook Time: 15 minutes)

Rinse the salmon filets and pat them dry with a paper towel. Then, toss the salmon filets with the Cajun spice mix, salt and black pepper. Cook the salmon filets in the preheated Air Fryer at 380 degrees F for 6 minutes; flip the salmon filets and cook for a further 6 minutes. Meanwhile, make the fennel slaw by stirring fennel, cucumber, red onion and tarragon in a salad bowl. Mix the remaining ingredients to make the dressing. Dress the salad and transfer to your refrigerator until ready to serve. Serve the warm fish with chilled fennel slaw. Enjoy!

476. Tuna Steaks with Pearl Onions
INGREDIENTS (4 Servings)

- 4 tuna steaks
- 1 pound pearl onions
- 4 teaspoons olive oil
- 1 teaspoon dried rosemary
- 1 teaspoon dried marjoram
- 1 tablespoon cayenne pepper
- 1/2 teaspoon sea salt
- 1/2 teaspoon black pepper, preferably freshly cracked
- 1 lemon, sliced

DIRECTIONS (Prep + Cook Time: 20 minutes)

Place the tuna steaks in the lightly greased cooking basket. Top with the pearl onions; add the olive oil, rosemary, marjoram, cayenne pepper, salt, and black pepper. Bake in the preheated Air Fryer at 400 degrees F for 9 to 10 minutes. Work in two batches. Serve warm with lemon slices and enjoy!

477. Tortilla-Crusted Haddock Fillets
INGREDIENTS (2 Servings)

- 2 haddock fillets
- 1/2 cup tortilla chips, crushed
- 2 tablespoons parmesan cheese, freshly grated
- 1 teaspoon dried parsley flakes
- 1 egg, beaten
- 1/2 teaspoon coarse sea salt
- 1/4 teaspoon ground black pepper
- 1/4 teaspoon cayenne pepper
- 2 tablespoons olive oil

DIRECTIONS (Prep + Cook Time: 20 minutes)

Start by preheating your Air Fryer to 360 degrees F. Pat dry the haddock fillets and set aside. In a shallow bowl, thoroughly combine the crushed tortilla chips with the parmesan and parsley flakes. Mix until everything is well incorporated. In a separate shallow bowl, whisk the egg with salt, black pepper, and cayenne pepper. Dip the haddock fillets into the egg. Then, dip the fillets into the tortilla/parmesan mixture until well coated on all sides. Drizzle the olive oil all over the fish fillets. Lower the coated fillets into the lightly greased Air Fryer basket. Cook for 11 to 13 minutes. Serve and enjoy!

478. English-Style Flounder Fillets
INGREDIENTS (2 Servings)

- 2 flounder fillets
- 1/4 cup all-purpose flour
- 1 egg
- 1/2 teaspoon Worcestershire sauce
- 1/2 cup bread crumbs
- 1/2 teaspoon lemon pepper
- 1/2 teaspoon coarse sea salt
- 1/4 teaspoon chili powder

DIRECTIONS (Prep + Cook Time: 20 minutes)

Rinse and pat dry the flounder fillets. Place the flour in a large pan. Whisk the egg and Worcestershire sauce in a shallow bowl. In a separate bowl, mix the bread crumbs with the lemon pepper, salt, and chili powder. Dredge the fillets in the flour, shaking off the excess. Then, dip them into the egg mixture. Lastly, coat the fish fillets with the breadcrumb mixture until they are coated on all sides. Spritz with cooking spray and transfer to the Air Fryer basket. Cook at 390 degrees for 7 minutes. Turn them over, spritz with cooking spray on the other side, and cook another 5 minutes. Serve and enjoy!

479. Smoked Halibut and Eggs in Brioche
INGREDIENTS (4 Servings)

- 4 brioche rolls
- 1 pound smoked halibut, chopped
- 4 eggs
- 1 teaspoon dried thyme
- 1 teaspoon dried basil
- Salt and black pepper, to taste

DIRECTIONS (Prep + Cook Time: 25 minutes)

Cut off the top of each brioche; then, scoop out the insides to make the shells. Lay the prepared brioche shells in the lightly greased cooking basket. Spritz with cooking oil; add the halibut. Crack an egg into each brioche shell; sprinkle with thyme, basil, salt, and black pepper. Bake in the preheated Air Fryer at 325 degrees F for 20 minutes. Serve and enjoy!

480. Quick-Fix Seafood Breakfast
INGREDIENTS (2 Servings)

- 1 tablespoon olive oil
- 2 garlic cloves, minced
- 1 small yellow onion, chopped
- 1/4 pound tilapia pieces
- 1/4 pound rockfish pieces
- 1/2 teaspoon dried basil
- Salt and white pepper, to taste
- 4 eggs, lightly beaten
- 1 tablespoon dry sherry
- 4 tablespoons cheese, shredded

DIRECTIONS (Prep + Cook Time: 30 minutes)

Start by preheating your Air Fryer to 350 degrees F; add the olive oil to a baking pan. Once hot, cook the garlic and onion for 2 minutes or until fragrant. Add the fish, basil, salt, and pepper. In a mixing dish, thoroughly combine the eggs with sherry and cheese. Pour the mixture into the baking pan. Cook at 360 degrees F approximately 20 minutes. Serve and enjoy!

481. Monkfish Fillets with Romano Cheese
INGREDIENTS (2 Servings)

- 2 monkfish fillets
- 1 teaspoon garlic paste
- 2 tablespoons butter, melted
- 1/2 teaspoon Aleppo chili powder
- 1/2 teaspoon dried rosemary
- 1/4 teaspoon cracked black pepper
- 1/2 teaspoon sea salt
- 4 tablespoons Romano cheese, grated

DIRECTIONS (Prep + Cook Time: 15 minutes)

Start by preheating the Air Fryer to 320 degrees F. Spritz the Air Fryer basket with cooking oil. Spread the garlic paste all over the fish fillets. Brush the monkfish fillets with the melted butter on both sides. Sprinkle with the chili powder, rosemary, black pepper, and salt. Cook for 7 minutes in the preheated Air Fryer. Top with the Romano cheese and continue to cook for 2 minutes more or until heated through. Serve and enjoy!

482. Grilled Hake with Garlic Sauce
INGREDIENTS (3 Servings)

3 hake fillets

6 tablespoons mayonnaise

1 teaspoon Dijon mustard

1 tablespoon fresh lime juice

1 cup panko crumbs Salt, to taste

1/4 teaspoon ground black pepper, or more to taste

Garlic Sauce:

1/4 cup Greek-style yogurt

2 tablespoons olive oil

2 cloves garlic, minced

1/2 teaspoon tarragon leaves, minced

DIRECTIONS (Prep + Cook Time: 20 minutes)

Pat dry the hake fillets with a kitchen towel. In a shallow bowl, whisk together the mayo, mustard, and lime juice. In another shallow bowl, thoroughly combine the panko crumbs with salt, and black pepper. Spritz the Air Fryer grill pan with non-stick cooking spray. Grill in the preheated Air Fry at 395 degrees F for 10 minutes, flipping halfway through the cooking time. Serve immediately.

483. Shrimp Scampi Linguine
INGREDIENTS (4 Servings)

1 ½ pounds shrimp, shelled and deveined

1/2 tablespoon fresh basil leaves, chopped

2 tablespoons olive oil

2 cloves garlic, minced

1/2 teaspoon fresh ginger, grated

1/4 teaspoon cracked black pepper

1/2 teaspoon sea salt

1/4 cup chicken stock

2 ripe tomatoes, pureed

8 ounces linguine pasta

1/2 cup parmesan cheese, preferably freshly grated

DIRECTIONS (Prep + Cook Time: 25 minutes)

Start by preheating the Air Fryer to 395 degrees F. Place the shrimp, basil, olive oil, garlic, ginger, black pepper, salt, chicken stock, and tomatoes in the casserole dish. Transfer the casserole dish to the cooking basket and bake for 10 minutes. Bring a large pot of lightly salted water to a boil. Cook the linguine for 10 minutes or until al dente; drain. Divide between four serving plates. Add the shrimp sauce and top with parmesan cheese. Enjoy!

484. Buttermilk Tuna fillets
INGREDIENTS (3 Servings)

1 pound tuna fillets

1/2 cup buttermilk

1/2 cup tortilla chips, crushed

1/4 cup parmesan cheese, grated

1/4 cup cassava flour

Salt and ground black pepper, to taste

1 teaspoon mustard seeds

1 teaspoon paprika

1 teaspoon garlic powder

1/2 teaspoon onion powder

DIRECTIONS (Prep + Cook Time: 50 minutes)

Place the tuna fillets and buttermilk in a bowl; cover and let it sit for 30 minutes. In a shallow bowl, thoroughly combine the remaining ingredients; mix until well combined. Dip the tuna fillets in the parmesan mixture until they are covered on all sides. Cook in the preheated Air Fryer at 380 degrees F for 12 minutes, turning halfway through the cooking time. Serve and enjoy!

485. Shrimp Scampi Dip with Cheese
INGREDIENTS (8 Servings)

2 teaspoons butter, melted

8 ounces shrimp, peeled and deveined

2 garlic cloves, minced

1/4 cup chicken stock

2 tablespoons fresh lemon juice

Salt and ground black pepper, to taste

1/2 teaspoon red pepper flakes

4 ounces cream cheese, at room temperature

1/2 cup sour cream

4 tablespoons mayonnaise

1/4 cup mozzarella cheese, shredded

DIRECTIONS (Prep + Cook Time: 25 minutes)

Start by preheating the Air Fryer to 395 degrees F. Grease the sides and bottom of a baking dish with the melted butter. Place the shrimp, garlic, chicken stock, lemon juice, salt, black pepper, and red pepper flakes in the baking dish. Transfer the baking dish to the cooking basket and bake for 10 minutes. Add the mixture to your food processor; pulse until the coarsely is chopped. Add the cream cheese, sour cream, and mayonnaise.Top with the mozzarella cheese and bake in the preheated Air Fryer at 360 degrees F for 6 to 7 minutes or until the cheese is bubbling. Serve immediately with breadsticks if desired.

486. King Prawns with Lemon Butter Sauce
INGREDIENTS (4 Servings)

King Prawns:

1 ½ pounds king prawns, peeled and deveined

2 cloves garlic, minced

1/2 cup Pecorino Romano cheese, grated

Sea salt and ground white pepper, to your liking

1/2 teaspoon onion powder

1 teaspoon garlic powder

1 teaspoon mustard seeds

2 tablespoons olive oil

Sauce:

2 tablespoons butter

2 tablespoons fresh lemon juice

1/2 teaspoon Worcestershire sauce

1/4 teaspoon ground black pepper

DIRECTIONS (Prep + Cook Time: 15 minutes)

In a plastic closeable bag, thoroughly combine all ingredients for the king prawns; shake to combine well. Transfer the coated king prawns to the lightly greased Air Fryer basket. Cook in the preheated Air Fryer at 390 degrees for 6 minutes, shaking the basket halfway through. Work in batches. In the meantime, heat a small saucepan over a moderate flame; melt the butter and add the remaining ingredients. Turn the temperature to low and whisk for 2 to 3 minutes until thoroughly heated. Spoon the sauce onto the warm king prawns. Serve and enjoy!

487. Creamed Trout Salad
INGREDIENTS (2 Servings)

1/2 pound trout fillets, skinless

2 tablespoons horseradish, prepared, drained

1/4 cup mayonnaise

1 tablespoon fresh lemon juice

1 teaspoon mustard

Salt and ground white pepper, to taste

6 ounces chickpeas, canned and drained

1 red onion, thinly sliced

1 cup Iceberg lettuce, torn into pieces

DIRECTIONS (Prep + Cook Time: 20 minutes)

Spritz the Air Fryer basket with cooking spray. Cook the trout fillets in the preheated Air Fryer at 395 degrees F for 10 minutes or until opaque. Make sure to turn them halfway through the cooking time. Break the fish into bite-sized chunks and place in the refrigerator to cool. Toss your fish with the remaining ingredients. Serve and enjoy!

488. Sea Bass with French Sauce Tartare
INGREDIENTS (2 Servings)

1 tablespoon olive oil

2 sea bass fillets

Sauce:

1/2 cup mayonnaise

1 tablespoon capers, drained and chopped

1 tablespoon gherkins, drained and chopped

2 tablespoons scallions, finely chopped

2 tablespoons lemon juice

DIRECTIONS (Prep + Cook Time: 15 minutes)

Start by preheating your Air Fryer to 395 degrees F. Drizzle olive oil all over the fish fillets. Cook the sea bass in the preheated Air Fryer for 10 minutes, flipping them halfway through the cooking time. Meanwhile, make the sauce by whisking the remaining ingredients until everything is well incorporated. Place in the refrigerator until ready to serve. Enjoy!

489. Double Cheese Fish Casserole
INGREDIENTS (4 Servings)

1 tablespoon avocado oil

1 pound hake fillets

1 teaspoon garlic powder

Sea salt and ground white pepper, to taste

2 tablespoons shallots, chopped

1 bell pepper, seeded and chopped

1/2 cup Cottage cheese

1/2 cup sour cream

1 egg, well whisked

1 teaspoon yellow mustard

1 tablespoon lime juice

1/2 cup Swiss cheese, shredded

DIRECTIONS (Prep + Cook Time: 30 minutes)

Brush the bottom and sides of a casserole dish with avocado oil. Add the hake fillets to the casserole dish and sprinkle with garlic powder, salt, and pepper. Add the chopped shallots and bell peppers. In a mixing bowl, thoroughly combine the Cottage cheese, sour cream, egg, mustard, and lime juice. Pour the mixture over fish and spread evenly. Cook in the preheated Air Fryer at 370 degrees F for 10 minutes. Top with the Swiss cheese and cook an additional 7 minutes. Let it rest for 10 minutes before slicing and serving. Enjoy!

490. Rosemary-Infused Butter Scallops
INGREDIENTS (4 Servings)

- 2 pounds sea scallops
- 1/2 cup beer
- 4 tablespoons butter
- 2 sprigs rosemary, only leaves
- Sea salt and freshly cracked black pepper, to taste

DIRECTIONS (Prep + Cook Time: 1 hour 10 minutes)

In a ceramic dish, mix the sea scallops with beer; let it marinate for 1 hour. Meanwhile, preheat your Air Fryer to 400 degrees F. Melt the butter and add the rosemary leaves. Stir for a few minutes. Discard the marinade and transfer the sea scallops to the Air Fryer basket. Season with salt and black pepper. Cook the scallops in the preheated Air Fryer for 7 minutes, shaking the basket halfway through the cooking time. Work in batches.

491. Italian-Style Crab Bruschetta
INGREDIENTS (2 Servings)

- 4 slices sourdough bread
- 2 tablespoons tomato ketchup
- 4 tablespoons mayonnaise
- 1 teaspoon fresh rosemary, chopped
- 8 ounces lump crabmeat
- 1 teaspoon granulated garlic
- 2 tablespoons shallots, chopped
- 4 tablespoons mozzarella cheese, crumbled

DIRECTIONS (Prep + Cook Time: 15 minutes)

Place the slices of sourdough bread on a flat surface. In a mixing bowl, thoroughly combine the tomato ketchup, mayo, rosemary, crabmeat, garlic, and shallots. Divide the crabmeat mixture between the slices of bread. Top with mozzarella cheese. Bake in the preheated Air Fryer at 370 degrees F for 10 minutes.

492. Greek Sardeles Psites
INGREDIENTS (2 Servings)

- 4 sardines, cleaned
- 1/4 cup all-purpose flour
- Sea salt and ground black pepper, to taste
- 4 tablespoons extra-virgin olive oil
- 1/2 red onion, chopped
- 1/2 teaspoon fresh garlic, minced
- 1/4 cup sweet white wine
- 1 tablespoon fresh coriander, minced
- 1/4 cup baby capers, drained
- 1 tomato, crushed
- 1/4 teaspoon chili paper flakes

DIRECTIONS (Prep + Cook Time: 40 minutes)

Coat your sardines with all-purpose flour until well coated on all sides. Season your sardines with salt and black pepper and arrange them in the cooking basket. Cook in your Air Fryer at 325 degrees F for 35 to 40 minutes until the skin is crispy. Meanwhile, heat olive oil in a frying pan over a moderate flame. Now, sauté the onion and garlic for 4 to 5 minutes or until tender and aromatic. Stir in the remaining ingredients, cover and let it simmer, for about 15 minutes or until the sauce has thickened and reduced. Spoon the sauce over the warm sardines and serve immediately. Enjoy!

493. Thai-Style Jumbo Scallops
INGREDIENTS (2 Servings)

- 8 jumbo scallops
- 1 teaspoon sesame oil
- Sea salt and red pepper flakes, to season
- 1 tablespoon coconut oil
- 1 Thai chili, deveined and minced
- 1 teaspoon garlic, minced
- 1 tablespoon oyster sauce
- 1 tablespoon soy sauce
- 1/4 cup coconut milk
- 2 tablespoons fresh lime juice

DIRECTIONS (Prep + Cook Time: 40 minutes)

Pat the jumbo scallops dry and toss them with 1 teaspoon of sesame oil, salt and red pepper. Cook the jumbo scallops in your Air Fryer at 400 degrees F for 4 minutes; turn them over and cook an additional 3 minutes. While your scallops are cooking, make the sauce in a frying pan. Heat the coconut oil in a pan over medium-high heat. Once hot, cook the Thai chili and garlic for 1 minute or so until just tender and fragrant. Add in the oyster sauce, soy sauce and coconut milk and continue to simmer, partially covered, for 5 minutes longer. Lastly, stir in fresh lime juice and stir to combine well. Add the warm scallops to the sauce and serve immediately.

494. Halibut Steak with Cremini Mushrooms
INGREDIENTS (3 Servings)

1 pound halibut steak	1 teaspoon butter, melted	1/2 teaspoon basil
1 teaspoon olive oil	1/4 teaspoon onion powder	1/2 teaspoon oregano
Sea salt and ground black pepper, to taste	1/4 teaspoon garlic powder	
7 ounces Cremini mushrooms	1/2 teaspoon rosemary	

DIRECTIONS (Prep + Cook Time: 15 minutes)

Toss the halibut steak with olive oil, salt and black pepper and transfer to the Air Fryer cooking basket. Toss the Cremini mushrooms with the other ingredients until well coated on all sides. Cook the halibut steak at 400 degrees F for 5 minutes. Turn the halibut steak over and top with mushrooms. Continue to cook an additional 5 minutes or until the mushrooms are fragrant. Serve warm and enjoy!

495. Marinated Flounder Filets
INGREDIENTS (3 Servings)

1 pound flounder filets	1/4 cup malt vinegar	1 egg
1 teaspoon garlic, minced	1 teaspoon granulated sugar	2 tablespoons milk
2 tablespoons soy sauce	Salt and black pepper, to taste	1/2 cup parmesan cheese, grated
1 teaspoon Dijon mustard	1/2 cup plain flour	

DIRECTIONS (Prep + Cook Time: 15 minutes + Marinating Time)

Place the flounder filets, garlic, soy sauce, mustard, vinegar and sugar in a glass bowl; cover and let it marinate in your refrigerator for at least 1 hour. Transfer the fish to a plate, discarding the marinade. Salt and pepper to taste. Place the plain flour in a shallow bowl; in another bowl, beat the egg and milk until pale and well combined; add parmesan cheese to the third bowl. Dip the flounder filets in the flour, then in the egg mixture; repeat the process and coat them with the parmesan cheese, pressing to adhere. Cook the flounder filets in the preheated Air Fryer at 400 degrees F for 5 minutes; turn the flounder filets over and cook on the other side for 5 minutes more. Enjoy!

496. Greek-Style Sea Bass
INGREDIENTS (2 Servings)

1/2 pound sea bass	1/2 teaspoon rigani (Greek oregano)	1/4 teaspoon ground cumin
1 garlic clove, halved	1/2 teaspoon dried dill weed	1/2 teaspoon shallot powder
Sea salt and ground black pepper, to taste	1/4 teaspoon ground bay leaf	

Greek sauce:

1/2 Greek yogurt	1/2 teaspoon Tzatziki spice mix	
1 teaspoon olive oil	1 teaspoon lime juice	

DIRECTIONS (Prep + Cook Time: 15 minutes)

Pat dry the sea bass with paper towels. Rub the fish with garlic halves. Toss the fish with salt, black pepper, rigani, dill, ground bay leaf, ground cumin and shallot powder. Cook the sea bass in your Air Fryer at 400 degrees F for 5 minutes; turn the filets over and cook on the other side for 5 to 6 minutes. In the meantime, make the sauce by simply blending the remaining ingredients. Serve the warm fish dolloped with Greek-style sauce. Enjoy!

497. Haddock Steaks with Decadent Mango Salsa
INGREDIENTS (2 Servings)

2 haddock steaks	1 tablespoon white wine	
1 teaspoon butter, melted	Sea salt and ground black pepper, to taste	

Mango salsa:

1/2 mango, diced	1 chili pepper, deveined and minced	2 tablespoons fresh lemon juice
1/4 cup red onion, chopped	1 teaspoon cilantro, chopped	

DIRECTIONS (Prep + Cook Time: 15 minutes)

Toss the haddock with butter, wine, salt and black pepper. Cook the haddock in your Air Fryer at 400 degrees F for 5 minutes. Flip the haddock and cook on the other side for 5 minutes more. Meanwhile, make the mango salsa by mixing all ingredients. Serve the warm haddock with the chilled mango salsa and enjoy!

498. Classic Fish Tacos
INGREDIENTS (3 Servings)

- 1 pound codfish
- 1 tablespoon olive oil
- 1 teaspoon Cajun spice mix
- Salt and red pepper, to taste
- 3 corn tortillas
- 1/2 avocado, pitted and diced
- 1 cup purple cabbage
- 1 jalapeño, minced

DIRECTIONS (Prep + Cook Time: 15 minutes)

Pat the codfish dry with paper towels; toss the codfish with olive oil, Cajun spice mix, salt and black pepper. Cook your codfish at 400 degrees F for 5 to 6 minutes. Then, turn the fish over and cook on the other side for 6 minutes until they are opaque. Let the fish rest for 5 minutes before flaking with a fork. Assemble the tacos: place the flaked fish over warmed tortillas; top with avocado, purple cabbage and minced jalapeño. Enjoy!

499. Halibut Steak with Zoodles and Lemon
INGREDIENTS (3 Servings)

- 1 pound halibut steak, cut into 3 pieces
- 1 garlic clove, halved
- 1 teaspoon avocado oil
- Sea salt and black pepper, to taste
- 1 pound zucchini, julienned
- 1/2 teaspoon onion powder
- 1/2 teaspoon granulated garlic
- 1 tablespoon fresh parsley, minced
- 1 teaspoon sage, minced
- 1 lemon, sliced

DIRECTIONS (Prep + Cook Time: 15 minutes)

Rub the halibut steaks with garlic and toss with avocado oil, salt and black pepper; then, transfer the halibut steaks to the Air Fryer cooking basket. Cook the halibut steak at 400 degrees F for 5 minutes. Turn the halibut steak over and continue to cook an additional 5 minutes or until it flakes easily when tested with a fork. Meanwhile, spritz a wok with a nonstick spray; heat the wok over medium-high heat. Once hot, stir fry the zucchini noodles along with the onion powder and granulated garlic; cook for 2 to 3 minutes or until just tender. Top your zoodles with the parsley and sage and stir to combine. Serve the hot zoodles with the halibut steaks and lemon slices. Enjoy!

500. Easy Lobster Tails
INGREDIENTS (5 Servings)

- 2 pounds fresh lobster tails, cleaned and halved, in shells
- 2 tablespoons butter, melted
- 1 teaspoon onion powder
- 1 teaspoon cayenne pepper
- Salt and ground black pepper, to taste
- 2 garlic cloves, minced
- 1 cup cornmeal
- 1 cup green olives

DIRECTIONS (Prep + Cook Time: 20 minutes)

In a plastic closeable bag, thoroughly combine all ingredients; shake to combine well. Transfer the coated lobster tails to the greased cooking basket. Cook in the preheated Air Fryer at 390 degrees for 6 to 7 minutes, shaking the basket halfway through. Work in batches. Serve with green olives and enjoy!

501. Saucy Garam Masala Fish
INGREDIENTS (2 Servings)

- 2 teaspoons olive oil
- 1/4 cup coconut milk
- 1/2 teaspoon cayenne pepper
- 1 teaspoon Garam masala
- 1/4 teaspoon Kala namak (Indian black salt)
- 1/2 teaspoon fresh ginger, grated
- 1 garlic clove, minced
- 2 catfish fillets
- 1/4 cup coriander, roughly chopped

DIRECTIONS (Prep + Cook Time: 25 minutes)

Preheat your Air Fryer to 390 degrees F. Then, spritz the baking dish with a nonstick cooking spray. In a mixing bowl, whisk the olive oil, milk, cayenne pepper, Garam masala, Kala namak, ginger, and garlic. Coat the catfish fillets with the Garam masala mixture. Cook the catfish fillets in the preheated Air Fryer approximately 18 minutes, turning over halfway through the cooking time. Garnish with fresh coriander and serve over hot noodles if desired. Enjoy!

502. Coconut Shrimp with Orange Sauce
INGREDIENTS (3 Servings)

1 pound shrimp, cleaned and deveined	1 egg	2 tablespoons olive oil
Sea salt and white pepper, to taste	1/4 cup shredded coconut, unsweetened	1 lemon, cut into wedges
1/2 cup all-purpose flour	3/2 cup fresh bread crumbs	

Dipping Sauce:

2 tablespoons butter	2 tablespoons soy sauce	1/2 teaspoon tapioca starch
1/2 cup orange juice	A pinch of salt	2 tablespoons fresh parsley, minced

DIRECTIONS (Prep + Cook Time: 1 hour 30 minutes)

Pat dry the shrimp and season them with salt and white pepper. Place the flour on a large tray; then, whisk the egg in a shallow bowl. In a third shallow bowl, place the shredded coconut and breadcrumbs. Dip the shrimp in the flour, then, dip in the egg. Lastly, coat the shrimp with the shredded coconut and bread crumbs. Refrigerate for 1 hour. Then, transfer to the cooking basket. Drizzle with olive oil and cook in the preheated Air Fryer at 370 degrees F for 6 minutes. Work in batches. Meanwhile, melt the butter in a small saucepan over medium-high heat; add the orange juice and bring it to a boil; reduce the heat and allow it to simmer approximately 7 minutes. Add the soy sauce, salt, and tapioca; continue simmering until the sauce has thickened and reduced. Spoon the sauce over the shrimp and garnish with lemon wedges and parsley. Serve immediately

503. Delicious Snapper en Papillote
INGREDIENTS (2 Servings)

2 snapper fillets	1 small-sized serrano pepper, sliced	1/2 teaspoon paprika
1 shallot, peeled and sliced	1 tomato, sliced	Sea salt, to taste
2 garlic cloves, halved	1 tablespoon olive oil	2 bay leaves
1 bell pepper, sliced	1/4 teaspoon freshly ground black pepper	

DIRECTIONS (Prep + Cook Time: 20 minutes)

Place two parchment sheets on a working surface. Place the fish in the center of one side of the parchment paper. Top with the shallot, garlic, peppers, and tomato. Drizzle olive oil over the fish and vegetables. Season with black pepper, paprika, and salt. Add the bay leaves. Fold over the other half of the parchment. Now, fold the paper around the edges tightly and create a half moon shape, sealing the fish inside. Cook in the preheated Air Fryer at 390 degrees F for 15 minutes. Serve warm

504. Dilled and Glazed Salmon Steaks
INGREDIENTS (2 Servings)

2 salmon steaks	1 tablespoon sesame oil	1/2 teaspoon smoked cayenne pepper
Coarse sea salt, to taste	Zest of 1 lemon	1/2 teaspoon dried dill
1/4 teaspoon freshly ground black pepper, or more to taste	1 tablespoon fresh lemon juice	
	1 teaspoon garlic, minced	
2 tablespoons honey		

DIRECTIONS (Prep + Cook Time: 20 minutes)

Preheat your Air Fryer to 380 degrees F. Pat dry the salmon steaks with a kitchen towel. In a ceramic dish, combine the remaining ingredients until everything is well whisked. Add the salmon steaks to the ceramic dish and let them sit in the refrigerator for 1 hour. Now, place the salmon steaks in the cooking basket. Reserve the marinade. Cook for 12 minutes, flipping halfway through the cooking time. Meanwhile, cook the marinade in a small sauté pan over a moderate flame. Cook until the sauce has thickened. Pour the sauce over the steaks and serve with mashed potatoes if desired. Enjoy!

Poultry

505. One-Tray Parmesan Chicken Wings
INGREDIENTS (4 Servings)

8 chicken wings	2 tbsp olive oil	2 tsp fresh parsley, chopped
1 tsp Dijon mustard	2 cloves garlic, crushed	
Salt to taste	4 tbsp Parmesan cheese, grated	

DIRECTIONS (Prep + Cook Time: 20 minutes)

Preheat air fryer to 380 F. Grease the frying basket. Season the wings with salt and black pepper. Brush them with mustard. On a plate, pour 2 tbsp of the Parmesan cheese. Coat the wings with Parmesan cheese, drizzle with olive oil, and place in the air fryer basket. AirFry for 15 minutes, turning once. Top with the remaining Parmesan cheese and parsley to serve.

506. South Asian Chicken Strips
INGREDIENTS (4 Servings)

1 lb chicken breasts, cut into strips	2 green onions, sliced	2 tbsp fresh cilantro, chopped
2 tomatoes, cubed	2 tbsp olive oil	Salt and black pepper to taste
1 green chili pepper, cut into stripes	1 tbsp yellow mustard	
½ tsp cumin	½ tsp ginger powder	

DIRECTIONS (Prep + Cook Time: 35 minutes)

Heat olive oil in a deep pan over medium heat and sauté mustard, green onions, ginger powder, cumin, and green chili pepper for 2-3 minutes. Stir in tomatoes, cilantro, and salt; set aside. Preheat the air fryer to 380 F. Season the chicken with salt and pepper, and place in the greased air fryer basket. AirFry for 15 minutes, shaking once. Top with the sauce and serve.

507. Crunchy Coconut Chicken Dippers
INGREDIENTS (4 Servings)

2 cups coconut flakes	½ cup cornstarch	2 eggs, beaten
4 chicken breasts, cut into strips	Salt and black pepper to taste	

DIRECTIONS (Prep + Cook Time: 25 minutes)

Preheat air fryer to 350 F. Mix salt, pepper, and cornstarch in a bowl. Line a frying basket with parchment paper. Dip the chicken first in the cornstarch, then into the eggs, and finally, coat with coconut flakes. Arrange in the air fryer and Bake for 16 minutes, flipping once until crispy. Serve with berry sauce.

508. Buffalo Chicken Tenders
INGREDIENTS (4 Servings)

1 cup breadcrumbs	½ tsp red chili pepper	1 tsp sweet paprika
½ cup yogurt	1 tbsp hot sauce	1 tsp garlic powder
1 lb chicken breasts, cut into strips	2 eggs, beaten	

DIRECTIONS (Prep + Cook Time: 25 minutes)

Preheat air fryer to 390 F. Whisk eggs with the hot sauce and yogurt. In a shallow bowl, combine the breadcrumbs, paprika, cayenne pepper, and garlic powder. Line a baking dish with parchment paper. Dip the chicken in the egg/yogurt mixture first, and then coat with breadcrumbs. Arrange on the sheet and Bake in the air fryer for 8-10 minutes. Flip the chicken over and bake for 6-8 more minutes. Serve.

509. Chicken Fillets with Sweet Chili Adobo
INGREDIENTS (4 Servings)

2 chicken breasts, halved	¼ cup sweet chili sauce
Salt and black pepper to taste	1 tsp turmeric

DIRECTIONS (Prep + Cook Time: 20 minutes)

Preheat air fryer to 390 F. In a bowl, add salt, black pepper, sweet chili sauce, and turmeric; mix well. Lightly brush the chicken with the mixture and place it in the frying basket. AirFry for 12-14 minutes, turning once halfway through. Serve with a side of steamed greens.

510. Jamaican Chicken Fajitas
INGREDIENTS (4 Servings)

- 1 lb chicken tenderloins
- 1 cup Jamaican jerk seasoning
- 2 tbsp lime juice
- 2 tbsp olive oil
- 4 large tortilla wraps
- 1 cup julienned carrots
- 1 cucumber, peeled, sliced
- 1 cup shredded lettuce
- 1 cup coleslaw mix
- ½ cup mango chutney

DIRECTIONS (Prep + Cook Time: 25 minutes + marinating time)

Whisk the olive oil, jerk seasoning, and lime juice in a bowl. Add in the chicken and toss to coat. Put in the fridge for 1 hour. Remove the chicken from the fridge, keeping the leftover marinade to the side. Preheat air fryer to 380 F. Arrange the chicken tenderloins on the greased fryer basket in a single layer. AirFry for 8 minutes. Flip the chicken and brush with more marinade. Fry for 5-7 more minutes. Divide the coleslaw mix carrots, cucumber, lettuce, and mango chutney between the tortillas. Add the chicken tenderloins on top and roll up the tortillas. Serve warm or cold.

511. Avocado & Mango Chicken Breasts
INGREDIENTS (2 Servings)

- 2 chicken breasts
- 1 mango, chopped
- 1 avocado, sliced
- 1 red pepper, chopped
- 1 tbsp balsamic vinegar
- 2 tbsp olive oil
- 2 garlic cloves, minced
- ½ tsp dried oregano
- 1 tsp mustard powder
- Salt and black pepper to taste

DIRECTIONS (Prep + Cook Time: 20 minutes + marinating time)

In a bowl, mix garlic, olive oil, and balsamic vinegar. Add in the breasts, cover, and marinate for 2 hours. Preheat the fryer to 360 F. Place the chicken in the frying basket and AirFry for 12-14 minutes, flipping once. Top with avocado, mango, and red pepper. Drizzle with balsamic vinegar and serve.

512. Easy Chicken Enchiladas
INGREDIENTS (4 Servings)

- 1 lb chicken breasts, chopped
- 1 cup mozzarella cheese, grated
- ½ cup salsa
- 1 can green chilies, chopped
- 8 flour tortillas
- 1 cup enchilada sauce

DIRECTIONS (Prep + Cook Time: 40 minutes)

Preheat the air fryer to 400 F. In a bowl, mix salsa and enchilada sauce. Toss in the chopped chicken to coat. Place the chicken in a baking dish and Bake in the air fryer for 14-18 minutes, shaking once. Remove and divide between the tortillas. Top with cheese and roll the tortillas. Place in the air fryer basket and Bake for 10 minutes. Serve with guacamole.

513. Ham & Cheese Filled Chicken Breasts
INGREDIENTS (4 Servings)

- 4 chicken breasts
- 4 ham slices
- 4 Swiss cheese slices
- 3 tbsp all-purpose flour
- 4 tbsp butter
- ½ tbsp paprika
- 1 tbsp chicken bouillon granules
- ¼ cup dry white wine
- 1 cup heavy whipping cream

DIRECTIONS (Prep + Cook Time: 25 minutes)

Preheat air fryer to 380 F. Pound the chicken breasts and put a slice of ham and cheese on each one. Fold the edges over the filling and seal them with toothpicks. In a bowl, combine paprika and flour, and coat the chicken. Transfer to the greased air fryer basket and Bake for 15 minutes, turning once. In a large skillet over medium heat, melt the butter and add the bouillon granules, wine, and heavy cream. Bring to a boil, reduce the heat to low, and simmer for 5 minutes. Serve the chicken with sauce.

514. Sweet Wasabi Chicken
INGREDIENTS (2 Servings)

- 2 tbsp wasabi
- 1 tbsp agave syrup
- 2 tsp black sesame seeds
- Salt and black pepper to taste
- 2 chicken breasts, cut into large chunks

DIRECTIONS (Prep + Cook Time: 20 minutes)

In a bowl, mix wasabi, agave syrup, sesame seed, salt, and pepper. Rub the mixture onto the breasts. Arrange the breasts on a greased frying basket and cook for 16 minutes, turning once halfway through.

515. Tasty Chicken Kiev
INGREDIENTS (4 Servings)

1 lb chicken breasts	2 garlic cloves, minced	1 cup panko breadcrumbs
4 tbsp butter, softened	1 tbsp lemon juice	1 cup plain flour
1 tbsp fresh dill, chopped	Salt and black pepper to taste	2 eggs, beaten

DIRECTIONS (Prep + Cook Time: 25 minutes)

Preheat air fryer to 390 F. In a bowl, mix butter, dill, garlic, lemon juice, salt, and pepper until a smooth paste is formed. Using a sharp knife, make a deep cut of each breast to create a large pocket. Stuff with the butter mixture and secure with toothpicks. Coat the breasts in the flour, then dip in the eggs, and finally in the breadcrumbs. Place chicken in the greased basket and Bake for 8-10 minutes. Turn over and cook for 6 more minutes. Serve sliced.

516. Tropical Coconut Chicken Thighs
INGREDIENTS (4 Servings)

1 tbsp curry powder	Salt and black pepper to taste	1 lb chicken thighs
4 tbsp mango chutney	¾ cup coconut, shredded	

DIRECTIONS (Prep + Cook Time: 20 minutes)

Preheat air fryer to 400 F. In a bowl, mix curry powder, mango chutney, salt, and black pepper. Brush the thighs with the glaze and roll the chicken thighs in shredded coconut. Grease a baking dish with cooking spray and arrange the thing in. Bake them in the air fryer for 12-14 minutes, turning once, until golden brown.

517. Sweet Mustard Chicken Thighs
INGREDIENTS (4 Servings)

4 chicken thighs, skin-on	1 tsp Dijon mustard
1 tbsp honey	Salt and garlic powder to taste

DIRECTIONS (Prep + Cook Time: 25 minutes)

In a bowl, mix honey, mustard, garlic powder, and salt. Brush the thighs with the mixture and AirFry them for 16 minutes at 400 F, turning once halfway through. Serve hot.

518. Crispy Drumsticks with Blue Cheese Sauce
INGREDIENTS (4 Servings)

Drumsticks:

1 lb drumsticks	1 tsp paprika	1 tsp onion powder
3 tbsp butter	¼ cup hot sauce	1 tsp garlic powder

Blue Cheese Sauce:

½ cup mayonnaise	½ tsp onion powder	2 tbsp buttermilk
1 cup blue cheese, crumbled	Salt and black pepper to taste	1 ½ tsp Worcestershire sauce
1 cup sour cream	½ tsp cayenne pepper	
½ tsp garlic powder	1 ½ tsp white wine vinegar	

DIRECTIONS (Prep + Cook Time: 30 minutes + marinating time)

Melt the butter in a skillet over medium heat and stir in the remaining drumstick ingredients, except for the drumsticks. Cook the mixture for 5 minutes or until the sauce reduces; then let cool. Place the drumsticks in a bowl, pour the cooled sauce over, and coat well. Refrigerate for 2 hours. In a jug, add sour cream, blue cheese, mayonnaise, garlic powder, onion powder, buttermilk, cayenne pepper, white wine vinegar, Worcestershire sauce, black pepper, and salt. Using a stick mixer, blend the ingredients until well mixed with no large lumps. Adjust the seasoning. Preheat air fryer to 350 F. Remove the drumsticks from the fridge and place them in the frying basket to Bake for 15 minutes. Turn the drumsticks with tongs every 5 minutes to ensure they cook evenly. Serve with blue cheese sauce and a side of celery sticks.

519. Thyme-Fried Chicken Legs
INGREDIENTS (4 Servings)

4 chicken legs	1 tbsp garlic powder	⅓ cup olive oil
2 lemons, halved	½ tsp dried oregano	Salt and black pepper to taste

DIRECTIONS (Prep + Cook Time: 50 minutes) Preheat the air fryer to 350 F. Brush the chicken legs with olive oil. Sprinkle with lemon juice and arrange in the frying basket. In a bowl, mix oregano, garlic powder, salt, and pepper. Scatter the seasoning mixture over the chicken and Bake the legs in the air fryer for 14-16 minutes, shaking once.

520. Tarragon & Garlic Roasted Chicken
INGREDIENTS (4 Servings)

1 chicken (around 3 lb)	2 tbsp butter, melted	1 lemon, cut into wedges
1 tsp fresh tarragon, chopped	Salt and black pepper to taste	1 garlic bulb

DIRECTIONS (Prep + Cook Time: 50 minutes) Preheat air fryer to 380 F. Brush the chicken with melted butter and season with salt and pepper. Put tarragon, garlic, and lemon into the cavity of the chicken and place in the air fryer basket. Bake for 40 minutes. Cover with foil and let rest for 10 minutes, then carve, and serve with fresh salad.

521. Honey-Glazed Turkey
INGREDIENTS (4 Servings)

1 ½ lb turkey tenderloins	½ tsp dried thyme	1 tbsp olive oil
¼ cup honey	½ tsp garlic powder	½ tbsp spicy brown mustard
2 tbsp Dijon mustard	½ onion powder	Salt and black pepper to taste

DIRECTIONS (Prep + Cook Time: 50 minutes)

Preheat air fryer to 375°F. Combine the honey, mustard, thyme, garlic powder, and onion powder in a bowl to make a paste. Season the turkey with salt and pepper, then spread the honey paste all over it. Put the turkey in the fryer basket and spray with olive oil, then air fry for 15 minutes. Turn it over and spray again before frying for 10-15 more minutes. Remove the turkey, cover loosely with foil and let stand 10 minutes before slicing. Serve and enjoy!

522. Turkey Tenderloins with Fattoush Salad
INGREDIENTS (4 Servings)

1 ½ lb turkey tenderloins	Salt and black pepper to taste	2 tbsp fresh mint, chopped
3 tbsp olive oil	1 tbsp lemon juice	6 radishes, thinly sliced
½ tsp paprika	1 tbsp pomegranate molasses	1 cucumber, deseeded and diced
½ tsp garlic powder	½ lb Roma tomatoes, chopped	5 oz pita crackers
½ tsp cayenne pepper	2 spring onions, sliced	

DIRECTIONS (Prep + Cook Time: 50 minutes)

In a bowl, mix the lemon juice, 2 tbsp of the olive oil, pomegranate molasses, and salt and whisk with a fork. Add in the tomatoes, spring onions, radishes, cucumber, fresh mint and toss to coat. Reserve. Preheat your Air Fryer to 375°F. Combine the paprika, garlic powder, salt, black pepper, and cayenne pepper in a small bowl, then rub the mixture all over the turkey. Put the turkey in the greased fryer basket and spray with olive oil, then air fry for 15 minutes. Turn it over and spray it again, then cook for 10-15 more minutes. Remove the turkey and let it sit for 5-8 minutes before slicing. Transfer the salad to a serving dish and top with pita crackers. Serve the turkey with the salad and enjoy!

523. Spice-Rubbed Jerk Chicken Wings
INGREDIENTS (4 Servings)

2 lb chicken wings	½ tsp allspice	3 tbsp lime juice
2 tbsp olive oil	1 habanero pepper, seeded	½ tbsp grated ginger
3 cloves garlic, minced	1 tbsp soy sauce	½ tbsp fresh thyme, chopped
1 tbsp chili powder	½ tbsp lemon pepper	⅓ tbsp sugar
½ tbsp cinnamon powder	¼ cup red wine vinegar	

DIRECTIONS (Prep + Cook Time: 25 minutes + marinating time) In a bowl, add olive oil, soy sauce, garlic, habanero pepper, allspice, cinnamon powder, chili powder, lemon pepper, sugar, thyme, ginger, lime juice, and red wine vinegar; mix well. Add the chicken wings to the mixture and toss to coat. Cover and refrigerate for 1 hour. Preheat air fryer to 380 F. Remove the chicken from the fridge, drain all the liquid, and pat dry with paper towels. Working in batches, cook the wings in the air fryer for 16 minutes in total. Shake once halfway through. Remove to a serving platter and serve with a blue cheese dip or ranch dressing.

524. Sweet Chili & Ginger Chicken Wings
INGREDIENTS (4 Servings)

- 1 lb chicken wings
- 1 tsp ginger root powder
- 1 tbsp tamarind powder
- ¼ cup sweet chili sauce

DIRECTIONS (Prep + Cook Time: 20 minutes)

Preheat air fryer to 390 F. Rub the chicken wings with tamarind and ginger root powders. Spray with cooking spray and place in the air fryer basket. Cook for 6 minutes. Slide-out the basket and cover with sweet chili sauce; cook for 8 more minutes. Serve warm.

525. Sweet Sesame Chicken Wings
INGREDIENTS (4 Servings)

- 1 lb chicken wings
- 2 tbsp sesame oil
- 1 tbsp maple syrup
- Salt and black pepper to taste
- 3 tbsp sesame seeds

DIRECTIONS (Prep + Cook Time: 25 minutes)

In a bowl, add wings, sesame oil, maple syrup, salt, and pepper and stir to coat. In another bowl, add the sesame seeds and roll up the wings in the seeds. Arrange the wings in an even layer inside your air fryer and cook for 12 minutes at 360 F, turning once halfway through. Serve.

526. Chicken Meatballs with Farfalle Pasta
INGREDIENTS (6 Servings)

- 1 lb ground chicken
- 3 tbsp olive oil
- 4 oz fresh spinach, chopped
- ½ cup panko bread crumbs
- ¼ tsp garlic powder
- 1 egg, beaten
- ⅓ cup feta cheese, crumbled
- 8 oz farfalle pasta, cooked
- 2 cups marinara sauce
- Salt and black pepper to taste

DIRECTIONS (Prep + Cook Time: 50 minutes)

Preheat air fryer to 360 F. Warm 2 tbsp of the olive oil in a large skillet over medium heat and add the spinach. Season with salt and cook for 2-3 minutes or until the spinach has wilted. Set aside. Mix the panko breadcrumbs, salt, pepper, and garlic powder in a bowl. Add the egg, ground chicken, spinach, and feta and stir to combine. Shape the mixture into 1-inch balls. Arrange them in a single layer on the greased fryer basket and spray with the remaining olive oil. Air fry for 7 minutes, shake them, and cook another 5-8 minutes or until golden. Serve the chicken meatballs on farfalle pasta and spoon over the marinara sauce. Enjoy!

527. Crispy Breaded Chicken Breasts
INGREDIENTS (4 Servings)

- 4 chicken breasts, sliced
- 1 tbsp Worcestershire sauce
- ¼ cup onions, chopped
- 1 tbsp brown sugar
- ¼ cup yellow mustard
- ½ cup ketchup

DIRECTIONS (Prep + Cook Time: 20 minutes)

Preheat air fryer to 360 F. In a bowl, mix sugar, 1 cup of water, ketchup, onions, mustard, Worcestershire sauce, and salt. Place the chicken into the mixture and let marinate for 10 minutes. Transfer the chicken to the frying basket and AirFry for 15 minutes, flipping once. Serve with the sauce.

528. Spanish-Style Crusted Chicken Fingers
INGREDIENTS (2 Servings)

- 2 chicken breasts, cut into strips
- Salt and black pepper to taste
- 1 tsp garlic powder
- 3 tbsp cornstarch
- 4 tbsp breadcrumbs
- 4 tbsp Manchego cheese, grated
- 1 egg, beaten

DIRECTIONS (Prep + Cook Time: 25 minutes + marinating time)

Mix salt, garlic, and black pepper in a bowl. Add in chicken and stir to coat. Marinate for 1 hour in the fridge. Mix the breadcrumbs with Manchego cheese evenly. Remove the chicken from the fridge, lightly toss in cornstarch, dip in egg and coat them gently in the cheese mixture. Preheat air fryer to 350 F. Place the chicken in the greased frying basket and Bake for 15 minutes, shaking once until nice and crispy. Serve with a side of vegetable fries. Yummy!

529. Crispy Chicken Tenderloins
INGREDIENTS (4 Servings)

8 chicken tenderloins   2 tbsp butter, melted   1 cup seasoned breadcrumbs

DIRECTIONS (Prep + Cook Time: 15 minutes)

Preheat air fryer to 380 F. Dip the chicken in the eggs, then coat with the seasoned crumbs. Coat the air fryer basket with some butter and place in the chicken. Brush with the remaining butter and cook for 14-16 minutes, shaking once halfway through. Serve with your favorite dip.

530. Herby Chicken Schnitzels with Mozzarella
INGREDIENTS (2 Servings)

2 chicken breasts   2 tbsp mixed herbs   1 cup breadcrumbs
2 eggs, beaten   2 cups mozzarella cheese, grated
4 tbsp tomato sauce   1 cup flour ¾ cup ham, shaved

DIRECTIONS (Prep + Cook Time: 25 minutes)

Flatten out each piece of the chicken breast using a rolling pin Place the chicken between 2 plastic sheets; flatten out it using a rolling pin. Place the eggs, flour, and crumbs in 3 different bowls. Coat the chicken in the flour, followed by the eggs, and finally the crumbs. Preheat air fryer to 350 F. Put the chicken in the greased frying basket and AirFry for 10 minutes. Remove them to a plate and top with ham, tomato sauce, mozzarella cheese, and mixed herbs. Return to the fryer and AirFry further for 5 minutes or until the mozzarella cheese melts. Serve warm.

531. Gluten-Free Crunchy Chicken
INGREDIENTS (4 Servings)

2 garlic cloves, minced   1 cup potato flakes   ½ cup mayonnaise
1 lb chicken breasts, sliced   Salt and black pepper to taste   1 lemon, zested
½ tsp dried thyme   ½ cup cheddar cheese, grated

DIRECTIONS (Prep + Cook Time: 25 minutes)

Preheat air fryer to 350 F. In a bowl, mix garlic, potato flakes, cheddar cheese, thyme, lemon zest, salt, and pepper. Brush the chicken with mayonnaise, then roll in the potato mixture. Place in the greased air fryer basket and AirFry for 18-20 minutes, shaking once halfway through. Serve warm.

532. Prosciutto-Wrapped Chicken Breasts
INGREDIENTS (2 Servings)

2 chicken breasts   Salt and black pepper to taste   2 brie cheese slices
1 tbsp olive oil   1 cup semi-dried tomatoes, sliced   4 thin prosciutto slices

DIRECTIONS (Prep + Cook Time: 25 minutes)

Preheat air fryer to 370 F. Put the chicken breasts on a chopping board and cut a small incision deep enough to make stuffing possible. Insert 1 slice of brie cheese and 4-5 tomato slices into each cut. Lay the prosciutto on the chopping board. Put the chicken on one side and roll the prosciutto over the breast, making sure that both ends of the prosciutto meet under the chicken. Drizzle with olive oil and sprinkle with salt and pepper. Place the chicken in the frying basket and Bake for 14-16 minutes, turning once halfway through. Slice each chicken breast in half and serve.

533. Gingery Chicken Wings
INGREDIENTS (4 Servings)

8 chicken drumsticks   1 tbsp honey   1 small knob fresh ginger, grated
1 tbsp olive oil   3 tbsp light soy sauce   2 tbsp black sesame seeds, toasted
1 tbsp sesame oil   2 crushed garlic clove

DIRECTIONS (Prep + Cook Time: 25 minutes)

Preheat air fryer to 400 F. Add all ingredients to a freezer bag, except for sesame seeds. Seal up and massage until the drumsticks are well coated. Place the drumsticks in the basket and cook for 10 minutes. Flip and cook for 10 more minutes. Sprinkle with sesame seeds and serve.

534. Air Fried Chicken Bowl with Black Beans
INGREDIENTS (4 Servings)

- 4 chicken breasts, cubed
- 1 can sweet corn
- 1 can black beans, rinsed and drained
- 1 cup red and green peppers, stripes, cooked
- 1 tbsp vegetable oil
- 1 tsp chili powder

DIRECTIONS (Prep + Cook Time: 18 minutes)

Coat the chicken with salt, black pepper, and a bit of oil. AirFry for 15 minutes at 380 F. In a deep skillet, pour 1 tbsp of oil and stir in chili powder, corn, peppers, and beans. Add a little bit of hot water and keep stirring for 3 minutes. Transfer the veggies to a serving platter and top with the fried chicken.

535. Rosemary & Oyster Chicken Breasts
INGREDIENTS (2 Servings)

- 2 chicken breasts
- 1 tbsp ginger paste
- 2 fresh rosemary sprigs, chopped
- 2 lemon wedges
- 1 tbsp soy sauce
- 1 tbsp olive oil
- 1 tbsp oyster sauce
- 1 tbsp brown sugar

DIRECTIONS (Prep + Cook Time: 25 minutes + marinating time)

Add ginger, soy sauce, and olive oil in a bowl. Add in the chicken and mix to coat well. Cover the bowl and refrigerate for 30 minutes. Preheat air fryer to 370 F. Transfer the marinated chicken to a baking dish and Bake in the fryer for 6 minutes. Mix oyster sauce, rosemary, and brown sugar in a bowl. Pour the sauce over the chicken. Return to the air fryer and Bake for 10 minutes. Remove the rosemary and serve with lemon wedges.

536. French-Style Chicken Thighs
INGREDIENTS (4 Servings)

- 1 tbsp herbes de Provence
- 1 lb bone-in, skinless chicken thighs
- Salt and black pepper to taste
- 2 garlic cloves, minced
- ½ cup honey
- ¼ cup Dijon mustard
- 2 tbsp butter
- 2 tbsp fresh dill, chopped

DIRECTIONS (Prep + Cook Time: 20 minutes)

Preheat air fryer to 390 F. In a bowl, mix herbes de Provence, salt, and pepper. Rub onto the chicken. Transfer to the greased air fryer basket and Bake for 15 minutes, flipping once halfway through. Melt butter in a saucepan over medium heat. Stir in honey, mustard, and garlic; cook until reduced to a thick consistency, about 3 minutes. Serve the chicken drizzled with the honey-mustard sauce.

537. Chicken Thighs with Parmesan Crust
INGREDIENTS (4 Servings)

- ½ cup Italian breadcrumbs
- 2 tbsp Parmesan cheese, grated
- 1 tbsp butter, melted
- 4 chicken thighs
- ½ cup marinara sauce
- ½ cup Monterrey jack cheese, shredded

DIRECTIONS (Prep + Cook Time: 25 minutes)

Preheat air fryer to 380 F. In a bowl, mix the crumbs with Parmesan cheese. Brush the thighs with butter. Dip each thigh into the crumb mixture. Arrange them on the greased air fryer basket. AirFry for 6-7 minutes at 380 F, flip, top with marinara sauce and shredded Monterrey Jack cheese, and continue to cook for another 4-5 minutes. Serve immediately

538. Thai Chicken Satay
INGREDIENTS (4 Servings)

- 1 lb chicken drumsticks
- 2 cloves garlic, minced
- 2 tbsp sesame oil
- ½ cup Thai peanut satay sauce
- 1 lime, zested and juiced
- 2 tbsp sesame seeds, toasted
- 4 scallions, chopped 1 red chili, sliced

DIRECTIONS (Prep + Cook Time: 25 minutes + marinating time)

In a bowl, mix the satay sauce, sesame oil, garlic, lime zest, and juice. Add in the chicken and toss to coat. Place in the fridge for 2 hours to marinate. Preheat air fryer to 380 F. Transfer the marinated chicken to the frying basket and AirFry for 18-20 minutes, flipping once halfway through. Garnish with sesame seeds, scallions, and red chili and serve.

539. Chicken & Baby Potato Traybake
INGREDIENTS (4 Servings)

1 lb chicken drumsticks, skin on and bone-in

3 shallots, quartered

Salt and black pepper to taste

1 tbsp cayenne pepper

1 lb baby potatoes, halved ½ tsp garlic powder

2 tbsp olive oil 1 cup cherry tomatoes

DIRECTIONS (Prep + Cook Time: 20 minutes)

Preheat air fryer to 360 F. Place the chicken in a baking tray and add in shallots, potatoes, oil, garlic powder, salt, and pepper; toss to coat. Place the tray in the fryer and Bake for 18-20 minutes, shaking once. Slide the basket out and add in the cherry tomatoes. Cook for another 5 minutes until charred.

540. Asian Sticky Chicken Wingettes
INGREDIENTS (4 Servings)

1 lb chicken wingettes

1 tbsp fresh cilantro, chopped

Salt and black pepper to taste

1 tbsp roasted peanuts, chopped

½ tbsp apple cider vinegar

1 garlic clove, minced

½ tbsp chili sauce

1 ginger, minced

1 ½ tbsp soy sauce

½ tbsp honey

DIRECTIONS (Prep + Cook Time: 25 minutes)

Preheat air fryer to 360 F. Season chicken wingettes with salt and pepper. In a bowl, mix ginger, garlic, chili sauce, honey, soy sauce, cilantro, and vinegar. Cover chicken with the mixture. Transfer to the air fryer basket and cook for 14-16 minutes, shaking once. Serve sprinkled with peanuts.

541. Portuguese Roasted Whole Chicken
INGREDIENTS (4 Servings)

1 (3 lb) whole chicken

1 lime, juiced

Portuguese seasoning:

Salt and black pepper to taste

1 tsp chili powder

1 tsp garlic powder

1 tsp oregano

1 tsp ground coriander

1 tsp cumin 2 tbsp olive oil

1 tsp paprika

DIRECTIONS (Prep + Cook Time: 50 minutes + marinating time)

In a bowl, pour oregano, garlic powder, chili powder, coriander, paprika, cumin, black pepper, salt, and olive oil and mix well. Rub onto the chicken and refrigerate the chicken for 20 minutes to marinate. Preheat air fryer to 350 F. Remove the chicken from the fridge, place it breast side down in the greased frying basket, and Bake for 30 minutes. After, flip the chicken breast-side up and continue cooking for 10-15 minutes. When over, let it rest for 10 minutes, then drizzle with lime juice and serve.

542. Turkey Burgers with Cabbage Slaw
INGREDIENTS (4 Servings)

1 lb ground turkey

¼ cup bread crumbs

1 tbsp olive oil

¼ cup hoisin sauce

4 buns

2 green onions, sliced

1 cup cabbage slaw

1 cup cherry tomatoes, halved

DIRECTIONS (Prep + Cook Time: 60 minutes)

Preheat air fryer to 375°F. Mix the turkey, breadcrumbs, and hoisin sauce in a bowl and create 4 equal patties. Put the patties in a single layer in the greased fryer basket, spray with olive oil, and air fry for 10 minutes. Turn the patties, spray with oil again, and cook for 5-10 more minutes or until golden. Put the burgers on buns and top with cherry tomatoes, green onions, and cabbage slaw. Serve and enjoy!

543. Turkey & Veggie Skewers
INGREDIENTS (4 Servings)

1 lb turkey breast, cubed

2 tbsp fresh rosemary, chopped

Salt and black pepper to taste

1 green bell pepper, cut into chunks

1 red bell pepper, cut into chunks

1 cup cherry tomatoes

1 red onion, cut into wedges

DIRECTIONS (Prep + Cook Time: 20 minutes)

Preheat air fryer to 350 F. Spray the air fryer basket with cooking spray. In a bowl, mix the turkey, salt, and black pepper. Thread the vegetables and turkey cubes alternately onto skewers. Spray with cooking spray and transfer to the frying basket. Bake for 15 minutes, flipping once halfway through. Serve sprinkled with fresh rosemary.

544. Turkey Strips with Garlic Mushrooms
INGREDIENTS (4 Servings)

2 lb portobello mushrooms, sliced	½ tsp garlic powder	2 tsp herbs
1 lb turkey breast strips	2 tbsp olive oil	Salt and black pepper to taste

DIRECTIONS (Prep + Cook Time: 20 minutes + marinating time)

In a bowl, mix turkey, mushrooms, olive oil, garlic powder, salt, pepper, and herbs and pour in vermouth. Mix to coat. Let marinate for 15 minutes. Preheat air fryer to 350 F. Place the turkey and mushrooms in a greased baking dish and Bake for 13-15 minutes, shaking once. Serve warm.

545. Chipotle Buttered Turkey
INGREDIENTS (4 Servings)

1 lb turkey breast, sliced	½ tsp chipotle chili pepper	1 stick butter, melted
2 cups panko breadcrumbs	Salt and black pepper to taste	

DIRECTIONS (Prep + Cook Time: 25 minutes)

In a bowl, combine panko and chipotle chili pepper. Sprinkle turkey with salt and black pepper, and brush with some butter. Coat the turkey with the panko mixture. Transfer to the frying basket dish and top with butter. AirFry for 10 minutes at 390 F. Shake, drizzle the remaining butter, and Bake for 5 more minutes, until nice and crispy. Serve with enchilada sauce.

546. Thai Tom Yum Wings
INGREDIENTS (2 Servings)

8 chicken wings	½ cup flour	2 tbsp tom yum paste
1 tbsp water	2 tbsp cornstarch	½ tbsp baking powder

DIRECTIONS (Prep + Cook Time: 20 minutes + marinating time)

Combine the tom yum paste and water in a small bowl. Place the wings in a large bowl, add the tom yum mixture, and mix to coat well. Cover the bowl and refrigerate for 2 hours. Preheat air fryer to 370 F. Mix baking powder, cornstarch, and flour. Dip the wings in the starch mixture. Place on the greased frying basket and AirFry for 7-8 minutes. Flip and cook for 5-6 minutes. Serve.

547. Sweet Curried Chicken Cutlets
INGREDIENTS (4 Servings)

1 lb chicken breasts, halved crosswise	½ tsp chili powder	½ tsp brown sugar
2 tbsp garlic mayonnaise	½ tsp curry powder	2 tbsp soy sauce

DIRECTIONS (Prep + Cook Time: 35 minutes + marinating time)

Put the chicken halves between 2 pieces of plastic wrap and gently pound them to ¼-inch thickness using a rolling pin. In a bowl, mix in soy sauce, brown sugar, curry powder, and chili powder. Add in the chicken and toss to coat. Cover with plastic wrap and refrigerate for 1 hour. Preheat air fryer to 350 F. Remove the chicken from the marinade and place it in the greased frying basket. AirFry for 8 minutes, flip, and cook further for 6 more minutes. Serve with garlic mayonnaise.

548. Almond-Fried Crispy Chicken
INGREDIENTS (4 Servings)

4 chicken breasts, cubed	3 whole eggs	Salt and black pepper to taste
2 cups almond meal	½ cup cornstarch	1 tbsp cayenne pepper

DIRECTIONS (Prep + Cook Time: 20 minutes)

Preheat air fryer to 350 F. In a bowl, mix salt, pepper, cornstarch, and cayenne pepper and coat the chicken. In another bowl, beat the eggs. In a third bowl, pour almond meal. Dredge chicken in the egg, then in almond meal, and place in the greased frying basket. AirFry for 14-16 minutes, shaking once.

549. Chicken Thighs with Herby Tomatoes
INGREDIENTS (2 Servings)

- 2 chicken thighs
- 2 ripe tomatoes, sliced
- 2 cloves garlic, minced
- ¼ tbsp dried tarragon
- ¼ tbsp olive oil
- ¼ tsp red pepper flakes
- Salt and black pepper to taste

DIRECTIONS (Prep + Cook Time: 25 minutes)

Preheat air fryer to 390 F. Add the tomatoes, red pepper flakes, tarragon, garlic, and olive oil to a bowl. Mix well. Season the chicken with salt and pepper and place in a greased baking dish. Bake in the fryer for 14 minutes, flipping once. Top with tomato mixture and Bake for 5 more minutes. Serve warm.

550. Chicken Quarters with Broccoli & Rice
INGREDIENTS (4 Servings)

- 4 chicken legs
- 1 cup long-grain rice
- 1 cup broccoli florets, chopped
- Salt and black pepper to taste
- 1 can condensed cream chicken soup
- 1 garlic clove, minced

DIRECTIONS (Prep + Cook Time: 30 minutes)

Preheat air fryer to 390 F. Season the chicken with salt and pepper and place in the greased air fryer basket. AirFry for 10 minutes, flipping once halfway through. Place a pot over medium heat and pour in the rice, 1 cup of water, garlic, and chicken soup; bring to a boil. Reduce the heat and simmer for 10 minutes. Fluff with a fork and add in broccoli. Spread the rice mixture on the bottom of a baking dish and top with chicken. Put in the air fryer and Bake for 5 minutes.

551. BBQ Whole Chicken
INGREDIENTS (3 Servings)

- 1 whole small chicken, cut into pieces
- Salt to taste
- ½ tsp smoked paprika
- ½ tsp garlic powder
- 1 cup BBQ sauce

DIRECTIONS (Prep + Cook Time: 35 minutes)

Mix salt, paprika, and garlic powder and coat the chicken pieces. Place in the air fryer basket and Bake for 18 minutes at 400 F. Remove to a plate and brush with barbecue sauce. Wipe the fryer clean from the chicken fat. Return the chicken to the fryer, skin-side up, and Bake for 5 more minutes at 340 F.

552. Whole Chicken with Prunes
INGREDIENTS (4-6 Servings)

- 1 (3 lb) whole chicken
- ½ cup prunes, pitted
- 3 garlic cloves, minced
- 2 tbsp capers
- 2 bay leaves
- 2 tbsp red wine vinegar
- 2 tbsp olive oil
- 1 tbsp dried oregano
- 1 tbsp brown sugar
- 1 tbsp chopped parsley
- Salt and black pepper to taste

DIRECTIONS (Prep + Cook Time: 55 minutes)

Preheat air fryer to 360 F. In a bowl, mix prunes, olives, capers, garlic, olive oil, bay leaves, oregano, wine vinegar, salt, and pepper. Spread the mixture on the bottom of a baking dish and place the chicken breast side down on top. Bake for 30 minutes in the fryer, turn it, breast side up, and sprinkle a little bit of brown sugar on top; cook for 10-15 minutes. Let sit for a few minutes before serving.

553. Thyme Turkey Nuggets
INGREDIENTS (2 Servings)

- ½ lb ground turkey
- 1 egg, beaten
- 1 cup breadcrumbs
- ½ tsp dried thyme
- ½ tsp fresh parsley, chopped
- Salt and black pepper to taste

DIRECTIONS (Prep + Cook Time: 20 minutes)

Preheat air fryer to 350 F. In a bowl, mix ground turkey, thyme, parsley, salt, and pepper. Shape the mixture into balls. Dip in the breadcrumbs, then in egg, and in the crumbs again. Place the nuggets in the air fryer basket, spray with cooking spray and AirFry for 12-14 minutes, shaking once. Serve hot.

554. Sticky Chicken Wings with Coleslaw
INGREDIENTS (2 Servings)

10 chicken wings	1 tsp tomato paste	½ white cabbage, shredded
2 tbsp hot chili sauce	Salt and black pepper to taste	1 carrot, grated
½ tbsp balsamic vinegar	4 tbsp mayonnaise	1 green onion, sliced
1 tbsp pomegranate molasses	½ cup yogurt	2 tbsp fresh parsley, chopped
1 tsp brown sugar	1 tbsp lemon juice	

DIRECTIONS (Prep + Cook Time: 20 minutes + marinating time)

Mix balsamic vinegar, pomegranate molasses, brown sugar, tomato paste, hot chili sauce, salt, and pepper in a bowl. Coat the chicken wings in the mixture, cover, and refrigerate for 30 minutes. In a salad bowl, combine the cabbage, carrot, green onion, and parsley and mix well. In a small bowl, whisk the mayonnaise, yogurt, lemon juice, salt, and pepper. Pour over the coleslaw and mix to combine. Keep in the fridge until ready to use. Preheat air fryer to 350 F. Put the chicken in the air fryer basket and AirFry for 15 minutes, turning once halfway through. Serve with the chilled coleslaw

555. .Hot Chili Chicken Wings
INGREDIENTS (2 Servings)

8 chicken wings	½ cup white wine	1-inch fresh ginger, grated
1 cup cornflour	1 tsp chili paste	1 tbsp olive oil

DIRECTIONS (Prep + Cook Time: 25 minutes + marinating time)

Preheat air fryer to 360 F. In a bowl, mix ginger, chili paste, and wine. Add in the chicken wings and marinate for 30 minutes. Remove the chicken, drain, and coat with cornflour. Brush with olive oil and place in the frying basket. AirFry for 14-16 minutes, shaking once until crispy on the outside. Serve

556. Italian Parmesan Wings with Herbs
INGREDIENTS (4 Servings)

1 lb chicken wings	2 cloves garlic, minced	Salt and black pepper to taste
¼ cup butter	½ tsp dried oregano	¼ tsp paprika
¼ cup Parmesan cheese, grated	½ tsp dried rosemary	

DIRECTIONS (Prep + Cook Time: 20 minutes)

Preheat air fryer to 370 F. Place the chicken on a plate and season with salt and pepper. Put in the greased air fryer basket and AirFry for 7-8 minutes, flipping once. Remove to a greased baking dish. Melt butter in a skillet over medium heat and cook garlic for 1 minute. Stir in paprika, oregano, and rosemary for another minute. Pour the mixture over the chicken, sprinkle with Parmesan cheese, and Bake in the air fryer for 5 minutes. Serve immediately.

557. Homemade Chicken Patties
INGREDIENTS (4 Servings)

1 lb ground chicken	1 egg, beaten	½ tbsp paprika
½ onion, chopped	½ cup breadcrumbs	½ tbsp coriander seeds, crushed
2 garlic cloves, chopped	½ tsp cumin	Salt and black pepper to taste

DIRECTIONS (Prep + Cook Time: 20 minutes)

In a bowl, mix chicken, onion, garlic, egg, breadcrumbs, cumin, paprika, coriander, salt, and black pepper. Use your hands to shape into 4 patties. Arrange on the greased air fryer basket and Bake for 10-12 minutes at 380 F, turning once halfway through. Serve and enjoy!

558. Rice Krispies Chicken Goujons
INGREDIENTS (2 Servings)

2 chicken breasts, cut into strips	½ cup rice Krispies	1 tbsp butter, melted
Salt and black pepper to taste	1 egg, beaten	
½ tsp tarragon	½ cup plain flour	

DIRECTIONS (Prep + Cook Time: 20 minutes)

Preheat air fryer to 390 F. Line the frying basket with baking paper and grease. Sprinkle the chicken with salt and pepper. Roll the strips in flour, then dip in the egg, and finally coat with rice Krispies. Place the strips in air fryer, drizzle with melted butter, and AirFry for 12-14 minutes, shaking once. Serve hot.

559. Chicken Pinchos with Salsa Verde
INGREDIENTS (4 Servings)

4 chicken breasts, cut into large cubes	1 tbsp maple syrup	1 green pepper, cut into sticks
Salt to taste	½ cup soy sauce	8 mushrooms, halved
1 tsp chili powder	2 red peppers, cut into sticks	2 tbsp sesame seeds

Salsa Verde:

1 garlic clove	1 lime	A bunch of skewers
2 tbsp olive oil Zest and juice from	¼ cup fresh parsley, chopped	

DIRECTIONS (Prep + Cook Time: 35 minutes)

In a bowl, mix chili powder, salt, maple syrup, soy sauce, and sesame seeds and toss in the chicken to coat. Start stacking up the ingredients, alternately, on skewers: red pepper, green pepper, a chicken cube, and a mushroom half, until the skewer is fully loaded. Repeat the process for all the ingredients. Preheat air fryer to 330 F. Brush the pinchos with soy sauce mixture and place them into the frying basket. Grease with cooking spray and cook for 20 minutes, flipping once halfway through. Blend all the salsa verde ingredients in a food processor until you obtain a chunky paste. Taste and adjust the seasoning with salt. Arrange the pinchos on a platter and serve with the salsa verde. Enjoy!

560. Crispy Chicken Tenders with Hot Aioli
INGREDIENTS (4 Servings)

1 lb chicken breasts, cut into strips	Salt and black pepper to taste	½ cup mayonnaise
4 tbsp olive oil	½ tbsp garlic powder	2 tbsp lemon juice
1 cup breadcrumbs	½ tbsp cayenne pepper	½ tbsp ground chili

DIRECTIONS (Prep + Cook Time: 20 minutes)

Preheat air fryer to 390 F. Mix breadcrumbs, salt, pepper, garlic powder, and cayenne pepper and spread onto a plate. Brush the chicken strips with some olive oil. Roll them in the breadcrumb mixture until well coated. Arrange the strips on a greased air fryer basket in an even layer and Bake for 12 minutes, turning once halfway through. To prepare the hot aioli: place the mayo with the lemon juice and ground chili in a small bowl and whisk to combine well. Serve with the chicken tenders and enjoy!

561. Juicy Chicken Fillets with Peppers
INGREDIENTS (2 Servings)

2 chicken fillets, cubed	½ tbsp ginger paste	1 red bell pepper, seeded, cut into strips
Salt and black pepper to taste	½ tbsp garlic paste	1 green bell pepper, seeded, cut into strips
1 cup flour	1 tbsp sugar	1 tbsp paprika
2 eggs	1 red chili, minced	4 tbsp water
½ cup apple cider vinegar	2 tbsp tomato puree	

DIRECTIONS (Prep + Cook Time: 35 minutes)

Preheat air fryer to 350 F. Pour the flour in a bowl, add in eggs, salt, and black pepper and whisk. Put chicken cubes in the flour mixture; mix to coat and place them in the frying basket. Spray with cooking spray and AirFry for 8 minutes. Shake the basket, and cook for 7 more minutes until golden and crispy. In a bowl, add water, apple cider vinegar, sugar, ginger paste, garlic paste, red chili, tomato puree, and paprika; mix with a fork. Place a skillet over medium heat and spray with cooking spray. Add the red and green pepper strips. Stir and cook until the peppers are sweaty but still crunchy. Pour the chili mixture over, stir, and simmer for 10 minutes. Serve the chicken drizzled with pepper-chili sauce.

562. Jerusalem Matzah & Chicken Schnitzels
INGREDIENTS (4 Servings)

4 chicken breasts	2 tbsp Parmesan cheese, grated	½ cup fine matzah meal
1 cup panko breadcrumbs	6 sage leaves, chopped	2 beaten eggs

DIRECTIONS (Prep + Cook Time: 10 minutes)

Pound the chicken to ¼-inch thickness using a rolling pin. In a bowl, add Parmesan cheese, sage, and breadcrumbs. Toss chicken with matzah meal, dip in eggs, then coat well with bread crumbs. Preheat air fryer to 390 F. Spray both sides of chicken breasts with cooking spray and AirFry in the frying basket for 14-16 minutes, turning once halfway through until golden. Serve warm.

563. Crumbed Sage Chicken Scallopini
INGREDIENTS (4 Servings)

4 chicken breasts	2 tbsp Parmesan cheese, grated	1 tbsp fresh sage, chopped
3 oz breadcrumbs	2 oz flour 2 eggs, beaten	1 lemon, cut into wedges

DIRECTIONS (Prep + Cook Time: 12 minutes) Preheat air fryer to 370 F. Place some plastic wrap underneath and on top of the breasts. Using a rolling pin, beat the meat until it becomes skinny. In a bowl, combine Parmesan cheese, sage, and breadcrumbs. Dip the chicken in the egg first, and then in the flour. Spray with cooking spray and AirFry for 14-16 minutes, flipping once halfway through. Serve with lemon wedges.

564. Creamy Asiago Chicken
INGREDIENTS (4 Servings)

4 chicken breasts, cubed	1 cup mayonnaise	Salt and black pepper to taste
½ tsp garlic powder	½ cup Asiago cheese, grated	2 tbsp fresh basil, chopped

DIRECTIONS (Prep + Cook Time: 25 minutes) Preheat air fryer to 380 F. In a bowl, mix Asiago cheese, mayonnaise, garlic powder, and salt. Add in the chicken and toss to coat. Place the coated chicken in the greased frying basket. Bake for 15 minutes, shaking once. Serve sprinkled with freshly chopped basil.

565. Hawaiian-Style Chicken
INGREDIENTS (4 Servings)

4 chicken breasts, cubed	½ tbsp ginger, minced	½ cup pineapple juice
2 garlic cloves, minced	½ cup soy sauce	2 tbsp apple cider vinegar
½ cup ketchup	2 tbsp sherry	½ cup brown sugar

DIRECTIONS (Prep + Cook Time: 20 minutes + marinating time)

Preheat air fryer to 360 F. In a bowl, mix in ketchup, pineapple juice, sugar, apple vinegar, and ginger. Heat the sauce in a pan over low heat. Cover the chicken with the soy sauce and sherry; pour the hot sauce on top. Let sit for 15 minutes. Place the chicken in the air fryer and cook for 15 minutes. Serve.

566. Creamy Onion Chicken
INGREDIENTS (4 Servings)

4 chicken breasts, cubed	1 cup mushroom soup
1 ½ cups onion soup mix	½ cup heavy cream

DIRECTIONS (Prep + Cook Time: 20 minutes + marinating time)

Preheat air fryer to 400 F. Warm mushroom soup, onion mix, and heavy cream in a frying pan over low heat for 1 minute. Pour the mixture over the chicken and let sit for 25 minutes. Transfer the chicken to the air fryer and Bake for 15 minutes, shaking once. Serve topped with the remaining sauce.

567. Garlicky Chicken on Green Bed
INGREDIENTS (2 Serving)

½ cup baby spinach	1 chicken breast, cut into cubes	1 garlic clove, minced
½ cup romaine lettuce, shredded	2 tbsp olive oil	Salt and black pepper to taste
3 large kale leaves, chopped	1 tsp balsamic vinegar	

DIRECTIONS (Prep + Cook Time: 20 minutes) Preheat air fryer to 390 F. In a bowl, add chicken, 1 tbsp olive oil, salt, garlic, and black pepper; mix well. Pour the mixture into a baking dish and fit in the fryer. Bake for 14 minutes. In a bowl, mix the greens, remaining olive oil, and balsamic vinegar and toss to coat. Place the chicken on top and serve.

568. Cauli-Oat Crusted Drumsticks
INGREDIENTS (4 Servings)

8 chicken drumsticks	2 oz oats	1 tsp ground cayenne pepper
½ tsp dried oregano	10 oz cauliflower florets, steamed	Salt and black pepper to taste
½ tsp dried thyme	1 egg	

DIRECTIONS (Prep + Cook Time: 25 minutes)

Preheat air fryer to 350 F. Rub the drumsticks with salt and pepper. Place all remaining ingredients, except for the egg, in a food processor. Process until smooth. Dip each drumstick in the egg first and then in the oat mixture. Arrange them on the frying basket and AirFry for 14-16 minutes, flipping once.

569. Hot Green Curry Chicken Drumsticks
INGREDIENTS (4 Servings)

4 chicken drumsticks, boneless, skinless	3 tbsp coconut cream	½ fresh habanero pepper, finely chopped
2 tbsp green curry paste	Salt and black pepper to taste	2 tbsp fresh parsley, roughly chopped

DIRECTIONS (Prep + Cook Time: 25 minutes) In a bowl, mix green curry paste, coconut cream, salt, black pepper, and habanero pepper. Add in the chicken drumsticks and toss to coat. Arrange the drumsticks in the greased air fryer and Bake for 13-16 minutes at 400 F, flipping once halfway through. Serve sprinkled with fresh parsley.

570. Chicken Asian Lollipop
INGREDIENTS (4 Servings)

1 lb mini chicken drumsticks	1 garlic clove, minced	1 egg, beaten
½ tbsp soy sauce	½ tbsp chili powder	1 tbsp flour
1 tbsp lime juice	½ tbsp fresh cilantro, chopped	1 tbsp maple syrup
Salt and black pepper to taste	½ tbsp garlic-ginger paste	
1 tbsp cornstarch	1 tbsp plain vinegar	

DIRECTIONS (Prep + Cook Time: 20 minutes)

Mix garlic-ginger paste, chili powder, maple syrup, soy sauce, cilantro, vinegar, egg, garlic, and salt in a bowl. Add the chicken and toss to coat. Stir in cornstarch, flour, and lime juice. Preheat air fryer to 350 F. Place the drumsticks in the greased frying basket and AirFry for 5-7 minutes. Turn and continue cooking for 5 more minutes. Remove to a serving platter and serve with tomato dip.

571. Whole Chicken with Sage & Garlic
INGREDIENTS (4 Servings)

1 (3 lb) whole chicken	1 cup breadcrumbs	1 onion, chopped
2 tbsp olive oil	⅓ cup sage, chopped	3 tbsp butter
Salt and black pepper to taste	4 cloves garlic, crushed	2 eggs, beaten

DIRECTIONS (Prep + Cook Time: 50 minutes) Melt butter in a pan over medium heat and sauté garlic and onion until browned, about 5 minutes. Add in eggs, sage, black pepper, and salt; mix well. Cook for 20 seconds and turn the heat off. Fill the chicken cavity with the mixture. Tie the legs with a butcher's twine and brush with olive oil. Rub the top and sides of the chicken generously with salt and black pepper. Preheat air fryer to 390 F. Place the chicken into the frying basket and Bake for 25 minutes. Turn the chicken over and continue cooking for 10-15 more minutes, checking regularly to ensure it doesn't dry or overcooks. After, wrap in aluminum foil and let rest for 10 minutes. Carve and serve.

572. Moroccan Turkey Meatballs
INGREDIENTS (6 Servings)

½ cup couscous	2 garlic cloves, minced	1 tsp sriracha sauce
1 cucumber, chopped	½ cup panko bread crumbs	Salt and black pepper to taste
1 egg, beaten	1 tbsp soy sauce ¼ cup +	
1 lb ground turkey	1 tbsp hoisin sauce	

DIRECTIONS (Prep + Cook Time: 30 minutes) In a bowl, mix couscous and 1 cup of boiling water. Cover and let sit for 8-10 minutes. Fluff with a fork. Preheat air fryer to 360 F. Mix the turkey, panko breadcrumbs, egg, soy sauce, 1 tablespoon of hoisin sauce, garlic, salt, and black pepper in a bowl. Make small balls with a tablespoon. Combine the remaining hoisin sauce and sriracha in a small bowl to make a glaze and set aside. Put the meatballs in the greased fryer basket in a single later and air fry for 8 minutes. Generously brush the meatballs with the glaze and cook 4-7 more minutes until cooked through. Season the couscous with salt and mix with the cucumber. Top with the meatballs and serve.

573. Parmesan Turkey Meatballs
INGREDIENTS (4 Servings)

1 lb ground turkey	1 tbsp garlic powder	¼ cup Parmesan cheese
1 egg	1 tbsp Italian seasoning	Salt and black pepper to taste
½ cup breadcrumbs	1 tbsp onion powder	

DIRECTIONS (Prep + Cook Time: 25 minutes)

Preheat air fryer to 400 F. In a bowl, mix ground turkey, egg, breadcrumbs, garlic powder, onion powder, Italian seasoning, Parmesan cheese, salt, and pepper. Make bite-sized balls out of the mixture. Add the balls to the greased frying basket and AirFry for 12-14 minutes, shaking once halfway through

574. Roasted Turkey with Brussels Sprouts
INGREDIENTS (6 Servings)

2 lb turkey breast	2 tsp Dijon mustard	Salt and black pepper to taste
2 garlic cloves, minced	1 ½ tsp rosemary	
1 tbsp olive oil	1 lb Brussels sprouts, halved	

DIRECTIONS (Prep + Cook Time: 60 minutes) Preheat your Air Fryer to 375°F. Mix the garlic, olive oil, Dijon mustard, rosemary, sage, thyme, salt, and pepper in a bowl and make a paste. Smear the paste all over the turkey breast. Put the turkey breast in the greased fryer basket and air fry for 20 minutes. Turn it over and baste it with any drippings from the bottom drawer. Add in the Brussels sprouts and air fry for 20 more minutes. Let the turkey sit for 10 minutes before slicing. Serve with Brussels sprouts.

575. Turkey Stuffed Bell Peppers
INGREDIENTS (4 Servings)

2 tbsp olive oil	1 (7-oz) can black beans, drained and rinsed	1 tsp chili powder
½ lb ground turkey		½ tsp ground cumin
4 bell peppers, stems and seeds removed	1 cup cooked long-grain brown rice	2 tbsp chopped fresh cilantro
1 cup mozzarella cheese, shredded	½ cup kernel corn	Salt and black pepper to taste
	1 cup mild salsa	

DIRECTIONS (Prep + Cook Time: 35 minutes)
Preheat air fryer to 360 F. Warm the olive oil in a large skillet over medium heat. Cook the turkey, breaking it up, until browned, about 5-6 minutes. Drain any excess fat and set aside. Combine the browned turkey, black beans, cheddar cheese, rice, corn, salsa, chili powder, salt, cumin, and black pepper in a bowl, then spoon the mixture into the bell peppers. Put the stuffed peppers in the greased fryer basket. Bake for about 10-15 minutes. Garnish with cilantro and serve.

576. Greek-Style Chicken Wings
INGREDIENTS (4 Servings)

1 lb chicken wings	1 tbsp cashew butter	1 tsp honey
1 tbsp fresh parsley, chopped	1 garlic clove, minced	½ tbsp vinegar
Salt and black pepper to taste	1 tbsp yogurt	½ tbsp garlic chili sauce

DIRECTIONS (Prep + Cook Time: 25 minutes)
Preheat air fryer to 360 F. Season the wings with salt and pepper and AirFry in the greased frying basket for 15 minutes, shaking once. In a bowl, mix the remaining ingredients. Transfer the wings to a greased baking dish, top with sauce, and cook in the air fryer basket for 5 minutes. Serve warm.

577. Authentic Mongolian Chicken Wings
INGREDIENTS (4 Servings)

1 lb chicken wings	4 tbsp canola oil	1 tbsp apple cider vinegar
1 cup flour	Salt and black pepper to taste	1 tbsp honey
1 cup breadcrumbs	2 tbsp sesame seeds	1 tbsp soy sauce
3 eggs, beaten	2 tbsp red pepper paste	

DIRECTIONS (Prep + Cook Time: 15 minutes) Preheat air fryer to 350 F. Separate the chicken wings into winglets and drummettes. In a bowl, mix salt, olive oil, and black pepper. Coat the chicken with flour, dip in the beaten eggs, and then in the breadcrumbs. Place the chicken in the frying basket and AirFry for 15 minutes, shaking once. Mix red pepper paste, vinegar, soy sauce, honey, and ¼ cup of water in a saucepan and bring to a boil. Simmer for 5-7 minutes until thickened. Pour the chicken over and sprinkle with sesame seeds. Serve.

578. Chicken & Jalapeño Quesadilla
INGREDIENTS (4 Servings)

8 tortillas	½ cup cooked chicken, shredded	1 beaten egg, to seal tortillas
2 cups Monterey Jack cheese, shredded	1 cup canned fire-roasted jalapeño peppers, chopped	

DIRECTIONS (Prep + Cook Time: 20 minutes)
Preheat air fryer to 390 F. Divide chicken, cheese, and jalapeño peppers between 4 tortillas. Seal the tortillas with beaten egg. Grease with cooking spray. In batches, place in the air fryer basket and Bake for 12 minutes, turning once halfway through. Serve with green salsa.

579. Spiced Chicken Tacos
INGREDIENTS (6 Servings)

1 tbsp buffalo sauce

2 cups shredded cooked chicken

8 oz cream cheese, softened

1 tbsp olive oil

1 tsp ground cumin

½ tsp smoked paprika

12 flour tortillas

DIRECTIONS (Prep + Cook Time: 25 minutes)

Preheat air fryer to 360 F. Stir the cream cheese and Buffalo sauce in a bowl until well-combined, then add the chicken and stir some more. On a clean workspace, lay the tortillas out flat and spoon 2-3 tablespoons of the chicken mixture down each tortilla center. Sprinkle with cumin and smoked paprika. Roll them up and put them in the air fryer, seam side down. Spray each tortilla with olive oil and air fry 5-10 minutes or until lightly golden and crisp. Arrange the tacos on plates and serve.

580. Chicken Fingers with Red Mayo Dip
INGREDIENTS (4 Servings)

1 lb chicken breasts, cut into finger-sized strips

1 tbsp olive oil

½ tsp paprika

½ tsp garlic powder

½ cup seasoned bread crumbs

1 tsp dried parsley

Salt and black pepper to taste

½ cup mayonnaise

2 tbsp ketchup

½ tsp garlic powder

½ tsp sweet chili sauce

DIRECTIONS (Prep + Cook Time: 35 minutes)

Preheat air fryer to 375 F. Toss the chicken with salt, pepper, paprika, and garlic powder in a bowl, coating the chicken evenly. Add olive oil and toss again. Mix the breadcrumbs and parsley in a shallow bowl and coat each piece of chicken.

Put the chicken in a single layer in the greased basket. AirFry for 10 minutes. Turn the chicken over, spray with olive oil again, and cook for 8-10 more minutes until golden and crisp. In a bowl, whisk the mayonnaise, ketchup, garlic powder, chili sauce, salt, and pepper. Pour the dip into a serving bowl and serve with the chicken fingers. Enjoy!

581. Harissa Chicken Sticks
INGREDIENTS (4 Servings)

4 chicken tenders, cut into strips

½ tsp ground cumin seeds

1 tbsp harissa powder

Salt and black pepper to taste

4 cup panko breadcrumbs

1 tbsp fresh parsley, chopped

2 large eggs, beaten

DIRECTIONS (Prep + Cook Time: 20 minutes)

Preheat air fryer to 400 F. In a bowl, mix breadcrumbs, harissa powder, cumin, salt, and black pepper. Dip the chicken strips in eggs and dredge in the harissa-crumb mixture. Place in the greased frying basket and AirFry for 15 minutes, flipping once halfway through. Serve immediately. Yummy!

582. Balsamic Chicken with Green Beans
INGREDIENTS (4 Servings)

1 lb chicken breasts, sliced

1 lb green beans, trimmed

¾ cup balsamic vinegar

2 tbsp olive oil

1 lb cherry tomatoes, halved

1 garlic clove, minced

DIRECTIONS (Prep + Cook Time: 40 minutes + marinating time)

In a bowl, add ½ cup of balsamic vinegar and chicken and stir to coat. Refrigerate for at least 1 hour. Preheat air fryer to 375 F. Mix the green beans, garlic, cherry tomatoes, and the remaining balsamic vinegar in a bowl and toss until well coated.

Put the veggies in the greased fryer basket and air fry for 8 minutes. Shake the basket and fry for 5-7 more minutes until the beans are crisp and tender and the tomatoes are soft and slightly charred.

Remove and cover with foil to keep warm. Spray the fryer basket with olive oil. Put the chicken in a single layer in the fryer basket and air fry for 7 minutes. Flip the chicken and cook for 5-8 more minutes. Serve the chicken with the veggies.

583. Chicken Breasts en Papillote
INGREDIENTS (4 Servings)

1 lb chicken breasts

2 tbsp butter, melted

Salt and black pepper to taste

½ tsp dried marjoram

DIRECTIONS (Prep + Cook Time: 25 minutes)

Preheat air fryer to 380 F. Place each chicken breast on a 12x12 inches aluminum foil wrap, and season with salt and black pepper. Top with marjoram and butter and wrap the foil around the breasts in a loose way to create a flow of air. Bake the in the fryer for 15 minutes. Unwrap, let cool, and serve.

584. Chicken Teriyaki
INGREDIENTS (4 Servings)

1 lb chicken tenderloins	½ tsp dried thyme	2 cups steamed broccoli florets
⅓ cup soy sauce	½ tsp cayenne pepper	1 tsp ground black pepper
⅓ cup honey	½ tsp ground allspice	1 tbsp fresh cilantro, chopped
3 tbsp white vinegar 1	2 cups cooked brown rice	2 green onions, chopped

DIRECTIONS (Prep + Cook Time: 20 minutes)
Mix soy sauce, honey, white vinegar, thyme, black pepper, cayenne pepper, and allspice in a bowl to make a marinade. Toss the tenderloins in the marinade to coat. Cover and refrigerate for 30 minutes. Preheat air fryer to 380 F. Remove the chicken the marinade; keep the marinade for later. Put the chicken in a single layer in the greased fryer basket and air fry for 6 minutes. Turn the chicken and brush with the remaining marinade. Cook for 5-7 more minutes. Divide the brown rice, steamed broccoli, and chicken tenderloins between 4 bowls. Top with cilantro and green onions and serve immediately.

585. Paprika Chicken Breasts
INGREDIENTS (4 Servings)

4 chicken breasts	¼ tsp garlic powder	2 tbsp butter, melted
Salt and black pepper to taste	1 tbsp paprika	2 tbsp fresh thyme, chopped

DIRECTIONS (Prep + Cook Time: 25 minutes)
Preheat air fryer to 360 F. Grease the frying basket with cooking spray. Rub the chicken with salt, black pepper, garlic powder, and paprika. Brush with butter. Place in the air fryer and AirFry for 15 minutes, flipping once halfway through cooking. Let cool slightly, then slice, and sprinkle with thyme to serve.

586. Spinach Loaded Chicken Breasts
INGREDIENTS (4 Servings)

1 cup spinach, chopped	2 chicken breasts Juice of	2 tbsp olive oil
4 tbsp cottage cheese, crumbled	½ lime 2 tbsp Italian seasoning	

DIRECTIONS (Prep + Cook Time: 15 minutes)
Preheat air fryer to 390 F. Grease the basket with cooking spray. Mix spinach and cottage cheese in a bowl. Halve the breasts with a knife and flatten them with a meat mallet. Season with Italian seasoning. Divide the spinach/cheese mixture between the chicken pieces. Roll up to form cylinders and use toothpicks to secure them. Brush with olive oil and place them in the frying basket. Bake for 7-8 minutes, flip, and cook for 6 minutes. Serve warm.

587. Caprese Chicken with Balsamic Sauce
INGREDIENTS (4 Servings)

4 chicken breasts, cubed	¼ cup balsamic vinegar	1 tbsp butter, melt
6 basil leaves, chopped	4 tomato slices	4 fresh mozzarella cheese slices

DIRECTIONS (Prep + Cook Time: 25 minutes + marinating time)
Preheat the air fryer to 400 F. Mix butter and balsamic vinegar and pour it over the chicken in a bowl. Let marinate for 30 minutes. Place the chicken in the frying basket and AirFry for 14-16 minutes, shaking once. Serve topped with basil, tomato, and fresh mozzarella cheese slices

588. Double Cheese Marinara Chicken
INGREDIENTS (2 Servings)

2 chicken fillets,	½ cup breadcrumbs	2 tbsp Grana Padano cheese, grated
½-inch thick	Salt and black pepper to taste	2 mozzarella cheese slices
1 egg, beaten	2 tbsp marinara sauce	

DIRECTIONS (Prep + Cook Time: 15 minutes)
Dip the fillets in the egg, then in the crumbs, and arrange on a greased baking dish. AirFry in the frying basket for 7-8 minutes at 400 F. Turn, top with marinara sauce, Grana Padano and mozzarella cheeses, and bake further for 5-6 more minutes. Serve warm.

589. Buttermilk Chicken Thighs
INGREDIENTS (4 Servings)

- 1 ½ lb chicken thighs
- ½ tbsp cayenne pepper
- Salt and black pepper to taste
- 1 cup flour
- ½ tsp paprika
- ½ tsp baking powder
- 2 cups buttermilk

DIRECTIONS (Prep + Cook Time: 25 minutes + marinating time)

Place the chicken thighs in a bowl. Stir in cayenne, salt, pepper, and buttermilk. Refrigerate for 2 hours. Preheat air fryer to 350 F. In another bowl, mix flour, paprika, salt, and baking powder. Dredge the chicken thighs in the flour, and then place them on a lined baking dish. Bake inside the fryer for 16-18 minutes, flipping once halfway through cooking. Serve hot.

590. Chicken Thighs with Marinara Sauce
INGREDIENTS (4 Servings)

- ½ cup panko breadcrumbs
- 2 tbsp Parmesan cheese, grated
- Salt and black pepper to taste
- 1 tbsp olive oil
- 1 tsp Italian seasoning
- 4 chicken thighs
- ½ cup spicy marinara sauce
- ½ cup mozzarella cheese

DIRECTIONS (Prep + Cook Time: 15 minutes)

Preheat air fryer to 350 F. In a bowl, combine breadcrumbs, Italian seasoning, and Parmesan cheese. Coat the chicken with olive oil, salt, and pepper. Dip in the breadcrumb/cheese mixture; shake off any excess. Place the thighs in the greased fryer and AirFry for 6-8 minutes. Slide the basket out and top with marinara sauce and mozzarella cheese. Slide back in, and cook for another 4-5 minutes. Serve.

591. Sweet & Sticky Chicken Drumsticks
INGREDIENTS (2 Servings)

- 2 chicken drumsticks, skin removed
- 2 tbsp canola oil
- 1 tbsp Agave nectar
- 1 garlic clove, minced

DIRECTIONS (Prep + Cook Time: 20 minutes + marinating time)

Add all ingredients to a resealable bag and massage until well-coated. Allow the chicken to marinate for 30 minutes. Preheat the air fryer to 380 F. Add the chicken to the frying basket and Bake for 15 minutes, shaking once. Serve warm

592. Whole Roasted Chicken
INGREDIENTS (4 Servings)

- 1 (3.5-ounce) whole chicken
- 2 tbsp olive oil
- 1 tsp garlic powder
- 1 tsp paprika
- ½ tsp oregano
- Salt and black pepper to taste
- 1 lemon, cut into quarters
- 5 garlic cloves

DIRECTIONS (Prep + Cook Time: 65 minutes)

In a bowl, combine olive oil, garlic powder, paprika, oregano, salt, and pepper, and mix well to make a paste. Rub the chicken with the paste and stuff lemon and garlic cloves into the cavity. Place the chicken in the air fryer, breast side down, and tuck the legs and wings tips under. Bake for 45 minutes at 360 F. Flip the chicken to breast side up and cook for another 15-20 minutes. Let rest for 5-6 minutes, then carve, and serve.

593. Turkey Fingers with Cranberry Glaze
INGREDIENTS (4 Servings)

- 1 lb turkey breast, cut into strips
- 1 tbsp chicken seasoning
- Salt and black pepper to taste
- ½ cup cranberry sauce

DIRECTIONS (Prep + Cook Time: 20 minutes)

Preheat air fryer to 390 F. Season the turkey with chicken seasoning, salt, and pepper. Spray with cooking spray and AirFry in the frying basket for 10-12 minutes, flipping once halfway through. Put a saucepan over low heat, and add the cranberry sauce and ¼ cup of water. Simmer for 5 minutes, stirring continuously. Serve the turkey drizzled with cranberry sauce. Yummy!

594. Quinoa Chicken Nuggets
INGREDIENTS (4 Servings)

2 chicken breasts, cut into bite-size chunks	½ cup flour 1 egg	Salt and black pepper to taste
½ cup cooked quinoa, cooled	½ tsp cayenne pepper	

DIRECTIONS (Prep + Cook Time: 15 minutes)

In a bowl, beat the egg with salt and black pepper. Spread flour on a plate and mix with cayenne pepper. Coat the chicken in flour, then in the egg, shake off and place in the quinoa. Press firmly such quinoa sticks on the chicken pieces. Spray with cooking spray and AirFry the nuggets in the greased frying basket for 14-16 minutes at 360 F, turning once halfway through. Serve hot.

595. Chicken Skewers with Yogurt Dip
INGREDIENTS (4 Servings)

1 lb chicken tenderloins	1 tbsp honey	2 tbsp fresh cilantro, chopped	8 wooden skewer, soaked in water for 30 minutes
1 tsp ground ginger	1 tbsp toasted sesame oil	1 lime, zested and juiced	
¼ cup soy sauce	2 tsp toasted sesame seeds	2 tbsp sweet chili sauce	
1 tbsp white vinegar	4 tbsp Greek yogurt		

DIRECTIONS (Prep + Cook Time: 20 minutes + marinating time)

Combine the soy sauce, white vinegar, honey, sesame oil, lime juice, and ginger in a zip-top bag to make a marinade. Toss the chicken in the bag, seal it, and put it in the fridge for a minimum of 2 hours to as long as overnight to marinate. Combine the Greek yogurt, cilantro, lime zest, and the remaining lime juice in a small bowl and mix to combine. Keep in the fridge until ready to use. Preheat air fryer to 380 F. Skewer each tenderloin on the wooden skewer and sprinkle with sesame seeds. Keep the excess marinade. Put the skewers in a single layer in the greased fryer basket and air fry for 6 minutes, flip the chicken, baste with more marinade, and cook 5-8 more minutes or until crispy. Serve the skewers hot with the yogurt dip on the side.

596. Tex-Mex Seasoned Chicken
INGREDIENTS (4 Servings)

3 mixed bell peppers, cut into chunks	1 lb chicken tenderloins, cut into strips	2 tbsp cilantro, chopped
1 red onion, sliced	1 tbsp olive oil	1 tbsp taco seasoning

DIRECTIONS (Prep + Cook Time: 25 minutes)

Preheat air fryer to 375 F. Mix the chicken, bell peppers, onion, 1 tbsp olive oil, and fajita seasoning mix in a large bowl and stir until the chicken is coated. Put the chicken and veggies in the greased fryer basket and spray with olive oil. Air fry for 7 minutes, shake the basket, and cook for 5-8 minutes, making sure the chicken is thoroughly cooked, and the veggies are starting to char. Serve topped with cilantro.

597. Popcorn Chicken Tenders
INGREDIENTS (4 Servings)

1 lb chicken tenders, cut into strips	½ cup panko breadcrumbs	½ tsp dried oregano	Salt and black pepper to taste
	2 eggs	2 tbsp butter, melted	
½ cup cooked popcorn	4 tbsp cornflour		

DIRECTIONS (Prep + Cook Time: 20 minutes)

Preheat the air fryer to 400 F. Pulse the popcorn in a blender until crumbs-like texture. In a bowl, combine the cornflour, oregano, salt, and black pepper. In another bowl, beat the eggs with some salt. In a third, mix panko crumbs with popcorn crumbs. Dip the chicken strips in the flour, then in the egg, and then coat with the breadcrumbs. Place in the air fryer basket. Drizzle with the melted butter and AirFry for 12-14 minutes, flipping once halfway through. Serve.

598. Cajun Chicken Tenders
INGREDIENTS (4 Servings)

1 lb chicken breasts, sliced	1 cup flour	½ tbsp garlic powder	1 tbsp Cajun seasoning
3 eggs	2 tbsp olive oil	1 tbsp salt	¼ cup milk

DIRECTIONS (Prep + Cook Time: 25 minutes)

Season the chicken with salt, black pepper, garlic powder, and Cajun seasoning. Pour the flour on a plate. In another bowl, whisk the eggs, milk, and olive oil. Preheat air fryer to 370 F. Line a baking sheet with parchment paper. Dip the chicken into the egg mixture, and then in the flour. Arrange on the sheet and Bake in the fryer for 12 minutes, shaking once

599. Greek Chicken Gyros
INGREDIENTS (4 Servings)

2 chicken breasts, cut into strips

Salt and black pepper to taste

1 cup flour

1 egg, beaten

½ cup breadcrumbs

4 flatbreads

2 cups white cabbage.

shredded 3 tbsp Greek yogurt dressing

DIRECTIONS (Prep + Cook Time: 20 minutes)

Preheat air fryer to 380 F. Spray the air fryer basket with cooking spray. Season the chicken with taco seasoning, salt, and black pepper. In 3 separate bowls, add breadcrumbs to one bowl, flour to another, and beaten egg to a third bowl. Dredge chicken in flour, then in egg, and then in the breadcrumbs. Spray with cooking spray and transfer to the frying basket. AirFry for 12-14 minutes, flipping once halfway through. Fill the taco shells with chicken strips, cabbage, and yogurt dressing to serve.

600. Gruyère Chicken with Lemon
INGREDIENTS (4 Servings)

½ cup seasoned breadcrumbs

¼ cup Gruyere cheese, grated

1 lb chicken breasts

½ cup flour

2 eggs, beaten

Salt and black pepper to taste

4 lemon slices

DIRECTIONS (Prep + Cook Time: 20 minutes)

Preheat air fryer to 370 F. Spray the air fryer basket with cooking spray. Mix the breadcrumbs with Gruyere cheese in a bowl, beat the eggs in another bowl, and add the flour to a third bowl. Toss the chicken in the flour, then in the eggs, and then in the breadcrumb mixture. Place in the frying basket and AirFry for 12-14 minutes. At the 6-minute mark, turn the chicken over. Once golden brown, remove to a plate and serve topped with lemon slices.

601. Lemony Chicken Breast
INGREDIENTS (2 Servings)

1 chicken breast

2 lemon, juiced and rind reserved

1 tbsp chicken seasoning

1 tbsp garlic puree

Salt and black pepper to taste

DIRECTIONS (Prep + Cook Time: 20 minutes)

Preheat the air fryer to 350 F. Place a silver foil sheet on a flat surface. Add all seasonings along with the lemon rind. Lay the chicken breast onto a chopping board and trim any fat. Season each side with the seasoning. Place in the silver foil sheet, seal, and flatten with a rolling pin. Place the breast in the basket and cook for 15 minutes, flipping once halfway through. Serve.

602. Apricot & Garlic Chicken Breasts
INGREDIENTS (4 Servings)

1 tsp yellow mustard

1 tbsp apricot jam

2 garlic cloves, minced

Salt and black pepper to taste

1 lb chicken breasts

3 tbsp butter, melted

DIRECTIONS (Prep + Cook Time: 22 minutes)

Preheat air fryer to 360 F. In a bowl, combine together mustard, butter, garlic, apricot jam, black pepper, and salt; mix well. Rub the chicken with the mixture and place it in the greased air fryer basket. Bake for 10 minutes, flip, and cook for 5-6 more minutes until crispy. Slice before serving.

603. Chicken Cheesy Divan Casserole
INGREDIENTS (4 Servings)

4 chicken breasts

Salt and black pepper to taste

1 cup cheddar cheese, shredded

1 broccoli head, cut into florets

½ cup cream of mushroom soup

½ cup croutons

DIRECTIONS (Prep + Cook Time: 30 minutes)

Preheat air fryer to 390 F. Rub the chicken breasts with salt and black pepper and place them in the greased frying basket. Bake for 14 minutes, flipping once. Let cool a bit and cut into bite-size pieces. To a bowl, add chicken pieces, broccoli florets, cheddar cheese, and mushroom soup cream; mix well. Scoop the mixture into a greased baking dish, add the croutons on top and spray with cooking spray. Put the dish in the frying basket and Bake for 10 minutes. Serve with a side of steamed greens.

604. Restaurant-Style Chicken with Yogurt
INGREDIENTS (4 Servings)

1 ¼ lb chicken tenders	1 tbsp fresh dill, chopped For Breading	½ cup all-purpose flour
1 cup Greek yogurt	2 whole eggs, beaten	Salt and black pepper to taste
1 tbsp lemon juice	½ cup breadcrumbs	2 tbsp olive oil

DIRECTIONS (Prep + Cook Time: 20 minutes)

Preheat air fryer to 380 F. Add breadcrumbs, eggs, and flour in three separate bowls. Season the chicken tenders with salt and pepper and dredge them first into flour, then into eggs, and finally into crumbs. AirFry them in the fryer for 10 minutes. Flip and cook for 5 more minutes until golden. Mix the yogurt with lemon juice, dill, salt, and pepper until smooth. Serve as a dip to the tenders.

605. Texas BBQ Chicken Thighs
INGREDIENTS (4 Servings)

8 chicken thighs	2 tsp Texas BBQ Jerky seasoning	2 tbsp fresh cilantro, chopped
Salt and black pepper to taste	1 tbsp olive oil	

DIRECTIONS (Prep + Cook Time: 30 minutes)

Preheat air fryer to 380 F. Grease the frying basket with cooking spray. Drizzle the chicken with olive oil, season with salt and black pepper, and sprinkle with BBQ seasoning. Place in the fryer and Bake for 15 minutes in total, flipping once. Top with fresh cilantro to serve.

606. Luscious Enchilada Chicken Thighs
INGREDIENTS (4 Servings)

4 chicken thighs, boneless	1 jalapeño pepper, finely chopped	Salt and black pepper to taste
2 garlic cloves, crushed	4 tbsp green enchilada sauce	

DIRECTIONS (Prep + Cook Time: 20 minutes)

In a bowl, add thighs, garlic, jalapeño pepper, enchilada sauce, salt, and pepper and stir to coat. AirFry the thighs in an even layer for 12-14 minutes at 380 F, turning once halfway through. Serve.

607. Honey Chicken Drumsticks
INGREDIENTS (2 Servings)

2 chicken drumsticks, skin removed	1 tsp honey
1 tbsp olive oil	½ tbsp garlic paste

DIRECTIONS (Prep + Cook Time: 50 minutes + marinating time)

Preheat air fryer to 400 F. Add garlic, oil, and honey in a zip bag. Add chicken and toss to coat; marinate for 30 minutes. Add the chicken to the air fryer basket and cook for 15 minutes, flipping once.

608. Easy Chicken Legs with Rice
INGREDIENTS (4 Servings)

1 lb chicken legs	3 tbsp butter, softened	1 onion, sliced
1 cup white rice	1 tbsp tomato paste	2 garlic cloves, minced
2 tomatoes, cubed	Salt and black pepper to taste	

DIRECTIONS (Prep + Cook Time: 40 minutes)

Brush chicken legs with butter. Sprinkle with salt and pepper and Bake in a greased baking dish in the air fryer for 12-14 minutes at 380 F, turning once halfway through cooking. Then, add onion, olive oil, tomatoes, tomato paste, and garlic, and cook for 5 more minutes. Meanwhile, in a pan, boil the rice in 2 cups of salted water for around 20 minutes. Serve with chicken.

609. Honey & Lemon-Glazed Stuffed Chicken
INGREDIENTS (6 Servings)

1 (3 lb) whole chicken

Stuffing:

2 red onions, chopped

2 tbsp olive oil

2 dry apricots, soaked and chopped

1 zucchini, chopped 1 apple, peeled and chopped

2 cloves finely chopped garlic

4 tbsp fresh thyme, chopped

Salt and black pepper to taste

Glaze:

5 oz honey Juice from

1 lemon 2 tbsp olive oil

Salt and black pepper to taste

DIRECTIONS (Prep + Cook Time: 55 minutes)

In a bowl, mix together all the stuffing ingredients. Fill the cavity of the chicken with the stuffing, without packing it tightly. Place the chicken breast-side down in the air fryer and Bake for 30 minutes at 380 F. Warm the honey and lemon juice in a large pan; season with salt and pepper. Slide the basket out and flip the chicken breast side up. Brush with some of the honey-lemon glaze and return to the fryer. Bake for another 15 minutes, brushing the chicken every 5 minutes with the glaze. Serve warm.

610. Greek-Style Whole Chicken
INGREDIENTS (4-6 Servings)

1 (3 lb) whole chicken, cut into pieces

3 garlic cloves, minced

2 tbsp olive oil

1 tbsp ouzo (anise-flavored aperitif)

1 tbsp fresh rosemary, chopped

1 tbsp fresh Greek oregano, chopped Juice from

1 lemon

Salt and black pepper to taste

DIRECTIONS (Prep + Cook Time: 45 minutes)

Preheat air fryer to 380 F. In a large bowl, combine garlic, ouzo, rosemary, olive oil, lemon juice, Greek oregano, salt, and pepper. Mix well and rub the mixture onto the chicken. Place the chicken in the dish, breast side down, and Bake in the fryer for 30-35 minutes. Turn the chicken, breast side up, and Broil for 10 more minutes. Let sit for a few minutes before carving.

611. Roasted Chicken with Pancetta & Thyme
INGREDIENTS (4 Servings)

1 (3,5 lb) whole chicken

1 lemon

4 slices pancetta, roughly chopped

1 onion, chopped 1 sprig fresh thyme, chopped

Salt and black pepper to taste

DIRECTIONS (Prep + Cook Time: 60 minutes)

In a bowl, mix pancetta, onion, thyme, salt, and black pepper. Insert the mixture into the chicken's cavity and press tight. Put the whole lemon in, and rub the top and sides of the chicken with salt and pepper. Transfer to the greased air fryer basket breast side down and Bake for 30 minutes at 360 F. Then, turn the breast side up, and bake for 15 more minutes until the skin is golden brown and crisp.

612. Chicken Parmigiana with Fresh Rosemary
INGREDIENTS (4 Servings)

1 lb chichen breasts, halved

1 cup seasoned breadcrumbs

½ cup Parmesan cheese, grated

Salt and black pepper to taste

2 eggs

2 sprigs rosemary, chopped

DIRECTIONS (Prep + Cook Time: 15 minutes)

Preheat air fryer to 380 F. Put the chicken halves on a clean flat surface and cover with clingfilm. Gently pound them to become thinner using a rolling pin. Beat the eggs in a bowl and season with salt and black pepper. In a separate bowl, mix breadcrumbs with Parmesan cheese. Dip the chicken in the eggs, then in the breadcrumbs. Spray with cooking spray and AirFry in the fryer for 6 minutes. Flip and cook for 6 more minutes. Sprinkle with rosemary and serve.

Pork Beff & Lamb

613. Pork Loin with Roasted Peppers
INGREDIENTS (3 Servings)

- 3 red bell peppers
- 1 ½ pounds pork loin
- 1 garlic clove, halved
- 1 teaspoon lard, melted
- 1/2 teaspoon cayenne pepper
- 1/4 teaspoon cumin powder
- 1/4 teaspoon ground bay laurel Kosher
- salt and ground black pepper, to taste

DIRECTIONS (Prep + Cook Time: 55 minutes)

Roast the peppers in the preheated Air Fryer at 395 degrees F for 10 minutes, flipping them halfway through the cooking time. Let them steam for 10 minutes; then, peel the skin and discard the stems and seeds. Slice the peppers into halves and add salt to taste. Rub the pork with garlic; brush with melted lard and season with spices until well coated on all sides. Place in the cooking basket and cook at 360 digress F for 25 minutes. Turn the meat over and cook an additional 20 minutes. Serve with roasted peppers. Enjoy!

614. Meatballs with Sweet and Sour Sauce
INGREDIENTS (3 Servings)

Meatballs:
- 1/2 pound ground pork
- 1/4 pound ground turkey
- 2 tablespoons scallions, minced
- 1/2 teaspoon garlic, minced
- 4 tablespoons tortilla chips, crushed
- 4 tablespoons parmesan cheese, grated
- 1 egg, beaten
- Salt and red pepper, to taste

Sauce:
- 6 ounces jellied cranberry
- 2 ounces hot sauce
- 2 tablespoons molasses
- 1 tablespoon wine vinegar

DIRECTIONS (Prep + Cook Time: 20 minutes)

In a mixing bowl, thoroughly combine all ingredients for the meatballs. Stir to combine well and roll the mixture into 8 equal meatballs. Cook in the preheated Air Fryer at 400 degrees F for 7 minutes. Shake the basket and continue to cook for 7 minutes longer. Meanwhile, whisk the sauce ingredients in a nonstick skillet over low heat; let it simmer, partially covered, for about 20 minutes. Fold in the prepared meatballs and serve immediately. Enjoy!

615. Korean Pork Bulgogi Bowl
INGREDIENTS (2 Servings)

- 2 pork loin chops
- 1 teaspoon stone-ground mustard
- 1 teaspoon cayenne pepper Kosher
- salt and ground black pepper, to taste
- 2 stalks green onion
- 1/2 teaspoon fresh ginger, grated
- 1 garlic clove, pressed
- 1 tablespoon rice wine
- 2 tablespoons gochujang chili paste
- 1 teaspoon sesame oil
- 1 tablespoon sesame seeds, lightly toasted

DIRECTIONS (Prep + Cook Time: 20 minutes)

Toss the pork loin chops with the mustard, cayenne pepper, salt and black pepper. Cook in the preheated Air Fryer at 400 degrees F for 10 minutes. Check the pork chops halfway through the cooking time. Add the green onions to the cooking basket and continue to cook for a further 5 minutes. In the meantime, whisk the fresh ginger, garlic, wine, gochujang chili paste and sesame oil. Simmer the sauce for about 5 minutes until thoroughly warmed. Slice the pork loin chops into bite-sized strips and top with green onions and sauce. Garnish with sesame seeds. Enjoy!

616. Pork and Mushroom Kabobs
INGREDIENTS (2 Servings)

- 1 pound pork butt, cut into bite-sized cubes
- 8 button mushrooms
- 1 red bell pepper, sliced
- 1 green bell pepper, sliced
- 2 tablespoons soy sauce
- 2 tablespoons lime juice
- Salt and black pepper, to taste

DIRECTIONS (Prep + Cook Time: 20 minutes)

Toss all ingredients in a bowl until well coated. Thread the pork cubes, mushrooms and peppers onto skewers. Cook in the preheated Air Fryer at 395 degrees F for 12 minutes, flipping halfway through the cooking time. Enjoy!

617. Chinese Five-Spice Pork Ribs
INGREDIENTS (3 Servings)

- 2 ½ pounds country-style pork ribs
- 1 teaspoon mustard powder
- 1 teaspoon cumin powder
- 1 teaspoon shallot powder
- 1 tablespoon Five-spice powder Coarse sea salt and ground black pepper
- 1 teaspoon sesame oil
- 2 tablespoons soy sauce

DIRECTIONS (Prep + Cook Time: 35 minutes)

Toss the country-style pork ribs with spices and sesame oil and transfer them to the Air Fryer cooking basket. Cook at 360 degrees F for 20 minutes; flip them over and continue to cook an additional 14 to 15 minutes. Drizzle with soy sauce just before serving. Enjoy!

618. Pork Cutlets with Pearl Onions
INGREDIENTS (2 Servings)

- 2 pork cutlets
- 1 teaspoon onion powder
- 1/2 teaspoon cayenne pepper Sea
- salt and black pepper, to taste
- 1/4 cup flour
- 1/4 cup Pecorino Romano cheese, grated
- 1 cup pearl onions

DIRECTIONS (Prep + Cook Time: 20 minutes)

Toss the pork cutlets with the onion powder, cayenne pepper, salt, black pepper, flour and cheese. Transfer the pork cutlets to the lightly oiled cooking basket. Scatter pearl onions around the pork. Cook in the preheated Air Fryer at 360 degrees for 15 minutes, turning over halfway through the cooking time. Enjoy!

619. Keto Crispy Pork Chops
INGREDIENTS (3 Servings)

- 3 center-cut pork chops, boneless
- 1/2 teaspoon paprika Sea salt and ground black pepper, to taste
- 1/4 cup Romano cheese, grated
- 1/4 cup crushed pork rinds
- 1/2 teaspoon garlic powder
- 1/2 teaspoon mustard seeds
- 1/2 teaspoon dried marjoram
- 1 egg, beaten 1 tablespoon buttermilk
- 1 teaspoon peanut oil

DIRECTIONS (Prep + Cook Time: 20 minutes)

Pat the pork chops dry with kitchen towels. Season them with paprika, salt and black pepper. Add the Romano cheese, crushed pork rinds, garlic powder, mustard seeds and marjoram to a rimmed plate. Beat the egg and buttermilk in another plate. Now, dip the pork chops in the egg, then in the cheese/pork rind mixture. Drizzle the pork with peanut oil. Cook in the preheated Air Fryer at 400 degrees F for 12 minutes, flipping pork chops halfway through the cooking time. Serve with keto-friendly sides such as cauliflower rice Enjoy!

620. Bacon with Onions Rings and Remoulade Sauce
INGREDIENTS (2 Servings)

- 2 thick bacon slices
- 8 ounces onion rings, frozen
- 1 teaspoon yellow mustard
- 2 tablespoons mayonnaise
- 1/4 teaspoon paprika
- 1 teaspoon hot sauce
- Salt and black pepper, to taste

DIRECTIONS (Prep + Cook Time: 15 minutes)

Place the slices of bacon and onion rings in the Air Fryer cooking basket. Cook the bacon and onion rings at 400 degrees F for 4 minutes; shake the basket and cook for a further 4 minutes or until cooked through. Meanwhile, make the Remoulade sauce by whisking the remaining ingredients. Arrange the bacon and onion rings on plates and garnish with Remoulade sauce. Enjoy!

621. Rustic Pizza with Ground Pork
INGREDIENTS (4 Servings)

- 1 (10-count) can refrigerator biscuits
- 4 tablespoons tomato paste
- 1 tablespoon tomato ketchup
- 2 teaspoons brown mustard
- 1/2 cup ground pork
- 1/2 cup ground beef sausage
- 1 red onion, thinly sliced
- 1/2 cup mozzarella cheese, shredded

DIRECTIONS (Prep + Cook Time: 30 minutes)

Spritz the sides and bottom of a baking pan with a nonstick cooking spray. Press five biscuits into the pan. Brush the top of biscuit with 2 tablespoons of tomato paste. Add 1/2 tablespoon of ketchup, 1 teaspoon of mustard, 1/4 cup of ground pork, 1/4 cup of beef sausage. Top with 1/2 of the red onion slices. Bake in the preheated Air Fryer at 360 degrees F for 10 minutes. Top with 1/4 cup of mozzarella cheese and bake another 5 minutes. Repeat the process with the second pizza. Slice the pizza into halves, serve and enjoy!

622. Easy Pork & Parmesan Meatballs
INGREDIENTS (3 Servings)

- 1 pound ground pork
- 2 tablespoons tamari sauce
- 1 teaspoon garlic, minced
- 2 tablespoons spring onions, finely chopped
- 1 tablespoon brown sugar
- 1 tablespoon olive oil
- 1/2 cup breadcrumbs
- 2 tablespoons parmesan cheese, preferably freshly grated

DIRECTIONS (Prep + Cook Time: 15 minutes)

Combine the ground pork, tamari sauce, garlic, onions, and sugar in a mixing dish. Mix until everything is well incorporated. Form the mixture into small meatballs. In a shallow bowl, mix the olive oil, breadcrumbs, and parmesan. Roll the meatballs over the parmesan mixture. Cook at 380 degrees F for 3 minutes; shake the basket and cook an additional 4 minutes or until meatballs are browned on all sides. enjoy!

623. Pork Shoulder with Molasses Sauce
INGREDIENTS (3 Servings)

- 2 tablespoons molasses
- 2 tablespoons soy sauce
- 2 tablespoons Shaoxing wine
- 2 garlic cloves, minced
- 1 teaspoon fresh ginger, minced
- 1 tablespoon cilantro stems and leaves, finely chopped
- 1 pound boneless pork shoulder
- 2 tablespoons sesame oil

DIRECTIONS (Prep + Cook Time: 25 minutes + Marinating Time)

In a large-sized ceramic dish, thoroughly combine the molasses, soy sauce, wine, garlic, ginger, and cilantro; add the pork shoulder and allow it to marinate for 2 hours in the refrigerator. Then, grease the cooking basket with sesame oil. Place the pork shoulder in the cooking basket; reserve the marinade. Cook in the preheated Air Fryer at 395 degrees F for 14 to 17 minutes, flipping and basting with the marinade halfway through. Let it rest for 5 to 6 minutes before slicing and serving. While the pork is roasting, cook the marinade in a preheated skillet over medium heat; cook until it has thickened. Brush the pork shoulder with the sauce and enjoy!

624. Boston Butt with Salsa Verde
INGREDIENTS (4 Servings)

- 1 pound Boston butt, thinly sliced across the grain into
- 2-inch-long strips
- 1/2 teaspoon red pepper flakes, crushed Sea
- salt and ground black pepper, to taste
- 1/2 pound tomatillos, chopped
- 1 small-sized onion, chopped
- 2 chili peppers, chopped
- 2 cloves garlic
- 2 tablespoons fresh cilantro, chopped
- 1 tablespoon olive oil
- 1 teaspoon sea salt

DIRECTIONS (Prep + Cook Time: 35 minutes)

Rub the Boston butt with red pepper, salt, and black pepper. Spritz the bottom of the cooking basket with a nonstick cooking spray. Roast the Boston butt in the preheated Air Fryer at 390 degrees F for 10 minutes. Shake the basket and cook another 10 minutes. While the pork is roasting, make the salsa. Blend the remaining ingredients until smooth and uniform. Transfer the mixture to a saucepan and add 1 cup of water. Bring to a boil; reduce the heat and simmer for 8 to 12 minutes. Serve the roasted pork with the salsa verde on the side. Enjoy!

625. Blade Steaks with Butter-Fried Broccoli
INGREDIENTS (4 Servings)

- 1 ½ pounds blade steaks skinless, boneless Kosher
- salt and ground black pepper, to taste
- 2 garlic cloves, crushed
- 2 tablespoons soy sauce
- 1 tablespoon oyster sauce
- 2 tablespoon lemon juice
- 1 pound broccoli, broken into florets
- 2 tablespoons butter, melted
- 1 teaspoon dried dill weed
- 2 tablespoons sunflower seeds, lightly toasted

DIRECTIONS (Prep + Cook Time: 30 minutes)

Start by preheating your Air Fryer to 385 degrees F. Spritz the bottom and sides of the cooking basket with cooking spray. Now, season the pork with salt and black pepper. Add the garlic, soy sauce, oyster sauce, and lemon juice. Cook for 20 minutes; turning over halfway through the cooking time. Toss the broccoli with the melted butter and dill. Add the broccoli to the cooking basket and cook at 400 degrees F for 6 minutes, shaking the basket periodically. Serve the warm pork with broccoli and garnish with sunflower seeds. Enjoy!

626. Party Pork and Bacon Skewers
INGREDIENTS (6 Servings)

- 1 cup cream of celery soup
- 1 (13.5-ounce) can coconut milk, unsweetened
- 2 tablespoons tamari sauce
- 1 teaspoon yellow mustard
- 1 tablespoon honey
- Salt and freshly ground white pepper, to taste
- 1/2 teaspoon cayenne pepper
- 1/2 teaspoon chili powder
- 1 teaspoon curry powder
- 2 pounds pork tenderloin, cut into bite-sized cubes
- 4 ounces bacon, cut into pieces
- 12 bamboo skewers, soaked in water

DIRECTIONS (Prep + Cook Time: 30 minutes + Marinating Time)

In a large pot, bring the cream of the celery soup, coconut milk, tamari sauce, mustard, honey, salt, white pepper, cayenne pepper, chili powder, and curry powder to a boil. Then, reduce the heat to simmer; cook until the sauce is heated through, about 13 minutes. Add the pork, gently stir, and place in your refrigerator for 2 hours. Thread the pork onto the skewers, alternating the cubes of meat with the pieces of bacon. Preheat your Air Fryer to 370 degrees F. Cook for 15 minutes, turning over a couple of times. Enjoy!

627. Pork Stuffed Peppers with Cheese
INGREDIENTS (3 Servings)

- 3 bell peppers, stems and seeds removed
- 1 tablespoon olive oil
- 3 scallions, chopped
- 1 teaspoon fresh garlic, minced
- 12 ounces lean pork, ground
- 1/2 teaspoon sea salt
- 1/2 teaspoon black pepper
- 1 tablespoon fish sauce
- 2 ripe tomatoes, pureed
- 3 ounces Monterey Jack cheese, grated

DIRECTIONS (Prep + Cook Time: 30 minutes)

Cook the peppers in boiling salted water for 4 minutes In a nonstick skillet, heat the olive oil over medium heat. Then, sauté the scallions and garlic until tender and fragrant. Stir in the ground pork and continue sautéing until the pork has browned; drain off the excess fat. Add the salt, black pepper, fish sauce, and 1 pureed tomato; give it a good stir. Divide the filling among the bell peppers. Arrange the peppers in a baking dish lightly greased with cooking oil. Place the remaining tomato puree around the peppers. Bake in the preheated Air Fryer at 380 degrees F for 13 minutes. Top with grated cheese and bake another 6 minutes. Serve warm and enjoy!

628. Festive Pork Fillets with Apples
INGREDIENTS (3 Servings)

- 1/4 cup chickpea flour
- 2 tablespoons Romano cheese, grated
- 1 teaspoon onion powder
- 1 teaspoon garlic powder
- 1/2 teaspoon ground cumin
- 1 teaspoon cayenne pepper
- 2 pork fillets (1 pound)
- 1 Granny Smiths apple, peeled and sliced
- 1 tablespoon lemon juice
- 1 ounce butter, cold

DIRECTIONS (Prep + Cook Time: 20 minutes)

Combine the flour, cheese, onions powder, garlic powder, cumin, and cayenne pepper in a ziploc bag; shake to mix well. Place the pork fillets in the bag. Shake to coat on all sides. Next, spritz the bottom of the Air Fryer basket with cooking spray. Cook in the preheated Air Fryer at 370 degrees F for 10 minutes. Add the apples and drizzle with lemon juice; place the cold butter on top and cook an additional 5 minutes. Serve immediately.

629. Pork Cutlets with Plum Sauce
INGREDIENTS (4 Servings)

- 4 pork cutlets
- 2 teaspoosn sesame oil
- 1/2 teaspoon ground
- black pepper Salt, to taste
- 1 tablespoon Creole seasoning
- 2 tablespoons aged balsamic vinegar
- 2 tablespoons soy sauce
- 6 ripe plums, pitted and diced

DIRECTIONS (Prep + Cook Time: 20 minutes)

Preheat your Air Fryer to 390 degrees F. Toss the pork cutlets with the sesame oil, black pepper, salt, Creole seasoning, vinegar, and soy sauce. Transfer them to a lightly greased baking pan; lower the pan onto the cooking basket. Cook for 13 minutes in the preheated Air Fryer, flipping them halfway through the cooking time. Serve warm.

630. Meatloaf Muffins with Sweet Potato Frosting
INGREDIENTS (4 Servings)

Meatloaf Muffins:

1 pound pork sausage, crumbled	1/2 cup oats	1 teaspoon dried basil
1 shallot, chopped	1/2 cup pasta sauce	Salt and ground black pepper, to taste
2 garlic cloves, minced	1 teaspoon dried oregano	1 egg

Sweet Potato Frosting:

1/2 pound sweet potatoes, cut into wedges	1/4 cup coconut milk	1 teaspoon salt
1/2 teaspoon garlic powder	1 tablespoon coconut oil	

DIRECTIONS (Prep + Cook Time: 1 hour)

Mix all ingredients for the meatloaf muffins until everything is well incorporated. Place the meat mixture in 4 cupcake liners. Bake at 220 degrees F for 23 minutes. Remove from the cooking basket and reserve keeping warm. Cook the sweet potatoes at 380 degrees F for 35 minutes, shaking the basket occasionally. When the sweet potatoes are cooled enough to handle, scoop out the flesh into a bowl. Add the garlic powder, coconut milk, coconut oil, and salt; mix to combine well. Beat with a wire whisk until everything is thoroughly mixed and fluffy. Pipe the potato mixture onto the sausage muffins using a pastry bag. Enjoy!

631. Tagliatelle al Ragu
INGREDIENTS (4 Servings)

1 tablespoon olive oil	1/2 pound ground pork	2 tablespoons cilantro leaves, chopped
1 shallot, chopped	1/2 pound smoked pork sausage, sliced	1 teaspoon dried basil
2 garlic cloves, minced	2 ripe medium-sized tomatoes, pureed	1 teaspoon dried oregano
2 bell peppers, sliced	2 tablespoons ketchup	Salt and ground black pepper, to taste
1 carrot, trimmed and sliced	1/4 cup red wine	1 package (16-ounce) tagliatelle

DIRECTIONS (Prep + Cook Time: 30 minutes)

Heat the oil in the baking pan at 380 degrees F. Then, sauté the shallots until tender about 4 minutes. Add the garlic, bell pepper, and carrots; cook an additional 2 minutes. Now, stir in ground pork and sausage and continue cooking for 5 minutes more, crumbling the meat with a spatula. Add tomato puree, ketchup, red wine, cilantro, basil, oregano, salt, and black pepper. Then, cook for 4 to 6 minutes longer or until everything is heated through. Meanwhile, bring a large pot of lightly salted water to a boil. Cook your tagliatelle for 10 to 12 minutes; drain. Top tagliatelle with the sauce and serve. Enjoy!

632. Greek Pork Loin with Tzatziki
INGREDIENTS (4 Servings)

Greek Pork:

2 pounds pork sirloin roast	1/2 teaspoon mustard seeds	1 teaspoon Ancho chili powder	2 tablespoons olive oil
Salt and black pepper, to taste	1/2 teaspoon celery seeds	1 teaspoon turmeric powder	2 cloves garlic, finely chopped
1 teaspoon smoked paprika	1 teaspoon fennel seeds	1/2 teaspoon ground ginger	

Tzatziki:

1/2 cucumber, finely chopped and squeezed	1 garlic clove, minced	1 teaspoon minced fresh dill
1 cup full-fat Greek yogurt	1 tablespoon extra virgin olive oil	A pinch of salt
	1 teaspoon balsamic vinegar	

DIRECTIONS (Prep + Cook Time: 55 minutes)

Toss all ingredients for Greek pork in a large mixing bowl. Toss until the meat is well coated. Cook in the preheated Air Fryer at 360 degrees F for 30 minutes; turn over and cook another 20 minutes. Meanwhile, prepare the tzatziki by mixing all the tzatziki ingredients. Place in your refrigerator until ready to use. Serve the pork sirloin roast with the chilled tzatziki on the side. Enjoy

633. Pork Ragout with Egg Noodles
INGREDIENTS (4 Servings)

- 2 pounds country pork ribs
- Sea salt, to your liking
- 1/2 teaspoon freshly cracked black pepper
- 1/2 teaspoon cayenne pepper
- 1 tablespoon yellow mustard
- 2 tablespoons sesame oil
- 1 shallot, diced
- 2 ripe tomatoes, pureed
- 1 cup vegetable broth
- 1/4 cup red wine
- 1 tablespoon fish sauce
- 1 tablespoon fresh lemon juice
- 1 teaspoon dried thyme
- 2 bay leaves
- 8 ounces egg noodles

DIRECTIONS (Prep + Cook Time: 50 minutes)

Place all ingredients, except the egg noodles, in a ceramic bowl; let it marinate at least 1 hour in your refrigerator. Discard the marinade and place the pork ribs in the lightly greased cooking basket. Cook at 365 degrees for 17 minutes. Turn the ribs over and cook an additional 14 to 15 minutes; reserve. Meanwhile, bring a large pot of lightly salted water to a boil. Cook the egg noodles for 10 to 12 minutes; drain and reserve, keeping warm. Then, heat the reserved marinade in a large nonstick skillet over a moderate flame; simmer the marinade for 5 to 7 minutes or until it has reduced by half. Add in the reserved meat and egg noodles; let it simmer an additional 3 to 4 minutes or until thoroughly heated. Enjoy!

634. Taco Casserole with Cheese
INGREDIENTS (4 Servings)

- 1 pound lean ground pork
- 1/2 pound ground beef
- 1/4 cup tomato puree Sea
- salt and ground black pepper, to taste
- 1 teaspoon smoked paprika
- 1/2 teaspoon dried oregano
- 1 teaspoon dried basil
- 1 teaspoon dried rosemary
- 2 eggs
- 1 cup Cottage cheese, crumbled, at room temperature
- 1/2 cup Cotija cheese, shredded

DIRECTIONS (Prep + Cook Time: 25 minutes)

Lightly grease a casserole dish with a nonstick cooking oil. Add the ground meat to the bottom of your casserole dish. Add the tomato puree. Sprinkle with salt, black pepper, paprika, oregano, basil, and rosemary. In a mixing bowl, whisk the egg with cheese. Place on top of the ground meat mixture. Place a piece of foil on top. Bake in the preheated Air Fryer at 350 degrees F for 10 minutes; remove the foil and cook an additional 6 minutes. Enjoy!

635. Ground Pork and Wild Rice Casserole
INGREDIENTS (3 Servings)

- 1 teaspoon olive oil
- 1 small-sized yellow onion, chopped
- 1 pound ground pork (84% lean)
- Salt and black pepper, to taste
- 1/2 cups cooked wild rice, uncooked
- 1/2 cup cream of mushroom soup
- 1/2 tomato paste
- 1 jalapeno pepper, minced
- 1 teaspoon Italian spice mix
- 1/2 cup Asiago cheese, shredded

DIRECTIONS (Prep + Cook Time: 25 minutes)

Start by preheating your Air Fryer to 350 degrees F. Heat the olive oil in a nonstick over medium-high heat. Then, sauté the onion and ground pork for 6 to 7 minutes, crumbling with a spatula. Season with salt and black pepper to your liking. Spoon the pork mixture into a lightly greased baking dish. Spoon the cooked rice over the pork layer. In a mixing dish, thoroughly combine the remaining ingredients. Bake for 15 minutes or until bubbly and heated through. Enjoy!

636. Fried Pork Loin Chops
INGREDIENTS (2 Servings)

- 1 egg
- 1/4 cup cornmeal
- 1/4 cup crackers, crushed
- 1/2 teaspoon garlic powder
- 1/2 teaspoon cayenne pepper
- Salt and black pepper, to taste
- 2 boneless pork loin chops, about 1-inch thick, 6 ounces each

DIRECTIONS (Prep + Cook Time: 15 minutes)

In a shallow mixing bowl, whisk the egg until pale and frothy. In another bowl, mix the cornmeal, crushed crackers, garlic powder, cayenne pepper, salt and black pepper. Dip each pork loin chop in the beaten egg. Then, roll them over the cornmeal mixture. Spritz the bottom of the cooking basket with cooking oil. Add the breaded pork cutlets and cook at 395 degrees F for 6 minutes. Flip and cook for 6 minutes on the other side. Serve warm.

637. Easy Munchy Pork Bites
INGREDIENTS (2 Servings)

- 1 pound pork stew meat, cubed
- 2 garlic cloves, crushed
- 1/4 cup dark rum
- 1/4 cup soy sauce
- 1 tablespoon lemon juice
- 1 tablespoon white vinegar
- 1 tablespoon olive oil
- 1/2 teaspoon sea salt
- 1 teaspoon mixed peppercorns
- 1/2 cup corn flakes, crushed

DIRECTIONS (Prep + Cook Time: 15 minutes + Marinating Time)

Place all ingredients, except for the cornflakes, in a ceramic dish. Stir to combine, cover and transfer to your refrigerator. Let it marinate at least 3 hours in your refrigerator. Discard the marinade and dredge the pork cubes in the crushed cornflakes, shaking off any residual coating. Now, cook the pork in your Air Fryer at 400 degrees F for 12 minutes. Shake the basket halfway through the cooking time. Serve warm.

638. Rustic Ground Pork-Stuffed Peppers
INGREDIENTS (4 Servings)

- 1 pound lean ground pork
- 1 small-sized shallot, chopped
- 2 cloves garlic, minced
- 2 tablespoons ketchup Sea
- salt and ground black pepper, to season
- 1/2 teaspoon cayenne pepper
- 4 bell peppers, tops and cores removed
- 1 teaspoon olive oil
- 1/2 cup Colby cheese, shredded

DIRECTIONS (Prep + Cook Time: 20 minutes)

Preheat a nonstick skillet over medium-high flame. Then, cook the pork and shallot for 3 minutes or until the meat is no longer pink. Add in the garlic and continue to cook until fragrant for 1 minute or so. Stir the ketchup into the skillet; season the meat mixture with salt, black pepper and cayenne pepper. Place the bell peppers cut side-up in the Air Fryer cooking basket and drizzle with oil. Spoon the meat mixture into each pepper. Cook in your Air Fryer at 360 degrees F for 12 minutes. Top with cheese and continue to bake for 4 minutes longer. Enjoy!

639. Country-Style Pork Goulash
INGREDIENTS (2 Servings)

- 1/2 pound pork stew meat, cut into bite-sized chunks
- 2 pork good quality sausages, sliced
- 1 small onion, sliced into rings
- 2 Italian peppers, sliced
- 1 Serrano pepper, sliced
- 2 garlic cloves, minced
- 1 tablespoon soy sauce
- 1/2 teaspoon ground cumin
- 1 bay leaf
- Salt and black pepper, to taste
- 1 cup beef stock

DIRECTIONS (Prep + Cook Time: 45 minutes)

Place the pork and sausage in the Air Fryer cooking basket. Cook the meat at 380 degrees F for 15 minutes, shaking the basket once or twice; place in a heavy-bottomed pot. Now, add the onion and peppers to the cooking basket; cook your vegetables at 400 degrees F for 10 minutes and transfer to the pot with the pork and sausage. Add in the remaining ingredients and cook, partially covered, for 15 to 20 minutes until everything is cooked through. Spoon into individual bowls and serve. Enjoy!

640. Delicious Chifa Chicharonnes
INGREDIENTS (4 Servings)

- 1/2 pound pork belly
- 2 cloves garlic, chopped
- 1 rosemary sprig, crushed
- 1 thyme sprig, crushed
- 1 teaspoon coriander
- 3 tablespoons kecap manis
- Salt and red pepper, to taste

DIRECTIONS (Prep + Cook Time: 40 minutes)

Put the pork belly, rind side up, in the cooking basket; add in the garlic, rosemary, thyme and coriander. Cook in the preheated Air Fryer at 350 degrees F for 20 minutes; turn it over and cook an additional 20 minutes. Turn the temperature to 400 degrees F, rub the pork belly with the kecap manis and sprinkle with salt and red pepper. Continue to cook for 15 to 20 minutes more. Let it rest on a wire rack for 10 minutes before slicing and serving. Enjoy!

641. Pineapple Pork Carnitas
INGREDIENTS (2 Servings)

1/2 pound pork loin	1/4 cup water	1 garlic clove, minced
1/2 teaspoon paprika Kosher	1/4 cup tomato paste	1 shallot, minced
salt and ground black pepper, to taste	1 tablespoon soy sauce	1 green chili pepper, minced
4 ounces fresh pineapple, crushed	1 teaspoon brown mustard	4 (6-inch) corn tortillas, warmed

DIRECTIONS (Prep + Cook Time: 55 minutes)

Pat the pork loin dry and season it with paprika, salt and black pepper. Then, cook the pork in your Air Fryer at 360 degrees F for 20 minutes; turn it over and cook an additional 25 minutes. Then, preheat a sauté pan over a moderately high heat. Combine the pineapple, water, tomato paste, soy sauce, mustard, garlic, shallot and green chili, bringing to a rolling boil. Turn the heat to simmer; continue to cook until the sauce has reduced by half, about 15 minutes. Let the pork rest for 10 minutes; then, shred the pork with two forks. Spoon the sauce over the pork and serve in corn tortillas. Enjoy!

642. Pork Sausage with Baby Potatoes
INGREDIENTS (3 Servings)

1 pound pork sausage, uncooked	1/4 teaspoon paprika	salt and black pepper, to taste
1 pound baby potatoes	1/2 teaspoon dried rosemary leaves, crushed Himalayan	

DIRECTIONS (Prep + Cook Time: 35 minutes)

Put the sausage into the Air Fryer cooking basket. Cook in the preheated Air Fryer at 380 degrees F for 15 minutes; reserve. Season the baby potatoes with paprika, rosemary, salt and black pepper. Add the baby potatoes to the cooking basket. Cook the potatoes at 400 degrees F for 15 minutes, shaking the basket once or twice. Serve warm sausages with baby potatoes and enjoy!

643. Easy Pork Pot Stickers
INGREDIENTS (2 Servings)

1/2 pound lean ground pork	1 tablespoon soy sauce	2 stalks scallions, chopped
1/2 teaspoon fresh ginger, freshly grated	1 tablespoon rice wine	1 tablespoon sesame oil
1 teaspoon chili garlic sauce	1/4 teaspoon Szechuan pepper	8 (3-inch) round wonton wrappers

DIRECTIONS (Prep + Cook Time: 10 minutes)

Cook the ground pork in a preheated skillet until no longer pink, crumbling with a fork. Stir in the other ingredients, except for the wonton wrappers; stir to combine well. Place the wonton wrappers on a clean work surface. Divide the pork filling between the wrappers. Wet the edge of each wrapper with water, fold the top half over the bottom half and pinch the border to seal. Place the pot stickers in the cooking basket and brush them with a little bit of olive oil. Cook the pot sticker at 400 degrees F for 8 minutes. Serve immediately.

644. Chinese Char Siu Pork
INGREDIENTS (3 Servings)

1 pound pork shoulder, cut into long strips	1 tablespoon hoisin sauce	1 tablespoon Shaoxing wine
1/2 teaspoon Chinese five-spice powder	2 tablespoons hot water	1 tablespoon molasses
1/4 teaspoon Szechuan pepper	1 teaspoon sesame oil	

DIRECTIONS (Prep + Cook Time: 25 minutes + Marinating Time)

Place all ingredients in a ceramic dish and let it marinate for 2 hours in the refrigerator. Cook in the preheated Air Fryer at 390 degrees F for 20 minutes, shaking the basket halfway through the cooking time. Heat the reserved marinade in a wok for about 15 minutes or until the sauce has thickened. Spoon the sauce over the warm pork shoulder and serve with rice if desired. Enjoy!

645. Perfect Meatball Hoagies
INGREDIENTS (2 Servings)

- 1/2 pound lean ground pork
- 1 teaspoon fresh garlic, minced
- 2 tablespoons fresh scallions, chopped
- 1 teaspoon dried basil
- 1/2 teaspoon dried oregano
- 1/2 teaspoon dried parsley flakes Sea
- salt and ground black pepper, to taste
- 1 tablespoon soy sauce
- 1 egg, beaten
- 1/4 cup Pecorino Romano cheese, grated
- 1/2 cup quick-cooking oats
- 2 hoagie rolls
- 1 medium-sized tomato, sliced
- 2 pickled cherry peppers

DIRECTIONS (Prep + Cook Time: 15 minutes)

In a mixing bowl, thoroughly combine the ground pork, garlic, scallions, basil, oregano, parsley, salt, black pepper, soy sauce, eggs, cheese and quick-cooking oats. Mix until well incorporated. Shape the mixture into 6 meatballs. Add the meatballs to the cooking basket and cook them at 360 degrees for 10 minutes. Turn the meatballs halfway through the cooking time. Cut the hoagie rolls lengthwise almost entirely through. Layer the meatballs onto the bottom of the roll. Top with the tomato and peppers. Close the rolls, cut in half and serve immediately. Enjoy!

646. Autumn Boston Butt with Acorn Squash
INGREDIENTS (3 Servings)

- 1 pound Boston butt
- 1 garlic clove, pressed
- 1/4 cup rice wine
- 1 teaspoon molasses
- 1 tablespoon Hoisin sauce
- 1/2 teaspoon red pepper flakes
- 1 teaspoon Sichuan pepper
- 1/2 teaspoon Himalayan salt
- 1/2 pound acorn squash, cut into
- 1/2-inch cubes

DIRECTIONS (Prep + Cook Time: 25 minutes + Marinating Time)

Place the Boston butt, garlic, rice wine, molasses, Hoisin sauce, red pepper flakes, Sichuan pepper and Himalayan salt in a ceramic dish. Cover and allow it to marinate for 2 hours in your refrigerator. Cook in the preheated Air Fryer at 400 degrees F for 10 minutes. Turn the Boston butt over and baste with the reserved marinade. Stir the squash cubes into the cooking basket and cook for 10 minutes on the other side. Taste, adjust seasonings and serve immediately.

647. Pork Cutlets with a Twist
INGREDIENTS (2 Servings)

- 1 cup water
- 1 cup red wine
- 1 tablespoon sea salt
- 2 pork cutlets
- 1/2 cup all-purpose flour
- 1 teaspoon shallot powder
- 1/2 teaspoon porcini powder
- Sea salt and ground black pepper, to taste
- 1 egg
- 1/4 cup yogurt
- 1 teaspoon brown mustard
- 1 cup tortilla chips, crushed

DIRECTIONS (Prep + Cook Time: 1 hour 20 minutes)

In a large ceramic dish, combine the water, wine and salt. Add the pork cutlets and put for 1 hour in the refrigerator. In a shallow bowl, mix the flour, shallot powder, porcini powder, salt, and ground pepper. In another bowl, whisk the eggs with yogurt and mustard. In a third bowl, place the crushed tortilla chips. Dip the pork cutlets in the flour mixture and toss evenly; then, in the egg mixture. Finally, roll them over the crushed tortilla chips. Spritz the bottom of the cooking basket with cooking oil. Add the breaded pork cutlets and cook at 395 degrees F and for 10 minutes. Flip and cook for 5 minutes more on the other side. Serve warm. Enjoy!

648. Cheesy Creamy Pork Casserole
INGREDIENTS (4 Servings)

- 2 tablespoons olive oil
- 2 pounds pork tenderloin, cut into serving-size pieces
- 1 teaspoon coarse sea salt
- 1/2 teaspoon freshly ground pepper
- 1/4 teaspoon chili powder
- 1 teaspoon dried marjoram
- 1 tablespoon mustard
- 1 cup Ricotta cheese
- 1 ½ cups chicken broth

DIRECTIONS (Prep + Cook Time: 25 minutes)

Start by preheating your Air Fryer to 350 degrees F. Heat the olive oil in a pan over medium-high heat. Once hot, cook the pork for 6 to 7 minutes, flipping it to ensure even cooking. Arrange the pork in a lightly greased casserole dish. Season with salt, black pepper, chili powder, and marjoram. In a mixing dish, thoroughly combine the mustard, cheese, and chicken broth. Pour the mixture over the pork chops in the casserole dish. Bake for another 15 minutes or until bubbly and heated through. Enjoy!

649. Mexican-Style Ground Pork with Peppers
INGREDIENTS (4 Servings)

2 chili peppers	2 ripe tomatoes, pureed	2 tablespoons fresh coriander, chopped
1 red bell pepper	1 teaspoon dried marjoram	Salt and ground black pepper, to taste
2 tablespoons olive oil	1/2 teaspoon mustard seeds	2 cups water
1 large-sized shallot, chopped	1/2 teaspoon celery seeds	1 tablespoon chicken bouillon granules
1 pound ground pork	1 teaspoon Mexican oregano	2 tablespoons sherry wine
2 garlic cloves, minced	1 tablespoon fish sauce	1 cup Mexican cheese blend

DIRECTIONS (Prep + Cook Time: 40 minutes)

Roast the peppers in the preheated Air Fryer at 395 degrees F for 10 minutes, flipping them halfway through cook time. Let them steam for 10 minutes; then, peel the skin and discard the stems and seeds. Slice the peppers into halves. Heat the olive oil in a baking pan at 380 degrees F for 2 minutes; add the shallots and cook for 4 minutes. Add the ground pork and garlic; cook for a further 4 to 5 minutes. After that, stir in the tomatoes, marjoram, mustard seeds, celery seeds, oregano, fish sauce, coriander, salt, and pepper. Add a layer of sliced peppers to the baking pan. Mix the water with the chicken bouillon granules and sherry wine. Add the mixture to the baking pan. Cook in the preheated Air Fryer at 395 degrees F for 10 minutes. Top with cheese and bake an additional 5 minutes until the cheese has melted. Serve immediately.

650. Smoky Mini Meatloaves with Cheese
INGREDIENTS (4 Servings)

1 pound ground pork	2 eggs	2 cloves garlic, finely chopped
1/2 pound ground beef	1 carrot, grated	2 tablespoons soy sauce sauce Sea
1 package onion soup mix	1 bell pepper, chopped	salt and black pepper, to your liking
1/2 cup seasoned bread crumbs	1 serrano pepper, minced	
4 tablespoons Romano cheese, grated	2 scallions, chopped	

Glaze:

1/2 cup tomato paste	1 tablespoon brown mustard	1 tablespoon honey
2 tablespoons ketchup	1 teaspoon smoked paprika	

DIRECTIONS (Prep + Cook Time: 50 minutes)

In a large mixing bowl, thoroughly combine all ingredients for the meatloaf. Mix with your hands until everything is well incorporated. Then, shape the mixture into four mini loaves. Transfer them to the cooking basket previously generously greased with cooking oil. Cook in the preheated Air Fryer at 385 degrees F approximately 43 minutes. Mix all ingredients for the glaze. Spread the glaze over mini meatloaves and cook for another 6 minutes. Enjoy!

651. Egg Noodles with Sausage-Pepper Sauce
INGREDIENTS (4 Servings)

1 tablespoon lard, at room temperature	1 pound pork sausages, sliced	Salt and black pepper, to taste
2 garlic cloves, smashed	2 ripe tomatoes, pureed	1 teaspoon basil
2 scallions, chopped	2 tablespoons tomato ketchup	1 teaspoon rosemary
1 red bell pepper, chopped	1 teaspoon molasses	1 teaspoon oregano
1 green bell pepper, chopped	1 tablespoon flax seed meal	1 package egg noodles

DIRECTIONS (Prep + Cook Time: 30 minutes)

Melt the lard in a baking pan at 380 degrees F. Once hot, sauté the garlic, scallions, and peppers until tender about 2 minutes. Add the sausages and cook an additional 5 minutes, stirring occasionally. Add the tomato puree, tomato ketchup, molasses, flax seed meal, and spices; cook for 4 to 5 minutes more or until everything is thoroughly warmed and the sauce has thickened. Meanwhile, bring a large pot of lightly salted water to a boil. Cook the egg noodles for 10 to 12 minutes; drain and divide between individual plates. Top with the warm sauce and serve. Enjoy!

652. Pork Loin with Mushroom Sauce
INGREDIENTS (4 Servings)

- 2 pounds top loin, boneless
- 1 tablespoon olive oil
- 1 teaspoon Celtic salt
- 1/4 teaspoon ground black pepper, or more to taste
- 2 shallots, sliced
- 2 garlic cloves, minced
- 1 cup mushrooms, chopped
- 2 tablespoons all-purpose flour
- 3/4 cup cream of mushroom soup
- 1 teaspoon chili powder
- Salt, to taste

DIRECTIONS (Prep + Cook Time: 30 minutes)

Pat dry the pork and drizzle with olive oil. Season with Celtic salt and pepper. Cook in the preheated Air Fryer at 370 degrees F for 10 minutes. Top with shallot slices and cook another 10 minutes. Test the temperature of the meat; it should be around 150 degrees F. Reserve the pork and onion, keeping warm. Add the cooking juices to a saucepan and preheat over medium-high heat. Cook the garlic and mushrooms until aromatic about 2 minutes. Combine the flour with the mushroom soup. Add the flour mixture to the pan along with the chili powder and salt. Gradually stir into the pan. Bring to a boil; immediately turn the heat to medium and cook for 2 to 3 minutes stirring frequently. Spoon the sauce over the reserved pork and onion. Enjoy!

653. St. Louis-Style Pork Ribs with Roasted Peppers
INGREDIENTS (2 Servings)

- 2 pounds St. Louis-style pork spareribs, individually cut
- 1 teaspoon seasoned salt
- 1/2 teaspoon ground black pepper
- 1 tablespoon sweet paprika
- 1/2 teaspoon mustard powder
- 2 tablespoons sesame oil
- 4 bell pepper, seeded

DIRECTIONS (Prep + Cook Time: 55 minutes)

Toss and rub the spices all over the pork ribs; drizzle with 1 tablespoon of sesame oil. Cook the pork ribs at 360 degrees F for 15 minutes; flip the ribs and cook an additional 20 minutes or until they are tender inside and crisp on the outside. Toss the peppers with the remaining 1 tablespoon of oil; season to taste and cook in the preheated Air Fryer at 390 degrees F for 15 minutes. Serve the warm spareribs with the roasted peppers on the side. Enjoy!

654. Elegant Pork Chops with Applesauce
INGREDIENTS (4 Servings)

- 4 pork chops, bone-in Sea
- salt and ground black pepper, to taste
- 1/2 teaspoon onion powder
- 1/2 teaspoon paprika
- 1/2 teaspoon celery seeds
- 2 cooking apples, peeled and sliced
- 1 tablespoon honey
- 1 tablespoon peanut oil

DIRECTIONS (Prep + Cook Time: 20 minutes)

Place the pork in a lightly greased baking pan. Season with salt and pepper, and transfer the pan to the cooking basket. Cook in the preheated Air Fryer at 370 degrees F for 10 minutes. Meanwhile, in a saucepan, simmer the remaining ingredients over medium heat for about 8 minutes or until the apples are softened. Pour the applesauce over the prepared pork chops. Add to the Air Fryer and bake for 5 minutes more. Enjoy!

655. Spanish-Style Pork with Padrón Peppers
INGREDIENTS (4 Servings)

- 1 tablespoon olive oil
- 8 ounces Padrón peppers
- 2 pounds pork loin, sliced
- 1 teaspoon Celtic salt
- 1 teaspoon paprika
- 1 heaped tablespoon capers, drained
- 8 green olives, pitted and halved

DIRECTIONS (Prep + Cook Time: 30 minutes)

Drizzle olive oil all over the Padrón peppers; cook them in the preheated Air Fryer at 400 degrees F for 10 minutes, turning occasionally, until well blistered all over and tender-crisp. Then, turn the temperature to 360 degrees F.

Season the pork loin with salt and paprika. Add the capers and cook for 16 minutes, turning them over halfway through the cooking time. Serve with olives and the reserved Padrón peppers.

656. Filipino Pork Adobo
INGREDIENTS (4 Servings)

- 1 tablespoon sesame oil
- 1 ½ pounds Boston butt, boneless and skinless, cut into
- 2 pieces Sea
- salt and ground black pepper, to taste
- 1 teaspoon paprika
- 1/2 teaspoon mustard seeds
- 1 teaspoon sesame oil
- 3 bell peppers, seeded and sliced
- 1 jalapeño pepper, seeded and sliced
- 1 red onion, sliced
- 2 garlic cloves, smashed
- 1/2 teaspoon curry
- 1/2 teaspoon ground bay leaf
- 1/4 cup soy sauce
- 1/4 cup apple cider vinegar
- 1 tablespoon cornstarch plus
- 2 tablespoons water

DIRECTIONS (Prep + Cook Time: 35 minutes)

Rub 1 tablespoon of sesame oil all over the Boston butt. Season with salt, pepper, paprika, and mustard seeds. Roast the Boston butt in the preheated Air Fryer at 390 degrees F for 10 minutes. Turn them over and cook another 10 minutes. Heat 1 teaspoon of sesame oil in a wok over medium-high heat. Once hot, cook the peppers until tender, about 2 minutes. Add the onion, garlic, curry, bay leaf, soy sauce, and vinegar. Cook an additional 5 minutes, stirring frequently. Add the cornstarch slurry and meat. Reduce the temperature to simmer and cook for 2 to 4 minute more or until everything is thoroughly heated. Enjoy!

657. Spanish Pork Skewers (Pinchos Morunos)
INGREDIENTS (4 Servings)

- 2 pounds center cut loin chop, cut into bite-sized pieces
- 1 teaspoon oregano
- 1/2 teaspoon ground turmeric
- 1/2 teaspoon ground coriander
- 1 teaspoon ground cumin
- 2 teaspoons sweet Spanish paprika
- Sea salt and freshly ground black pepper, to taste
- 2 garlic cloves, minced
- 2 tablespoons extra virgin olive oil
- 1/4 cup dry red wine
- 1 lemon,
- 1/2 juiced
- 1/2 wedges

DIRECTIONS (Prep + Cook Time: 35 minutes + Marinating Time)

Mix all ingredients, except the lemon wedges, in a large ceramic dish. Allow it to marinate for 2 hours in your refrigerator. Discard the marinade. Now, thread the pork pieces on to skewers and place them in the cooking basket. Cook in the preheated Air Fryer at 360 degrees F for 15 to 17 minutes, shaking the basket every 5 minutes. Work in batches. Serve immediately garnished with lemon wedges. Enjoy!

658. Porterhouse Steak for Two
INGREDIENTS (2 Servings)

- **1 pound porterhouse steak,** cut meat from bone in 2 pieces
- 1/2 teaspoon ground black pepper
- 1 teaspoon cayenne pepper
- 1/2 teaspoon salt
- 1 teaspoon garlic powder
- 1/2 teaspoon dried thyme
- 1/2 teaspoon dried marjoram
- 1 teaspoon Dijon mustard
- 1 tablespoon butter, melted

DIRECTIONS (Prep + Cook Time: 25 minutes)

Sprinkle the porterhouse steak with all the seasonings. Spread the mustard and butter evenly over the meat. Cook in the preheated Air Fryer at 390 degrees F for 12 to 14 minutes. Taste for doneness with a meat thermometer and serve immediately.

659. Dijon Mustard and Honey Roasted Pork Cutlets
INGREDIENTS (2 Servings)

- 1 pound pork cutlets
- 1 teaspoon cayenne pepper Kosher
- salt and ground black pepper, to season
- 1/2 teaspoon garlic powder
- 1 tablespoon honey
- 1 teaspoon Dijon mustard

DIRECTIONS (Prep + Cook Time: 15 minutes)

Spritz the sides and bottom of the cooking basket with a nonstick cooking spray. Place the pork cutlets in the cooking basket; sprinkle with cayenne pepper, salt, black pepper and garlic powder. In a mixing dish, thoroughly combine the honey and Dijon mustard. Cook the pork cutlets at 390 degrees F for 6 minutes. Flip halfway through, rub with the honey mixture and continue to cook for 6 minutes more. Serve immediately.

660. BBQ-Glazed Meatloaf Muffins
INGREDIENTS (3 Servings)

- 1 pound lean ground pork
- 1 small onion, chopped
- 2 cloves garlic, crushed
- 1/4 cup carrots, grated
- 1 serrano pepper, seeded and minced
- 1 teaspoon stone-ground mustard
- 1/4 cup crackers, crushed
- 1 egg, lightly beaten Sea
- salt and ground black pepper, to taste
- 1/2 cup BBQ sauce

DIRECTIONS (Prep + Cook Time: 45 minutes)

Mix all ingredients, except for the BBQ sauce, until everything is well incorporated. Brush a muffin tin with vegetable oil. Use an ice cream scoop to spoon the meat mixture into the cups. Top each meatloaf cup with a spoonful of BBQ sauce. Bake in the preheated Air Fryer at 395 degrees F for about 40 minutes. Transfer to a cooling rack. Wait for a few minutes before unmolding and serving. Enjoy!

661. Pork Tenderloin with Brussels Sprouts
INGREDIENTS (3 Servings)

- 1 pound Brussels sprouts, halved
- 1 ½ pounds tenderloin
- 1 teaspoon peanut oil
- 1 teaspoon garlic powder
- 1 tablespoon coriander, minced
- 1 teaspoon smoked paprika
- Sea salt and ground black pepper, to taste

DIRECTIONS (Prep + Cook Time: 20 minutes)

Toss the Brussels sprouts and pork with oil and spices until well coated. Place in the Air Fryer cooking basket. Cook in the preheated Air Fryer at 370 degrees F for 15 minutes. Taste and adjust seasonings. Eat warm. Enjoy!

662. Perfect Pork Wraps
INGREDIENTS (2 Servings)

- 1/2 pound pork loin
- 1 teaspoon butter, melted
- Salt and black pepper, to season
- 1/2 teaspoon marjoram
- 1/2 teaspoon hot paprika
- 2 tortillas

Sauce:

- 2 tablespoons tahini
- 1 tablespoon sesame oil
- 2 tablespoons soy sauce
- 1 tablespoon lime juice
- 1 tablespoon white vinegar
- 1 teaspoon fresh ginger, peeled and grated
- 2 garlic cloves, pressed
- 1 teaspoon honey

DIRECTIONS (Prep + Cook Time: 55 minutes)

Rub the pork with melted butter and season with salt, pepper, marjoram and hot paprika. Place in the cooking basket and cook at 360 digress F for 25 minutes. Turn the meat over and cook an additional 20 minutes. Place the roasted pork loin on a cutting board. Slice the roasted pork loin into strips using a sharp kitchen knife. In the meantime, mix the sauce ingredients with a wire whisk. Turn the temperature to 390 degrees F. Spoon the pork strips and sauce onto each tortilla; wrap them tightly. Drizzle with a nonstick cooking spray and bake about 6 minutes. Serve warm. Enjoy!

663. Authentic Balkan-Style Cevapi
INGREDIENTS (3 Servings)

- 1/2 pound lean ground pork
- 1/2 pound ground chuck
- 2 cloves garlic, minced
- 2 tablespoons green onions, chopped
- 1 tablespoon parsley, finely chopped
- 1 tablespoon coriander, finely chopped
- 1/2 teaspoon smoked paprika
- Sea salt and ground black pepper, to taste
- 2 ciabatta bread

DIRECTIONS (Prep + Cook Time: 55 minutes)

Mix the ground meat with the garlic, green onion, herbs and spices. Roll the mixture into small sausages, about 3 inches long. Spritz a cooking basket with a nonstick cooking spray. Cook cevapi at 380 degrees F for 10 minutes, shaking the basket periodically to ensure even cooking. Serve in ciabatta bread with some extra onions, mustard or ketchup. Enjoy!

664. Sunday Meatball Sliders
INGREDIENTS (2 Servings)

- 1/2 pound lean ground pork
- 1 shallot, chopped
- 1 teaspoon garlic, pressed
- 1 tablespoon soy sauce
- 1/2 cup quick-cooking oats
- 1 tablespoon Italian parsley, minced
- 1/2 teaspoon fresh ginger, ground
- 1/4 teaspoon ground bay laurel
- 1/2 teaspoon red pepper flakes, crushed
- Sea salt and ground black pepper, to taste
- 4 dinner rolls

DIRECTIONS (Prep + Cook Time: 15 minutes)

In a mixing bowl, thoroughly combine the ground pork, shallot, garlic, soy sauce, oats, parsley, ginger and spices; stir until everything is well incorporated. Shape the mixture into 4 meatballs. Add the meatballs to the cooking basket and cook them at 360 degrees for 10 minutes. Check the meatballs halfway through the cooking time. Place one meatball on top of the bottom half of one roll. Top with the other half of the roll and serve immediately. Enjoy!

665. Mexican Pork Quesadillas
INGREDIENTS (2 Servings)

- 1/2 pound pork tenderloin, cut into strips
- 1 teaspoon peanut oil
- 1/2 teaspoon onion powder
- 2 flour tortillas
- 1/2 teaspoon garlic powder
- 1/2 teaspoon red pepper flakes
- 1/4 teaspoon dried basil
- 1/2 teaspoon Mexican oregano
- 1/2 teaspoon dried marjoram
- Sea salt and ground black pepper, to taste

Pico de Gallo:

- 1 tomato, diced
- 3 tablespoons onion, chopped
- 3 tablespoons cilantro, chopped
- 3 tablespoons lime juice

DIRECTIONS (Prep + Cook Time: 25 minutes)

Toss the pork tenderloin strips with peanut oil and spices. Cook in the preheated Air Fryer at 370 degrees F for 15 minutes, shaking the cooking basket halfway through the cooking time. Meanwhile, make the Pico de Gallo by whisking the ingredients or it. Assemble your tortillas with the meat mixture and Pico de Gallo; wrap them tightly. Turn the temperature to 390 degrees F. Drizzle the tortillas with a nonstick cooking spray and bake about 6 minutes. Eat warm. Enjoy!

666. Warm Pork Salad
INGREDIENTS (3 Servings)

- 1 pound pork shoulder, cut into strips
- 1/4 teaspoon fresh ginger, minced
- 1 teaspoon garlic, pressed
- 1 tablespoon olive oil
- 1 tablespoon honey
- 2 teaspoons fresh cilantro, chopped
- 1 tablespoon Worcestershire sauce
- 1 medium-sized cucumber, sliced
- 1 cup arugula
- 1 cup baby spinach
- 1 cup Romaine lettuce
- 1 tomato, diced
- 1 shallot, sliced

DIRECTIONS (Prep + Cook Time: 20 minutes)

Spritz the Air Fryer cooking basket with a nonstick spray. Place the pork in the Air Fryer cooking basket. Cook at 400 degrees F for 13 minutes, shaking the basket halfway through the cooking time. Transfer the meat to a serving bowl and toss with the remaining ingredients. Enjoy!

667. Classic Fried Bacon
INGREDIENTS (4 Servings)

- 1/2 pound bacon slices
- 1/2 cup tomato ketchup
- 1/4 teaspoon cayenne pepper
- 1/4 teaspoon dried marjoram
- 1 teaspoon Sriracha sauce

DIRECTIONS (Prep + Cook Time: 10 minutes)

Place the bacon slices in the cooking basket. Cook the bacon slices at 400 degrees F for about 8 minutes. Meanwhile, make the sauce by mixing the remaining ingredients. Serve the warm bacon with the sauce on the side. Enjoy!

668. Herb-Crusted Pork Roast

INGREDIENTS (2 Servings)

- 1/2 pound pork loin
- Salt and black pepper, to taste
- 1/2 teaspoon onion powder
- 1/2 teaspoon parsley flakes
- 1/2 teaspoon oregano
- 1/2 teaspoon thyme
- 1/2 teaspoon grated lemon peel
- 1 teaspoon garlic, minced
- 1 teaspoon butter, softened

DIRECTIONS (Prep + Cook Time: 1 hour)

Pat the pork loin dry with kitchen towels. Season it with salt and black pepper. In a bowl, mix the remaining ingredients until well combined. Coat the pork with the herb rub, pressing to adhere well. Cook in the preheated Air Fryer at 360 degrees F for 30 minutes; turn it over and cook on the other side for 25 minutes more. Enjoy!

669. Balsamic Pork Chops with Asparagus

INGREDIENTS (2 Servings)

- 2 pork loin chops
- 1 pound asparagus spears, cleaned and trimmed
- 1 teaspoon sesame oil
- 2 tablespoons balsamic vinegar
- 1 teaspoon yellow mustard
- 1/2 teaspoon garlic, minced
- 1/2 teaspoon smoked pepper
- 1/4 teaspoon dried dill
- Salt and black pepper, to taste

DIRECTIONS (Prep + Cook Time: 15 minutes)

Toss the pork loin chops and asparagus with the other ingredients until well coated on all sides. Place the pork in the Air Fryer cooking basket and cook at 400 degrees F for 7 minutes; turn them over, top with the asparagus and continue to cook for a further 5 minutes. Serve warm with mayo, sriracha sauce, or sour cream if desired. Enjoy!

670. Spicy Bacon-Wrapped Tater Tots

INGREDIENTS (5 Servings)

- 10 thin slices of bacon
- 1 teaspoon cayenne pepper
- 10 tater tots, frozen

Sauce:

- 1/4 cup mayo
- 4 tablespoons ketchup
- 1 teaspoon rice vinegar
- 1 teaspoon chili powder

DIRECTIONS (Prep + Cook Time: 25 minutes)

Lay the slices of bacon on your working surface. Place a tater tot on one end of each slice; sprinkle with cayenne pepper and roll them over. Cook in the preheated Air Fryer at 390 degrees F for 15 to 16 minutes. Whisk all ingredients for the sauce in a mixing bowl and store in your refrigerator, covered, until ready to serve. Serve Bacon-Wrapped Tater Tots with the sauce on the side. Enjoy!

671. Tender Spare Ribs

INGREDIENTS (4 Servings)

- 1 rack pork spareribs, fat trimmed and cut in half
- 2 tablespoons fajita seasoning
- 2 tablespoons smoked paprika
- Sea salt and pepper, to taste
- 1 tablespoon prepared brown mustard
- 3 tablespoons Worcestershire sauce
- 1/2 cup beer
- 1 tablespoon peanut oil

DIRECTIONS (Prep + Cook Time: 35 minutes + Marinating Time)

Toss the spareribs with the fajita seasoning, paprika, salt, pepper, mustard, and Worcestershire sauce. Pour in the beer and let it marinate for 1 hour in your refrigerator. Rub the sides and bottom of the cooking basket with peanut oil. Cook the spareribs in the preheated Air Fryer at 365 degrees for 17 minutes. Turn the ribs over and cook an additional 14 to 15 minutes. Serve warm. Enjoy!

672. Pork Belly with New Potatoes

INGREDIENTS (4 Servings)

- 1 ½ pounds pork belly, cut into
- 4 pieces Kosher
- salt and ground black pepper, to taste
- 1 teaspoon smoked paprika
- 1/2 teaspoon turmeric powder
- 2 tablespoons oyster sauce
- 2 tablespoons green onions
- 4 cloves garlic, sliced
- 1 pound new potatoes, scrubbed

DIRECTIONS (Prep + Cook Time: 50 minutes)

Preheat your Air Fryer to 390 degrees F. Pat dry the pork belly and season with all spices listed above. Add the oyster sauce and spritz with a nonstick cooking spray on all sides. Now, cook in the preheated Air Fryer for 30 minutes. Turn them over every 10 minutes. Increase the temperature to 400 degrees F. Add the green onions, garlic, and new potatoes. Cook another 15 minutes, shaking occasionally. Serve warm.

673. Authentic Spaghetti Bolognese
INGREDIENTS (4 Servings)

2 tablespoons olive oil	1 cup tomato puree	1 teaspoon rosemary
1 shallot, peeled and chopped	2 tablespoons apple cider vinegar	Salt and black pepper, to taste
1 teaspoon fresh garlic, minced	1 teaspoon oregano	1 package spaghetti
1 pound lean ground pork	1 teaspoon basil	1 tablespoon fresh parsley

DIRECTIONS (Prep + Cook Time: 30 minutes)

Heat the oil in a baking pan at 380 degrees F. Then, sauté the shallots until tender about 4 minutes. Add the garlic and ground pork; cook an additional 6 minutes, stirring and crumbling meat with a spatula. Add the tomato puree, vinegar, and spices; cook for 4 to 6 minutes longer or until everything is heated through. Meanwhile, bring a large pot of lightly salted water to a boil. Cook your spaghetti for 10 to 12 minutes; drain and divide between individual plates. Top with the Bolognese sauce and serve garnished with fresh parsley. Enjoy!

674. Perfect Sloppy Joes
INGREDIENTS (4 Servings)

1 tablespoon olive oil	1 pound ground pork	Dash ground allspice
1 shallot, chopped	2 ripe medium-sized tomatoes, pureed	6 hamburger buns
2 garlic cloves, minced	1 tablespoon Worcestershire sauce	
1 bell pepper, chopped	1 tablespoon poultry seasoning blend	

DIRECTIONS (Prep + Cook Time: 30 minutes)

Start by preheating your Air Fryer to 390 degrees F. Heat the olive oil for a few minutes. Once hot, sauté the shallots until just tender. Add the garlic and bell pepper; cook for 4 minutes more or until they are aromatic. Add the ground pork and cook for 5 minutes more, crumbling with a fork. Next step, stir in the pureed tomatoes, Worcestershire sauce, and spices. Decrease the temperature to 365 degrees F and cook another 10 minutes. Spoon the meat mixture into hamburger buns and transfer them to the cooking basket. Cook for 7 minutes or until thoroughly warmed. Enjoy!

675. Sausage and Mushroom Chili
INGREDIENTS (4 Servings)

1 tablespoon olive oil	2 cups tomato puree	Salt and ground black pepper, to taste
1 shallot, chopped	2 tablespoons tomato ketchup	1 (16-ounce) can pinto beans, rinsed and drained
2 garlic cloves, smashed	1 teaspoon yellow mustard	
10 ounces button mushrooms, sliced	1 cup chicken broth	1/2 cup cream cheese
1/2 pound pork sausages, chopped	2 teaspoons ancho chili powder	

DIRECTIONS (Prep + Cook Time: 35 minutes)

Start by preheating your Air Fryer to 360 degrees F. Heat the oil in a baking pan for a few minutes and cook the shallot until tender about 4 minutes. Add the garlic and mushrooms; cook another 4 minutes or until tender and fragrant. Next, stir in sausage and cook for a further 9 minutes. Add tomato puree, ketchup, mustard, and broth. Stir to combine and cook another 6 minutes. Add spices and beans; cook an additional 7 minutes. Divide between individual bowls and top each bowl with cream cheese. Enjoy!

676. Cracker Pork Chops with Mustard
INGREDIENTS (3 Servings)

1/4 cup all-purpose flour	1 teaspoon mustard Kosher salt, to taste	1/2 teaspoon porcini powder
1 teaspoon turmeric powder	1/4 teaspoon freshly ground black pepper	1 teaspoon shallot powder
1 egg	2 cups crackers, crushed	3 center-cut loin pork chops

DIRECTIONS (Prep + Cook Time: 20 minutes)

Place the flour and turmeric in a shallow bowl. In another bowl, whisk the eggs, mustard, salt, and black pepper. In the third bowl, mix the crushed crackers with the porcini powder and shallot powder. Preheat your Air Fryer to 390 degrees F. Dredge the pork chops in the flour mixture, then in the egg, followed by the cracker mixture. Cook the pork chops for 7 minutes per side, spraying with cooking oil. Enjoy!

677. Hawaiian Cheesy Meatball Sliders
INGREDIENTS (4 Servings)

- 1 pound ground pork
- 2 tablespoons bacon, chopped
- 2 garlic cloves, minced
- 2 tablespoons scallions, chopped
- Salt and ground black pepper, to taste
- 1/2 cup Romano cheese, grated
- 1 cup tortilla chips, crushed
- 1 ½ cups marinara sauce
- 8 Hawaiian rolls
- 1 cup Cheddar cheese, shredded

DIRECTIONS (Prep + Cook Time: 20 minutes)

Mix the ground pork with the bacon, garlic, scallions, salt, black pepper, cheese, and tortilla chips. Shape the mixture into 8 meatballs. Add the meatballs to the lightly greased baking pan. Pour in the marinara sauce and lower the pan onto the cooking basket. Cook the meatballs in the preheated Air Fryer at 380 degrees for 10 minutes. Check the meatballs halfway through the cooking time. Place one meatball on top of the bottom half of one roll. Spoon the marinara sauce on top of each meatball. Top with cheese and bake in your Air Fryer at 370 degrees F for 3 to 4 minutes. Top with the other half of the roll and serve immediately. Enjoy!

678. Omelet with Prosciutto and Ricotta Cheese
INGREDIENTS (2 Servings)

- 2 tablespoons olive oil
- 4 eggs
- 2 tablespoons scallions, chopped
- 4 tablespoons Ricotta cheese
- 1/4 teaspoon black pepper, freshly cracked
- Salt, to taste
- 6 ounces prosciutto, chopped
- 1 tablespoon Italian parsley, roughly chopped

DIRECTIONS (Prep + Cook Time: 15 minutes)

Generously grease a baking pan with olive oil. Then, whisk the eggs, and add the scallions, cheese, black pepper, and salt. Fold in the chopped prosciutto and mix to combine well. Spoon into the prepared baking pan. Cook in the preheated Air Fryer at 360 F for 6 minutes. Serve immediately garnished with Italian parsley.

679. Pork Leg with Candy Onions
INGREDIENTS (4 Servings)

- 1 rosemary sprig, chopped
- 1 thyme sprig, chopped
- 1 teaspoon dried sage, crushed
- Sea salt and ground black pepper, to taste
- 1 teaspoon cayenne pepper
- 2 teaspoons sesame oil
- 2 pounds pork leg roast, scored
- 1 pound candy onions, peeled
- 2 chili peppers, minced
- 4 cloves garlic, finely chopped

DIRECTIONS (Prep + Cook Time: 1 hour)

Start by preheating your Air Fryer to 400 degrees F. Then, mix the seasonings with the sesame oil. Rub the seasoning mixture all over the pork leg. Cook in the preheated Air Fryer for 40 minutes. Add the candy onions, peppers and garlic and cook an additional 12 minutes. Slice the pork leg. Afterwards, spoon the pan juices over the meat and serve with the candy onions. Enjoy!

680. Honey and Herb Roasted Pork Tenderloin
(Ready in about 20 minutes + marinating time | Servings 3)

INGREDIENTS (3 Servings)

- 1 garlic clove, pressed
- 2 tablespoons honey
- 2 tablespoons Worcestershire sauce
- 2 tablespoons tequila
- 2 tablespoons yellow mustard
- 1 pound pork tenderloin, sliced into 3 pieces
- 1 teaspoon rosemary
- 1 teaspoon basil
- 1/2 teaspoon oregano
- 1/2 teaspoon parsley flakes
- Salt and black pepper, to taste

DIRECTIONS (Prep + Cook Time: 20 minutes + Marinating Time)

In a glass bowl, thoroughly combine the garlic, honey, Worcestershire sauce, tequila and mustard. Add in the pork tenderloin pieces, cover and marinate in your refrigerator for about 1 hour. Transfer the pork tenderloin to the cooking basket, discarding the marinade. Sprinkle the pork tenderloin with herbs, salt and black pepper. Cook in your Air Fryer at 370 degrees F for 15 minutes, checking periodically and basting with the reserved marinade. Serve warm.

681. Pork Loin with Greek-Style Sauce
INGREDIENTS (2 Servings)

- 1/2 pound boneless pork loin, well-trimmed
- 1 garlic clove, halved
- 1 teaspoon grainy mustard Kosher
- salt and ground black pepper, to taste
- 1/2 teaspoon lard, melted
- 1/4 cup mayonnaise
- 1/4 cup Greek-style yogurt
- 1/4 teaspoon dried dill
- 1/2 teaspoon garlic, pressed

DIRECTIONS (Prep + Cook Time: 55 minutes)

Rub the pork with garlic halves on all sides; then, rub the pork with mustard. Season it with salt and pepper and drizzle with melted lard. Transfer to the Air Fryer cooking basket and cook at 360 degrees F for 45 minutes, turning over halfway through the cooking time. In the meantime, make the sauce by whisking all ingredients. Let it rest for 8 to 10 minutes before carving and serving. Serve the warm pork loin with the sauce on the side. Enjoy!

682. German-Style Pork with Sauerkraut
INGREDIENTS (3 Servings)

- 1 pound pork butt
- 2 teaspoons olive oil
- 1 teaspoon dried thyme
- Salt and black pepper, to taste
- 1 tart apple, thinly sliced
- 1 onion, thinly sliced
- 2 garlic cloves, minced
- 1 bay leaf
- 1/2 teaspoon cayenne pepper
- 1 pound sauerkraut, drained

DIRECTIONS (Prep + Cook Time: 15 minutes)

Toss the pork butt with 1 teaspoon of olive oil, thyme, salt and black pepper. Place the pork in the Air Fryer cooking basket. Cook the pork at 400 degrees F for 7 minutes. Top with apple slices and cook for a further 7 minutes. Meanwhile, heat the olive oil in a large saucepan over medium-high heat. Now, sauté the onion for 2 to 3 minutes or until just tender and translucent. Add in the garlic, bay leaf, cayenne pepper and sauerkraut and continue to cook for 10 minutes more or until cooked through. Slice the pork into 3 portions; top the warm sauerkraut with the pork. Enjoy!

683. Tacos Al Pastor
INGREDIENTS (3 Servings)

Pork:
- 1 pound pork loin
- 1 tablespoon honey
- Sea salt and ground black pepper, to taste
- 1/2 teaspoon cayenne pepper
- 1/2 teaspoon garlic powder
- 1/2 teaspoon thyme
- 1 teaspoon olive

oil Tacos:
- 1 tablespoon annatto seeds
- 1 tablespoon olive oil
- 1/2 teaspoon coriander seeds
- 3 corn tortillas
- 1 clove garlic, crushed
- 1 tablespoon apple cider vinegar
- 1 dried guajillo chili, deseeded and crushed

DIRECTIONS (Prep + Cook Time: 50 minutes)

Pat dry pork loin; toss the pork with the remaining ingredients until well coated on all sides. Cook in the preheated Air Fryer at 360 degrees F for 45 minutes, turning over halfway through the cooking time. In the meantime, make the achiote paste by mixing the annatto seeds, olive oil, coriander seeds, garlic, apple cider vinegar and dried guajillo chili in your blender. Slice the pork into bite-sized pieces. Spoon the pork and achiote onto warmed tortillas. Enjoy!

684. Italian Nonna's Polpette
INGREDIENTS (3 Servings)

- 1 teaspoon olive oil
- 2 tablespoons green onions, chopped
- 1/2 teaspoon garlic, pressed
- 1/2 pound sweet Italian pork sausage, crumbled
- 1 tablespoon parsley, chopped
- 1/2 teaspoon cayenne pepper
- Sea salt and ground black pepper, to taste
- 1 egg
- 2 tablespoons milk
- 1 crustless bread slice

DIRECTIONS (Prep + Cook Time: 15 minutes)

Mix the olive oil, green onions, garlic, sausage, parsley, cayenne pepper, salt and black pepper in a bowl. Whisk the egg and milk until pale and frothy. Soak the bread in the milk mixture. Add the soaked bread to the sausage mixture. Mix again to combine well. Shape the mixture into 8 meatballs. Add the meatballs to the cooking basket and cook them at 360 degrees for 5 minutes. Then, turn them and cook the other side for 5 minutes more. You can serve these meatballs over spaghetti. Enjoy!

685. Caprese Pork Chops
INGREDIENTS (3 Servings)

- 1 pound center-cut pork chops, boneless
- 1/4 cup balsamic vinegar
- 1 tablespoon honey
- 1 tablespoon whole-grain mustard
- 1/2 teaspoon olive oil
- 1/2 teaspoon smoked paprika
- Salt and black pepper, to taste
- 1/2 teaspoon shallot powder
- 1/2 teaspoon porcini powder
- 1/2 teaspoon granulated garlic
- 3 slices fresh mozzarella
- 3 thick slices tomatoes
- 2 tablespoons fresh basil leaves, chopped

DIRECTIONS (Prep + Cook Time: 15 minutes + Marinating Time)

Place the pork chops, balsamic vinegar, honey, mustard, olive oil and spices in a bowl. Cover and let it marinate in your refrigerator for 1 hour. Cook in the preheated Air Fryer at 400 degrees F for 7 minutes. Top with cheese and continue to cook for 5 minutes more. Top with sliced tomato and basil and serve immediately.

686. The Best BBQ Ribs Ever
INGREDIENTS (2 Servings)

- 1/2 pound ribs
- Sea salt and black pepper, to taste
- 1/2 teaspoon red chili flakes
- 1 tablespoon agave syrup
- 1/2 teaspoon garlic powder
- 1/2 cup tomato paste
- 1 teaspoon brown mustard
- 1 tablespoon balsamic vinegar
- 1 tablespoon Worcestershire sauce

DIRECTIONS (Prep + Cook Time: 40 minutes)

Place the pork ribs, salt, black pepper and red pepper flakes in a Ziplock bag; shake until the ribs are coated on all sides. Roast in the preheated Air Fryer at 350 degrees F for 35 minutes. In a saucepan over medium heat, heat all sauce ingredients, bringing to a boil. Turn the heat to a simmer until the sauce has reduced by half. Spoon the sauce over the ribs and serve warm. Enjoy!

687. Texas Pulled Pork
INGREDIENTS (3 Servings)

- 1 pound pork shoulder roast
- 1 teaspoon butter, softened
- 1 teaspoon Italian seasoning mix
- 1/2 cup barbecue sauce
- 1/4 cup apple juice
- 1 teaspoon garlic paste
- 2 tablespoons soy sauce
- 2 hamburger buns, split

DIRECTIONS (Prep + Cook Time: 1 hour)

Brush the pork shoulder with butter and sprinkle with Italian seasoning mix on all sides. Cook in the preheated Air Fryer at 360 degrees F for 1 hour, shaking the basket once or twice. Meanwhile, warm the barbecue sauce, apple juice, garlic paste and soy sauce in a small saucepan. Remove the pork shoulder from the basket and shred the meat with two forks. Spoon the sauce over the pork and stir to combine well. Spoon the pork into the toasted buns and eat warm. Enjoy!

688. Authentic Greek Pork Gyro
INGREDIENTS (2 Servings)

- 3/4 pound pork butt
- Sea salt and ground black pepper, to taste
- 1/2 teaspoon red pepper flakes, crushed
- 1 teaspoon ground coriander
- 1/2 teaspoon mustard seeds
- 1/2 teaspoon granulated garlic
- 1/2 teaspoon oregano
- 1/2 teaspoon basil
- 1 teaspoon olive oil
- 2 pita bread, warmed
- 4 lettuce leaves
- 1 small tomato, diced
- 2 tablespoons red onion, chopped

Tzatziki:

- 1/2 cup Greek-style yogurt
- 1 tablespoon cucumber, minced and drained
- 1 teaspoon fresh lemon juice
- 1 teaspoon fresh dill, minced
- 1/4 teaspoon fresh garlic, pressed

DIRECTIONS (Prep + Cook Time: 20 minutes)

Toss the pork butt with salt, black pepper, red pepper flakes, coriander, mustard seeds, granulated garlic, oregano, basil and olive oil. Transfer the pork butt to the Air Fryer cooking basket. Cook the pork at 400 degrees F for 7 minutes. Turn the pork over and cook for a further 7 minutes. Shred the meat with two forks. In the meantime, make the Tzatziki sauce by whisking all ingredients until everything is well combined. Spoon the pork onto each pita bread; top with Tzatziki, lettuce, tomato and red onion. Serve immediately and enjoy!

689. Pork Koftas with Yoghurt Sauce
INGREDIENTS (4 Servings)

- 2 teaspoons olive oil
- 1/2 pound ground pork
- 1/2 pound ground beef
- 1 egg, whisked
- Sea salt and ground black pepper, to taste
- 1 teaspoon paprika
- 2 garlic cloves, minced
- 1 teaspoon dried marjoram
- 1 teaspoon mustard seeds
- 1/2 teaspoon celery seeds

Yogurt Sauce:

- 2 tablespoons olive oil
- 2 tablespoons fresh lemon juice Sea salt, to taste
- 1/4 teaspoon red pepper flakes, crushed
- 1/2 cup full-fat yogurt
- 1 teaspoon dried dill weed

DIRECTIONS (Prep + Cook Time: 25 minutes)

Spritz the sides and bottom of the cooking basket with 2 teaspoons of olive oil. In a mixing dish, thoroughly combine the ground pork, beef, egg, salt, black pepper, paprika, garlic, marjoram, mustard seeds, and celery seeds. Form the mixture into kebabs and transfer them to the greased cooking basket. Cook at 365 degrees F for 11 to 12 minutes, turning them over once or twice. In the meantime, mix all the sauce ingredients and place in the refrigerator until ready to serve. Serve the pork koftas with the yogurt sauce on the side. Enjoy!

690. Herbed Pork Loin with Carrot Chips
INGREDIENTS (4 Servings)

- 1 tablespoon peanut oil
- 1 ½ pounds pork loin, cut into 4 pieces Coarse
- sea salt and ground black pepper, to taste
- 1/2 teaspoon onion powder
- 1 teaspoon garlic powder
- 1/2 teaspoon cayenne pepper
- 1/2 teaspoon dried rosemary
- 1/2 teaspoon dried basil
- 1/2 teaspoon dried oregano
- 1 pound carrots, cut into matchsticks
- 1 tablespoon coconut oil, melted

DIRECTIONS (Prep + Cook Time: 1 hour 15 minutes)

Drizzle 1 tablespoon of peanut oil all over the pork loin. Season with salt, black pepper, onion powder, garlic powder, cayenne pepper, rosemary, basil, and oregano. Cook in the preheated Air Fryer at 360 degrees F for 55 minutes; make sure to turn the pork over every 15 minutes to ensure even cooking. Test for doneness with a meat thermometer. Toss the carrots with melted coconut oil; season to taste and cook in the preheated Air Fryer at 380 degrees F for 15 minutes. Serve the warm pork loin with the carrots on the side. Enjoy!

691. Italian-Style Honey Roasted Pork
INGREDIENTS (4 Servings)

- 1 teaspoon Celtic sea salt
- 1/2 teaspoon black pepper, freshly cracked
- 1/4 cup red wine
- 2 tablespoons mustard
- 2 tablespoons honey
- 2 garlic cloves, minced
- 1 pound pork top loin
- 1 tablespoon Italian herb seasoning blend

DIRECTIONS (Prep + Cook Time: 50 minutes)

In a ceramic bowl, mix the salt, black pepper, red wine, mustard, honey, and garlic. Add the pork top loin and let it marinate at least 30 minutes. Spritz the sides and bottom of the cooking basket with a nonstick cooking spray. Place the pork top loin in the basket; sprinkle with the Italian herb seasoning blend. Cook the pork tenderloin at 370 degrees F for 10 minutes. Flip halfway through, spraying with cooking oil and cook for 5 to 6 minutes more. Serve immediately.

692. Ground Pork and Cheese Casserole
INGREDIENTS (4 Servings)

- 1 tablespoon olive oil
- 1 ½ pounds pork, ground
- Sea salt and ground black pepper, to taste
- 1 medium-sized leek, sliced
- 1 teaspoon fresh garlic, minced
- 2 carrots, trimmed and sliced
- 1 (2-ounce) jar pimiento, drained and chopped
- 1 can (10 ¾-ounces) condensed cream of mushroom soup
- 1 cup water
- 1/2 cup ale
- 1 cup cream cheese
- 1/2 cup soft fresh breadcrumbs
- 1 tablespoon fresh cilantro, chopped

DIRECTIONS (Prep + Cook Time: 45 minutes)

Start by preheating your Air Fryer to 320 degrees F. Add the olive oil to a baking dish and heat for 1 to 2 minutes. Add the pork, salt, pepper and cook for 6 minutes, crumbling with a fork. Add the leeks and cook for 4 to 5 minutes, stirring occasionally. Add the garlic, carrots, pimiento, mushroom soup, water, ale, and cream cheese. Gently stir to combine. Turn the temperature to 370 degrees F. Top with the breadcrumbs. Place the baking dish in the cooking basket and cook approximately 30 minutes or until everything is thoroughly cooked. Serve garnished with fresh cilantro. Enjoy!

693. Asian Sticky Ribs
INGREDIENTS (4 Servings)

- 1 teaspoon salt
- 1 teaspoon cayenne pepper
- 1/2 teaspoon ground black pepper
- 2 teaspoons raw honey 2 garlic cloves, minced
- 1 (1-inch) piece ginger, peeled and grated
- 1/2 teaspoon onion powder
- 1/2 teaspoon porcini powder
- 1 teaspoon mustard seeds
- 1 tablespoon sweet chili sauce
- 1 tablespoon balsamic vinegar
- 1 ½ pounds pork country-style ribs

DIRECTIONS (Prep + Cook Time: 40 minutes)

In a mixing bowl, combine the salt, cayenne pepper, black pepper, honey, garlic, ginger, onion powder, porcini powder, mustard seeds, sweet chili sauce, and balsamic vinegar. Toss and rub the seasoning mixture all over the pork ribs. Cook the country-style ribs at 360 degrees F for 15 minutes; flip the ribs and cook an additional 20 minutes or until they are tender inside and crisp on the outside. Serve warm, garnished with fresh chives if desired.

694. Smoked Sausage with Sauerkraut
INGREDIENTS (4 Servings)

- 4 pork sausages, smoked
- 2 tablespoons canola oil
- 2 garlic cloves, minced
- 1 pound sauerkraut 1 teaspoon cayenne pepper
- 1/2 teaspoon black peppercorns
- 2 bay leaves

DIRECTIONS (Prep + Cook Time: 35 minutes)

Start by preheating your Air Fryer to 360 degrees F. Prick holes into the sausages using a fork and transfer them to the cooking basket. Cook approximately 14 minutes, shaking the basket a couple of times. Set aside. Now, heat the canola oil in a baking pan at 380 degrees F. Add the garlic and cook for 1 minute. Immediately stir in the sauerkraut, cayenne pepper, peppercorns, and bay leaves. Let it cook for 15 minutes, stirring every 5 minutes. Serve in individual bowls with warm sausages on the side!

695. Easy Pork Sandwiches
INGREDIENTS (3 Servings)

2 teaspoons peanut oil

1 ½ pounds pork sirloin Coarse

sea salt and ground black pepper, to taste

1 tablespoon smoked paprika

1/4 cup prepared barbecue sauce

3 hamburger buns, split

DIRECTIONS (Prep + Cook Time: 55 minutes)

Start by preheating your Air Fryer to 360 degrees F. Drizzle the oil all over the pork sirloin. Sprinkle with salt, black pepper, and paprika. Cook for 50 minutes in the preheated Air Fryer. Remove the roast from the Air Fryer and shred with two forks. Mix in the barbecue sauce. Serve over hamburger buns. Enjoy!

696. Sticky Dijon Pork Chops
INGREDIENTS (4 Servings)

1/4 cup soy sauce

2 tablespoons brown sugar

1/4 cup rice vinegar

1 pound pork loin center rib chops, bone-in Celtic

salt and ground black pepper, to taste

1 tablespoon Dijon mustard

DIRECTIONS (Prep + Cook Time: 20 minutes)

Thoroughly combine the soy sauce, brown sugar, and vinegar; add the pork and let it marinate for 1 hour in the refrigerator. Sprinkle the pork chops with salt and black pepper. Spread the mustard, all over the pork chops. Cook in the preheated Air Fryer at 400 degrees F for 12 minutes. Serve warm with mashed potatoes if desired. Enjoy!

697. Easy Keto Pork Rinds
INGREDIENTS (10 Servings)

2 pounds pork belly, trim the fat layer and cut into cubes

1 teaspoon Celtic salt

1 tablespoon red pepper flakes, crushed

DIRECTIONS (Prep + Cook Time: 30 minutes)

Add the pork, salt, and red pepper to the baking pan. Bake at 395 degrees F for 10 minutes. Pat it dry and transfer to your refrigerator to cool for 15 minutes. Process the pork fat in the blender until it resembles coarse breadcrumbs. Use with your favorite keto creations!

698. Sri Lankan Pork Curry
INGREDIENTS (4 Servings)

2 cardamom pods, only the seeds, crushed

1 teaspoon fennel seeds

1 teaspoon cumin seeds

1 teaspoon coriander seeds

2 teaspoons peanut oil

2 scallions, chopped

2 garlic cloves, smashed

2 jalapeno peppers, minced

1/2 teaspoon ginger, freshly grated

1 pound pork loin, cut into bite-sized cubes

1 cup coconut milk

1 cup chicken broth

1 teaspoon turmeric powder

1 tablespoon tamarind paste

1 tablespoon fresh lime juice

DIRECTIONS (Prep + Cook Time: 35 minutes) Place the cardamom, fennel, cumin, and coriander seeds in a nonstick skillet over medium-high heat. Stir for 6 minutes until the spices become aromatic and start to brown. Stir frequently to prevent the spices from burning. Set aside. Preheat your Air Fryer to 370 degrees F. Then, in a baking pan, heat the peanut oil for 2 minutes. Once hot, sauté the scallions for 2 to 3 minutes until tender. Stir in the garlic, peppers, and ginger; cook an additional minute, stirring frequently. Next, cook the pork for 3 to 4 minutes. Pour in the coconut milk and broth. Add the reserved seeds, turmeric, and tamarind paste. Let it cook for 15 minutes in the preheated Air Fryer. Divide between individual bowls; drizzle fresh lime juice over the top and serve immediately.

699. Herbed and Garlicky Pork Belly
INGREDIENTS (4 Servings)

1 pound pork belly

2 garlic cloves, halved

1 teaspoon shallot powder

1 teaspoon sea salt

1 teaspoon dried basil

1 teaspoon dried oregano

1 teaspoon dried thyme

1 teaspoon dried marjoram

1 teaspoon ground black pepper

1 lime, juiced

DIRECTIONS (Prep + Cook Time: 1 hour 15 minutes + Marinating Time)

Blanch the pork belly in a pot of boiling water for 10 to 13 minutes. Pat it dry with a kitchen towel. Now, poke holes all over the skin by using a fork. Then, mix the remaining ingredients to make the rub. Massage the rub all over the pork belly.

Drizzle lime juice all over the meat; place the pork belly in the refrigerator for 3 hours. Preheat your Air Fryer to 320 degrees F. Cook the pork belly for 35 minutes. Turn up the temperature to 360 degrees F and continue cooking for 20 minutes longer. Serve warm. Enjoy!

700. Ranchero Pork Kebabs
INGREDIENTS (3 Servings)

1 pound lean pork, ground	1 teaspoon mustard	4 tablespoons ranch-flavored tortilla chips, finely crushed
1 onion, chopped	Salt and ground black pepper, to taste	
1 garlic clove, smashed		

DIRECTIONS (Prep + Cook Time: 25 minutes)

Mix all ingredients using your hands. Knead until everything is well incorporated. Shape the meat mixture around flat skewers (sausage shapes). Cook at 365 degrees F for 11 to 12 minutes, turning them over once or twice. Work in batches. Serve!

701. Enchilada Bake with Corn and Cheese
INGREDIENTS (3 Servings)

1 tablespoon butter, melted	1 tablespoon California chili powder	2 tablespoons fish sauce
2 scallions, chopped	1 cup tomato sauce	3 corn tortillas
1 teaspoon fresh garlic, minced	1 cup chicken stock	1 cup corn
1 pound ground pork	1/4 teaspoon ground cumin	1 cup Colby cheese, shredded

DIRECTIONS (Prep + Cook Time: 30 minutes)

Melt the butter in a saucepan over medium heat. Now, add the scallions and garlic and cook for 2 minutes or until tender. Add the ground pork and cook for a further 3 minutes, crumbling with a spatula. To make the enchilada sauce, in a mixing bowl, thoroughly combine the chili powder, tomato sauce, chicken stock, cumin, and fish sauce. Place little sauce on the bottom of a baking pan. Add one tortilla and 1/3 of the tomato sauce; top with 1/3 of the ground pork mixture. Add 1/3 cup of the corn and 1/3 cup of the shredded Colby cheese. Repeat these steps 2 more times, finishing with cheese.

Cover the top of the casserole with a piece of foil and place in the cooking basket. Cook for 16 minutes at 250 degrees F. Enjoy!

702. Dijon Ribs with Cherry Tomatoes
INGREDIENTS (2 Servings)

1 rack ribs, cut in half to fit the Air Fryer	1 tablespoon Dijon mustard	1 teaspoon dried rosemary
1/4 cup dry white wine	Sea salt and ground black pepper, to taste	
2 tablespoons soy sauce	1 cup cherry tomatoes	

DIRECTIONS (Prep + Cook Time: 35 minutes)

Toss the pork ribs with wine, soy sauce, mustard, salt, and black pepper. Add the ribs to the lightly greased cooking basket. Cook in the preheated Air Fryer at 370 degrees F for 25 minutes. Turn the ribs over, add the cherry tomatoes and rosemary; cook an additional 5 minutes. Serve immediately.

703. Country-Style Pork and Mushroom Patties
INGREDIENTS (4 Servings)

1 tablespoon canola oil	1/2 pound brown mushrooms, chopped	1/2 teaspoon dried dill
1 onion, chopped	Salt and black pepper, to taste	4 slices Cheddar cheese
2 garlic cloves, minced	1 teaspoon cayenne pepper	
1 pound ground pork	1/2 teaspoon dried rosemary	

DIRECTIONS (Prep + Cook Time: 30 minutes)

Start by preheating your Air Fryer to 370 degrees F. In a mixing bowl, thoroughly combine the oil, onions, garlic, ground pork, mushrooms, salt, black pepper, cayenne pepper, rosemary, and dill. Shape the meat mixture into four patties.

Spritz the bottom of the cooking basket with cooking spray. Cook the meatballs in the preheated Air Fryer at 370 degrees for 20 minutes, flipping them halfway through cooking. Top the warm patties with cheese and serve. Enjoy!

704. Japanese Ribs (Supearibu no Nikomi)
INGREDIENTS (4 Servings)

- 2 pounds pork ribs
- 1/2 cup tomato puree
- 1/2 cup ketchup
- 1 teaspoon orange zest
- 1 tablespoon Worcestershire sauce
- 2 tablespoons brown sugar
- 1 teaspoon garlic powder
- 1 tablespoon instant dashi
- 1 tablespoon mirin
- 1 tablespoon black sesame seeds

DIRECTIONS (Prep + Cook Time: 25 minutes)

Preheat your Air Fryer to 370 degrees F. Toss the pork ribs with all ingredients, except the sesame seeds, in a nonstick grill pan. Grill your ribs approximately 18 minutes at 390 degrees F, turning them periodically. Serve with the sauce and black sesame seeds and enjoy!

705. Easy Minty Meatballs
INGREDIENTS (4 Servings)

- 1/2 pound ground pork
- 1/2 pound ground beef
- 1 shallot, chopped
- 2 garlic cloves, minced
- 1 tablespoon coriander, chopped
- 1 teaspoon fresh mint, minced
- Sea salt and ground black pepper, to taste
- 1/2 teaspoon mustard seeds
- 1 teaspoon fennel seeds
- 1 teaspoon ground cumin
- 1 cup mozzarella, sliced

DIRECTIONS (Prep + Cook Time: 20 minutes)

In a mixing bowl, combine all ingredients, except the mozzarella. Shape the mixture into balls and transfer them to a lightly greased cooking basket. Cook the meatballs in the preheated Air Fryer at 380 degrees for 10 minutes. Check the meatballs halfway through the cooking time. Top with sliced mozzarella and bake for 3 minutes more. To serve, arrange on a nice serving platter. Enjoy!

706. Italian Sausage Meatball Casserole
INGREDIENTS (4 Servings)

- 1 pound Italian pork sausage, crumbled
- 1 egg
- 1 cup regular rolled oat
- 1 teaspoon cayenne pepper
- Sea salt and ground black pepper, to taste
- 1 tablespoon olive oil
- 1 leek, chopped
- 1 teaspoon fresh garlic, minced
- 1 chili pepper, chopped
- 1 teaspoon dried oregano
- 1 teaspoon dried basil
- 1 teaspoon celery seeds
- 1 teaspoon brown mustard
- 2 cups tomato puree

DIRECTIONS (Prep + Cook Time: 35 minutes) In a mixing bowl, thoroughly combine the pork sausage with egg, oats, cayenne pepper, salt, and black pepper. Form the sausage mixture into meatballs. Spritz the Air Fryer basket with cooking oil. Cook the meatballs in the preheated Air Fryer at 380 degrees for 10 minutes, shaking the basket halfway through the cooking time. Reserve. Meanwhile, heat the olive oil in a pan over medium-high heat. Sauté the leeks until tender and aromatic. Stir in the garlic, pepper, and seasonings and cook for a further 2 minutes. Add the brown mustard and tomato puree and cook another 5 minutes. Transfer the tomato sauce to the baking pan. Add the meatballs and cook in the preheated Air Fryer at 350 degrees F for 10 minutes. Serve warm.

707. Pigs in a Blanket with a Twist
INGREDIENTS (4 Servings)

- 12 refrigerator biscuits
- 8 hot dogs, cut into
- 3 pieces
- 1 egg yolk
- 2 tablespoons poppy seeds
- 1 tablespoon oregano

DIRECTIONS (Prep + Cook Time: 15 minutes) Flatten each biscuit slightly; cut in half. Now, mix the egg yolk with the poppy seeds and oregano. Wrap the biscuits around the hot dog pieces sealing the edges and brushing with the egg mixture to adhere. Bake in the preheated Air Fryer at 395 degrees F for 8 minutes, Enjoy!

708. Mayo Roasted Sirloin Steak
INGREDIENTS (3 Servings)

- 1 pound sirloin steak, cubed
- 1/2 cup mayonnaise
- 1 tablespoon red wine vinegar
- 1/2 teaspoon dried basil
- 1 teaspoon garlic, minced
- 1/2 teaspoon cayenne pepper Kosher
- salt and ground black pepper, to season

DIRECTIONS (Prep + Cook Time: 20 minutes)

Pat dry the sirloin steak with paper towels. In a small mixing dish, thoroughly combine the remaining ingredients until everything is well incorporated. Toss the cubed steak with the mayonnaise mixture and transfer to the Air Fryer cooking basket. Cook in the preheated Air Fryer at 400 degrees F for 7 minutes. Shake the basket and continue to cook for a further 7 minutes. Enjoy!

709. Porterhouse Steak with Tangy Sauce
INGREDIENTS (2 Servings)

- 1/2 pound Porterhouse steak, cut into four thin pieces
- Salt and pepper, to season
- 1 teaspoon sesame oil
- 1 teaspoon garlic paste
- 1 teaspoon ginger juice
- 1 tablespoon fish sauce
- 1 tablespoon soy sauce
- 1 habanero pepper, minced
- 2 tablespoons brown sugar

DIRECTIONS (Prep + Cook Time: 20 minutes)

Pat the steak dry and generously season it with salt and black pepper. Cook in the preheated Air Fryer at 400 degrees F for 7 minutes; turn on the other side and cook an additional 7 to 8 minutes. To make the sauce, heat the remaining ingredients in a small saucepan over medium-high heat; let it simmer for a few minutes until heated through. Spoon the sauce over the steak and serve over hot cooked rice or egg noodles. Enjoy!

710. Filet Mignon and Green Bean Salad
INGREDIENTS (2 Servings)

- 1/2 pound filet mignon
- Salt and ground black pepper, to taste
- 1/2 pound green beans
- 1/2 teaspoon butter, melted
- 1 red bell pepper, sliced
- 1 green bell pepper, sliced
- 1 cup mixed greens
- 1/4 cup walnuts, roughly chopped
- 1/4 cup feta cheese, crumbled
- 2 tablespoons tahini
- 1 tablespoon Dijon mustard
- 1 tablespoon sesame oil
- 1 tablespoon balsamic vinegar
- 2 tablespoons pomegranate seeds

DIRECTIONS (Prep + Cook Time: 25 minutes)

Season the fillet mignon with salt and pepper to taste. Cook in the preheated Air Fryer at 400 degrees F for 18 minutes, turning them over halfway through the cooking time. Set aside. Then, add the green beans to the cooking basket and drizzle it with melted butter. Cook at 400 degrees F for 5 minutes, shaking the basket once or twice. Slice the beef into bite-sized strips and transfer to a nice salad bowl. Toss the beef and green beans with bell peppers, mixed greens, walnuts and feta cheese. Then, make the dressing by whisking tahini, mustard, sesame oil and balsamic vinegar; dress your salad and serve garnished with pomegranate seeds. Enjoy!

711. Grandma's Roast Beef with Harvest Vegetables
INGREDIENTS (3 Servings)

- 1 pound beef roast
- 1 teaspoon brown mustard
- 1/4 cup apple juice
- 1 tablespoon fish sauce
- 1 tablespoon honey
- 1/2 teaspoon dried dill
- 1/2 teaspoon dried thyme
- 2 medium-sized carrots, sliced
- 1 parsnip, sliced
- 1 red onion, sliced
- Sea salt and ground black pepper, to taste
- 1 teaspoon paprika

DIRECTIONS (Prep + Cook Time: 45 minutes) Toss the beef roast with the mustard, apple juice, fish sauce, honey, dill and thyme in a glass bowl. Cover and let it marinate in your refrigerator overnight. Add the marinated beef roast to the cooking basket, discarding the marinade. Roast in your Air Fryer at 400 degrees F for 40 minutes. Turn the beef over and baste with the reserved marinade. Add the carrots, parsnip and onion to the cooking basket; continue to cook for 12 minutes more. Season the beef and vegetables with salt, black pepper and paprika. Serve warm.

712. Mediterranean Burgers with Onion Jam
INGREDIENTS (2 Servings)

- 1/2 pound ground chuck
- 2 tablespoons scallions, chopped
- 1/2 teaspoon garlic, minced
- 1 teaspoon brown mustard Kosher
- salt and ground black pepper, to taste
- 2 burger buns
- 2 ounces Haloumi cheese
- 1 medium tomato, sliced
- 2 Romaine lettuce leaves

Onion jam:

- 2 tablespoons butter, at room temperature
- 2 red onions, sliced
- Sea salt and ground black pepper, to taste
- 1 cup red wine
- 2 tablespoons honey
- 1 tablespoon fresh lemon juice

DIRECTIONS (Prep + Cook Time: 20 minutes) Mix the ground chuck, scallions, garlic, mustard, salt and black pepper until well combined; shape the mixture into two equal patties. Spritz a cooking basket with a nonstick cooking spray. Air fry your burgers at 370 degrees F for about 11 minutes or to your desired degree of doneness. Meanwhile, make the onion jam. In a small saucepan, melt the butter; once hot, cook the onions for about 4 minutes. Turn the heat to simmer, add salt, black pepper and wine and cook until liquid evaporates. Stir in the honey and continue to simmer until the onions are a jam-like consistency; afterwards, drizzle with freshly squeezed lemon juice. Top the bottom halves of the burger buns with the warm beef patty. Top with haloumi cheese, tomato, lettuce and onion jam. Set the bun tops in place and serve right now. Enjoy!

713. Traditional Italian Beef Braciole
INGREDIENTS (4 Servings)

- 1 pound round steak, pounded 1/4 inch thick
- Sea salt and ground black pepper, to taste
- 1 tablespoon olive oil
- 1 red onion, sliced
- 1/4 cup provolone cheese, shredded
- 2 tablespoons marinara sauce
- 1 tablespoon fresh cilantro, chopped
- 1 tablespoon fresh Italian parsley, chopped
- 1 large Italian pepper, deveined and sliced

DIRECTIONS (Prep + Cook Time: 15 minutes)

Pat the round steak dry with paper towels and generously season it with salt and black pepper. Heat the olive oil in a small skillet over a moderate heat; once hot, sauté the onion until just tender and translucent. Add in the cheese, marinara, cilantro, parsley and pepper; stir to combine well. Spoon the mixture onto the center of the steak. Roll the steak jelly-roll style and secure with toothpicks. Cook your Braciole in the preheated Air Fryer at 400 degrees F for about 10 minutes, checking the meat halfway through the cooking time. Serve with hot cooked orecchiette pasta or polenta. Enjoy!

714. Mediterranean-Style Beef Steak and Zucchini
INGREDIENTS (4 Servings)

- 1 ½ pounds beef steak
- 1 pound zucchini
- 1 teaspoon dried rosemary
- 1 teaspoon dried basil
- 1 teaspoon dried oregano
- 2 tablespoons extra-virgin olive oil
- 2 tablespoons fresh chives, chopped

DIRECTIONS (Prep + Cook Time: 20 minutes)

Start by preheating your Air Fryer to 400 degrees F. Toss the steak and zucchini with the spices and olive oil. Transfer to the cooking basket and cook for 6 minutes. Now, shale the basket and cook another 6 minutes. Serve immediately garnished with fresh chives. Enjoy!

715. Scotch Fillet with Sweet 'n' Sticky Sauce
INGREDIENTS (4 Servings)

- 2 pounds scotch fillet, sliced into strips
- 4 tablespoons tortilla chips, crushed
- 2 green onions, chopped
- Sauce:
- 1 tablespoon butter
- 2 garlic cloves, minced
- 1/2 teaspoon dried rosemary
- 1/2 teaspoon dried dill
- 1/2 cup beef broth
- 1 tablespoons fish sauce
- 2 tablespoons honey

DIRECTIONS (Prep + Cook Time: 40 minutes)

Start by preheating your Air Fryer to 390 degrees F. Coat the beef strips with the crushed tortilla chips on all sides. Spritz with cooking spray on all sides and transfer them to the cooking basket. Cook for 30 minutes, shaking the basket every 10 minutes. Meanwhile, heat the sauce ingredient in a saucepan over medium-high heat. Bring to a boil and reduce the heat; cook until the sauce has thickened slightly. Add the steak to the sauce; let it sit approximately 8 minutes. Serve over the hot egg noodles if desired. Enjoy!

716. Beef Taco Roll-Ups with Cotija Cheese
INGREDIENTS (4 Servings)

- 1 tablespoon sesame oil
- 2 tablespoons scallions, chopped
- 1 garlic clove, minced
- 1 bell pepper, chopped
- 1/2 pound ground beef
- 1/2 teaspoon Mexican oregano
- 1/2 teaspoon dried marjoram
- 1 teaspoon chili powder
- 1/2 cup refried beans
- Sea salt and ground black pepper, to taste
- 1/2 cup Cotija cheese, shredded
- 8 roll wrappers

DIRECTIONS (Prep + Cook Time: 25 minutes)

Start by preheating your Air Fryer to 395 degrees F. Heat the sesame oil in a nonstick skillet over medium-high heat. Cook the scallions, garlic, and peppers until tender and fragrant. Add the ground beef, oregano, marjoram, and chili powder. Continue cooking for 3 minutes longer or until it is browned. Stir in the beans, salt, and pepper. Divide the meat/bean mixture between wrappers that are softened with a little bit of water. Top with cheese. Roll the wrappers and spritz them with cooking oil on all sides. Cook in the preheated Air Fryer for 11 to 12 minutes, flipping them halfway through the cooking time. Enjoy!

717. Meatballs with Cranberry Sauce
INGREDIENTS (4 Servings)

Meatballs:

1 ½ pounds ground chuck	1/2 teaspoon dried basil	2 garlic cloves, minced
1 egg 1 cup rolled oats	1/2 teaspoon dried oregano	2 tablespoons scallions, chopped
1/2 cup Romano cheese, grated	1 teaspoon paprika	Sea salt and cracked black pepper, to taste

Cranberry Sauce:

10 ounces BBQ sauce	8 ounces cranberry sauce

DIRECTIONS (Prep + Cook Time: 40 minutes)

In a large bowl, mix all ingredients for the meatballs. Mix until everything is well incorporated; then, shape the meat mixture into 2-inch balls using a cookie scoop. Transfer them to the lightly greased cooking basket and cook at 380 degrees F for 10 minutes. Shake the basket occasionally and work in batches. Add the BBQ sauce and cranberry sauce to a saucepan and cook over moderate heat until you achieve a glaze-like consistency; it will take about 15 minutes. Gently stir in the air fried meatballs and cook an additional 3 minutes or until heated through. Enjoy!

718. Kid-Friendly Mini Meatloaves
INGREDIENTS (4 Servings)

2 tablespoons bacon, chopped	1 pound ground beef	Salt and black pepper, to taste
1 small-sized onion, chopped	1/2 teaspoon dried basil	1/2 cup panko crumbs
1 bell pepper, chopped	1/2 teaspoon dried mustard seeds	4 tablespoons tomato puree
1 garlic clove, minced	1/2 teaspoon dried marjoram	

DIRECTIONS (Prep + Cook Time: 30 minutes)

Heat a nonstick skillet over medium-high heat; cook the bacon for 1 to 2 minutes; add the onion, bell pepper, and garlic and cook another 3 minutes or until fragrant. Heat off. Stir in the ground beef, spices, and panko crumbs. Stir until well combined. Shape the mixture into four mini meatloaves. Preheat your Air Fryer to 350 degrees F. Spritz the cooking basket with nonstick spray. Place the mini meatloaves in the cooking basket and cook for 10 minutes; turn them over, top with the tomato puree and continue to cook for 10 minutes more.

719. Mayonnaise and Rosemary Grilled Steak
INGREDIENTS (4 Servings)

1 cup mayonnaise	2 tablespoons Worcestershire sauce	1/2 teaspoon ground black pepper	1 teaspoon garlic, minced
1 tablespoon fresh rosemary, finely chopped	Sea salt, to taste	1 teaspoon smoked paprika	1 ½ pounds short loin steak

DIRECTIONS (Prep + Cook Time: 20 minutes)

Combine the mayonnaise, rosemary, Worcestershire sauce, salt, pepper, paprika, and garlic; mix to combine well. Now, brush the mayonnaise mixture over both sides of the steak. Lower the steak onto the grill pan. Grill in the preheated Air Fryer at 390 degrees F for 8 minutes. Turn the steaks over and grill an additional 7 minutes. Check for doneness with a meat thermometer. Serve warm and enjoy!

720. New York Strip with Pearl Onions
INGREDIENTS (4 Servings)

1 ½ pounds New York strip, cut into strips	1 (1-pound) head cauliflower, broken into florets	1 cup pearl onion, sliced

Marinade:

1/4 cup tamari sauce	2 cloves garlic, minced	1/4 cup tomato paste
1 tablespoon olive oil	1 teaspoon of ground ginger	1/4 cup red wine

DIRECTIONS (Prep + Cook Time: 20 minutes + Marinating Time)

Mix all ingredients for the marinade. Add the beef to the marinade and let it sit in your refrigerator for 1 hour. Preheat your Air Fryer to 400 degrees F.

Transfer the meat to the Air Fryer basket. Add the cauliflower and onions. Drizzle a few tablespoons of marinade all over the meat and vegetables. Cook for 12 minutes, shaking the basket halfway through the cooking time. Serve warm.

721. Grilled London Broil with Mustard
INGREDIENTS (4 Servings)

For the marinade:

- 2 tablespoons Worcestershire sauce
- 2 garlic cloves, minced
- 1 tablespoon oil
- 2 tablespoons rice vinegar
- 1 tablespoon molasses

London Broil:

- 2 pounds London broil
- 2 tablespoons tomato paste
- Sea salt and cracked black pepper, to taste
- 1 tablespoon mustard

DIRECTIONS (Prep + Cook Time: 30 minutes + Marinating Time) Combine all the marinade ingredients in a mixing bowl; add the London boil to the bowl. Cover and let it marinate for 3 hours. Preheat the Air Fryer to 400 degrees F. Spritz the Air Fryer grill pan with cooking oil. Grill the marinated London broil in the preheated Air Fryer for 18 minutes. Turn London broil over, top with the tomato paste, salt, black pepper, and mustard. Continue to grill an additional 10 minutes. Serve immediately.

722. Beef Skewers with Pearl Onions and Eggplant
INGREDIENTS (4 Servings)

- 1 ½ pounds beef stew meat cubes
- 1/4 cup mayonnaise
- 1/4 cup sour cream
- 1 tablespoon yellow mustard
- 1 tablespoon Worcestershire sauce
- 1 cup pearl onions
- 1 medium-sized eggplant,
- 1 ½-inch cubes
- Sea salt and ground black pepper, to taste

DIRECTIONS (Prep + Cook Time: 1 hour 30 minutes) In a mixing bowl, toss all ingredients until everything is well coated. Place in your refrigerator, cover, and let it marinate for 1 hour. Soak wooden skewers in water for 15 minutes Thread the beef cubes, pearl onions and eggplant onto skewers. Cook in preheated Air Fryer at 395 degrees F for 12 minutes, flipping halfway through the cooking time. Serve warm.

723. Beef and Sausage Meatloaf with Peppers
INGREDIENTS (4 Servings)

- 1/2 pound beef sausage, crumbled
- 1/2 pound ground beef
- 1/4 cup pork rinds
- 2 tablespoons Parmesan, preferably freshly grated
- 1 shallot, finely chopped
- 2 garlic cloves, minced
- Sea salt and ground black pepper, to taste
- 1 red bell pepper, finely chopped
- 1 serrano pepper, finely chopped

DIRECTIONS (Prep + Cook Time: 35 minutes) Start by preheating your Air Fryer to 390 degrees F. Mix all ingredients in a bowl. Knead until everything is well incorporated. Shape the mixture into a meatloaf and place in the baking pan that is previously greased with cooking oil. Cook for 24 minutes in the preheated Air Fryer. Let it stand on a cooling rack for 6 minutes before slicing and serving. Enjoy!

724. Korean Beef Bowl with Rice
INGREDIENTS (4 Servings)

- 2 tablespoons bacon, chopped
- 1 ½ pounds ground chuck
- 1 leek, chopped
- 2 garlic cloves, minced
- 1 tablespoon daenjang (soybean paste)
- 1 teaspoon kochukaru (chili pepper flakes)
- Sea salt and ground black pepper, to taste
- 2 cups white rice, hot cooked

DIRECTIONS (Prep + Cook Time: 20 minutes) Start by preheating your Air Fryer to 360 degrees. Then, add the bacon to the baking pan; cook the bacon just until it starts to get crisp. Add the ground chuck and cook for 2 minutes more, crumbling with a spatula. Add the leeks, garlic, and spices. Cook for 12 minutes more. Stir in the hot rice; stir well to combine and serve. Enjoy!

725. Birthday Party Cheeseburger Pizza
INGREDIENTS (4 Servings)

- Nonstick cooking oil
- 1 pound ground beef Kosher
- salt and ground black pepper, to taste
- 1/2 teaspoon oregano
- 1/2 teaspoon basil
- 1/4 teaspoon red pepper flakes
- 1/4 cup marinara sauce
- 2 spring onions, chopped
- 4 burger buns
- 1 cup mozzarella cheese, shredded

DIRECTIONS (Prep + Cook Time: 20 minutes) Start by preheating your Air Fryer to 370 degrees F. Spritz the Air Fryer basket with cooking oil. Add the ground beef and cook for 10 minutes, crumbling with a spatula. Season with salt, black pepper, oregano, basil, and red peppers. Spread the marinara pasta on each half of burger bun. Place the spring onions and ground meat mixture on the buns equally. Set the temperature to 350 degrees F. Place the burger pizza in the Air Fryer basket. Top with mozzarella cheese. Bake approximately 4 minutes or until cheese is bubbling. Top with another half of burger bun and serve. Enjoy!

726. Roasted Blade Steak with Green Beans
INGREDIENTS (4 Servings)

2 garlic cloves, smashed	1 tablespoon Cajun seasoning	1/2 teaspoon Tabasco pepper sauce
2 teaspoons sunflower oil	1 ½ pounds blade steak	Sea salt and ground black pepper, to taste
1/2 teaspoon cayenne pepper	2 cups green beans	

DIRECTIONS (Prep + Cook Time: 25 minutes)

Start by preheating your Air Fryer to 330 degrees F. Mix the garlic, oil, cayenne pepper, and Cajun seasoning to make a paste. Rub it over both sides of the blade steak. Cook for 13 minutes in the preheated Air Fryer. Now, flip the steak and cook an additional 8 minutes. Heat the green beans in a saucepan. Add a few tablespoons of water, Tabasco, salt, and black pepper; heat until it wilts or about 10 minutes. Serve the roasted blade steak with green beans on the side. Enjoy!

727. Polish Sausage and Sourdough Kabobs
INGREDIENTS (4 Servings)

1 pound smoked Polish beef sausage, sliced	1 tablespoon olive oil	2 cups sourdough bread, cubed
	2 tablespoons Worcestershire sauce	Salt and ground black pepper, to taste
1 tablespoon mustard	2 bell peppers, sliced	

DIRECTIONS (Prep + Cook Time: 20 minutes)

Toss the sausage with the mustard, olive, and Worcestershire sauce. Thread sausage, peppers, and bread onto skewers. Sprinkle with salt and black pepper. Cook in the preheated Air Fryer at 360 degrees F for 11 minutes. Brush the skewers with the reserved marinade. Enjoy!

728. Grilled Vienna Sausage with Broccoli
INGREDIENTS (4 Servings)

1 pound beef Vienna sausage	1 teaspoon yellow mustard	1 teaspoon garlic powder	1 pound broccoli
1/2 cup mayonnaise	1 tablespoon fresh lemon juice	1/4 teaspoon black pepper	

DIRECTIONS (Prep + Cook Time: 25 minutes)

Start by preheating your Air Fryer to 380 degrees F. Spritz the grill pan with cooking oil. Cut the sausages into serving sized pieces. Cook the sausages for 15 minutes, shaking the basket occasionally to get all sides browned. Set aside. In the meantime, whisk the mayonnaise with mustard, lemon juice, garlic powder, and black pepper. Toss the broccoli with the mayo mixture. Turn up temperature to 400 degrees F. Cook broccoli for 6 minutes, turning halfway through the cooking time. Serve the sausage with the grilled broccoli on the side. Enjoy!

729. Steak Fingers with Lime Sauce
INGREDIENTS (4 Servings)

1 ½ pounds sirloin steak	1 teaspoon celery seeds	1 cup breadcrumbs
1/4 cup soy sauce	1 teaspoon mustard seeds Coarse	1/4 cup parmesan cheese
1/4 cup fresh lime juice	sea salt and ground black pepper, to taste	1 teaspoon paprika
1 teaspoon garlic powder	1 teaspoon red pepper flakes	
1 teaspoon shallot powder	2 eggs, lightly whisked	

DIRECTIONS (Prep + Cook Time: 20 minutes + Marinating Time) Place the steak, soy sauce, lime juice, garlic powder, shallot powder, celery seeds, mustard seeds, salt, black pepper, and red pepper in a large ceramic bowl; let it marinate for 3 hours. Tenderize the cube steak by pounding with a mallet; cut into 1-inch strips. In a shallow bowl, whisk the eggs. In another bowl, mix the breadcrumbs, parmesan cheese, and paprika. Dip the beef pieces into the whisked eggs and coat on all sides. Now, dredge the beef pieces in the breadcrumb mixture. Cook at 400 degrees F for 14 minutes, flipping halfway through the cooking time. Meanwhile, make the sauce by heating the reserved marinade in a saucepan over medium heat; let it simmer until thoroughly warmed. Serve the steak fingers with the sauce on the side. Enjoy!

730. Classic Beef Ribs
INGREDIENTS (4 Servings)

2 pounds beef back ribs	1 teaspoon red pepper flakes
1 tablespoon sunflower oil	1 teaspoon dry mustard Coarse
1/2 teaspoon mixed peppercorns, cracked	sea salt, to taste

DIRECTIONS (Prep + Cook Time: 35 minutes)

Trim the excess fat from the beef ribs. Mix the sunflower oil, cracked peppercorns, red pepper, dry mustard, and salt. Rub over the ribs. Cook in the preheated Air Fryer at 395 degrees F for 11 minutes Turn the heat to 330 degrees F and continue to cook for 18 minutes more. Serve warm.

731. Spicy Short Ribs with Red Wine Sauce
INGREDIENTS (4 Servings)

1 ½ pounds short ribs	1 teaspoon fresh ginger, grated	1 teaspoon chipotle chili powder
1 cup red wine	1 teaspoon salt	1 cup ketchup
1/2 cup tamari sauce	1 teaspoon black pepper	1 teaspoon garlic powder
1 lemon, juiced	1 teaspoon paprika	1 teaspoon cumin

DIRECTIONS (Prep + Cook Time: 20 minutes + Marinating Time)

In a ceramic bowl, place the beef ribs, wine, tamari sauce, lemon juice, ginger, salt, black pepper, paprika, and chipotle chili powder. Cover and let it marinate for 3 hours in the refrigerator. Discard the marinade and add the short ribs to the Air Fryer basket. Cook in the preheated Air fry at 380 degrees F for 10 minutes, turning them over halfway through the cooking time. In the meantime, heat the saucepan over medium heat; add the reserved marinade and stir in the ketchup, garlic powder, and cumin. Cook until the sauce has thickened slightly. Pour the sauce over the warm ribs and serve immediately. Enjoy!

732. Beef Nuggets with Cheesy Mushrooms
INGREDIENTS (4 Servings)

2 eggs, beaten	salt and ground black pepper, to taste	1 cup Swiss cheese, shredded
4 tablespoons yogurt	1/2 teaspoon onion powder	
1 cup tortilla chips, crushed	1 pound cube steak, cut into bite-size pieces	
1 teaspoon dry mesquite flavored seasoning mix Coarse	1 pound button mushrooms	

DIRECTIONS (Prep + Cook Time: 25 minutes)

In a shallow bowl, beat the eggs and yogurt. In a resealable bag, mix the tortilla chips, mesquite seasoning, salt, pepper, and onion powder. Dip the steak pieces in the egg mixture; then, place in the bag, and shake to coat on all sides. Cook at 400 degrees F for 14 minutes, flipping halfway through the cooking time. Add the mushrooms to the lightly greased cooking basket. Top with shredded Swiss cheese. Bake in the preheated Air Fryer at 400 degrees F for 5 minutes. Serve with the beef nuggets. Enjoy!

733. Asian-Style Beef Dumplings
INGREDIENTS (5 Servings)

1/2 pound ground chuck	2 garlic cloves, minced	2 teaspoons sesame oil
1/2 pound beef sausage, chopped	1 medium-sized egg, beaten	2 teaspoons sesame seeds, lightly toasted
1 cup Chinese cabbage, shredded	Sea salt and ground black pepper, to taste	2 tablespoons seasoned rice vinegar
1 bell pepper, chopped	20 wonton wrappers	1/2 teaspoon chili sauce
1 onion, chopped	2 tablespoons soy sauce	

DIRECTIONS (Prep + Cook Time: 25 minutes)

To make the filling, thoroughly combine the ground chuck, sausage, cabbage, bell pepper, onion, garlic, egg, salt, and black pepper. Place the wrappers on a clean and dry surface. Now, divide the filling among the wrappers. Then, fold each dumpling in half and pinch to seal. Transfer the dumplings to the lightly greased cooking basket. Bake at 390 degrees F for 15 minutes, turning over halfway through. In the meantime, mix the soy sauce, sesame oil, sesame seeds, rice vinegar, and chili sauce. Serve the beef dumplings with the sauce on the side. Enjoy!

734. Paprika Porterhouse Steak with Cauliflower
INGREDIENTS (4 Servings)

1 pound Porterhouse steak, sliced	1/2 teaspoon shallot powder	1 pound cauliflower, torn into florets
1 teaspoon butter, room temperature Coarse	1/2 teaspoon porcini powder	
sea salt and ground black pepper, to taste	1 teaspoon granulated garlic	
	1 teaspoon smoked paprika	

DIRECTIONS (Prep + Cook Time: 20 minutes)

Brush the steak with butter on all sides; season it with all spices. Season the cauliflower with salt and pepper to taste. Place the steak in the cooking basket and roast at 400 degrees F for 12 minutes; turn over halfway through the cooking time. Remove the cauliflower from the basket and continue to cook your steak for 2 to 3 minutes if needed. Serve the steak garnished with the cauliflower. Eat warm. Enjoy!

735. Rustic Mini Meatloaves
INGREDIENTS (3 Servings)

- 2 slices bacon
- 1 onion, chopped
- 1 bell pepper, chopped
- 3/4 pound lean ground beef
- 1/2 teaspoon rosemary
- 1/4 teaspoon basil
- 1/2 teaspoon oregano Coarse
- sea salt and ground black pepper, to taste
- 1 teaspoon fresh garlic, minced
- 1 teaspoon mustard
- 1 egg, beaten
- 1/2 cup tomato paste

DIRECTIONS (Prep + Cook Time: 20 minutes)

Het up a frying pan over medium-high heat. Cook the bacon for 2 to 3 minutes, crumbling with a fork or wide spatula; reserve, leaving the bacon fat in the pan. Now, sauté the onion and pepper until just tender and fragrant. Add in the ground beef and cook for 2 to 3 minutes longer until no longer pink. Stir in the spices, garlic, mustard, egg and 1/4 of tomato paste. Add in the reserved bacon. Stir to combine well. Divide the mixture between three ramekins. Divide the remaining tomato paste between the ramekins. Then, air fry at 380 degrees F for 10 minutes. Let it rest for a few minutes before serving. Enjoy!

736. Kansas City-Style Ribs
INGREDIENTS (3 Servings)

- 1 pound beef ribs
- 1/4 cup ketchup
- 1/4 cup rum
- 1 tablespoon mustard
- 1 tablespoon olive oil
- 1 tablespoon brown sugar
- 1 teaspoon garlic powder
- 1/2 teaspoon onion powder
- 1/2 teaspoon chili powder
- 1 teaspoon liquid smoke
- Sea salt and ground black pepper, to season

DIRECTIONS (Prep + Cook Time: 35 minutes + Marinating Time)

Place all ingredients in a ceramic bowl, cover and allow it to marinate for 3 to 4 hours. Roast in your Air Fryer at 400 degrees F for 10 minutes. Reduce heat to 330 degrees F and cook an additional 20 minutes. Warm the remaining marinade in a nonstick skillet over a moderate flame to make the sauce. Drizzle the sauce over the beef ribs and eat warm. Enjoy!

737. Greek-Style Roast Beef
INGREDIENTS (3 Servings)

- 1 clove garlic, halved
- 1 ½ pounds beef eye round roast
- 1 zucchini, sliced lengthwise
- 2 teaspoons olive oil
- 1 teaspoon
- Greek spice mix Sea salt, to season
- 1/2 cup Greek-style yogurt

DIRECTIONS (Prep + Cook Time: 55 minutes)

Rub the beef eye round roast with garlic halves. Brush the beef eye round roast and zucchini with olive oil. Sprinkle with spices and place the beef in the cooking basket. Roast in your Air Fryer at 400 degrees F for 40 minutes. Turn the beef over. Add the zucchini to the cooking basket and continue to cook for 12 minutes more or until cooked through. Serve warm, garnished with Greek-style yogurt. Enjoy!

738. Argentinian Beef Empanadas
INGREDIENTS (2 Servings)

- 1/2 pound ground chuck
- 1/2 yellow onion
- 1 teaspoon fresh garlic, minced
- 2 tablespoons piri piri sauce
- 1 tablespoon mustard
- 6 cubes Cotija cheese
- 6 Goya discos pastry dough

DIRECTIONS (Prep + Cook Time: 20 minutes)

Heat a nonstick skillet over medium-high heat. Once hot, cook the ground beef, onion and garlic until tender, about 6 minutes. Crumble with a fork and stir in the piri piri sauce; stir to combine. Divide the sauce between empanadas. Top with mustard and cheese. Fold each of them in half and seal the edges. Bake in the preheated Air Fryer at 340 degrees F for about 8 minutes, flipping them halfway through the cooking time. Serve with salsa sauce if desired. Enjoy!

739. Authentic Greek Souvlaki with Sauce
INGREDIENTS (2 Servings)

- 1/2 pound sirloin steak, cut into bite-sized pieces
- 1 tablespoon olive oil
- 2 tablespoons Worcestershire sauce
- 4 tablespoons wine vinegar
- 1 tablespoon molasses
- 1 tablespoon mustard
- 2 garlic cloves, pressed
- 1 teaspoon dried oregano
- 1/4 teaspoon sea salt
- 1 teaspoon black peppercorns
- 4 tablespoons Greek-style yogurt
- 1/2 teaspoon tzatziki spice mix
- 2 tablespoons mayonnaise
- 4 wooden skewer sticks, soaked in water

DIRECTIONS (Prep + Cook Time: 15 minutes + Marinating Time)

Place the sirloin steak, olive oil, Worcestershire sauce, vinegar, molasses, mustard, garlic, oregano, salt and black peppercorns in a ceramic dish. Place in your refrigerator and let it marinate overnight. Thread the beef cubes onto skewers. Cook in preheated Air Fryer at 395 degrees F for 12 minutes, flipping halfway through the cooking time. In the meantime, mix the Greek yogurt with the tzatziki spice mix and mayo. Serve the souvlaki with the sauce on the side. Enjoy!

740. BBQ Glazed Beef Riblets
INGREDIENTS (3 Servings)

- 1 pound beef riblets
- Sea salt and red pepper, to taste
- 1/4 cup tomato paste
- 1/4 cup Worcestershire sauce
- 2 tablespoons hot sauce
- 1 tablespoon oyster sauce
- 2 tablespoons rice vinegar
- 1 tablespoon stone-ground mustard

DIRECTIONS (Prep + Cook Time: 15 minutes + Marinating Time)

Combine all ingredients in a glass dish, cover and marinate at least 2 hours in your refrigerator. Discard the marinade and place riblets in the Air Fryer cooking basket. Cook in the preheated Air Fryer at 360 degrees F for 12 minutes, shaking the basket halfway through to ensure even cooking. Heat the reserved marinade in a small skillet over a moderate flame; spoon the glaze over the riblets and serve immediately.

741. Beef Sausage-Stuffed Zucchini
INGREDIENTS (2 Servings)

- 1/2 pound beef sausage, crumbled
- 1/2 cup tortilla chips, crushed
- 1/2 teaspoon garlic, pressed
- 1/4 cup tomato paste
- 2 small-sized zucchini, halved lengthwise and seeds removed
- 1/2 cup sharp cheddar cheese, grated

DIRECTIONS (Prep + Cook Time: 30 minutes)

In a mixing bowl, thoroughly combine the beef sausage, tortilla chips, garlic and tomato paste. Divide the sausage mixture between the zucchini halves. Bake in the preheated Air Fryer at 400 degrees F for 20 minutes. Top with grated cheddar cheese and cook an additional 5 minutes. Enjoy!

742. Italian-Style Steak with Cremini Mushrooms
INGREDIENTS (2 Servings)

- 1/2 pound flank steak, cut into bite-sized pieces
- 8 ounces Cremini mushrooms, sliced
- 2 tablespoons tamari sauce
- 1 tablespoon peanut oil
- 1 teaspoon Italian seasoning blend
- Salt and black pepper, to taste

DIRECTIONS (Prep + Cook Time: 15 minutes)

Toss the steak and mushrooms with tamari sauce, peanut oil, Italian spices, salt and black pepper. Toss until the steak and mushrooms are well coated on all sides. Transfer the beef to the Air Fryer cooking basket. Cook at 400 degrees F for 7 minutes. Then, shake the basket and stir in the mushrooms. Continue to cook for 5 minutes longer. Serve immediately.

743. Tex-Mex Taco Pizza
INGREDIENTS (1 Servings)

- 1 teaspoon lard, melted
- 4 ounces ground beef sirloin
- 4 ounces pizza dough
- 2 tablespoons jarred salsa
- 1/4 teaspoon Mexican oregano
- 1/2 teaspoon basil
- 1/2 teaspoon granulated garlic
- 2 ounces cheddar cheese grated
- 1 plum tomato, sliced

DIRECTIONS (Prep + Cook Time: 20 minutes)

Melt the lard in a skillet over medium-high heat; once hot, cook the beef until no longer pink, about 5 minutes. Roll the dough out and transfer it to the Air Fryer cooking basket. Spread the jarred salsa over the dough. Sprinkle Mexican oregano, basil, garlic and cheese over the salsa. Top with the sautéed beef, then with the sliced tomato. Bake in your Air Fryer at 375 degrees F for about 11 minutes until the bottom of crust is lightly browned.

744. Doubly Cheesy Meatballs
INGREDIENTS (4 Servings)

- 1 pound ground beef
- 1/4 cup Grana Padano, grated
- 2 tablespoons scallion, chopped
- 2 garlic cloves, minced
- 2 stale crustless bread slices
- 1 tablespoon Italian seasoning mix
- 1 egg, beaten
- 1/4 cup Mozzarella cheese, shredded Kosher
- salt and ground black pepper, to taste

DIRECTIONS (Prep + Cook Time: 15 minutes) In a mixing bowl, combine all ingredients. Then, shape the mixture into 8 meatballs. Cook the meatballs at 370 degrees F for 10 minutes, shaking the basket halfway through the cooking time. Serve the meatballs in a sandwich if desired. Enjoy!

745. Taco Stuffed Avocados
INGREDIENTS (3 Servings)

- 1/3 pound ground beef
- 2 tablespoons shallots, minced
- 1/2 teaspoon garlic, minced
- 1 tomato, chopped
- 1/3 teaspoon Mexican oregano
- Salt and black pepper, to taste
- 1 chipotle pepper in adobo sauce, minced
- 1/4 cup cilantro
- 3 avocados, cut into halves and pitted
- 1/2 cup Cotija cheese, grated

DIRECTIONS (Prep + Cook Time: 15 minutes)

Preheat a nonstick skillet over medium-high heat. Cook the ground beef and shallot for about 4 minutes. Stir in the garlic and tomato and continue to sauté for a minute or so. Add in the Mexican oregano, salt, black pepper, chipotle pepper and cilantro. Then, remove a bit of the pulp from each avocado half and fill them with the taco mixture. Cook in the preheated Air Fryer at 400 degrees F for 5 minutes. Top with Cotija cheese and continue to cook for 4 minutes more or until cheese is bubbly. Enjoy!

746. Roasted Ribeye with Garlic Mayo
INGREDIENTS (3 Servings)

- 1 ½ pounds ribeye, bone-in
- 1 tablespoon butter, room temperature
- Salt, to taste
- 1/2 teaspoon crushed black pepper
- 1/2 teaspoon dried dill
- 1/2 teaspoon cayenne pepper
- 1/2 teaspoon garlic powder
- 1/2 teaspoon onion powder
- 1 teaspoon ground coriander
- 3 tablespoons mayonnaise
- 1 teaspoon garlic, minced

DIRECTIONS (Prep + Cook Time: 20 minutes)

Start by preheating your Air Fryer to 400 degrees F. Pat dry the ribeye and rub it with softened butter on all sides. Sprinkle with seasonings and transfer to the cooking basket. Cook in the preheated Air Fryer for 15 minutes, flipping them halfway through the cooking time. In the meantime, simply mix the mayonnaise with garlic and place in the refrigerator until ready to serve. Enjoy!

747. Quick Sausage and Veggie Sandwiches
INGREDIENTS (4 Servings)

- 4 bell peppers
- 2 tablespoons canola oil
- 4 medium-sized tomatoes, halved
- 4 spring onions
- 4 beef sausages
- 4 hot dog buns
- 1 tablespoon mustard

DIRECTIONS (Prep + Cook Time: 35 minutes) Start by preheating your Air Fryer to 400 degrees F. Add the bell peppers to the cooking basket. Drizzle 1 tablespoon of canola oil all over the bell peppers. Cook for 5 minutes. Turn the temperature down to 350 degrees F. Add the tomatoes and spring onions to the cooking basket and cook an additional 10 minutes. Reserve your vegetables. Then, add the sausages to the cooking basket. Drizzle with the remaining tablespoon of canola oil. Cook in the preheated Air Fryer at 380 degrees F for 15 minutes, flipping them halfway through the cooking time. Add the sausage to a hot dog bun; top with the air-fried vegetables and mustard; serve. Enjoy!

748. Tender Marinated Flank Steak
INGREDIENTS (4 Servings)

- 1 ½ pounds flank steak
- 1/2 cup red wine
- 1/2 cup apple cider vinegar
- 2 tablespoons soy sauce Salt, to taste
- 1/2 teaspoon ground black pepper
- 1/2 teaspoon red pepper flakes, crushed
- 1/2 teaspoon dried basil
- 1 teaspoon thyme

DIRECTIONS (Prep + Cook Time: 20 minutes + Marinating Time)

Add all ingredients to a large ceramic bowl. Cover and let it marinate for 3 hours in your refrigerator. Transfer the flank steak to the Air Fryer basket that is previously greased with nonstick cooking oil. Cook in the preheated Air Fryer at 400 degrees F for 12 minutes, flipping over halfway through the cooking time. Enjoy!

749. Korean-Style Breakfast Patties
INGREDIENTS (4 Servings)

- 1 ½ pounds ground beef
- 1 teaspoon garlic, minced
- 2 tablespoons scallions, chopped
- Sea salt and cracked black pepper, to taste
- 1 teaspoon Gochugaru (Korean chili powder)
- 1/2 teaspoon dried marjoram
- 1 teaspoon dried thyme
- 1 teaspoon mustard seeds
- 1/2 teaspoon shallot powder
- 1/2 teaspoon cumin powder
- 1/2 teaspoon paprika
- 1 tablespoon liquid smoke flavoring

DIRECTIONS (Prep + Cook Time: 20 minutes)

In a mixing bowl, thoroughly combine all ingredients until well combined. Shape into four patties and spritz them with cooking oil on both sides. Bake at 357 degrees F for 18 minutes, flipping over halfway through the cooking time. Serve on hamburger buns if desired. Enjoy!

750. Indonesian Beef with Peanut Sauce
INGREDIENTS (4 Servings)

- 2 pounds filet mignon, sliced into bite-sized strips
- 1 tablespoon oyster sauce
- 2 tablespoons sesame oil
- 2 tablespoons tamari sauce
- 1 tablespoon ginger-garlic paste
- 1 tablespoon mustard 1 tablespoon honey
- 1 teaspoon chili powder
- 1/4 cup peanut butter
- 2 tablespoons lime juice
- 1 teaspoon red pepper flakes
- 2 tablespoons water

DIRECTIONS (Prep + Cook Time: 25 minutes + Marinating Time)

Place the beef strips, oyster sauce, sesame oil, tamari sauce, ginger-garlic paste, mustard, honey, and chili powder in a large ceramic dish. Cover and allow it to marinate for 2 hours in your refrigerator. Cook in the preheated Air Fryer at 400 degrees F for 18 minutes, shaking the basket occasionally. Mix the peanut butter with lime juice, red pepper flakes, and water. Spoon the sauce onto the air fried beef strips and serve warm. Enjoy!

751. Authentic Dum Kebab with Raita Sauce
INGREDIENTS (4 Servings)

- 1 ½ pounds ground chuck
- 1 egg
- 1 medium-sized leek, chopped
- 2 garlic cloves, smashed
- 2 tablespoons fresh parsley, chopped
- 1 teaspoon fresh rosemary, chopped
- Sea salt, to taste
- 1/2 teaspoon ground black pepper
- 1/2 teaspoon chili powder
- 1 teaspoon garam masala
- 1 teaspoon papaya paste
- 1 teaspoon ginger paste
- 1/2 teaspoon ground cumin

Raita Sauce:

- 1 small-sized cucumber, grated and squeezed
- A pinch of salt
- 1 cup full-fat yogurt
- 1/4 cup fresh cilantro, coarsely chopped
- 1 tablespoon fresh lime juice

DIRECTIONS (Prep + Cook Time: 25 minutes)

Combine all ingredients until everything is well incorporated. Press the meat mixture into a baking pan. Cook in the preheated Air Fryer at 360 degrees F for 15 minutes. Taste for doneness with a meat thermometer. Meanwhile, mix all ingredients for the sauce. Serve the warm meatloaf with the sauce on the side. Enjoy!

752. Moroccan-Style Steak Salad
INGREDIENTS (4 Servings)

- 2 pounds flank steak
- 1/4 cup soy sauce
- 4 tablespoons dry red wine
- Salt, to taste
- 1/2 teaspoon ground black pepper
- 2 parsnips, peeled and sliced lengthways
- 1 teaspoon paprika
- 1 teaspoon onion powder
- 1 teaspoon garlic powder
- 1/2 teaspoon ground coriander
- 1/4 teaspoon ground allspice 2 tablespoons olive oil
- 2 tablespoons lime juice
- 1 teaspoon honey
- 1 cup lettuce leaves, shredded
- 1/2 cup pomegranate seeds

DIRECTIONS (Prep + Cook Time: 20 minutes)

Place the flank steak, soy sauce, wine, salt, and black pepper in a ceramic bowl. Let it marinate for 2 hours in your refrigerator. Transfer the meat to a lightly greased cooking basket. Top with parsnips. Add the paprika, onion powder, garlic powder, coriander, and allspice. Cook in the preheated Air Fryer at 400 degrees F for 7 minutes; turn over and cook an additional 5 minutes. In the meantime, make the dressing by mixing olive oil with lime juice and honey. Put the lettuce leaves and roasted parsnip in a salad bowl; toss with the dressing. Slice the steaks and place on top of the salad. Sprinkle over the pomegranate seeds and serve. Enjoy!

753. Best Pretzel Sliders
INGREDIENTS (4 Servings)

- 3/4 pound ground beef
- 1 smoked beef sausage, chopped
- 4 scallions, chopped
- 1 garlic clove, minced
- 2 tablespoons fresh coriander, chopped
- 4 tablespoons rolled oats
- 2 tablespoons tomato paste
- Himalayan salt and ground black pepper, to taste
- 8 small pretzel rolls
- 4 tablespoons mayonnaise
- 8 thin slices of tomato

DIRECTIONS (Prep + Cook Time: 40 minutes)

Start by preheating your Air Fryer to 370 degrees F. In a mixing bowl, thoroughly combine the ground beef, sausage, scallions, garlic, coriander, oats, tomato paste, salt, and black pepper. Knead with your hands until everything is well combined. Form the mixture into eight patties and cook them for 18 to 20 minutes. Work in batches. Place the burgers on slider buns; top with mayonnaise and tomato slices. Enjoy!

754. Pastrami and Cheddar Quiche
INGREDIENTS (2 Servings)

- 4 eggs
- 1 bell pepper, chopped
- 2 spring onions, chopped
- 1 cup pastrami, sliced
- 1/4 cup Greek-style yogurt
- 1/2 cup Cheddar cheese, grated
- Sea salt, to taste
- 1/4 teaspoon ground black pepper

DIRECTIONS (Prep + Cook Time: 20 minutes)

Start by preheating your Air Fryer to 330 degrees F. Spritz the baking pan with cooking oil. Then, thoroughly combine all ingredients and pour the mixture into the prepared baking pan. Cook for 7 to 9 minutes or until the eggs have set. Place on a cooling rack and let it sit for 10 minutes before slicing and serving. Enjoy!

755. Hungarian Oven Stew (Marha Pörkölt)
INGREDIENTS (4 Servings)

- 4 tablespoons all-purpose flour
- Sea salt and cracked black pepper, to taste
- 1 teaspoon Hungarian paprika
- 1 pound beef chuck roast, boneless, cut into bite-sized cubes
- 2 teaspoons sunflower oil
- 1 medium-sized leek, chopped
- 2 garlic cloves, minced
- 2 bay leaves
- 1 teaspoon caraway seeds.
- 2 cups roasted vegetable broth
- 2 ripe tomatoes, pureed
- 2 tablespoons red wine
- 2 bell peppers, chopped
- 2 medium carrots, sliced
- 1 celery stalk, peeled and diced

DIRECTIONS (Prep + Cook Time: 1 hour 10 minutes)

Add the flour, salt, black pepper, paprika, and beef to a resealable bag; shake to coat well. Heat the oil in a Dutch oven over medium-high flame; sauté the leeks, garlic, bay leaves, and caraway seeds about 4 minutes or until fragrant. Transfer to a lightly greased baking pan. Then, brown the beef, stirring occasionally, working in batches. Add to the baking pan. Add the vegetable broth, tomatoes, and red wine. Lower the pan onto the Air Fryer basket. Bake at 325 degrees F for 40 minutes. Add the bell peppers, carrots, and celery. Cook an additional 20 minutes. Serve immediately and enjoy!

756. Ranch Meatloaf with Peppers
INGREDIENTS (5 Servings)

- 1 pound beef, ground
- 1/2 pound veal, ground
- 1 egg
- 4 tablespoons vegetable juice
- 1 cup crackers, crushed
- 2 bell peppers, chopped
- 1 onion, chopped
- 2 garlic cloves, minced
- 2 tablespoons tomato paste
- 2 tablespoons soy sauce
- 1 (1-ounce) package ranch dressing mix Sea salt, to taste
- 1/2 teaspoon ground black pepper, to taste
- 7 ounces tomato paste
- 1 tablespoon Dijon mustard

DIRECTIONS (Prep + Cook Time: 35 minutes)

Start by preheating your Air Fryer to 330 degrees F. In a mixing bowl, thoroughly combine the ground beef, veal, egg, vegetable juice, crackers, bell peppers, onion, garlic, tomato paste, soy sauce, ranch dressing mix, salt, and ground black pepper. Mix until everything is well incorporated and press into a lightly greased meatloaf pan. Cook approximately 25 minutes in the preheated Air Fryer. Whisk the tomato paste with the mustard and spread the topping over the top of your meatloaf. Continue to cook 2 minutes more. Let it stand on a cooling rack for 6 minutes before slicing and serving. Enjoy!

757. Cube Steak with Cowboy Sauce
INGREDIENTS (4 Servings)

- 1 ½ pounds cube steak Salt, to taste
- 1/4 teaspoon ground black pepper, or more to taste
- 4 ounces butter
- 2 garlic cloves, finely chopped
- 2 scallions, finely chopped
- 2 tablespoon fresh parsley, finely chopped
- 1 tablespoon fresh horseradish, grated
- 1 teaspoon cayenne pepper

DIRECTIONS (Prep + Cook Time: 20 minutes)

Pat dry the cube steak and season it with salt and black pepper. Spritz the Air Fryer basket with cooking oil. Add the meat to the basket. Cook in the preheated Air Fryer at 400 degrees F for 14 minutes. Meanwhile, melt the butter in a skillet over a moderate heat. Add the remaining ingredients and simmer until the sauce has thickened and reduced slightly. Top the warm cube steaks with Cowboy sauce and serve immediately. Enjoy!

758. Beef Kofta Sandwich
INGREDIENTS (4 Servings)

- 1/2 cup leeks, chopped
- 2 garlic cloves, smashed
- 1 pound ground chuck
- 1 slice of bread, soaked in water until fully tender Salt, to taste
- 1/4 teaspoon ground black pepper, or more to taste
- 1 teaspoon cayenne pepper
- 1/2 teaspoon ground sumac
- 3 saffron threads
- 2 tablespoons loosely packed fresh continental parsley leaves
- 4 tablespoons tahini sauce
- 4 warm flatbread
- 4 ounces baby arugula
- 2 tomatoes, cut into slices

DIRECTIONS (Prep + Cook Time: 30 minutes)

In a bowl, mix the chopped leeks, garlic, ground meat, soaked bread, and spices; knead with your hands until everything is well incorporated. Now, mound the beef mixture around a wooden skewer into a pointed-ended sausage. Cook in the preheated Air Fryer at 360 degrees F for 25 minutes. To make the sandwiches, spread the tahini sauce on the flatbread; top with the kofta kebabs, baby arugula and tomatoes. Enjoy!

759. Beef Schnitzel with Buttermilk Spaetzle
INGREDIENTS (2 Servings)

- 1 egg, beaten
- 1/2 teaspoon ground black pepper
- 1 teaspoon paprika
- 1/2 teaspoon coarse sea salt
- 1 tablespoon ghee, melted
- 1/2 cup tortilla chips, crushed
- 2 thin-cut minute steaks

Buttermilk Spaetzle:

- 2 eggs
- 1/2 cup buttermilk
- 1/2 cup all-purpose flour
- 1/2 teaspoon salt

DIRECTIONS (Prep + Cook Time: 20 minutes) Start by preheating your Air Fryer to 360 degrees F. In a shallow bowl, whisk the egg with black pepper, paprika, and salt. Thoroughly combine the ghee with the crushed tortilla chips and coarse sea salt in another shallow bowl. Using a meat mallet, pound the schnitzel to 1/4-inch thick. Dip the schnitzel into the egg mixture; then, roll the schnitzel over the crumb mixture until coated on all sides. Cook for 13 minutes in the preheated Air Fryer. To make the spaetzle, whisk the eggs, buttermilk, flour, and salt in a bowl. Bring a large saucepan of salted water to a boil. Push the spaetzle mixture through the holes of a potato ricer into the boiling water; slice them off using a table knife. Work in batches. When the spaetzle float, take them out with a slotted spoon. Repeat with the rest of the spaetzle mixture. Serve with warm schnitzel. Enjoy!

760. Mom's Toad in the Hole
INGREDIENTS (4 Servings)

- 6 beef sausages
- 1 tablespoon butter, melted
- 1 cup plain flour
- A pinch of salt
- 2 eggs
- 1 cup semi-skimmed milk

DIRECTIONS (Prep + Cook Time: 45 minutes) Cook the sausages in the preheated Air Fryer at 380 degrees F for 15 minutes, shaking halfway through the cooking time. Meanwhile, make up the batter mix. Tip the flour into a bowl with salt; make a well in the middle and crack the eggs into it. Mix with an electric whisk; now, slowly and gradually pour in the milk, whisking all the time. Place the sausages in a lightly greased baking pan. Pour the prepared batter over the sausages. Cook in the preheated Air Fryer at 370 degrees F approximately 25 minutes, until golden and risen. Serve with gravy if desired. Enjoy!

761. Chuck Roast with Sweet 'n' Sticky Sauce
INGREDIENTS (3 Servings)

- 1 pound chuck roast
- Sea salt and ground black pepper, to taste
- 2 tablespoons butter, softened
- 1 tablespoon coriander, chopped
- 1 tablespoon fresh scallions, chopped
- 1 teaspoon soy sauce
- 1 tablespoon fish sauce
- 2 tablespoons honey

DIRECTIONS (Prep + Cook Time: 35 minutes) Season the chuck roast with salt and pepper; spritz a nonstick cooking oil all over the beef. Air fry at 400 degrees F for 30 to 35 minutes, flipping the chuck roast halfway through the cooking time. While the roast is cooking, heat the other ingredients in a sauté pan over medium-high heat. Bring to a boil and reduce the heat; let it simmer, partially covered, until the sauce has thickened and reduced. Slice the chuck roast into thick cuts and serve garnished with sweet 'n' sticky sauce. Enjoy!

762. Flank Steak with Dijon Honey Butter
INGREDIENTS (3 Servings)

- 1 pound flank steak
- 1/2 teaspoon olive oil
- Sea salt and red pepper flakes, to taste
- 3 tablespoons butter
- 1 teaspoon Dijon mustard
- 1 teaspoon honey

DIRECTIONS (Prep + Cook Time: 15 minutes) Brush the flank steak with olive oil and season with salt and pepper. Cook at 400 degrees F for 6 minutes. Then, turn the steak halfway through the cooking time and continue to cook for a further 6 minutes. In the meantime, prepare the Dijon honey butter by whisking the remaining ingredients. Serve the warm flank steak dolloped with the Dijon honey butter. Enjoy!

763. Ritzy Cheesy Meatballs
INGREDIENTS (2 Servings)

- 1/2 pound ground chuck
- 1/4 pound ground pork
- 1/3 cup shallots, chopped
- 2 tablespoons Italian parsley, chopped
- 1 teaspoon garlic, minced
- 1/3 cup parmesan cheese, grated
- 1 tablespoon flaxseed meal
- 1/3 cup saltines (e.g. Ritz crackers), crushed
- 1 tablespoon oyster sauce
- 1/2 teaspoon cayenne pepper Kosher
- salt and ground black pepper, to taste

DIRECTIONS (Prep + Cook Time: 15 minutes) In a mixing bowl, thoroughly combine all ingredients until everything is well incorporated. Shape the mixture into 6 equal meatballs. Spritz a cooking basket with a nonstick cooking spray. Cook the meatballs at 360 degrees F for 10 to 11 minutes, shaking the basket occasionally to ensure even cooking. An instant thermometer should read 165 degrees F. Enjoy!

764. Classic Filet Mignon with Mushrooms
INGREDIENTS (2 Servings)

- 1 pound filet mignon
- 2 garlic cloves, halved
- Salt and black pepper, to season
- 1 bell pepper, sliced
- 6 ounces button mushrooms, cleaned and halved
- 1 teaspoon olive oil

DIRECTIONS (Prep + Cook Time: 20 minutes)

Rub your filet mignon with garlic halves. Season it with the salt and black pepper to taste. Place the filet mignon in a lightly greased cooking basket. Top with peppers and air fry them at 400 degrees F for 10 minutes. Turn them over. Now, add in the mushrooms. Drizzle olive oil over the mushrooms and continue to cook for 8 minutes more. Serve warm. Enjoy!

765. Masala Dum Kabab
INGREDIENTS (3 Servings)

- 1 ½ pounds ground beef
- 1/2 cup breadcrumbs
- 1 teaspoon garam masala
- 1 teaspoon garlic paste
- 1/2 teaspoon turmeric powder
- 1/2 teaspoon coriander powder
- Sea salt and ground black pepper, to taste

DIRECTIONS (Prep + Cook Time: 20 minutes)

In a mixing bowl, combine all ingredients. Divide the mixture into three pieces and roll them into kabab shape. Spritz each kabab with a nonstick spray and place them in the cooking basket. Cook in the preheated Air Fryer at 380 degrees F for 10 minutes. Flip them over and cook an additional 5 minutes. Serve immediately with warm chapati. Enjoy!

766. Marinated London Broil
INGREDIENTS (2 Servings)

- 2 tablespoons soy sauce
- 2 garlic cloves, minced
- 1 teaspoon mustard
- 1 tablespoon olive oil
- 2 tablespoons wine vinegar
- 1 tablespoon honey
- 1 pound London broil
- 1/2 teaspoon paprika
- Salt and black pepper, to taste

DIRECTIONS (Prep + Cook Time: 25 minutes + Marinating Time)

In a ceramic dish, mix the soy sauce, garlic, mustard, oil, wine vinegar and honey. Add in the London broil and let it marinate for 2 hours in your refrigerator. Season the London broil with paprika, salt and pepper. Cook in the preheated Air Fryer at 400 degrees F for 10 minutes; turn over and continue to cook for a further 10 minutes. Slice the London broil against the grain and eat warm. Enjoy!

767. Easy Beef Burritos
INGREDIENTS (3 Servings)

- 1 pound rump steak
- Sea salt and crushed red pepper, to taste
- 1/2 teaspoon shallot powder
- 1/2 teaspoon porcini powder
- 1/2 teaspoon celery seeds
- 1/2 teaspoon dried Mexican oregano
- 1 teaspoon piri piri powder
- 1 teaspoon lard, melted
- 3 (approx 7-8" dia) whole-wheat tortillas

DIRECTIONS (Prep + Cook Time: 25 minutes)

Toss the rump steak with the spices and melted lard. Cook in your Air Fryer at 390 degrees F for 20 minutes, turning it halfway through the cooking time. Place on a cutting board to cool slightly. Slice against the grain into thin strips. Spoon the beef strips onto wheat tortillas; top with your favorite fixings, roll them up and serve. Enjoy!

768. Grandma's Meat Tarts
INGREDIENTS (3 Servings)

- 6 ounces refrigerated pie crusts
- 3/4 pound lean ground beef
- 1/2 onion
- 1 clove garlic, finely chopped
- Sea salt and ground black pepper, to taste
- 1/2 cup tomato paste
- 3 Swiss cheese slices
- 1 egg white, beaten

DIRECTIONS (Prep + Cook Time: 20 minutes)

Start by preheating your Air Fryer to 360 degrees F. Cook the ground beef, onion and garlic in a nonstick skillet until the beef is no longer pink and the onion is translucent. Season with salt and pepper; fold in the tomato paste and stir to combine. Unroll the pie crust and use a round cookie cutter to make 3 even rounds. Fill the pie crust rounds with the beef mixture. Top with cheese. Moisten the outside of each round with beaten egg white. Fold the pie crust rounds in half and use a fork to gently press the edges. Cook at 360 degrees F for about 15 minutes. Serve immediately. Enjoy!

769. Beef Parmigiana Sliders
INGREDIENTS (2 Servings)

- 1/2 pound lean ground chuck
- 1 ounce bacon bits
- 2 tablespoons tomato paste
- 3 tablespoons shallots, chopped
- 1 garlic clove, minced
- 1/4 cup parmesan cheese, grated
- 1 teaspoon cayenne pepper
- Salt and black pepper, to taste
- 4 pretzel rolls

DIRECTIONS (Prep + Cook Time: 15 minutes)

Thoroughly combine the ground chuck, bacon bits, tomato paste, shallots, garlic, parmesan cheese, cayenne pepper, salt, black pepper. Shape the mixture into 4 equal patties. Spritz your patties with a nonstick cooking spray. Air fry your burgers at 380 degrees F for about 11 minutes or to your desired degree of doneness. Place your burgers on pretzel rolls and serve with favorite toppings. Enjoy!

770. Dad's Barbecued Ribs
INGREDIENTS (3 Servings)

- 1 pound beef ribs
- 1/4 cup ketchup
- 1/4 cup tequila
- 1 tablespoon brown mustard
- 1 tablespoon brown sugar
- 2 tablespoons soy sauce
- 1/2 red onion, sliced
- 2 garlic cloves, pressed

DIRECTIONS (Prep + Cook Time: 20 minutes +Marinating Time)

Cut the ribs into serving size portions and transfer them to a ceramic dish. Add in the remaining ingredients, cover and allow it to marinate in your refrigerator overnight. Discard the marinade. Grill in the preheated Air Fryer at 400 degrees F for 10 minutes. Turn them over and continue to cook for 10 minutes more. Meanwhile, make the sauce by warming the marinade ingredients in a nonstick pan. Spoon over the warm ribs and serve immediately.

771. London Broil with Herb Butter
INGREDIENTS (3 Servings)

- 1 pound London broil

Herb butter:

- 2 tablespoons butter, at room temperature
- 1 teaspoon basil, chopped
- 1 tablespoon cilantro, chopped
- 1 tablespoon chives, chopped
- 1 tablespoon lemon juice
- Coarse sea salt and crushed black peppercorns, to taste

DIRECTIONS (Prep + Cook Time: 30 minutes)

Pat the London broil dry with paper towels. Mix all ingredients for the herb butter. Cook in the preheated Air Fryer at 400 degrees F for 14 minutes; turn over, brush with the herb butter and continue to cook for a further 12 minutes. Slice the London broil against the grain and serve warm.

772. American-Style Roast Beef
INGREDIENTS (3 Servings)

- 1 pound beef eye of round roast
- 1 teaspoon sesame oil
- 1 teaspoon red pepper flakes
- 1/4 teaspoon dried bay laurel
- 1/2 teaspoon cumin powder
- Sea salt and black pepper, to taste
- 1 sprig thyme, crushed

DIRECTIONS (Prep + Cook Time: 30 minutes) Simply toss the beef with the remaining ingredients; toss until well coated on all sides. Cook in the preheated Air Fryer at 390 degrees F for 15 to 20 minutes, flipping the meat halfway through to cook on the other side. Remove from the cooking basket, cover loosely with foil and let rest for 15 minutes before carving and serving. Enjoy!

773. Beef and Broccoli Stir-Fry
INGREDIENTS (2 Servings)

- 1/2 pound beef stew meat, cut into bite-sized cubes
- 1/2 pound broccoli, cut into florets
- 1 small shallot, sliced
- 1 teaspoon peanut oil
- 1/2 teaspoon garlic powder
- Salt and red pepper, to taste
- 1 teaspoon Five-spice powder
- 1 tablespoon fish sauce
- 1 tablespoon tamari sauce
- 1 teaspoon sesame seed oil
- 1 teaspoon Chiu Chow chili sauce

DIRECTIONS (Prep + Cook Time: 20 minutes)

Toss all ingredients until the beef and veggies are well coated. Cook in the preheated Air Fryer at 400 degrees F for 6 minutes; shake the basket and continue to air fry for 6 minutes more. Now, test the meat for doneness, remove the vegetables and cook the meat for 5 minutes more if needed. Taste and adjust seasonings. Serve immediately.

774. Cuban Mojo Beef
INGREDIENTS (3 Servings)

3/4 pound blade steak, cut into cubes	1 teaspoon olive oil	Salt and red pepper flakes, to season

Mojo sauce:

1 teaspoon garlic, smashed	2 tablespoons fresh parsley, chopped	1/2 lime, freshly squeezed
2 tablespoons extra-virgin olive oil	2 tablespoons fresh cilantro, chopped	1 green chili pepper, minced

DIRECTIONS (Prep + Cook Time: 15 minutes)

Toss the steak with olive oil, salt and red pepper. Cook in your Air Fryer at 400 degrees F for 12 minutes, turning them over halfway through the cooking time. Meanwhile, make the sauce by mixing all ingredients in your food processor or blender. Serve the warm blade steak with the Mojo sauce on the side. Enjoy!

775. Chicago-Style Beef Sandwich
INGREDIENTS (2 Servings)

1/2 pound chuck, boneless	1/2 teaspoon shallot powder	salt and ground black pepper, to taste
1 tablespoon olive oil	1/4 teaspoon porcini powder	1 cup pickled vegetables, chopped
1 tablespoon soy sauce	1/2 teaspoon garlic powder	2 ciabatta rolls, sliced in half
1/4 teaspoon ground bay laurel	1/2 teaspoon cayenne pepper Kosher	

DIRECTIONS (Prep + Cook Time: 25 minutes)

Toss the chuck roast with olive oil, soy sauce and spices until well coated. Cook in the preheated Air Fryer at 400 degrees F for 20 minutes, turning over halfway through the cooking time. Shred the meat with two forks and adjust seasonings. Top the bottom halves of the ciabatta rolls with a generous portion of the meat and pickled vegetables. Place the tops of the ciabatta rolls on the sandwiches. Serve immediately and enjoy!

776. Classic Beef Jerky
INGREDIENTS (4 Servings)

6 ounces top round steak, cut into 1/8-inch thick strips	1 teaspoon onion powder	1 teaspoon liquid smoke
	2 tablespoons Worcestershire sauce	1 teaspoon hot sauce
1/2 teaspoon fresh garlic, crushed	1/2 tablespoon honey	

DIRECTIONS (Prep + Cook Time: 4 hours 30 minutes)

Transfer the strips of steak to a large Ziplock bag; add in the other ingredients, seal the bag and shake to combine well. Refrigerate for at least 30 minutes. Cook in the preheated Air Fryer at 160 degrees F for about 4 hours, until it is dry and firm. Refrigerate in an airtight container for up to 1 month. Enjoy!

777. Dad's Meatloaf with a Twist
INGREDIENTS (2 Servings)

1 tablespoon olive oil	1 Serrano pepper, deveined and chopped	1/2 cup crushed corn flakes
1 onion, chopped	1/2 pound ground beef	4 tablespoons tomato paste
1/2 teaspoon garlic, minced	1 tablespoon soy sauce	1 teaspoon Italian seasoning mix
1 Italian pepper, deveined and chopped	1 tablespoon Dijon mustard	1/2 teaspoon liquid smoke

DIRECTIONS (Prep + Cook Time: 35 minutes)

Start by preheating your Air Fryer to 350 degrees F. In a mixing bowl, thoroughly combine the onion, garlic, peppers, ground beef, soy sauce, mustard and crushed corn flakes. Salt to taste. Mix until everything is well incorporated and press into a lightly greased meatloaf pan. Air fry for about 25 minutes. Whisk the tomato paste with the Italian seasoning mix and liquid smoke; spread the mixture over the top of your meatloaf. Continue to cook for 3 minutes more. Let it rest for 6 minutes before slicing and serving. Enjoy!

778. Italian Piadina Sandwich
INGREDIENTS (2 Servings)

1/2 pound ribeye steak	Sea salt and red pepper, to taste	2 ounces Fontina cheese, grated
1 teaspoon sesame oil	2 medium-sized piadinas	4 tablespoons Giardiniera

DIRECTIONS (Prep + Cook Time: 20 minutes)

Brush the ribeye steak with sesame oil and season with salt and red pepper. Cook at 400 degrees F for 6 minutes. Then, turn the steak halfway through the cooking time and continue to cook for a further 6 minutes. Slice the ribeye steak into bite-sized strips. Top the piadinas with steak strips and cheese. Heat the sandwich in your Air Fryer at 380 degrees F for about 3 minutes until the cheese melts. Top with Giardiniera and serve. Enjoy!

779. Sunday Beef Schnitzel
INGREDIENTS (2 Servings)

2 beef schnitzel	1 egg, beaten	1 teaspoon olive oil
Salt and black pepper, to taste	1/2 cup breadcrumbs	1/2 lemon, cut into wedges to serve
2 ounces all-purpose flour	1/2 teaspoon paprika	

DIRECTIONS (Prep + Cook Time: 15 minutes) Pat the beef dry and generously season it with salt and black pepper. Add the flour to a rimmed plate. Place the egg in a shallow bowl and mix the breadcrumbs and paprika in another bowl. Dip the meat in the flour first, then the egg, then the paprika/breadcrumb mixture. Drizzle olive oil over each beef schnitzel. Cook in the preheated Air Fryer at 390 degrees F for about 10 minutes, flipping the meat halfway through the cooking time. Enjoy!

---

780. Dijon Top Chuck with Herbs
INGREDIENTS (3 Servings)

1 ½ pounds top chuck	Dijon mustard	1 teaspoon dried thyme
2 teaspoons olive oil	Sea salt and ground black pepper, to taste	1/2 teaspoon fennel seeds
1 tablespoon	1 teaspoon dried marjoram	

DIRECTIONS (Prep + Cook Time: 1 hours) Start by preheating your Air Fryer to 380 degrees F Add all ingredients in a Ziploc bag; shake to mix well. Next, spritz the bottom of the Air Fryer basket with cooking spray. Place the beef in the cooking basket and cook for 50 minutes, turning every 10 to 15 minutes. Let it rest for 5 to 7 minutes before slicing and serving. Enjoy!

---

781. Peperonata with Beef Sausage
INGREDIENTS (4 Servings)

2 teaspoons canola oil	1 shallot, sliced	1/2 teaspoon mustard seeds
2 bell peppers, sliced	Sea salt and pepper, to taste	1 teaspoon fennel seeds
1 green bell pepper, sliced	1/2 dried thyme	2 pounds thin beef parboiled sausage
1 serrano pepper, sliced	1 teaspoon dried rosemary	

DIRECTIONS (Prep + Cook Time: 35 minutes)

Brush the sides and bottom of the cooking basket with 1 teaspoon of canola oil. Add the peppers and shallot to the cooking basket. Toss them with the spices and cook at 390 degrees F for 15 minutes, shaking the basket occasionally. Reserve. Turn the temperature to 380 degrees F Then, add the remaining 1 teaspoon of oil. Once hot, add the sausage and cook in the preheated Air Frye for 15 minutes, flipping them halfway through the cooking time. Serve with reserved pepper mixture. Enjoy!

---

782. New York Strip with Mustard Butter
INGREDIENTS (4 Servings)

1 tablespoon peanut oil	Sea salt and freshly cracked black pepper, to taste	1 teaspoon whole-grain mustard
2 pounds New York Strip		1/2 teaspoon honey
1 teaspoon cayenne pepper	1/2 stick butter, softened	

DIRECTIONS (Prep + Cook Time: 20 minutes) Rub the peanut oil all over the steak; season with cayenne pepper, salt, and black pepper. Cook in the preheated Air Fryer at 400 degrees F for 7 minutes; turn over and cook an additional 7 minutes. Meanwhile, prepare the mustard butter by whisking the butter, whole-grain mustard, and honey. Serve the roasted New York Strip dolloped with the mustard butter. Enjoy!

---

783. Crustless Beef and Cheese Tart
INGREDIENTS (4 Servings)

1 tablespoon canola oil	1/2 pound Chorizo sausage, crumbled	1 cup cream cheese, room temperature
1 onion, finely chopped	1 cup pasta sauce Sea salt, to taste	1/2 cup Swiss cheese, shredded
2 fresh garlic cloves, minced	1/4 teaspoon ground black pepper	1 egg
1/2 pound ground chuck	1/2 teaspoon red pepper flakes, crushed	1/2 cup crackers, crushed

DIRECTIONS (Prep + Cook Time: 25 minutes)

Start by preheating your Air Fryer to 370 degrees F. Grease a baking pan with canola oil. Add the onion, garlic, ground chuck, sausage, pasta sauce, salt, black pepper, and red pepper. Cook for 9 minutes. In the meantime, combine cheese with egg. Place the cheese-egg mixture over the beef mixture. Sprinkle with crushed crackers and cook for 10 minutes. Serve warm and enjoy!

784. Barbecue Skirt Steak
INGREDIENTS (5 Servings)

- 2 pounds skirt steak
- 2 tablespoons tomato paste
- 1 tablespoon tomato ketchup
- 1 tablespoon olive oil
- 1 tablespoon soy sauce
- 1/4 cup rice vinegar
- 1 tablespoon fish sauce
- Sea salt, to taste
- 1/2 teaspoon dried dill
- 1/2 teaspoon dried rosemary
- 1/4 teaspoon black pepper, freshly cracked
- 1 tablespoon brown sugar

DIRECTIONS (Prep + Cook Time: 20 minutes + Marinating Time)

Place all ingredients in a large ceramic dish; let it marinate for 3 hours in your refrigerator. Coat the sides and bottom of the Air Fryer with cooking spray. Add your steak to the cooking basket; reserve the marinade. Cook the skirt steak in the preheated Air Fryer at 400 degrees F for 12 minutes, turning over a couple of times, basting with the reserved marinade. Serve warm with roasted new potatoes, if desired. Enjoy!

785. Cheesy Beef Burrito
INGREDIENTS (4 Servings)

- 1 pound rump steak
- 1 teaspoon garlic powder
- 1/2 teaspoon onion powder
- 1/2 teaspoon cayenne pepper
- 1 teaspoon piri piri powder
- 1 teaspoon Mexican oregano
- Salt and ground black pepper, to taste
- 1 cup Mexican cheese blend
- 4 large whole wheat tortillas
- 1 cup iceberg lettuce, shredded

DIRECTIONS (Prep + Cook Time: 20 minutes)

Toss the rump steak with the garlic powder, onion powder, cayenne pepper, piri piri powder, Mexican oregano, salt, and black pepper. Cook in the preheated Air Fryer at 390 degrees F for 10 minutes. Slice against the grain into thin strips. Add the cheese blend and cook for 2 minutes more. Spoon the beef mixture onto the wheat tortillas; top with lettuce; roll up burrito-style and serve. Enjoy!

786. Beef and Vegetable Stir Fry
INGREDIENTS (4 Servings)

- 2 pounds top round, cut into bite-sized strips
- 2 garlic cloves, sliced
- 1 teaspoon dried marjoram
- 1/4 cup red wine
- 1 tablespoon tamari sauce
- Salt and black pepper, to taste
- 1 tablespoon olive oil
- 1 red onion, sliced
- 2 bell peppers, sliced
- 1 carrot, sliced

DIRECTIONS (Prep + Cook Time: 35 minutes + Marinating Time)

Place the top round, garlic, marjoram, red wine, tamari sauce, salt and pepper in a bowl, cover and let it marinate for 1 hour. Preheat your Air Fryer to 390 degrees F and add the oil. Once hot, discard the marinade and cook the beef for 15 minutes. Add the onion, peppers, carrot, and garlic and continue cooking until tender about 15 minutes more. Open the Air Fryer every 5 minutes and baste the meat with the remaining marinade. Serve immediately.

787. Homemade Beef Empanadas
INGREDIENTS (5 Servings)

- 1 teaspoon olive oil
- 1/2 onion, chopped
- 1 garlic clove, minced
- 1/2 pound ground beef chuck 1 tablespoon raisins
- 1/2 teaspoon dried oregano
- 1/2 cup tomato paste
- 1/2 cup vegetable broth
- Salt and ground pepper, to taste
- 10 Goya discs pastry dough
- 2 egg whites, beaten

DIRECTIONS (Prep + Cook Time: 35 minutes)

Heat the oil in a saucepan over medium-high heat. Once hot, sauté the onion and garlic until tender, about 3 minutes. Then, add the beef and continue to sauté an additional 4 minutes, crumbling with a fork. Add the raisins, oregano, tomato paste, vegetable broth, salt, and black pepper. Reduce the heat to low and cook an additional 15 minutes. Preheat the Air Fryer to 330 degrees F. Brush the Air Fryer basket with cooking oil. Divide the sauce between discs. Fold each of the discs in half and seal the edges. Brush the tops with the beaten eggs. Bake for 7 to 8 minutes, working with batches. Serve with salsa sauce if desired. Enjoy!

788. Sunday Tender Skirt Steak
INGREDIENTS (4 Servings)

- 1/3 cup soy sauce
- 4 tablespoon molasses
- 2 garlic cloves, minced
- 2 tablespoons champagne vinegar
- 1 teaspoon shallot powder
- 1 teaspoon porcini powder
- 1 teaspoon celery seeds
- 1 teaspoon paprika
- 1 ½ pounds skirt steak, cut into slices
- Sea salt and ground black pepper, to taste

DIRECTIONS (Prep + Cook Time: 20 minutes + Marinating Time)

Place the soy sauce, molasses, garlic, vinegar, shallot powder, porcini powder, celery seeds, paprika, and beef in a large resealable plastic bag. Shake well and let it marinate overnight. Discard the marinade and place the beef in the Air Fryer basket. Season with salt and black pepper to taste. Cook in the preheated Air Fryer at 400 degrees F for 12 minutes, flipping and basting with the reserved marinade halfway through the cooking time. Enjoy!

789. Beef with Creamed Mushroom Sauce
INGREDIENTS (5 Servings)

- 2 tablespoons butter
- 2 pounds sirloin, cut into four pieces
- Salt and cracked black pepper, to taste
- 1 teaspoon cayenne pepper
- 1/2 teaspoon dried rosemary
- 1/2 teaspoon dried dill
- 1/4 teaspoon dried thyme
- 1 pound Cremini mushrooms, sliced
- 1 cup sour cream
- 1 teaspoon mustard
- 1/2 teaspoon curry powder

DIRECTIONS (Prep + Cook Time: 20 minutes)

Start by preheating your Air Fryer to 396 degrees F. Grease a baking pan with butter. Add the sirloin, salt, black pepper, cayenne pepper, rosemary, dill, and thyme to the baking pan. Cook for 9 minutes. Next, stir in the mushrooms, sour cream, mustard, and curry powder. Continue to cook another 5 minutes or until everything is heated through. Spoon onto individual serving plates. Enjoy!

790. Burgers with Caramelized Onions
INGREDIENTS (4 Servings)

- 1 pound ground beef
- Salt and ground black pepper, to taste
- 1 teaspoon garlic powder
- 1/2 teaspoon cumin powder
- 1 tablespoon butter
- 1 red onion, sliced
- 1 teaspoon brown sugar
- 1 tablespoon balsamic vinegar
- 1 tablespoon vegetable stock
- 4 hamburger buns
- 8 tomato slices
- 4 teaspoons mustard

DIRECTIONS (Prep + Cook Time: 30 minutes) Start by preheating your Air Fryer to 370 degrees F. Spritz the cooking basket with nonstick cooking oil. Mix the ground beef with salt, pepper, garlic powder, and cumin powder. Shape the meat mixture into four patties and transfer them to the preheated Air Fryer. Cook for 10 minutes; turn them over and cook on the other side for 8 to 10 minutes more. While the burgers are frying, melt the butter in a pan over medium-high heat. Then, add the red onion and sauté for 4 minutes or until soft. Add the brown sugar, vinegar, and stock and cook for 2 to 3 minute more. To assemble your burgers, add the beef patties to the hamburger buns. Top with the caramelized onion, tomato, and mustard. Serve immediately and enjoy!

791. Easy Asian Gyudon
INGREDIENTS (4 Servings)

- 1 shallot, chopped
- 1/2 cup dashi
- 1 tablespoon mirin
- 1 teaspoon agave syrup
- 2 tablespoons Shoyu sauce
- 1/2 teaspoon wasabi
- 1 pound rib eye, sliced

DIRECTIONS (Prep + Cook Time: 20 minutes) Add all ingredients to a lightly greased baking pan. Gently stir to combine. Cook in the preheated Air Fryer at 400 degrees F for 7 minutes. Stir again and cook for a further 7 minutes. Serve with Japanese ramen noodles if desired. Enjoy!

792. Juicy Strip Steak
INGREDIENTS (4 Servings)

- 1 ½ pounds strip steak, sliced
- 1/4 cup chickpea flour
- 1/3 cup Shoyu sauce
- 2 tablespoons honey
- 1 teaspoon mustard seeds
- 2 tablespoons champagne vinegar
- 1 teaspoon ginger-garlic paste
- 1/2 teaspoon coriander seeds
- 1 tablespoon cornstarch

DIRECTIONS (Prep + Cook Time: 30 minutes) Start by preheating your Air Fryer to 395 degrees F. Spritz the Air Fryer basket with cooking oil. Toss the strip steak with chickpea flour. Cook the strip steak for 12 minutes; flip them over and cook an additional 10 minutes.

In the meantime, heat the saucepan over medium-high heat. Add the Shoyu sauce, honey, mustard seeds, champagne vinegar, ginger-garlic paste, and coriander seeds. Reduce the heat and simmer until the sauce is heated through. Make the slurry by whisking the cornstarch with 1 tablespoon of water. Now, whisk in the cornstarch slurry and continue to simmer until the sauce has thickened. Spoon the sauce over the steak and serve. Enjoy!

793. Filipino Tortang Giniling
INGREDIENTS (3 Servings)

- 1 teaspoon lard
- 2/3 pound ground beef
- 1/4 teaspoon chili powder
- 1/2 teaspoon ground bay leaf
- 1/2 teaspoon ground pepper
- Sea salt, to taste
- 1 green bell pepper, seeded and chopped
- 1 red bell pepper, seeded and chopped
- 6 eggs
- 1/3 cup double cream
- 1/2 cup Colby cheese, shredded
- 1 tomato, sliced

DIRECTIONS (Prep + Cook Time: 20 minutes) Melt the lard in a cast-iron skillet over medium-high heat. Add the ground beef and cook for 4 minutes until no longer pink, crumbling with a spatula. Add the ground beef mixture, along with the spices to the baking pan. Now, add the bell peppers. In a mixing bowl, whisk the eggs with double cream. Spoon the mixture over the meat and peppers in the pan. Cook in the preheated Air Fryer at 355 degrees F for 10 minutes. Top with the cheese and tomato slices. Continue to cook for 5 minutes more or until the eggs are golden and the cheese has melted. Enjoy!

794. Minty Tender Filet Mignon
INGREDIENTS (4 Servings)

- 2 tablespoons olive oil
- 2 tablespoons Worcestershire sauce
- 1 lemon, juiced
- 1/4 cup fresh mint leaves, chopped
- 4 cloves garlic, minced
- Sea salt and ground black pepper, to taste
- 2 pounds filet mignon

DIRECTIONS (Prep + Cook Time: 20 minutes + Marinating Time) In a ceramic bowl, place the olive oil, Worcestershire sauce, lemon juice, mint leaves, garlic, salt, black pepper, and cayenne pepper. Add the fillet mignon and let it marinate for 2 hours in the refrigerator. Roast in the preheated Air Fryer at 400 degrees F for 18 minutes, basting with the reserved marinade and flipping a couple of times. Serve warm. Enjoy!

795. Easy Beef Jerky
INGREDIENTS (4 Servings)

- 1 cup beer
- 1/2 cup tamari sauce
- 1 teaspoon liquid smoke
- 2 garlic cloves, minced
- Sea salt and ground black pepper
- 1 teaspoon ancho chili powder
- 2 tablespoons honey
- 3/4 pound flank steak, slice into strips

DIRECTIONS (Prep + Cook Time: 1 hours + Marinating Time) Place all ingredients in a ceramic dish; let it marinate for 3 hours in the refrigerator. Slice the beef into thin strips Marinate the beef in the refrigerator overnight. Now, discard the marinade and hang the meat in the cooking basket by using skewers. Air Fry at 190 degrees F degrees for 1 hour. Store it in an airtight container for up to 2 weeks. Enjoy!

796. Indian Beef Samosas
INGREDIENTS (8 Servings)

- 1 tablespoon sesame oil
- 4 tablespoons shallots, minced
- 2 cloves garlic, minced
- 2 tablespoons green chili peppers, chopped
- 1/2 pound ground chuck
- 4 ounces bacon, chopped
- Salt and ground black pepper, to taste
- 1 teaspoon cumin powder
- 1 teaspoon turmeric
- 1 teaspoon coriander
- 1 cup frozen peas, thawed
- 1 (16-ounce) package phyllo dough
- 1 egg, beaten with
- 2 tablespoons of water (egg wash)

DIRECTIONS (Prep + Cook Time: 35 minutes) Heat the oil in a saucepan over medium-high heat. Once hot, sauté the shallots, garlic, and chili peppers until tender, about 3 minutes. Then, add the beef and bacon; continue to sauté an additional 4 minutes, crumbling with a fork. Season with the salt, pepper, cumin powder, turmeric, and coriander. Stir in peas. Then, preheat your Air Fryer to 330 degrees F. Brush the Air Fryer basket with cooking oil. Place 1 to 2 tablespoons of the mixture onto each phyllo sheet. Fold the sheets into triangles, pressing the edges. Brush the tops with egg wash. Bake for 7 to 8 minutes, working with batches. Serve with Indian tomato sauce if desired. Enjoy!

797. Aromatic T-Bone Steak with Garlic
INGREDIENTS (3 Servings)

- 1 pound T-bone steak
- 4 garlic cloves, halved
- 1/4 cup all-purpose flour
- 2 tablespoons olive oil
- 1/4 cup tamari sauce
- 2 teaspoons brown sugar
- 4 tablespoons tomato paste
- 1 teaspoon Sriracha sauce
- 2 tablespoons white vinegar
- 1 teaspoon dried rosemary
- 1/2 teaspoon dried basil
- 2 heaping tablespoons cilantro, chopped

DIRECTIONS (Prep + Cook Time: 20 minutes) Rub the garlic halves all over the T-bone steak. Toss the steak with the flour. Drizzle the oil all over the steak and transfer it to the grill pan; grill the steak in the preheated Air Fryer at 400 degrees F for 10 minutes. Meanwhile, whisk the tamari sauce, sugar, tomato paste, Sriracha, vinegar, rosemary, and basil. Cook an additional 5 minutes Serve garnished with fresh cilantro. Enjoy!

798. Sausage Scallion Balls
INGREDIENTS (4 Servings)

- 1 ½ pounds beef sausage meat
- 1 cup rolled oats
- 4 tablespoons scallions, chopped
- 1 teaspoon Worcestershire sauce
- Flaky sea salt and freshly ground black pepper, to taste
- 1 teaspoon paprika
- 1/2 teaspoon granulated garlic
- 1 teaspoon dried basil
- 1/2 teaspoon dried oregano
- 4 teaspoons mustard
- 4 pickled cucumbers

DIRECTIONS (Prep + Cook Time: 20 minutes)

Start by preheating your Air Fryer to 380 degrees F. Spritz the Air Fryer basket with cooking oil. In a mixing bowl, thoroughly combine the sausage meat, oats, scallions, Worcestershire sauce, salt, black pepper, paprika, garlic, basil, and oregano. Then, form the mixture into equal sized meatballs using a tablespoon. Place the meatballs in the Air Fryer basket and cook for 15 minutes, turning halfway through the cooking time. Serve with mustard and cucumbers. Enjoy!

799. Beef Sausage Goulash
INGREDIENTS (2 Servings)

- 1 tablespoon lard, melted
- 1 shallot, chopped
- 1 bell pepper, chopped
- 2 red chilies, finely chopped
- 1 teaspoon ginger-garlic paste
- Sea salt, to taste
- 1/4 teaspoon ground black pepper
- 4 beef good quality sausages, thinly sliced
- 2 teaspoons smoked paprika
- 1 cup beef bone broth
- 1/2 cup tomato puree
- 2 handfuls spring greens, shredded

DIRECTIONS (Prep + Cook Time: 40 minutes)

Melt the lard in a Dutch oven over medium-high flame; sauté the shallots and peppers about 4 minutes or until fragrant. Add the ginger-garlic paste and cook an additional minute. Season with salt and black pepper and transfer to a lightly greased baking pan.

Then, brown the sausages, stirring occasionally, working in batches. Add to the baking pan. Add the smoked paprika, broth, and tomato puree. Lower the pan onto the Air Fryer basket. Bake at 325 degrees F for 30 minutes. Stir in the spring greens and cook for 5 minutes more or until they wilt. Serve over the hot rice if desired. Enjoy!

800. Char Siew Pork Ribs
INGREDIENTS (4 Servings)

- 2 lb pork ribs
- 2 tbsp char siew sauce
- 2 tbsp minced ginger
- 2 tbsp hoisin sauce
- 2 tbsp sesame oil
- 1 tsp honey
- 4 garlic cloves, minced
- 1 tbsp soy sauce

DIRECTIONS (Prep + Cook Time: 35 minutes + marinating time)

Whisk together all ingredients, except for the ribs, in a small bowl. Coat the ribs with the mixture. Place in a container, cover with a lid, and refrigerate for 2 hours. Preheat air fryer to 390 F. Put ribs in a greased baking dish and place in the fryer basket; do not throw away the liquid from the container. Bake for 15 minutes, pour in the juice, and cook for 10 minutes.

801. Pork & Pear Blue Cheese Patties
INGREDIENTS (2 Servings)

- ½ lb ground pork
- 1 pear, peeled and grated
- 1 cup breadcrumbs
- 2 oz blue cheese, crumbled
- ½ tsp ground cumin
- Salt and black pepper to taste

DIRECTIONS (Prep + Cook Time: 20 minutes)

In a bowl, add ground pork, pear, breadcrumbs, cumin, blue cheese, salt, and black pepper, and mix with hands. Shape into 2 even-sized burger patties. Arrange the patties on the greased air fryer basket and AirFry for 14 minutes at 380 F, turning once halfway through. Serve warm.

802. Maple Mustard Pork Balls
INGREDIENTS (4 Servings)

- 1 lb ground pork
- 1 large onion, chopped
- ½ tsp maple syrup
- 1 tsp yellow mustard
- ½ cup basil leaves, chopped
- Salt and black pepper to taste
- 2 tbsp cheddar cheese, grated

DIRECTIONS (Prep + Cook Time: 20 minutes)

In a bowl, add ground pork, onion, maple syrup, mustard, basil leaves, salt, pepper, and cheddar cheese; mix well. Form bite-sized balls. Place in the frying basket and AirFry for 10 minutes at 400 F. Slide the basket out and shake the meatballs. Slide in and cook further for 5 minutes. When ready, remove them and serve with zoodles and marinara sauce.

803. Fennel & Sage Pork Sausage Balls
INGREDIENTS (4 Servings)

1 lb pork sausage meat

1 whole egg, beaten

1 onion, chopped

2 tbsp fresh sage, chopped

2 tbsp ground almonds

¼ head fennel bulb, chopped

Salt and black pepper to taste

DIRECTIONS (Prep + Cook Time: 40 minutes)

Preheat air fryer to 350 F. In a bowl, combine sausage meat, onion, almonds, fennel, egg, black pepper, and salt. Mix to coat well and let sit for 15 minutes. Shape the mixture into balls. Add them to the greased air fryer basket and Bake for 15 minutes, shaking once. Serve sprinkled with fresh sage.

804. Pork, Red Pepper & Mushroom Pinchos
INGREDIENTS (4 Servings)

1 lb pork tenderloin, cubed

2 tbsp olive oil

1 lime, juiced and zested

2 cloves garlic, minced

1 tsp chili powder

1 tsp ground fennel seeds

½ tsp ground cumin

Salt and white pepper to taste

1 red pepper, cut into chunks

½ cup mushrooms, quartered

DIRECTIONS (Prep + Cook Time: 20 minutes+ marinating time)

In a bowl, mix half of the olive oil, lime zest and juice, garlic, chili, ground fennel, cumin, salt, and white pepper. Add in the pork and stir to coat. Cover with cling film and place in the fridge for 1 hour. Preheat air fryer to 380 F. Season the mushrooms and red pepper with salt and pepper and drizzle with the remaining olive oil. Thread alternate the pork, mushroom, and red pepper pieces onto short skewers. Place in the fryer's basket. AirFry for 15 minutes, turning once. Serve warm.

805. Stuffed Pork Tenderloin
INGREDIENTS (4 Servings)

16 bacon slices

1 lb pork tenderloin, butterflied

Salt and black pepper to taste

1 cup spinach

3 oz cream cheese

1 small onion, sliced

1 tbsp olive oil

1 clove garlic, minced

½ tsp dried thyme

½ tsp dried rosemary

DIRECTIONS (Prep + Cook Time: 40 minutes)

Place the tenderloin on a chopping board, cover it with a plastic wrap and pound it using a kitchen hammer to a 2-inches flat and square piece. Trim the uneven sides with a knife to have a perfect square; remove to a plate. On the same chopping board, place and weave the bacon slices into a square the size of the pork. Place the pork on the bacon weave and set aside. Heat olive oil in a skillet over medium heat and sauté onion and garlic until transparent, about 3 minutes. Add in spinach, rosemary, thyme, salt, and pepper and cook until the spinach wilts. Stir in cream cheese until the mixture is even. Turn the heat off. Preheat air fryer to 360 F. Spread the spinach mixture onto the pork loin. Roll up bacon and pork over the spinach stuffing. Secure the ends with toothpicks. Place in the fryer's basket and Bake for 15 minutes. Turn them and cook for 5 more minutes until golden. Let sit for 4 minutes before slicing.

806. Sage-Rubbed Pork Loin
INGREDIENTS (4 Servings)

1 lb boneless pork tenderloin

1 tbsp olive oil

1 tbsp lime juice

½ tbsp soy sauce

½ tbsp chili powder

1 garlic clove, minced

2 tbsp fresh sage, minced

½ tsp ground coriander

DIRECTIONS (Prep + Cook Time: 40 minutes+ marinating time)

Combine the lime juice, olive oil, soy sauce, chili powder, garlic, sage, and ground coriander in a bowl. Add in the pork and toss to coat. Cover with foil and refrigerate for a minimum of 1 hour up to overnight. Preheat air fryer to 390 F. Remove the pork from the bag, shaking off any extra marinade. Place in the greased fryer basket. Air fry for 15 minutes. Flip the pork over and continue cooking for another 5 minutes. Leave the pork to sit for 10 minutes so that it can retain its juices before cutting. Serve warm.

807. Pork Chops with Mustard-Apricot Glaze
INGREDIENTS (4 Servings)

- 4 pork chops, ½-inch thick
- Salt and black pepper to taste
- 1 tbsp apricot jam
- 1 ½ tbsp minced garlic
- 2 tbsp wholegrain mustard

DIRECTIONS (Prep + Cook Time: 15 minutes)

In a bowl, add maple syrup, garlic, mustard, salt, and black pepper; mix well. Add the pork and toss to coat. Place the chops in a greased air fryer basket and Bake for 10 minutes at 350 F. Work in batches. Flip the chops with a spatula and cook further for 8 minutes. Once ready, remove them to a serving platter and serve with a side of steamed green veggies.

808. French Pork Chops with Blue Cheese Butter
INGREDIENTS (4 Servings)

- 3 tsp olive oil 1 tsp butter, softened
- ¼ cup blue cheese, crumbled
- 2 tbsp hot mango chutney
- 4 thin-cut pork chops 1 tbsp fresh thyme, chopped

DIRECTIONS (Prep + Cook Time: 25 minutes+ marinating time)

Preheat air fryer to 390 F. In a bowl, mix together butter, mango chutney, and blue cheese; set aside. Season the pork with salt and pepper and drizzle with olive oil. Place the chops in the fryer and AirFry for 14-16 minutes, flipping once. Remove to a plate and spread the blue cheese mixture on each pork chop. Let sit covered with foil for 3-5 minutes. Sprinkle with fresh thyme and serve.

809. Italian Pork Scaloppini
INGREDIENTS (4 Servings)

- 4 pork loin thin steaks
- Salt and black pepper to taste
- ¼ cup Parmesan cheese, grated
- 2 tbsp Italian breadcrumbs

DIRECTIONS (Prep + Cook Time: 20 minutes)

Preheat air fryer to 390 F. Spray the air fryer basket with cooking spray. In a bowl, mix Italian breadcrumbs and Parmesan cheese. Season the pork with salt and black pepper. Coat in the breadcrumb mixture and spray with cooking spray. Transfer to the air fryer basket and AirFry for 15 minutes, turning once halfway through. Serve immediately.

810. Thyme Pork Escalopes
INGREDIENTS (4 Servings)

- 4 pork loin steaks
- 2 tbsp olive oil
- Salt and black pepper to taste
- 2 eggs 1 tbsp flour
- 1 cup breadcrumbs
- 1 tbsp fresh thyme, chopped

DIRECTIONS (Prep + Cook Time: 25 minutes + marinating time)

In a bowl, mix olive oil, salt, and pepper to form a marinade. Place the pork into the marinade, 15 minutes. Preheat air fryer to 400 F. Beat the eggs in a separate bowl and add the crumbs to a plate. Dip the meat into the eggs and then roll in the breadcrumbs. Place the steaks in the air fryer and Bake for 16-18 minutes, shaking every 5 minutes. Sprinkle with thyme and serve.

811. Tangy Pork Belly with Herbs
INGREDIENTS (4 Servings)

- 1 ½ lb pork belly, boiled
- ½ tsp garlic powder
- ½ tsp coriander powder
- Salt and black pepper to taste
- ½ tsp dried thyme
- ½ tsp dried oregano
- ½ tsp cumin powder
- 1 lemon, halved

DIRECTIONS (Prep + Cook Time: 45 minutes)

In a bowl, add garlic powder, coriander powder, salt, black pepper, thyme, oregano, and cumin powder. Poke holes all around the belly using a fork. Smear the herb, rub thoroughly on all sides with your hands, and squeeze the lemon juice all over. Let sit for 5 minutes. Put the pork in the center of the frying basket and Bake for 15-20 minutes. Then flip it, increase the temperature to 350 F, and continue to cook for 15 minutes. Remove to a chopping board to sit for 4-5 minutes before slicing. Serve the pork slices with a side of sautéed asparagus and hot sauce.

812. Healthy Burgers
INGREDIENTS (4 Servings)

1 ½ lb ground beef

½ tsp onion powder

Salt and black pepper to taste

½ tsp dried oregano

1 tbsp Worcestershire sauce

½ tsp garlic powder

1 tsp Maggi seasoning sauce

1 tbsp olive oil

DIRECTIONS (Prep + Cook Time: 20 minutes)

Preheat the air fryer to 350 F. In a bowl, combine Worcestershire and Maggi sauces, onion and garlic powders, oregano, salt, and pepper. Add in ground beef and mix until well combined. Divide the meat mixture into four equal pieces to form patties. Brush with olive oil and place the patties in the air fryer basket to AirFry for 14-16 minutes, turning once halfway through. Serve immediately.

813. Mexican Beef Cabbage Wraps
INGREDIENTS (4 Servings)

1 lb ground beef

8 savoy cabbage leaves

1 small onion, chopped

1 tsp taco seasoning

1 tbsp cilantro-lime rotel

⅔ cup Mexican cheese, shredded

2 tbsp olive oil

Salt and black pepper to taste

2 garlic cloves, minced

1 tbsp fresh cilantro, chopped

DIRECTIONS (Prep + Cook Time: 30 minutes)

Preheat the air fryer to 400 F. Heat olive oil in a skillet over medium heat and sauté onion and garlic until fragrant, about 3 minutes. Add in ground beef, salt, black pepper, and taco seasoning. Cook until the beef browns while breaking it with a vessel as it cooks. Add cilantro rotel and stir to combine. Lay 4 savoy cabbage leaves on a flat surface and scoop ¼ of the beef mixture in the center; sprinkle with Mexican cheese. Wrap diagonally and double wrap with the remaining cabbage leaves. Arrange the rolls on the greased air fryer basket and Bake for 8 minutes. Flip the rolls and cook for 5 more minutes. Remove to a plate, garnish with cilantro, and let cool before serving.

814. Mexican Chorizo & Beef Empanadas
INGREDIENTS (4 Servings)

2 garlic cloves, minced

½ cup green bell pepper, chopped

1 red onion, chopped

4 oz chorizo, chopped

½ lb ground beef

4 dough discs

1 cup Mexican blend cheese, shredded

2 tbsp vegetable oil

¼ cup chunky salsa

Salt and black pepper to taste

DIRECTIONS (Prep + Cook Time: 35 minutes)

Heat the vegetable oil in a pan over medium heat and sauté bell pepper, garlic, and onion for 4 minutes until tender. Add the ground beef and chorizo and stir-fry for 5-6 minutes. Season with salt and pepper. Pour in chunky salsa and cook, stirring occasionally, until the sauce thickens, 5 minutes. Preheat air fryer to 390 F. Divide the meat mixture and cheese between the dough discs. Fold them in half over the filling; press and seal the edges with a fork. Spritz with cooking spray and transfer to the air fryer basket. Bale for 12-15 minutes, turning once until golden. Let cool slightly before serving.

815. Italian Beef Meatloaf with Basil & Cheese
INGREDIENTS (4 Servings)

1 lb ground beef

2 tbsp fresh basil, chopped

1 onion, diced

1 tbsp Worcestershire sauce

2 tbsp tomato paste

Salt and black pepper to taste

1 cup breadcrumbs

3 tbsp mozzarella cheese, grated

DIRECTIONS (Prep + Cook Time: 35 minutes)

Preheat air fryer to 350 F. In a bowl, add all ingredients except for the cheese. Mix with hands until well combined. Place in a greased baking dish and shape into a loaf. Place in the air fryer basket and Bake for 15-18 minutes. Top with cheese 3-4 minutes before it's cooked. Let cool slightly and slice.

816. Chimichurri New York Steak
INGREDIENTS (4 Servings)

½ cup chimichurri salsa

2 tbsp olive oil

1 ½ lb New York strip steak

1 tbsp smoked paprika

Salt and black pepper to taste

1 jar (16-oz) roasted peppers, sliced

DIRECTIONS (Prep + Cook Time: 20 minutes + cooling time)

Preheat air fryer to 380 F. Rub the steak with smoked paprika, sea salt, and pepper. Drizzle with olive oil and Bake in the air fryer for 12-14 minutes, turning once halfway through. Transfer to a cutting board and let it sit for a few minutes. Slice, drizzle the chimichurri salsa, and serve immediately.

817. Chipotle Rib-Eye Steak with Avocado Salsa
INGREDIENTS (4 Servings)

- 1 ½ lb rib-eye steak
- 2 tsp olive oil
- 1 tbsp chipotle chili pepper
- Salt and black pepper to taste
- 1 avocado, diced Juice from ½ lime

DIRECTIONS (Prep + Cook Time: 25 minutes + marinating time)

Place the steak on a chopping board. Drizzle with olive oil and sprinkle with chipotle pepper, salt, and pepper. Use hands to rub the spices onto the meat. Leave it to sit to incorporate flavors for 30 minutes. Preheat air fryer to 400 F. Pull out the frying basket and place the meat inside. Bake for 10 minutes. Turn the steak and continue cooking for 6 minutes. Remove the steak, cover with foil, and let it sit for 5 minutes before slicing. Mash avocado in a bowl and mix in lime juice. Serve with the sliced beef.

818. Beef Veggie Mix with Hoisin Sauce
INGREDIENTS (4 Servings)

Hoisin Sauce:

- 2 tbsp soy sauce
- 1 tbsp peanut butter
- ½ tsp sriracha sauce
- 1 tsp sugar
- 1 tsp rice vinegar
- 3 cloves garlic, minced

Beef Veggie Mix:

- 1 ½ lb beef sirloin steak, cut into strips
- 1 yellow pepper, cut into strips
- 1 green pepper, cut into strips
- 1 white onion, cut into strips
- 1 red onion, cut into strips
- 1 lb broccoli, cut into florets
- 1 tbsp soy sauce
- 2 tsp sesame oil
- 3 tsp minced garlic
- 1 tsp ground ginger
- 1 tbsp olive oil

DIRECTIONS (Prep + Cook Time: 55 minutes)

Place a pan over low heat and add all hoisin sauce ingredients. Bring to a simmer and cook until reduced, about 3-4 minutes; let cool. To the chilled hoisin sauce, add garlic, sesame oil, soy sauce, ginger, and ½ cup of water; mix well. Stir in the beef, cover, and refrigerate for 20 minutes to marinade. In a greased baking dish, combine broccoli, peppers, onions, and olive oil. Place the dish in the fryer. Bake for 10 minutes at 400 F, shaking once. Transfer to a plate and cover with foil to keep warm. Remove the meat from the fridge and drain the liquid into a bowl. Add the beef into the fryer and Bake at 380 F for 10 minutes, shake, and cook for 7 more minutes. Transfer to the veggie plate, season with salt and pepper, and pour the hoisin sauce over. Serve immediately.

819. Korean Beef Bulgogi
INGREDIENTS (4 Servings)

- 1 lb flank steak
- 2 cups cooked brown rice
- 2 cups steamed broccoli florets
- ½ cup soy sauce
- 1 tbsp gochujang
- 1 tbsp grated fresh ginger
- 2 spring onion, sliced diagonally
- 2 tbsp brown sugar
- 2 tbsp red wine vinegar
- 1 tbsp olive oil
- 1 tbsp sesame oil
- 3 tsp slurry (2 tsp cornstarch mixed with 1 tsp water)

DIRECTIONS (Prep + Cook Time: 35 minutes + marinating time) Slice the flat steak across the grain into about ¼-inch strips. Whisk the soy sauce, gochujang, ginger, brown sugar, vinegar, olive oil, and sesame oil in a large bowl. Add in the beef strips and toss to coat. Cover the bowl with plastic wrap and refrigerate for a minimum of 30 minutes or a maximum of 2 hours. Preheat your Air Fryer to 390 F. Remove the steak from the marinade. Put any leftover marinade to the side. Put the steak in the greased fryer basket in a single layer. Air fry for 10 minutes. Turn the pieces of steak over and cook until they reach the level of preferred doneness according to the internal temperature. Rare is 120°F, medium-rare is 130°F, the medium is 140°F, and medium well is 150°F. Put the reserved marinade in a small saucepan over medium heat and bring to a boil. Pour the slurry into the saucepan and simmer until the sauce thickens, about 2-3 minutes. Add in the pieces of steak and stir to coat. Remove from the heat. Divide the brown rice and steamed broccoli between 4 bowls.

820. Spicy Sweet Beef with Veggie Topping
INGREDIENTS (4 Servings)

- 2 beef steaks, sliced into thin strips
- 2 garlic cloves, minced
- 2 tsp maple syrup
- 1 tsp oyster sauce
- 1 tsp cayenne pepper
- ½ tsp olive oil Juice of
- 1 lime Salt and black pepper to taste
- 1 cauliflower, cut into florets
- 2 carrots, cut into chunks
- 1 cup green peas

DIRECTIONS (Prep + Cook Time: 20 minutes)

In a bowl, add beef, garlic, maple syrup, oyster sauce, cayenne pepper, olive oil, lime juice, salt, and black pepper and stir to combine. Place the beef mixture in a baking dish. Preheat air fryer to 400 F. Top with the veggies and Bake for 12-14 minutes, shaking once during cooking. Serve warm.

821. Mexican Beef Quesadillas
INGREDIENTS (4 Servings)

2 tbsp olive oil	1 cup mozzarella cheese, grated	1 cup corn kernels, canned
8 soft round taco shells	½ cup fresh cilantro, chopped	Salt and black pepper to taste
1 lb beef steak, sliced	1 jalapeño chili, chopped	

DIRECTIONS (Prep + Cook Time: 30 minutes)

Heat olive oil in a skillet over medium heat and brown the beef for 6-8 minutes, stirring occasionally. Place the cooked beef on each taco shell, top with cheese, cilantro, jalapeño, corn, salt, and pepper. Fold in half and secure with toothpicks. Arrange the quesadillas on the greased air fryer basket and Bake at 380 F for 14-16 minutes, turning once halfway through. Serve with guacamole.

822. Thyme Lamb Chops with Asparagus
INGREDIENTS (4 Servings)

1 lb lamb chops	2 tsp fresh thyme, chopped	Salt and black pepper to taste
2 tbsp olive oil	1 garlic clove, minced	1 lb asparagus spears, trimmed

DIRECTIONS (Prep + Cook Time: 20 minutes)

Preheat air fryer to 400 F. Drizzle the asparagus with some olive oil and sprinkle with salt. Season the lamb with salt and pepper. Brush with the remaining olive oil and place in the air fryer basket. AirFry for 10 minutes, turn and add the asparagus. Cook for another 5 minutes. Serve topped with thyme.

823. LAMB Honey Barbecue Pork Ribs
INGREDIENTS (2 Servings)

1 lb pork ribs	2 garlic cloves, minced	4 tbsp barbecue sauce
½ tsp five-spice powder	1 tsp sesame oil	1 tsp soy sauce
Salt and black pepper to taste	1 tbsp honey + for brushing	

DIRECTIONS (Prep + Cook Time: 25 minutes + marinating time)

Chop the ribs into smaller pieces and place them in a large bowl. In another bowl, whisk all other ingredients in a bowl. Drizzle over the meat and mix until well coated. Cover and refrigerate for 1 hour. Preheat air fryer to 350 F. Place the ribs in the frying basket and AirFry for 8 minutes. Slide the basket out and brush the ribs with some honey. Cook for another 12614 minutes. Serve immediately

824. Sweet & Hot Pork Ribs
INGREDIENTS (2 Servings)

1 lb pork ribs	½ tbsp maple syrup	1 tbsp cayenne pepper
1 tsp soy sauce	3 tbsp barbecue sauce	1 tsp sesame oil
¼ tsp dried oregano	1 garlic clove, minced	

DIRECTIONS (Prep + Cook Time: 25 minutes + marinating time)

Put the ribs on a chopping board and cut them into pieces. Put them in a mixing bowl and add the soy sauce, oregano, maple syrup, barbecue sauce, garlic, cayenne, and sesame oil. Mix well and place the pork in the fridge to marinate for 1 hour. Preheat air fryer to 350 F. Place the ribs in the frying basket and Bake for 16-18 minutes, turn, and continue cooking for 10 minutes. Serve hot.

825. Swedish Meatballs
INGREDIENTS (4 Servings)

1 lb ground pork	⅓ cup seasoned breadcrumbs	2 tbsp butter
1 tbsp fresh dill, chopped	1 egg, beaten	⅓ cup sour cream
½ tsp жидкха nutmeg	Salt and white pepper to taste	2 tbsp flour

DIRECTIONS (Prep + Cook Time: 25 minutes)

Preheat air fryer to 360 F. In a bowl, combine ground pork, dill, nutmeg, breadcrumbs, egg, salt, and pepper and mix well. Shape the mixture into small balls. AirFry for 12 minutes, flipping once. Melt butter in a saucepan over medium heat and stir in the flour until lightly browned, about 1-2 minutes. Gradually add in 1 cup of water and whisk until the sauce thickens. Stir in sour cream and cook for 1 minute. Serve the meatballs covered with the sauce.

826. Pork Sausage with Butter Bean Ratatouille
INGREDIENTS (4 Servings)

- 4 pork sausages For Ratatouille
- 1 red bell pepper, chopped
- 2 zucchinis, chopped
- 1 eggplant, chopped
- 1 medium red onion, chopped
- 2 tbsp olive oil
- 1 cup canned butter beans, drained 15 oz canned tomatoes,
- chopped 2 tbsp fresh thyme,
- chopped 1 tbsp balsamic vinegar
- 2 garlic cloves, minced
- 1 red chili, minced

DIRECTIONS (Prep + Cook Time: 40 minutes)

Preheat air fryer to 390 F. Add sausages to a greased air fryer basket and AirFry for 12-15 minutes, turning once, halfway through cooking. Cover with foil to keep warm. Mix all ratatouille ingredients in a baking dish and Bake in the fryer for 15-18 minutes, shaking once. Serve the sausages with ratatouille.

827. Paprika Pork Kabobs
INGREDIENTS (4 Servings)

- 1 lb pork tenderloin, cubed
- Salt and black pepper to taste
- 1 green bell pepper, cut into chunks
- 1 red onion, sliced
- ½ tsp oregano
- ½ tsp smoked paprika
- 1 zucchini, cut into chunks

DIRECTIONS (Prep + Cook Time: 25 minutes)

Preheat air fryer to 350 F. In a bowl, mix the pork, paprika, salt, and black pepper. Thread the vegetables and pork cubes alternately onto small bamboo skewers. Spray with cooking spray and transfer to the frying basket. Bake for 15-18 minutes, flipping once halfway through. Serve sprinkled with oregano.

828. Zesty Breaded Chops
INGREDIENTS (4 Servings)

- 4 lean pork chops
- Salt and black pepper to taste
- 2 eggs
- 1 cup breadcrumbs
- ½ tsp garlic powder
- 1 tsp paprika
- ½ tsp dried oregano
- ½ tsp cayenne pepper
- ¼ tsp dry mustard
- 1 lemon, zested

DIRECTIONS (Prep + Cook Time: 25 minutes)

In a bowl, whisk the eggs with 1 tbsp of water. In another bowl, add the breadcrumbs, salt, pepper, garlic powder, paprika, oregano, cayenne pepper, lemon zest, and dry mustard and mix evenly. Preheat air fryer to 380 F. In the egg mixture, dip each pork chop and then dip in the crumb mixture. Place the chops in a greased air fryer basket and AirFry for 10 minutes. Flip and cook for another 5 minutes until golden. Remove the chops to a chopping board and let rest for 3 minutes before slicing.

829. Southeast-Asian Pork Chops
INGREDIENTS (4 Servings)

- 4 pork chops
- 2 garlic cloves, minced
- ½ tbsp sugar
- 4 stalks lemongrass, trimmed and chopped
- 2 shallots, chopped
- 2 tbsp olive oil
- 1 ¼ tsp soy sauce
- 1 ¼ tsp fish sauce
- Salt and black pepper to taste

DIRECTIONS (Prep + Cook Time: 20 minutes + marinating time)

In a bowl, add garlic, sugar, lemongrass, shallots, olive oil, soy sauce, fish sauce, salt, and pepper; mix well. Add the pork chops, coat them well in the mixture and marinate for 2 hours to get nice and savory. Preheat air fryer to 400 F. Remove the chops from the marinade and lay them in the air fryer basket. Bake for 10 minutes. Turn the chops and cook for 5 more minutes. Serve with sautéed asparagus.

830. Roasted Pork Chops with Mushrooms
INGREDIENTS (4 Servings)

- 1 lb boneless pork chops
- 2 carrots, cut into sticks
- 1 cup mushrooms, sliced
- 2 tbsp olive oil
- 2 garlic cloves, minced
- 1 tsp cayenne pepper
- 1 tsp dried thyme
- Salt and black pepper to taste

DIRECTIONS (Prep + Cook Time: 25 minutes)

Preheat air fryer to 360 F. Season the chops with cayenne pepper, thyme, salt, and pepper. In a bowl, combine carrots, olive oil, mushrooms, and salt. Place the veggies in a greased baking dish and then in the air fryer basket. Top with pork chops and Bake for 15-18 minutes, turning once. Serve.

831. Juicy Double Cut Pork Chops
INGREDIENTS (4 Servings)

4 pork chops	2 tbsp corn syrup	2 tbsp ketchup
½ cup green mole sauce	1 tbsp olive oil	2 tbsp water
2 tbsp tamarind paste	2 tbsp molasses	
1 garlic clove, minced	4 tbsp southwest seasoning	

DIRECTIONS (Prep + Cook Time: 25 minutes + marinating time)

In a bowl, mix all ingredients, except for pork chops and mole sauce. Add in the pork chops to marinate for 30 minutes. Preheat air fryer to 350 F. Place the chops in the greased frying basket. Bake for 16-18 minutes, turning once. Serve the pork chops drizzled with mole sauce.

832. Stuffed Pork Chops
INGREDIENTS (4 Servings)

4 thick pork chops	Salt and black pepper to taste	2 garlic cloves, minced
½ cup mushrooms, sliced	1 tbsp olive oil	2 tbsp sage, chopped
1 shallot, chopped	2 tbsp butter	

DIRECTIONS (Prep + Cook Time: 35 minutes)

Melt butter in a skillet over medium heat and sauté shallot, garlic, mushrooms, sage, salt, and pepper for 4-5 minutes until tender. Preheat air fryer to 350 F. Cut a pocket in each pork chop to create a cavity and fill the chops with the mushroom mixture. Secure with toothpicks. Season the stuffed chops with salt and pepper and brush with olive oil. Place them in the frying basket and Bake for 18-20 minutes, turning once. Remove the toothpicks and serve.

833. Pork Sandwiches with Bacon & Cheddar
INGREDIENTS (2 Servings)

½ lb pork steak	5 thick bacon slices	2 burger buns, halved
1 tsp steak seasoning	½ cup cheddar cheese, grated	
Salt and black pepper to taste	½ tbsp Worcestershire sauce	

DIRECTIONS (Prep + Cook Time: 40 minutes)

Preheat air fryer to 400 F. Season the pork steak with black pepper, salt, and steak seasoning. Place in the air fryer and Bake for 15 minutes, turn, and continue cooking for 6 minutes. Remove the steak to a chopping board, let cool slightly, and using two forks, shred into small pieces. Place the bacon in the frying basket and AirFry at 370 F for 5-8 minutes. Chop the bacon and transfer to a bowl. Mix in the pulled pork, Worcestershire sauce, and cheddar cheese. Adjust the seasoning and spoon the mixture into the halved buns to serve.

834. Smoked Beef Burgers with Hoisin Sauce
INGREDIENTS (4 Servings)

1 lb ground beef	1 tsp garlic powder	4 tbsp mayonnaise
Salt and black pepper to taste	1 ½ tbsp hoisin sauce	1 large tomato, sliced
¼ tsp liquid smoke	4 buns, halved	4 slices cheddar cheese
2 tsp onion powder	4 trimmed lettuce leaves	

DIRECTIONS (Prep + Cook Time: 25 minutes)

Preheat air fryer to 370 F. In a bowl, combine beef, salt, pepper, liquid smoke, onion powder, garlic powder, and Worcestershire sauce with your hands. Form 4 patties out of the mixture. Place the patties in the fryer basket, making sure to leave enough space between them. Cook for 10 minutes, turn and cook further for 5 minutes. Assemble the burgers in the buns with lettuce, mayonnaise, sliced cheese, sliced tomato, and patties. Serve.

835. Beef & Tomato Meatball Bake
INGREDIENTS (4 Servings)

1 small onion, chopped	½ tbsp fresh thyme leaves, chopped	Salt and black pepper to taste
1 lb grounded beef	1 whole egg, beaten	1 cup tomato sauce
1 tbsp fresh parsley, chopped	3 tbsp breadcrumbs	

DIRECTIONS (Prep + Cook Time: 25 minutes)

Preheat air fryer to 390 F. In a bowl, mix all ingredients except for the tomato sauce. Roll the mixture into 10-12 balls. Place the balls in a greased baking dish and Bake in the air fryer for 8 minutes. Pour the tomato sauce over the balls and cook for 5 more minutes at 300 F. Gently stir and serve.

836. Argentinian-Style Beef Empanadas
INGREDIENTS (4 Servings)

- 1 lb ground beef
- ½ onion, diced
- 1 garlic clove, minced
- ¼ cup tomato salsa
- 4 empanada shells
- 1 egg yolk
- 2 tsp milk
- ½ tsp cumin
- Salt and black pepper to taste
- 2 tbsp olive oil

DIRECTIONS (Prep + Cook Time: 30 minutes)

Heat olive oil in a pan over medium heat and cook ground beef, onion, cumin, garlic, salt, and black pepper for 5-6 minutes, stirring occasionally. Stir in tomato salsa and cook for 3 minutes, and set aside. Preheat air fryer to 350 F. In a bowl, whisk the egg yolk with milk. Divide the beef mixture between empanada shells, fold the shells and seal the ends with a fork. Brush with the egg mixture. Place empanadas in the greased frying basket and AirFry for 10 minutes, flipping once. Serve warm.

837. Chili Beef & Bean Casserole
INGREDIENTS (4 Servings)

- 1 ½ lb ground beef
- ½ tbsp chili powder
- Salt and black pepper to taste
- 1 can (8 oz) cannellini beans, drained
- 1 tbsp fresh cilantro, chopped
- 1 tbsp olive oil
- ½ cup celery, chopped
- 1 onion, chopped
- 2 garlic cloves, minced
- 1 ½ cups vegetable broth
- 1 can tomatoes, diced
- ½ cup red bell pepper, finely chopped

DIRECTIONS (Prep + Cook Time: 30 minutes)

Heat olive oil in a skillet over medium heat and sauté garlic, onion, bell pepper, and celery for 5 minutes. Add in the beef and cook for 6 more minutes. Stir in broth, tomatoes, chili powder, and cilantro. Let cook for 10 minutes and transfer to a baking dish. Preheat the air fryer to 350 F. Stir the beans into the dish and season with salt and pepper. Place in the air fryer basket and Bake for 12-14 minutes. Let cool slightly before serving.

838. Effortless Beef Short Ribs
INGREDIENTS (4 Servings)

- 1 ½ lb bone-in beef short ribs
- ½ cup soy sauce
- ¼ cup white wine vinegar
- 1 brown onion, chopped
- 1 tbsp ginger powder
- 2 garlic cloves, minced
- 1 tbsp olive oil
- 2 tbsp chives, chopped
- Salt and black pepper to taste

DIRECTIONS (Prep + Cook Time: 15 minutes + marinating time)

In a shallow bowl, mix short ribs, soy sauce, wine vinegar, onion, ginger powder, garlic, olive oil, salt, and black pepper. Cover and allow to marinate in the fridge for at least 2 hours or overnight if preferred. Preheat air fryer to 390 F. Arrange the ribs on the frying basket and Bake for 12 minutes. Slide the basket out, flip, and cook for another 7-8 minutes. Serve sprinkled with freshly chopped chives.

839. Tender Rib Eye Steak
INGREDIENTS (2 Servings)

- 2 beef rib-eye steaks
- 1 tbsp balsamic vinegar
- ½ tbsp Italian seasoning
- 2 tbsp olive oil
- Salt and black pepper to taste

DIRECTIONS (Prep + Cook Time: 25 minutes + marinating time)

Preheat air fryer to 360 F. In a bowl, combine all ingredients, cover it, and place in the fridge for 30 minutes. Transfer the beef to the frying basket and Bake for 20 minutes, flipping once halfway through.

840. Sausage-Stuffed Beef Steak
INGREDIENTS (4 Servings)

- ½ lb beef sausage, sliced
- 1 tbsp olive oil
- 1 ½ lb sirloin steak, sliced
- 2 bell peppers, cut into thin strips
- 2 tbsp Worcestershire sauce
- ½ tbsp garlic powder
- ½ tbsp onion powder
- Salt and black pepper to taste

DIRECTIONS (Prep + Cook Time: 50 minutes + marinating time) Pound steaks very thin using a meat mallet. Mix the Worcestershire sauce, garlic powder, and onion powder in a bowl. Add in the steaks and stir to coat. Cover with foil and refrigerate for a minimum of 30 minutes. While steaks are marinating, soak 8 toothpicks in water, about 15 to 20 minutes. Preheat your Air Fryer to 390 F. Take the steaks out of the refrigerator and bag. Place the bell peppers and beef sausage in the middle, then sprinkle with salt and pepper. Roll up the beef tightly and secure using toothpicks. Spray fryer basket with a light coating of olive oil. In a single layer, place beef roll up in the greased basket with the toothpick side down. Air fry for 10 minutes. Turn the steaks over and continue cooking for another 7 to 10 minutes or until the internal temperature is at least 150°F. Allow beef roll-ups to rest for 10 minutes. Serve warm.

841. Spice-Coated Beef Steaks
INGREDIENTS (2 Servings)

2 beef steaks,	1 tbsp olive oil	Salt and black pepper to taste
1-inch thick ½ tsp cayenne pepper	½ tsp paprika	

DIRECTIONS (Prep + Cook Time: 15 minutes)

Preheat air fryer to 390 F. In a bowl, mix olive oil, black pepper, cayenne pepper, paprika, and salt. Rub the mixture onto the steaks. Place them in the greased air frying basket. Bake for 12 minutes, turning once halfway through. Transfer to a plate, cover with foil and let it sit for 10 minutes. Serve.

842. Thai Roasted Beef
INGREDIENTS (4 Servings)

1 lb beef steak, sliced	2 garlic cloves, chopped	1 tbsp fresh basil, chopped
Salt and black pepper to taste	1 tsp brown sugar Juice of	2 tbsp sesame oil
2 tbsp soy sauce	1 lime	2 tbsp fish sauce
1 tbsp fresh ginger, minced	2 tbsp mirin	
2 chilies, seeded and chopped	1 tbsp fresh cilantro, chopped	

DIRECTIONS (Prep + Cook Time: 20 minutes + marinating time)

Place all ingredients, except for the beef, in a blender and process until smooth. Transfer to a zipper bag and add in the beef; shake to combine and refrigerate for 1 hour. Preheat air fryer to 350 F. Place in the marinated beef. Bake for 12-14 minutes, depending on whether you want it well done. Let sit for a couple of minutes before serving. Serve with fresh salad

843. Boeuf Stroganoff
INGREDIENTS (4 Servings)

1 lb beef steak, thinly sliced	1 cup sour cream	2 cups cooked egg noodles
4 tbsp butter, melted	8 oz mushrooms, sliced	
1 whole onion, chopped	2 cups beef broth	

DIRECTIONS (Prep + Cook Time: 20 minutes + marinating time)

Preheat air fryer to 400 F. In a bowl, mix the butter, mushrooms, sour cream, onion, and beef broth. Pour the mixture over the steak and set aside for 30 minutes. Place the marinated beef in a baking dish and Bake in the air fryer for 14 minutes, shaking once halfway through. Serve with egg noodles.

844. Beef with Cauliflower & Carrots
INGREDIENTS (4 Servings)

1 lb circular beef steak, cut into strips	⅓ cup sherry	1 tbsp olive oil
½ cauliflower head, cut into florets	1 tsp soy sauce	1 garlic clove, minced
⅓ cup oyster sauce	1 tsp white sugar	2 tbsp pine nuts, toasted
2 tbsp sesame oil	1 tsp cornstarch	

DIRECTIONS (Prep + Cook Time: 20 minutes)

In a bowl, mix all ingredients except for the beef, cauliflower, and carrots. Add in the beef strips and stir to coat. Transfer to a greased air fryer basket. Bake for 14-16 minutes at 390 F, shaking once. Blanch the cauliflower and carrots in salted water in a pot over medium heat for 3-4 minutes. Drain and place on a serving plate. Top with pine nuts. When the beef is ready, add it to the cauliflower and serve.

845. Crunchy Beef Escalopes
INGREDIENTS (4 Servings)

4 beef schnitzel cutlets	Salt and black pepper to taste	2 butter slices
½ cup flour	1 cup breadcrumbs	
2 eggs, beaten	2 tbsp olive oil	

DIRECTIONS (Prep + Cook Time: 25 minutes)

Coat the cutlets in flour and shake off any excess. Dip into the beaten eggs, season with salt and black pepper, and dip into the crumbs to coat well. Brush with olive oil and AirFry for 16 minutes at 360 F, turning once halfway through. Serve topped with butter slices.

846. African Minty Lamb Kofta
INGREDIENTS (4 Servings)

1 lb ground lamb	1 tsp garlic powder	½ tsp dried coriander
1 tsp cumin	1 tsp onion powder	4 bamboo skewers
2 tbsp mint, chopped	1 tbsp ras el hanout	Salt and black pepper to taste

DIRECTIONS(Prep + Cook Time: 15 minutes + marinating time)

In a bowl, mix ground lamb, cumin, garlic and onion powders, mint, ras el hanout, coriander, salt, and pepper. Mold into sausage shapes and place onto skewers. Let sit for 15 minutes in the fridge. Preheat air fryer to 380 F. Grease the frying basket with cooking spray. Arrange the skewers on the basket and AirFry for 10-12 minutes, turning once halfway through. Serve with yogurt dip.

847. Traditional Lamb Kabobs
INGREDIENTS (4 Servings)

1 ½ lb ground lamb	2 tsp coriander seeds	½ tsp ground ginger
1 green onion, chopped	½ tsp cayenne pepper	1 red bell pepper, cut into 2-inch pieces
2 tbsp mint leaves, chopped	1 tsp salt	
3 garlic cloves, minced	1 tbsp fresh parsley, chopped	1 sweet onion, cut into wedges
1 tsp paprika	1 tsp cumin	1 cup whole small mushrooms

DIRECTIONS(Prep + Cook Time: 35 minutes)

Combine all ingredients, except for the bell pepper, sweet onion, and mushrooms in a bowl. Mix well with hands until the herbs and spices are evenly distributed, and the mixture is well incorporated; let sit for 10 minutes. Form the mixture into sausage shapes. Preheat air fryer to 380 F. Thread the meat and vegetables onto the skewers, alternately, and place them in the greased frying basket. AirFry for 12-15 minutes, turning once. Serve hot with green salad.

848. Thyme Lamb Steaks with Potatoes
INGREDIENTS (2 Servings)

2 lamb steaks	2 garlic cloves, crushed	2 tbsp fresh thyme, chopped
2 tbsp olive oil	Salt and black pepper to taste	2 red potatoes, sliced

DIRECTIONS (Prep + Cook Time: 25 minutes)

Rub the steaks with 1 tbsp olive oil, garlic, salt, and pepper. Place them in the greased air fryer basket. Season the potatoes with olive oil, salt, pepper, and thyme. Arrange the potatoes next to the steaks and cook at 360 F for 14-16 minutes, turning once halfway through cooking. Serve immediately.

849. Lamb Taquitos
INGREDIENTS (4 Servings)

1 lb lamb meat, sliced into strips	2 tsp fresh cilantro, chopped	2 tbsp queso fresco, crumbled
2 tbsp olive oil	2 tsp fire-roasted green chilies	4 corn tortillas

DIRECTIONS (Prep + Cook Time: 20 minutes)

Warm olive oil in a skillet over medium heat and stir-fry the lamb for 5-6 minutes. Remove and stir in green chilies. Preheat air fryer to 400 F. Divide the mixture between tortillas and roll up them. Spritz with cooking spray and AirFry for 8 minutes, turning once. Top with queso fresco and cilantro to serve.

850. Roasted Pork Rack with Macadamia Nuts
INGREDIENTS (2 Servings)

1 lb pork rack	Salt and black pepper to taste	1 egg, beaten in a bowl
2 tbsp olive oil	1 cup macadamia nuts, thinly chopped	1 tbsp rosemary, chopped
1 clove garlic, minced	1 tbsp breadcrumbs	

DIRECTIONS (Prep + Cook Time: 50 minutes)

Add the olive oil and garlic to a bowl. Mix vigorously with a spoon to make garlic oil. Place the rack of pork on a chopping board and brush with the garlic oil. Sprinkle with salt and black pepper. Preheat air fryer to 370 F. In a bowl, add breadcrumbs, macadamia nuts, and rosemary. Brush the meat with the egg on all sides and sprinkle the nut mixture generously all over. Place the coated pork in the frying basket and Bake for 30 minutes. Flip over and cook further for 5-8 minutes. Remove the meat onto a chopping board. Let it rest for 10 minutes before slicing. Serve with a salad.

851. Baby Back Pork Ribs with BBQ Sauce
INGREDIENTS (4 Servings)

½ tsp smoked paprika

1 tsp cayenne pepper

1 rack baby back pork ribs, cut into individual pieces

1 tsp onion powder

1 tsp garlic powder

1 tsp pomegranate molasses

½ tsp dried oregano

½ cup barbecue sauce

Salt and black pepper to taste

2 scallions, chopped

DIRECTIONS (Prep + Cook Time: 25 minutes + marinating time)

In a bowl, combine paprika, cayenne pepper, garlic powder, pomegranate molasses, onion powder, oregano, salt, and pepper. Add in the ribs and toss to coat. Cover and let in the fridge for 30 minutes. Preheat air fryer to 360 F. Spray ribs with cooking spray and place in the fryer basket. Cook for 15-18 minutes, flipping once halfway through. Drizzle with barbecue sauce, scatter scallions over, and serve.

852. Pork Meatball Noodle Bowl
INGREDIENTS (4 Servings)

2 lb ground pork

2 eggs, beaten

1 tbsp olive oil

1cup panko bread crumbs

1 shallot, chopped

2 tsp soy sauce

2 garlic cloves, minced

½ tsp ground ginger

2 cups rice noodles, cooked

1 gem lettuce, torn

1 carrot, shredded 1

cucumber, peeled, thinly sliced

1 cup Asian sesame dressing

1 lime, cut into wedges

DIRECTIONS (Prep + Cook Time: 30 minutes)

Preheat air fryer to 390 F. Mix pork, eggs, bread crumbs, shallot, soy sauce, garlic, and ginger in a large mixing bowl. Divide the mixture into 24 balls. Place them i into the greased fryer basket. Air fry for about 10 to 15 minutes, shaking the basket every 5 minutes to ensure even cooking. Cook until the meatballs are golden brown. Divide the rice noodles, lettuce, carrots, and cucumber between 4 bowls. Top with meatballs and drizzle with sesame dressing. Serve with lime wedges.

853. Best Ever Pork Burgers
INGREDIENTS (2 Servings)

½ lb ground pork

½ medium onion, chopped

½ tsp mixed herbs

½ tsp garlic powder

½ tsp dried basil

½ tsp mustard

Salt and black pepper to taste

2 bread buns, halved

Assembling:

½ onion, sliced in

2-inch rings

1 large tomato, sliced in

2-inch rings

1 small lettuce leave, cleaned

4 slices Cheddar cheese

DIRECTIONS (Prep + Cook Time: 20 minutes)

In a bowl, add ground pork, onion, mixed herbs, garlic powder, basil, mustard, salt, and pepper and mix evenly. Form 2 patties out of the mixture and place on a flat plate. Preheat the air fryer to 370 F. Place the pork patties in the greased air fryer basket and Bake for 10 minutes. Slide-out the basket and turn the patties. Continue cooking for 5 minutes. Place the two halves of the buns on a clean flat surface. Place lettuce leaves on both, then a patty each, followed by an onion ring each, a tomato ring each, and 2 slices of cheddar cheese. Cover the buns with the other halves. Serve with ketchup and french fries.

854. Pork Kofta Kebabs with Yogurt Sauce
INGREDIENTS (4 Servings)

1 lb pork sausage meat

Salt and black pepper to taste

1 onion, chopped

½ tsp garlic puree

1 tsp ground cumin

1 cup Greek yogurt

2 tbsp walnuts, chopped

1 tbsp fresh dill, chopped

DIRECTIONS (Prep + Cook Time: 20 minutes)

Preheat air fryer to 340 F. In a bowl, mix onion, sausage meat, ground cumin, salt, and pepper. Form patties out the mixture, about ½ inch thick, and lay them on the greased frying basket and AirFry for 15 minutes, shaking once or twice. Mix yogurt, walnuts, garlic, dill, and salt in a small bowl until a sauce forms. Serve the kofta with the yogurt sauce and enjoy.

855. Sausage Sticks Rolled in Bacon
INGREDIENTS (4 Servings)

Sausage:

8 bacon strips	8 pork sausages

Relish:

8 large tomatoes, chopped	3 tbsp fresh parsley, chopped	1 tsp smoked paprika
1 clove garlic, peeled	Salt and black pepper to taste	1 tbsp white wine vinegar
1 small onion, peeled	2 tbsp sugar	

DIRECTIONS (Prep + Cook Time: 30 minutes + chilling time)

Pulse the tomatoes, garlic, and onion in a food processor until the mixture is pulpy. Transfer to a saucepan over medium heat and add vinegar, salt, and pepper; simmer for 10 minutes. Stir in paprika, parsley, and sugar and cook for 10 more minutes until thick. Let cool for 1 hour. Wrap each sausage in a bacon strip neatly and stick in a bamboo skewer at the end of the sausage to secure the bacon ends. Place in a greased air fryer basket and AirFry for 12 minutes at 350 F, turning once halfway through. Serve the sausages with the cooled relish.

856. Spicy Tricolor Pork Kebabs
INGREDIENTS (4 Servings)

1 lb pork steak, cut into cubes	1 tsp powdered chili	1 tbsp white wine vinegar
¼ cup soy sauce	1 tsp garlic salt	3 tbsp steak sauce
2 tsp smoked paprika	1 tsp red chili flakes	

Skewing:

1 green pepper, cut into cubes	1 yellow squash, seeded and cut into cubes	Salt and black pepper to taste
1 red pepper, cut into cubes	1 green squash, seeded and cut into cubes	A bunch of skewers

DIRECTIONS (Prep + Cook Time: 20 minutes + marinating time)

In a mixing bowl, add the pork cubes, soy sauce, paprika, chili, garlic salt, red chili flakes, white wine vinegar, and steak sauce. Mix with a spoon and refrigerate to marinate for 1 hour. Preheat air fryer to 370 F. On each skewer, stick the pork cubes and vegetables in the order that you prefer. Arrange the skewers on the frying basket and Bake them for 12-14 minutes, flipping once.

857. Sweet Pork Tenderloin
INGREDIENTS (4 Servings)

1 lb pork tenderloin, sliced	1 orange, juiced and zested	1 tbsp soy sauce
2 tbsp quince preserve	2 tbsp olive oil	Salt and black pepper to taste

DIRECTIONS (Prep + Cook Time: 20 minutes)

Brush the pork tenderloin slices with some olive oil and season with salt and pepper. Put them into the air fryer and Bake for 14 minutes at 380 F, turning once halfway through. Heat the remaining olive oil in a skillet over low heat and add in orange juice, soy sauce, orange zest, and quince preserve. Simmer until the sauce thickens slightly, about 2-3 minutes. Season to taste with salt and pepper. Arrange the pork on a platter and pour the quince sauce over to serve.

858. Pork Lettuce Cups
INGREDIENTS (4 Servings)

1 tbsp sesame oil	2 Little Gem lettuces, leaves separated	1 tsp honey
1 lb pork tenderloin, sliced	1 cup radishes, cut into matchsticks	Salt and black pepper to taste
½ white onion, sliced	1 tsp red chili flakes	
2 tbsp sesame seeds, toasted	2 tbsp teriyaki sauce	

DIRECTIONS (Prep + Cook Time: 25 minutes + marinating time)

In a bowl, combine teriyaki sauce, red chili flakes, honey, sesame oil, salt, and pepper. Add in the pork, toss to coat, and place in the fridge covered for 30 minutes. Preheat air fryer to 360 F. Remove the pork from the marinade and place it in the greased frying basket, reserving the marinade liquid. AirFry for 12 minutes, turning once halfway through. Arrange the lettuce leaves on a serving platter and divide the pork between them. Top with onion, radishes, and sesame seeds. Drizzle with the reserved marinade and serve.

859. Hungarian-Style Pork Chops
INGREDIENTS (4 Servings)

1 lb pork chops, boneless	½ ground bay leaf	Salt and black pepper to taste
2 tbsp olive oil	½ tsp dried thyme	¼ cup yogurt
2 tsp Hungarian paprika	1 tsp garlic powder	2 garlic cloves, minced

DIRECTIONS (Prep + Cook Time: 15 minutes)

Preheat air fryer to 380 F. Spray the air fryer basket with cooking spray. Mix the Hungarian paprika, ground bay leaf, thyme, garlic powder, salt, and black pepper in a bowl. Rub the pork with the mixture, drizzle with some olive oil and place them in the fryer's basket. AirFry for 15 minutes, turning once. Mix yogurt with garlic, the remaining oil, and salt. Serve with the chops.

860. Mexican Pork Chops
INGREDIENTS (4 Servings)

4 pork chops	2 tbsp olive oil	1 tsp chipotle chili pepper
1 lime, juiced	½ cup tomato sauce	1 cup long-grain rice
Salt and black pepper to taste	1 onion, chopped	1 tbsp butter
1 tsp garlic powder	3 garlic cloves, minced	1 cup canned black beans, drained
1 tsp onion powder	½ tsp oregano	

DIRECTIONS (Prep + Cook Time: 40 minutes + marinating time)

Preheat air fryer to 350 F. In a bowl, mix onion and garlic powder, chipotle pepper, oregano, lime juice, olive oil, salt, pepper, and tomato sauce. Coat the pork with the mixture. Let marinate for 1 hour. Place butter, rice, tomato sauce, onion, salt, and 2 cups of water in a medium saucepan over medium heat and bring to a boil. Reduce heat to low, cover, and simmer 20 minutes or until rice is tender. Stir in black beans. Remove the meat from the marinade, shake off, and place it in the air fryer. Bake for 15-18 minutes, turning once halfway through. Serve with cooked rice and black beans.

861. Apple Pork Chops
INGREDIENTS (4 Servings)

1 small onion, sliced	¼ tsp brown sugar	4 pork chops
3 tbsp olive oil	1 sliced apple	Salt and black pepper to taste
2 tbsp apple cider vinegar	½ tsp rosemary	
½ tsp thyme	¼ tsp smoked paprika	

DIRECTIONS (Prep + Cook Time: 25 minutes)

Preheat air fryer to 350. Heat 2 tbsp olive oil in a skillet over medium heat and cook onion, apple slices, 1 tbsp apple cider vinegar, sugar, thyme, and rosemary for 4 minutes; set aside. In a bowl, mix the remaining olive oil, apple cider vinegar, paprika, salt, and pepper. Add in the pork chops and toss to coat. Place in the fryer and Bake for 10 minutes, flipping once halfway through. When ready, top with the sautéed apples, return to the fryer, and cook for 5 more minutes. Serve warm

862. Spicy-Sweet Pork Chops
INGREDIENTS (4 Servings)

4 thin boneless pork chops	½ tsp ancho chili powder	½ cup hot sauce
3 tbsp brown sugar	½ tsp garlic powder	Salt and black pepper to taste
½ tsp cayenne pepper	1 tbsp olive oil	

DIRECTIONS (Prep + Cook Time: 25 minutes)

Preheat your Air Fryer to 375 F. To make the marinade, mix brown sugar, olive oil, cayenne pepper, garlic powder, salt, and pepper in a small bowl. Dip each pork chop into the marinade, shaking off any excess or drips before placing it into the air fryer in a single layer. Air fry for 7 minutes. Turn the pork chops. Brush with marinade, then cook for another 5 to 8 minutes. Remove to a plate and top with hot sauce to serve.

863. Pork Escalopes with Beet & Cabbage Salad
INGREDIENTS (4 Servings)

- 2 eggs, beaten
- 4 boneless pork chops
- 1 tbsp olive oil
- ½ cup panko bread crumbs
- ½ tsp garlic powder
- Salt and black pepper to taste
- 1 cup white cabbage, shredded
- 1 red beet, grated
- 1 apple, sliced into matchsticks
- 2 tbsp Italian Dressing

DIRECTIONS (Prep + Cook Time: 30 minutes)

In a bowl, combine the cabbage, beet, apple, and Italian dressing; toss to coat. Keep in the fridge until ready to use. Preheat your Air Fryer to 390 F. Divide the pork chops between two sheets of plastic wrap. Pound with a meat mallet or rolling pin until thin, about ¼ inch in thickness. In a shallow bowl or pie plate, combine panko and garlic powder. In a second shallow bowl or pie plate, whisk eggs with 1 teaspoon of water until combined. First, coat the pork chop in the egg mixture. Shake off extra mixture or drips before dredging the pork in the bread crumb mixture. Put dredged pork chops in a single layer on the greased fryer basket. Spray chops with a little bit of olive oil. Air fry for 8 minutes. Turn the chops over and spray again with olive oil. Continue to cook for another 4 to 7 minutes. Serve with the salad and enjoy!

864. Crispy Pork Schnitzel
INGREDIENTS (4 Servings)

- 4 pork chops, center-cut
- 1 egg, beaten
- 1 tsp chili powder
- 2 tbsp flour
- 2 tbsp sour cream
- Salt and black pepper to taste
- ½ cup breadcrumbs
- 2 tbsp olive oil

DIRECTIONS (Prep + Cook Time: 20 minutes)

Preheat air fryer to 380 F. Using a meat tenderizer, pound the chops until ¼-inch thickness. Whisk the egg and sour cream in a bowl. Mix the breadcrumbs with chili powder, salt, and pepper in another. Coat the chops with flour, egg mixture, and breadcrumbs in that order. Brush with olive oil and arrange them on the air fryer basket. AirFry for 14 minutes at 380 F, turning once until golden brown. Serve.

865. Provençal Pork Medallions
INGREDIENTS (4 Servings)

- 1 lb pork medallions
- 1 tbsp olive oil
- 1 tbsp herbes de Provence
- ½ cup dry white wine
- ½ lemon, juiced and zested
- Salt and black pepper to taste

DIRECTIONS (Prep + Cook Time: 25 minutes + marinating time)

Preheat air fryer to 360 F. Season the pork medallions with salt and black pepper and drizzle with olive oil. Place in the air fryer basket and AirFry for 12614 minutes, flipping once. In a saucepan over medium heat, bring white wine and 2 tbsp of water to a boil. Reduce the heat and add in the lemon zest and juice and herbs de Provence; season with salt and pepper. Simmer until the sauce thickens, about 2-3 minutes. Pour the sauce over the medallions and serve.

866. Pork Belly the Philippine Style
INGREDIENTS (4 Servings)

- 2 lb pork belly, cut in half, blanched
- 1 bay leaf, crushed
- 2 tbsp soy sauce
- 3 garlic cloves, minced
- 1 tbsp peppercorns
- 1 tbsp peanut oil
- ½ tsp salt

DIRECTIONS (Prep + Cook Time: 50 minutes + marinating time)

Take a mortar and pestle and place bay leaf, garlic, salt, peppercorns, and peanut oil in it. Smash until paste-like consistency forms. Whisk the paste with soy sauce. Pierce the skin of the belly with a fork. Rub the mixture onto the meat, wrap the pork with a plastic foil and refrigerate for 2 hours. Preheat the fryer to 350 F. Place the pork in the fryer and AirFry for 30 minutes, flipping once halfway through.

867. South American Burgers
INGREDIENTS (4 Servings)

- 1 ½ lb ground beef
- 1 green chili, chopped
- 2 tbsp fresh cilantro, chopped
- Salt and black pepper to taste
- 4 hamburger buns, halved
- 4 tomato slices
- 2 tbsp mayonnaise
- Lettuce leaves, for serving

DIRECTIONS (Prep + Cook Time: 20 minutes)

Preheat the Air Fryer to 350 F. In a bowl, combine ground beef, green chili, cilantro, salt, and black pepper. Mold the mixture into four patties. Spray them lightly on both sides with cooking spray and place in the air fryer basket. AirFry for 8 minutes, slide the basket out, flip, and cook for another 6 minutes until browned. Fill the buns with lettuce, mayonnaise, burger patties, and tomatoes. Serve hot.

868. Beef Meatballs in Tomato Sauce
INGREDIENTS (4 Servings)

1 lb ground beef	tbsp breadcrumbs	10 oz of tomato sauce
1 medium onion, chopped	1 tbsp fresh parsley, chopped	Salt and black pepper to taste
1 egg 4	½ tbsp thyme leaves, chopped	

DIRECTIONS (Prep + Cook Time: 20 minutes) Place all ingredients into a bowl and mix well, except for tomato sauce. Shape the mixture into 10 to 12 medium-sized balls. Preheat the fryer to 380 F. Place the meatballs in the greased frying basket. AirFry for 12-14 minutes, shaking once. Remove them to a baking dish that fits in the fryer. Pour in tomato sauce, fit in the fryer, lower the temperature to 300 F, and Bake for 6 more minutes. Serve.

869. Greek-Style Beef Meatballs
INGREDIENTS (4 Servings)

1 lb ground beef	1 red onion, chopped	½ cup feta cheese, crumbled
2 tbsp olive oil	1 garlic clove, minced	Salt and black pepper to taste
1 tsp ground cumin	1 egg, beaten	
¼ cup Kalamata olives, pitted and chopped	1 lb tomatoes, chopped	

DIRECTIONS (Prep + Cook Time: 40 minutes) Preheat air fryer to 350 F. Mix ground beef, onion, garlic, olives, and egg in a bowl and season with cumin, salt, and pepper. Shape the meat mixture into golf-sized balls. Place them in the greased air fryer basket and AirFry for 12 minutes, shaking once halfway through. Heat the olive oil in a saucepan over medium heat and add in the tomatoes, salt, and pepper. Bring to a boil and simmer for 8-10 until the sauce starts to thicken. Reduce the heat to low and gently stir in the meatballs; cook for 2 minutes. Transfer to a plate and scatter with the feta cheese all over to serve.

870. California-Style Street Beef Taco Rolls
INGREDIENTS (4 Servings)

2 tbsp olive oil	½ tbsp chili powder	1 cup cheddar cheese, shredded
1 lb ground beef	2 tbsp creole seasoning	Salt and black pepper to taste
1 onion, chopped	1 (15-oz) can diced tomatoes	½ cup Pico de gallo
2 garlic cloves, minced	4 taco shells	2 tbsp fresh cilantro, chopped

DIRECTIONS (Prep + Cook Time: 30 minutes) Heat the olive oil in a pan over medium heat. Sauté garlic and onion for 3 minutes until soft. Add the ground beef and stir-fry for 6 minutes until no longer pink. Season with chili powder, creole seasoning, salt, and pepper. Pour in the tomatoes and stir-fry for another 5-6 minutes. Mix in the cheese. Divide the meat mixture between taco shells and roll up them, sealing the edges. Spray each roll with cooking spray and place them in the greased frying basket. Bake for 10 minutes at 390 F, turning once halfway through. Garnish with Pico de gallo and cilantro. Serve immediately.

871. Classic Beef Meatloaf
INGREDIENTS (4 Servings)

1 lb ground beef	2 garlic cloves, minced	1 tsp mixed dried herbs
2 eggs, lightly beaten	1 onion, finely chopped	
½ cup breadcrumbs	2 tbsp ketchup	

DIRECTIONS (Prep + Cook Time: 30 minutes + cooling time) Line a loaf pan that fits in the air fryer with baking paper. In a bowl, mix ground beef, eggs, breadcrumbs, garlic, onion, and mixed herbs. Gently press the mixture into the pan and top with ketchup. Slide in the air fryer. Bake for 25 minutes on 380 F. Let cool for 10-15 minutes before slicing and serving.

872. Stefania Beef Meatloaf
INGREDIENTS (4 Servings)

1 cup tomato basil sauce	2 tbsp minced ginger	1 tsp paprika
1 ½ lb ground beef	½ cup breadcrumbs	½ tsp dried basil
1 diced onion	3 hardboiled eggs, peeled	2 tbsp fresh parsley, chopped
2 garlic cloves, minced	Salt and black pepper to taste	2 egg whites

DIRECTIONS (Prep + Cook Time: 40 minutes) Preheat air fryer to 360 F. In a bowl, add the beef, onion, garlic, ginger, breadcrumbs, paprika, salt, pepper, basil, parsley, and egg whites; mix well. Shape half of the mixture into a long oblong form. Arrange the boiled eggs in a row in the center. Cover the eggs with the remaining meat dough. Scoop the meat mixture into a greased baking pan. Shape the meat into the pan while pressing firmly. Brush the tomato sauce onto the meat. Place the pan in the frying basket and Bake for 25 minutes.

873. Mini Beef Sausage Rolls
INGREDIENTS (4 Servings)

1 lb beef sausage meat	8 mini puff pastry squares	Salt and black pepper to taste
3 green onions, thinly sliced	1 cup flour 1 egg, beaten	

DIRECTIONS (Prep + Cook Time: 30 minutes)

Preheat air fryer to 360 F. Grease the frying basket with cooking spray. In a bowl, mix beef sausage meat with green onions. Lay the pastry squares on a floured surface. Divide the sausage mixture in the center of the pastry squares. Brush the edges with some of the beaten egg. Fold the squares and seal them. Transfer to the frying basket and brush the top of the rolls with the remaining egg. AirFry for 20 minutes, flipping once, until crisp and golden. Serve warm.

---

874. Ginger-Garlic Beef Ribs with Hot Sauce
INGREDIENTS (2 Servings)

1 rack rib steak	½ tsp garlic powder	½ tsp ginger powder
Salt and white pepper to taste	½ tsp red pepper flakes	3 tbsp hot sauce

DIRECTIONS (Prep + Cook Time: 25 minutes)

Preheat air fryer to 360 F. Season the rib rack with salt, garlic, ginger, white pepper, and red pepper flakes. Place in the frying basket and Bake for 10 minutes. Turn the meat and cook further for 5-7 minutes. Let sit for 3 minutes before slicing. Plate and drizzle hot sauce over to serve.

---

875. Garlic Steak with Mexican Salsa
INGREDIENTS (4 Servings)

2 rib-eye steaks tbsp olive oil	1 avocado, roughly chopped	2 tbsp chopped cilantro
1 tsp garlic	7oz canned sweetcorn	1 chili, minced
salt Black pepper to taste	½ red onion, sliced	1 lime, zested and juiced
½ cup heavy cream	10 cherry tomatoes, quartered	

DIRECTIONS (Prep + Cook Time: 20 minutes)

Preheat your Air Fryer to 390 F. Place the steaks on a plate and rub with olive oil on all sides. Season with garlic salt, salt, and pepper. Rub both sides to coat and massage the seasoning into the meat. Lay the steaks into the greased air fryer. Air fry for 16-18 minutes, turning once halfway through. In a bowl, mix the avocado, corn, cherry tomatoes, onion, cilantro, chili, lime juice, and zest. Season to taste. Serve the steaks with the Mexican salsa and a dollop of heavy cream on the side.

---

876. Gorgonzola Rib Eye Steak
INGREDIENTS (4 Servings)

2 lb rib-eye steak	1 cup gorgonzola cheese, crumbled	Salt and black pepper to taste
1 tbsp steak rub	2 tbsp fresh chives, chopped	
1 cup heavy cream	1 tbsp olive oil	

DIRECTIONS (Prep + Cook Time: 20 minutes)

Preheat air fryer to 400 F. In a bowl, combine olive oil, salt, and black pepper. Rub the steak with the seasoning and place it in the frying basket. Bake for 10 minutes, flip, and cook for 5 more minutes. Heat heavy cream in a skillet over medium heat. Add in the cheese; stir until you obtain a smooth sauce, and the cheese is melted, 3 minutes. Drizzle the sauce over steaks and scatter chives all over. Yummy!

---

877. Parsley Crumbed Beef Strips
INGREDIENTS (2 Servings)

2 tbsp vegetable oil	2 oz breadcrumbs	1 thin beef sirloin steak, cut into strips
½ tsp fresh parsley, chopped	1 whole egg, whisked	1 lemon, juiced

DIRECTIONS (Prep + Cook Time: 25 minutes)

Preheat air fryer to 370 F. In a bowl, add breadcrumbs, parsley, and vegetable oil and stir well to get a loose mixture. Dip beef in egg, then coat well in breadcrumb mixture. Place the strips in the greased frying basket and Bake for 14-16 minutes, flipping once. Serve with a drizzle of lemon juice.

878. Homemade Hot Beef Satay
INGREDIENTS (4 Servings)

2 lb flank steaks, cut into long strips	2 tbsp sugar	2 tsp hot sauce
2 tbsp fish sauce	1 ½ tsp garlic powder	1 cup fresh cilantro, chopped
2 tbsp soy sauce	1 ½ tsp ground ginger	½ cup roasted peanuts, chopped

DIRECTIONS (Prep + Cook Time: 20 minutes)

Preheat air fryer to 400 F. In a zipper bag, add the beef, fish sauce, sugar, garlic, soy sauce, ginger, half of the cilantro, and hot sauce. Zip the bag and massage the ingredients to mix well. Open the bag, remove the beef, shake off the excess marinade, and place in the frying basket in a single layer. Avoid overlapping. AirFry for 6 minutes, turn the beef, and cook further for 6 minutes. Dish the meat and garnish with roasted peanuts and the remaining cilantro.

879. Pesto Beef Steaks
INGREDIENTS (4 Servings)

4 boneless beef steaks	alt and black pepper to taste
1 tbsp smoked paprika S	4 tbsp pesto sauce

DIRECTIONS (Prep + Cook Time: 25 minutes + marinating time)

Preheat the Air fryer to 390 F. Season the steaks with paprika, salt, and pepper. Let the meat incorporate the flavors for 30 minutes. Place in the frying basket and Bake for 14-16 minutes, flipping once halfway through. Remove to a cutting board to cool slightly before slicing. Top with pesto sauce and serve.

880. Beef Steak Fingers
INGREDIENTS (4 Servings)

1 lb beef steak, cut into strips	¼ tsp cayenne pepper	1 lb chopped tomatoes
1 tbsp olive oil	2 eggs, beaten	1 tbsp tomato paste
½ cup flour	½ cup milk	1 tsp honey
½ cup panko breadcrumbs	Salt and black pepper to taste	1 tbsp white wine vinegar

DIRECTIONS (Prep + Cook Time: 30 minutes) Place the tomatoes, tomato paste, honey, and vinegar in a deep skillet over medium heat. Cook for 6-8 minutes, stirring occasionally until the sauce thickens. Set aside to cool. Preheat your Air Fryer to 390 F. Spray the fryer basket with a light coating of olive oil. In a shallow bowl or pie plate, combine flour, salt, black pepper, and cayenne. In a second shallow bowl or pie plate, whisk eggs and milk until combined. Dredge steak strips first in flour mixture, then coat with the egg mixture, and finally in the breadcrumbs until completely coated. Arrange the steak strips in a single layer on the fryer basket and spray lightly with olive oil. AirFry for 8 minutes. Turn them over and spray with a little bit of olive oil. Continue to air fry for another 5-7 minutes until they are golden and crispy. Spoon into paper cones and serve warm with the tomato sauce.

881. Bloody Mary Beef Steak with Avocado
INGREDIENTS (4 Servings)

1 ½ lb flank steaks	2 tbsp vodka	salt and black pepper to taste
2 tbsp tomato juice	1 tsp Worcestershire sauce	
1 lemon, juiced and zested	1 tsp hot sauce Celery	

DIRECTIONS (Prep + Cook Time: 20 minutes + marinating time) Combine the tomato juice, vodka, Worcestershire sauce, hot sauce, lemon juice and zest, celery salt, and black pepper in a bowl. Add in steaks and toss to coat. Allow marinating for 30 minutes. Preheat air fryer to 360 F. Grease the frying basket. Place in the steaks and Bake for 13-15 minutes, turning once halfway through. Cook in batches if needed. Let them cool slightly before slicing.

882. Burgundy Beef Casserole
INGREDIENTS (4 Servings)

1 ½ lb beef steak	1 can (14.5 oz) cream mushroom soup	½ cup beef broth
1 package egg noodles, cooked	2 cups mushrooms, sliced	¼ cup Pinot Noir red wine
1 oz dry onion soup mix	1 whole onion, chopped	3 garlic cloves, minced

DIRECTIONS (Prep + Cook Time: 35 minutes) Preheat air fryer to 360 F. Drizzle onion soup mix all over the meat and transfer to a baking dish. In a bowl, mix mushroom soup, garlic, beef broth, red wine, onion, and mushrooms. Top the meat with the mixture and place the dish in the air fryer. Bake for 25 minutes until golden. Serve with egg noodles.

883. Delicious Beef with Rice & Broccoli
INGREDIENTS (4 Servings)

1 lb beef steak, cut into strips	1 ½ tbsp soy sauce	2 tsp vinegar
Salt and black pepper to taste	2 tsp sesame oil	1 garlic clove, minced
2 cups cooked rice	2 tsp minced ginger	½ head steamed broccoli, chopped

DIRECTIONS (Prep + Cook Time: 40 minutes)

Season the beef with salt and black pepper. Preheat air fryer to 400 F. Bake in the beef for 12 minutes, turning once. Once ready, remove to a plate. In a skillet, heat sesame oil and sauté ginger and garlic for 2-3 minutes until tender. Add vinegar, rice, broccoli, garlic, and soy sauce. Stir-fry for 1 minute or until heated through. Serve the strips over a bed of the rice mixture.

884. Simple Roast Beef with Herbs
INGREDIENTS (2 Servings)

2 tsp olive oil	½ tsp dried rosemary	½ tsp dried oregano
1 lb beef roast	½ tsp dried thyme	Salt and black pepper to taste

DIRECTIONS (Prep + Cook Time: 55 minutes)

Preheat air fryer to 400 F. Drizzle olive oil over the beef, and sprinkle with salt, black pepper, and herbs. Rub onto the meat with hands and Bake in the fryer for 15 minutes for medium-rare and 18 minutes for well-done. Check halfway through and flip to ensure it cooks evenly. Wrap the beef in foil for 10 minutes after cooking to allow the juices to reabsorb into the meat. Serve sliced.

885. Wiener Beef Schnitzel
INGREDIENTS (1 Serving)

1 thin beef cutlet	2 oz panko breadcrumbs	1 parsley butter slice
1 egg, beaten	2 tbsp flour Lemon slices	Salt and black pepper to taste
	¼ tsp garlic powder	

DIRECTIONS (Prep + Cook Time: 20 minutes)

Preheat air fryer to 350 F. Combine breadcrumbs, garlic, salt, and pepper in a bowl. Dredge the cutlet in the flour, then dip in the beaten egg, and finally oat it with the breadcrumb mixture. Place in the greased air fryer basket and AirFry for 12 minutes, turning once. Top with parsley butter and lemon.

886. Beer-Dredged Corned Beef
INGREDIENTS (4 Servings)

2 tbsp olive oil	2 carrots, julienned	1 lb corned beef
1 tbsp beef seasoning	4 oz bottle beer	
1 whole onion, chopped	1 cup chicken broth	

DIRECTIONS (Prep + Cook Time: 40 minutes + marinating time)

Preheat air fryer to 380 F. Cover the beef with beer and let sit for 20 minutes. Heat olive oil in a pot over medium heat and sauté carrots and onions for 3 minutes. Add in the beef and broth and bring to a boil. Simmer for 5 minutes. Remove the meat with a slotted spoon and place it in the frying basket. Cook for 10-15 minutes until richly browned. Serve poured with veggies and sauce.

887. Beef Liver with Onions
INGREDIENTS (2 Servings)

1lb beef liver, sliced	1tbsp black pepper to taste	1tbsp fresh parslay, chopped
2 onions, sliced	1 garlic clove, mindced	

Directions (Prep + Cook Time: 25 minutes)

Preheat air fryer to 360 F. Season the liver with salt and pepper and brush with truffle oil. Spread the onion slices on a greased baking dish. Bake in the fryer for 5 minutes. Arrange the liver on top of the onions. Bake for 12 minutes, turning the liver over halfway through. Serve topped with garlic and parsley.

Vegetables & Side Dishes

888. Serve Roasted Tomatoes with Cheese Topping
INGREDIENTS (4 Servings)

½ cup cheddar cheese, shredded

¼ cup Parmesan cheese, grated

1 tsp olive oil

4 tomatoes, cut into ½ inch slices

2 tbsp parsley, chopped

Salt and black pepper to taste

DIRECTIONS (Prep + Cook Time: 30 minutes) Preheat your Air Fryer to 380 F. Lightly salt the tomato slices and put them in the greased fryer basket in a single layer. Top with mozzarella and Parmesan cheeses and sprinkle with black pepper. AirFry for 5-6 minutes until the cheese is melted and bubbly. Serve topped with parsley and enjoy!

889. Authentic Spanish Patatas Bravas
INGREDIENTS (4 Servings)

1 lb waxy potatoes, into bite-size chunks

4 tbsp olive oil

1 tsp smoked paprika

1 shallot, chopped

2 tomatoes, chopped

1 tbsp tomato paste

1 tbsp flour

2 tbsp sriracha hot chili sauce

1 tsp sugar

2 tbsp fresh parsley, chopped

Salt to taste

DIRECTIONS (Prep + Cook Time: 40 minutes) Heat 2 tbsp of the olive oil in a skillet over medium heat and sauté the shallot for 3 minutes until fragrant. Stir in the flour for 2 more minutes. Add in the remaining ingredients and 1 cup of water. Bring to a boil, reduce the heat, and simmer for 6-8 minutes until the sauce becomes pulpy. Remove to a food processor and blend until smooth. Let cool completely. Preheat air fryer to 400 F. Coat potatoes with the remaining olive oil and AirFry in the fryer for 20-25 minutes, shaking once halfway through. Sprinkle with salt and spoon over the sauce to serve. enjoy!

890. Curly Coconut Fries
INGREDIENTS (2 Servings)

2 potatoes, spiralized

1 tbsp tomato ketchup

2 tbsp olive oil

Salt and black pepper to taste

2 tbsp coconut oil

DIRECTIONS (Prep + Cook Time: 20 minutes)

air fryer to 360 F. In a bowl, coat potatoes with coconut oil, salt, and pepper. Place in the frying basket and AirFry for 20 minutes, shaking once halfway through. Serve topped with mango sauce. enjoy!

891. Crispy Bell Peppers with Tartare Sauce
INGREDIENTS (4 Servings)

1 egg, beaten

2 bell peppers, cut into ½-inch-thick slices

⅔ cup panko breadcrumbs

½ tsp paprika

½ tsp garlic powder

Salt to taste

1 tsp lime juice

¼ tsp Dijon mustard

½ cup mayonnaise

2 tbsp capers, chopped

2 tbsp fresh parsley

2 dill pickles, chopped

DIRECTIONS (Prep + Cook Time: 25 minutes)

Preheat your Air Fryer to 390 F. Mix the panko breadcrumbs, paprika, garlic powder, and salt in a shallow bowl. In a separate bowl, whisk the egg with 1 ½ teaspoons of water to make an egg wash. Coat the bell pepper slices in the egg wash, then roll them in the panko mixture until fully covered. Put the peppers in the greased air basket in a single layer and spray with olive oil, then air 4-7 minutes until light brown. In a bowl, mix the mayonnaise, lime juice, capers, pickles, parsley, and salt. Remove the peppers from the fryer and serve with the tartare sauce. Enjoy!

892. Crunchy Parmesan Zucchini
INGREDIENTS (4 Servings)

4 small zucchinis, cut lengthwise

½ cup Parmesan cheese, grated

½ cup breadcrumbs

¼ cup melted butter

¼ cup fresh parsley, chopped

4 garlic cloves, minced

Salt and black pepper to taste

DIRECTIONS (Prep + Cook Time: 20 minutes) Preheat air fryer to 370 F. In a bowl, mix breadcrumbs, Parmesan cheese, garlic, and parsley. Season with salt and pepper and stir in the melted butter. Scoop out the seeds with a spoon. Spoon the mixture into the zucchini. Arrange the zucchini on the greased frying basket and Bake for 12 minutes. Serve. enjoy!

---

893. Russian-Style Eggplant Caviar
INGREDIENTS (4 Servings)

2 eggplants

½ red onion, chopped

2 tbsp balsamic vinegar

1 tbsp olive oil

Salt to taste

DIRECTIONS (Prep + Cook Time: 20 minutes) Arrange the eggplants in the greased frying basket and Bake for 15 minutes at 380 F. Remove and let cool. Then, cut the eggplants in half, lengthwise, and empty their insides with a spoon. Transfer the flesh to a food processor and add in red onion and olive oil; process until smooth. Season with balsamic vinegar and a bit of salt. Serve cold on a bread slice. enjoy!

---

894. Avocado Fries with Pico de Gallo
INGREDIENTS (4 Servings)

3 eggs, beaten in a bowl

4 avocados, cut in half, pits removed

2 tbsp olive oil

1 ½ cups panko breadcrumbs

1 ½ tsp paprika

Salt and black pepper to taste

2 tbsp cilantro, chopped

2 tomatoes, chopped

1 jalapeño pepper, minced

¼ cup red onions, finely chopped

1 lime, juiced

6 corn tortillas

DIRECTIONS (Prep + Cook Time: 30 minutes) In a mixing bowl, thoroughly combine the cilantro, tomatoes, jalapeño pepper, red onion, lime juice, and salt. Place in the fridge to allow the flavors to combine until ready to use. Preheat air fryer to 360 F. Remove the skin from the avocado, leaving the flesh intact. Cut the halves into 5-6 lengthwise slices. Mix the breadcrumbs, salt, pepper, and paprika in a bowl. Dip each avocado slice in the eggs, then in the panko mixture. Press the panko mixture gently into the avocado, so it sticks. Put the avocado slices in a single layer on the greased fryer basket and brush with some olive oil. Air fry for 8-10 minutes, turning once until light brown and crispy. Serve with pico de gallo on the side. enjoy!

---

895. Cheese & Cauliflower Tater Tot Bites
INGREDIENTS (4 Servings)

1 large egg

¼ cup Pecorino cheese, grated

¼ cup sharp cheddar cheese, shredded

1 lb cauliflower florets

1 garlic clove, minced

½ cup seasoned breadcrumbs

1 tbsp olive oil

2 tbsp scallions, chopped

Salt and black pepper to taste

DIRECTIONS (Prep + Cook Time: 35 minutes)

Cook the cauliflower in boiling salted water until al dente. Drain well and let it dry on absorbent paper for 10 minutes. Then finely chop cauliflower and put it into a bowl. Add in the egg, garlic, Pecorino cheese, cheddar cheese, breadcrumbs, salt, and pepper and stir to combine. Chill for 10 minutes. Preheat your Air Fryer to 380 F. Shape the cauliflower mixture into bite-sized oval 'tater tots.' Lay them in a single layer in the greased fryer basket, giving them plenty of space. Brush the tots with oil and air fry for 15 minutes, turning halfway through the cooking time until crispy and browned. Top with scallions and serve with your favorite sauce for dipping. Enjoy!

896. Broccoli with Parmesan Cheese
INGREDIENTS (4 Servings)

1 head broccoli, cut into florets	Salt and black pepper to taste
1 tbsp olive oil	1 oz Parmesan cheese, grated

DIRECTIONS (Prep + Cook Time: 25 minutes)

Preheat your air fryer to 360 F. In a bowl, mix all the ingredients. Add the mixture to a greased baking dish and Bake in the air fryer for 20 minutes. Serve warm. enjoy!

897. Spicy Vegetable Skewers
INGREDIENTS (2 Servings)

2 large sweet potatoes	1 tsp chili flakes	¼ tsp garlic powder
1 beetroot	Salt and black pepper to taste	¼ tsp paprika
1 green bell pepper	½ tsp turmeric	1 tbsp olive oil

DIRECTIONS (Prep + Cook Time: 25 minutes) Preheat air fryer to 350 F. Peel the veggies and cut them into bite-sized chunks. Place the chunks in a bowl along with the remaining ingredients and mix until completely coated. Thread the vegetables, alternately, onto skewers in this order: potato, pepper, and beetroot. Place in the greased frying basket and Bake for 18-20 minutes, turning once. Serve with yogurt dip. enjoy!

898. Roasted Balsamic Veggies
INGREDIENTS (4 Servings)

2 lb chopped veggies:	potatoes, parsnips, zucchini, pumpkin, carrot, leeks 3 tbsp olive oil 1 tbsp balsamic vinegar 1 tbsp agave syrup	Salt and black pepper to taste

DIRECTIONS (Prep + Cook Time: 30 minutes) In a bowl, add olive oil, balsamic vinegar, agave syrup, salt, and black pepper; mix well. Arrange the veggies on a baking tray and place them in the frying basket. Drizzle with the dressing and massage with hands until well-coated. AirFry for 18-22 minutes at 360 F, tossing once halfway through. Serve. enjoy!

899. Classic French Ratatouille
INGREDIENTS (2 Servings)

2 tbsp olive oil	1 zucchini, thinly sliced	2 tbsp herbs de Provence
2 Roma tomatoes, thinly sliced	2 yellow bell peppers, sliced	Salt and black pepper to taste
2 garlic cloves, minced	1 tbsp vinegar	

DIRECTIONS (Prep + Cook Time: 30 minutes) Preheat air fryer to 390 F. Place all ingredients in a bowl. Season with salt and pepper and stir to coat. Arrange them on a baking dish and place them inside the air fryer. Bake for 15 minutes. Serve warm. enjoy!

900. Middle Eastern Veggie Kofta
INGREDIENTS (4 Servings)

2 tbsp cornflour	¼ cup fresh mint leaves, chopped	3 garlic cloves, chopped
1 cup canned white beans	½ tsp ras el hanout powder	A bunch of skewers, soaked in water
⅓ cup carrots, grated	2 tbsp pine nuts	Salt to taste
2 potatoes, boiled and mashed	½ cup fresh mozzarella, chopped	

DIRECTIONS (Prep + Cook Time: 20 minutes)

Preheat air fryer to 390 F. Place the beans, carrots, pine nuts, garlic, mozzarella, and mint in a food processor. Blend until smooth, then transfer to a bowl. Add in the mashed potatoes, cornflour, salt, and ras el hanout and mix until fully incorporated. Divide the mixture into equal shaped-patties, about 3 inches long by 1 inch thick. Thread shapes on skewers and Bake in the greased frying basket for 10 minutes, turning once halfway through. Serve warm. enjoy!

901. Chili Falafel with Cheesy Sauce
INGREDIENTS (4 Servings)

1 (14-oz) can chickpeas, drained	¼ tsp chili powder	2 tbsp olive oil
2 tbsp fresh parsley, chopped	1 cup cream cheese, softened	2 tbsp plain yogurt
6 spring onions, sliced	1 clove garlic, chopped	1 tsp apple cider vinegar
1 tsp garlic powder	½ tsp dried dill	
Salt to taste	1 tsp hot paprika	

DIRECTIONS (Prep + Cook Time: 25 minutes)

Place the cream cheese, minced garlic, dill, hot paprika, olive oil, yogurt, and vinegar in a bowl and whisk until you obtain a smooth and homogeneous sauce consistency. Keep covered in the fridge. In a blender, place chickpeas, parsley, spring onions, garlic powder, chili powder, and salt and process until crumbly. Place the mixture in a bowl and refrigerate covered for 20 minutes. For each falafel, take 2 tablespoons to form a round ball, flattened around the edges. Preheat air fryer to 370 F and arrange falafels on the greased frying basket. AirFry for 14-16 minutes, flipping once until lightly browned and cooked through. Serve with the cream cheese sauce. enjoy!

902. African Vegetables with Fontina Cheese
INGREDIENTS (4 Servings)

2 tbsp olive oil	1 lemon, juiced	1 red onion, cut into wedges
1 tsp cayenne pepper	2 yellow bell peppers, cut into chunks	2 garlic cloves, minced
2 tsp ground cumin	1 zucchini, sliced	6 oz fontina cheese, grated
1 tbsp tomato purée	1 eggplant, cut into chunks	10 green olives

DIRECTIONS (Prep + Cook Time: 20 minutes)

Preheat air fryer to 370 F. In a small bowl, combine the cayenne pepper, garlic, ground cumin, tomato purée, lemon juice, and olive oil. Add in the bell peppers, zucchini, eggplant, and onion and mix well. Transfer to a baking dish and place in the air fryer. Bake for 18-20 minutes until golden. Sprinkle with fontina cheese and green olives and Bake for a further 5 minutes until the cheese is melted. Serve. enjoy!

903. Italian-Style Stuffed Mushrooms
INGREDIENTS (4 Servings)

4 oz mascarpone cheese, softened	¾ cup shredded Italian blend cheese	Salt and black pepper to taste
1 egg 1 cup fresh baby spinach	¼ cup breadcrumbs	
20 large mushrooms, stems removed	1 tbsp olive oil	

DIRECTIONS (Prep + Cook Time: 25 minutes) Preheat your Air Fryer to 375 F. Whisk the mascarpone cheese, Italian blend cheese, breadcrumbs, egg, salt, and pepper with an electric mixer. Stir in the spinach with a spoon until everything is well combined. Divide the mixture between the mushrooms, leaving some popping out of the top. Put the mushrooms in the greased fryer basket and drizzle them with olive oil. AirFry for 7-10 minutes, until the mushrooms have begun to brown and the cheese on top is light brown. Serve warm. enjoy!

904. Egg & Cauliflower Rice Casserole
INGREDIENTS (4 Servings)

1 head cauliflower, cut into florets	1 cup okra, chopped	1 tbsp soy sauce
2 tbsp olive oil	½ onion, chopped	2 eggs, beaten
1 yellow bell pepper, chopped	Salt and black pepper to taste	

DIRECTIONS (Prep + Cook Time: 20 minutes) Preheat air fryer to 380 F. Grease a baking dish with cooking spray. Pulse cauliflower in a food processor until it resembles rice. Add the cauli rice to the baking dish and mix in bell pepper, okra, onion, soy sauce, salt, and pepper. Pour over the beaten eggs and drizzle with olive oil. Place the dish in the air fryer and Bake for 12 minutes. Serve warm. enjoy!

905. Air Fried Veggie Sushi
INGREDIENTS (4 Servings)

2 cups cooked sushi rice	1 avocado, sliced	2 tbsp sesame seeds
4 nori sheets	1 tbsp olive oil	Soy sauce, wasabi, and pickled ginger to serve
1 carrot, sliced lengthways	1 tbsp rice wine vinegar	
1 red bell pepper, sliced	1 cup panko crumbs	

DIRECTIONS (Prep + Cook Time: 30 minutes) Prepare a clean working board, a small bowl of lukewarm water, and a sushi mat. Wet your hands, and lay a nori sheet onto the sushi mat, and spread a half cup of sushi rice, leaving a half-inch of nori clear, so you can seal the roll. Place carrot, pepper, and avocado sideways to the rice. Roll sushi tightly and rub warm water along the clean nori strip to seal. In a bowl, mix oil and rice vinegar. In another bowl, mix crumbs and sesame seeds. Roll each sushi log in the vinegar mixture and then straight to the sesame bowl to coat. Arrange sushi in the air fryer and Bake for 14 minutes at 360 F, turning once. Slice and serve with soy sauce, pickled ginger, and wasabi. enjoy!

906. Cheesy English Muffins
INGREDIENTS (2 Servings)

2 English muffins, halved and toasted	2 tbsp ranch-style salad dressing	½ sweet onion, chopped
½ cup cheddar cheese, shredded	½ cup alfalfa sprouts	1 tbsp sesame seeds, toasted
1 ripe avocado, mashed	1 tomato, chopped	

DIRECTIONS (Prep + Cook Time:15 minutes) Arrange the muffins open-faced in a greased baking dish. Spread the mashed avocado on each half of the cupcakes. Top with sprouts, tomatoes, onion, dressing, and cheese. Bake in the air fryer for 7-8 minutes at 350 F. Serve sprinkled with sesame seeds. enjoy!

907. Crispy Mozzarella Rolls
INGREDIENTS (4 Servings)

1 lb mozzarella cheese, chopped	1 tbsp butter, softened	1 tsp poppy seeds
3 packages Pepperidge farm rolls	1 tsp mustard seeds	1 small onion, chopped

DIRECTIONS (Prep + Cook Time: 20 minutes) In a bowl, mix butter, mustard seeds, onion, and poppy seeds. Spread the mixture on top of the rolls. Cover with cheese, roll up, and arrange on the greased frying basket. Bake at 350 F for 15 minutes. enjoy!

908. Romanian Polenta Fries
INGREDIENTS (4 Servings)

2 cups milk	Salt and black pepper to taste
1 cup instant polenta	2 tbsp fresh thyme, chopped

DIRECTIONS (Prep + Cook Time: 30 minutes) Line a baking dish with parchment paper. Pour 2 cups of milk and 2 cups of water into a saucepan and let simmer. Keep whisking as you pour in the polenta. Continue to whisk until polenta thickens and bubbles; season to taste. Add polenta into the lined dish and spread out. Refrigerate for 45 minutes. Slice the cold polenta into batons. Arrange the chips on the greased frying basket and AirFry for 14-16 minutes at 380 F, turning once halfway through. Make sure the fries are golden and crispy. Serve. enjoy!

909. Brussels Sprouts with Raisins & Pine Nuts
INGREDIENTS (4 Servings)

1 lb Brussels sprouts, stems cut off and halved	¾ oz raisins, soaked and drained	Salt to taste
2 tbsp olive oil 1	Juice of 1 orange	2 tbsp pine nuts, toasted

DIRECTIONS (Prep + Cook Time: 20 minutes)

Preheat air fryer to 390 F. In a bowl, toss the Brussels sprouts with olive oil and salt and stir to combine. Place in the frying and Bake for 15 minutes, shaking once halfway through. Top with toasted pine nuts and raisins. Drizzle with orange juice to serve. Serve. enjoy!

910. Mushroom Balls with Tomato Sauce
INGREDIENTS (4 Servings)

- ⅓ cup cooked rice
- 1 lb mushrooms, chopped
- ½ onion, chopped
- ½ green bell peppers, chopped
- Celery salt to taste
- 1 tbsp Worcestershire sauce
- 1 garlic clove, minced
- 2 cups tomato juice
- 1 tsp oregano

DIRECTIONS (Prep + Cook Time: 30 minutes)

In a food processor, blend the mushrooms until they resemble large crumbs. In a bowl, combine rice, ground mushrooms, onion, celery salt, green peppers, and garlic. Shape into balls, and arrange them on the greased frying basket. Bake for 18 minutes at 370 degrees, shaking once. In a saucepan over medium heat, pour tomato juice, oregano, celery salt, and Worcestershire sauce and cook until reduced by half. Pour the sauce over the balls and serve. enjoy!

911. Spicy Sweet Potato French Fries
INGREDIENTS (4 Servings)

- ½ tsp salt
- ½ tsp garlic powder
- ½ tsp chili powder
- ¼ tsp cumin
- 3 tbsp olive oil
- 4 sweet potatoes, cut into thick strips

DIRECTIONS (Prep + Cook Time: 30 minutes)

In a bowl, mix salt, garlic powder, chili powder, and cumin and whisk in olive oil. Coat the strips in the mixture and place them in the frying basket. AirFry for 20 minutes at 380 F, shaking once, until crispy. Traditional Jacket Potatoes INGREDIENTS (4 Servings) 1 lb potatoes 2 garlic cloves, minced Salt and black pepper to taste 1 tsp dried rosemary 2 tsp butter, melted DIRECTIONS (Prep + Cook Time: 30 minutes) Preheat air fryer to 360 F. Prick the potatoes with a fork. Place them in the greased frying basket and Bake for 23-25 minutes, turning once halfway through. Remove and cut in half. Drizzle with melted butter and season with salt and black pepper. Sprinkle with rosemary and serve. enjoy!

912. Brussels Sprouts with Garlic Aioli
INGREDIENTS (4 Servings)

- 3 garlic cloves, peel-on
- 1 lb Brussels sprouts, trimmed and halved
- 2 cups water
- Salt and black pepper to taste
- 2 tbsp olive oil
- 2 tsp lemon juice
- ¾ cup mayonnaise

DIRECTIONS (Prep + Cook Time: 25 minutes)

Place a skillet over medium heat and roast the garlic cloves until lightly brown and fragrant. Remove the skillet and place a pot with water; bring to a boil. Blanch in Brussels sprouts for 3 minutes; drain. Preheat air fryer to 350 F. Drizzle the Brussels sprouts with olive oil and season with pepper and salt. Pour them into frying basket and AirFry for 5 minutes, shaking once. Peel garlic and crush it in a bowl. Add in mayonnaise, lemon juice, black pepper, and salt; mix well. Remove the Brussels sprouts onto a serving bowl and serve with the garlic aioli. enjoy!

913. Green Cabbage with Blue Cheese Sauce
INGREDIENTS (4 Servings)

- 1 head green cabbage, cut into wedges
- 1 cup mozzarella cheese, shredded
- 4 tbsp butter, melted
- Salt and black pepper to taste
- ½ cup blue cheese sauce

DIRECTIONS (Prep + Cook Time: 25 minutes)

Preheat air fryer to 380 F. Brush cabbage wedges with butter and sprinkle with mozzarella. Transfer to a greased baking dish and Bake in the air fryer for 20 minutes. Serve with blue cheese sauce. enjoy!

914. Eggplant Steaks with Garlic & Parsley
INGREDIENTS (4 Servings)

- 2 eggplants, sliced
- 2 cups breadcrumbs
- 1 tsp Italian seasoning
- 1 cup flour Salt to taste
- 4 eggs
- 2 garlic cloves, sliced
- 2 tbsp fresh parsley, chopped

DIRECTIONS (Prep + Cook Time: 20 minutes)

Preheat air fryer to 390 F. In a bowl, beat the eggs with salt. In a separate bowl, mix breadcrumbs and Italian seasoning. In a third bowl, pour the flour. Dip eggplant steaks in the flour, followed by a dip in the eggs, and finally, coat in the breadcrumbs. Place in the greased air fryer basket and AirFry for 10-12 minutes, flipping once. Remove to a platter and sprinkle with garlic and parsley to serve. enjoy!

915. Eggplant & Zucchini Chips
INGREDIENTS (4 Servings)

- 1 large eggplant, cut into strips
- 1 zucchini, cut into strips
- ½ cup cornstarch
- 3 tbsp olive oil
- Salt to season

DIRECTIONS (Prep + Cook Time: 20 minutes) Preheat air fryer to 390 F. In a bowl, stir in cornstarch, salt, pepper, olive oil, eggplants, and zucchini. Place the coated veggies in the greased frying basket and AirFry for 12 minutes, shaking once. enjoy!

916. Breaded Italian Green Beans
INGREDIENTS (4 Servings)

- 1 cup panko breadcrumbs
- 2 eggs, beaten
- ½ cup Parmesan cheese, grated
- ½ cup flour
- 1 tsp cayenne pepper
- 1 ½ lb green beans
- 1 cup tomato pasta sauce
- Salt and black pepper to taste

DIRECTIONS (Prep + Cook Time: 20 minutes) Preheat air fryer to 400 F. In a bowl, mix breadcrumbs, Parmesan cheese, cayenne pepper, salt, and pepper. Coat the green beans in the flour, followed by the beaten egg and finally the Parmesan-panko crumbs. AirFry in the fryer for 15 minutes, turning once halfway through. Serve with tomato sauce. enjoy!

917. Cholula Seasoned Broccoli
INGREDIENTS (4 Servings)

- 1 lb broccoli florets
- ½ tsp lemon zest
- 1 garlic clove, minced
- 1 tsp olive oil
- 1 ½ tbsp soy sauce
- 1 tsp lemon juice
- 1 tsp cholula hot sauce
- Salt and black pepper to taste

DIRECTIONS (Prep + Cook Time: 30 minutes) Preheat your Air Fryer to 390 F. Put the broccoli florets, olive oil, and garlic in a bowl and season with salt. Toss together, then put the broccoli in the greased fryer basket, giving the florets plenty of space. Air fry for 15-20 minutes or until light brown and crispy. Shake the basket every 5 minutes. Whisk the soy sauce, white vinegar, cholula sauce, and lemon juice in a bowl. Toss the broccoli and sauce mixture in a large bowl and mix well. Sprinkle with lemon zest, salt, and pepper, and serve. enjoy!

918. Tempura Veggies with Sesame Soy Sauce
INGREDIENTS (4 Servings)

2 lb chopped veggies:

carrot, parsnip, green beans, zucchini, onion rings, asparagus, cauliflower

Dipping sauce:

4 tbsp soy sauce Juice of

1 lemon

1 ½ cups plain flour

Salt and black pepper to taste

½ tsp sesame oil

½ tsp sugar

1 ½ tbsp cornstarch

¾ cup cold water

½ garlic clove, chopped

½ tsp sweet chili sauce

DIRECTIONS (Prep + Cook Time: 20 minutes)

Line the air fryer basket with baking paper. In a bowl, mix flour, salt, pepper, and cornstarch; whisk to combine. Keep whisking as you add in water, so a smooth batter is formed. Dip each veggie piece into the batter and place it into the frying basket. AirFry for 12 minutes at 360 F, turning once; cook until crispy. Mix all dipping ingredients in a bowl. Serve with the crispy veggies. enjoy!

919. Spicy Mixed Veggie Bake
INGREDIENTS (4 Servings)

1 cauliflower, cut into florets	1 leek, sliced thinly	1 tsp dried coriander
1 carrot, diced	1 small zucchini, chopped	1 tsp ground cumin
1 broccoli, cut into florets	1 tbsp garlic paste	1 cup vegetable broth
1 onion, chopped	2 tbsp olive oil	1 tsp ginger paste
½ cup garden peas	1 tbsp curry paste	Salt and black pepper to taste

DIRECTIONS (Prep + Cook Time: 35 minutes) Preheat air fryer to 350 F. Heat olive oil in a saucepan over medium heat and sauté onion, leek, ginger paste, carrot, curry paste, and garlic for 5 minutes. Stir in the remaining ingredients and transfer to a baking dish. Bake in the air fryer for 10-15 minutes. Serve warm. enjoy!

920. Turmeric Crispy Chickpeas
INGREDIENTS (4 Servings)

1 (15-oz) can chickpeas, rinsed

1 tbsp butter, melted

½ tsp dried rosemary

¼ tsp turmeric

DIRECTIONS (Prep + Cook Time: 20 minutes) Preheat air fryer to 380 F. In a bowl, combine together chickpeas, butter, rosemary, turmeric, and salt; toss to coat. Place the in the greased frying basket and AirFry for 6 minutes. Shake, and cook for 6 more minutes until crispy. enjoy!

921. Air Fried Ravioli
INGREDIENTS (4 Servings)

1 package cheese ravioli	¼ cup Pecorino cheese, grated	2 tsp olive oil
2 cup Italian breadcrumbs	1 cup buttermilk	¼ tsp garlic powder

DIRECTIONS (Prep + Cook Time: 15 minutes) Preheat air fryer to 390 F. In a small bowl, combine breadcrumbs, Pecorino cheese, garlic powder, and olive oil. Dip the ravioli in the buttermilk and then coat them with the breadcrumb mixture. Line a baking tray with parchment paper and arrange the ravioli on it. Place in the air fryer and Bake for 5-6 minutes. Serve with marinara or carbonara sauce. enjoy!

922. Easy Vegetable Croquettes
INGREDIENTS (4 Servings)

1 lb red potatoes	½ cup baby spinach, chopped	1 carrot, grated
1 ¼ cups milk	½ lb mushrooms, chopped	⅓ cup flour
Salt to taste	½ lb broccoli florets, chopped	2 eggs, beaten
3 tbsp butter	1 green onion, sliced	1 ½ cups breadcrumbs
2 tsp olive oil	1 red onion, chopped	
1 red bell pepper, chopped	2 garlic cloves, minced	

DIRECTIONS (Prep + Cook Time: 45 minutes) Cover the potatoes with salted water in a pot over medium heat and cook for about 15-18 minutes. Drain and place in a bowl. Add in 2 tbsp of butter, 1 cup of milk, and salt. Mash with a potato masher. In a food processor, place onion, garlic, bell pepper, broccoli, mushrooms, green onion, spinach, olive oil, salt, and remaining milk and pulse until a breadcrumb texture is formed. Mix with mashed potatoes. Using your hands, create oblong balls out of the mixture and place them on a baking sheet in a single layer. Refrigerate for 30 minutes. Preheat air fryer to 390 F. Take 3 separate bowls, pour breadcrumbs in one, flour in another, and eggs in a third bowl. Remove the croquettes from the fridge. Dredge the croquettes in flour, then in the eggs, and finally in the crumbs. Arrange them on the greased frying basket without overlapping. AirFry for 12-14 minutes, shaking once. Remove to a wire rack. Let cool and serve. enjoy!

923. Hoisin Spring Rolls
INGREDIENTS (4 Servings)

½ lb shiitake mushrooms, chopped	2 cups green cabbage, shredded	1 tbsp hoisin sauce
2 tbsp canola oil	1 carrot, shredded	12 wonton wrappers
1 clove garlic, minced	1 green onion, thinly sliced	
1-inch piece ginger, grated	1 tbsp soy sauce	

DIRECTIONS (Prep + Cook Time: 25 minutes) Warm 1 tbsp of the canola oil in a pan over medium heat and sauté green onion, garlic, and ginger for 30 seconds. Add in shiitake mushrooms, carrots, and cabbage and cook, stirring occasionally until tender, about 4 minutes. Stir in the soy sauce and hoisin sauce. Preheat air fryer to 390 F. Distribute the mixture across the wrappers and roll-up. Place the rolls in the greased frying basket and Bake for 14-16 minutes, turning once until golden and crisp. Serve warm. enjoy!

924. Chili Roasted Pumpkin with Orzo
INGREDIENTS (4 Servings)

1 lb pumpkin, peeled and cubed	1 red chili pepper, minced	Salt and black pepper to taste
2 red bell peppers, diced	1 tsp ground caraway seeds	
2 shallots, quartered	1 cup orzo	

DIRECTIONS (Prep + Cook Time: 35 minutes) Preheat air fryer to 380 F. In a bowl, place the pumpkin, bell peppers, shallots, chili pepper, ground caraway seeds, salt, and pepper; toss to coat. Transfer to the greased frying basket. Bake for 20-25 minutes, shaking once until golden. Place a pot filled with salted water over medium heat and bring to a boil. Add in the orzo and cook for 4 minutes. Drain and place on a serving platter. Spread the baked pumpkin all over. Serve and enjoy!

925. Greek-Style Stuffed Bell Peppers
INGREDIENTS (4 Servings)

4 red bell peppers, tops sliced off	1 tbsp Greek seasoning	Salt and black pepper to taste
2 cups cooked rice	¼ cup Kalamata olives, pitted and sliced	1 cup feta cheese, crumbled
1 onion, chopped	¾ cup tomato sauce	2 tbsp fresh dill, chopped

DIRECTIONS (Prep + Cook Time: 20 minutes) Preheat air fryer to 360 F. Microwave the bell peppers for 1-2 minutes until soft. In a bowl, combine rice, onion, Greek seasoning, feta cheese, olives, tomato sauce, salt, and pepper. Divide the mixture between the bell peppers and arrange them on a greased baking dish. Place in the air fryer and Bake for 15 minutes. When ready, remove to a serving plate, scatter with dill and serve. enjoy!

926. Vegetable & Goat Cheese Tian
INGREDIENTS (4 Servings)

- 2 tbsp butter
- 1 garlic clove, minced
- 2 tomatoes, sliced
- 1 cup canned chickpeas, drained
- ¼ cup black olives, pitted and chopped
- 1 fennel bulb, sliced
- 1 zucchini, sliced into rounds
- 4 oz goat cheese, sliced into rounds
- 1 tsp dried thyme
- Salt and black pepper to taste

DIRECTIONS (Prep + Cook Time: 45 minutes) Preheat air fryer to 360 F. Melt the butter in a skillet over medium heat and sauté the fennel, garlic, and chickpeas for 5-6 minutes, stirring often until soft. Season with thyme, salt, and pepper. Transfer to a baking dish and arrange tomato, zucchini, and cheese slices on top. Scatter with black olives. Place the dish in the fryer and Bake for 20-25 minutes until the cheese is melted and golden. Remove and let sit for a few minutes before serving. enjoy!

927. Cheesy Vegetable Quesadilla
INGREDIENTS (1 Servings)

- 2 flour tortillas
- ¼ cup gouda cheese, shredded
- ¼ yellow bell pepper, sliced
- ¼ zucchini, sliced
- ½ green onion, sliced
- 1 tbsp fresh cilantro, chopped
- 1 tsp olive oil

DIRECTIONS (Prep + Cook Time: 15 minutes)

Preheat air fryer to 390 F. Grease the air fryer basket with cooking spray. Place a flour tortilla in the greased frying basket and top with gouda cheese, bell pepper, zucchini, cilantro, and green onion. Cover with the other tortilla and brush with olive oil. Cook for 10 minutes until lightly browned. Cut into 4 wedges and serve. enjoy!

928. Dilled Zucchini Egg Cakes
INGREDIENTS (4 Servings)

- 12 oz thawed puff pastry
- 4 large eggs
- 1 medium zucchini, sliced
- 4 oz feta cheese, drained and crumbled
- 2 tbsp fresh dill, chopped
- Salt and black pepper to taste

DIRECTIONS (Prep + Cook Time: 25 minutes)

Preheat air fryer to 360 F. In a bowl, whisk the eggs with salt and pepper. Stir in zucchini, dill, and feta cheese. Grease a muffin tin tray with cooking spray. Roll pastry and arrange them to cover the sides of the muffin holes. Divide the egg mixture evenly between the holes. Place the muffin tray in your air fryer and Bake for 13-15 minutes, until golden. enjoy!

929. Cheesy Broccoli & Egg Cups
INGREDIENTS (4 Servings)

- 1 lb broccoli florets, steamed and chopped
- 4 eggs, beaten
- 1 cup sharp cheese, shredded
- 1 cup heavy cream
- ½ tsp nutmeg
- ½ tsp ginger powder
- Salt and black pepper to taste

DIRECTIONS (Prep + Cook Time: 15 minutes)

Place the broccoli in a bowl and mix in eggs, heavy cream, nutmeg, ginger, salt, and black pepper. Divide the mixture between 4 greased ramekins. Top with the cheese and Bake in the air fryer for 12-14 minutes at 330 F. Remove and let cool for a few minutes before serving. enjoy!

930. Vegetable Tortilla Pizza
INGREDIENTS (1 Servings)

- ¼ tbsp tomato paste
- 1 tbsp cheddar cheese, grated
- 1 tbsp mozzarella cheese, grated
- 1 tbsp cooked sweet corn
- 4 zucchini slices
- 4 eggplant slices
- 4 red onion rings
- ½ green bell pepper, chopped
- 1 tortilla
- ¼ tsp basil

DIRECTIONS (Prep + Cook Time: 15 minutes)

Preheat air fryer to 350 F. Spread the tomato paste on the tortilla. Arrange zucchini and eggplant slices first, then green peppers and onion rings. Sprinkle the corn all over. Top with cheddar and mozzarella. Place on a greased baking tray and fit in the fryer. Bake for 10-12 minutes. Sprinkle with basil to serve. enjoy!

931. Potato Filled Bread Rolls
INGREDIENTS (4 Servings)

- 8 slices sandwich bread
- 4 large potatoes, boiled and mashed
- ½ tsp turmeric
- Salt to taste
- 2 green chilies, seeded and chopped
- 1 onion, finely chopped
- ½ tsp mustard seeds
- 1 tbsp olive oil

DIRECTIONS (Prep + Cook Time: 25 minutes)

Preheat air fryer to 350 F. In a skillet over medium heat, warm olive oil, and stir-fry onion and mustard seeds for 3 minutes. Remove to a bowl and add in potatoes, chilies, turmeric, and salt; mix well. Trim the crust sides of the bread, and roll out with a rolling pin. Spread a spoonful of the potato mixture on each bread sheet, and roll the bread over the filling, sealing the edges. Place the rolls in the greased frying basket and Bake for 12 minutes. Serve warm. enjoy!

932. Easy Fried Green Tomatoes
INGREDIENTS (2 Servings)

- 1 green tomato, sliced
- ¼ tbsp creole seasoning
- Salt and black pepper to taste
- ¼ cup flour
- ½ cup buttermilk
- 1 cup breadcrumbs

DIRECTIONS (Prep + Cook Time: 15 minutes)

Add flour to one bowl and buttermilk to another. Season tomatoes with salt and pepper. Make a mix of creole seasoning and breadcrumbs. Roll tomato slices up in the flour, dip in buttermilk, and then into the breadcrumbs. AirFry in the greased frying basket for 5 minutes at 400 F, turning once. enjoy!

933. Roasted Brussels Sprouts
INGREDIENTS (4 Servings)

- 1 lb Brussels sprouts
- 1 tsp garlic powder
- 2 tbsp olive oil
- Salt and black pepper to taste

DIRECTIONS (Prep + Cook Time: 25 minutes)

Trim off the outer leaves, keeping only the head of the Brussels sprouts. In a bowl, mix olive oil, garlic powder, salt, and pepper. Add in the sprouts and coat well. Transfer them to the greased frying basket and AirFry for 15 minutes, shaking once halfway through. Serve warm. enjoy!

934. Honey Baby Carrots
INGREDIENTS (4 Servings)

1 lb baby carrots	2 tbsp olive oil	Salt and black pepper to taste
1 tsp dried dill	1 tbsp honey	

DIRECTIONS (Prep + Cook Time: 20 minutes)

Preheat air fryer to 350 F. In a bowl, mix olive oil, carrots, and honey; stir to coat. Season with dill, pepper, and salt. Place coated carrots in the greased frying basket and AirFry for 12 minutes, shaking once. Serve warm or chilled. enjoy!

935. Sesame Balsamic Asparagus
INGREDIENTS (4 Servings)

1 ½ lb asparagus, trimmed	4 tbsp olive oil	Salt and black pepper to taste
4 tbsp balsamic vinegar	2 tbsp fresh rosemary, chopped	2 tbsp sesame seeds

DIRECTIONS (Prep + Cook Time: 25 minutes)

Preheat your Air Fryer to 360 F. Whisk the olive oil, sesame seeds, and balsamic vinegar to make a marinade in a bowl. Place the asparagus on a baking dish and pour over the asparagus the marinade.Toss to coat and let them sit for 10 minutes. Then AirFry for 10-12 minutes, shaking halfway through the cooking time until tender and lighty charred. Serve asparagus topped with rosemary. Enjoy!

936. Homemade Cipollini Onions
INGREDIENTS (4 Servings)

2 lb cipollini onions, cut into flowers	2 cups flour	1 tbsp ketchup
2 tbsp olive oil	Salt and black pepper to taste	¼ cup mayonnaise
1 tsp cayenne pepper	1 tbsp paprika	¼ cup sour cream
1 tsp garlic powder	¼ cup mayonnaise	

DIRECTIONS (Prep + Cook Time: 20 minutes)

Preheat your air fryer to 360 F. In a bowl, mix salt, pepper, paprika, flour, garlic powder, and cayenne pepper. Stir in mayonnaise, ketchup, and sour cream. Coat the onions with the prepared mixture and spray with olive oil. Add the coated onions to a baking dish and Bake in the air fryer for 15 minutes. enjoy!

937. Easy Roasted Cauliflower
INGREDIENTS (4 Servings)

1 head cauliflower, cut into florets	1 tsp turmeric	1 tbsp olive oil
1 tsp garlic powder	1 tsp cumin	Salt and black pepper to taste

DIRECTIONS (Prep + Cook Time: 30 minutes) Preheat your Air Fryer to 390 F. Thoroughly combine the cauliflower florets, turmeric, cumin, and garlic powder in a mixing bowl; toss to coat the florets well. Add salt and pepper to taste. Add the cauliflower to the greased fryer basket and brush with olive oil. Air fry until browned and crispy, about 20 minutes. Be sure to shake the basket every 5 minutes or so. Serve hot. enjoy!

938. Party Crispy Nachos
INGREDIENTS (2 Servings)

1 cup sweet corn	1 tbsp butter	Salt to taste
1 cup all-purpose flour	½ tsp chili powder	

DIRECTIONS (Prep + Cook Time: 30 minutes)

Add a small amount of water to the sweet corn and grind until you obtain a very fine paste. In a bowl, mix flour, salt, chili powder, and butter; add corn and stir. Knead with your palm until you obtain a stiff dough. Preheat air fryer to 350 F. On a working surface, dust a little bit of flour and spread the dough with a rolling pin. Make it around ½ inch thick. Cut into tringle-shape and AirFry in the greased frying basket for around 10 minutes. Serve with guacamole salsa. enjoy!

939. Winter Vegetable Delight
INGREDIENTS (2 Servings)

1 parsnip, sliced	½ celery stalk, chopped	2 tsp olive oil
1 cup sliced butternut squash	1 tbsp fresh thyme, chopped	
1 small red onion, cut into wedges	Salt and black pepper to taste	

DIRECTIONS (Prep + Cook Time: 20 minutes)

Preheat air fryer to 380 F. In a bowl, add turnip, squash, onion, celery, thyme, pepper, salt, and olive oil; mix well. Pour the vegetables into the frying basket and AirFry for 16 minutes, tossing once. Serve. enjoy!

940. Green Vegetable Rotini Pasta Bake
INGREDIENTS (4 Servings)

1 cup green peas	2 tbsp flour	3 tbsp butter
1 lb broccoli florets, steamed	2 cups milk	1 tbsp fresh basil, chopped
1 cup kale, chopped	¼ cup mozzarella cheese, grated	Salt and black pepper to taste
1 garlic clove, minced	16 oz rotini pasta	

DIRECTIONS (Prep + Cook Time: 30 minutes)

Bring a large saucepan of salted water to a boil. Add in the rotini pasta and cook following pack instructions. Drain and set aside. Melt butter in a skillet over medium heat and sauté garlic for 1 minute. Stir in flour for 1 minute. Gradually add in the milk and simmer until slightly thickened, 3 minutes. Preheat air fryer to 350 F. Transfer the milk mixture to a baking dish and add in the pasta, broccoli, kale, green peas, salt, and pepper; stir to combine. Top with the mozzarella cheese and sprinkle with basil. Place in the air fryer and Bake for 10-12 minutes until the cheese is golden. Serve warm. enjoy!

941. Roasted Veggies with Penne Pasta
INGREDIENTS (4 Servings)

1 lb penne pasta	½ cup mushrooms, sliced	1 cup grape tomatoes, halved
1 zucchini, sliced	½ cup Kalamata olives, pitted and halved	3 tbsp balsamic vinegar
1 bell pepper, sliced	¼ cup olive oil	2 tbsp fresh basil, chopped
½ lb acorn squash, sliced	1 tsp Italian seasoning	Salt and black pepper to taste

DIRECTIONS (Prep + Cook Time: 45 minutes) Fill a pot with salted water and bring to a boil over medium heat. Add in the penne pasta and cook until al dente, about 8 minutes. Drain and place in a bowl; set aside. Preheat air fryer to 380 F. In a baking dish, combine bell pepper, zucchini, acorn squash, mushrooms, and olive oil. Season with salt and pepper. Bake in the air fryer for 15 minutes, shaking once. Remove the veggies to the pasta bowl. Mix in tomatoes, olives, Italian seasoning, and balsamic vinegar. Sprinkle with basil and serve. enjoy!

942. Tomato Sandwiches with Feta & Pesto
INGREDIENTS (2 Servings)

1 heirloom tomato	1 garlic clove	2 tbsp fresh parsley, chopped
1 (4-oz) block Feta cheese	Salt to taste 2 tsp + ¼ cup olive oil	¼ cup Parmesan cheese, grated
1 small red onion, thinly sliced	1 ½ tbsp pine nuts, toasted	¼ cup fresh basil, chopped

DIRECTIONS (Prep + Cook Time: 25 minutes)

Add basil, pine nuts, garlic, Parmesan cheese, and salt to a food processor. Pulse while slowly adding ¼ cup of olive oil. Preheat air fryer to 390 F. Slice feta cheese and tomato into ½-inch slices. Spread the obtained pesto sauce on the tomato slices. Top with feta cheese and onion and drizzle the remaining olive oil. Place the tomato in the greased frying basket and Bake for 6-8 minutes. Remove to a serving platter, sprinkle lightly with salt, and top with fresh parsley. Serve chilled. enjoy!

943. Mexican Chile Relleno
INGREDIENTS (4 Servings)

2 (8-oz) cans whole green chiles, drained	1 cup flour	½ cup milk
2 cups Mexican cheese, shredded	2 large eggs, beaten	

DIRECTIONS (Prep + Cook Time: 20 minutes) Preheat air fryer to 380 F. Lay the green chilies on a plate and fill them with cheese. In a bowl, whisk eggs, milk, and half of the flour. Pour the remaining flour on a flat plate. Dip the chilies in the flour first, then in the egg mixture, and arrange them on the greased frying basket. AirFry for 8-10 minutes, flipping once halfway through. Serve with slices of avocado. enjoy!

944. Homemade Pie with Root Vegetables
INGREDIENTS (4 Servings)

1 lb potatoes, cubed	½ cup Parmesan cheese, grated	½ tsp dried sage
3 tbsp pine nuts	1 cup crème fraiche	2 tbsp butter
1 parsnip, chopped	1 bread slice, diced	1 tsp yellow mustard

DIRECTIONS (Prep + Cook Time: 40 minutes) Boil potatoes and parsnip in a pot filled with salted water over medium heat for 15 minutes. Drain and place in a bowl. Add in mustard, crème fraiche, sage, butter, salt, and pepper and mash them using a potato masher. Mix in bread and Parmesan cheese. Preheat air fryer to 360 F. Add the resulting batter to a greased baking dish and place it in the air fryer. Bake for 15 minutes. Serve warm or chilled. enjoy!

945. Plantain Fritters
INGREDIENTS (4 Servings)

3 bananas, sliced diagonally	1 egg white	Salt and black pepper to taste
2 tbsp cornflour	¼ cup breadcrumbs	

DIRECTIONS (Prep + Cook Time: 15 minutes) Preheat air fryer to 340 F. Pour breadcrumbs on a plate. Season with salt and pepper. Coat the plantain slices with the cornflour first, brush with egg white, and roll in the breadcrumbs. Arrange on a greased baking tray and lightly spray with oil. Bake in the air fryer for 8 minutes, flipping once. Serve. enjoy!

946. Baked Mediterranean Shakshuka
INGREDIENTS (4 Servings)

1 onion, sliced	2 tsp paprika	4 eggs
2 garlic cloves, minced	¼ tsp chili powder	2 tbsp fresh parsley, chopped
2 tbsp olive oil	1 red bell pepper, seeded and diced	4 tbsp feta cheese, crumbled
1 tsp ground cumin	2 (14.5-oz) cans tomatoes, diced	Salt and black pepper to taste

DIRECTIONS (Prep + Cook Time: 25 minutes) Heat olive oil in a skillet over medium heat and sauté bell pepper, onion, and garlic for 5 minutes until tender. Stir in paprika, chili powder, cumin, salt, and pepper and pour in the tomatoes. Simmer for 10 minutes and transfer to a baking pan. Crack in the eggs. Bake in the air fryer for 12 minutes at 370 F enjoy!

947. Spanish-Style Huevos Rotos (Broken Eggs)
INGREDIENTS (2 Servings)

½ tsp salt	3 tbsp olive oil	2 russet potatoes, cut into wedges
½ tsp garlic powder	1 tsp sweet paprika	2 eggs

DIRECTIONS (Prep + Cook Time: 36 minutes)

In a bowl, mix salt, garlic powder, and 1 tbsp olive oil. Add in the potatoes and toss to coat. Arrange them on the frying basket without overcrowding and AirFry for 20-25 minutes at 380 F. Shake regularly to get crispy on all sides. Heat the remaining olive oil in a pan over medium heat and fry the eggs until the whites are firm and the yolks are still runny, about 5 minutes. Place the potatoes on a serving bowl and top with the fried eggs and paprika. Break the eggs with a fork and serve. enjoy!

948. Delicious Potato Patties
INGREDIENTS (4 Servings)

4 potatoes, shredded	¼ cup milk	Salt and black pepper to taste
1 onion, chopped	2 tbsp butter	3 tbsp flour
1 egg, beaten	½ tsp garlic powder	

DIRECTIONS (Prep + Cook Time: 20 minutes) Preheat air fryer to 390 F. In a bowl, add the egg, potatoes, onion, milk, butter, black pepper, flour, garlic powder, and salt and mix well to form a batter. Mold the mixture into four patties. Place the patties in a greased frying basket and AirFry for 14-16 minutes, flipping once. Serve warm. enjoy!

949. Traditional Jacket Potatoes
INGREDIENTS (4 Servings)

1 lb potatoes	Salt and black pepper to taste	2 tsp butter, melted
2 garlic cloves, minced	1 tsp dried rosemary	

DIRECTIONS (Prep + Cook Time: 30 minutes) Preheat air fryer to 360 F. Prick the potatoes with a fork. Place them in the greased frying basket and Bake for 23-25 minutes, turning once halfway through. Remove and cut in half. Drizzle with melted butter and season with salt and black pepper. Sprinkle with rosemary and serve enjoy!.

950. Cheesy Potatoes & Asparagus
INGREDIENTS (5 Servings)

4 potatoes, cut into wedges	¼ cup buttermilk	Salt and black pepper to taste
1 bunch asparagus, trimmed	¼ cup cottage cheese, crumbled	
2 tbsp olive oil	1 tbsp whole-grain mustard	

DIRECTIONS (Prep + Cook Time: 30 minutes) Preheat air fryer to 400 F. Place the potatoes in a greased frying basket and Bake for 20-22 minutes; remove and cover with foil to keep warm. Drizzle asparagus with olive oil and season with salt and black pepper. Bake them in the air fryer for 6-8 minutes, shaking halfway through the cooking time. In a bowl, mix the cottage cheese, buttermilk, and whole-grain mustard. Arrange potatoes and asparagus on a serving platter and drizzle with the cheese sauce. Serve and enjoy!

951. Easy Cabbage Steaks
INGREDIENTS (3 Servings)

1 cabbage head	2 tbsp olive oil	2 tsp fennel seeds
1 tbsp garlic paste	Salt and black pepper to taste	

DIRECTIONS (Prep + Cook Time:25 minutes) Preheat air fryer to 350 F. Cut the cabbage into 1 ½-inch thin slices. In a small bowl, combine all the other ingredients and brush cabbage with the mixture. Arrange the steaks on the greased frying basket and Bake for 15 minutes, flipping once halfway through. Serve warm or chilled. enjoy!

952. Bulgarian Red Pepper "Burek"
INGREDIENTS (4 Servings)

4 red bell peppers, roasted	4 garlic cloves, chopped	Salt and black pepper to taste
1 cup feta cheese, crumbled	1 tomato, peeled and chopped	1 tbsp olive oil
4 eggs	1 tsp fresh dill, chopped	½ cup flour
1 cup breadcrumbs	1 tbsp fresh parsley, chopped	1 cup plain yogurt

DIRECTIONS (Prep + Cook Time: 25 minutes) In a small bowl, mix the yogurt with olive oil, half of the garlic, and dill. Keep the sauce in the fridge. Preheat air fryer to 350 F. In a bowl, beat 3 eggs with salt and pepper. Add in feta cheese, the remaining garlic, tomato, and parsley and mix to combine. Fill the peppers with the mixture. Beat the remaining egg with salt and pepper in a bowl. Coat the peppers with flour first, then dip in the egg, and finally in the crumbs. Arrange on the greased frying basket and AirFry for 10-12 minutes until golden brown. Serve the peppers with the yogurt sauce on the side. enjoy!

953. Zesty Bell Pepper Bites
INGREDIENTS (4 Servings)

1 red bell pepper, cut into small portions	3 tbsp balsamic vinegar	½ tsp dried parsley
1 yellow pepper, cut into small portions	2 tbsp olive oil	Salt and black pepper to taste
1 green bell pepper, cut into small portions	1 garlic clove, minced	½ cup garlic mayonnaise
	½ tsp dried basil	

DIRECTIONS (Prep + Cook Time: 20 minutes)

Preheat air fryer to 390 F. In a bowl, mix bell peppers, olive oil, garlic, balsamic vinegar, basil, and parsley and season with salt and black pepper. Transfer to a greased baking dish and Bake in the air fryer for 12-15 minutes, tossing once or twice. Serve with garlic mayonnaise. enjoy!

954. Green Pea Arancini with Tomato Sauce
INGREDIENTS (4 Servings)

1 cup rice, rinsed	2 garlic cloves, minced	2 tbsp olive oil
½ green peas	1 egg	Salt and black pepper to taste
1 tbsp butter	3 tbsp Parmesan cheese, shredded	1 lb Roma tomatoes, chopped
1 onion, chopped	½ cup breadcrumbs	2 tbsp fresh basil, chopped

DIRECTIONS (Prep + Cook Time: 60 minutes)

Fill a shallow saucepan with water and place over medium heat. Bring to a boil and add in the rice, salt, and pepper. Cook for 20-22 minutes, stirring often. Drain rice and place in a bowl; mix in green peas. Melt the butter in a skillet over medium heat and sauté onion and garlic for 3 minutes until soft. Remove the mixture to the rice bowl and add in Parmesan cheese and egg; mix well. Mold the mixture into golf-size balls and roll them in breadcrumbs. Place on a baking sheet and refrigerate for 1 hour. Heat the olive oil in the skillet and cook the tomatoes for 6-8 minutes, stirring occasionally until the sauce thickens. Season with salt and pepper. Scatter basil on top and set aside. Preheat air fryer to 360 F. Remove the arancini from the fridge and arrange them on the greased frying basket. AirFry for 14-16 minutes, shaking from time to time until nicely browned. Serve with the sauce. enjoy!

955. Indian Fried Okra
INGREDIENTS (4 Servings)

1 tbsp chili powder	1 cup cornmeal	½ lb okra, trimmed and halved lengthwise
2 tbsp garam masala	¼ cup flour Salt to taste	1 egg

DIRECTIONS (Prep + Cook Time: 20 minutes)

Preheat air fryer to 380 F. In a bowl, mix cornmeal, flour, chili powder, garam masala, salt, and pepper. In another bowl, whisk the egg; season with salt and pepper. Dip the okra in the egg and then coat in cornmeal mixture. Spray okra with cooking spray and place in the frying basket. AirFry for 6 minutes, slide the basket out, shake and cook for another 6 minutes until golden brown. Serve with hot sauce. enjoy!

956. Zucchini Fries with Tabasco Dip
INGREDIENTS (4 Servings)

2 zucchinis, sliced

2 egg whites

½ cup seasoned breadcrumbs

2 tbsp Parmesan cheese, grated

¼ tsp garlic powder

Salt and black pepper to taste

1 cup mayonnaise

¼ cup heavy cream

1 tbsp Tabasco sauce

1 tsp lime juice

DIRECTIONS (Prep + Cook Time: 25 minutes)

Preheat air fryer to 400 F. In a bowl, beat egg whites with salt and pepper. In another bowl, mix garlic powder, Parmesan cheese, and breadcrumbs. Dip zucchini in the egg whites, followed by breadcrumbs. Add to the greased frying basket and AirFry for 14 minutes, turning once halfway through. In a small bowl, mix mayonnaise, heavy cream, Tabasco sauce, and lime juice. Serve on the side of the zucchini. enjoy!

957. Cheesy Eggplant Schnitzels
INGREDIENTS (4 Servings)

2 eggplants

½ cup mozzarella cheese, grated

2 tbsp milk

1 egg, beaten

2 cups breadcrumbs

2 tomatoes, sliced

DIRECTIONS (Prep + Cook Time:15 minutes)

Preheat air fryer to 400 F. Cut the eggplants lengthways into ½-in thick slices. In a bowl, mix egg and milk. In another bowl, combine breadcrumbs and mozzarella cheese. Dip eggplant slices in the egg mixture, followed by the crumb mixture. Place in the greased frying basket and AirFry for 10-12 minutes, turning once halfway through. Top with tomato slices and serve. enjoy!

958. Effortless Eggplant Cheeseburger
INGREDIENTS (1 Servings)

1 hamburger bun

2-inch eggplant slice, cut along the round axis

1 mozzarella slice

1 red onion cut into

3 rings

1 lettuce leaf

½ tbsp tomato sauce

1 pickle, sliced

DIRECTIONS (Prep + Cook Time: 10 minutes)

Preheat air fryer to 330 F. Place the eggplant in a greased frying basket and Bake for 6 minutes, flipping once. Top with the mozzarella slice and cook for 30 more seconds. Spread the tomato sauce on one half of the bun. Lay the lettuce leaf on top, then lay the cheesy eggplant, onion rings, and sliced pickles. Finish with the other bun half. Serve immediately. enjoy!

959. Air Fried Eggplant Toast
INGREDIENTS (2 Servings)

2 large eggplant slices

1 large spring onion, finely sliced

2 white bread slices

½ cup sweet corn

1 egg white, whisked

1 tbsp black sesame seeds

DIRECTIONS (Prep + Cook Time: 12 minutes)

In a bowl, place corn, spring onion, egg white, and sesame seeds and mix well. Spread the mixture over the bread slices. Top with eggplants and place in the greased air fryer basket. Bake for 8-10 minutes at 370 F until golden. Serve enjoy!

960. Quick Beetroot Chips
INGREDIENTS (2 Servings)

2 golden beetroots, thinly sliced	1 tbsp yeast flakes	Salt to taste
2 tbsp olive oil	1 tsp Italian seasoning	

DIRECTIONS (Prep + Cook Time: 20 minutes)

Preheat air fryer to 360 F. In a bowl, add olive oil, beetroot slices, Italian seasoning, and yeast and mix well. Dump the coated chips in the greased frying basket and AirFry for 12 minutes, shaking once. enjoy!

961. Tasty Balsamic Beets
INGREDIENTS (2 Servings)

2 beets, cubed	2 tbsp olive oil	Salt and black pepper to taste
⅓ cup balsamic vinegar	1 tbsp honey	2 springs rosemary, chopped

DIRECTIONS (Prep + Cook Time: 25 minutes)

Preheat air fryer to 400 F. In a bowl, mix beets, olive oil, rosemary, pepper, and salt and toss to coat. Bake the beets in the frying basket for 15 minutes, shaking once halfway through. Pour the balsamic vinegar and honey into a pan over medium heat; bring to a boil and cook until reduced by half. Drizzle the beets with balsamic sauce and serve. enjoy!

962. Aunt's Shallot & Carrot Bake
INGREDIENTS (4 Servings)

2 tsp olive oil	Salt to taste	2 tbsp fresh parsley, chopped
2 shallots, chopped	¼ cup yogurt	
3 carrots, sliced	2 garlic cloves, minced	

DIRECTIONS (Prep + Cook Time: 25 minutes)

Preheat air fryer to 370 F. In a bowl, mix carrots, salt, garlic, shallots, parsley, and yogurt. Drizzle with olive oil. Transfer to a greased baking dish and Bake in the air fryer for 15 minutes, shaking once. enjoy!

963. Teriyaki Cauliflower
INGREDIENTS (4 Servings)

1 big cauliflower head, cut into florets	1 tsp sesame oil	1 tsp cornstarch
½ cup soy sauce	½ chili powder	
1 tbsp brown sugar	2 cloves garlic, chopped	

DIRECTIONS (Prep + Cook Time:20 minutes)

In a bowl, whisk soy sauce, sugar, sesame oil, ⅓ cup of water, chili powder, garlic, and cornstarch until smooth. In a bowl, add cauliflower and pour teriyaki sauce over the top, toss to coat. Place the cauliflower in the greased frying basket and AirFry for 14 minutes at 340 F, turning once halfway through. When ready, check if the cauliflower is cooked but not too soft. Serve warm. enjoy!

964. Air Fried Parmesan Cauliflower
INGREDIENTS (4 Servings)

1 head of cauliflower, cut into florets	4 tbsp Parmesan cheese, grated
2 tbsp olive oil	Salt and black pepper to taste

DIRECTIONS (Prep + Cook Time: 15 minutes)

In a bowl, mix cauliflower, olive oil, salt, and black pepper. Transfer to the greased frying basket and Bake for 8-10 minutes at 360 F, shaking once, until crispy. Serve sprinkled with Parmesan cheese. enjoy!

965. Chili Corn on the Cob
INGREDIENTS (4 Servings)

4 ears of sweet corn, shucked

1 clove garlic, minced

1 green chili, minced

1 lemon, zested

2 tbsp olive oil

2 tbsp butter, melted

Salt to taste

DIRECTIONS (Prep + Cook Time: 25 minutes)

Preheat air fryer to 380 F. in a bowl, mix olive oil, garlic, lemon zest, and green chili. Rub the mixture on all sides. Place the ears in the frying basket; work in batches. AirFry for 14-16 minutes, turning once until lightly browned. Remove to a platter and drizzle with melted butter. Scatter with salt and serve. enjoy!

966. Zucchini & Turnip Bake
INGREDIENTS (4 Servings)

1 lb turnips, sliced

1 large red onion, cut into rings

1 large zucchini, sliced

Salt and black pepper to taste

2 cloves garlic, crushed

2 tbsp olive oil

DIRECTIONS (Prep + Cook Time: 30 minutes)

Preheat air fryer to 330 F. Place turnips, red onion, garlic, and zucchini in a baking pan. Drizzle with olive oil and season with salt and pepper. Place in the frying and Bake for 18-20 minutes, turning once. enjoy!

967. Vegetable Bean Burgers
INGREDIENTS (4 Servings)

1 parsnip, chopped

1 carrot, chopped

½ lb mushrooms, chopped

1 (15-oz) can black beans, drained and rinsed

2 tbsp olive oil

1 egg, beaten

2 tbsp tomato paste

2 garlic cloves, minced

½ tsp onion powder

½ cup breadcrumbs

Salt and black pepper to taste

4 hamburger buns

DIRECTIONS (Prep + Cook Time: 45 minutes)

Preheat your Air Fryer to 360 F. Put the parsnip and carrot in the greased fryer basket, drizzle with some olive oil, and season with salt and pepper. AirFry for 8 minutes. Toss the mushrooms in the fryer basket with the veggies, spray with oil, and season with salt and pepper. AirFry for 5 more minutes. Mash the black beans in a bowl with a fork. Mix in the egg, tomato paste, garlic, onion powder, salt, cooked carrots, and mushrooms and mash the veggies with a fork. Add the breadcrumbs and stir to combine. Make 4 patties out of the mixture. Put the patties in the fryer basket, giving each patty plenty of room. AirFry for 5 minutes, flip and spray with oil, then air fry for 5-7 more minutes. Serve on buns. enjoy!

968. Roasted Squash with Goat Cheese
INGREDIENTS (2 Servings)

1 lb butternut squash, cut into wedges

½ tsp dried rosemary

2 tbsp olive oil

1 tbsp maple syrup

1 cup goat cheese, crumbled

Salt to season

DIRECTIONS (Prep + Cook Time: 30 minutes)

Preheat air fryer to 350 F. Brush the squash with olive oil and season with salt and rosemary. Place in the frying basket and Bake for 20 minutes, flipping once halfway through. Top with goat cheese and drizzle with maple syrup. Serve warm. enjoy!

969. Nutty Pumpkin with Blue Cheese
INGREDIENTS (2 Servings)

½ small pumpkin, chopped

2 oz blue cheese, crumbled

2 tbsp pine nuts, toasted

1 tbsp olive oil

½ cup baby spinach, packed

1 spring onion, sliced

2 radishes, thinly sliced

1 tsp white wine vinegar

DIRECTIONS (Prep + Cook Time: 30 minutes)

Preheat air fryer to 390 F. Place the pumpkin on a baking dish and drizzle with the olive oil; toss well. Bake in the air fryer for 20 minutes, shaking once. Remove to a serving bowl. Add in baby spinach, radishes, and spring onion; drizzle with vinegar. Top with blue cheese and pine nuts to serve warm. enjoy!

970. Indian Aloo Tikki
INGREDIENTS (2 Servings)

4 boiled potatoes, shredded

3 tbsp lemon juice

1 roasted bell pepper, chopped

Salt and black pepper to taste

2 onions, chopped

¼ cup fennel, chopped

5 tbsp flour

2 tbsp ginger-garlic paste

1 tbsp mint leaves, chopped

1 tbsp fresh cilantro, chopped

DIRECTIONS (Prep + Cook Time: 30 minutes)

Preheat your air fryer to 360 F. In a bowl, mix cilantro, mint, fennel, ginger-garlic paste, flour, salt, and lemon juice. Add in potatoes, bell pepper, and onions, and mix to combine. Make the mixture into balls and flatten them to form patties. Place into the greased frying basket and Bake for 15 minutes, flipping once. Serve with mint chutney. enjoy!

971. Garlicky Vegetable Spread
INGREDIENTS (6 Servings)

1 lb green peppers

1 lb tomatoes

1 medium onion

3 tbsp olive oil

½ tbsp salt

4 galic cloves, peeled

DIRECTIONS (Prep + Cook Time: 20 minutes)

Preheat air fryer to 360 F. Place green peppers, tomatoes, and onion in the greased frying basket and Bake for 5 minutes, flip, and cook for 10 more minutes. Remove and peel the skin. Place the vegetables in a blender and add the garlic, olive oil, and salt and pulse until smooth. Serve. enjoy!

972. Root Vegetable Medley
INGREDIENTS (4 Servings)

8 shallots, halved

2 carrots, sliced

1 turnip, cut into chunks

1 rutabaga, cut into chunks

2 potatoes, cut into chunks

1 beet, cut into chunks

Salt and black pepper to taste

2 tbsp fresh thyme, chopped

2 tbsp olive oil

2 tbsp tomato pesto

DIRECTIONS (Prep + Cook Time: 30 minutes)

Preheat air fryer to 400 F. In a bowl, combine all the root vegetables, salt, pepper, and olive oil. Toss to coat and transfer to the frying basket. AirFry for 10 minutes, then shake and continue cooking for another 10 minutes. Combine the pesto with 2 tbsp of water and drizzle over the vegetables, sprinkle with thyme, and serve enjoy!

973. Crispy Fried Tofu
INGREDIENTS (4 Servings)

14 oz firm tofu, cut into ½-inch thick strips

2 tbsp olive oil

½ cup flour

½ cup crushed cornflakes

Salt and black pepper to taste

DIRECTIONS (Prep + Cook Time: 20 minutes)

On a plate, mix flour, cornflakes, salt, and black pepper. Dip each tofu strip into the mixture to coat, brush with oil, and arrange them on the frying basket. Bake for 14 minutes at 360 F, turning once. enjoy!

974. Cashew & Chickpea Balls
INGREDIENTS (4 Servings)

2 tbsp olive oil

2 tbsp soy sauce

1 tbsp flax meal

2 cups cooked chickpeas

½ cup sweet onions, chopped

½ cup carrots, grated

½ cup cashews, roasted Juice of 1 lemon

½ tsp turmeric

1 tsp cumin

1 tsp garlic powder

1 cup rolled oats

DIRECTIONS (Prep + Cook Time: 30 minutes) Combine olive oil, sweet onions, and carrots in a baking dish and Bake in the air fryer for 6 minutes at 350 F. Ground the oats and cashews in a food processor. Remove to a large bowl. Process the chickpeas with the lemon juice and soy sauce in the food processor until smooth. Add them to the cashew bowl as well. Add onions and carrots to the same bowl. Stir in the remaining ingredients, and mix well. Make meatballs out of the mixture. Place the balls in the greased frying basket and Bake for 12 minutes to 370 F, shaking once, until nice and crispy. Serve warm. enjoy!

975. Fava Bean Falafel with Tzatziki
INGREDIENTS (4 Servings)

2 cups cooked fava beans

½ cup flour

2 tbsp fresh parsley, chopped

Juice of 1 lemon

2 garlic cloves, chopped

1 onion, chopped

½ tsp ground cumin

1 cup tzatziki sauce

4 pita wraps, warm

Salt and black pepper to taste

DIRECTIONS (Prep + Cook Time: 25 minutes) In a blender, add chickpeas, flour, parsley, lemon juice, garlic, onion, cumin, salt, and pepper and blend until well-combined but not too battery; there should be some lumps. Shape the mixture into balls. Press them with hands, making sure they are still around. Spray with olive oil and arrange on a paper-lined air fryer basket. AirFry for 14 minutes at 360 F, turning once halfway through until crunchy and golden. Serve in the pita wraps drizzled with tzatziki sauce. enjoy!

976. Halloumi Cheese with Veggies
INGREDIENTS (4 Servings)

6 oz halloumi cheese, cubed

2 zucchinis, cut into even chunks

1 carrot, cut into chunks

1 eggplant, peeled, cut into chunks

2 tsp olive oil

1 tsp dried mixed herbs

Salt and black pepper to taste

DIRECTIONS (Prep + Cook Time: 15 minutes)

In a bowl, add halloumi, zucchinis, carrot, eggplant, olive oil, herbs, salt, and pepper. Transfer to the frying basket and AirFry for 14 minutes at 340 F, shaking once. Top with mixed herbs to serve. enjoy!

977. Eggplant Gratin with Mozzarella Crust
INGREDIENTS (2 Servings)

- 1 cup eggplants, cubed
- ¼ cup red peppers, chopped
- ¼ cup green peppers, chopped
- ¼ cup onion, chopped
- ⅓ cup tomatoes, chopped
- 1 garlic clove, minced
- 1 tbsp sliced pimiento-stuffed olives
- 1 tsp capers
- ¼ tsp dried basil
- ¼ tsp dried marjoram
- Salt and black pepper to taste
- ¼ cup mozzarella cheese, grated
- 1 tbsp breadcrumbs

DIRECTIONS (Prep + Cook Time: 30 minutes) Preheat air fryer to 300 F. In a bowl, add eggplants, green peppers, red peppers, onion, tomatoes, olives, garlic, basil, marjoram, capers, salt, and pepper; mix well. Spoon the eggplant mixture into a greased baking dish and level it using the vessel. Sprinkle mozzarella cheese on top and cover with breadcrumbs. Place the dish in the air fryer and Bake for 15-20 minutes. Serve warm. enjoy!

978. Quinoa & Veggie Stuffed Peppers
INGREDIENTS (2 Servings)

- 1 cup cooked quinoa
- 2 red bell peppers, cored and cleaned
- ½ onion, diced
- ½ cup tomatoes, diced
- ¼ tsp smoked paprika
- Salt and black pepper to taste
- 1 tsp olive oil
- ¼ tsp basil

DIRECTIONS (Prep + Cook Time: 30 minutes) Preheat air fryer to 350 F. In a bowl, combine quinoa, onion, basil, diced tomatoes, paprika, salt, and pepper and stir. Stuff the peppers with the filling and brush them with olive oil. Place the peppers in a greased baking dish and Bake in the fryer for 12 minutes. Serve warm enjoy!

979. Poblano & Tomato Stuffed Squash
INGREDIENTS (4 Servings)

- 1 butternut squash
- 6 grape tomatoes, halved
- 1 poblano pepper, cut into strips
- ¼ cup mozzarella cheese, grated
- 2 tsp olive oil
- Salt and black pepper to taste

DIRECTIONS (Prep + Cook Time: 30 minutes) Preheat air fryer to 350 F. Trim the ends and cut the squash lengthwise. You will only need one half for this recipe. Scoop the flesh out to make room for the filling. Brush the squash with olive oil. Place in the air fryer and Bake for 15 minutes. Combine the remaining olive oil with tomatoes and poblano pepper, season with salt and pepper. Fill the squash half with the mixture and Bake for 12 more minutes. Top with mozzarella cheese and cook further for 3 minutes until the cheese melts. enjoy!

980. Chickpea & Spinach Casserole
INGREDIENTS (4 Servings)

- 2 tbsp olive oil
- 1 onion, chopped
- Salt and black pepper to taste
- 2 garlic cloves, minced
- 1 can coconut milk
- 1 tbsp ginger, minced
- 1 lb spinach
- ½ cup dried tomatoes, chopped
- 1 (14-oz) can chickpeas, drained
- 1 chili pepper, minced

DIRECTIONS (Prep + Cook Time: 20 minutes)

Heat olive oil in a saucepan over medium heat and sauté onion, garlic, chili pepper, ginger, salt, and pepper for 3 minutes. Add in spinach and stir for 3-4 minutes until wilted. Transfer to a baking dish. Mix in the remaining ingredients. Preheat air fryer to 370 F. Place the baking dish in the air fryer. Bake for 15 minutes until golden on top. Serve warm enjoy!

981. Jalapeño & Bean Tacos
INGREDIENTS (4 Servings)

4 soft taco shells, warm	1 fresh jalapeño pepper, chopped	½ tsp cayenne pepper
½ cup kidney beans, drained	2 tbsp fresh cilantro, chopped	Salt and black pepper to taste
½ cup black beans, drained	1 cup corn kernels	1 cup mozzarella cheese, grated
1 tbsp tomato puree	½ tsp cumin	Guacamole to serve

DIRECTIONS (Prep + Cook Time: 25 minutes)

In a bowl, add kidney and black beans, tomato puree, jalapeño, cilantro, corn, cumin, cayenne, salt, and pepper and stir. Fill taco shells with the bean mixture and sprinkle with mozzarella. Lay the tacos on the greased frying basket and Bake for 14 minutes at 360 F, turning once. Serve with guacamole. enjoy!

982. Southern-Style Corn Cakes
INGREDIENTS (4-6 Servings)

2 cups corn kernels, canned, drained	¼ cup parsley, chopped	Salt and black pepper to taste
2 eggs, lightly beaten	1 cup flour	
⅓ cup green onions, finely chopped	½ tsp baking powder	

DIRECTIONS (Prep + Cook Time:25 minutes)

In a bowl, add corn kernels, eggs, parsley, and green onions, and season with salt and pepper; mix well. Sift flour and baking powder into the bowl and stir. Line the frying basket with parchment paper and spoon batter dollops, making sure they are separated by at least one inch. Bake for 10 minutes at 400 F, turning once halfway through. Serve with sour cream. enjoy!

Desserts

983. French Sour Cherry Clafoutis
INGREDIENTS (4 Servings)

½ lb sour cherries, pitted

½ cup all-purpose flour

¼ tsp salt 2 tbsp sugar

2 eggs + 2 yolks

1 tsp vanilla extract

1 tbsp lemon zest

2 tbsp butter, melted

1 ¼ cups milk Icing sugar to dust

DIRECTIONS (Prep + Cook Time: 30 minutes + cooling time)

Preheat air fryer to 380 F. In a bowl, mix the flour, sugar, and salt. Whisk in the eggs, egg yolks, vanilla extract, lemon zest, and melted butter until creamy. Gradually, add in the milk and stir until bubbly. Spread the sour cherries on a greased baking dish and pour over the batter. Bake in the air fryer for 25-30 minutes until a lovely golden crust is formed. Dust the top with icing sugar and serve warm.Enjoy!

984. Classic Crème Brûlée
INGREDIENTS (4 Servings)

1 cup whipped cream

1 cup milk

2 vanilla pods

10 egg yolks

4 tbsp sugar + extra for topping

DIRECTIONS (Prep + Cook Time: 30 minutes)

In a pan, add the milk and whipped cream. Cut the vanilla pods open and scrape the seeds into the pan along with the pods. Place the pan over medium heat on a stovetop until almost boiled, stirring regularly. Turn off the heat. Beat egg yolks in a bowl and whisk in sugar, but not too bubbly. Remove the vanilla pods from the milk mixture; pour the mixture onto the egg mixture, stirring constantly. Let rest for 15 minutes. Fill 4 ramekins with the mixture and cover tightly with foil. Place them in the frying basket and Bake at 170 F for 25 minutes. Remove the ramekins and discard the foil; let cool at room temperature, then refrigerate for 1 hour. Sprinkle the remaining sugar over the crème brûlée and use a torch to caramelize the top. Serve immediately or chilled. Enjoy!

985. Apple Caramel Relish
INGREDIENTS (4 Servings)

1 vanilla box cake mix

2 apples, peeled, sliced

3 oz butter, melted

½ cup brown sugar

1 tsp cinnamon

½ cup flour

1 cup caramel sauce

DIRECTIONS (Prep + Cook Time: 30 minutes)

Line a cake tin with baking paper. In a bowl, mix butter, sugar, cinnamon, and flour until you obtain a crumbly texture. Prepare the cake mix according to the instructions (no baking). Pour the obtained batter into the tin and arrange the apple slices on top. Spoon the caramel over the apples and pour the crumbly flour mixture over the sauce. Bake in the preheated air fryer for 18-20 minutes at 360 F. Check halfway through to avoid overcooking. Serve chilled. Enjoy!

986. White Chocolate Pudding
INGREDIENTS (2 Servings)

3 oz white chocolate

4 egg whites

2 egg yolks, at room temperature

¼ cup sugar

1 tbsp melted butter

1 tbsp cold butter

¼ tsp vanilla extract

1 ½ tbsp flour

DIRECTIONS (Prep + Cook Time: 30 minutes) Coat two ramekins with melted butter. Swirl in 2 tbsp of sugar to coat the butter. Melt the cold butter with the chocolate in a microwave; set aside. In another bowl, beat the egg yolks vigorously. Add the vanilla and the remaining sugar; beat to incorporate fully. Mix in the melted chocolate. Add the flour and mix until there are no lumps. Preheat air fryer to 330 F. Whisk the egg whites in another bowl until the mixture holds stiff peaks. Fold in the chocolate mixture and divide the mixture between the ramekins. Place them in the frying basket, and Bake for 14-16 minutes, until cooked through. Enjoy!

987. Madrid-Style Almond Meringues
INGREDIENTS (4 Servings)

8 egg whites	⅓ cups sugar	½ tsp vanilla extract
½ tsp almond extract 1	2 tsp lemon juice 1	Melted dark chocolate, to drizzle

DIRECTIONS (Prep + Cook Time: 30 minutes)

In a bowl, beat egg whites and lemon juice with an electric mixer until foamy. Slowly beat in the sugar until thoroughly combined. Add almond and vanilla extracts. Beat until stiff peaks form and glossy. Line a baking tray with parchment paper. Fill a piping bag with the meringue mixture and pipe as many mounds on the baking sheet as you can, leaving 2-inch spaces between each mound. Place the baking tray in the frying basket and Bake at 250 F for 5 minutes. Reduce the temperature to 220 F and bake for 15 more minutes. Then, reduce the temperature to 190 F and cook for 13-15 more minutes. Let the meringues cool. Drizzle with dark chocolate and serve. Enjoy!

988. Cinnamon Grilled Pineapples
INGREDIENTS (2 Servings)

1 tsp cinnamon	½ cup brown sugar	1 tbsp honey
5 pineapple slices	1 tbsp mint, chopped	

DIRECTIONS (Prep + Cook Time: 30 minutes)

Preheat air fryer to 340 F. In a small bowl, mix sugar and cinnamon. Drizzle the sugar mixture over pineapple slices. Place them in the greased frying basket and Bake for 5 minutes. Flip the pineapples and cook for 5 more minutes. Drizzle with honey and sprinkle with fresh mint. Enjoy!

989. Dark Rum Pear Pie
INGREDIENTS (4 Servings)

1 cup flour	3 tbsp butter, softened	2 pears, sliced
5 tbsp sugar	1 tbsp dark spiced rum	

DIRECTIONS (Prep + Cook Time: 30 minutes)

Preheat air fryer to 370 F. In a bowl, place 3 tbsp of the sugar, butter, and flour and mix to form a batter. Roll out the butter on a floured surface and transfer to the greased baking dish. Arrange the pears slices on top and sprinkle with sugar and dark rum. Bake in the air fryer for 20 minutes. Serve cooled. Enjoy!

990. Tropical Pineapple Fritters
INGREDIENTS (5 Servings)

1 ½ cups flour	3 tbsp sesame seeds	1 tsp baking powder
1 pineapple, sliced into rings	2 eggs, beaten	½ tbsp sugar

DIRECTIONS (Prep + Cook Time: 30 minutes)

Preheat air fryer to 350 F. In a bowl, mix salt, sesame seeds, flour, baking powder, eggs, sugar, and 1 cup water. Dip sliced pineapple in the flour mixture and arrange them on the greased frying basket. AirFryer for 15 minutes, turning once. Enjoy!

991. Chocolate Soufflé
INGREDIENTS (2 Servings)

2 eggs, whites and yolks separated	2 tbsp flour	3 oz chocolate, melted
¼ cup butter, melted	3 tbsp sugar	½ tsp vanilla extract

DIRECTIONS (Prep + Cook Time: 30 minutes)

Preheat air fryer to 320 F. In a bowl, beat the yolks along with sugar and vanilla extract until creamy. Stir in butter, chocolate, and flour. In another bowl, whisk the whites until stiff peak forms. Working in batches, gently combine the egg whites with the chocolate mixture. Divide the batter between two greased ramekins. Bake in the air fryer for 14 minutes. Serve warm or at room temperature. Enjoy!

992. Apricot & Lemon Flapjacks
INGREDIENTS (4 Servings)

- ¼ cup butter
- 2 tbsp maple syrup
- 2 tbsp pure cane sugar
- 1 ¼ cups rolled oats
- 2 tsp lemon zest
- 3 apricots, stoned and sliced

DIRECTIONS (Prep + Cook Time: 30 minutes)

Preheat air fryer to 350 F. Line a baking dish with parchment paper. Melt the butter in a skillet over medium heat and stir in pure cane sugar and maple syrup until the sugar dissolves, about 2 minutes. Mix in the remaining ingredients and transfer to the baking dish. Bake for 18-20 minutes or until golden. Let cool for a few minutes before cutting into flapjacks Enjoy!

993. Molten Lava Cake
INGREDIENTS (4 Servings)

- 2 tbsp butter, melted
- 3 ½ tbsp sugar
- 1 ½ tbsp self-rising flour
- 3 ½ oz dark chocolate, melted
- 2 eggs

DIRECTIONS (Prep + Cook Time: 30 minutes)

Preheat air fryer to 360 F. In a bowl, beat the eggs and sugar until frothy. Stir in butter and chocolate and gently fold in the flour. Divide the mixture between 4 greased ramekins and Bake in the air fryer for 18 minutes. Let cool for a few minutes before inverting the lava cakes onto serving plates. Enjoy!

994. Blueberry Muffins
INGREDIENTS (6 Servings)

- 1 ½ cups flour
- ½ tsp salt
- ½ cup sugar
- ¼ cup vegetable oil
- 2 tsp vanilla extract
- 1 cup fresh blueberries
- 1 egg
- 2 tsp baking powder

DIRECTIONS (Prep + Cook Time: 30 minutes)

Preheat air fryer to 340 F. In a bowl, combine flour, salt, and baking powder. In another bowl, add vegetable oil, vanilla extract, and egg and whisk the mixture until fully incorporated. Combine the wet and dry ingredients; gently fold in the blueberries. Divide the mixture between a greased 6-hole muffin tray. Bake in the air fryer for 10-12 minutes until set and golden. Serve cooled. Enjoy!

995. Spanish Churros con Chocolate
INGREDIENTS (4 Servings)

- 1 tsp vanilla extract
- ¼ cup butter
- ½ cup water
- 1 pinch of salt
- ½ cup all-purpose flour
- 2 eggs
- ¼ cup white sugar
- ½ tsp ground cinnamon
- 4 oz dark chocolate chips
- ¼ cup milk

DIRECTIONS (Prep + Cook Time: 30 minutes)

In a skillet over medium heat, pour water, sugar, butter, and a pinch of salt; bring to a boil. Stir in the flour until the mixture is thick, about 3 minutes. Remove to a bowl, mix in vanilla, and let cool slightly. Preheat air fryer to 360 F. Gently stir in the eggs, one at a time, until glossy and smooth. Place the dough in a piping bag and grease the frying basket with cooking spray. Pipe in the batter into strips. Place in the air fryer and AirFry for 8-10 minutes until golden. Mix the chocolate with cinnamon in a heatproof bowl and microwave for 60-90 seconds until the chocolate is melted. Stir in milk until smooth. Serve the churros with hot chocolate. Enjoy!

996. Mock Cherry Pie
INGREDIENTS (4-6 Servings)

2 store-bought pie crusts

21 oz cherry pie filling

1 egg yolk, beaten

DIRECTIONS (Prep + Cook Time: 30 minutes) (Prep + Cook Time: 30 minutes) Preheat air fryer to 340 F. Place one pie crust in a greased pie pan. Poke holes into the crust and Bake for 5 minutes in the air fryer. Remove the pan and spread the cherry pie filling on top. Cut the other crust into strips and make a lattice over the filling. Brush the lattice with the yolk and Bake the pie in the fryer for 15-20 minutes until golden. If you fancy, dust with powdered sugar and serve chilled. Enjoy!

---

997. Vanilla & Chocolate Brownies
INGREDIENTS (10 Servings)

6 oz dark chocolate

3 eggs

¼ cup cocoa powder

6 oz butter

2 tsp vanilla extract

1 cup walnuts, chopped

¾ cup white sugar

¾ cup flour

1 cup white chocolate chips

DIRECTIONS (Prep + Cook Time: 30 minutes)

Line a baking dish with baking paper. Place a saucepan over low heat and melt the dark chocolate and butter, stirring constantly until a smooth mixture is obtained; let cool slightly. In a bowl, whisk eggs, sugar, and vanilla. Sift flour and cocoa and stir in the egg mixture to combine. Sprinkle the walnuts over and add white chocolate chips and melted dark chocolate into the batter; stir well. Spread the batter onto the dish and Bake in the preheated air fryer for 20 minutes at 340 F. Enjoy!

---

998. Orange Sponge Cake
INGREDIENTS (4 Servings)

1 cup sugar

1 tsp vanilla extract

4 tbsp superfine sugar

1 cup self-rising flour

Zest and juice from 1 orange

½ cup ground walnuts

3 eggs

2 egg whites

DIRECTIONS (Prep + Cook Time: 30 minutes)

Preheat air fryer to 360 F. In a bowl, beat sugar, flour, eggs, vanilla, and half of the orange zest with an electric mixer until creamy and fluffy, about 8 minutes. Transfer half of the batter into a greased and floured cake pan and Bake in the air fryer for 15 minutes. Repeat the process for the remaining batter. Meanwhile, prepare the frosting by beating egg whites, orange juice, and superfine sugar together. Spread half of the frosting mixture on top of one cooled cake. Top with the other cake and spread the remaining frosting all over. Top with walnuts, slice, and serve. Enjoy!

---

999. Chocolate & Raspberry Cake
INGREDIENTS (6 Servings)

1 cup flour

¼ cup brown sugar

2 eggs, beaten

⅓ cup cocoa powder

½ cup butter, melted

1 cup raspberries

1 tsp baking powder

1 tsp vanilla extract

1 cup chocolate chips

½ cup white sugar

⅔ cup milk

DIRECTIONS (Prep + Cook Time: 30 minutes) Line a cake tin with baking paper. In a bowl, sift flour, cocoa powder, and baking powder. In another bowl, whisk butter, white and brown sugar, vanilla, and milk until creamy. Mix in the eggs. Pour the wet ingredients into the dry ones, and fold to combine. Add in the raspberries and chocolate chips. Pour the batter into the lined tin and Bake in the air fryer for 20 minutes at 350 F. Serve cooled. Enjoy!

1000. Lemon-Glazed Cupcakes
INGREDIENTS (6 Servings)

- 1 cup flour
- ½ cup sugar
- 1 egg
- 1 tsp lemon zest
- ¾ tsp baking powder
- 2 tbsp vegetable oil
- ½ cup milk
- ½ tsp vanilla extract
- ½ cup powdered sugar
- 2 tsp lemon juice

DIRECTIONS (Prep + Cook Time: 30 minutes)

Preheat air fryer to 360 F. In a bowl, combine flour, sugar, lemon zest, and baking powder. In another bowl, whisk together egg, vegetable oil, milk, and vanilla extract. Gently combine the two mixtures to obtain a smooth batter. Divide the batter between greased muffin tins or 6-hole muffin tray. Place the muffin tins or tray in the fryer and Bake for 12-14 minutes. Remove muffins and let cool. Whisk powdered sugar with lemon juice until smooth. Pour the glaze on top of the muffins and serve. Enjoy!

1001. Peach Almond Flour Cake
INGREDIENTS (4 Servings)

- 3 tbsp butter, melted
- 1 cup peaches, chopped
- 3 tbsp sugar
- 1 cup almond flour
- 1 cup heavy cream
- 1 tsp vanilla extract
- 2 eggs, whisked
- 1 tsp baking soda

DIRECTIONS (Prep + Cook Time: 30 minutes) Preheat air fryer to 360 F. In a bowl, mix all the ingredients and stir well. Pour the mixture into a greased baking dish and insert it in the air fryer basket. Bake for 25 minutes until golden. Cool, slice, and serve. Enjoy!

1002. Air Fried Donuts
INGREDIENTS (4 Servings)

- 1 cup self-rising flour
- 1 tsp baking powder
- ½ cup milk
- 2 ½ tbsp butter, softened
- 1 egg, beaten
- 4 tbsp brown sugar

DIRECTIONS (Prep + Cook Time: 30 minutes)

Preheat air fryer to 350 F. In a bowl, whisk butter with brown sugar until smooth. Mix in eggs and milk to combine. In another bowl, combine flour with baking powder. Fold the flour into the butter mixture. Form donut shapes and cut off the center with cookie cutters. Arrange on a lined baking sheet and Bake in the fryer for 15 minutes. Serve with whipped cream or drizzled with maple syrup. Enjoy!

1003. Mom's Lemon Curd
INGREDIENTS (2 Servings)

- 3 tbsp butter
- 3 tbsp sugar
- 1 egg
- 1 egg yolk
- ¾ lemon, juiced

DIRECTIONS (Prep + Cook Time: 30 minutes) Add sugar and butter to a medium-size ramekin and beat evenly. Slowly whisk in egg and egg yolk until fresh yellow color is obtained. Mix in the lemon juice. Place the ramekin in the preheated air fryer and Bake at 220 F for 6 minutes. Increase the temperature to 320 F and cook for 13-15 minutes. Remove the ramekin and use a spoon to check for any lumps. Serve chilled. Enjoy!

1004. Snickerdoodle Poppers
INGREDIENTS (4 Servings)

- 1 box instant vanilla
- Jell-O mix 1 can
- Pillsbury Grands Flaky Layers Biscuits
- 1 ½ cups cinnamon sugar
- 2 tbsp butter, melted

DIRECTIONS (Prep + Cook Time: 30 minutes) Preheat air fryer to 340 F. Unroll the flaky biscuits and cut them into fourths. Roll each ¼ into a ball. Arrange the balls on a paper-lined baking sheet and Bake in the air fryer for 7 minutes or until golden. Prepare the Jell-O following the package's instructions. Using an injector, insert some of the vanilla pudding into each ball. Brush the balls with melted butter and then coat with cinnamon sugar. Enjoy!

1005. Chocolate & Peanut Butter Fondants
INGREDIENTS (4 Servings)

¾ cup dark chocolate	½ cup sugar, divided	1 tsp salt
½ cup peanut butter, crunchy	4 eggs, room temperature	¼ cup water
2 tbsp butter	⅛ cup flour, sieved	

DIRECTIONS (Prep + Cook Time: 30 minutes)

Make the praline by adding ¼ cup of sugar, 1 tsp of salt, and water in a saucepan over low heat. Stir and bring to a boil. Simmer until the mixture reduces by half, about 5 minutes. Spread on a baking tray to let cool and harden. Then break into pieces and set aside the pralines. Preheat air fryer to 300 F. Place a pot of water over medium heat and place a heatproof bowl on top. Add in chocolate, butter, and peanut butter. Stir continuously until fully melted, combined, and smooth. Remove the bowl, and let cool slightly. Whisk in the eggs, add flour and remaining sugar; mix well. Grease 4 small loaf pans with cooking spray and divide the chocolate mixture between them. Place them in the air fryer and Bake for 7 minutes. Remove and serve with a piece of praline. Enjoy!

1006. Awesome Chocolate Fudge
INGREDIENTS (4-6 Servings)

1 cup sugar	¼ cup milk	2 eggs
1 cup plain flour	1 tsp vanilla extract	½ cup butter, softened
1 tbsp honey	1 tbsp cocoa powder	1 orange, juice and zest

Icing:

1 oz butter, melted	1 tbsp milk
4 oz powdered sugar	2 tsp honey

DIRECTIONS (Prep + Cook Time: 35 minutes)

Preheat air fryer to 350 F. In a bowl, mix sugar, flour, orange zest, and cocoa powder. In another bowl, beat eggs, butter, honey, milk, vanilla, and orange juice until creamy. Combine the two mixtures. Transfer the batter to a greased cake pan and Bake in the air fryer for 23-26 minutes, until set and golden. Remove and let cool. Whisk together all icing ingredients in a bowl. When the cake is chilled, top with the icing, slice, and serve. Enjoy!

1007. Easy Lemony Cheesecake
INGREDIENTS (8 Servings)

8 oz graham crackers, crushed	3 eggs	Zest of 2 lemons
4 oz butter, melted	3 tbsp sugar	
16 oz plain cream cheese	1 tbsp vanilla extract	

DIRECTIONS (Prep + Cook Time: 40 minutes) Line a cake tin that fits in your air fryer with baking paper. Mix together the crackers and butter and press at the bottom of the tin. In a bowl, add cream cheese, eggs, sugar, vanilla, and lemon zest and beat with a hand mixer until well combined and smooth. Pour the mixture on top of the cracker's base. Bake in the air fryer for 20 minutes at 350 F. Regularly check to ensure it's set but still a bit wobbly. Let cool, then refrigerate overnight. Serve at room temperature or chilled. Enjoy!

1008. Oat & Walnut Granola
INGREDIENTS (4 Servings)

¼ cup walnuts, chopped	3 tbsp canola oil	2 tbsp muscovado sugar
½ cup oats	½ cup maple syrup	1 cup fresh blueberries

DIRECTIONS (Prep + Cook Time: 30 minutes)

Preheat air fryer to 380 F. In a bowl, place oil, maple syrup, muscovado sugar, and vanilla and mix. Coat in the oats. Spread out the mixture on a greased baking tray and Bake for 20-25 minutes. Sprinkle with blueberries and bake for another 3 minutes. Leave to cool before breaking up and storing in a jar. Enjoy!

1009. Soft Buttermilk Biscuits
INGREDIENTS (10 Servings)

1 cup all-purpose flour

½ tsp baking powder

1 tsp sugar

¾ tsp salt

4 tbsp butter, cubed

¾ cup buttermilk

DIRECTIONS (Prep + Cook Time: 30 minutes) Preheat air fryer to 360 F. In a bowl, whisk flour, baking powder, sugar, and salt until well combined. Add in butter and rub it into the flour mixture until crumbed. Stir in the buttermilk until a dough is formed. Flour a flat and dry surface and roll out the dough until half-inch thick. Cut out 10 rounds with a small cookie cutter. Arrange the biscuits on a greased baking tray. Working in batches, Bake in the air fryer for 16-18 minutes. Let cool for a few minutes before serving. Enjoy!

1010. Easy Chocolate Squares
INGREDIENTS (2 Servings)

1 whole egg, beaten

2 tbsp white sugar

¼ cup cocoa powder

¼ cup chocolate chips

⅓ cup flour 2 tbsp olive oil

DIRECTIONS (Prep + Cook Time: 30 minutes) Preheat air fryer to 330 F. In a bowl, mix the egg, sugar, and olive oil until creamy. In another bowl, mix the cocoa powder and flour. Add the flour mixture to the egg mixture and stir until fully incorporated. Pour the mixture into a greased baking dish. Sprinkle chocolate chips on top and Bake in the fryer for 20 minutes. Let cool, slice into squares, and serve. Enjoy!

1011. White Chocolate Cookies
INGREDIENTS (4 Servings)

1 cup self-rising flour

1 tbsp honey

½ cup butter, softened

4 tbsp brown sugar

1 ½ tbsp milk

1 egg 2 oz white chocolate chips

1 tsp baking soda

DIRECTIONS (Prep + Cook Time: 30 minutes) Preheat air fryer to 350 F. In a bowl, beat butter and sugar until fluffy. Mix in honey, egg, and milk. In a separate bowl, mix flour and baking soda and gradually add to the butter while stirring constantly. Gently fold in the chocolate cookies. Drop spoonfuls of the mixture onto a greased cookie sheet and press down slightly to flatten. Bake in the air fryer for 18 minutes. Remove to a wire rack to cool completely before serving. Enjoy!

1012. Effortless Pecan Pie
INGREDIENTS (4 Servings)

¾ cup maple syrup

2 tbsp almond butter

1 (8-inch) pie dough

2 eggs

2 tbsp brown sugar

¾ tsp vanilla extract

¼ tsp ground nutmeg

½ cup pecans, chopped

½ tsp cinnamon

1 tbsp butter, melted

DIRECTIONS (Prep.40 minutes + Cook Time: 30 minutes) Preheat air fryer to 360 F. Coat the pecans with melted butter. Place them in the frying basket and Bake for 8-10 minutes, shaking once. Place the pie crust into a 7-inch round pie pan and pour the pecans over. Whisk together all the remaining ingredients in a bowl. Spread the maple syrup mixture over the pecans. Set the air fryer to 320 F and Bake the pie for 25 minutes. Serve chilled. Enjoy!

1013. Pineapple Cake
INGREDIENTS (4 Servings)

2 oz dark chocolate, grated

7 oz pineapple chunks

2 tbsp milk

8 oz self-rising flour

½ cup pineapple juice

½ cup sugar

4 oz butter

1 egg

DIRECTIONS (Prep + Cook Time: 30 minutes) Preheat air fryer to 350 F. Place the butter and flour into a bowl and rub the mixture with your fingers until crumbed. Stir in pineapple chunks, sugar, chocolate, and pineapple juice. Beat eggs and milk separately and add to the batter. Transfer the batter to a greased cake pan and Bake in the air fryer for 25 minutes. Let cool for a few minutes before serving. Enjoy!

1014. Simple Coffee Cake
INGREDIENTS (2 Servings)

¼ cup butter	1 egg ¼ cup sugar	Powdered sugar, for icing
½ tsp instant coffee	¼ cup flour	
1 tbsp black coffee, brewed	1 tsp cocoa powder	

DIRECTIONS (Prep + Cook Time: 30 minutes) Preheat air fryer to 320 F. In a bowl, beat sugar and egg until creamy. Mix in cocoa, instant and black coffees; stir in flour. Transfer the batter to a greased baking dish. Bake in the air fryer for 15 minutes. Let cool for at least 1 hour at room temperature. Dust with powdered sugar, slice and serve.

1015. Yummy Moon Pie
INGREDIENTS (4 Servings)

4 graham cracker sheets, snapped in half	8 large marshmallows	8 squares each of dark, milk, and white chocolate

DIRECTIONS (Prep + Cook Time: 30 minutes) Arrange the crackers on a cutting board. Put 2 marshmallows onto half of the graham cracker halves. Place 2 squares of chocolate on top of the crackers with marshmallows. Put the remaining crackers on top to create 4 sandwiches. Wrap each one in baking paper, so it resembles a parcel. Bake in the preheated air fryer for 5 minutes at 340 F. Serve at room temperature or chilled. Enjoy!

1016. Honey & Cherry Rice
INGREDIENTS (4 Servings)

1 cup long-grain rice	½ cup cherries, chopped	1 tsp vanilla extract
2 cups milk	3 tbsp honey	1/3 cup heavy cream

DIRECTIONS (Prep + Cook Time: 30 minutes) Preheat air fryer to 360 F. In a baking dish, combine all the ingredients, except for the cherries. Place the dish in the air fryer and Bake for 20 minutes. Spoon into glass cups and top with cherries to serve. Enjoy!

1017. No Flour Lime Cupcakes
INGREDIENTS (4 Servings)

2 eggs +	1 cup yogurt	1 tsp vanilla extract
1 egg yolk	¼ cup superfine sugar	
Juice and zest of 1 lime	8 oz cream cheese	

DIRECTIONS (Prep + Cook Time: 30 minutes) Preheat air fryer to 300 F. In a bowl, mix yogurt and cream cheese until uniform. In another bowl, beat eggs, egg yolk, sugar, vanilla, lime juice, and zest. Gently fold the in the cheese mixture. Divide the batter between greased muffin tins. Bake in the fryer for 15 minutes until golden. Serve chilled.

1018. Cheat Apple Pie
INGREDIENTS (4 Servings)

2 apples, diced	1 tbsp brown sugar	2 large puff pastry sheets
2 tbsp butter, melted	1 tsp cinnamon	¼ tsp salt
2 tbsp white sugar	1 egg, beaten	

DIRECTIONS (Prep + Cook Time: 30 minutes)

Whisk white sugar, brown sugar, cinnamon, salt, and butter. Place the apples in a greased baking dish and coat them with the mixture. Place the dish in the air fryer and Bake for 10 minutes at 350 F. Meanwhile, roll out the pastry on a floured flat surface and cut each sheet into 6 equal pieces. Divide the apple filling between the pieces. Brush the edges of the pastry squares with the egg. Fold the squares and seal the edges with a fork. Place on a lined baking sheet and Bake in the fryer at 350 F for 8 minutes. Flip over, increase the heat to 320 F, and cook for 2 more minutes. Serve chilled. Enjoy!

1019. Fruit Skewers
INGREDIENTS (2 Servings)

1 cup blueberries	1 mango, peeled and cut into cubes	2 kiwi fruit, peeled and quartered
1 banana, sliced	1 peach, cut into wedges	2 tbsp caramel sauce

DIRECTIONS (Prep + Cook Time: 30 minutes) (Prep + Cook Time: 15 minutes) Preheat air fryer to 340 F. Thread the fruit through your skewers. Transfer to the greased frying basket and AirFry for 6-8 minutes, turning once until the fruit caramelize slightly. Drizzle with the caramel sauce and serve. Enjoy!

1020. Homemade Chelsea Currant Buns
INGREDIENTS (4 Servings)

1/2 pound cake flour	A pinch of sea salt	4 tablespoons butter
1 teaspoon dry yeast	1/2 cup milk, warm	1/2 cup dried currants
2 tablespoons granulated sugar	1 egg, whisked	1 ounce icing sugar

DIRECTIONS (Prep + Cook Time: 50 minutes)

Mix the flour, yeast, sugar and salt in a bowl; add in milk, egg and 2 tablespoons of butter and mix to combine well. Add lukewarm water as necessary to form a smooth dough. Knead the dough until it is elastic; then, leave it in a warm place to rise for 30 minutes. Roll out your dough and spread the remaining 2 tablespoons of butter onto the dough; scatter dried currants over the dough. Cut into 8 equal slices and roll them up. Brush each bun with a nonstick cooking oil and transfer them to the Air Fryer cooking basket. Cook your buns at 330 degrees F for about 20 minutes, turning them over halfway through the cooking time. Dust with icing sugar before serving.

1021. Chocolate Mug Cake
INGREDIENTS (2 Servings)

1/2 cup self-rising flour	4 tablespoons coconut oil	A pinch of grated nutmeg
6 tablespoons brown sugar	4 tablespoons unsweetened cocoa powder	A pinch of salt
5 tablespoons coconut milk	2 eggs	

DIRECTIONS (Prep + Cook Time:10 minutes)

Mix all the ingredients together; divide the batter between two mugs. Place the mugs in the Air Fryer cooking basket and cook at 390 degrees F for about 10 minutes. Enjoy!

1022. Mini Apple and Cranberry Crisp Cakes
INGREDIENTS (3 Servings)

2 Bramley cooking apples, peeled, cored and chopped	1 tablespoon golden caster sugar	1/2 cup rolled oats
	1 teaspoon apple pie spice mix	1/3 cup brown bread crumbs
1/4 cup dried cranberries	A pinch of coarse salt	1/4 cup butter, diced
1 teaspoon fresh lemon juice		

DIRECTIONS (Prep + Cook Time: 40 minutes)

Divide the apples and cranberries between three lightly greased ramekins. Drizzle your fruits with lemon juice and sprinkle with caster sugar, spice mix and salt. Then, make the streusel by mixing the remaining ingredients in a bowl. Spread the streusel batter on top of the filling. Bake the mini crisp cakes in the preheated Air Fryer at 330 degrees F for 35 minutes or until they're a dark golden brown around the edges. Enjoy!

1023. Old-Fashioned Baked Pears
INGREDIENTS (2 Servings)

- 2 large pears, halved and cored
- 1 teaspoon lemon juice
- 2 teaspoons coconut oil
- 1/2 cup rolled oats
- 1/4 cup walnuts, chopped
- 1/4 cup brown sugar
- 1 teaspoon apple pie spice mix

DIRECTIONS (Prep + Cook Time:10 minutes) Drizzle the pear halves with lemon juice and coconut oil. In a mixing bowl, thoroughly combine the rolled oats, walnuts, brown sugar and apple pie spice mix. Cook in the preheated Air Fryer at 360 degrees for 8 minutes, checking them halfway through the cooking time. Dust with powdered sugar if desired. Enjoy!

1024. Honey-Drizzled Banana Fritters
INGREDIENTS (3 Servings)

- 3 ripe bananas, peeled
- 1 egg, whisked
- 1/4 cup almond flour
- 1/4 cup plain flour
- 1/2 teaspoon baking powder
- 1 teaspoon canola oil
- 1 tablespoon honey

DIRECTIONS (Prep + Cook Time:15 minutes) Mash your bananas in a bowl. Now, stir in the egg, almond flour, plain flour and baking powder. Drop spoonfuls of the batter into the preheated Air Fryer cooking basket. Brush the fritters with canola oil. Cook the banana fritters at 360 degrees F for 10 minutes, flipping them halfway through the cooking time. Drizzle with some honey just before serving. Enjoy!

1025. Easy Monkey Rolls
INGREDIENTS (4 Servings)

- 8 ounces refrigerated buttermilk biscuit dough
- 1/2 cup brown sugar
- 4 ounces butter, melted
- 1/4 teaspoon grated nutmeg
- 1/2 teaspoon ground cinnamon
- 1/4 teaspoon ground cardamom

DIRECTIONS (Prep + Cook Time: 25 minutes) Spritz 4 standard-size muffin cups with a nonstick spray. Thoroughly combine the brown sugar with the melted butter, nutmeg, cinnamon and cardamom. Spoon the butter mixture into muffins cups. Separate the dough into biscuits and divide your biscuits between _ cups. Bake the Monkey rolls at 340 degrees F for about 15 minutes or until golden brown. Turn upside down just before serving. Enjoy!

1026. Dessert French Toast with Blackberries
INGREDIENTS (2 Servings)

- 2 tablespoons butter, at room temperature
- 1 egg
- 2 tablespoons granulated sugar
- 1/4 teaspoon ground cinnamon
- 1/4 teaspoon vanilla extract
- 6 slices French baguette
- 1 cup fresh blackberries
- 2 tablespoons powdered sugar

DIRECTIONS (Prep + Cook Time:20 minutes) Start by preheating your Air Fryer to 375 degrees F. In a mixing dish, whisk the butter, egg, granulated sugar, cinnamon and vanilla. Dip all the slices of the French baguette in this mixture. Transfer the French toast to the baking pan. Bake in the preheated Air Fryer for 8 minutes, turning them over halfway through the cooking time to ensure even cooking. To serve, divide the French toast between two warm plates. Arrange the blackberries on top of each slice. Dust with powdered sugar and serve immediately. Enjoy!

1027. Chocolate Apple Chips
INGREDIENTS (6 Servings)

- 1 large Pink Lady apple, cored and sliced
- 1 tablespoon light brown sugar
- A pinch of kosher salt
- 2 tablespoons lemon juice
- 2 teaspoons cocoa powder

DIRECTIONS (Prep + Cook Time: 15 minutes) Toss the apple slices with the other ingredients. Bake at 350 degrees F for 5 minutes; shake the basket to ensure even cooking and continue to cook an additional 5 minutes. Enjoy!

1028. Peppermint Chocolate Cheesecake
INGREDIENTS (6 Servings)

- 1 cup powdered sugar
- 1/2 cup all-purpose flour
- 1/2 cup butter
- 1 cup mascarpone cheese, at room temperature
- 4 ounces semisweet chocolate, melted
- 1 teaspoon vanilla extract
- 2 drops peppermint extract

DIRECTIONS (Prep + Cook Time: 40 minutes) Beat the sugar, flour, and butter in a mixing bowl. Press the mixture into the bottom of a lightly greased baking pan. Bake at 350 degrees F for 18 minutes. Place it in your freezer for 20 minutes. Then, make the cheesecake topping by mixing the remaining ingredients. Place this topping over the crust and allow it to cool in your freezer for a further 15 minutes. Serve well chilled.

1029. Chocolate Biscuit Sandwich Cookies
INGREDIENTS (10 Servings)

- 2 ½ cups self-rising flour
- 4 ounces brown sugar
- 1 ounce honey
- 5 ounces butter, softened
- 1 egg, beaten
- 1 teaspoon vanilla essence
- 4 ounces double cream
- 3 ounces dark chocolate
- 1 teaspoon cardamom seeds, finely crushed

DIRECTIONS (Prep + Cook Time: 20 minutes) Start by preheating your Air Fryer to 350 degrees F. In a mixing bowl, thoroughly combine the flour, brown sugar, honey, and butter. Mix until your mixture resembles breadcrumbs. Gradually, add the egg and vanilla essence. Shape your dough into small balls and place in the parchment-lined Air Fryer basket. Bake in the preheated Air Fryer for 10 minutes. Rotate the pan and bake for another 5 minutes. Transfer the freshly baked cookies to a cooling rack. As the biscuits are cooling, melt the double cream and dark chocolate in an air-fryer safe bowl at 350 degrees F. Add the cardamom seeds and stir well. Spread the filling over the cooled biscuits and sandwich together. Enjoy!

1030. Country Pie with Walnuts
INGREDIENTS (6 Servings)

- 1 cup coconut milk
- 2 eggs
- 1/2 stick butter, at room temperature
- 1 teaspoon vanilla essence
- 1/4 teaspoon ground cardamom
- 1/4 teaspoon ground cloves
- 1/2 cup walnuts, ground
- 1/2 cup sugar
- 1/3 cup almond flour

DIRECTIONS (Prep + Cook Time: 20 minutes) Begin by preheating your Air Fryer to 360 degrees F. Spritz the sides and bottom of a baking pan with nonstick cooking spray. Mix all ingredients until well combined. Scrape the batter into the prepared baking pan. Bake approximately 13 minutes; use a toothpick to test for doneness. Enjoy!

1031. Rustic Baked Apples
INGREDIENTS (4 Servings)

- 4 Gala apples
- 1/4 cup rolled oats
- 1/4 cup sugar
- 2 tablespoons honey
- 1/3 cup walnuts, chopped
- 1 teaspoon cinnamon powder
- 1/2 teaspoon ground cardamom
- 1/2 teaspoon ground cloves
- 2/3 cup water

DIRECTIONS (Prep + Cook Time: 25 minutes) Use a paring knife to remove the stem and seeds from the apples, making deep holes. In a mixing bowl, combine together the rolled oats, sugar, honey, walnuts, cinnamon, cardamom, and cloves. Pour the water into an Air Fryer safe dish. Place the apples in the dish. Bake at 340 degrees F for 17 minutes. Serve at room temperature. Enjoy!

1032. Coconut Chip Cookies
INGREDIENTS (12 Servings)

1 cup butter, melted	1 teaspoon coconut extract	1/2 teaspoon baking soda
1 ¾ cups granulated sugar	1 teaspoon vanilla extract	1/2 teaspoon fine table salt
3 eggs	2 ¼ cups all-purpose flour	2 cups coconut chips
2 tablespoons coconut milk	1/2 teaspoon baking powder	

DIRECTIONS (Prep + Cook Time: 20minutes)

Begin by preheating your Air Fryer to 350 degrees F. In the bowl of an electric mixer, beat the butter and sugar until well combined. Now, add the eggs one at a time, and mix well; add the coconut milk, coconut extract, and vanilla; beat until creamy and uniform. Mix the flour with baking powder, baking soda, and salt. Then, stir the flour mixture into the butter mixture and stir until everything is well incorporated. Finally, fold in the coconut chips and mix again. Scoop out 1 tablespoon size balls of the batter on a cookie pan, leaving 2 inches between each cookie. Bake for 10 minutes or until golden brown, rotating the pan once or twice through the cooking time. Let your cookies cool on wire racks. Enjoy!

1033. Chocolate Birthday Cake
INGREDIENTS (6 Servings)

2 eggs, beaten	1/4 cup honey	1 ½ teaspoons baking powder
2/3 cup sour cream	1/3 cup coconut oil, softened	1 teaspoon vanilla extract
1 cup flour	1/4 cup cocoa powder	1/2 teaspoon pure rum extract
1/2 cup sugar	2 tablespoons chocolate chips	

Chocolate Frosting:

1/2 cup butter, softened	2 cups powdered sugar	
1/4 cup cocoa powder	2 tablespoons milk	

DIRECTIONS (Prep + Cook Time: 35 minutes)

Mix all ingredients for the chocolate cake with a hand mixer on low speed. Scrape the batter into a cake pan. Bake at 330 degrees F for 25 to 30 minutes. Transfer the cake to a wire rack Meanwhile, whip the butter and cocoa until smooth. Stir in the powdered sugar. Slowly and gradually, pour in the milk until your frosting reaches desired consistency. Whip until smooth and fluffy; then, frost the cooled cake. Place in your refrigerator for a couple of hours. Serve well chilled. Enjoy!

1034. Baked Fruit Compote with Coconut Chips
INGREDIENTS (6 Servings)

1 tablespoon butter	1/3 cup packed brown sugar	1 teaspoon pure vanilla extract
8 ounces canned apricot halves, drained	1/4 teaspoon grated nutmeg	1/2 cup coconut chips
8 ounces canned pear halves, drained	1/4 teaspoon ground cloves	
16 ounces pineapple slices, undrained	1/2 teaspoon ground cinnamon	

DIRECTIONS (Prep + Cook Time: 25 minutes)

Start by preheating your Air Fryer to 330 degrees F. Grease a baking pan with butter. Place all ingredients, except for the coconut chips, in a baking pan. Bake in the preheated Air Fryer for 20 minutes. Serve in individual bowls, garnished with coconut chips. Enjoy!

1035. Greek-Style Griddle Cakes
INGREDIENTS (4 Servings)

3/4 cup self-raising flour	2 tablespoons sugar	2 eggs, lightly beaten
1/4 teaspoon fine sea salt	1/2 cup milk	1 tablespoon butter

Topping:

1 cup Greek-style yogurt	1 banana, mashed	2 tablespoons honey

DIRECTIONS (Prep + Cook Time: 25 minutes) Mix the flour, salt, and sugar in a bowl. Then, stir in the milk, eggs, and butter. Mix until smooth and uniform. Drop tablespoons of the batter into the Air Fryer pan. Cook at 300 degrees F for 4 to 5 minutes or until bubbles form on top of the griddle cakes. Repeat with the remaining batter. Meanwhile, mix all ingredients for the topping. Place in your refrigerator until ready to serve. Serve the griddle cakes with the chilled topping. Enjoy!

1036. Coconut Pancake Cups
INGREDIENTS (4 Servings)

1/2 cup flour	1 tablespoon coconut oil, melted	1/2 cup coconut chips
1/3 cup coconut milk	1 teaspoon vanilla	
2 eggs	A pinch of ground cardamom	

DIRECTIONS (Prep + Cook Time: 30 minutes) Mix the flour, coconut milk, eggs, coconut oil, vanilla, and cardamom in a large bowl. Let it stand for 20 minutes. Spoon the batter into a greased muffin tin. Cook at 230 degrees F for 4 to 5 minutes or until golden brown. Repeat with the remaining batter. Decorate your pancakes with coconut chips. Enjoy!

1037. Classic Butter Cake
INGREDIENTS (8 Servings)

1 stick butter, at room temperature	1 teaspoon baking powder	A pinch of ground star anise
1 cup sugar	1/2 teaspoon baking soda	1/4 cup buttermilk
2 eggs	1/4 teaspoon salt	1 teaspoon vanilla essence
1 cup all-purpose flour	A pinch of freshly grated nutmeg	

DIRECTIONS (Prep + Cook Time: 35 minutes)

Begin by preheating your Air Fryer to 320 degrees F. Spritz the bottom and sides of a baking pan with cooking spray. Beat the butter and sugar with a hand mixer until creamy. Then, fold in the eggs, one at a time, and mix well until fluffy. Stir in the flour along with the remaining ingredients. Mix to combine well. Scrape the batter into the prepared baking pan. Bake for 15 minutes; rotate the pan and bake an additional 15 minutes, until the top of the cake springs back when gently pressed with your fingers. Enjoy!

1038. Pop Tarts with Homemade Strawberry Jam
INGREDIENTS (8 Servings)

1 cup strawberries, sliced	2 tablespoons chia seeds	1 tablespoon of water (egg wash)
1 tablespoon fresh lemon juice	1 (14-ounce) box refrigerated pie crust	1/2 cup powdered sugar
1 teaspoon maple syrup	1 egg, whisked with	

DIRECTIONS (Prep + Cook Time: 45 minutes)

In a saucepan, heat the strawberries until they start to get syrupy. Mash them and add the lemon juice and maple syrup. Remove from the heat and stir in the chia seeds. Let it stand for 30 minutes or until it thickens up. Unroll the pie crusts and cut them into small rectangles. Spoon the strawberry jam in the center of a rectangle; top with another piece of crust. Repeat until you run out of ingredients. Line the Air Fryer basket with parchment paper. Brush the pop tarts with the egg wash and bake at 400 degrees F for 6 minutes or until slightly brown. Work in batches and transfer to cooling racks. Dust with powdered sugar and enjoy!

1039. Old-Fashioned Plum Dumplings
INGREDIENTS (4 Servings)

1 (14-ounce) box pie crusts	2 tablespoons coconut oil	1 egg white, slightly beaten
2 cups plums, pitted	1/4 teaspoon ground cardamom	
2 tablespoons granulated sugar	1/2 teaspoon ground cinnamon	

DIRECTIONS (Prep + Cook Time: 40 minutes)

Place the pie crust on a work surface. Roll into a circle and cut into quarters. Place 1 plum on each crust piece. Add the sugar, coconut oil, cardamom, and cinnamon. Roll up the sides into a circular shape around the plums. Repeat with the remaining ingredients. Brush the edges with the egg white. Place in the lightly greased Air Fryer basket. Bake in the preheated Air Fryer at 360 degrees F for 20 minutes, flipping them halfway through the cooking time. Work in two batches, decorate and serve at room temperature.

1040. White Chocolate Rum Molten Cake
INGREDIENTS (4 Servings)

2 ½ ounces butter, at room temperature	1/2 cup powdered sugar	1 teaspoon vanilla extract
3 ounces white chocolate	1/3 cup self-rising flour	
2 eggs, beaten	1 teaspoon rum extract	

DIRECTIONS (Prep + Cook Time: 20 minutes)

Begin by preheating your Air Fryer to 370 degrees F. Spritz the sides and bottom of four ramekins with cooking spray. Melt the butter and white chocolate in a microwave-safe bowl. Mix the eggs and sugar until frothy. Pour the butter/chocolate mixture into the egg mixture. Stir in the flour, rum extract, and vanilla extract. Mix until everything is well incorporated. Scrape the batter into the prepared ramekins. Bake in the preheated Air Fryer for 9 to 11 minutes. Let stand for 2 to 3 minutes. Invert on a plate while warm and serve. Enjoy!

1041. Coconut Cheesecake Bites
INGREDIENTS (8 Servings)

1 ½ cups Oreo cookies, crushed	4 ounces double cream	1 cup toasted coconut
4 ounces granulated sugar	2 eggs, lightly whisked	
4 tablespoons butter, softened	1 teaspoon pure vanilla extract	
12 ounces cream cheese	1 teaspoon pure coconut extract	

DIRECTIONS (Prep + Cook Time: 30 minutes)

Start by preheating your Air Fryer to 350 degrees F. Mix the crushed Oreos with sugar and butter; press the crust into silicone cupcake molds. Bake for 5 minutes and allow them to cool on wire racks. Using an electric mixer, whip the cream cheese and double cream until fluffy; add one egg at a time and continue to beat until creamy. Finally, add the vanilla and coconut extract. Pour the topping mixture on top of the crust. Bake at 320 degrees F for 13 to 15 minutes. Afterwards, top with the toasted coconut. Allow the mini cheesecakes to chill in your refrigerator before serving. Enjoy!

1042. Old-Fashioned Pinch-Me Cake with Walnuts
INGREDIENTS (4 Servings)

1 (10-ounces) can crescent rolls	1/2 cup caster sugar	1 tablespoon dark rum
1/2 stick butter	1 teaspoon pumpkin pie spice blend	1/2 cup walnuts, chopped

DIRECTIONS (Prep + Cook Time: 20 minutes)

Start by preheating your Air Fryer to 350 degrees F. Roll out the crescent rolls. Spread the butter onto the crescent rolls; scatter the sugar, spices and walnuts over the rolls. Drizzle with rum and roll them up. Using your fingertips, gently press them to seal the edges. Bake your cake for about 13 minutes or until the top is golden brown. Enjoy!

1043. Air Grilled Peaches with Cinnamon-Sugar Butter
INGREDIENTS (2 Servings)

2 fresh peaches, pitted and halved

1 tablespoon butter

2 tablespoons caster sugar

1/4 teaspoon ground cinnamon

DIRECTIONS (Prep + Cook Time: 25 minutes)

Mix the butter, sugar and cinnamon. Spread the butter mixture onto the peaches and transfer them to the Air Fryer cooking basket. Cook your peaches at 320 degrees F for about 25 minutes or until the top is golden. Serve with vanilla ice cream, if desired. Enjoy!

1044. Crunchy French Toast Sticks
INGREDIENTS (3 Servings)

1 egg

1/4 cup double cream

1/4 cup milk

1 tablespoon brown sugar

1/4 teaspoon ground cloves

1/4 teaspoon ground cinnamon

1/4 vanilla paste 3

thick slices of brioche bread, cut into thirds

1 cup crispy rice cereal

DIRECTIONS (Prep + Cook Time: 10 minutes)

Thoroughly combine the egg, cream, milk, sugar, ground cloves, cinnamon and vanilla. Dip each piece of bread into the cream mixture and then, press gently into the cereal, pressing to coat all sides. Arrange the pieces of bread in the Air Fryer cooking basket and cook them at 380 degrees F for 2 minutes; flip and cook on the other side for 2 to 3 minutes longer. Enjoy!

1045. Blueberry Fritters with Cinnamon Sugar
INGREDIENTS (4 Servings)

1/2 cup plain flour

1/2 teaspoon baking powder

1 teaspoon brown sugar

A pinch of grated nutmeg

1/4 teaspoon ground star anise

A pinch of salt

1 egg

1/4 cup coconut milk

1 cup fresh blueberries

1 tablespoon coconut oil, melted

4 tablespoons cinnamon sugar

DIRECTIONS (Prep + Cook Time: 20minutes) Combine the flour, baking powder, brown sugar, nutmeg, star anise and salt. In another bowl, whisk the eggs and milk until frothy. Add the wet mixture to the dry mixture and mix to combine well. Fold in the fresh blueberries. Carefully place spoonfuls of batter into the Air Fryer cooking basket. Brush them with melted coconut oil. Cook your fritters in the preheated Air Fryer at 370 degrees for 10 minutes, flipping them halfway through the cooking time. Repeat with the remaining batter. Dust your fritters with the cinnamon sugar and serve at room temperature. Enjoy!

1046. Summer Fruit Pie
INGREDIENTS (4 Servings)

2 (8-ounce) refrigerated pie crusts

2 cups fresh blackberries

1/4 cup caster sugar

2 teaspoons cornstarch

A pinch of sea salt

1/4 teaspoon ground nutmeg

1/4 teaspoon ground cinnamon

1/4 teaspoon vanilla extract

DIRECTIONS (Prep + Cook Time: 35 minutes)

Start by preheating your Air Fryer to 350 degrees F. Place the pie crust in a lightly greased pie plate. In a bowl, combine the fresh blackberries with caster sugar, cornstarch, salt, nutmeg, cinnamon and vanilla extract. Spoon the blackberry filling into the prepared pie crust. Top the blackberry filling with second crust and cut slits in pastry. Bake your pie in the preheated Air Fryer for 35 minutes or until the top is golden brown. Enjoy!

1047. Cinnamon-Streusel Coffeecake
INGREDIENTS (4 Servings)

Cake:

1/2 cup unbleached white flour	3 tablespoons white sugar	3 tablespoons coconut oil
1/4 cup yellow cornmeal	1 tablespoon unsweetened cocoa powder	
1 teaspoon baking powder	A pinch of kosher salt	
1/4 cup milk 1 egg		

Topping:

2 tablespoons polenta	1 teaspoon ground cinnamon	2 tablespoons coconut oil
1/4 cup brown sugar	1/4 cup pecans, chopped	

DIRECTIONS (Prep + Cook Time: 35 minutes) In a large bowl, combine together the cake ingredients. Spoon the mixture into a lightly greased baking pan. Then, in another bowl, combine the topping ingredients. Spread the topping ingredients over your cake. Bake the cake at 330 degrees F for 12 to 15 minutes until a tester comes out dry and clean. Allow your cake to cool for about 15 minutes before cutting and serving. Enjoy!

1048. Chocolate Chip Banana Crepes
INGREDIENTS (2 Servings)

1 small ripe banana	1/4 cup chocolate chips
1/8 teaspoon baking powder	1 egg, whisked

DIRECTIONS (Prep + Cook Time: 30 minutes) Mix all ingredients until creamy and fluffy. Let it stand for about 20 minutes. Spritz the Air Fryer baking pan with cooking spray. Pour 1/2 of the batter into the pan using a measuring cup. Cook at 230 degrees F for 4 to 5 minutes or until golden brown. Repeat with another crepe. Enjoy!!

1049. Sweet Dough Dippers
INGREDIENTS (4 Servings)

8 ounces bread dough	2 tablespoons butter, melted	2 ounces powdered sugar

DIRECTIONS (Prep + Cook Time: 10 minutes)

Cut the dough into strips and twist them together 3 to 4 times. Then, brush the dough twists with melted butter and sprinkle sugar over them. Cook the dough twists at 350 degrees F for 8 minutes, tossing the basket halfway through the cooking time. Serve with your favorite dip. Enjoy!

1050. Baked Banana with Chocolate Glaze
INGREDIENTS (2 Servings)

2 bananas, peeled and cut in half lengthwise	1 tablespoon coconut oil, melted	1 tablespoon agave syrup
	1 tablespoon cocoa powder	

DIRECTIONS (Prep + Cook Time: 15 minutes) Bake your bananas in the preheated Air Fryer at 370 degrees F for 12 minutes, turning them over halfway through the cooking time. In the meantime, microwave the coconut oil for 30 seconds; stir in the cocoa powder and agave syrup. Serve the baked bananas with a few drizzles of the chocolate glaze. Enjoy!

1051. Classic Brownie Cupcakes
INGREDIENTS (3 Servings)

1/3 cup all-purpose flour	1/3 cup caster sugar	1/2 teaspoon rum extract
1/4 teaspoon baking powder	2 ounces butter, room temperature	A pinch of ground cinnamon
3 tablespoons cocoa powder	1 large egg	A pinch of salt

DIRECTIONS (Prep + Cook Time: 25 minutes) Mix the dry ingredients in a bowl. In another bowl, mix the wet ingredients. Gradually, stir in the wet ingredients into the dry mixture. Divide the batter among muffin cups and transfer them to the Air Fryer cooking basket. Bake your cupcakes at 330 degrees for 15 minuets until a tester comes out dry and clean. Transfer to a wire rack and let your cupcakes sit for 10 minutes before unmolding. Enjoy!

1052. Old-Fashioned Donuts
INGREDIENTS (4 Servings)

8 ounces refrigerated buttermilk biscuits	1/2 tablespoon cinnamon	A pinch of salt
2 tablespoons butter, unsalted and melted	4 tablespoons caster sugar	A pinch of grated nutmeg

DIRECTIONS (Prep + Cook Time: 15 minutes) Separate the biscuits and cut holes out of the center of each biscuit using a 1-inch round biscuit cutter; place them on a parchment paper. Lower your biscuits into the Air Fryer cooking basket. Brush them with 1 tablespoon of melted butter. Air fry your biscuits at 340 degrees F for about 8 minutes or until golden brown, flipping them halfway through the cooking time. Meanwhile, mix the sugar with cinnamon, salt and nutmeg. Brush your donuts with remaining 1 tablespoon of melted butter; roll them in the cinnamon-sugar and serve. Enjoy!

1053. Apricot and Almond Crumble
INGREDIENTS (3 Servings)

1 cup apricots, pitted and diced	4 tablespoons granulated sugar	1/2 teaspoon ground cardamom
1/4 cup flaked almonds	1/2 teaspoon ground cinnamon	2 tablespoons butter
1/3 cup self-raising flour	1 teaspoon crystallized ginger	

DIRECTIONS (Prep + Cook Time: 35 minutes) Place the sliced apricots and almonds in a baking pan that is lightly greased with a nonstick cooking spray. In a mixing bowl, thoroughly combine the remaining ingredients. Sprinkle this topping over the apricot layer. Bake your crumble in the preheated Air Fryer at 330 degrees F for 35 minutes. Enjoy!

1054. Greek Roasted Figs with Yiaourti me Meli
INGREDIENTS (3 Servings)

1 teaspoon coconut oil, melted	1/4 teaspoon ground cloves	1/2 cup Greek yogurt
6 medium-sized figs	1/4 teaspoon ground cinnamon	
1/4 teaspoon ground cardamom	3 tablespoon honey	

DIRECTIONS (Prep + Cook Time: 20 minutes)

Drizzle the melted coconut oil all over your figs. Sprinkle cardamom, cloves and cinnamon over your figs. Roast your figs in the preheated Air Fryer at 330 degrees F for 15 to 16 minutes, shaking the basket occasionally to promote even cooking. In the meantime, thoroughly combine the honey with the Greek yogurt to make the yiaourti me meli. Divide the roasted figs between 3 serving bowls and serve with a dollop of yiaourti me meli. Enjoy!

1055. Panettone Pudding Tart
INGREDIENTS (3 Servings)

3 cups panettone bread, crusts trimmed, bread cut into 1-inch cubes

1/2 cup creme fraiche

1/2 cup coconut milk

2 tablespoons orange marmalade

1 tablespoon butter

2 tablespoons amaretto liqueur

1/2 teaspoon vanilla extract

1/4 cup sugar

A pinch of grated nutmeg

A pinch of sea salt

1 egg, whisked

DIRECTIONS (Prep + Cook Time: 45minutes)

Put the panettone bread cubes into a lightly greased baking pan. Then, make the custard by mixing the remaining ingredients. Pour the custard over your panettone. Let it rest for 30 minutes, pressing with a wide spatula to submerge. Cook the panettone pudding in the preheated Air Fryer at 370 degrees F degrees for 7 minutes; rotate the pan and cook an additional 5 to 6 minutes. Enjoy!

1056. Banana Chips with Chocolate Glaze
INGREDIENTS (2 Servings)

2 banana, cut into slices

1/4 teaspoon lemon zest

1 tablespoon agave syrup

1 tablespoon cocoa powder

1 tablespoon coconut oil, melted

DIRECTIONS (Prep + Cook Time: 2 0minutes)

Toss the bananas with the lemon zest and agave syrup. Transfer your bananas to the parchment-lined cooking basket. Bake in the preheated Air Fryer at 370 degrees F for 12 minutes, turning them over halfway through the cooking time. In the meantime, melt the coconut oil in your microwave; add the cocoa powder and whisk to combine well. Serve the baked banana chips with a few drizzles of the chocolate glaze. Enjoy!

1057. Favorite Apple Crisp
INGREDIENTS (4 Servings)

4 cups apples, peeled, cored and sliced

1/2 cup brown sugar

1 tablespoon honey

1 tablespoon cornmeal

1/4 teaspoon ground cloves

1/2 teaspoon ground cinnamon

1/4 cup water 1/2 cup quick-cooking oats

1/2 cup all-purpose flour

1/2 cup caster sugar

1/2 teaspoon baking powder

1/3 cup coconut oil, melted

DIRECTIONS (Prep + Cook Time: 40minutes)

Toss the sliced apples with the brown sugar, honey, cornmeal, cloves, and cinnamon. Divide between four custard cups coated with cooking spray. In a mixing dish, thoroughly combine the remaining ingredients. Sprinkle over the apple mixture. Bake in the preheated Air Fryer at 330 degrees F for 35 minutes. Enjoy!

1058. Cinnamon and Sugar Sweet Potato Fries
INGREDIENTS (2 Servings)

1 large sweet potato, peeled and sliced into sticks

1 teaspoon ghee

1 tablespoon cornstarch

1/4 teaspoon ground cardamom

1/4 cup sugar

1 tablespoon ground cinnamon

DIRECTIONS (Prep + Cook Time: 30 minutes)

Toss the sweet potato sticks with the melted ghee and cornstarch. Cook in the preheated Air Fryer at 380 degrees F for 20 minutes, shaking the basket halfway through the cooking time. Sprinkle the cardamom, sugar, and cinnamon all over the sweet potato fries and serve. Enjoy!

1059. Chocolate Raspberry Wontons
INGREDIENTS (6 Servings)

1 (12-ounce) package wonton wrappers	1/2 cup raspberries, mashed	1 tablespoon of water (egg wash)
6 ounces chocolate chips	1 egg, lightly whisked +	1/4 cup caster sugar

DIRECTIONS (Prep + Cook Time: 15minutes)

Divide the chocolate chips and raspberries among the wonton wrappers. Now, fold the wrappers diagonally in half over the filling; press the edges with a fork. Brush with the egg wash and seal the edges. Bake at 370 degrees F for 8 minutes, flipping them halfway through the cooking time. Work in batches. Sprinkle the caster sugar over your wontons and enjoy!

1060. Sunday Banana Chocolate Cookies
INGREDIENTS (8 Servings)

1 stick butter, at room temperature	1 2/3 cups all-purpose flour	1/4 teaspoon crystallized ginger
1 ¼ cups caster sugar	1/3 cup cocoa powder	1 ½ cups chocolate chips
2 ripe bananas, mashed	1 ½ teaspoons baking powder	
1 teaspoon vanilla paste	1/4 teaspoon ground cinnamon	

DIRECTIONS (Prep + Cook Time: 30 minutes)

In a mixing dish, beat the butter and sugar until creamy and uniform. Stir in the mashed bananas and vanilla. In another mixing dish, thoroughly combine the flour, cocoa powder, baking powder, cinnamon, and crystallized ginger. Add the flour mixture to the banana mixture; mix to combine well. Afterwards, fold in the chocolate chips. Drop by large spoonfuls onto a parchment-lined Air Fryer basket. Bake at 365 degrees F for 11 minutes or until golden brown on the top. enjoy!

1061. Chocolate and Peanut Butter Brownies
INGREDIENTS (10 Servings)

1 cup peanut butter	1 cup all-purpose flour	1 cup dark chocolate, broken into chunks
1 ¼ cups sugar	1 teaspoon baking powder	
3 eggs	1/4 teaspoon kosher salt	

DIRECTIONS (Prep + Cook Time: 30 minutes)

Start by preheating your Air Fryer to 350 degrees F. Now, spritz the sides and bottom of a baking pan with cooking spray. In a mixing dish, thoroughly combine the peanut butter with the sugar until creamy. Next, fold in the egg and beat until fluffy. After that, stir in the flour, baking powder, salt, and chocolate. Mix until everything is well combined. Bake in the preheated Air Fryer for 20 to 22 minutes. Transfer to a wire rack to cool before slicing and serving. Enjoy!

1062. English-Style Scones with Raisins
INGREDIENTS (6 Servings)

1 ½ cups all-purpose flour	1/4 teaspoon ground cloves	6 tablespoons butter, cooled and sliced
1/4 cup brown sugar	1/2 teaspoon ground cardamom	1/2 cup double cream
1 teaspoon baking powder	1 teaspoon ground cinnamon	2 eggs, lightly whisked
1/4 teaspoon sea salt	1/2 cup raisins	1/2 teaspoon vanilla essence

DIRECTIONS (Prep + Cook Time: 20 minutes)

In a mixing bowl, thoroughly combine the flour, sugar, baking powder, salt, cloves, cardamom cinnamon, and raisins. Mix until everything is combined well. Add the butter and mix again. In another mixing bowl, combine the double cream with the eggs and vanilla; beat until creamy and smooth. Stir the wet ingredients into the dry mixture. Roll your dough out into a circle and cut into wedges. Bake in the preheated Air Fryer at 360 degrees for 11 minutes, rotating the pan halfway through the cooking time. Enjoy!

1063. Spanish-Style Doughnut Tejeringos
INGREDIENTS (4 Servings)

- 3/4 cup water
- 1 tablespoon sugar
- 1/4 teaspoon sea salt
- 1/4 teaspoon grated nutmeg
- 1/4 teaspoon ground cloves
- 6 tablespoons butter
- 3/4 cup all-purpose flour
- 2 eggs

DIRECTIONS (Prep + Cook Time: 30 minutes)

To make the dough, boil the water in a pan over medium-high heat; now, add the sugar, salt, nutmeg, and cloves; cook until dissolved. Add the butter and turn the heat to low. Gradually stir in the flour, whisking continuously, until the mixture forms a ball. Remove from the heat; fold in the eggs one at a time, stirring to combine well. Pour the mixture into a piping bag with a large star tip. Squeeze 4-inch strips of dough into the greased Air Fryer pan. Cook at 410 degrees F for 6 minutes, working in batches. Enjoy!

1064. Banana Crepes with Apple Topping
INGREDIENTS (2 Servings)

Banana Crepes:

- 1 large banana, mashed
- 2 eggs, beaten
- 1/4 teaspoon baking powder
- 1 shot dark rum
- 1/2 teaspoon vanilla extract
- 1 teaspoon butter, melted
- 2 tablespoons brown sugar

Topping:

- 2 apples, peeled, cored, and chopped
- 2 tablespoons sugar
- 1/2 teaspoon cinnamon
- 3 tablespoons water

DIRECTIONS (Prep + Cook Time: 40 minutes)

Mix all ingredients for the banana crepes until creamy and fluffy. Let it stand for 15 to 20 minutes. Spritz the Air Fryer baking pan with cooking spray. Pour the batter into the pan using a measuring cup. Cook at 230 degrees F for 4 to 5 minutes or until golden brown. Repeat with the remaining batter. To make the pancake topping, place all ingredients in a heavy-bottomed skillet over medium heat. Cook for 10 minutes, stirring occasionally. Spoon on top of the banana crepes and enjoy!

1065. Butter Rum Cookies with Walnuts
INGREDIENTS (6 Servings)

- 1 cup all-purpose flour
- 1/2 teaspoon baking powder
- 1/4 teaspoon fine sea salt
- 1 stick butter, unsalted and softened
- 1/2 cup sugar
- 1 egg
- 1/2 teaspoon vanilla
- 1 teaspoon butter rum flavoring
- 3 ounces walnuts, finely chopped

DIRECTIONS (Prep + Cook Time: 35 minutes) Begin by preheating the Air Fryer to 360 degrees F. In a mixing dish, thoroughly combine the flour with baking powder and salt. Beat the butter and sugar with a hand mixer until pale and fluffy; add the whisked egg, vanilla, and butter rum flavoring; mix again to combine well. Now, stir in the dry ingredients. Fold in the chopped walnuts and mix to combine. Divide the mixture into small balls; flatten each ball with a fork and transfer them to a foil-lined baking pan. Bake in the preheated Air Fryer for 14 minutes. Work in a few batches and transfer to wire racks to cool completely. Enjoy!

1066. Fall Harvest Apple Cinnamon Buns
INGREDIENTS (6 Servings)

- 1/2 cup milk
- 1/2 cup granulated sugar
- 1 tablespoon yeast
- 1/2 stick butter, at room temperature
- 1 egg, at room temperature
- 1/4 teaspoon salt
- 2 1/4 cups all-purpose flour

Filling:

- 3 tablespoons butter, at room temperature
- 1/4 cup brown sugar
- 1/2 teaspoon ground cardamom
- 1/2 teaspoon ground cloves
- 1 teaspoon ground cinnamon
- 1 apple, peeled, cored, and chopped
- 1/2 cup powdered sugar

DIRECTIONS (Prep + Cook Time: 1 hour 20 minutes) Heat the milk in a microwave safe bowl and transfer the warm milk to the bowl of a stand electric mixer. Add the granulated sugar and yeast, and mix to combine well. Cover and let sit until the yeast is foamy. Then, beat the butter on low speed. Fold in the the egg and mix again. Add the salt and flour. Mix on medium speed until a soft dough forms. Knead the dough on a lightly floured surface. Cover it loosely and let sit in a warm place about 1 hour or until doubled in size. Then, spritz the bottom and sides of a baking pan with cooking oil (butter flavored). Roll your dough out into a rectangle. Spread 3 tablespoons of butter all over the dough. In a mixing dish, combine the brown sugar, cardamom, cloves, and cinnamon; sprinkle evenly over the dough. Top with the chopped apples. Then, roll up your dough to form a log. Cut into 6 equal rolls and place them in the parchment-lined Air Fryer basket. Bake at 350 degrees for 12 minutes, turning them halfway through the cooking time. Dust with powdered sugar. Enjoy!

1067. Summer Fruit Pie with Cinnamon Streusel
INGREDIENTS (4 Servings)

1 (14-ounce) box pie crusts Filling:

- 1/3 cup caster sugar
- 1/3 cup all-purpose flour
- 1/4 teaspoon ground cardamom
- 1/2 teaspoon ground cinnamon
- 1 teaspoon pure vanilla extract
- 2 cups apricots, pitted and sliced peeled
- 2 cups peaches, pitted and sliced peeled

Streusel:

- 1 cup all-purpose flour
- 1/2 cup brown sugar
- 1 teaspoon ground cinnamon
- 1/3 cup cold salted butter

DIRECTIONS (Prep + Cook Time: 30 minutes)

Place the pie crust in a lightly greased pie plate. In a mixing bowl, thoroughly combine the caster sugar, 1/3 cup of flour, cardamom, cinnamon, and vanilla extract. Add the apricots and peaches and mix until coated. Spoon into the prepared pie crust. Make the streusel by mixing 1 cup of flour, brown sugar, and cinnamon. Cut in the cold butter and continue to mix until the mixture looks like coarse crumbs. Sprinkle over the filling. Bake at 350 degrees F for 35 minutes or until topping is golden brown. Enjoy!

1068. Authentic Swedish Kärleksmums
INGREDIENTS (3Servings)

- 2 tablespoons Swedish butter, at room temperature
- 4 tablespoons brown sugar
- 1 egg
- 1 tablespoon lingonberry jam
- 5 tablespoons all-purpose flour
- 1/2 teaspoon baking powder
- 2 tablespoons cocoa powder
- A pinch of grated nutmeg
- A pinch of coarse sea salt

DIRECTIONS (Prep + Cook Time: 20 minutes)

Cream the butter and sugar using an electric mixer. Fold in the egg and lingonberry jam and mix to combine well. Stir in the flour, baking powder, cocoa powder, grated nutmeg and salt; mix again to combine well. Pour the batter into a lightly buttered baking pan. Bake your cake at 330 degrees F for about 15 minutes until a tester inserted into the center of the cake comes out dry and clean. Enjoy!

1069. Strawberry Dessert Dumplings
INGREDIENTS (3 Servings)

9 wonton wrappers	1/3 strawberry jam	2 ounces icing sugar

DIRECTIONS (Prep + Cook Time: 10 minutes)

Start by laying out the wonton wrappers. Divide the strawberry jam between the wonton wrappers. Fold the wonton wrapper over the jam; now, seal the edges with wet fingers. Cook your wontons at 400 degrees F for 8 minutes; working in batches. Enjoy!

1070. Old-Fashioned Apple Crumble
INGREDIENTS (4 Servings)

2 baking apples, peeled, cored and diced	1/2 teaspoon ground cinnamon	1/4 cup brown sugar
2 tablespoons brown sugar	1/2 teaspoon vanilla essence	1/2 teaspoon baking powder
1 tablespoon cornstarch	1/4 cup apple juice	1/4 cup coconut oil
1/4 teaspoon grated nutmeg	1/2 cup quick-cooking oats	
1/4 teaspoon ground cloves	1/4 cup self-rising flour	

DIRECTIONS (Prep + Cook Time: 35 minutes) Toss the apples with 2 tablespoons of brown sugar and cornstarch. Place the apples in a baking pan that is previously lightly greased with a nonstick cooking spray. In a mixing dish, thoroughly combine the remaining topping ingredients. Sprinkle the topping ingredients over the apple layer. Bake your apple crumble in the preheated Air Fryer at 330 degrees F for 35 minutes. Enjoy!

1071. Banana and Pecan Muffins
INGREDIENTS (4 Servings)

1 extra-large ripe banana, mashed	1/4 cup brown sugar	4 tablespoons pecans, chopped
1/4 cup coconut oil	1/2 teaspoon vanilla essence	1/2 cup self-rising flour
1 egg	1/2 teaspoon ground cinnamon	

DIRECTIONS (Prep + Cook Time: 25 minutes) Start by preheating your Air Fryer to 330 degrees F. In a mixing bowl, combine the banana, coconut oil, egg, brown sugar, vanilla and cinnamon. Add in the chopped pecans and flour and stir again to combine well. Spoon the mixture into a lightly greased muffin tin and transfer to the Air Fryer cooking basket. Bake your muffins in the preheated Air Fryer for 15 to 17 minutes or until a tester comes out dry and clean. Sprinkle some extra icing sugar over the top of each muffin if desired. Serve and enjoy!

1072. Air Grilled Apricots with Mascarpone
INGREDIENTS (2 Servings)

6 apricots, halved and pitted	2 ounces mascarpone cheese	1 tablespoon confectioners' sugar
1 teaspoon coconut oil, melted	1/2 teaspoon vanilla extract	
A pinch of sea salt		

DIRECTIONS (Prep + Cook Time: 30 minutes) Place the apricots in the Air Fryer cooking basket. Drizzle the apricots with melted coconut oil. Cook the apricots at 320 degrees F for about 25 minutes or until the top is golden. In a bowl, whisk the mascarpone, vanilla extract, confectioners' sugar by hand until soft and creamy. Remove the apricots from the cooking basket. Spoon the whipped mascarpone into the cavity of each apricot. Sprinkle with coarse sea salt and enjoy!

1073. Lemon-Glazed Crescent Ring
INGREDIENTS (6 Servings)

8 ounces refrigerated crescent dough	1/2 teaspoon vanilla paste	2 ounces caster sugar
2 ounces mascarpone cheese, at room temperature	1 tablespoon coconut oil, at room temperature	

Glaze:

1/3 cup powdered sugar	1 tablespoon fresh lemon juice	1 tablespoon full-fat coconut milk

DIRECTIONS (Prep + Cook Time: 25minutes) Separate the crescent dough sheet into 8 triangles. Then, arrange the triangles in a sunburst pattern so it should look like the sun. Mix the mascarpone cheese, vanilla, coconut oil and caster sugar in a bowl. Place the mixture on the bottom of each triangle; fold triangle tips over filling and tuck under base to secure. Bake the ring at 360 degrees F for 20 minutes until dough is golden. In small mixing dish, whisk the powdered sugar, lemon juice and coconut milk. Drizzle over warm crescent ring and garnish with grated lemon peel. Enjoy!

1074. Authentic Spanish Churros
INGREDIENTS (4 Servings)

1/2 cup water	A pinch of ground cinnamon	1/2 cup plain flour
1/4 cup butter, cut into cubes	A pinch of salt	1 egg
1 tablespoon granulated sugar	1/2 teaspoon lemon zest	

Chocolate Dip:

2 ounces dark chocolate	1/2 cup milk	1 teaspoon ground cinnamon

DIRECTIONS (Prep + Cook Time: 20 minutes) Boil the water in a saucepan over medium-high heat; now, add the butter, sugar, cinnamon, salt and lemon zest; cook until the sugar has dissolved. Next, remove the pan from the heat. Gradually stir in the flour, whisking continuously until the mixture forms a ball; let it cool slightly. Fold in the egg and continue to beat using an electric mixer until everything comes together. Pour the dough into a piping bag with a large star tip. Squeeze 4-inch strips of dough into the greased Air Fryer pan. Cook your churros at 380 degrees F for about 10 minutes, shaking the basket halfway through the cooking time. In the meantime, melt the chocolate and milk in a saucepan over low heat. Add in the cinnamon and cook on low heat for about 5 minutes. Serve the warm churros with the chocolate dip and enjoy!

1075. Indian-Style Donuts (Gulgulas)
INGREDIENTS (2 Servings)

1/3 cup whole wheat flour	1 teaspoon ghee	1 tablespoon apple juice
1/3 cup sugar	1 tablespoon Indian dahi	

DIRECTIONS (Prep + Cook Time: 10 minutes) Mix the ingredients until everything is well incorporated. Drop a spoonful of batter onto the greased Air Fryer pan. Cook Indian gulgulas at 360 degrees F for 5 minutes or until golden brown, flipping them halfway through the cooking time. Repeat with the remaining batter. Serve with hot Indian tea and enjoy!

1076. Perfect English-Style Scones
INGREDIENTS (4 Servings)

1 ½ cups cake flour	1 teaspoon baking soda	1/2 stick butter
1/4 cup caster sugar	1/4 teaspoon salt	1 egg, beaten
1 teaspoon baking powder	1/2 teaspoon vanilla essence	1/2 cup almond milk

DIRECTIONS (Prep + Cook Time: 15minutes)

Start by preheating your Air Fryer to 360 degrees F. Thoroughly combine all dry ingredients. In another bowl, combine all wet ingredients. Then, add the wet mixture to the dry ingredients and stir to combine well. Roll your dough out into a circle and cut into wedges. Bake the scones in the preheated Air Fryer for about 11 minutes, flipping them halfway through the cooking time. Enjoy!

1077. Sherry Roasted Sweet Cherries
INGREDIENTS (4 Servings)

- 2 cups dark cherries
- 1/4 cup granulated sugar
- 1 tablespoon honey
- 3 tablespoons sherry
- A pinch of sea salt
- A pinch of grated nutmeg

DIRECTIONS (Prep + Cook Time: 35minutes)

Arrange your cherries in the bottom of a lightly greased baking dish. Whisk the remaining ingredients; spoon this mixture into the baking dish. Air fry your cherries at 370 degrees F for 35 minutes. Enjoy!

1078. Apple Fries with Snickerdoodle Dip
INGREDIENTS (2 Servings)

- 1 Gala apple, cored and sliced
- 1 teaspoon peanut oil
- 1 teaspoon butter, room temperature
- 2 ounces cream cheese, room temperature
- 2 ounces
- Greek yogurt
- 2 ounces caster sugar
- 1 teaspoon ground cinnamon

DIRECTIONS (Prep + Cook Time: 10 minutes)

Drizzle peanut oil all over the apple slices; transfer the apple slices to the Air Fryer. Bake the apple slices at 350 degrees F for 5 minutes; shake the basket and continue cooking an additional 5 minutes. In the meantime, mix the remaining ingredients until everything is well incorporated. Serve the apple fries with Snickerdoodle dip on the side. Enjoy!

1079. Classic Vanilla Mini Cheesecakes
INGREDIENTS (6 Servings)

- 1/2 cup almond flour
- 1 ½ tablespoons unsalted butter, melted
- 1 tablespoon white sugar
- 1 (8-ounce) package cream cheese, softened
- 1/4 cup powdered sugar
- 1/2 teaspoon vanilla paste
- 1 egg, at room temperature

Topping:

- 1 ½ cups sour cream
- 3 tablespoons white sugar
- 1 teaspoon vanilla extract
- 1/4 cup maraschino cherries

DIRECTIONS (Prep + Cook Time: 40 minutes) Thoroughly combine the almond flour, butter, and sugar in a mixing bowl. Press the mixture into the bottom of lightly greased custard cups. Then, mix the cream cheese, 1/4 cup of powdered sugar, vanilla, and egg using an electric mixer on low speed. Pour the batter into the pan, covering the crust. Bake in the preheated Air Fryer at 330 degrees F for 35 minutes until edges are puffed and the surface is firm. Mix the sour cream, 3 tablespoons of white sugar, and vanilla for the topping; spread over the crust and allow it to cool to room temperature. Transfer to your refrigerator for 6 to 8 hours. Decorate with maraschino cherries and serve well chilled. Enjoy!

1080. Light and Fluffy Chocolate Cake
INGREDIENTS (6Servings)

- 1/2 stick butter, at room temperature
- 1/2 cup chocolate chips
- 2 tablespoons honey
- 2/3 cup almond flour
- A pinch of fine sea salt
- 1 egg, whisked
- 1/2 teaspoon vanilla extract

DIRECTIONS (Prep + Cook Time: 20 minutes)

Begin by preheating your Air Fryer to 330 degrees F. In a microwave-safe bowl, melt the butter, chocolate, and honey. Add the other ingredients to the cooled chocolate mixture; stir to combine well. Scrape the batter into a lightly greased baking pan. Bake in the preheated Air Fryer for 15 minutes or until the center is springy and a toothpick comes out dry. Enjoy!

1081. Cocktail Party Fruit Kabobs
INGREDIENTS (6 Servings)

- 2 pears, diced into bite-sized chunks
- 2 apples, diced into bite-sized chunks
- 2 mangos, diced into bite-sized chunks
- 1 tablespoon fresh lemon juice
- 1 teaspoon vanilla essence
- 2 tablespoons maple syrup 1 teaspoon ground cinnamon
- 1/2 teaspoon ground cloves

DIRECTIONS (Prep + Cook Time: 30 minutes

Toss all ingredients in a mixing dish. Tread the fruit pieces on skewers. Cook at 350 degrees F for 5 minutes. Enjoy!

1082. The Ultimate Berry Crumble
INGREDIENTS (6 Servings)

- 18 ounces cherries
- 1/2 cup granulated sugar
- 2 tablespoons cornmeal
- 1/4 teaspoon ground star anise
- 1/2 teaspoon ground cinnamon
- 2/3 cup all-purpose flour
- 1 cup demerara sugar
- 1/2 teaspoon baking powder
- 1/3 cup rolled oats
- 1/2 stick butter, cut into small pieces

DIRECTIONS (Prep + Cook Time: 40 minutes)

Toss the cherries with the granulated sugar, cornmeal, star anise, and cinnamon. Divide between six custard cups coated with cooking spray. In a mixing dish, thoroughly combine the remaining ingredients. Sprinkle over the berry mixture. Bake in the preheated Air Fryer at 330 degrees F for 35 minutes. Enjoy!

1083. Easy Chocolate and Coconut Cake
INGREDIENTS (10 Servings)

- 1 stick butter
- 1 ¼ cups dark chocolate, broken into chunks
- 1/4 cup tablespoon agave syrup
- 1/4 cup sugar
- 2 tablespoons milk
- 2 eggs, beaten
- 1/3 cup coconut, shredded

DIRECTIONS (Prep + Cook Time: 20 minutes) Begin by preheating your Air Fryer to 330 degrees F. In a microwave-safe bowl, melt the butter, chocolate, and agave syrup. Allow it to cool to room temperature. Add the remaining ingredients to the chocolate mixture; stir to combine well. Scrape the batter into a lightly greased baking pan. Bake in the preheated Air Fryer for 15 minutes or until a toothpick comes out dry and clean. Enjoy!

1084. Baked Peaches with Oatmeal Pecan Streusel
INGREDIENTS (3 Servings)

- 2 tablespoons old-fashioned rolled oats
- 3 tablespoons golden caster sugar
- 1/2 teaspoon ground cinnamon
- 1 egg
- 2 tablespoons cold salted butter, cut into pieces
- 3 tablespoons pecans, chopped
- 3 large ripe freestone peaches, halved and pitted

DIRECTIONS (Prep + Cook Time: 20 minutes)

Mix the rolled oats, sugar, cinnamon, egg, and butter until well combined. Add a big spoonful of prepared topping to the center of each peach. Pour 1/2 cup of water into an Air Fryer safe dish. Place the peaches in the dish. Top the peaches with the roughly chopped pecans. Bake at 340 degrees F for 17 minutes. Serve at room temperature. Enjoy!

1085. Nana's Famous Apple Fritters
INGREDIENTS (4 Servings)

2/3 cup all-purpose flour	A pinch of freshly grated nutmeg	1/4 cup milk
3 tablespoons granulated sugar	1 teaspoon baking powder	2 apples, peeled, cored and diced
A pinch of sea salt	2 eggs, whisked	1/2 cup powdered sugar

DIRECTIONS (Prep + Cook Time: 20 minutes)

Mix the flour, sugar, salt, nutmeg and baking powder. In a separate bowl whisk the eggs with the milk; add this wet mixture into the dry ingredients; mix to combine well. Add the apple pieces and mix again. Cook in the preheated Air Fryer at 370 degrees for 3 minutes, flipping them halfway through the cooking time. Repeat with the remaining batter. Dust with powdered sugar and serve at room temperature. Enjoy!

1086. Salted Caramel Cheesecake
INGREDIENTS (10 Servings)

1 cup granulated sugar	3/4 cup heavy cream	1 teaspoon vanilla extract
1/3 cup water	2 tablespoons butter	1/2 teaspoon coarse sea salt

Crust:

1 ½ cups graham cracker crumbs	1/3 cup salted butter, melted	2 tablespoons brown sugar

Topping:

20 ounces cream cheese, softened	1 cup granulated sugar	1/4 teaspoon ground star anise
1 cup sour cream	1 teaspoon vanilla essence	3 eggs

DIRECTIONS (Prep + Cook Time: 1 hour + chilling time)

To make the caramel sauce, cook the sugar in a saucepan over medium heat; shake it to form a flat layer. Add the water and cook until the sugar dissolves. Raise the heat to medium-high, and continue to cook your caramel for a further 10 minutes until it turns amber colored. Turn the heat off; immediately stir in the heavy cream, butter, vanilla extract, and salt. Stir to combine well. Let the salted caramel sauce cool to room temperature. Beat all ingredients for the crust in a mixing bowl. Press the mixture into the bottom of a lightly greased baking pan. Bake at 350 degrees F for 18 minutes. Place it in your freezer for 20 minutes. Then, make the cheesecake topping by mixing the remaining ingredients. Pour the prepared topping over the cooled crust and spread evenly. Bake in the preheated Air Fryer at 330 degrees F for 25 to 30 minutes; leave it in the Air Fryer to keep warm for another 30 minutes. Refrigerate your cheesecake until completely cool and firm or overnight. Prior to serving, pour the salted caramel sauce over the cheesecake. Enjoy!

1087. Pecan Fudge Brownies
INGREDIENTS (6 Servings)

1/2 cup butter, melted	1/2 cup flour	1/4 teaspoon fine sea salt
1/2 cup sugar	1/2 teaspoon baking powder	1 ounce semisweet chocolate, coarsely chopped
1 teaspoon vanilla essence	1/4 cup cocoa powder	1/4 cup pecans, finely chopped
1 egg	1/2 teaspoon ground cinnamon	

DIRECTIONS (Prep + Cook Time: 30 minutes)

Start by preheating your Air Fryer to 350 degrees F. Now, lightly grease six silicone molds. In a mixing dish, beat the melted butter with the sugar until fluffy. Next, stir in the vanilla and egg and beat again. After that, add the flour, baking powder, cocoa powder, cinnamon, and salt. Mix until everything is well combined. Fold in the chocolate and pecans; mix to combine. Bake in the preheated Air Fryer for 20 to 22 minutes. Enjoy!

1088. Pear Fritters with Cinnamon and Ginger
INGREDIENTS (4 Servings)

2 pears, peeled, cored and sliced	A pinch of fine sea salt	2 eggs
1 tablespoon coconut oil, melted	A pinch of freshly grated nutmeg	4 tablespoons milk
1 ½ cups all-purpose flour	1/2 teaspoon ginger	
1 teaspoon baking powder	1 teaspoon cinnamon	

DIRECTIONS (Prep + Cook Time: 30 minutes)

Mix all ingredients, except for the pears, in a shallow bowl. Dip each slice of the pears in the batter until well coated. Cook in the preheated Air Fryer at 360 degrees for 4 minutes, flipping them halfway through the cooking time. Repeat with the remaining ingredients. Dust with powdered sugar if desired. Enjoy!

1089. Mom's Orange Rolls
INGREDIENTS (6 Servings)

1/2 cup milk	1/2 stick butter, at room temperature	2 cups all-purpose flour
1/4 cup granulated sugar	1 egg, at room temperature	2 tablespoons fresh orange juice
1 tablespoon yeast	1/4 teaspoon salt	

Filling:

2 tablespoons butter	1 teaspoon ground star anise	1 teaspoon vanilla paste
4 tablespoons white sugar	1/4 teaspoon ground cinnamon	1/2 cup confectioners' sugar

DIRECTIONS (Prep + Cook Time: 1 hour 20 minutes)

Heat the milk in a microwave safe bowl and transfer the warm milk to the bowl of a stand electric mixer. Add the granulated sugar and yeast, and mix to combine well. Cover and let it sit until the yeast is foamy. Then, beat the butter on low speed. Fold in the egg and mix again. Add salt and flour. Add the orange juice and mix on medium speed until a soft dough forms. Knead the dough on a lightly floured surface. Cover it loosely and let it sit in a warm place about 1 hour or until doubled in size. Then, spritz the bottom and sides of a baking pan with cooking oil (butter flavored). Roll your dough out into a rectangle. Spread 2 tablespoons of butter all over the dough. In a mixing dish, combine the white sugar, ground star anise, cinnamon, and vanilla; sprinkle evenly over the dough. Then, roll up your dough to form a log. Cut into 6 equal rolls and place them in the parchment-lined Air Fryer basket. Bake at 350 degrees for 12 minutes, turning them halfway through the cooking time. Dust with confectioners' sugar and enjoy!

1090. Sweet Potato Boats
INGREDIENTS (2 Servings)

2 sweet potatoes, pierce several times with a fork	2 tablespoons peanut butter	1/4 teaspoon ground cloves
	1 tablespoon agave nectar	1/2 teaspoon ground cinnamon
1/4 cup quick-cooking oats	1/2 teaspoon vanilla essence	A pinch of salt

DIRECTIONS (Prep + Cook Time: 25 minutes)

Cook the sweet potatoes in the preheated Air Fryer at 380 degrees F for 20 to 25 minutes. Then, scrape the sweet potato flesh using a spoon; mix the sweet potato flesh with the remaining ingredients. Stuff the potatoes and place them in the Air Fryer cooking basket. Bake the sweet potatoes for a further 10 minutes or until cooked through. Enjoy!

1091. Classic Flourless Cake
INGREDIENTS (4 Servings)

Crust:

1 teaspoon butter	1 tablespoon flaxseed meal	1 teaspoon caster sugar
1/3 cup almond meal	1 teaspoon pumpkin pie spice	

Filling:

6 ounces cream cheese	1/2 teaspoon pure vanilla extract
1 egg	2 tablespoons powdered sugar

DIRECTIONS (Prep + Cook Time: 2 hour) Mix all the ingredients for the crust and then, press the mixture into the bottom of a lightly greased baking pan. Bake the crust at 350 degrees F for 18 minutes. Transfer the crust to the freezer for about 25 minutes. Now, make the cheesecake topping by mixing the remaining ingredients. Spread the prepared topping over the cooled crust. Bake your cheesecake in the preheated Air Fryer at 320 degrees F for about 30 minutes; leave it in the Air Fryer to keep warm for another 30 minutes. Serve well chilled. Enjoy!

1092. Mini Molten Lava Cakes
INGREDIENTS (2 Servings)

1/2 cup dark chocolate chunks	1 egg	1 tablespoon self-rising flour
3 tablespoons butter	1 ounce granulated sugar	2 tablespoons almonds, chopped

DIRECTIONS (Prep + Cook Time: 12 minutes) Microwave the chocolate chunks and butter for 30 to 40 seconds until the mixture is smooth. Then, beat the eggs and sugar; stir in the egg mixture into the chocolate mixture. Now, stir in the flour and almonds. Pour the batter into two ramekins. Bake your cakes at 370 degrees for about 10 minutes and serve at room temperature. Enjoy!

1093. Chocolate Peppermint Cream Pie
INGREDIENTS (2 Servings)

12 cookies, crushed into fine crumbs	1/2 cup heavy whipping cream	1/4 teaspoon ground cinnamon
2 ounces butter, melted	4 tablespoons brown sugar	1/4 teaspoon ground cloves
2 ounces dark chocolate chunks	2 drops peppermint extract	

DIRECTIONS (Prep + Cook Time: 40minutes) In a mixing bowl, thoroughly combine crushed cookies and butter to make the crust. Press the crust into the bottom of a lightly oiled baking dish. Bake the crust at 350 degrees F for 18 minutes. Transfer it to your freezer for 20 minutes. Then, microwave the chocolate chunks for 30 seconds; stir in the heavy whipping cream, brown sugar, peppermint extract, cinnamon and cloves. Spread the mousse evenly over the crust. Refrigerate until firm for about 3 hours. Enjoy!

1094. Fluffy Chocolate Chip Cookies
INGREDIENTS (6 Servings)

1/2 cup butter, softened	1/2 teaspoon coconut extract	1/2 cup all-purpose flour
1/2 cup granulated sugar	1/2 teaspoon vanilla paste	1/2 teaspoon baking powder
1 large egg	1 cup quick-cooking oats	6 ounces dark chocolate chips

DIRECTIONS (Prep + Cook Time: 20 minutes)

Start by preheating your Air Fryer to 330 degrees F. In a mixing bowl, beat the butter and sugar until fluffy. Beat in the egg, coconut extract and vanilla paste. In a second mixing bowl, whisk the oats, flour and baking powder. Add the flour mixture to the egg mixture. Fold in the chocolate chips and gently stir to combine. Drop 2-tablespoon scoops of the dough onto the parchment paper and transfer it to the Air Fryer cooking basket. Gently flatten each scoop to make a cookie shape. Cook in the preheated Air Fryer for about 10 minutes. Work in batches. Enjoy!

1095. Baked Fruit Salad
INGREDIENTS (2 Servings)

- 1 banana, peeled
- 1 cooking pear, cored
- 1 cooking apple, cored
- 1 tablespoon freshly squeezed lemon juice
- 1/2 teaspoon ground star anise
- 1/4 teaspoon ground cinnamon
- 1/2 teaspoon granulated ginger
- 1/4 cup brown sugar
- 1 tablespoon coconut oil, melted

DIRECTIONS (Prep + Cook Time: 15 minutes)

Toss your fruits with lemon juice, star anise, cinnamon, ginger, sugar and coconut oil. Transfer the fruits to the Air Fryer cooking basket. Bake the fruit salad in the preheated Air Fryer at 330 degrees F for 15 minutes. Serve in individual bowls, garnished with vanilla ice cream. Enjoy!

1096. Chocolate Puff Pastry Sticks
INGREDIENTS (3 Servings)

- 8 ounces frozen puff pastry, thawed, cut into strips
- 1/2 stick butter, melted
- 1/2 teaspoon ground cinnamon
- 1/2 cup chocolate hazelnut spread

DIRECTIONS (Prep + Cook Time: 15 minutes)

Brush the strips of the puff pastry with melted butter. Arrange the strips in the Air Fryer cooking basket and bake them at 380 degrees F for 2 minutes; flip and cook on the other side for 2 to 3 minutes longer. Top the pastry sticks with cinnamon and chocolate hazelnut spread. Enjoy!

1097. Red Velvet Pancakes
INGREDIENTS (3 Servings)

- 1 cup all-purpose flour
- 1/2 teaspoon baking soda
- 1 teaspoon granulated sugar
- 1/8 teaspoon sea salt
- 1/8 teaspoon freshly grated nutmeg
- 2 tablespoons ghee, melted
- 1 small-sized egg, beaten
- 1/2 cup milk
- 1 teaspoon red paste food color
- 2 ounces cream cheese, softened
- 1 tablespoon butter, softened
- 1/2 cup powdered sugar

DIRECTIONS (Prep + Cook Time: 15 minutes)

Thoroughly combine the flour, baking soda, granulated sugar, salt and nutmeg in a large bowl. Gradually add in the melted ghee, egg, milk and red paste food color, stirring into the flour mixture until moistened. Allow your batter to rest for about 30 minutes. Spritz the Air Fryer baking pan with cooking spray. Pour the batter into the pan using a measuring cup. Set the pan into the Air Fryer cooking basket. Cook at 330 degrees F for about 5 minutes or until golden brown. Repeat with the other pancakes. Meanwhile, mix the remaining ingredients until creamy and fluffy. Decorate your pancakes with cream cheese topping. Enjoy!

1098. Chocolate Lava Cake
INGREDIENTS (4 Servings)

- 4 ounces butter, melted
- 4 ounces dark chocolate
- 2 eggs, lightly whisked
- 4 tablespoons granulated sugar
- 2 tablespoons cake flour
- 1 teaspoon baking powder
- 1/2 teaspoon ground cinnamon
- 1/4 teaspoon ground star anise

DIRECTIONS (Prep + Cook Time: 20 minutes) Begin by preheating your Air Fryer to 370 degrees F. Spritz the sides and bottom of a baking pan with nonstick cooking spray. Melt the butter and dark chocolate in a microwave-safe bowl. Mix the eggs and sugar until frothy. Pour the butter/chocolate mixture into the egg mixture. Stir in the flour, baking powder, cinnamon, and star anise. Mix until everything is well incorporated. Scrape the batter into the prepared pan. Bake in the preheated Air Fryer for 9 to 11 minutes. Let stand for 2 minutes. Invert on a plate while warm and serve. Enjoy!

1099. Grandma's Butter Cookies
INGREDIENTS (4 Servings)

- 8 ounces all-purpose flour
- 2 ½ ounces sugar
- 1 teaspoon baking powder
- A pinch of grated nutmeg
- A pinch of coarse salt
- 1 large egg, room temperature
- 1 stick butter, room temperature
- 1 teaspoon vanilla extract

DIRECTIONS (Prep + Cook Time: 25minutes) Mix the flour, sugar, baking powder, grated nutmeg, and salt in a bowl. In a separate bowl, whisk the egg, butter, and vanilla extract. Stir the egg mixture into the flour mixture; mix to combine well or until it forms a nice, soft dough. Roll your dough out and cut out with a cookie cutter of your choice. Bake in the preheated Air Fryer at 350 degrees F for 10 minutes. Decrease the temperature to 330 degrees F and cook for 10 minutes longer. Enjoy!

1100. Cinnamon Dough Dippers
INGREDIENTS (6 Servings)

- 1/2 pound bread dough
- 1/4 cup butter, melted
- 1/2 cup caster sugar
- 1 tablespoon cinnamon
- 1/2 cup cream cheese, softened
- 1 cup powdered sugar
- 1/2 teaspoon vanilla
- 2 tablespoons milk

DIRECTIONS (Prep + Cook Time: 20 minutes) Roll the dough into a log; cut into 1-1/2 inch strips using a pizza cutter. Mix the butter, sugar, and cinnamon in a small bowl. Use a rubber spatula to spread the butter mixture over the tops of the dough dippers. Bake at 360 degrees F for 7 to 8 minutes, turning them over halfway through the cooking time. Work in batches. Meanwhile, make the glaze dip by whisking the remaining ingredients with a hand mixer. Beat until a smooth consistency is reached. Serve at room temperature and enjoy!

1101. Baked Coconut Doughnuts
INGREDIENTS (6 Servings)

- 1 ½ cups all-purpose flour
- 1 teaspoon baking powder
- A pinch of kosher salt
- A pinch of freshly grated nutmeg
- 1/2 cup white sugar
- 2 eggs
- 2 tablespoons full-fat coconut milk
- 2 tablespoons coconut oil, melted
- 1/4 teaspoon ground cardamom
- 1/4 teaspoon ground cinnamon
- 1 teaspoon coconut essence
- 1/2 teaspoon vanilla essence
- 1 cup coconut flakes

DIRECTIONS (Prep + Cook Time: 20 minutes) In a mixing bowl, thoroughly combine the all-purpose flour with the baking powder, salt, nutmeg, and sugar. In a separate bowl, beat the eggs until frothy using a hand mixer; add the coconut milk and oil and beat again; lastly, stir in the spices and mix again until everything is well combined. Then, stir the egg mixture into the flour mixture and continue mixing until a dough ball forms. Try not to over-mix your dough. Transfer to a lightly floured surface. Roll out your dough to a 1/4-inch thickness using a rolling pin. Cut out the doughnuts using a 3-inch round cutter; now, use a 1-inch round cutter to remove the center. Bake in the preheated Air Fryer at 340 degrees F approximately 5 minutes or until golden. Repeat with remaining doughnuts. Decorate with coconut flakes and serve. Enjoy!

1102. Bakery-Style Hazelnut Cookies
INGREDIENTS (6 Servings)

- 1 ½ cups all-purpose flour
- 1 teaspoon baking soda
- 1 teaspoon fine sea salt
- 1 stick butter
- 1 cup brown sugar
- 2 teaspoons vanilla
- 2 eggs, at room temperature
- 1 cup hazelnuts, coarsely chopped

DIRECTIONS (Prep + Cook Time: 20 minutes) Begin by preheating your Air Fryer to 350 degrees F. Mix the flour with the baking soda, and sea salt. In the bowl of an electric mixer, beat the butter, brown sugar, and vanilla until creamy. Fold in the eggs, one at a time, and mix until well combined. Slowly and gradually, stir in the flour mixture. Finally, fold in the coarsely chopped hazelnuts. Divide the dough into small balls using a large cookie scoop; drop onto the prepared cookie sheets. Bake for 10 minutes or until golden brown, rotating the pan once or twice through the cooking time. Work in batches and cool for a couple of minutes before removing to wire racks. Enjoy!

1103. Easy Chocolate Brownies
INGREDIENTS (8 Servings)

1 stick butter, melted	1 teaspoon vanilla essence	A pinch of salt
1/2 cup caster sugar	1/2 cup all-purpose flour	A pinch of ground cardamom
1/2 cup white sugar	1 teaspoon baking powder	
1 egg	1/2 cup cocoa powder	

DIRECTIONS (Prep + Cook Time: 30 minutes) Start by preheating your Air Fryer to 350 degrees F. Now, spritz the sides and bottom of a baking pan with cooking spray. In a mixing dish, beat the melted butter with sugar until fluffy. Next, fold in the egg and beat again. After that, add the vanilla, flour, baking powder, cocoa, salt, and ground cardamom. Mix until everything is well combined. Bake in the preheated Air Fryer for 20 to 22 minutes. Enjoy!

1104. Easy Blueberry Muffins
INGREDIENTS (10 Servings)

1 ½ cups all-purpose flour	1/4 teaspoon kosher salt	1/2 cup milk 1/4 cup coconut oil, melted
1/2 teaspoon baking soda	1/2 cup granulated sugar	1/2 teaspoon vanilla paste
1 teaspoon baking powder	2 eggs, whisked	1 cup fresh blueberries

DIRECTIONS (Prep + Cook Time: 20 minutes) In a mixing bowl, combine the flour, baking soda, baking powder, sugar, and salt. Whisk to combine well. In another mixing bowl, mix the eggs, milk, coconut oil, and vanilla. Now, add the wet egg mixture to dry the flour mixture. Then, carefully fold in the fresh blueberries; gently stir to combine. Scrape the batter mixture into the muffin cups. Bake your muffins at 350 degrees F for 12 minutes or until the tops are golden brown. Sprinkle some extra icing sugar over the top of each muffin if desired. Serve and enjoy!

1105. Mocha Chocolate Espresso Cake
INGREDIENTS (8 Servings)

1 ½ cups flour	1/4 teaspoon salt	1/2 teaspoon vanilla
2/3 cup sugar	1 stick butter, melted	
1 teaspoon baking powder	1/2 cup hot strongly brewed coffee	
1 egg		

Topping:

1/4 cup flour	1/2 teaspoon ground cardamom	3 tablespoons coconut oil
1/2 cup sugar	1 teaspoon ground cinnamon	

DIRECTIONS (Prep + Cook Time: 30 minutes) Mix all dry ingredients for your cake; then, mix in the wet ingredients. Mix until everything is well incorporated. Spritz a baking pan with cooking spray. Scrape the batter into the baking pan. Then make the topping by mixing all ingredients. Place on top of the cake. Smooth the top with a spatula. Bake at 330 degrees F for 30 minutes or until the top of the cake springs back when gently pressed with your fingers. Serve with your favorite hot beverage. Enjoy!

1106. Grilled Banana Boats
INGREDIENTS (3 Servings)

3 large bananas	2 tablespoons mini chocolate chips	3 tablespoons crushed vanilla wafers
1 tablespoon ginger snaps	3 tablespoons mini marshmallows	

DIRECTIONS (Prep + Cook Time: 15minutes)

In the peel, slice your banana lengthwise; make sure not to slice all the way through the banana. Divide the remaining ingredients between the banana pockets. Place in the Air Fryer grill pan. Cook at 395 degrees F for 7 minutes. Let the banana boats cool for 5 to 6 minutes, and then eat with a spoon. Enjoy!

1107. Favorite New York Cheesecake
INGREDIENTS (8 Servings)

1 ½ cups digestive biscuits crumbs	32 ounces full-fat cream cheese	1 tablespoon vanilla essence
2 ounces white sugar	1/2 cup heavy cream	1 teaspoon grated lemon zest
1 ounce demerara sugar	1 ¼ cups caster sugar	
1/2 stick butter, melted	3 eggs, at room temperature	

DIRECTIONS (Prep + Cook Time: 40 minutes) Coat the sides and bottom of a baking pan with a little flour. In a mixing bowl, combine the digestive biscuits, white sugar, and demerara sugar. Add the melted butter and mix until your mixture looks like breadcrumbs. Press the mixture into the bottom of the prepared pan to form an even layer. Bake at 330 degrees F for 7 minutes until golden brown. Allow it to cool completely on a wire rack. Meanwhile, in a mixer fitted with the paddle attachment, prepare the filling by mixing the soft cheese, heavy cream, and caster sugar; beat until creamy and fluffy. Crack the eggs into the mixing bowl, one at a time; add the vanilla and lemon zest and continue to mix until fully combined. Pour the prepared topping over the cooled crust and spread evenly. Bake in the preheated Air Fryer at 330 degrees F for 25 to 30 minutes; leave it in the Air Fryer to keep warm for another 30 minutes. Cover your cheesecake with plastic wrap. Place in your refrigerator and allow it to cool at least 6 hours or overnight. Serve well chilled. Enjoy!

1108. Red Velvet Pancakes
INGREDIENTS (3 Servings)

1/2 cup flour	2 tablespoons white sugar	1 egg
1 teaspoon baking powder	1/2 teaspoon cinnamon	1/2 cup milk
1/4 teaspoon salt	1 teaspoon red paste food color	1 teaspoon vanilla

Topping:

2 ounces cream cheese, softened	2 tablespoons butter, softened	3/4 cup powdered sugar

DIRECTIONS (Prep + Cook Time: 35 minutes) Mix the flour, baking powder, salt, sugar, cinnamon, red paste food color in a large bowl. Gradually add the egg and milk, whisking continuously, until well combined. Let it stand for 20 minutes. Spritz the Air Fryer baking pan with cooking spray. Pour the batter into the pan using a measuring cup. Cook at 230 degrees F for 4 to 5 minutes or until golden brown. Repeat with the remaining batter. Meanwhile, make your topping by mixing the ingredients until creamy and fluffy. Decorate your pancakes with topping. Enjoy!

1109. Summer Peach Crisp
INGREDIENTS (4 Servings)

2 cups fresh peaches, pitted and sliced	1 teaspoon pure vanilla extract	1 stick cold butter
1/4 cup cornmeal	1/2 teaspoon ground cinnamon	1/2 cup rolled oats
1/4 cup brown sugar	A pinch of fine sea salt	

DIRECTIONS (Prep + Cook Time: 40 minutes) Toss the sliced peaches with the cornmeal, brown sugar, vanilla extract, cinnamon, and sea salt. Place in a baking pan coated with cooking spray. In a mixing dish, thoroughly combine the cold butter and rolled oats. Sprinkle the mixture over each peach. Bake in the preheated Air Fryer at 330 degrees F for 35 minutes. Enjoy!

1110. Authentic Indian Gulgulas
INGREDIENTS (3 Servings)

1 banana, mashed	1/2 teaspoon vanilla essence	1/2 milk
1/4 cup sugar	1/4 teaspoon ground cardamom	3/4 cup all-purpose flour
1 egg	1/4 teaspoon cinnamon	1 teaspoon baking powder

DIRECTIONS (Prep + Cook Time: 20 minutes) In a mixing bowl, whisk the mashed banana with the sugar and egg; add the vanilla, cardamom, and cinnamon and mix to combine well. Gradually pour in the milk and mix again. Stir in the flour and baking powder. Mix until everything is well incorporated. Drop a spoonful of batter onto the greased Air Fryer pan. Cook in the preheated Air Fryer at 360 degrees F for 5 minutes, flipping them halfway through the cooking time. Repeat with the remaining batter and serve warm. Enjoy!

1111. Apricot and Walnut Crumble
INGREDIENTS (8 Servings)

2 pounds apricots, pitted and sliced	1 cup brown sugar	2 tablespoons cornstarch

Topping:

1 ½ cups old-fashioned rolled oats	1 teaspoon crystallized ginger	1 stick butter, cut into pieces
½ cup brown sugar	½ teaspoon ground cardamom	1/2 cup walnuts, chopped
2 tablespoons agave nectar	A pinch of salt	1/2 cup dried cranberries

DIRECTIONS (Prep + Cook Time: 40 minutes)

Toss the sliced apricots with the brown sugar and cornstarch. Place in a baking pan lightly greased with nonstick cooking spray. In a mixing dish, thoroughly combine all the topping ingredients. Sprinkle the topping ingredients over the apricot layer. Bake in the preheated Air Fryer at 330 degrees F for 35 minutes. Enjoy!

1112. Fried Honey Banana
INGREDIENTS (2 Servings)

2 ripe bananas, peeled and sliced	3 tablespoons desiccated coconut	1/4 teaspoon cardamom powder
2 tablespoons honey	A pinch of fine sea salt	
3 tablespoons rice flour	1/2 teaspoon baking powder	

DIRECTIONS (Prep + Cook Time: 20 minutes)

Preheat the Air Fryer to 390 degrees F. Drizzle honey over the banana slices. In a mixing dish, thoroughly combine the rice flour, coconut, salt, baking powder, and cardamom powder. Roll each slice of banana over the flour mixture. Bake in the preheated Air Fryer approximately 13 minutes, flipping them halfway through the cooking time. Enjoy!

1113. Almond Chocolate CupCakes
INGREDIENTS (6 Serving)

¾ cup self-raising flour	1 tablespoon cocoa powder	½ teaspoon vanilla extract
1 cup powdered sugar	2 ounces butter, softender	1 ½ ounces dark chocolate chunks
¼ teaspoon salt	1 egg, whisked	½ cup almonds, chopped
¼ teaspoon nutmeg, preferably freshly grated	2 tablespoons almond milk	

DIRECTIONS (Prep + Cook Time: 20 minutes) In a mixing bowl, combine the flour, sugar, salt, nutmeg, and cocoa powder. Mix to combine well. In another mixing bowl, whisk the butter, egg, almond milk, and vanilla. Now, add the wet egg mixture to the dry ingredients. Then, carefully fold in the chocolate chunks and almonds; gently stir to combine. Scrape the batter mixture into muffin cups. Bake your cupcakes at 350 degrees F for 12 minutes until a toothpick comes out clean. Decorate with chocolate sprinkles if desired. Serve and enjoy!

Other Air Fryer Favorites

1114. Air-Fried Guacamole Balls
INGREDIENTS (4 Serving)

- 2 avocados, pitted, peeled and mashed
- 2 tablespoons shallots, finely chopped
- 2 tablespoons fresh cilantro, chopped
- 2 eggs, whisked
- 1/2 teaspoon paprika
- Himalayan
- salt and ground black pepper, to taste
- 1 cup tortilla chips, crushed

DIRECTIONS (Prep + Cook Time: 20 minutes)

In a mixing bowl, thoroughly combine the avocado, shallots, cilantro, eggs, paprika, salt and black pepper. Scoop the mixture onto a parchment-lined cookie sheet; freeze for about 3 hours or until hardened.

Shape the mixture into balls and roll them in crushed tortilla chips. Cook the guacamole balls in the preheated Air Fryer at 400 degrees F for about 4 minutes; shake the basket and continue to cook an additional 3 minutes.

Work in batches. Enjoy!

1115. Greek-Style Frittata
INGREDIENTS (1 Serving)

- 1/2 teaspoon olive oil
- 2 eggs
- 4 tablespoons Greek-style yogurt
- 1 scallion stalk, chopped
- 1 bell pepper, divined and chopped
- 1/4 teaspoon oregano
- Coarse sea
- salt and ground black pepper, to season
- 1 small tomato, sliced
- 2 ounces feta cheese, crumbled
- 1 tablespoon fresh basil leaves

DIRECTIONS (Prep + Cook Time: 15 minutes)

Brush the sides and bottoms of a baking dish with olive oil. In a mixing dish, beat the eggs until frothy; then, stir in Greek yogurt, scallion, bell pepper, oregano, salt and black pepper.

Cook your frittata at 350 degrees for 10 minutes; top with tomatoes and continue to cook for 5 minutes more; check for doneness. Garnish with feta cheese and fresh basil leaves, serve warm. Enjoy!

1116. Cornbread Muffins with Raisins
INGREDIENTS (3 Serving)

- 1/2 cup yellow cornmeal
- 1/2 cup plain flour
- 1 teaspoon baking powder
- 1/3 cup brown sugar
- 1/2 teaspoon salt
- A pinch of grated nutmeg
- A pinch of ground cinnamon
- 1/2 cup whole milk
- 1 egg, beaten
- 2 ounces butter, melted
- 1/2 cup raisins

DIRECTIONS (Prep + Cook Time: 25 minutes)

In a mixing bowl, thoroughly combine the dry ingredients. In another bowl, mix the wet ingredients. Then, stir the wet mixture into the dry mixture. Pour the batter into a lightly buttered muffin tin. Now, bake your cornbread muffins at 350 degrees F for about 20 minutes. Check for doneness and transfer to a wire rack to cool slightly before serving.Enjoy!

1117. Classic French Potato Galette
INGREDIENTS (2 Serving)

- 1/2 pound potatoes, thinly sliced
- 3 tablespoons butter, melted
- 2 tablespoons white onion, finely chopped
- Kosher
- salt and freshly ground black pepper, to season
- 1/4 teaspoon rosemary
- 1/4 teaspoon allspices
- 4 ounces goat cheese

DIRECTIONS (Prep + Cook Time: 40 minutes)

Toss the potato slices with melted butter, onion, salt, black pepper, rosemary and allspice. Place 1/2 of the potato mixture on a foil-lined cooking basket. Top with 2 ounces of goat cheese.

Then, cover it with a layer of the potato slices. Top with goat cheese and fold the foil loosely over it. Bake your galette at 380 degrees F for 25 to 30 minutes. Now, turn the temperature to 340 degrees F, open the foil and continue to cook for 5 to 7 minutes more until the potatoes are tender. Cut your galette into wedges and serve warm. Enjoy!

1118. Taco Rolls with A Twist
INGREDIENTS (3 Serving)

1/2 pound ground turkey	1 small-sized shallot, finely chopped	2 ounces Cotija cheese, shredded
2 cloves garlic, minced	1 tablespoon taco seasoning	1 tablespoon butter, melted
1 teaspoon jalapeno pepper, chopped	6 ounces refrigerated crescent rolls	1/2 cup salsa

DIRECTIONS (Prep + Cook Time: 15 minutes)

Cook the ground turkey in a frying pan for about 3 minutes until no longer pink. Now, add in the garlic, jalapeno and shallot and cook for a minute or so until fragrant. Stir the taco seasoning into the cooked taco meat. Lay the crescent rolls flat on a piece of parchment paper; divide the cooked taco meat between the crescent rolls. Top with the shredded cheese and roll them up. Brush the top of each roll with melted butter and transfer them to the Air Fryer cooking basket. Air fry your taco rolls at 370 degrees F for about 7 minutes, checking them for doneness. Serve with salsa and enjoy!

1119. Easy Greek Revithokeftedes
INGREDIENTS (3 Serving)

12 ounces canned chickpeas, drained	1 tablespoon fresh coriander	Sea salt and freshly ground pepper, to taste
1 red onion, sliced	2 tablespoons all-purpose flour	
2 cloves garlic	1/2 teaspoon cayenne pepper	3 large (6 ½ -inch) pita bread
1 chili pepper		

DIRECTIONS (Prep + Cook Time: 30 minutes)

Pulse the chickpeas, onion, garlic, chili pepper and coriander in your food processor until the chickpeas are ground. Add the all-purpose flour, cayenne pepper, salt, and black pepper; stir to combine well. Form the chickpea mixture into balls and place them in the lightly greased Air Fryer basket. Cook at 380 degrees F for about 15 minutes, shaking the basket occasionally to ensure even cooking. Warm the pita bread in your Air Fryer at 390 degrees F for around 6 minutes. Serve the revithokeftedes in pita bread with tzatziki or your favorite Greek topping. Enjoy!

1120. Rosemary Roasted Mixed Nuts
INGREDIENTS (6 Serving)

2 tablespoons butter, at room temperature	1 teaspoon coarse sea salt	1 cup pecans
	1/2 teaspoon paprika	1/2 cup hazelnuts
1 tablespoon dried rosemary	1/2 cup pine nuts	

DIRECTIONS (Prep + Cook Time: 20 minutes)

Toss all the ingredients in the mixing bowl. Line the Air Fryer basket with baking parchment. Spread out the coated nuts in a single layer in the basket. Roast at 350 degrees F for 6 to 8 minutes, shaking the basket once or twice. Work in batches. Enjoy!

1121. Jamaican Cornmeal Pudding
INGREDIENTS (6 Serving)

3 cups coconut milk	1 cup sugar	1/2 cup water
2 ounces butter, softened	1/2 teaspoon fine sea salt	½ cup raisins
1 teaspoon cinnamon	1 ½ cups yellow cornmeal	1 teaspoon rum extract
1/2 teaspoon grated nutmeg	1/4 cup all-purpose flour	1 teaspoon vanilla extract

Custard:

1/2 cup full-fat coconut milk	1/4 cup honey
1 ounce butter	1 dash vanilla

DIRECTIONS (Prep + Cook Time: 1 hour + chilling time)

Place the coconut milk, butter, cinnamon, nutmeg, sugar, and salt in a large saucepan; bring to a rapid boil. Heat off. In a mixing bowl, thoroughly combine the cornmeal, flour and water; mix to combine well. Add the milk/butter mixture to the cornmeal mixture; mix to combine. Bring the cornmeal mixture to boil; then, reduce the heat and simmer approximately 7 minutes, whisking continuously. Remove from the heat. Now, add the raisins, rum extract, and vanilla. Place the mixture into a lightly greased baking pan and bake at 325 degrees F for 12 minutes. In a saucepan, whisk the coconut milk, butter, honey, and vanilla; let it simmer for 2 to 3 minutes. Now, prick your pudding with a fork and top with the prepared custard. Return to your Air Fryer and bake for about 35 minutes more or until a toothpick inserted comes out dry and clean. Place in your refrigerator until ready to serve. Enjoy!

1122. Traditional Onion Bhaji
INGREDIENTS (3 Serving)

- 1 egg, beaten
- 2 tablespoons olive oil
- 2 onions, sliced
- 1 green chili, deseeded and finely chopped
- 2 ounces chickpea flour
- 1 ounce all-purpose flour
- Salt and black pepper, to taste
- 1 teaspoon cumin seeds
- 1/2 teaspoon ground turmeric

DIRECTIONS (Prep + Cook Time: 40 minutes) Place all ingredients, except for the onions, in a mixing dish; mix to combine well, adding a little water to the mixture. Once you've got a thick batter, add the onions; stir to coat well. Cook in the preheated Air Fryer at 370 degrees F for 20 minutes flipping them halfway through the cooking time. Work in batches and transfer to a serving platter. Enjoy!

1123. Baked Eggs Florentine
INGREDIENTS (2 Serving)

- 1 tablespoon ghee, melted
- 2 cups baby spinach, torn into small pieces
- 2 tablespoons shallots, chopped
- 1/4 teaspoon red pepper flakes
- Salt, to taste
- 1 tablespoon fresh thyme leaves, roughly chopped
- 4 eggs

DIRECTIONS (Prep + Cook Time: 20 minutes) Start by preheating your Air Fryer to 350 degrees F. Brush the sides and bottom of a gratin dish with the melted ghee. Put the spinach and shallots into the bottom of the gratin dish. Season with red pepper, salt, and fresh thyme. Make four indents for the eggs; crack one egg into each indent. Bake for 12 minutes, rotating the pan once or twice to ensure even cooking. Enjoy!

1124. Classic Egg Salad
INGREDIENTS (3 Serving)

- 6 eggs
- 1 teaspoon mustard
- 1/2 cup mayonnaise
- 1 tablespoons white vinegar
- 2 carrots, trimmed and sliced
- 1 red bell pepper, seeded and sliced
- 1 green bell pepper, seeded and sliced
- 1 shallot, sliced
- Sea salt and ground black pepper, to taste

DIRECTIONS (Prep + Cook Time: 20 minutes) Place the wire rack in the Air Fryer basket; lower the eggs onto the wire rack. Cook at 270 degrees F for 15 minutes. Transfer them to an ice-cold water bath to stop the cooking. Peel the eggs under cold running water; coarsely chop the hard-boiled eggs and set aside. Toss with the remaining ingredients and serve well chilled. Enjoy!

1125. Southwest Bean Potpie
INGREDIENTS (5 Serving)

- 1 tablespoon olive oil
- 2 sweet peppers, seeded and sliced
- 1 carrot, chopped
- 1 onion, chopped
- 2 garlic cloves, minced
- 1 cup cooked bacon, diced
- 1 ½ cups beef bone broth
- 20 ounces canned red kidney beans, drained
- Sea salt and freshly ground black pepper, to taste
- 1 package (8 1/2-ounce) cornbread mix
- 1/2 cup milk
- 2 tablespoons butter, melted

DIRECTIONS (Prep + Cook Time: 30 minutes)

Heat the olive oil in a saucepan over medium-high heat. Now, cook the peppers, carrot, onion, and garlic until they have softened, about 7 minutes Add the bacon and broth. Bring to a boil and cook for 2 minutes more. Stir in the kidney beans, salt and black pepper; continue to cook until everything is heated through. Transfer the mixture to the lightly greased baking pan. In a small bowl, combine the muffin mix, milk, and melted butter. Stir until well mixed and spoon evenly over the bean mixture. Smooth it with a spatula and transfer to the Air Fryer cooking basket. Bake in the preheated Air Fryer at 400 degrees F for 12 minutes. Place on a wire rack to cool slightly before slicing and serving. Enjoy!

1126. French Toast with Blueberries and Honey
INGREDIENTS (6 Serving)

- 1/4 cup milk
- 2 eggs
- 2 tablespoons butter, melted
- 1/2 teaspoon ground cinnamon
- 1/4 teaspoon ground cloves
- 1 teaspoon vanilla extract
- 6 slices day-old French baguette
- 2 tablespoons honey
- 1/2 cup blueberries

DIRECTIONS (Prep + Cook Time: 20 minutes) In a mixing bowl, whisk the milk eggs, butter, cinnamon, cloves, and vanilla extract. Dip each piece of the baguette into the egg mixture and place in the parchment-lined Air Fryer basket. Cook in the preheated Air Fryer at 360 degrees F for 6 to 7 minutes, turning them over halfway through the cooking time to ensure even cooking. Serve garnished with honey and blueberries. Enjoy!

1127. Famous Western Eggs
INGREDIENTS (6 Serving)

6 eggs	1/4 teaspoon ground black pepper	1/3 cup cheddar cheese, shredded
3/4 cup milk	1/4 teaspoon paprika	
1 ounce cream cheese, softened Sea salt, to your liking	6 ounces cooked ham, diced	
	1 onion, chopped	

DIRECTIONS (Prep + Cook Time:20 minutes)

Begin by preheating the Air Fryer to 360 degrees F. Spritz the sides and bottom of a baking pan with cooking oil. In a mixing dish, whisk the eggs, milk, and cream cheese until pale. Add the spices, ham, and onion; stir until everything is well incorporated. Pour the mixture into the baking pan; top with the cheddar cheese. Bake in the preheated Air Fryer for 12 minutes. Serve warm and enjoy!

1128. Easy Roasted Hot Dogs
INGREDIENTS (6Serving)

6 hot dogs	1 tablespoon mustard	6 lettuce leaves
6 hot dog buns	6 tablespoons ketchup	

DIRECTIONS (Prep + Cook Time: 25 minutes)

Place the hot dogs in the lightly greased Air Fryer basket. Bake at 380 degrees F for 15 minutes, turning them over halfway through the cooking time to promote even cooking. Place on the bun and add the mustard, ketchup, and lettuce leaves. Enjoy!

1129. Bourbon Glazed Mango with Walnuts
INGREDIENTS (4 Serving)

2 ripe mangos, peeled and diced	2 tablespoons coconut oil, melted	1/4 teaspoon pure coconut extract
2 tablespoons bourbon whiskey	1/4 teaspoon ground cardamom	1/2 cup walnuts, coarsely chopped
2 tablespoons sugar	1 teaspoon vanilla essence	

DIRECTIONS (Prep + Cook Time: 20 minutes)

Start by preheating your Air Fryer to 400 degrees F. Toss all ingredients in a baking dish and transfer to the Air fryer basket. Now, bake for 10 minutes, or until browned on top. Serve with whipped cream if desired. Enjoy!

1130. Salted Pretzel Crescents
INGREDIENTS (4 Serving)

1 can crescent rolls	1 egg, whisked with	2 tablespoons sesame seed
10 cups water	1 tablespoon water	1 teaspoon coarse sea salt
1/2 cup baking soda	1 tablespoon poppy seeds	

DIRECTIONS (Prep + Cook Time: 20 minutes)

Unroll the dough onto your work surface; separate into 8 triangles. In a large saucepan, bring the water and baking soda to a boil over high heat. Cook each roll for 30 seconds. Remove from the water using a slotted spoon; place on a kitchen towel to drain. Repeat with the remaining rolls. Now, brush the tops with the egg wash; sprinkle each roll with the poppy seeds, sesame seed and coarse sea salt. Cover and let rest for 10 minutes. Arrange the pretzels in the lightly greased Air Fryer basket. Bake in the preheated Air Fryer at 340 degrees for 7 minutes or until golden brown. Enjoy!

1131. Party Pancake Kabobs
INGREDIENTS (4 Serving)

Pancakes:

1 cup all-purpose flour	1/4 teaspoon salt	1/2 teaspoon vanilla extract
1 teaspoon baking powder	1 large egg, beaten	2 tablespoons unsalted butter, melted
1 tablespoon sugar	1/2 cup milk	

Kabobs:

1 banana, diced	1 Granny Smith apples, diced	1/4 cup maple syrup, for serving

DIRECTIONS (Prep + Cook Time: 40minutes)

Mix all ingredients for the pancakes until creamy and fluffy. Let it stand for 20 minutes. Spritz the Air Fryer baking pan with cooking spray. Drop the pancake batter on the pan with a small spoon. Cook at 230 degrees F for 4 minutes or until golden brown. Repeat with the remaining batter. Tread the mini pancakes and the fruit onto bamboo skewers, alternating between the mini pancakes and fruit. Drizzle maple syrup all over the kabobs and serve immediately. Enjoy!

1132. Red Currant Cupcakes
INGREDIENTS (3 Serving)

- 1 cup all-purpose flour
- 1/2 cup sugar
- 1 teaspoon baking powder
- A pinch of kosher salt
- A pinch of grated nutmeg
- 1/4 cup coconut, oil melted
- 1 egg
- 1/4 cup full-fat coconut milk
- 1/4 teaspoon ground cardamom
- 1/4 teaspoon ground cinnamon
- 1 teaspoon vanilla extract
- 6 ounces red currants

DIRECTIONS (Prep + Cook Time: 20 minutes)

Mix the flour with the sugar, baking powder, salt, and nutmeg. In a separate bowl, whisk the coconut oil, egg, milk, cardamom, cinnamon, and vanilla. Add the egg mixture to the dry ingredients; mix to combine well. Now, fold in the red currants; gently stir to combine. Scrape the batter into lightly greased 6 standard-size muffin cups. Bake your cupcakes at 360 degrees F for 12 minutes or until the tops are golden brown. Sprinkle some extra icing sugar over the top of each muffin if desired. Enjoy!

1133. Cranberry Cornbread Muffins
INGREDIENTS (4 Serving)

- 3/4 cup all-purpose flour
- 3/4 cup cornmeal
- 1 teaspoon baking powder
- 1/2 teaspoon baking soda
- 1/2 teaspoon salt
- 3 tablespoons honey
- 1 egg, well whisked
- 1/4 cup olive oil
- 3/4 cup milk
- 1/2 cup fresh cranberries, roughly chopped

DIRECTIONS (Prep + Cook Time: 35 minutes)

In a mixing dish, thoroughly combine the flour, cornmeal, baking powder, baking soda, and salt. In a separate bowl, mix the honey, egg, olive oil, and milk. Next, stir the liquid mixture into the dry ingredients; mix to combine well. Fold in the fresh cranberries and stir to combine well. Pour the batter into a lightly greased muffin tin; cover with aluminum foil and poke tiny little holes all over the foil. Now, bake for 15 minutes. Remove the foil and bake for 10 minutes more. Transfer to a wire rack to cool slightly before cutting and serving. Enjoy!

1134. Sweet Corn and Kernel Fritters
INGREDIENTS (4 Serving)

- 1 medium-sized carrot, grated
- 1 yellow onion, finely chopped
- 4 ounces canned sweet corn kernels, drained
- 1 teaspoon sea salt flakes
- 1 heaping tablespoon fresh cilantro, chopped
- 1 medium-sized egg, whisked
- 2 tablespoons plain milk
- 1 cup of Parmesan cheese, grated
- 1/4 cup of self-rising flour
- 1/3 teaspoon baking powder
- 1/3 teaspoon brown sugar

DIRECTIONS (Prep + Cook Time: 20 minutes)

Press down the grated carrot in the colander to remove excess liquid. Then, spread the grated carrot between several sheets of kitchen towels and pat it dry. Then, mix the carrots with the remaining ingredients in the order listed above. Roll 1 tablespoon of the mixture into a ball; gently flatten it using the back of a spoon or your hand. Now, repeat with the remaining ingredients. Spitz the balls with a nonstick cooking oil. Cook in a single layer at 350 degrees for 8 to 11 minutes or until they're firm to touch in the center. Serve warm and enjoy!

1135. Creamed Cajun Chicken
INGREDIENTS (6 Serving)

- 3 green onions, thinly sliced
- ½ tablespoon Cajun seasoning
- 1 ½ cup buttermilk
- 2 large-sized chicken breasts, cut into strips
- 1/2 teaspoon garlic powder
- 1 teaspoon salt
- 1 cup cornmeal mix
- 1 teaspoon shallot powder
- 1 ½ cup flour
- 1 teaspoon ground
- black pepper, or to taste

DIRECTIONS (Prep + Cook Time: 10 minutes)

Prepare three mixing bowls. Combine 1/2 cup of the plain flour together with the cornmeal and Cajun seasoning in your bowl. In another bowl, place the buttermilk. Pour the remaining 1 cup of flour into the third bowl. Sprinkle the chicken strips with all the seasonings. Then, dip each chicken strip in the 1 cup of flour, then in the buttermilk; finally, dredge them in the cornmeal mixture. Cook the chicken strips in the air fryer baking pan for 16 minutes at 365 degrees F. Serve garnished with green onions. enjoy!

1136. Grilled Chicken Tikka Masala
INGREDIENTS (4 Serving)

- 1 teaspoon Tikka Masala
- 1 teaspoon fine sea salt
- 2 heaping teaspoons whole grain mustard
- 2 teaspoons coriander, ground
- 2 tablespoon olive oil
- 2 large-sized chicken breasts, skinless and halved lengthwise
- 2 teaspoons onion powder
- 1 ½ tablespoons cider vinegar
- Basmati rice, steamed
- 1/3 teaspoon red pepper flakes, crushed

DIRECTIONS (Prep + Cook Time: 35 minutes + marinating time)

Preheat the air fryer to 335 degrees for 4 minutes. Toss your chicken together with the other ingredients, minus basmati rice. Let it stand at least 3 hours. Cook for 25 minutes in your air fryer; check for doneness because the time depending on the size of the piece of chicken. Serve immediately over warm basmati rice. Enjoy!

1137. Tangy Paprika Chicken
INGREDIENTS (4 Serving)

- 1 ½ tablespoons freshly squeezed lemon juice
- 2 small-sized chicken breasts, boneless
- 1/2 teaspoon ground cumin
- 1 teaspoon dry mustard powder
- 1 teaspoon paprika
- 2 teaspoons cup pear cider vinegar
- 1 tablespoon olive oil
- 2 garlic cloves, minced
- Kosher salt and freshly ground mixed peppercorns, to savor

DIRECTIONS (Prep + Cook Time: 30minutes)

Warm the olive oil in a nonstick pan over a moderate flame. Sauté the garlic for just 1 minutes. Remove your pan from the heat; add cider vinegar, lemon juice, paprika, cumin, mustard powder, kosher salt, and black pepper. Pour this paprika sauce into a baking dish. Pat the chicken breasts dry; transfer them to the prepared sauce. Bake in the preheated air fryer for about 28 minutes at 335 degrees F; check for doneness using a thermometer or a fork. Allow to rest for 8 to 9 minutes before slicing and serving. Serve with dressing. Enjoy!

1138. Roasted Turkey Sausage with Potatoes
INGREDIENTS (6 Serving)

- 1/2 pound red potatoes, peeled and diced
- 1/2 teaspoon onion salt
- 1/2 teaspoon dried sage
- 1/2 pound ground turkey
- 1/3 teaspoon ginger, ground
- 1 sprig rosemary, chopped
- 1 ½ tablespoons olive oil
- 1/2 teaspoon paprika
- 2 sprigs thyme, chopped
- 1 teaspoon ground black pepper

DIRECTIONS (Prep + Cook Time: 40 minutes)

In a bowl, mix the first six ingredients; give it a good stir. Heat a thin layer of vegetable oil in a nonstick skillet that is placed over a moderate flame. Form the mixture into patties; fry until they're browned on all sides, or about 12 minutes. Arrange the potatoes at the bottom of a baking dish. Sprinkle with the rosemary and thyme; add a drizzle of olive oil. Top with the turkey. Roast for 32 minutes at 365 degrees F, turning once halfway through. Eat warm. Enjoy!

1139. Super Easy Sage and Lime Wings
INGREDIENTS (4 Serving)

- 1 teaspoon onion powder
- 1/3 cup fresh lime juice
- 1/2 tablespoon corn flour
- 1/2 heaping tablespoon fresh chopped parsley
- 1/3 teaspoon mustard powder
- 1/2 pound turkey wings, cut into smaller pieces
- 2 heaping tablespoons fresh chopped sage
- 1/2 teaspoon garlic powder
- 1/2 teaspoon seasoned salt
- 1 teaspoon freshly cracked black or white peppercorns

DIRECTIONS (Prep + Cook Time: 23 minutes + marinating time)

Simply dump all of the above ingredients into a mixing dish; cover and let it marinate for about 1 hours in your refrigerator. Air-fry turkey wings for 28 minutes at 355 degrees F. Enjoy!

1140. Cajun Turkey Meatloaf
INGREDIENTS (6 Serving)

- 1 1/3 pounds turkey breasts, ground
- 1/2 cup vegetable stock
- 2 eggs, lightly beaten
- 1/2 sprig thyme, chopped
- 1/2 teaspoon
- Cajun seasonings
- 1/2 sprig coriander, chopped
- 1/2 cup seasoned breadcrumbs
- 2 tablespoons butter, room temperature
- 1/2 cup scallions, chopped
- 1/3 teaspoon ground nutmeg
- 1/3 cup tomato ketchup
- 1/2 teaspoon table salt
- 2 teaspoons whole grain mustard
- 1/3 teaspoon mixed peppercorns, freshly cracked

DIRECTIONS (Prep + Cook Time: 45 minutes)

Firstly, warm the butter in a medium-sized saucepan that is placed over a moderate heat; sauté the scallions together with the chopped thyme and coriander leaves until just tender. While the scallions are sautéing, set your air fryer to cook at 365 degrees F. Combine all the ingredients, minus the ketchup, in a mixing dish; fold in the sautéed mixture and mix again. Shape into a meatloaf and top with the tomato ketchup. Air-fry for 50 minutes. Enjoy!

1141. Cornbread with Pulled Pork
INGREDIENTS (2 Serving)

- 2 1/2 cups pulled pork, leftover works well too
- 1 teaspoon dried rosemary 1
- /2 teaspoon chili powder
- 3 cloves garlic, peeled and pressed
- 1/2 recipe cornbread
- 1/2 tablespoon brown sugar
- 1/3 cup scallions, thinly sliced
- 1 teaspoon sea salt

DIRECTIONS (Prep + Cook Time: 24 minutes)

Preheat a large-sized nonstick skillet over medium heat; now, cook the scallions together with the garlic and pulled pork. Next, add the sugar, chili powder, rosemary, and salt. Cook, stirring occasionally, until the mixture is thickened. Preheat your air fryer to 335 degrees F. Now, coat two mini loaf pans with a cooking spray. Add the pulled pork mixture and spread over the bottom using a spatula. Spread the previously prepared cornbread batter over top of the spiced pulled pork mixture. Bake this cornbread in the preheated air fryer until a tester inserted into the center of it comes out clean, or for 18 minutes. Enjoy!

1142. Easiest Pork Chops Ever
INGREDIENTS (6 Serving)

- 1/3 cup Italian breadcrumbs
- Roughly chopped fresh cilantro, to taste
- 2 teaspoons Cajun seasonings
- Nonstick cooking spray
- 2 eggs, beaten
- 3 tablespoons white flour
- 1 teaspoon seasoned salt
- Garlic & onion spice blend, to taste
- 6 pork chops
- 1/3 teaspoon freshly cracked black pepper

DIRECTIONS (Prep + Cook Time: 22 minutes)

Coat the pork chops with Cajun seasonings, salt, pepper, and the spice blend on all sides. Then, add the flour to a plate. In a shallow dish, whisk the egg until pale and smooth. Place the Italian breadcrumbs in the third bowl. Dredge each pork piece in the flour; then, coat them with the egg; finally, coat them with the breadcrumbs. Spritz them with cooking spray on both sides. Now, air-fry pork chops for about 18 minutes at 345 degrees F; make sure to taste for doneness after first 12 minutes of cooking. Lastly, garnish with fresh cilantro. Enjoy!

1143. Sausage, Pepper and Fontina Frittata
INGREDIENTS (5 Serving)

- 3 pork sausages, chopped
- 5 well-beaten eggs
- 1 1/2 bell peppers, seeded and chopped
- 1 teaspoon smoked cayenne pepper
- 2 tablespoons Fontina cheese
- 1/2 teaspoon tarragon
- 1/2 teaspoon ground black pepper
- 1 teaspoon salt

DIRECTIONS (Prep + Cook Time: 14 minutes)

In a cast-iron skillet, sweat the bell peppers together with the chopped pork sausages until the peppers are fragrant and the sausage begins to release liquid. Lightly grease the inside of a baking dish with pan spray. Throw all of the above ingredients into the prepared baking dish, including the sautéed mixture; stir to combine. Bake at 345 degrees F approximately 9 minutes. Serve right away with the salad of choice. Enjoy!

1144. The Best London Broil Ever
INGREDIENTS (8 Serving)

2 pounds London broil

3 large garlic cloves, minced

3 tablespoons balsamic vinegar

3 tablespoons whole-grain mustard

2 tablespoons olive oil

Sea salt and ground black pepper, to taste

1/2 teaspoon dried hot red pepper flakes

DIRECTIONS (Prep + Cook Time: 30 minutes+ marinating time)

Score both sides of the cleaned London broil. Thoroughly combine the remaining ingredients; massage this mixture into the meat to coat it on all sides. Let it marinate for at least 3 hours. Set the Air Fryer to cook at 400 degrees F; Then cook the London broil for 15 minutes. Flip it over and cook another 10 to 12 minutes. Enjoy!

1145. All-In-One Spicy Spaghetti with Beef
INGREDIENTS (4 Serving)

3/4 pound ground chuck

1 onion, peeled and finely chopped

1 teaspoon garlic paste

1 bell pepper, chopped

1 small-sized habanero pepper, deveined and finely minced

1/2 teaspoon dried rosemary

1/2 teaspoon dried marjoram

1 ¼ cups crushed tomatoes, fresh or canned

1/2 teaspoon sea salt flakes

1/4 teaspoon ground black pepper, or more to taste

1 package cooked spaghetti, to serve

DIRECTIONS (Prep + Cook Time: 30 minutes)

In the Air Fryer baking dish, place the ground meat, onion, garlic paste, bell pepper, habanero pepper, rosemary, and the marjoram. Air-fry, uncovered, for 10 to 11 minutes. Next step, stir in the tomatoes along with salt and pepper; cook 17 to 20 minutes. Serve over cooked spaghetti. Enjoy!

1146. Beef and Kale Omelet
INGREDIENTS (4 Serving)

Non-stick cooking spray

1/2 pound leftover beef, coarsely chopped

2 garlic cloves, pressed

1 cup kale, torn into pieces and wilted

1 tomato, chopped

1/4 teaspoon brown sugar

4 eggs, beaten

4 tablespoons heavy cream

1/2 teaspoon turmeric powder

Salt and ground black pepper, to your liking

1/8 teaspoon ground allspice

DIRECTIONS (Prep + Cook Time: 20 minutes)

Spritz the inside of four ramekins with a cooking spray. Divide all of the above ingredients among the prepared ramekins. Stir until everything is well combined. Air-fry at 360 degrees F for 16 minutes; check with a wooden stick and return the eggs to the Air Fryer for a few more minutes as needed. Serve immediately. Enjoy!

1147. Spanish Bolitas de Queso
INGREDIENTS (3 Serving)

1/2 cup plain flour

2 tablespoons cornstarch

2 eggs 1 garlic clove minced

1/2 teaspoon red pepper flakes, crushed

1/2 teaspoon pimentón

6 ounces goat cheese, shredded

1 cup tortilla chips, crushed

DIRECTIONS (Prep + Cook Time: 15 minutes)

In a mixing bowl, thoroughly combine all ingredients, except for the crushed tortilla chips. Shape the mixture into bite-sized balls. Roll your balls into the crushed tortilla chips and transfer them to a lightly greased cooking basket. Cook the balls at 390 degrees F for about 8 minutes, shaking the basket halfway through the cooking time to promote even cooking. Enjoy!

1148. Pumpkin Griddle Cake
INGREDIENTS (3 Serving)

1/3 cup almond butter

2/3 cup pumpkin puree

1/2 cup all-purpose flour

1/2 teaspoon baking powder

2 eggs, beaten

1/2 teaspoon crystalized ginger

1 teaspoon pumpkin pie spice

4 tablespoons honey

DIRECTIONS (Prep + Cook Time: 20minutes)

Start by preheating your Air Fryer to 340 degrees F. In a mixing bowl, thoroughly combine all ingredients. Working in batches, drop batter, 1/2 cup at a time, into a lightly oiled baking dish. Cook the griddle cake for about 8 minutes or until golden brown. Repeat with the other cake and serve with some extra honey, if desired. Enjoy!

1149. Coconut Chip Cookies
INGREDIENTS (3 Serving)

- 1/4 cup almond flour
- 1/2 cup plain flour
- 1/2 teaspoon baking powder
- 1/3 cup granulated sugar
- 1/8 teaspoon coarse sea slat
- 1 tablespoon butter, melted
- 1 egg, beaten
- 1/2 teaspoon vanilla extract
- 1/2 teaspoon coconut extract
- 1/4 cup coconut chips

DIRECTIONS (Prep + Cook Time: 40 minutes)

Begin by preheating your Air Fryer to 350 degrees F. In a mixing bowl, combine the flour, baking powder, sugar and salt. Add in the butter and egg and continue stirring into the flour mixture until moistened. Stir in the vanilla and coconut extract. Lastly, fold in the coconut chips and mix again. Allow your batter to rest for about 30 minutes. Scoop out 1 tablespoon size balls of the batter on a cookie pan, leaving 2 inches between each cookie. Bake for 10 minutes or until golden brown, rotating the pan once or twice through the cooking time. Enjoy!

1150. Apple Oatmeal Cups
INGREDIENTS (3 Serving)

- 1 cup rolled oats
- 1/4 teaspoon ground cardamom
- 1/4 teaspoon ground cinnamon
- 1/2 teaspoon baking powder
- 1/4 teaspoon sea salt
- 1/2 cup milk
- 2 tablespoons honey
- 1/2 teaspoon vanilla extract
- 1 apple, peeled, cored and diced
- 2 tablespoons peanut butter

DIRECTIONS (Prep + Cook Time: 10 minutes)

In a mixing bowl, thoroughly combine the rolled oats, cardamom, cinnamon, baking powder, sea salt, milk, honey and vanilla. Lastly, fold in the apple and spoon the mixture into an Air Fryer safe baking dish. Bake in the preheated Air Fryer at 395 degrees F for about 9 minutes. Spoon into individual bowls and serve with peanut butter. Enjoy!

1151. Mini Banana Bread Loaves
INGREDIENTS (4 Serving)

- 1 cup all-purpose flour
- 1/2 teaspoon baking powder
- A pinch of salt
- 1 teaspoon apple spice
- 2 bananas, peeled
- 3 tablespoons date syrup
- 4 tablespoons coconut oil
- 2 eggs, whisked

DIRECTIONS (Prep + Cook Time: 40 minutes)

Start by preheating your Air Fryer to 320 degrees F. Then, grease bottoms of mini loaf pans with a nonstick cooking spray. In a mixing bowl, combine the flour with baking powder, salt and apple spice. In another bowl, mash your bananas with date syrup, coconut oil and eggs until everything is well incorporated. Fold the banana mixture into the flour mixture. Spoon the mixture into prepared mini loaf pans and transfer them to the Air Fryer cooking basket. Bake your loaves in the preheated Air Fryer for 35 minutes or until a tester comes out dry and clean. Sprinkle some extra icing sugar over the top of banana bread, if desired. Enjoy!

1152. Air-Fried Popcorn
INGREDIENTS (1 Serving)

- 3 tablespoons corn kernels
- 1 teaspoon butter, melted Sea salt, to taste

DIRECTIONS (Prep + Cook Time: 15 minutes)

Start by preheating your Air Fryer to 390 degrees F. Now, line the bottom and sides of the cooking basket with aluminum foil. Add the kernels to the Air Fryer cooking basket. Air fry your popcorn in the preheated Air Fryer for 15 minutes, shaking the basket every 5 minutes to ensure the kernels are not burning. Toss your popcorn with melted butter and sea salt. Enjoy!

1153. Spicy Polenta Fries
INGREDIENTS (2 Serving)

- 8 ounces pre-cooked polenta
- 1 teaspoon canola oil
- 1/2 teaspoon red chili flakes
- Salt and black pepper, to taste

DIRECTIONS (Prep + Cook Time: 35 minutes)

Pour the polenta onto a large lined baking tray; now, let it cool and firm up. Using a sharp knife, cut chilled polenta into sticks. Sprinkle canola oil, red chili flakes, salt and black pepper onto polenta sticks. Air fry the polenta fries at 400 degrees F for about 30 minutes, turning them over once or twice. Enjoy!

1154. Salted Pretzel Croissants
INGREDIENTS (3 Serving)

1 (8-ounce) can refrigerated crescent rolls	1 egg, whisked with	2 tablespoons sesame seed
1/2 cup baking soda	1 tablespoon of water	1 teaspoon coarse sea salt

DIRECTIONS (Prep + Cook Time: 20 minutes)

Unroll the dough and separate it into triangles. Roll them up to make a croissant shape. Bring 6 cups of water and the baking soda to a boil in a medium saucepan. Cook each croissant for 30 seconds and carefully remove from the water with a slotted spoon; pat dry with a kitchen towel. Now, brush the tops of your croissants with the egg wash; sprinkle each roll with sesame seed and coarse sea salt. Allow them to rest for about 10 minutes. Now, place your croissants in the lightly greased Air Fryer cooking basket. Bake your croissants in the preheated Air Fryer at 330 degrees for about 6 minutes or until golden brown. Enjoy!

1155. Air-Grilled Sweet English Muffin
INGREDIENTS (1 Serving)

1 English muffin, split in half	1 ounce milk	1/4 teaspoon ground cinnamon
1 teaspoon butter	1 ounce double cream	1 tablespoon icing sugar
2 egg	1 tablespoon brown sugar	

DIRECTIONS (Prep + Cook Time: 10 minutes)

Spread the butter onto the bottom half of the English muffin. In a mixing bowl, beat the eggs with milk, double cream, brown sugar and cinnamon. Dip the English muffin into the egg/cream mixture and place it in the lightly greased Air Fryer cooking basket. Cook the English muffin in the preheated Air Fryer at 380 degrees F for 5 minutes, turning it over halfway through the cooking time. Dust with icing sugar and serve immediately. Enjoy!

1156. Mediterranean Keto Bread
INGREDIENTS (1 Serving)

1/2 cup provolone cheese, shredded	1/2 teaspoon oregano	1/2 teaspoon garlic powder
1 egg, whisked	1/4 teaspoon basil	

DIRECTIONS (Prep + Cook Time: 10 minutes)

Thoroughly combine all ingredients in a mixing bowl. Press the batter into a round circle on a piece of parchment paper. Transfer it to the Air Fryer cooking basket. Bake the keto bread at 350 degrees F for 9 to 10 minutes. Eat warm and enjoy!

1157. Baked Eggs in Dinner Rolls
INGREDIENTS (2 Serving)

4 dinner rolls	4 eggs 1/4 teaspoon cayenne pepper
2 tablespoons butter	Sea salt and ground black pepper, to taste

DIRECTIONS (Prep + Cook Time: 15minutes)

Scoop out the insides of dinner rolls to make the shells. Brush them with melted butter on all sides. Crack an egg into each roll shell; sprinkle with cayenne pepper, salt and black pepper. Bake your rolls in the preheated Air Fryer at 330 degrees F for about 10 minutes until eggs are set. Cook for a few more minutes to achieve your desired level of doneness, if needed. Enjoy!

1158. Mini Raspberry Pies
INGREDIENTS (4 Serving)

11 ounces flaky-style biscuit dough	8 ounces canned raspberry pie filling	1/2 cup powdered sugar

DIRECTIONS (Prep + Cook Time: 20 minutes)

Roll each section of the biscuit dough into a round circle. Divide the raspberry pie filling among the circles. Roll them up and transfer to the Air Fryer cooking basket. Brush the rolls with a nonstick cooking oil. Air fry your pies at 330 degrees F for about 12 minutes, work in batches. Roll the warm pies in powdered sugar until well coated on all sides. Transfer them to a wire rack to cool before serving. Enjoy!

1159. Farmer's Breakfast Deviled Eggs
INGREDIENTS (3 Serving)

- 6 eggs
- 6 slices bacon
- 2 tablespoons mayonnaise
- 1 teaspoon hot sauce
- 1/2 teaspoon Worcestershire sauce
- 2 tablespoons green onions, chopped
- 1 tablespoon pickle relish
- Salt and ground black pepper, to taste
- 1 teaspoon smoked paprika

DIRECTIONS (Prep + Cook Time: 25minutes) Place the wire rack in the Air Fryer basket; lower the eggs onto the wire rack. Cook at 270 degrees F for 15 minutes. Transfer them to an ice-cold water bath to stop the cooking. Peel the eggs under cold running water; slice them into halves. Cook the bacon at 400 degrees F for 3 minutes; flip the bacon over and cook an additional 3 minutes; chop the bacon and reserve. Mash the egg yolks with the mayo, hot sauce, Worcestershire sauce, green onions, pickle relish, salt, and black pepper; add the reserved bacon and spoon the yolk mixture into the egg whites. Garnish with smoked paprika. Enjoy!

1160. Brown Rice Bowl
INGREDIENTS (4 Serving)

- 1 cup brown rice
- 1 tablespoon peanut oil
- 2 tablespoons soy sauce
- 1/2 cup scallions, chopped
- 2 bell pepper, chopped 2 eggs, beaten
- Sea salt and ground black pepper, to taste
- 1/2 teaspoon granulated garlic

DIRECTIONS (Prep + Cook Time: 55 minutes) Heat the brown rice and 2 ½ cups of water in a saucepan over high heat. Bring it to a boil; turn the stove down to simmer and cook for 35 minutes. Grease a baking pan with nonstick cooking spray. Add the hot rice and the other ingredients. Cook at 370 degrees F for 15 minutes, checking occasionally to ensure even cooking. Enjoy!

1161. Delicious Hot Fruit Bake
INGREDIENTS (4 Serving

- 2 cups blueberries
- 2 cups raspberries
- 1 tablespoon cornstarch
- 3 tablespoons maple syrup
- 2 tablespoons coconut oil, melted
- A pinch of freshly grated nutmeg
- A pinch of salt
- 1 cinnamon stick
- 1 vanilla bean

DIRECTIONS (Prep + Cook Time: 40 minutes) Place your berries in a lightly greased baking dish. Sprinkle the cornstarch onto the fruit. Whisk the maple syrup, coconut oil, nutmeg, and salt in a mixing dish; add this mixture to the berries and gently stir to combine. Add the cinnamon and vanilla. Bake in the preheated Air Fryer at 370 degrees F for 35 minutes. Serve warm or at room temperature. Enjoy!

1162. Country-Style Apple Fries
INGREDIENTS (4 Serving)

- 1/2 cup milk
- 1 egg
- 1/2 all-purpose flour
- 1 teaspoon baking powder
- 4 tablespoons brown sugar
- 1 teaspoon vanilla extract
- 1/2 teaspoon ground cloves
- A pinch of kosher salt
- A pinch of grated nutmeg
- 1 tablespoon coconut oil, melted
- 2 Pink Lady apples, cored, peeled, slice into pieces (shape and size of French fries)
- 1/3 cup granulated sugar
- 1 teaspoon ground cinnamon

DIRECTIONS (Prep + Cook Time: 20 minutes) In a mixing bowl, whisk the milk and eggs; gradually stir in the flour; add the baking powder, brown sugar, vanilla, cloves, salt, nutmeg, and melted coconut oil. Mix to combine well. Dip each apple slice into the batter, coating on all sides. Spritz the bottom of the cooking basket with cooking oil. Cook the apple fries in the preheated Air Fryer at 395 degrees F approximately 8 minutes, turning them over halfway through the cooking time. Cook in small batches to ensure even cooking. In the meantime, mix the granulated sugar with the ground cinnamon; sprinkle the cinnamon sugar over the apple fries. Serve warm. Enjoy!

1163. Italian Sausage and Veggie Bake
INGREDIENTS (4 Serving)

- 1 pound Italian sausage
- 2 red peppers, seeded and sliced
- 2 green peppers, seeded and sliced
- 1 cup mushrooms, sliced
- 1 shallot, sliced
- 4 cloves garlic
- 1 teaspoon dried basil
- 1 teaspoon dried oregano
- 1/4 teaspoon black pepper
- 1/4 teaspoon cayenne pepper
- Sea salt, to taste
- 2 tablespoons Dijon mustard
- 1 cup chicken broth

DIRECTIONS (Prep + Cook Time: 20minutes)

Toss all ingredients in a lightly greased baking pan. Make sure the sausages and vegetables are coated with the oil and seasonings. Bake in the preheated Air Fryer at 380 degrees F for 15 minutes. Divide between individual bowls and serve warm. Enjoy!

1164. Quinoa with Baked Eggs and Bacon
INGREDIENTS (4 Serving)

- 1/2 cup quinoa
- 1/2 pound potatoes, diced
- 1 onion, diced
- 6 slices bacon, precooked
- 1 tablespoon butter, melted
- Sea salt and ground black pepper, to taste
- 6 eggs

DIRECTIONS (Prep + Cook Time: 40 minutes) Rinse the quinoa under cold running water. Place the rinsed quinoa in a pan and add 1 cup of water. Bring it to the boil. Turn the heat down and let it simmer for 13 to 15 minutes or until tender; reserve. Place the diced potatoes and onion in a lightly greased casserole dish. Add the bacon and the reserved quinoa. Drizzle the melted butter over the quinoa and sprinkle with salt and pepper. Bake in the preheated Air Fryer at 390 degrees F for 10 minutes. Turn the temperature down to 350 degrees F. Make six indents for the eggs; crack one egg into each indent. Bake for 12 minutes, rotating the pan once or twice to ensure even cooking. Enjoy!

1165. English Muffins with a Twist
INGREDIENTS (4 Serving)

- 4 English muffins, split in half
- 2 eggs
- 1/3 cup milk
- 1/4 cup heavy cream
- 2 tablespoons honey
- 1 teaspoon pure vanilla extract
- 1/4 cup confectioners' sugar

DIRECTIONS (Prep + Cook Time: 15 minutes)

Cut the muffins crosswise into strips. In a mixing bowl, whisk the eggs, milk, heavy cream, honey, and vanilla extract. Dip each piece of muffins into the egg mixture and place in the parchment-lined Air Fryer basket. Cook in the preheated Air Fryer at 360 degrees F for 6 to 7 minutes, turning them over halfway through the cooking time to ensure even cooking. Dust with confectioners' sugar and serve warm. Enjoy!

1166. Mediterranean Roasted Vegetable and Bean Salad
INGREDIENTS (4 Serving)

- 1 red onion, sliced
- 1 pound cherry tomatoes
- 1/2 pound asparagus 1 cucumber, sliced
- 2 cups baby spinach
- 2 tablespoons white vinegar
- 1/4 cup extra-virgin olive oil
- 2 tablespoons fresh parsley
- Sea salt and pepper to taste
- 8 ounces canned red kidney beans, rinsed
- 1/2 cup Kalamata olives, pitted and sliced

DIRECTIONS (Prep + Cook Time: 20minutes) Begin by preheating your Air Fryer to 400 degrees F. Place the onion, cherry tomatoes, and asparagus in the lightly greased Air Fryer basket. Bake for 5 to 6 minutes, tossing the basket occasionally. Transfer to a salad bowl. Add the cucumber and baby spinach. Then, whisk the vinegar, olive oil, parsley, salt, and black pepper in a small mixing bowl. Dress your salad; add the beans and olives. Toss to combine well and serve. Enjoy!

1167. Crunch-Crunch Party Mix
INGREDIENTS (8 Serving)

- 1 cup whole-grain Rice Chex
- 2 cups cheese squares
- 1 cup pistachios
- 1/2 cup almonds
- 1 cup cheddar-flavored mini pretzel twists
- 2 tablespoons butter, melted
- 1/4 cup poppy seeds
- 1/2 cup sunflower seeds
- 1 tablespoon coarse sea salt
- 1 tablespoon garlic powder
- 1 tablespoon paprika

DIRECTIONS (Prep + Cook Time: 25 minutes)

Mix all ingredients in a large bowl. Toss to combine well. Place in a single layer in the parchment-lined cooking basket. Bake in the preheated Air Fryer at 310 degrees F for 13 to 16 minutes. Allow it to cool completely before serving. Store in an airtight container for up to 3 months. Enjoy!

1168. Easy Fried Button Mushrooms
INGREDIENTS (4 Serving)

- 1 pound button mushrooms
- 1 cup cornstarch
- 1 cup all-purpose flour
- 1/2 teaspoon baking powder
- 2 eggs, whisked
- 2 cups seasoned breadcrumbs
- 1/2 teaspoon salt
- 2 tablespoons fresh parsley leaves, roughly chopped

DIRECTIONS (Prep + Cook Time: 15 minutes) Pat the mushrooms dry with a paper towel. To begin, set up your breading station. Mix the cornstarch, flour, and baking powder in a shallow dish. In a separate dish, whisk the eggs. Finally, place your breadcrumbs and salt in a third dish. Start by dredging the mushrooms in the flour mixture; then, dip them into the eggs. Press your mushrooms into the breadcrumbs, coating evenly. Spritz the Air Fryer basket with cooking oil. Add the mushrooms and cook at 400 degrees F for 6 minutes, flipping them halfway through the cooking time. Serve garnished with fresh parsley leaves. Enjoy!

1169. Creamed Asparagus and Egg Salad
INGREDIENTS (4 Serving)

- 2 eggs
- 1 pound asparagus, chopped
- 2 cup baby spinach
- 1/2 cup mayonnaise
- 1 teaspoon mustard
- 1 teaspoon fresh lemon juice
- Sea salt and ground black pepper, to taste

DIRECTIONS (Prep + Cook Time: 25 minutes)

Place the wire rack in the Air Fryer basket; lower the eggs onto the wire rack. Cook at 270 degrees F for 15 minutes. Transfer them to an ice-cold water bath to stop the cooking. Peel the eggs under cold running water; coarsely chop the hard-boiled eggs and set aside. Increase the temperature to 400 degrees F. Place your asparagus in the lightly greased Air Fryer basket. Cook for 5 minutes or until tender. Place in a nice salad bowl. Add the baby spinach. In a mixing dish, thoroughly combine the remaining ingredients. Drizzle this dressing over the asparagus in the salad bowl and top with the chopped eggs. Enjoy!

1170. Spring Chocolate Doughnuts
INGREDIENTS (6 Serving)

- 1 can (16-ounce) can buttermilk biscuits
- Chocolate

Glaze:

- 1 cup powdered sugar
- 4 tablespoons unsweetened baking cocoa
- 2 tablespoon butter, melted
- 2 tablespoons milk

DIRECTIONS (Prep + Cook Time: 20 minutes)

Bake your biscuits in the preheated Air Fryer at 350 degrees F for 8 minutes, flipping them halfway through the cooking time. While the biscuits are baking, make the glaze. Beat the ingredients with whisk until smooth, adding enough milk for the desired consistency; set aside. Dip your doughnuts into the chocolate glaze and transfer to a cooling rack to set. Enjoy!

1171. Scrambled Eggs with Spinach and Tomato
INGREDIENTS (2 Serving)

- 2 tablespoons olive oil, melted
- 4 eggs, whisked
- 5 ounces fresh spinach, chopped
- 1 medium-sized tomato, chopped
- 1 teaspoon fresh lemon juice
- 1/2 teaspoon coarse salt
- 1/2 teaspoon ground black pepper
- 1/2 cup of fresh basil, roughly chopped

DIRECTIONS (Prep + Cook Time: 15 minutes)

Add the olive oil to an Air Fryer baking pan. Make sure to tilt the pan to spread the oil evenly. Simply combine the remaining ingredients, except for the basil leaves; whisk well until everything is well incorporated. Cook in the preheated Air Fryer for 8 to 12 minutes at 280 degrees F. Garnish with fresh basil leaves. Serve warm with a dollop of sour cream if desired. Enjoy!

1172. Potato Appetizer with Garlic-Mayo Sauce
INGREDIENTS (4 Serving)

- 2 tablespoons vegetable oil of choice

For the Dipping Sauce:

- 2 teaspoons dried rosemary, crushed
- 3 garlic cloves, minced
- Kosher salt and freshly ground black pepper, to taste
- 1/3 teaspoon dried marjoram, crushed
- 1/4 cup sour cream
- 3 Russet potatoes, cut into wedges
- 1/3 cup mayonnaise

DIRECTIONS (Prep + Cook Time: 19 minutes)

Lightly grease your potatoes with a thin layer of vegetable oil. Season with salt and ground black pepper. Arrange the seasoned potato wedges in an air fryer cooking basket. Bake at 395 degrees F for 15 minutes, shaking once or twice. In the meantime, prepare the dipping sauce by mixing all the sauce ingredients. Serve the potatoes with the dipping sauce and enjoy! Enjoy!

1173. Potato and Kale Croquettes
INGREDIENTS (6 Serving)

- 4 eggs, slightly beaten
- 1/3 cup flour
- 1/3 cup goat cheese, crumbled
- 1 ½ teaspoons fine sea salt
- 4 garlic cloves, minced
- 1 cup kale, steamed
- 1/3 cup breadcrumbs
- 1/3 teaspoon red pepper flakes
- 3 potatoes, peeled and quartered
- 1/3 teaspoon dried dill weed

DIRECTIONS (Prep + Cook Time: 9 minutes)

Firstly, boil the potatoes in salted water. Once the potatoes are cooked, mash them; add the kale, goat cheese, minced garlic, sea salt, red pepper flakes, dill and one egg; stir to combine well. Now, roll the mixture to form small croquettes. Grab three shallow bowls. Place the flour in the first shallow bowl. Beat the remaining 3 eggs in the second bowl. After that, throw the breadcrumbs into the third shallow bowl. Dip each croquette in the flour; then, dip them in the eggs bowl; lastly, roll each croquette in the breadcrumbs. Air fry at 335 degrees F for 7 minutes or until golden. Tate, adjust for seasonings and serve warm. Enjoy!

1174. Cheese and Chive Stuffed Chicken Rolls
INGREDIENTS (6 Serving)

- 2 eggs, well-whisked Tortilla chips, crushed
- 1 1/2 tablespoons extra-virgin olive oil
- 1 ½ tablespoons fresh chives, chopped
- 3 chicken breasts, halved lengthwise
- 1 ½ cup soft cheese
- 2 teaspoons sweet paprika
- 1/2 teaspoon whole grain mustard
- 1/2 teaspoon cumin powder
- 1/3 teaspoon fine sea salt
- 1/3 cup fresh cilantro, chopped
- 1/3 teaspoon freshly ground black pepper, or more to taste

DIRECTIONS (Prep + Cook Time: 20 minutes)

Flatten out each piece of the chicken breast using a rolling pin. Then, grab three mixing dishes. In the first one, combine the soft cheese with the cilantro, fresh chives, cumin, and mustard. In another mixing dish, whisk the eggs together with the sweet paprika. In the third dish, combine the salt, black pepper, and crushed tortilla chips. Spread the cheese mixture over each piece of chicken. Repeat with the remaining pieces of the chicken breasts; now, roll them up. Coat each chicken roll with the whisked egg; dredge each chicken roll into the tortilla chips mixture. Lower the rolls onto the air fryer cooking basket. Drizzle extra-virgin olive oil over all rolls. Air fry at 345 degrees F for 28 minutes, working in batches. Serve warm, garnished with sour cream if desired. Enjoy!

1175. Dinner Avocado Chicken Sliders
INGREDIENTS (4 Serving)

- ½ pounds ground chicken meat
- 4 burger buns
- 1/2 cup Romaine lettuce, loosely packed
- ½ teaspoon dried parsley flakes
- 1/3 teaspoon mustard seeds
- 1 teaspoon onion powder
- 1 ripe fresh avocado, mashed
- 1 teaspoon garlic powder
- 1 ½ tablespoon extra-virgin olive oil
- 1 cloves garlic, minced Nonstick cooking spray
- Salt and cracked black pepper (peppercorns), to taste

DIRECTIONS (Prep + Cook Time: 10 minutes)

Firstly, spritz an air fryer cooking basket with a nonstick cooking spray. Mix ground chicken meat, mustard seeds, garlic powder, onion powder, parsley, salt, and black pepper until everything is thoroughly combined. Make sure not to overwork the meat to avoid tough chicken burgers. Shape the meat mixture into patties and roll them in breadcrumbs; transfer your burgers to the prepared cooking basket. Brush the patties with the cooking spray. Air-fry at 355 F for 9 minutes, working in batches. Slice burger buns into halves. In the meantime, combine olive oil with mashed avocado and pressed garlic. To finish, lay Romaine lettuce and avocado spread on bun bottoms; now, add burgers and bun tops. Enjoy!

1176. Cheesy Pasilla Turkey
INGREDIENTS (2 Serving)

- 1/3 cup Parmesan cheese, shredded
- 2 turkey breasts, cut into four pieces
- 1/3 cup mayonnaise 1 ½ tablespoons sour cream
- 1/2 cup crushed crackers
- 1 dried Pasilla peppers
- 1 teaspoon onion salt
- 1/3 teaspoon mixed peppercorns, freshly cracked

DIRECTIONS (Prep + Cook Time: 30 minutes)

In a shallow bowl, mix the crushed crackers, Parmesan cheese, onion salt, and the cracked mixed peppercorns together. In a food processor, blitz the mayonnaise, along with the cream and dried Pasilla peppers until there are no lumps. Coat the turkey breasts with this mixture, ensuring that all sides are covered. Then, coat each piece of turkey in the Parmesan/cracker mix. Now, preheat the air fryer to 365 degrees F; cook for 28 minutes until thoroughly cooked. Enjoy!

1177. Creamy Lemon Turkey
INGREDIENTS (4 Serving)

- 1/3 cup sour cream
- 2 cloves garlic, finely minced
- 1/3 teaspoon lemon zest
- 2 small-sized turkey breasts, skinless and cubed
- 1/3 cup thickened cream
- 2 tablespoons lemon juice
- 1 teaspoon fresh marjoram, chopped
- Salt and freshly cracked mixed peppercorns, to taste
- 1/2 cup scallion, chopped
- 1/2 can tomatoes, diced
- 1 ½ tablespoons canola oil

DIRECTIONS (Prep + Cook Time: 2 hour 25 minutes)

Firstly, pat dry the turkey breast. Mix the remaining items; marinate the turkey for 2 hours. Set the air fryer to cook at 355 degrees F. Brush the turkey with a nonstick spray; cook for 23 minutes, turning once. Serve with naan and enjoy!

1178. Easy Pork Burgers with Blue Cheese
INGREDIENTS (6 Serving)

- 1/3 cup blue cheese, crumbled
- 6 hamburger buns, toasted
- 2 teaspoons dried basil
- 1/3 teaspoon smoked paprika
- 1 pound ground pork
- 2 tablespoons tomato puree
- 2 small-sized onions, peeled and chopped
- 1/2 teaspoon ground black pepper
- 3 garlic cloves, minced
- 1 teaspoon fine sea salt

DIRECTIONS (Prep + Cook Time: 44minutes)

Start by preheating your air fryer to 385 degrees F. In a mixing dish, combine the pork, onion, garlic, tomato puree, and seasonings; mix to combine well. Form the pork mixture into six patties; cook the burgers for 23 minutes. Pause the machine, turn the temperature to 365 degrees F and cook for 18 more minutes. Place the prepared burger on the bottom bun; top with blue cheese; assemble the burgers and serve warm. enjoy!

1179. Grilled Lemony Pork Chops
INGREDIENTS (5 Serving)

- 5 pork chops
- 1/3 cup vermouth
- 1/2 teaspoon paprika
- 2 sprigs thyme, only leaves, crushed
- 1/2 teaspoon dried oregano Fresh parsley, to serve
- 1 teaspoon garlic salt
- ½ lemon, cut into wedges
- 1 teaspoon freshly cracked black pepper
- 3 tablespoons lemon juice
- 3 cloves garlic, minced
- 2 tablespoons canola oil

DIRECTIONS (Prep + Cook Time: 34minutes)

Firstly, heat the canola oil in a sauté pan over a moderate heat. Now, sweat the garlic until just fragrant. Remove the pan from the heat and pour in the lemon juice and vermouth. Now, throw in the seasonings. Dump the sauce into a baking dish, along with the pork chops. Tuck the lemon wedges among the pork chops and air-fry for 27 minutes at 345 degrees F. enjoy!

1180. Old-Fashioned Beef Stroganoff
INGREDIENTS (4 Serving)

- 3/4 pound beef sirloin steak, cut into small-sized strips
- 1/4 cup balsamic vinegar
- 1 tablespoon brown mustard
- 2 tablespoons all-purpose flour
- 1 tablespoon butter
- 1 cup beef broth
- 1 cup leek, chopped
- 2 cloves garlic, crushed
- 1 teaspoon cayenne pepper
- Sea salt flakes and crushed red pepper, to taste
- 1 cup sour cream
- 2 ½ tablespoons tomato paste

DIRECTIONS (Prep + Cook Time: 20minutes)

Place the beef along with the balsamic vinegar and the mustard in a mixing dish; cover and marinate in your refrigerator for about 1 hour. Then, coat the beef strips with the flour; butter the inside of a baking dish and put the beef into the dish. Add the broth, leeks and garlic. Cook at 380 degrees for 8 minutes. Pause the machine and add the cayenne pepper, salt, red pepper, sour cream and tomato paste; cook for additional 7 minutes. Check for doneness and serve with warm egg noodles, if desired. enjoy!

1181. Beer-Braised Short Loin
INGREDIENTS (4 Serving)

1 ½ pounds short loin

2 tablespoons olive oil 1 bottle beer

2-3 cloves garlic, finely minced

2 Turkish bay leaves

DIRECTIONS (Prep + Cook Time: 15 minutes)

Pat the beef dry; then, tenderize the beef with a meat mallet to soften the fibers. Place it in a large-sized mixing dish. Add the remaining ingredients; toss to coat well and let it marinate for at least 1 hour. Cook about 7 minutes at 395 degrees F; after that, pause the Air Fryer. Flip the meat over and cook for another 8 minutes, or until it's done. enjoy!

1182. Traditional Greek Revithokeftedes
INGREDIENTS (4 Serving)

2 cups chickpeas, soaked overnight

1 teaspoon fresh garlic, minced

1 red onion, chopped

2 boiled potatoes, peeled and mashed

2 tablespoons all-purpose flour

1 teaspoon Greek spice mix

1 teaspoon olive oil

DIRECTIONS (Prep + Cook Time: 20minutes)

In a mixing bowl, thoroughly combine all ingredients until everything is well incorporated. Shape the mixture into equal patties. Then, transfer the patties to the Air Fryer cooking basket. Cook the patties at 380 degrees F for about 15 minutes, turning them over halfway through the cooking time. Serve your revithokeftedes in pita bread with toppings of your choice. Enjoy!

1183. Malaysian Sweet Potato Balls
INGREDIENTS (4 Serving)

1/2 pound sweet potatoes

1/2 cup rice flour

1 tablespoon milk

2 tablespoons honey

1/2 teaspoon vanilla extract

1/2 cup icing sugar, for dusting

DIRECTIONS (Prep + Cook Time: 23 minutes)

Steam the sweet potatoes until fork-tender and mash them in a bowl. Add in the rice flour, milk, honey and vanilla. Then, shape the mixture into bite-sized balls. Bake the sweet potato balls in the preheated Air Fryer at 360 degrees F for 15 minutes or until thoroughly cooked and crispy. Dust the sweet potato balls with icing sugar. Enjoy!

1184. Broccoli and Ham Croquettes
INGREDIENTS (3Serving)

1/2 pound broccoli florets, grated

1 teaspoon olive oil

2 tablespoons shallot, chopped

2 ounces ham, chopped

1/2 teaspoon garlic, pressed

1/2 cup all-purpose flour

1 egg

Sea salt and ground black pepper, to taste

DIRECTIONS (Prep + Cook Time: 12 minutes)

In a mixing bowl, thoroughly combine all ingredients. Shape the mixture into small patties and transfer them to the lightly oiled Air Fryer cooking basket. Cook your croquettes in the preheated Air Fryer at 365 degrees F for 6 minutes. Turn them over and cook for a further 6 minutes Serve immediately and Enjoy!

1185. Easy Fluffy Flapjacks
INGREDIENTS (4 Serving)

1/2 cup all-purpose flour

1/2 cup quick-cooking oats

1/2 teaspoon baking powder

1/2 teaspoon baking soda

A pinch of granulated sugar

A pinch of sea salt

1/2 teaspoon lemon zest

1 egg, whisked

1/2 cup milk

DIRECTIONS (Prep + Cook Time: 15 minutes)

In a mixing bowl, thoroughly combine the dry ingredients; in another bowl, mix the wet ingredients. Then, stir the wet mixture into the dry mixture and stir again to combine well. Allow your batter to rest for 20 minutes in the refrigerator. Spoon the batter into a greased muffin tin. Bake your flapjacks in the Air Fryer at 330 degrees F for 6 to 7 minutes or until golden brown. Repeat with the remaining batter. Enjoy!

1186. Air-Grilled Fruit Skewers
INGREDIENTS (2 Serving)

- 2 ounces pear chunks
- 2 ounces apple chunks
- 2 ounces peach chunks
- 2 ounces pineapple chunks
- 1 teaspoon fresh lemon juice
- 1/2 teaspoon apple pie spice
- 1 teaspoon coconut oil, melted

DIRECTIONS (Prep + Cook Time: 10minutes)

Toss your fruit with the fresh lemon juice, apple pie spice and coconut oil. Then, thread the pieces of fruit onto bamboo skewers. Bake the fruit skewers in the preheated Air Fryer at 330 degrees F for 10 minutes. Serve with vanilla ice cream, if desired. Enjoy!

1187. Air Grilled Yam Skewers
INGREDIENTS (3 Serving)

- 1 pound yams, peeled and cut into bite-sized chunks
- 1 teaspoon olive oil
- 1/4 teaspoon cayenne pepper
- Kosher salt and ground white pepper, to taste

DIRECTIONS (Prep + Cook Time: 35 minutes)

Toss the pieces of yams with olive oil, cayenne pepper, salt and white pepper. Thread the pieces of yams onto bamboo skewers and transfer them to the Air Fryer cooking basket. Air fry your skewers at 380 degrees F for 15 minutes; turn them over and continue to cook an additional 15 minutes. Enjoy!

1188. Mini Espresso Brownies
INGREDIENTS (3 Serving)

- 1/3 cup granulated sugar
- 1/3 cup cocoa powder
- 1 tablespoon instant espresso powder
- 1/3 cup cake flour
- 1/2 teaspoon baking powder
- 1/4 teaspoon ground cinnamon
- A pinch of grated nutmeg
- A pinch of kosher salt
- 1/2 teaspoon lime zest
- 1 egg
- 1/3 cup butter, melted

DIRECTIONS (Prep + Cook Time: 30 minutes)

Brush a muffin tin with a nonstick cooking spray. In a bowl, thoroughly combine the sugar, cocoa powder, instant espresso powder, cake flour, baking powder, cinnamon, nutmeg, salt and lime zest. In another bowl, beat the egg with the melted butter until smooth. Then, stir the egg/butter mixture into the dry flour mixture and stir until everything is well combined. Divide the brownie batter between muffin cups and smooth top with a spatula. Cook your brownies at 350 degrees F for about 17 minutes. Allow your brownies to cool for 8 to 10 minutes before unmolding and serving. Enjoy!

1189. Philadelphia Mushroom Omelet
INGREDIENTS (2 Serving)

- 1 tablespoon olive oil
- 1/2 cup scallions, chopped
- 1 bell pepper, seeded and thinly sliced
- 6 ounces button mushrooms, thinly sliced
- 4 eggs
- 2 tablespoons milk
- Sea salt and freshly ground black pepper, to taste
- 1 tablespoon fresh chives, for serving

DIRECTIONS (Prep + Cook Time: 20minutes)

Heat the olive oil in a skillet over medium-high heat. Now, sauté the scallions and peppers until aromatic. Add the mushrooms and continue to cook an additional 3 minutes or until tender. Reserve. Generously grease a baking pan with nonstick cooking spray. Then, whisk the eggs, milk, salt, and black pepper. Spoon into the prepared baking pan. Cook in the preheated Air Fryer at 360 F for 4 minutes. Flip and cook for a further 3 minutes. Place the reserved mushroom filling on one side of the omelet. Fold your omelet in half and slide onto a serving plate. Serve immediately garnished with fresh chives. Enjoy!

1190. Fingerling Potatoes with Cashew Sauce
INGREDIENTS (4 Serving)

1 pound fingerling potatoes

1 tablespoon butter, melted

Cashew Sauce:

1/2 cup raw cashews

1 teaspoon cayenne pepper

3 tablespoons nutritional yeast

Sea salt and ground black pepper, to your liking

1 teaspoon shallot powder

2 teaspoons white vinegar

4 tablespoons water

1/4 teaspoon dried rosemary

1 teaspoon garlic powder

1/4 teaspoon dried dill

DIRECTIONS (Prep + Cook Time: 20 minutes)

Toss the potatoes with the butter, salt, black pepper, shallot powder, and garlic powder. Place the fingerling potatoes in the lightly greased Air Fryer basket and cook at 400 degrees F for 6 minutes; shake the basket and cook for a further 6 minutes. Meanwhile, make the sauce by mixing all ingredients in your food processor or high-speed blender. Drizzle the cashew sauce over the potato wedges. Bake at 400 degrees F for 2 more minutes or until everything is heated through. Enjoy!

1191. Grilled Cheese Sandwich
INGREDIENTS (1 Serving)

2 slices artisan bread

1 tablespoon butter, softened

1 tablespoon tomato ketchup

1/2 teaspoon dried oregano

2 slices Cheddar cheese

DIRECTIONS (Prep + Cook Time: 15 minutes)

Brush one side of each slice of the bread with melted butter. Add the tomato ketchup, oregano, and cheese. Make the sandwich and grill at 360 degrees F for 9 minutes or until cheese is melted. Enjoy!

1192. Scrambled Eggs with Sausage
INGREDIENTS (6 Serving)

1 teaspoon lard

1/2 pound turkey sausage

6 eggs

1 scallion, chopped

1 garlic clove, minced

1 sweet pepper, seeded and chopped

1 chili pepper, seeded and chopped

Sea salt and ground black pepper, to taste

1/2 cup Swiss cheese, shredded

DIRECTIONS (Prep + Cook Time: 25 minutes)

Start by preheating your Air Fryer to 330 degrees F. Now, spritz 6 silicone molds with cooking spray. Melt the lard in a saucepan over medium-high heat. Now, cook the sausage for 5 minutes or until no longer pink. Coarsely chop the sausage; add the eggs, scallions, garlic, peppers, salt, and black pepper. Divide the egg mixture between the silicone molds. Top with the shredded cheese. Bake in the preheated Air Fryer at 340 degrees F for 15 minutes, checking halfway through the cooking time to ensure even cooking. Enjoy!

1193. Easiest Vegan Burrito Ever
INGREDIENTS (6 Serving)

2 tablespoons olive oil

1 small onion, chopped

2 sweet peppers, seeded and chopped

1 chili pepper, seeded and minced

Sea salt and ground black pepper, to taste

1 teaspoon red pepper flakes, crushed

1 teaspoon dried parsley flakes

10 ounces cooked pinto beans

12 ounces canned sweet corn, drained

6 large corn tortillas

1/2 cup vegan sour cream

DIRECTIONS (Prep + Cook Time: 35 minutes)

Begin by preheating your Air Frye to 400 degrees F. Heat the olive oil in a baking pan. Once hot, cook the onion and peppers until they are tender and fragrant, about 15 minutes. Stir in the salt, black pepper, red pepper, parsley, beans, and sweet corn; stir to combine well. Divide the bean mixture between the corn tortillas. Roll up your tortillas and place them on the parchment-lined Air Fryer basket. Bake in the preheated Air Fryer at 350 degrees F for 15 minutes. Serve garnished with sour cream. Enjoy!

1194. Mozzarella Stick Nachos
INGREDIENTS (4 Serving)

- 1 (16-ounce) package mozzarella cheese sticks
- 2 eggs
- 1/2 cup flour
- 1/2 (7 12-ounce) bag multigrain tortilla chips, crushed
- 1 teaspoon garlic powder
- 1 teaspoon dried oregano
- 1/2 cup salsa, preferably homemade

DIRECTIONS (Prep + Cook Time: 40 minutes)

Set up your breading station. Put the flour into a shallow bowl; beat the eggs in another shallow bowl; in a third bowl, mix the crushed tortilla chips, garlic powder, and oregano. Coat the mozzarella sticks lightly with flour, followed by the egg, and then the tortilla chips mixture. Place in your freezer for 30 minutes. Place the breaded cheese sticks in the lightly greased Air Fryer basket. Cook at 380 degrees F for 6 minutes. Serve with salsa on the side and Enjoy!

1195. Easy Zucchini Chips
INGREDIENTS (4 Serving)

- 3/4 pound zucchini, peeled and sliced
- 1 egg, lightly beaten
- 1/2 cup seasoned breadcrumbs
- 1/2 cup parmesan cheese, preferably freshly grated

DIRECTIONS (Prep + Cook Time: 20 minutes)

Pat the zucchini dry with a kitchen towel. In a mixing dish, thoroughly combine the egg, breadcrumbs, and cheese. Then, coat the zucchini slices with the breadcrumb mixture. Cook in the preheated Air Fryer at 400 degrees F for 9 minutes, shaking the basket halfway through the cooking time. Work in batches until the chips is golden brown. Enjoy!

1196. Sweet Mini Monkey Rolls
INGREDIENTS (6 Serving)

- 3/4 cup brown sugar
- 1 stick butter, melted
- 1/4 cup granulated sugar
- 1 teaspoon ground cinnamon
- 1/4 teaspoon ground cardamom
- 1 (16-ounce) can refrigerated buttermilk biscuit dough

DIRECTIONS (Prep + Cook Time: 25 minutes)

Spritz 6 standard-size muffin cups with nonstick spray. Mix the brown sugar and butter; divide the mixture between muffin cups. Mix the granulated sugar with cinnamon and cardamom.

Separate the dough into 16 biscuits; cut each in 6 pieces. Roll the pieces over the cinnamon sugar mixture to coat. Divide between muffin cups. Bake at 340 degrees F for about 20 minutes or until golden brown. Turn upside down and serve. Enjoy!

1197. Crispy Wontons with Asian Dipping Sauce
INGREDIENTS (4 Serving

- 1 teaspoon sesame oil
- 3/4 pound ground beef Sea salt, to taste
- Dipping Sauce:
- 2 tablespoons low-sodium soy sauce
- 1 tablespoon honey
- 1/4 teaspoon Sichuan pepper
- 20 wonton wrappers
- 1 teaspoon Gochujang
- 1 teaspoon rice wine vinegar
- ½ teaspoon sesame oil

DIRECTIONS (Prep + Cook Time: 23 minutes)

Heat 1 teaspoon of sesame oil in a wok over medium-high heat. Cook the ground beef until no longer pink. Season with salt and Sichuan pepper. Lay a piece of the wonton wrapper on your palm; add the beef mixture in the middle of the wrapper. Then, fold it up to form a triangle; pinch the edges to seal tightly. Place your wontons in the lightly greased Air Fryer basket. Cook in the preheated Air Fryer at 360 degrees F for 10 minutes. Work in batches. Meanwhile, mix all ingredients for the sauce. Serve warm.

1198. Spicy Cheesy Risotto Balls
INGREDIENTS (4 Serving)

3 ounces cooked rice

1/2 cup roasted vegetable stock

1 egg, beaten

1 cup white mushrooms, finely chopped

1/2 cup seasoned breadcrumbs

3 garlic cloves, peeled and minced

1/2 yellow onion, finely chopped

1/3 teaspoon ground black pepper, or more to taste

1 ½ bell peppers, seeded minced

1/2 chipotle pepper, seeded and minced

1/2 tablespoon Colby cheese, grated

1 ½ tablespoons canola oil Sea salt, to savor

DIRECTIONS (Prep + Cook Time: 26 minutes)

Heat a saucepan over a moderate heat; now, heat the oil and sweat the garlic, onions, bell pepper and chipotle pepper until tender. Throw in the mushrooms and fry until they are fragrant and the liquid has almost evaporated. Throw in the cooked rice and stock; boil for 18 minutes. Now, add the cheese and spices; mix to combine. Allow the mixture to cool completely. Shape the risotto mixture into balls. Dip the risotto balls in the beaten egg; then, roll them over the breadcrumbs. Air-fry risotto balls for 6 minutes at 400 degrees F. Serve with marinara sauce and enjoy!

1199. Spicy Potato Wedges
INGREDIENTS (4 Serving)

1 ½ tablespoons melted butter

1 teaspoon dried parsley flakes

1 teaspoon ground coriander

1 teaspoon seasoned salt

3 large-sized red potatoes, cut into wedges

1/2 teaspoon chili powder

1/3 teaspoon garlic pepper

DIRECTIONS (Prep + Cook Time: 23 minutes)

Dump the potato wedges into the air fryer cooking basket. Drizzle with melted butter and cook for 20 minutes at 380 degrees F. Make sure to shake them a couple of times during the cooking process. Add the remaining ingredients; toss to coat potato wedges on all sides. Enjoy!

1200. Lamb Meat Balls whit Roasted Veggie Salad
INGREDIENTS (2 Servings)

½ lb ground lamb

1 shallot, chopped

½ tsp garlic powder

Salt and black pepper to taste

1 egg, beaten

½ tsp turmeric

1 potato, chopped

¼ red onion, sliced

1 carrot, sliced diagonally

½ small beetroot, sliced

1 cup cherry tomatoes, halved

Juice of 1 lemon

A handful of rocket salad

A handful of baby spinach

3 tbsp canned chickpeas

½ tsp cumin

2 tbsp olive oil

Parmesan shavings

DIRECTIONS (Prep + Cook Time: 25 minutes)

Preheat air fryer to 370 F. In a bowl, mix red onion, potato, tomatoes, carrot, beetroot, cumin, salt, and 1 tbsp olive oil. Place in a greased baking dish and Bake in the fryer for 10 minutes, shaking once. Meanwhile, in another bowl, mix the ground lamb, shallot, garlic clove, salt, and pepper. Shape the mixture into balls. Place the meatballs over the vegetables in the air fryer and AirFry for 12-14 minutes. Place the rocket salad, spinach, lemon juice, and the remaining olive oil into a serving bowl; mix to combine. Stir in the cooled roasted veggies. Top with chickpeas and Parmesan shavings and serve

1201. Sweet & Sour Lamb Strips
INGREDIENTS (4 Servings)

1 cup cornflour

1 tsp garlic powder

For the sauce

6 tbsp ketchup

½ lemon, juiced

1 tsp allspice

Salt and black pepper to taste

1 tsp honey

2 tbsp soy sauce

2 eggs

1 lb lean lamb, cut into strips

DIRECTIONS (Prep + Cook Time: 20 minutes)

Preheat air fryer to 350 F. In a bowl, whisk all the sauce ingredients with ½ cup of water until smooth; reserve. In another bowl, mix garlic powder, cornflour, allspice, salt, and black pepper. In a third bowl, beat the eggs with some salt. Coat the lamb in the cornflour mixture, then dip in the eggs, then again in the cornflour mixture. Spray with cooking spray and place in the frying basket. AirFry for 15 minutes, shaking once halfway through. Serve drizzled with the prepared sauce.

1202. Italian Sausace Peperonata Pomodoro
INGREDIENTS (2 Servings)

- 2 bell peppers, sliced
- 1 chili pepper
- 1 yellow onion, sliced
- 2 smoked beef sausages
- 1 teaspoon olive oil
- 2 medium-sized tomatoes, peeled and crushed
- 1 garlic clove, minced
- 1 teaspoon Italian spice mix

DIRECTIONS (Prep + Cook Time: 15 minutes)

Spritz the sides and bottom of the cooking basket with a nonstick cooking oil. Add the peppers, onion and sausage to the cooking basket. Cook at 390 degrees F for 10 minutes, shaking the basket periodically. Reserve. Heat the olive oil in a medium-sized saucepan over medium-high flame until sizzling; add in the tomatoes and garlic; let it cook for 2 to 3 minutes. Stir in the peppers, onion and Italian spice mix. Continue to cook for 1 minute longer or until heated through. Fold in the sausages and serve warm. Enjoy

1203. Easy Homemade Hamburgers
INGREDIENTS (2 Servings)

- 3/4 pound lean ground chuck
- Kosher salt and ground black pepper, to taste
- 3 tablespoons onion, minced
- 1 teaspoon garlic, minced
- 1 teaspoon soy sauce
- 1/2 teaspoon smoked paprika
- 1/4 teaspoon ground cumin
- 1/2 teaspoon cayenne pepper
- 1/2 teaspoon mustard seeds
- 2 burger buns

DIRECTIONS (Prep + Cook Time: 15 minutes)

Thoroughly combine the ground chuck, salt, black pepper, onion, garlic and soy sauce in a mixing dish. Season with smoked paprika, ground cumin, cayenne pepper and mustard seeds. Mix to combine well. Shape the mixture into 2 equal patties. Spritz your patties with a nonstick cooking spray. Air fry your burgers at 380 degrees F for about 11 minutes or to your desired degree of doneness. Place your burgers on burger buns and serve with favorite toppings. Enjoy

Made in the USA
Middletown, DE
26 January 2021